'READING' GREEK DEATH

'Reading' Greek Death
To the End of the Classical Period

Christiane Sourvinou-Inwood

CLARENDON PRESS · OXFORD

*This book has been printed digitally and produced in a standard specification
in order to ensure its continuing availability*

OXFORD
UNIVERSITY PRESS

Great Clarendon Street, Oxford OX2 6DP

Oxford University Press is a department of the University of Oxford.
It furthers the University's objective of excellence in research, scholarship,
and education by publishing worldwide in

Oxford New York

Auckland Cape Town Dar es Salaam Hong Kong Karachi
Kuala Lumpur Madrid Melbourne Mexico City Nairobi
New Delhi Shanghai Taipei Toronto
With offices in
Argentina Austria Brazil Chile Czech Republic France Greece
Guatemala Hungary Italy Japan South Korea Poland Portugal
Singapore Switzerland Thailand Turkey Ukraine Vietnam

Oxford is a registered trade mark of Oxford University Press
in the UK and in certain other countries

Published in the United States
by Oxford University Press Inc., New York

ISBN 978-0-19-815069-5

Printed and bound by CPI Antony Rowe, Eastbourne

with Mainland Greeks. In my view, complexity is the second (correlative with the first) universal characteristic of this type of interaction, which operates in complex ways and results in complex religious forms that bear complex relationships to their forms of origin.[44]

These modalities of religious change have important methodological implications. The projection of Greek data into the Minoan period, which more recently has been aided by the discovery of names of historical Greek deities in the Knossos tablets, has traditionally rested on the alleged 'recognition' of Minoan elements in historical Greek religion: the presence of non-Greek names (especially ones with Cretan associations) in Greek religion; the apparent similarities between some elements of historical Greek belief, myth, and ritual (again, especially ones with Cretan associations) and certain Minoan data, or rather, certain particular readings and interpretations of certain Minoan data; and finally, on the vaguely defined and subjective notion that certain features in historical Greek religion have a 'Minoan' or 'non-Greek' character. As we saw, this approach relies implicitly on a fallacious assumption: that the presence in a religious system of an element belonging to a later system shows that the whole nexus to which that element had belonged in the later system was present in the earlier one and in the same form. The fallaciousness of this assumption will be confirmed in the remaining part of this section. At this point I must unpack a culturally constructed mirage: sometimes, the assumption

---

[44] The following are some examples of complex developments and interactions between religious systems. On the complex relationship between Greek culture and Jewish religion cf. briefly Momigliano 1978: 57–9 (cf. p. 49 on the influence of Iranian religion on Judaism). The history of sufism in India provides a good illustration of the complex interactions of a religious system, in this case a sect, with a different religion and with the orthodox mainstream of Islam, in the context of, and determined by, and interacting with, specific historical circumstances (social, economic, political, and so on): Ata 1980: 39–45. On sufism and its interaction with other religious systems cf. also briefly J. R. Hinnels (ed.), *The Penguin Dictionary of Religions* (Harmondsworth 1984), 313–14, s.v. 'Sufism, Sufis'. Cf. for the graftings on to, and reshaping of, North Algonkian eschatology under the influence of Christianity: Hultkrantz 1980: 161–83. An example of interaction between two religions resulting in changes in both is the interaction between Islam and traditional African religions: cf. Gilliland 1979: 241–57. Finally, the following is an example illustrating the emergence of a new religion in circumstances in which the process of formation and the elements that went into it can be studied: H. Welch and Chün-Fang Yü (1980: 222–46), on the syncretic new Chinese religion 'The Holy Teaching of Heaven's virtue' (T'ien-te sheng-chiao) which combined elements from Buddhism, Taoism, and the already existing syncretic Chinese religious systems.

that certain practices are Minoan in origin appears to be confirmed by the Minoan evidence; but in reality this confirmation is not independent, for the assumption which purports to be being examined and tested has in fact centred the investigation and shaped the filters through which the Minoan data have been read. Arguments of this kind, like the strategy of model-testing, of which they are a crude version, contain hidden circularity and are self-validating.[45]

I will now say something about the historical circumstances in the 'Dark Ages'; this will provide first, a very broad framework in which to consider whether such circumstances were conducive to religious change, and second, a background for the empirical analyses in the following sections. I shall be very brief and bland, and as far as possible neutral; for since a proper investigation of this topic is beyond my scope here, I will limit myself to the absolute minimum that is generally accepted.

No one, I believe, would deny that the historical circumstances of the Greek communities underwent dramatic upheavals and transformations, affecting the economic, political, and social spheres, in the course of the centuries separating the Mycenaean world from the historical Greek period. The collapse and disintegration of Mycenaean palatial society, and with it of the structures that had supported cult in the Mycenaean kingdoms, inevitably brought about changes in practices and discontinuities.[46] The Dark Ages were impoverished when compared to the Mycenaean period, though in their later part there was increasing prosperity which eventually led to the 'Renaissance' of the eighth century. The large Mycenaean kingdoms with their palatial bureaucracy were replaced by a pattern of villages, generally poor and small in the Early Dark Ages, more prosperous and better populated subsequently. Writing and many craft skills were lost. In the early part of the period conditions were unsettled, and at least some population movements took place. The minimalist view of such movements would be to accept only small-scale population movements within the area of

---

[45] I discuss this question in the Appendix.

[46] This collapse and disintegration did not happen overnight; in many places in LHIIIC palatial society had not come to a halt, its disintegration was gradual, and followed different rhythms, and probably took different forms in different places. Hence objections against the notion that society changed after the collapse of the palaces which are based on the detected continuities between LHIIIB and LHIIIC do not invalidate the basic proposition. For what matters for our purposes is something that no one, I think, would deny, the view of the Dark Ages summarized in the statement that follows this note.

the Mycenaean kingdoms—and perhaps also outwards from it. The maximalist view is that besides these there were also (small-scale) movements into the area that had been Mycenaean Greece from areas at its northern fringes in the late Mycenaean period and Early Dark Ages. In my own view there was a series of small-scale movements over a long period and through a variety of routes which later became glorified under the concept of 'Dorian Invasion'. The situation in Dark-Age Crete was even more complex, for even more complex factors come into play. The Minoan/Mycenaean religious syncretism testified to by the Linear B tablets of Knossos is one of the major strands that went into the making of Cretan religion. The disintegration of the structures that had generated and supported it, and the inevitable interactions with a series of other religious strands on the island (such as, perhaps, different variants of relatively 'pure' Minoan beliefs and practices that may have survived in certain areas outside the immediate sphere of influence of palatial culture and cult structures) would lead us to expect that this 'syncretic koine' developed through very complex processes, perhaps into different variants resulting from different local developments and diversifications after the breakdown of palatial cult control. These, then, were very complex processes, and they became even more complex with the arrival of the subsequent waves of Greek-speakers, first, it would appear, fleeing Mycenaeans at the end of the thirteenth century and again in the late twelfth and subsequently (whenever that may have been) speakers of Doric. These new arrivals came into contact, and so their religious systems entered into a relationship, with the different religious strands then found on the island. All these interacted and developed in a variety of ways, which were then affected by each other, and these complex operations shaped the Cretan religion of the historical period.

This state of affairs in Dark-Age Crete would be conducive to a change in cult activities, a retrenchment in scale, quantity, and quality. For fewer resources were now available, and thus fewer than before for dedication—even if there had been no change in the proportion of resources dedicated to those available. There was also no powerful central authority, no king, or polis institutions, with surpluses, part of which they would turn into gifts to the gods as they did in the Mycenaean kingdoms and in historical Greece. Another change in the articulation of cult likely to have arisen in the situation of the Dark Ages was a reduction in the geographical

scale of the religious system: while in the Mycenaean kingdoms there was—whatever the situation at the very local level—a wider framework, that of the whole kingdom, within which cult was articulated, and a pantheon set into place, in the Dark Ages we would expect cult to be articulated at the local level, with the settlement-unit, the village. This does not exclude inter-community relationships, such as religious leagues, both small-scale ones between neighbouring villages, and larger-scale ones involving wider geographical areas, at least after the unsettled Early Dark Ages. In fact, I believe that some Dark-Age sanctuaries did involve people from different localities, and did play the role of centres of interaction between different communities. But the basic unit, the basic framework—comparable to the role of the polis and polis religion in historical Greek times[47]—was likely to have been the village, interacting with other villages but setting into place a pantheon and set of cults, inherited from the Mycenaean period (both cults that had been locally based and the important cults of the wider kingdom it partook in), and shaped to fit the particular circumstances and needs of the group. In this context we should expect divergent local developments according to the different local needs and circumstances, with the religious leagues providing a 'centripetal' trend towards some cohesion in some parts of the religious system within each league.

A change in the circumstances of the worshipping group that affects religion in important ways is the influx of new population groups. If people from the fringes of Mycenaean Greece had indeed moved into what had been the Mycenaean world over a long period, they would have brought with them new religious practices and concepts, expressing the realities, and catering for the needs, of simpler societies than those of the Mycenaeans (by whom, of course, these putative simpler societies may not have been entirely unaffected, for they had been in contact with them). This would have set in motion complex interactions between the religious systems, leading to changes. The new religious practices and beliefs may have had an important impact because they corresponded more closely to the simpler realities of the Dark-Age communities than did the legacy of the Mycenaean religious tradition—though the latter, we saw, would have developed to fit the new circumstances.

[47] Which I have discussed in Sourvinou-Inwood 1990b: 295–322.

We should postulate, then, a complex process of development and interaction.

In these circumstances, we conclude that the consideration of certain universal characteristics of religion in conjunction with the historical circumstances of the worshipping group in the period under consideration allows us to make the following deductions. First, we should expect the Greek religious system to have undergone significant changes and developments between the Bronze Age and the historical Greek period. Second, given the modalities of religious change, the presence in a Minôan or Mycenaean nexus of one element (for example, a divine name) which is the same as, or corresponds closely to, a historical Greek element, does not entail that the whole nexus to which that element belonged in the historical period (for example, the whole divine personality) had existed, in that (or any other) form in Minoan or Mycenaean religion. Third, since every element acquires its meanings through complex networks of relationships with the other elements of the system, it is fallacious to attribute the meanings of the historical Greek element to the corresponding Minoan or Mycenaean one—let alone to attribute the values of the whole Greek nexus (ritual, divine personality, and so on) to the Minoan or Mycenaean nexus.

Certain correlatives of this picture can indeed be detected in the data. First, and perhaps most strikingly, some cult practices previously detected in the archaeological record now disappear. In the earlier part of the Dark Ages sanctuaries are almost entirely invisible, and dedications which leave an archaeological record have clearly ceased. Second, the divergences in, for example, the panthea or the calendars of the different *poleis* or the particular modalities of cult such as the form of particular festivals, even festivals bearing the same name in the different poleis, presents the image of diversity that would ensue if the religious developments in the Dark Ages were indeed of the kind postulated here. Most importantly, there are very significant differences in the panthea of deities worshipped on the one hand in Mycenaean Greece, for which we have the evidence of the Linear B tablets, and on the other the Greek poleis of the historical period. It must be clear from what has been said above that such differences in the panthea are both important religious changes in themselves and also part of, and indices for, fundamental changes in the religious system as a whole; they also

entail that even deities with the same name cannot be 'the same' in the two different panthea. Third, important facets of historical Greek religion are inextricably connected with the historical and institutional realities of the polis and were therefore set in place in the context of the emergence of the polis and its development from the eighth century onwards.[48] Finally, there may indeed be evidence for Dark-Age leagues. This is a very complex question. Here I shall only mention that, in my view, it is not impossible that it was the religious associations of the Dark Ages which provided the most common and regular framework for other forms of interaction in this period[49] in which inter-community contacts—and contacts with the outside world—were less intensive and extensive than they had been before or were to be after it.[50]

When the Minoan evidence is studied separately, and then its conclusions compared to the historical Greek phenomena which appear to be related, the relationship that emerges from the comparison is precisely of the type inferred from the considerations set out here.[51] The historical Greek religious elements which are related to Minoan elements reveal themselves to be complex and varied *transformations* of the Minoan phenomena—rather than unchanged (or almost unchanged) 'survivals'. This, I hope, will become clear in the case of Elysion. In these circumstances, it is clearly fallacious to collapse highly complex phenomena into simplistic schemata by making facile identifications of 'Minoan religious survivals'.

[48] On this cf. e.g. Vernant 1976: 27–8; and cf. Polignac 1984: *passim* on the relationship between religion and the emerging polis.

[49] Thus, e.g., it is possible that they provided the framework for coping with the uncertain and uneven agricultural production, for exchanging agricultural products when some areas may have had a food shortage and others a surplus—hence, perhaps, the advantage of the larger-scale leagues which covered large geographical areas.

[50] Prof. W. G. Forrest in a lecture in 1987 in Oxford also expressed, independently, the view that religious leagues were of importance in the Dark Ages and in the process of polis formation.

[51] I argue elsewhere (*Reading Dumb Images: A Study in Minoan Iconography and Religion*, in preparation) that the model of complex religious developments in Crete from the Neopalatial period onwards presented here (which entails the inadvisability of attempting to 'cut through' these developments to reconstruct original forms, and of using later Greek data in the study of the Minoan period) is confirmed empirically when the results of the analyses of a Minoan ritual in which only Minoan data are taken into account are considered in relation to comparable elements of historical Greek religion which, I suggest, are their (highly complex and not logically reconstructable on the basis of the historical data) later transformations.

A Note on 'Systems'. The view that societies are interlocking and interacting systems and that cultural details can only be understood in context originated with Durkheim.[52] But the fact that this view originated in, and has been closely associated with, functionalism

[52] On Durkheim cf. Boon 1982: 54–68 (and cf. 143); cf. also Lukes 1973. On Durkheim's theory of religion cf. Evans-Pritchard 1965: 51–70. On Durkheim's followers cf. ibid. 70–7. (This view of religion was first applied to the classical world by L. Gernet; for a discussion of Gernet's work and place in the history of classical studies cf. Humphreys 1978: 76–96. On the interdependence between religion and all other aspects of Greek life and thought cf. also Vernant 1974: 110–11.) The interdependence between all facets of society is a point at which the functionalist school and the structuralist approach converge; see briefly Leach 1976: 5; 1973: 38–9. On the relationship between functionalism and structuralism on this point cf. Mair 1965: 28–35, where the concept of function is also discussed, with bibliog. on p. 47; cf. also p. 234. On the concept of function cf. also Hallpike 1979: 64. On the convergences and the differences between functionalism and structuralism on this point (with a critique of functionalism) cf. also Hodder 1982b: 7. On function and functional value and their relationship to culture cf. Hodder 1982b: 3–4, cf. also 7; Sahlins 1976: 206. On religion as part of the social structure in structuralism cf. the writings of Lévi-Strauss, *passim*; cf. e.g. Lévi-Strauss 1972: 313–14. On the various and manifold ways in which society and religion are interrelated, and on the various perspectives on this relationship, cf. e.g. the essays, by various authors, in R. Robertson 1969. On the close relationship between religion and society cf. also Douglas 1975: *passim*, esp. 144, 150, 161, 183, 204, 212, 309–12 (and more generally 276–316); 1980: 60–1. On the interaction between religion and social structure cf. also Winter 1966: 155–74, esp. 155–7; Morton-Williams 1968: 1–24, esp. 4–6; Yalman 1967: 87. For an example of the way in which religious elements interlock with various facets of the society's other systems cf. e.g. how, among the Fulani of Nigeria, the pilgrimage to Mecca, a religious act, is (not surprisingly) affected by, and interacts with, social, political, and economic factors (Hickey, Staats, and McGaw 1979: 217–30). The authors suggest that the same is also true of Islamic pilgrimage in general. On the social significance of Islamic pilgrimage in a different ethnic group cf. Scupin 1982: 25–33.

Functionalists, 'naïve' and more sophisticated, and their critics differ in the degree of complexity, sophistication, flexibility and openness they ascribe to the notion of 'social system'. For the modified, looser, version of the notion of 'social systems' cf. Gluckman and Eggan 1966: pp. xxx–xxxii. Reductionist, closed models of the social system take no account of interactions with other societies and cultures, as Lévi-Strauss pointed out in his critique of functionalism (Lévi-Strauss 1975: ii. 118–19). What is desirable is an open (and complex) model in which are also inscribed the interactions with other systems, other societies and cultures. For recent critiques of functionalism cf. e.g. Boon 1982: pp. xi, 9–21, 114; Hallpike 1979: 63–5; Hodder 1982b: 3–6, where New Archaeology is also criticized for its functionalism. For a discussion and reassessment of functionalism, and of criticisms of functionalism (esp. Hempel's) cf. Burhenn 1980: 350–60. Humphreys (1978: 9) criticizes the value of 'the structural-functional approach in its conventional, positivist form' for the analysis of, esp., more complex societies, and in particular those of ancient Greece; cf. also Willey 1974: 145–6. All these criticisms do not, of course, invalidate the notion that a society's world-system is a system of interconnected systems, but point out the need for more sophisticated and complex models, which must be used in circumscribed ways and for circumscribed purposes (cf. Burhenn 1980: 359–60). For some specialized facets of the correlation between historical circumstances and religion cf. Hallpike 1979: 65; Asad 1983: 237–59.

does not entail[53] that to agree with it involves taking on the reductionist tendencies of functionalism.[54] Most importantly, acceptance of the principle that social phenomena—including religion—are interdependent does not entail acceptance of a reductionist belief that religion is to be reduced to a set of representations of the social order.[55] The use I am making of the model of religion as a system that interlocks and interacts with the society's other systems is limited and circumscribed: I am not deploying it in an attempt to explain specific religious phenomena; I am using it simply as a basic representation of religion and its operation, which brings out the basic parameters for the investigation of religious phenomena and especially of change, by placing those phenomena within the context in which they function. This placing does not 'explain' the religious system, but it constitutes a fundamental parameter for the understanding of that system and its operation, and for the understanding of religious change.[56]

(d) *Elysion*

The Hypothesis of Minoan Origin. We saw that in *Odyssey* 4. 561–5 Menelaos is told by Proteus that he will not die, but, because he is Zeus' son-in-law, he will be sent by the gods to a paradise with ideal weather, the Elysian fields at the ends of the earth, where Rhadamanthys dwells.[57] I suggested above that the widely held modern belief that this Paradise is an afterlife concept of Minoan origin is mistaken; in this section I will set out my case in detail. We saw that the notion that the later Greek evidence creates a presumption in favour of the view that Elysion originated in Minoan Crete is fallacious and that it is illegitimate to project later Greek beliefs to the Minoan or Mycenaean period. In my doctoral dissertation[58] I attempted to set the basic parameters[59] for the reconstruction of Minoan and Mycenaean afterlife beliefs through an

---

[53] Cf. previous note.

[54] Or the rather mechanistic conceptions of culture which have been associated with New Archaeology; cf. n. 52 for references to critiques of functionalism and New Archaeology.

[55] On this fallacy cf. e.g. Douglas 1980: 106. Cf. also, on a related point, Boon 1982: 114. '(F)unctionalists overstep their bounds when they imply that by mapping the mechanisms one captures the culture.'

[56] Cf. also Willey 1974: 146.

[57] On the formulations through which Elysion is described cf. Davies 1987: 266–80.

[58] Completed in 1973; foolishly, I did not publish it.

[59] Though I did not call it that.

investigation from which I excluded all later Greek evidence. I tried to reconstruct Bronze-Age beliefs only in so far as this can be done on the basis of contemporary evidence seen in its historical background, and to reach some conclusions mostly in the form of plausible hypotheses and exclusions of some possibilities. It is beyond my scope here to discuss the complex problems involved in such an enterprise; I will only summarize some of the conclusions that suggest certain possibilities and exclude others. After the relevant Homeric beliefs have been considered in themselves I shall briefly consider the relationship between those conclusions and the tentative conclusions pertaining to the Bronze-Age beliefs—or, rather, the parameters of determination of such beliefs—and then attempt to determine what the relationship is between them. Given what was said above, if a detectable relationship exists, we would expect it to have involved bricolage, reinterpretations and modifications.

S. West[60] has recently restated the traditional position on Elysion as follows. 'The Cretan provenance of this conception, so much at odds with the normal Greek belief in a shadow-like afterlife in Hades, is indicated by the brief reference *othi xanthos Rhadamanthys*; the association of Rhadamanthys with Elysium was evidently familiar. Rhadamanthys ... bears a pre-Greek name (*-nth-*) and is closely associated with Crete.' I shall now consider the Rhadamanthys–Elysion association. I shall discuss below the notion that the conception of Elysion, is 'so much at odds with the normal Greek belief in a shadow-like afterlife in Hades'. As for West's statement 'This view of the afterlife accords with what little may be inferred about Minoan beliefs from their funerary monuments ...' it is, we shall see, incorrect. On the contrary, what has happened is that the Minoan data have been interpreted in the light of the projection of certain assumptions about historical Greek beliefs. I cited West's restatement of the case because it summarizes the most important arguments on which the traditional thesis about Elysion relies. I shall now set out to answer them.

I shall start with West's formulation of the argument concerning the association between Elysion and Rhadamanthys. Even leaving aside the fact that this reading, which assumes prior knowledge of Rhadamanthys in Elysion, is only one possible reading of the

---

[60] S. West 1988: 227 *ad Od.* 4. 563 ff.

verses—and, in my view, a far from compelling one—the argument that Rhadamanthys' association with Elysion in *Odyssey* 4. 563 ff. indicates that the whole nexus was originally Cretan can be shown to be invalid. It was Malten who first argued, on the basis of the *Odyssey* passage, that the concept of Elysion is a Minoan heritage because in Homer it is associated with Rhadamanthys who is pre-Greek on the evidence of his -*nth*- name and Cretan on the evidence of myth and genealogies.[61] He also tried to prove that the word *Elysion* itself is Minoan, but this suggestion has not met with approval; I shall return to it. The one element in the Elysion nexus that is Minoan is Rhadamanthys, whose persona in myth is consistently that of a Minoan king. However, we saw that this does not entail that the Elysion/paradise concept was of Minoan origin; for the modalities of religious development make it illegitimate to assume that Rhadamanthys' significant association in Homer with a specific kind of Land of the Dead, a paradise for the chosen few, entails that he had been associated with a similar paradise in the Minoan period. On the contrary, both the modalities of religious development and of the generation and transmission of oral poetry[62] were highly conducive to radical change. Thus, the belief that Rhadamanthys had been associated with a paradise in the Minoan period because he was associated with Elysion in Homer is dependent on culturally determined expectations that are in violent conflict with the expectations constructed as a result of the consideration of the modalities of religious development and the nature of the text in which the belief is articulated.

Moreover, the notion that Rhadamanthys' association with Elysion proves that the latter is of Minoan origin depends on a very selective use of evidence. For Rhadamanthys is not the only Minoan ruler associated with a Land of the Dead in Homer. Minos, Rhadamanthys' brother of *Iliad* 14. 321–2, is significantly associated with Hades in *Odyssey* 11. 567–71, a Land of the Dead very different from Elysion. What the two have in common is a significant association of a Minoan ruler with a Land of the Dead (or 'Dead'). Given what we have seen about bricolage and transformation, the

---

[61] Malten 1913: 35–51. Malten 1912: 264 suggested an emendation in Rhadamanthys' genealogies which, if accepted (and it generally has been accepted), shows Rhadamanthys associated with Phaestus.

[62] Which, we saw, can lead to phenomena such as the conflation of elements applying to, say, different types of shields, from different periods, to describe one and the same shield.

association of two different Minoan rulers with two different Lands of the Dead in Homer may generate the hypothesis that these two mythemes are different transformations of a Minoan conceptual schema 'association of Minoan rulers with a Land of the Dead'. Since it seems that such a modality of multiple transformations of Minoan elements and schemata did indeed govern relationships between Minoan and historical Greek mythico-cultic nexuses[63] it is legitimate to suggest that the most convincing interpretation of the data is that the two are transformations of a Minoan schema 'Minoan ruler in a prominent/significant position in a Land of the Dead'. It is not legitimate to assume that one of the two represents the original Minoan form of the schema, unless there is strong evidence to support such a view, which is far from being the case. I must stress that the two transformations interpretation is only a hypothesis, and it would be methodologically dangerous simply to set out to 'test' it.[64] We must leave it aside and only return to it in order to consider how it relates to the (independently derived) results of the other parts of our investigation.

The Minoan Evidence.   Since the later evidence does not create a presumption in favour of the Minoan origin of Elysion, we must try to determine what, if anything, the Minoan evidence allows us to reconstruct with regard to eschatology and funerary ideology and whether it offers any reason for thinking that Elysion was a Minoan belief. I followed this procedure in my thesis, but I cannot set out the whole argument here; I shall summarize some general conclusions pertaining to kingship and death and concentrate on the Elysion question. In my view, what had been in pre-palatial times a 'cult of the dead'[65] which (at least in some places) was offered to all (or most of) the dead of each community[66] eventually

---

[63] Cf. Sourvinou-Inwood 1991: 226–7, 235–6.

[64] On these methodological dangers see Appendix.

[65] I use this term conventionally, to indicate offerings to the dead on fixed occasions for some years after burial, such as the offerings made by the Athenians of the classical period.

[66] Pini (1968: 28–32) argued in favour of a prepalatial cult of the dead; Branigan (1970*b*: 102, 119–20) disagreed (cf. also Renfrew 1972: 432). In Branigan 1970*a*, written before 1970*b* (cf. 1970*a*, p. xvi and 1970*b*, p. xv), Branigan was more willing to accept the possibility of a cult of the dead in connection with the Messara tholoi. In my thesis I argued against Branigan's arguments and concluded that cult of the dead in association with a ritual addressed to divinities on behalf of the dead had been practised in the pre-palatial period. On this question now cf. also Petit 1987: 35–42. Cf. also on the funerary practices of the Messara tholoi Branigan 1987: 43–50.

became focused on, and crystallized into, cult offered to the royal dead only. This development fits the modality that has been observed to govern the creation of royal ceremonial everywhere: they are constructed of building blocks consisting of earlier ritual materials.[67] At the beginning of the palatial period began a long process of decline of the cult of the dead for the common dead, while the practice became focused on the royal dead—after a long period of coexistence of the royal cult of the dead with cult of the dead offered to the common dead.[68] This transformation should be seen in the context of, and as one particular aspect of, the clearly observable trend in Minoan palatial society[69] of a progressively greater control of cult—as of some crafts—by the palaces, especially in the Neopalatial period, when it is combined with the decentralization of some economic and administrative functions. The palaces were the location of religious activities open to the public. This control of cult as one of the most important aspects of public life allows a symbolic underpinning of central authority and the symbolic manipulation of reality.[70]

As to whether the Minoan evidence offers any reason for thinking that Elysion was a Minoan afterlife belief, it will become clear that the answer is negative, and that scholars have only been able to sustain the opposite view because their case implicitly relied on centring the interpretation of the Minoan data on the presumption of Minoan origin based on later evidence; by structuring the data to fit that central assumption on the basis of what appear logical connections to modern scholars but which comparative studies show to be no more than culturally determined expectations; by privileging one possible interpretation of each individual element among many,[71] because it is the one that can be made to fit the

---

[67] Cannadine 1987: 15–16; Bloch 1987: 271–2 (cf. also 271–97).

[68] I argued this, and its modalities, circumstances, and possible motivations, in detail in my thesis, but I do not think that this simple statement of development as it stands in this bare form is controversial (cf. Pini 1968: 72).

[69] Cf. a brief survey, with a discussion of some recent papers, in my review of R. Hägg and N. Marinatos (eds.), *The Function of the Minoan Palaces*, CR 39 (1989), 337.

[70] The fact that the palace controlled cult is very far from implying theocracy or anything of that kind (cf. previous note).

[71] e.g. by assuming that the fact that a terracotta figurine of a boat was found in some Minoan graves can only be interpreted as fulfilling the need of a boat to go to a paradise beyond the sea (cf. Davaras 1984: 55–95) despite the fact that, as we shall see, not only is it entirely unsupported by the evidence, but in fact, in so far as the scarce and ambiguous evidence can indicate anything it shows that this was not the case.

central hypothesis of Minoan origin of Elysion, then taking this as fact and proceeding to the next hypothesis; and by blurring important distinctions, so that a series of highly speculative hypotheses are bound together in a mutually supporting whole which appears convincing because the fallaciousness of its central assumption and the circularity of the relationship between the different parts of the case are hidden. I shall demonstrate these contentions by investigating further the case made for the Minoan origin of Elysion.

Nilsson[72] accepted Malten's theories enthusiastically—except for the etymology of *Elysion* on which he is non-committal; for he could use them to explain what he calls a contradiction in Greek afterlife beliefs, the coexistence of Elysion with the Underworld as pictured in the main part of *Odyssey* 11. If, Nilsson argues, the former is a Minoan heritage the contradiction can be explained. He creates a neat picture of Greek afterlife beliefs on the basis of an illegitimate *petitio principii* involving an arbitrary distinction based on race, a principle already criticized by Guthrie[73] and wholly discredited in modern scholarship. Unfortunately, it is often the case that views derived from interpretations based on discredited principles seep into, and become part of, the established discourse, without regard to their origins, though few would accept the premises on which those views are ultimately based. Nilsson's claim is that[74] the 'conception of the dark and gloomy Hades with its pale and fluttering shadows' was 'the natural result of the innate Greek character'; and also that it is a common belief of seafaring people that the dead travel beyond the seas to a remote Land of the Dead, and therefore such a concept would be 'natural' for the Minoans, but not for the Greeks who learnt to navigate late. It is unclear what length of time in navigation experience Nilsson considered necessary for such ideas to develop, and why he confidently decides that the Minoans had had, while the Greeks had not had, the time to adopt such beliefs. In this distinction, he clearly takes the Bronze Age as the determining period for afterlife beliefs associated with seafaring, since by Homer's time the 'Greeks' cannot be denied some seven centuries of seafaring activities. But that it was the Bronze Age that was the determining period for this type of afterlife belief is in fact part of the point which Nilsson purports to prove:

[72] Nilsson 1950: 623–5, 630.
[73] Guthrie 1950: 302–4.
[74] Nilsson 1950: 620.

that Elysion originated in the Bronze Age, in Minoan Crete. Thus, there is circularity even in the deployment of this argument, which is itself highly dubious. In the context of her expression of support for the thesis that Elysion originated in Crete West also states that this conception is 'so much at odds with the normal Greek belief in a shadow-like afterlife in Hades'.[75]

The notion that Elysion is at odds with the normal Greek belief in a shadow-like afterlife in Hades is, in my view, misconceived. First, it is untrue that such an afterlife was the normal Greek belief; even in *Odyssey* 11 not all afterlife is shadow-like, and in the archaic period many 'happier versions' were generated, especially in Mysteric and sectarian contexts—which can only be thought of as marginal if one ignores the intimate intertwining of the Eleusinian Mysteries with Athenian polis religion. Then, the notion that the two sets of beliefs were 'at odds' is based on a culturally determined judgement, and needs serious rethinking. It consists of two distinct facets. First, the contrast between the paradisiac afterlife of Elysion and the shadow-like afterlife in Hades described in *Odyssey* 11; and second, the conflict between the belief in a paradise for a few who do not die and the belief (deeply rooted in the epics) that everyone dies and goes to Hades. But what is the basis for believing that this conflict indicates that Elysion must have originated in the non-Greek world? That it can best be explained in terms of different origins of the conflicting beliefs may seem logical to the modern mind; but the fact that both were part of Homeric eschatology entails that their coexistence made some sort of sense to both the poet and his audience. Thus, instead of beginning the investigation by structuring the data through *a priori* assumptions, we must focus on this coexistence. For, whatever their origin what we need to understand is how the two sets of beliefs appeared, and were made sense of, in that system.

Let us look at the pattern of the appearance and development of their coexistence. As we saw, the balance between the two beliefs changes. After Homer the Elysion-type strand (most often in the Isles of the Blest version) increased in importance; in general, the importance of the escape from death strand grew dramatically; at the same time life in Hades itself came to accommodate a happy strand. The importance of the strand that was 'in conflict' with

[75] S. West 1988: 227 (*ad* 563 ff.).

Elysion, the belief 'everyone dies', significantly decreased. Thus, there were pressures in the system pulling up the former and pushing down the latter. Hence, there is every reason for thinking that the Elysion-type strand was generated within this system. Even if it had been taken over from another system, it would have been in order to fulfil a need; religious beliefs are not just borrowed like fashions, they fill a need within the borrowing system, even though the need itself would not have been unaffected by the interaction with the 'exporting' system, which may have helped crystallize an emerging need. The fact that the trend in question grew steadily in importance confirms that there was growing pressure within the system in its direction. Thus, the presumption is in favour of the view that the paradise strand was generated within the same system as the 'everyone dies' one. Even if it had been brought from the outside, since religious interaction and borrowing operate in a bricolage modality, the concept of Elysion would not have been taken over as a 'fixed essence' but would have been adapted to fit the Greek system.

Let us return to Nilsson's case, which has formed the centre of the modern orthodoxy of the Minoan origin of Elysion. He[76] tried to corroborate his view of the relationship between Greek and Minoan afterlife beliefs cited above by arguing that the Minoans adopted a different attitude towards the afterlife from the Greeks. This thesis, based on his own interpretation of the Haghia Triada sarcophagus, claims that the deification of men, of rulers, was thought possible in Minoan Crete, while it is inconsistent with classical Greek beliefs. A first objection to this schema is the fact that in Homer Rhadamanthys is not said to be divine, nor is Menelaos promised such divinity. Paradisiac immortality is what they have, but this is not the same as divinity. Then, the notion that Minoan rulers were deified needs serious rethinking. It is based on the symbiotic combination of the following arguments.[77] (1) A particular interpretation of the representations on the Haghia Triada sarcophagus, according to which they represent the deification of a

---

[76] Nilsson 1950: 625.

[77] That these are the arguments on the combination of which this thesis is based is not always explicitly set out by its adherents. Nor are these arguments always presented together, as making up a coherent mutually supporting case; often one or the other forms an implicit, unstated, background providing implicit support, and creating an appropriate perceptual cast for the reception of this notion. This is why the fallaciousness of the foundations on which the notion of the divinity of the Minoan rulers rests has been less obvious than one might have expected.

dead man. (2) A particular interpretation of the 'cult of the royal dead'. (3) The fact that a discredited undifferentiated model of the divine king[78] or the very different historical model of the Roman emperor has (sometimes implicitly sometimes explicitly) informed the interpretation of the Minoan data. Other bits and pieces of evidence interpreted in certain specific ways are also brought in support of this notion; they will be mentioned below.

The intrusion of (3) is arbitrary and threatens to corrupt our reading of the culture; I shall return to this. As for the Haghia Triada sarcophagus, it will become clear that it cannot support the theory which has been built on it. First, and very importantly, the Haghia Triada sarcophagus[79] does not belong to the period of Minoan hegemony and independence; it was not the product of Minoan palatial society but of the period of Mycenaean rule.[80] This was a period of Minoan/Mycenaean syncretism in religion, as is shown, for example, by the presence of the clearly Minoan goddess *pi-pi-tu-na* in the Linear B tablets, side by side with the Mycenaean deities, and also by the fact that worship is offered to *pa-si-te-o-i*, all the gods, which is a concept known in syncretic religious systems; therefore it is not legitimate to assume that the beliefs reflected in these scenes—whatever they may have been—were Minoan, rather than products of this syncretism. Second, Nilsson's reading of the sarcophagus images is based on a flawed methodology; not surprisingly for the period, there is no attempt to construct a strategy aimed at limiting the intrusion of culturally determined assumptions to the minimum when reading the images of a society to which our access is highly restricted. I cannot, of course, discuss this here, so I will only point out that one of the things we do not know, is the parameters of selection determining what was shown on such sarcophagi. Not only is the interpretation of the whole scenes problematic, but also, even when we know that some of the objects represented are, for example, religious symbols, we cannot know whether they were represented as generic religious symbols or because they had a connection with the death ritual, or for whatever

---

[78] On this notion cf. the critical discussion of Price 1984: 235–6, cf. 236–9, with bibliog.; cf. also, against the notion of Minoan priest-kings, Bennett 1961–2: 327–35.

[79] There is a vast literature on the Haghia Triada sarcophagus; cf. esp. Long 1974: with bibliog.

[80] According to the generally accepted chronological and historical framework.

other reason.[81] Our culturally determined logic tells us that they must have been related to death and the dead; this may well be right, but we cannot know what this relationship was. For example, the possibility that some images may be articulating the deceased's social persona, like those on the archaic funerary monuments we shall be discussing in Chapter III § ii, has generally been ignored. But it cannot be assumed that a man on a chariot or a hunting scene may not be simply an image of the deceased's social persona in life, through which he is defined as a hunter. Even when a scene can be unambiguously identified as ritual, we cannot be certain that it was represented because it was part of the burial ritual, or whether it was a generic religious scene painted on the sarcophagus in order to provide a generic 'protection', a crystallized act of worship on behalf of the deceased—or even because the deceased was a priest, and the scene articulated his social persona (as well as representing a crystallized act of worship). In Nilsson's view,[82] the Haghia Triada sarcophagus represents acts of worship towards the deified dead. This view is the result of an interpretative operation based on culturally determined assumptions and expectations. He recognized that elements of divine cult were depicted; but because he expected the scenes to be referring directly to the dead he connected the two in the only way that seemed to him logically possible: 'I see only one way out of this dilemma, and that is to suppose that the dead was deified and consequently worshipped in the forms of the divine cult'.[83] I cannot offer a proper reading of the scenes here, I shall only make a few remarks relevant to our investigation.

Nauert[84] has pointed out that certain elements are associated with the cult of a young male god; my own analyses lead me to the conclusion that some other elements are also associated with the young male god who was involved in a ritual I am trying to reconstruct systematically elsewhere.[85] Three offerings are presented

---

[81] It is not legitimate to take Minoan sarcophagi together with the Mycenaean Tanagra sarcophagi; the assumption of unaltered cultural borrowing that this would entail would be in conflict with what we saw about the modalities of religious interaction.

[82] Nilsson 1950: 426–43.

[83] Ibid. 438.

[84] Nauert 1965: 91–8.

[85] *Reading Dumb Images: A Study in Minoan Iconography and Religion* (in preparation). The other elements relating to the ritual nexus in question is the juxtaposition of stepped altar and tree and their combination in the same scene as a boat (cf. the same combination on the Mochlos ring: Sourvinou-Inwood 1973b: 149–58; 1989b: 97–100), and perhaps also as the offerings of cattle—but this is another story.

to the figure usually identified as the dead man, a boat and two heads of cattle, perhaps bulls despite the fact that the penis is omitted.[86] The three males presenting the offerings are very similar to each other. At Haghia Triada itself the boat is associated with the divine cult practised in the cult unit of the Piazzale dei Sacelli.[87] With the same cult unit are associated chariot wheels,[88] fantastic beasts,[89] double axes,[90] horns of consecration,[91] and animals,[92] all elements that appear on the sarcophagus. In my view, the Haghia Triada sarcophagus scenes represent cult practices belonging to the cult of a divinity, almost certainly the young male god who disappeared for part of a year; the bull sacrifice belongs primarily to a divinity cult, the boat is associated with the divinity worshipped at Haghia Triada, the double axe and the horns of consecration are primarily divine symbols. The chariots drawn by griffins and wild goats have been traced in the historical cult of the young dying god Hyakinthos[93]—who is, in my view, one of the Minoan young god's later transformations, and whose cult incorporated some religious elements from the Minoan god's nexus in a modified form. No element can be shown to have a non-divine or a funerary, connection; it is the context that makes the scenes funerary, the fact that they are painted on a sarcophagus. But all this is capable of a more plausible interpretation, that the person shown receiving the offerings is the priest who receives them on behalf of the god. His dress is made of hide, the same material as the skirt of the three men who bring the offerings and one (or perhaps two, the second has minor variations) of the women participating in the ritual. This material is worn by figures with a cult function. In design his dress is a version of the enveloping cloak often worn by men involved in cultic contexts.[94] Neither this type of cloak, nor a garment made of hide are, to my knowledge, ever worn by a male who may be a god. If this is right, the ritual may have been represented on the sarcophagus either because images from divine ritual functioned as

[86] Long (1974: 46) thinks both cattle and boat were models.
[87] Banti 1941–4: 63; 65 fig. 65.
[88] Ibid. 57.
[89] Ibid. 54–6.
[90] Ibid. 58.
[91] Ibid. 58–62.
[92] Ibid. 52–4.
[93] Nauert 1965: 91–8.
[94] On this type of garment cf. Morgan 1988: 93–6.

general protection images, or because this god who disappeared for part of the year and returned (which may have been perceived as a metaphorical death, a metaphor for death) was an appropriate deity for a sarcophagus because the most appropriate protector of the dead; or possibly, the most appropriate deity to look after transitions. It is also possible that the deceased may have been a priest in the cult of this god, and that the representation of the ritual on his sarcophagus combined religious protection with the representation of his social persona.

In any case, and most importantly,[95] whatever the meanings of these images, the link between the mutually sustaining arguments (1) and (2), the deification reading of the Haghia Triada scenes and the interpretation of the 'cult of the royal dead' as entailing deification, can be conclusively proved wrong. For the deification allegedly represented on the sarcophagus cannot be taken to correspond to the practice of cult of the royal dead. For, irrespective of how we interpret the images on the Haghia Triada sarcophagus, the deceased whose sarcophagus this was was not a ruler[96] and did not receive cult of the dead.[97] Thus, these scenes are not the iconographical correlative of the cult offered to the royal dead; the two cannot be put together into a nexus of evidence to support the notion of a deified dead ruler. On the contrary, the association of elements of divine cult with a non-royal funerary context here shows that when such elements are associated with a royal funerary context they must not be assumed to be indicating the divinity facet of the rulers; they may be more plausibly interpreted as indicating a divine cult component in the funerary ritual, probably involving cult offered to divinities connected with death, partly on behalf of the deceased, to obtain these deities' blessings and protection for them, and partly on behalf of the community as a whole. We shall consider briefly in Chapter III § ii.4c the comparable phenomenon of shrines dedicated to deities in archaic cemeteries. Elements of divine cult are also observable in the pre-palatial cult of the community dead out of which the cult of the royal dead had developed. Consequently, any divine cult facet detected in the cult of the royal dead can most plausibly be seen as belonging to, and reflecting, this 'cult addressed to deities' facet associated with the

---

[95] Despite Nilsson's attempts at mental acrobatics (1950: 441–2).
[96] The tomb is unpretentious (Long 1974: 11).
[97] Long 1974: 80.

cult of the dead; it cannot be taken as proof of the divinity of the Minoan rulers. This is also valid for some of the grander manifestations of the cult of the royal dead, such as in the Temple Tomb, a two-storeyed royal tomb at Knossos which combines a burial section and a 'shrine' section.[98]

At the beginning of the palatial period, we saw, began a long process of decline of the practice of cult to the common dead, as this cult became focused on the royal dead. This, and the long period of coexistence of the royal ceremonial with cult of the dead offered to the common dead, provides some support for the view that the cult offered to the royal dead should not be seen as correlative with an alleged divine status, but as one of the ritual practices that went into the making of the nexus of 'social markers' that made up the royal ceremonial that articulated the ideology of Minoan monarchy; that it did not have any implications of divinity, only of grand hierarchical superiority. I do not deny that this differential post-burial behaviour may have had an eschatological correlative. On the contrary, the fact that it (and the other parts of the royal ceremonial) was a social marker and ideological correlative of the differential status of the deceased in life makes it more likely that it was also a social marker and ideological correlative of a perceived differential status of the deceased in afterlife. But (as cross-cultural comparisons confirm) such a differential status can take many different forms; deification is by far the least plausible in the circumstances. Thus, the notion that this correlative is the deification of the Minoan rulers, far from being, as has been assumed, a privileged interpretation that can be taken for granted and become the basis for further hypotheses entirely dependent on its validity, is in fact not an adequate or convincing interpretation of the observable behaviour. But even if we were to suppose for the sake of the argument that the Minoan rulers were indeed believed to become divine after death, it does not follow that their existence can be equated with that of the inhabitants of the Homeric Elysion. For they may have been believed to have joined the gods on their death, or to have become deities in a common Land of the Dead. The

---

[98] Cf. Evans 1935: 962–1018; Platon 1954: 446–7; Long 1959: 60–1. The same interpretation would pertain to other royal graves which are associated with the same phenomenon of cult of the dead associated with elements of divine cult, such as, for example, Arkhanes tholos B (cf. Sakellarakis 1970: 140). I am assuming that Arkhanes is a royal cemetery associated with Knossos.

meanings from the text by means of a series of strategies—for example, at the most elementary level, the selection (or emphasizing), with the help of the context, of one set of meanings rather than another for a given term which carries both.[7] Apart from linguistic competence[8] the writer also shares with his intended audience a fund of general knowledge to which they refer in the process of recreating the meanings he has inscribed. This type of knowledge is encoded in a text by means of 'frames', which refer the reader to a particular segment of encyclopaedic knowledge and invite him to bring it to bear in the decoding and interpretation of the text. 'Frames are cognitive knowledge representations about the "world", which enable us to perform such basic cognitive acts as perception, language comprehension and actions.'[9] There are two types of frames, 'common frames' and 'intertextual frames'. Common frames are representations of a stereotyped situation deriving from, and referring to, general encyclopaedic knowledge including everyday experience, for example, 'school'. Intertextual frames are derived from, and refer the reader to, his fund of 'intertextual knowledge',[10] the knowledge and experience which his reading of other texts has deposited in his mind. This experience cannot be shut out, but the text may or may not signal that it is to be called up and emphasized—positively or negatively.[11] Intertextual knowledge is encoded in the text by means of intertextual frames, such as, for example, genre rules, or thematic topoi, or narrative schemata.[12] The following example will illustrate the way in which frames function and the difference between common and intertextual frames, and between a reader who shares with the author the knowledge from which the frames are derived and one who does not. It is derived from the popular film genre, which is highly codified. Let us take the narrative sequence which shows a woman returning home late at night alone, and going up the stairs while we hear a certain type of music which is always associated (in this genre) with suspense and impending catastrophe. The intertextual

---

[7] Cf. Eco 1981: 19.

[8] Cf. Lyons 1977: ii. 573–89.

[9] Eco 1981: 20–1.

[10] On intertextual knowledge and intertextuality cf. Kristeva 1981: 170; Culler 1981: 12, 38, 100–18; Eco 1981: 21–2, 32; Culler 1975: 139–40.

[11] As when it is 'challenged', when the expectations created by the intertextual knowledge are overturned, subverted, as part of the creation of particular meanings.

[12] Cf. Eco 1981: 21, 32.

frame activated by this sequence leads us to expect that something horrible is going to happen, that, for example, the woman will be attacked, or will discover a dead body. The film will either fulfil these expectations or frustrate them, for example, by having this sequence followed by a comic anticlimax. In either case, the creation of these expectations as part of the readers' strategy is part of the writer's strategy, through which he inscribes certain meanings, a certain foreseen interpretation, into the text which the reader then creates. Eco calls these moves that involve the formulation by the reader of certain predictions on the basis of, and activated by, intertextual frames 'inferential walks'.[13] But this is only valid for readers who possess the intertextual knowledge to formulate these expectations. A reader who does not will read the sequence through common frames, derived from everyday-life experience: a woman returns home late at night and goes up the stairs while somewhere in the house music is playing.[14] An extra-terrestrial in whose world beings can propel themselves vertically through space will not even possess the common frame 'stairs', and will have to try to make sense of the sequence through different strategies, which would include the attempt to make certain deductions which would allow him to understand the action 'going up the stairs'.

Consequently, when we aim at reconstructing the meanings which a text had for its contemporaries, we must first try, as far as possible, to reconstruct its circumstances of production, its historical social and cultural milieu, its function and audience, which will provide the matrix for the reconstruction of the assumptions, the codes, and strategies operated by the writer and the audience he was addressing—including the common and intertextual frames encoding the encyclopaedic and intertextual knowledge of a particular historical moment and social group. Classical scholarship does try to reconstruct the ancient assumptions. But until recently the full implications of the differences in assumptions between the ancients and ourselves had not been fully explored.

The decoding moves that belong to the basic level of reading operations can be said in a very general way to take place in the early stages of the interpretative process, but there is no linear

---

[13] Ibid. 31–3.

[14] As Eco has noted (1981: 22), intertextual frames are more reduced than common ones; the intertextual frame 'the great train robbery' involves fewer actions, characters, and other properties than the common frame 'train robbery'.

progression from one level of operations to another, there is a continuous coming and going between the different levels. Such, for example, is the movement between the identification of intertextual frames and the formulation of predictions and expectations activated by these frames.[15] The fact that the formulation of certain hypotheses concerning higher levels affects the decoding strategies at the lower levels[16] is important. The circumstances of utterance (context) are among the factors shaping the formulation of the presuppositions which direct the decoding operations at the lower level.[17] If we read a text outside its context we are leaving out a set of parameters that would have directed its readings by its ancient contemporaries. Other reading operations[18] are concerned with the selection of the textually relevant semantic properties of each word and concept, so that in each case some of these are stressed and others neutralized;[19] with the reduction of frames and selection of the right frames, and most importantly, with the individuation of the topic or topics, a selection that is procedurally and hierarchically primary, since it directs and governs all the others. The topics are often hidden and have to be recovered by the reader—with or without the help of topic-markers such as titles. At this level also, then, the reader makes certain selections and so extracts/imposes certain organizing structures—structures and selections constantly interact and determine each other. It is thus inevitable that here also readers can make choices different from those that were conceivable for the writer and his contemporaries (that is, from those shaped by the parameters of determination shaped by their shared cultural assumptions) if, approaching the text from a different perspective, they import different priorities and/or assess the 'clues' differently, and thus identify different topics and organize the other semantic disclosures on that basis. This kind of operation illustrates how a fallacious central hypothesis[20] determines the reading of all

---

[15] On forecasts and inferential walks cf. Eco 1981: 31–2.

[16] Cf. ibid. 15.

[17] Cf. ibid. 16. On the importance of the wider context in literary criticism cf. Suleiman 1980: 5. On how context affects interpretation in linguistics cf. Lyons 1981: 201–6, 217–19; cf. also 105–8. On context in linguistics cf. Lyons 1977: ii. 570–635.

[18] Eco groups these operations together under the heading 'semantic disclosures' (Eco 1981: 23–7).

[19] 'Narcotized' is the term used by Eco (ibid.).

[20] Fallacious when one is concerned with the recovery of the original meanings inscribed by the author and read by his contemporaries who shared his assumptions.

the elements which it organizes. A comparable interaction, also involving the potential of contamination from fallacious assessments, takes place between the different 'levels' of the reading operations. At one of the deeper levels the reader compares the world presented in the text—even a fictional text—with the 'real' world of his own experience.[21] Readers approach texts from a personal ideological perspective, with their own ideological bias, even if this is a simple axiological system. This bias determines their perception of the text's ideological structures, whether, for example, certain aspects of its ideology will be discovered or ignored.[22] At a more basic level of ideology, because the ways in which different societies classify the world, perceive, understand and structure it, are culturally determined,[23] the ways in which one perceives, understands, and reacts to, others' classifications inscribed in a text, are also culturally determined.[24]

This brief survey has illuminated some of the mechanics of the cultural determination of reading. A basic modal tendency in the cultural determination of perception is that selections favour and stress the familiar as determined by the perceiver's cultural tradition: the starting point of perception is the established conceptual schemata which organize the sense-data,[25] and this has the effect of focusing attention on the common and familiar elements and understressing the unique and unfamiliar. Thus the tendency is

---

[21] Eco 1981: 17, 37.

[22] Cf. Eco 1981: 22–3; on the role of ideology in reading cf. also Eco 1976: 289–90; Eagleton 1978: 11–43, esp. 20.

[23] Cf. e.g. Douglas 1975: 51–3, 209 (cf. also 203–8, 150–1; Abrams 1971: 65–6; Maranda 1980: 183–204, esp. 187).

[24] Cf. e.g. Boon 1982: 27–46.

[25] Sensory perception is achieved by means of the imposition of organizing patterns which allow us to make sense of the vast numbers of stimuli; these organizing patterns are not bias-free, they are shaped by implicit culturally determined expectations through which we build and test hypotheses and thus perceive, and these operations include filling in missing units so as to recognize the expected 'shape' of things and ignoring others which are there but do not fit the perceiver's assumptions and expectations: Gregory 1966: *passim*, cf. 204–19; cf. esp. 220–8; Douglas 1975: 51; Hebb 1949; 1958; Gombrich 1971: 158; 1982: 28, 272–7, 297; 1977: 76–7, 171–2, 231. Perception is conditioned by cultural habits: Eco 1976: 204–5. Thus, recognition of resemblance between an iconic sign representing a certain object and the object which it represents is frequently based on our knowledge of certain cultural conventions of interpretation (Lyons 1977: i. 102–5; Peirce 1931–3: ii. paras. 276–82; Culler 1981: 24; cf. also Kaplan 1970: 275–6). Perception and artistic expression are determined by pre-existing mental schemata (cf. Gombrich 1977: 76–7, 126, 231), determined by cultural traditions and codes, assumptions and expectations (cf. Gombrich 1977: *passim*, cf. esp. 53–78; 1971: 33–4).

towards standardization, it is to approximate forms to standard types established within the perceiver's tradition.[26]

It is clear, then, that, in order to read an ancient text as nearly as possible in the ways in which it was read by its contemporaries it is necessary to reconstruct the latter's reading operations, for which the first step is to reconstruct the assumptions which formed their perceptual filters, recover their 'horizon of expectations'.[27] The notion that such a reconstruction should be a first step in reading does not imply a simplistic approach to reading. Culler[28] makes a not entirely fair criticism of Jauss when, having remarked that Jauss concentrates on beliefs and commonplaces rather than on interpretative operations, he goes on to observe that 'a reader's response is not simply a process of comparing the statements of a work with his own beliefs or the beliefs of his time'. This is of course correct. But the following considerations should be taken into account—and this touches upon an important aspect of the problem of reading ancient texts. First, as the survey of the reading process has shown, the reconstruction of beliefs and attitudes is a necessary *first* step for any interpretative operation concerning a text produced in a society different from ours, however complex the interaction between on the one hand systems of beliefs and attitudes and on the other text and responses to it. Jauss's procedure may be incomplete,[29] but a concern with systems of belief and attitudes does not imply a simplistic relationship between this system and the text. Indeed, it is only after the referential framework constituted by this system has been reconstructed that the diversity of interpretative operations can be explored. Second, in the absence of information about contemporary reception and interpretation, the (even partial) reconstruction of the cultural assumptions and the horizon of expectations pertaining to the text, though methodologically an incomplete framework for the proper recovery of the

[26] Cf. Gombrich 1977: 72; see also Douglas 1975: 51–2.

[27] The horizon of expectations is 'the set of cultural, ethical and literary (generic, stylistic, thematic) expectations of the work's readers in the historical moment of its appearance' (Suleiman 1980: 35). One particular trend in audience-centred post-structuralist literary theory, Rezeptionsaesthetik, concentrates on the changing horizon of expectations through which a text is received and made sense of, at different times and in different societies. On Rezeptionsaesthetik: cf. esp. Jauss 1974*a*; 1974*b*. Cf. also: Warning 1975: *passim*; Suleiman 1980: 35–7; Culler 1981: 54–8.

[28] Culler (1981: 57–8).

[29] Culler himself (1981: 57) notes that lack of information is probably an important reason for this.

original readings, nevertheless represents a great methodological improvement over its inevitable, default, alternative: the 'timeless' reading, which involves the implicit intromission of assumptions and expectations alien to the writer and his contemporaries and thus conducive to the production of different readings from theirs. The strategy advocated here at least allows us to set in place the basic parameters determining the reception of a text by its contemporaries. Of course, a certain diversity in the horizon of expectations, a kind of multiplication of horizons, rather than one homogeneous one, can be recognized in any period and society, even when the society in question is a simple one.[30] Such distinctions need to be made, especially when what is investigated is the complex meanings of complex texts, but for such a process to be feasible it is necessary to possess adequate information about the contemporary audience with its various segments.

It is a good strategy to focus on the reconstruction of the ways in which a text was made sense of by its contemporaries. For we can reconstruct at least the basic parameters determining this process; while the writer's 'intentions'—however these are defined, at whatever segment of the conscious–unconscious spectrum they are situated—are mostly beyond our grasp. We can (up to a point) reconstruct certain parameters determining the writer's selections—which are part of the set of assumptions the writer shares with his readers and which help determine his reception.[31] This does not belittle the importance of individual creativity: I have set out some of the implications of the fact that creativity is situated within, and shaped by, the parameters of the society's cultural systems through which it operates. In recent years, research in linguistics, anthropology, and the study of mentalities, psychology, and psychoanalysis has eroded the notion of the subject as a controlling consciousness which is the source of meaning, 'decentred

---

[30] Jauss 1974a: 32–3; Suleiman 1980: 32–5, 37. Cf. also Eco 1981: 141. A writer shares with all his contemporaries, the members of his social group in the wider sense (e.g. Englishmen) many of the cultural assumptions through which he produces the text. He shares all, or most, of these only with a more restricted group (e.g. English middle-class male liberal urban intellectual)—the more complex the society, the more restricted the group. Actually, in a very complex and fragmented society such as ours, a writer is likely to be sharing different parts of his horizon of expectations with different groups (in function of, e.g. his educational achievement, political affiliation, religious affiliation, etc.).

[31] Cf. Sourvinou-Inwood (1991: 32–41) for an example of such a reconstruction pertaining to images.

the subject', as the subject's various functions—including the creation of meaning—were seen to operate by means of cultural-semantic systems, structured networks of conventions through which the outside world is perceived, conceptualized, expressed in, and related to through communication.[32] This does not entail that the self actually dissolves into these component cultural systems. Only that these systems mould and shape it and form the parameters determining, among other things, its creativity. We shall see in Chapters II and V that the Homeric epics and other texts, when investigated through a neutral methodology (that does not depend on the validity of the notion that creativity operated within parameters determined by the society's assumptions) will confirm that a poet's selections are not purely 'personal', divorced from collective assumptions—a notion in any case difficult to sustain in the case of the Homeric epics, shaped as they were by parameters determined by collective beliefs and attitudes. The reconstruction of these parameters is partly accessible to us and it is this operation that I consider an appropriate focus for the attempts to read ancient texts through ancient eyes and to recover their attitudes, beliefs, and mentalities.

[32] On the individual as a cultural construct cf. Gluckmann 1949–50. Reality is socially constructed: Douglas 1973 (*passim*, esp. p. 9); for the history of the concept: ibid. 9–13; cf. also Berger and Luckmann 1971: *passim*. On decentring the subject cf. Foucault 1972: 12–14; Derrida 1967: 293–340, cf. esp. 335, 339; 1972: 122–3; Lévi-Strauss 1966: 245–69; Maranda 1980: 184–5, 193; Culler 1981: 31–3; 1979: 174; Bowie 1979: 131–5. In fact, Marx, Freud, and Durkheim had already shown 'that individual experience is made possible by the symbolic systems of collectivities, whether these systems be social ideologies, languages, or structures of the unconscious' (Culler 1981: 26).

II.

Afterlife in the Homeric Poems: Text and Belief[1]

i. Text and Belief

The extent and the ways in which it is legitimate to use literary texts as evidence for ancient beliefs is a problem that needs discussing. As far as religious practices are concerned, the texts must clearly not be treated as though they were documents containing straightforward information which can be simply extracted. For the ancient authors manipulated ritual stuff according to their aims and writing modes, which determined their selections, and thus the ways in which the material out of which the texts were created was shaped. This material sometimes included cultic knowledge functioning as a point of reference, as a given, the manipulations of which were registered by the contemporary audience (in which I am including the notion 'readers'), who shared in that knowledge, as manipulation, distortion, polarization, or reversal. This awareness was part of the process through which meanings were created. For example, exaggeration and polarization are part of the comic mode through which cultic facts are manipulated in Aristophanes. In order to reconstruct the ritual knowledge which underlies, for example, Aristophanes' selections in *Lysistrata* 641–7, where mention is made of the *arrhephoroi* and the Brauronian bears, it is necessary to reconstruct the text's writing modes and aims; these, together with the

[1] Because the bibliography on things Homeric is colossal I have had to be highly selective in citing it. As is the case elsewhere in the book, except in the case of the more significant discussions of a topic or problem (in the sense of discussions that are correct and/or interesting and/or influential, or interestingly wrong, or that demand refutation), in the selection of 'informative references' directing the reader to further discussions, I give preference to the more recent studies, for they also include the earlier bibliography.

context of the passage and its role in the play, provide the parameters for understanding how the information to be reconstructed was manipulated, and thus the parameters for reconstructing the ancient readings, and also (with caution and preferably in combination with other evidence) the ritual knowledge, the shared cultic assumptions which underlie the text. On this passage, my analyses suggested[2] that in *Lysistrata* 641–7 the text keeps within what was ritually possible, while distorting normal custom, through exaggeration and polarization.

Clearly, the same problems and strategies pertain to the reconstruction of beliefs, which, however, is even more difficult, not least because while cult practices were something concrete and determinate, beliefs were—within certain parameters—more fluid and variable, ambiguous, ambivalent, and also perceived to be uncertain, to be ultimately but one set of representations of, and responses to, a divine world which was ultimately unknowable. Thus formulations concerning beliefs must not be read (implicitly) as though they were banal statements. They are articulations of particular perceptions, determined by a variety of factors, including their place and role in the texts, and the nature, conventions and aims of the texts of which they are part. For the latter are not documentary reports or photographic records—and of course these categories of document themselves are not as neutral and 'objective' as it was once assumed; they may be exploring the interstices of established belief and/or giving a particular form to an ambiguous concept—or stressing one facet of an ambivalent one. As we saw in Chapter I, a writer's creativity operates within the parameters of the society's assumptions. In the realm of religious belief too, creativity operates within the parameters of established belief.[3] I hope that the present study will confirm this. It is the reconstruction of these parameters within which poetic creativity operated at a particular time that is partly accessible to us. We can better answer the question 'what are the parameters determining the Homeric articulations of the afterlife?' than 'what exactly did eighth-century Greeks believe about the afterlife?' Greek religion was not crystallized dogma, but an open system, transversed by the fundamental Greek notion of the ultimate unknowability of the divine world,

---

[2] Sourvinou-Inwood 1988: 23–4, 137–48.
[3] Though the precise modalities of the interaction are less unproblematic; cf. e.g. de Mourges 1967: 120, 67; Goldman 1970: 103–4.

so there was great scope for poets to present new representations of the world beyond human experience. Thus, poetry articulated theology and mythology, but of course the versions it offered were not authoritative. Though poets were inspired by the Muses, the Muses also lied.[4] This gives us one of the parameters of determination of the relationship between texts and beliefs. Beliefs were—within certain parameters—fluid and variable, ambiguous, ambivalent, and also perceived to be uncertain; thus it was less problematic for poetry to articulate change. The notion that poetic creativity operates within the parameters of established belief may have seemed to render problematic the generation of change. For what would be the locus of its articulation, given the absence of appropriate vehicles other than poetic texts? On my view, the character of Greek religion enabled changes in Greek eschatology to be articulated in the framework of, and in interaction with, new attitudes (themselves shifting in complex and interactive ways),[5] beginning with, and in, the interstices of established belief. These articulations helped crystallize and develop the beliefs and attitudes they reflected and set off a process of further interaction between beliefs and poetic creativity. This model of possible relationship between texts and beliefs will turn out to correspond to the pattern indicated by the conclusions of the sets of analyses pertaining to eschatology, funerary ideology and behaviour conducted in this book. Since the analyses are independent of this model, and the investigation does not involve model-testing,[6] this convergence provides some support for the validity of both.

The Homeric poems involve an especially complex relationship between texts and beliefs. For they are the end-product of a long tradition of oral poetry which began probably in the Mycenaean, or conceivably in the Early 'Dark Age' period; and the world they describe, its material culture and social institutions, does not have a correlative in a real historical society but is a conflated picture made up of elements derived from many societies,[7] each time inevitably perceived, handled, and made sense of, through the perceptual filters of each generation of poets. They were thus manipulated and

---

[4] Cf. Hes. *Theog.* 27–8.
[5] Cf. on this Ch. IV.
[6] On the methodological fallacies of which cf. Appendix.
[7] Cf. Gray 1947: 109–21; 1954: 1–15; Snodgrass 1974: 114–25; Sherratt 1990: 807–24.

combined to create this stratified picture over the centuries during which the epic material was expanded, compressed, and modified by the successive generations of bards. My position concerning the date and circumstances of production of the *Iliad* and the *Odyssey* is that they were given their final form, a form which is substantially that in which we know them, and perhaps written down, in the eighth century in Ionia. Whether they were composed by one poet or two, the two final-version poems are intimately connected and are the products of the same cultural environment. I shall be referring to their creator(s) as 'Homer'. As we shall see, the Homeric 'system' of afterlife beliefs, like the other Homeric 'systems', is conflated and artificial: a composite eschatology made up of elements which had originated in different historical societies; these were perceived, and channelled through, the viewpoint of the poet's own funerary ideology and religious–mythological mentality, which provided the matrices for both the understanding, and the reshaping and elaboration, of the traditional material which Homer deployed. In this chapter I will consider Homeric eschatology as one system, with a separate consideration of *Odyssey* 24. In Chapter V below I will consider various later articulations of the journey to Hades up to, and including, the fifth century. I shall examine its pattern of appearance and attempt to determine its implication if it is taken at face value, if we assume, as a working hypothesis, that it is a more or less accurate reflection of the ancient realities. The alternative hypothesis, formulated by several scholars with regard to one of the mythological figures involved in this journey, Charon, is that that pattern is deceptive, that it reflects only one part of the picture, the rest of which was suppressed. Thus, for example, Alexiou has recently revived the view that Charon was an old popular god, a pre-Olympian death-god as she puts it, who was neglected in the Olympian pantheon.[8] There are, we shall see, many arguments against her thesis; but what concerns us here is that this is a recent reformulation of the notion that Charon 'must have been' older than Homer, and that Homer simply 'leaves him out'. There is no evidence whatsoever in favour of such hypotheses, which are simply projections of what appears to some scholars to be the 'logical' way of making sense of fragmentary data—a perception inevitably dependent on culturally determined implicit assumptions. I will try

---

[8] Cf. Ch. V. § iv below.

to show that the pattern of appearance of the beliefs under discussion in the extant texts corresponds to the beliefs of the texts' period of production; and also that it makes excellent sense in the context of other developments in funerary ideology and behaviour: that the changes that are detected when this pattern is taken at face value correspond to similar changes in the wider nexus to which these beliefs belong and can thus be seen as one facet of a complex development. If this is right, the poet's selections do provide valid evidence for the study of belief and are not purely 'personal' selections unaffected by contemporary collective representations—a notion in any case difficult to sustain in the case of the Homeric poems; they were determined by the parameters of the collective beliefs and attitudes. This does not exclude innovations, new articulations; on the contrary. But such new articulations were not arbitrarily created, in one man's creative vacuum; they were shaped by the parameters of existing belief in interaction with the shifting representations; this interactive (shifting) ideological nexus created the parameters within which old and new articulations of belief in literary texts took place.

There are in the Homeric epics broadly two types of reference to what is believed to happen after death. First, random and brief references throughout the epics—some of which are crystallized into formulae—which articulate, and are articulated by, perceptions that need to be recovered and taken account of in the consideration of Homeric eschatology. And second, segments of the text which are either located in the world of the dead or involve some contact with that world. Because of the nature of my enterprise and the nature of the evidence, which in combination generate both goals and constraints, my investigation will have two foci, of unequal length: the general picture of the situation in the two epics as a whole;[9] and certain segments of the poems, namely the whole of *Odyssey* 11, *Iliad* 23. 65–101, and *Odyssey* 4. 561–9, which are especially relevant to our investigation, and which shall be considered in some detail. *Odyssey* 24 will also be considered, in a separate section, since I consider it to be the work of a Continuator in the archaic period—a question that will be further discussed in that section.

Odysseus' narration in Phaeacia from the beginning of book 9

[9] Excluding *Od.* 24.

to the end of 12 is what in narratological terms[10] is called a character-text, a text presented by a character in the narrative rather than by the primary, external narrator and focalizer;[11] the character presenting the text—here Odysseus—functions as a secondary, internal, narrator and focalizer. This secondary, internal, narrator/focalizer may, and in the case of the text under consideration frequently does, embed in his character-text the speech of another character, who thus functions as a tertiary narrator/focalizer. This character-text that is Odysseus' narration in Phaeacia from the beginning of book 9 to the end of 12 is an external *analepsis*,[12] a flashback outside the time span of the primary fabula, that is of the chronological series of events caused or experienced by the characters in the narrative.[13] The whole of the Nekyia is part of this long external *analepsis*; it is presented and focalized not by the primary narrator (that is, the 'author's fictional delegate in the text'[14]) but by the poem's main character Odysseus. The primary narrator only reports on his own authority that Odysseus said all this; the question of the veracity of the tale is left open and ambiguous.[15] The narrator of the Homeric poems that is Homer's constructed voice does not tell us that the Underworld is like this and that Odysseus went there. He tells us that this is what Odysseus told the Phaeacians.

Since Hades is the unseeable place, it must not be assumed that this distancing between the poet and his articulation of the Land of the Dead is without significance. It is possible that it was only obliquely and through the voice of a character to whom the narrator does not lend his authority in guaranteeing the truth of what is said that the terrible unseeable realm of death can be verbally articulated in the epics. Certainly, we find this same modality of presentation in the description of the circumstances of Patroklos' shade and its attempts to enter Hades in *Iliad* 23. 65 ff.: they are also articulated in a character text in which Patroklos is the secondary narrator/focalizer. Of course, Patroklos is a shade, albeit an unburied

---

[10] Cf. e.g. De Jong 1987: 37.

[11] On the notion of focalizer cf. De Jong 1987: pp. xiv, 31–6.

[12] Cf. on *analepses* De Jong 1987: 81–4, and esp. on external *analepses* in a character-text pp. 160–8.

[13] On the fabula cf. De Jong 1987: pp. xiv, 31–2, 35.

[14] Cf. on this question De Jong 1987: 29–30, 32.

[15] On the status of this narration and the fact that its authority (its status as true or false) is ambiguous, not marked cf. also Goldhill 1991: 54–6.

one who could move about in the upper world, and we have it on
the narrator's authority that he appeared to Achilles and said these
things—as we have it elsewhere that people go to Hades. But what
Hades is really like, and what the shades are like after they were
buried and they joined the community of the dead we only have
obliquely. In the *Odyssey* the first description of the Underworld[16]
is in a speech embedded in the character text that is Odysseus'
narration, a speech by Circe the supernatural witch who is thus a
tertiary narrator/focalizer. The Phaeacians, then, first hear about
Hades from a double distance that would generate a matrix of
reception on the lines: 'This is what he is telling us she told him he
would find; who knows if it is true?' Then the distancing is somewhat reduced in that Hades is then presented as Odysseus' experience—with the ambiguous authority mentioned above. Menelaos'
narration in *Odyssey* 4. 332–592 is a minor version of Odysseus'
narration, a character-text in which the (internal secondary)
narrator/focalizer is Menelaos; in this case it is not the unseeable,
but the alternative to the unseeable, Elysion, the notion, in the
form of a prophecy, that Menelaos will go to Elysion, that is
articulated in an embedded speech, Proteus', who is thus a tertiary
narrator/focalizer.

Thus it is possible that in the epic tradition, the poets' parameters
of selection determined that the unseeable realm of death was
articulated only obliquely and without the narrator's authority,
leaving the question of authority open, presenting the articulation
as a possibility. And that it is only after this Homeric articulation
became familiar and ultimately acquired a certain amount of authority or at least prestige, and became involved in an interaction with
religious beliefs, came to provide a filter that helped crystallize and
partly shape such beliefs, that the notion of articulating the unseeable realm became commonplace and so the parameters of selection
altered, and the primary external narrator could choose to describe
the Underworld in his own voice.[17]

---

[16] *Od.* 10. 507–38.

[17] This fits the situation in *Od.* 24. 1 ff. The fact that in *Od.* 24. 1 ff. the descent of the
shades to Hades is presented by the primary narrator is one of the many ways in which this
book is at odds with normal Homeric usage, a strong cumulative case which, we shall see,
leaves no doubt as to the inauthenticity of the present ending of the *Odyssey.* The Continuator
would not have taken pains to imitate the Homeric epics in this respect because, once the
distinction lost its importance, it would not have registered as significant to the (Continuator)
reader or indeed his audience.

ii. Death and the World of the Dead in Homer

1. INTRODUCTION

The consideration of the texts themselves, of Greek eschatology in general, and of afterlife beliefs and funerary attitudes cross-culturally, suggest that the following are important questions to be explored in the investigation of Homeric funerary ideology and eschatology. First, mortality and immortality: does everyone die or do some people escape death? Is there what one may call a consistent picture on this throughout the epics? Second, what happens at death and where does what survives of the dead person go after death and how do they get there? What is the nature of this Land of the Dead, and where is it located? Is the image consistent throughout the epics? Third, the destiny of the shades: is it a collective destiny, the same for all the shades, or are there differentiations such as rewards and punishments, depending on conduct in life? Is the image consistent throughout the epics? Finally, what is the nature of the shades and of existence in the Land of the Dead? Is the image consistent throughout the epics?

2. MORTALITY AND IMMORTALITY: ELYSION AND OTHER STORIES

(a) *Mortality and Immortality*

'All men must die' is a constant motif in the epics.[18] In *Odyssey* 3. 236–8 the disguised Athena tells Telemachos that 'death is common to all men, and not even the gods can keep it off a man they love, when the portion of death which brings long woe destroys him'. Everybody dies and goes to Hades, even the children of the gods, even the great Herakles.[19] This is a central tenet of mainstream Homeric eschatology in all its strands. But there is also a very thin layer of belief, not integrated within the remaining funerary ideology, according to which a few select people connected with the gods escape death and gain some sort of immortality. Menelaos, who is Zeus' son-in-law, will go to a paradise with ideal weather,

---

[18] Cf. *Il.* 18. 115–19; *Od.* 3. 236–8.
[19] *Il.* 18. 117–19.

the Elysian fields at the ends of the earth.[20] The Dioscuri were given a kind of eternal life on alternating days.[21] These are the first signs of a divergence from the inescapable fate of death; in the archaic period this divergent trend will grow and develop into an important new eschatological strand that will provide the common man with a model of hope for a better life after death. Already in Hesiod the theme of paradise is more developed than in Homer. Part of the 'heroic' race which included the Homeric heroes went to the Islands of the Blest, a paradise where the earth produces crops three times a year.[22]

The image I have just presented radically challenges a notion often taken for granted in modern scholarship, that Elysion is of Minoan origin. I shall investigate the concept of Elysion and attempt to determine the status of this hypothesis.

(b) *Introduction to Elysion*

I begin with a recent restatement of that theory, which can serve as a preliminary introduction to our investigation. Edwards states[23] that the notion of a Land of the Blessed for the select few 'is generally agreed to go back at least to Minoan/Mycenaean times'. He adds[24] that Nilsson's discussions are 'still fundamental to discussion of this problem'. I shall consider Nilsson's arguments in a moment. As for the notion (implicit in Edwards' formulation) that general agreement among scholars in a particular cultural period constitutes in itself an argument for the validity of the thesis, its persuasive power has been seriously undermined by our understanding of the cultural determination of perception and reception, which shows how a theory that has convinced everyone and may be wrong gives a false picture of the ancient realities. Once the investigation of scarce data has become structured and centred through a theory that has gained general acceptance, the data can be fitted around it and appear to make logical sense, even when in

---

[20] *Od.* 4. 561–5.
[21] *Od.* 11. 300–4. A third case, Calypso's promise of immortality to Odysseus is mentioned in a part of the *Odyssey* (23. 333–6) which is almost certainly post-Homeric (cf on this question below, § iii.1); but of course, even if it were Homeric, the main argument here is not affected.
[22] *Works and Days*, 157–69.
[23] Edwards 1985: 218.
[24] Ibid. 218 n. 9.

fact the discourse has radically falsified the ancient realities.[25] It is thus methodologically dangerous to allow a cast of mind centred (unconsciously) on the implicit assumption that the discourse of earlier scholarship is right unless it is conclusively and beyond doubt proved to be wrong. Because very few things can be conclusively and beyond doubt proved to be wrong in this area of investigation, this cast of mind privileges the established discourse —despite the methodological shortcomings and the much more limited data that had been involved in its generation. Edwards' notion of a Land of the Blessed for the select few 'going back to the Minoan/Mycenaean period' is, we shall now see, dependent on fundamental misconceptions about the nature of religion and religious development, to which I now turn.[26]

The investigation of the relationship between Bronze-Age and historical Greek religion is often centred on the notion of 'continuity': the question is asked, whether or not there is continuity between the two. But this notion is not precise and can be a source of confusion. There is the risk that a vague—and correct—notion that not all the elements of Minoan religion had disappeared and been totally forgotten by the historical Greek period, may slide into a notion of continuity in the religious system which would legitimately allow the projection of Greek data back into the Bronze Age to illuminate Minoan religion. Thus continuity in one part of the religious systems, for example in the use of a few cult-places, or the presence of names of Greek deities in the Linear B tablets, has sometimes (implicitly or explicitly) been thought to sanction the introduction of Greek evidence in the study of Minoan or Mycenaean religion. The basic assumption on which this approach (implicitly) relies is that the presence of an element belonging to a certain religious nexus is an index denoting the presence of the whole nexus; that, for example, the presence of a Greek divine name in the Linear B tablets of Knossos entails that the deity's whole divine personality as it is known from historical Greece were part of her divine personality in Mycenaean Knossos; or that continuity in the use of a cult-place entails that cult-practices and

---

[25] Cf. also Appendix.

[26] I discuss this question, and its implications for the study of Greek religion, elsewhere (*Mutant in the Shadow: Religion in the Greek 'Dark Ages'* (in preparation)); cf. also very briefly my review of B. C. Dietrich, *Tradition in Greek Religion*, in *CR* 39 (1989), 51–8.

beliefs, the whole religious system associated with that cult-place, and, by extension, the whole religious system of which the cult-place is a part, have remained unchanged. As we shall see, this assumption and the related assumptions it generates is demonstrably wrong. Some scholars who use data from historical Greek religion in their study of Bronze-Age religion do acknowledge that changes and developments have taken place, but do not draw the correct implications. For they assume the change to be of a simple, unilinear type, such as, for example, the simple addition of oriental elements; while in reality such changes are extremely complex. They also assume that it is possible to 'cut through' the later developments and recover the original form. This assumption depends both on the presumption of simple changes and on the implicit refusal to acknowledge that the researcher's assumptions about organization patterns and logical operations deployed in the course of the analysis, which appear 'logical', are in fact inevitably culturally determined and thus lead to the creation of a cultural construct, rather than an accurate reconstruction of the ancient process of change. Even if the likelihood of such a distortion were not so well established, the mere fact that the possibility exists at all entails that it is unsound to adopt an approach that is so vulnerable to corruption. It is necessary to opt for a methodology which is, as far as possible, bias-free, and certainly one which is not dependent on the validity of prior assumptions, and thus excessively vulnerable to distortion. This is what I have tried to do here; in addition, in order to have some sort of control, I shall be cross-checking the conclusions of my empirical analyses against those resulting from the consideration of the interactions between the general modalities of religious development and change and the historical circumstances in the relevant societies, which will be conducted separately, and to which I now turn.

(c) *The Modalities of Religious Development and Interaction*

There are some fundamental characteristics pertaining to the nature of religion that seem to be universal, and they entail certain general tendencies in the nature of religious development and change. Their consideration can allow us to recover the basic parameters governing such processes.

A fundamental characteristic of religion, as of all other facets of

society's culture,[27] is that it forms a structured, articulated system of interacting elements, each of which is defined by its relationship to the others. Cultural artefacts, including texts, myths, rituals, and whole religious systems, are articulated systems of interdependent elements, each of which acquires value through the networks of relationships of association and opposition in which they are implicated. No element (no belief or cult act, no deity or facet of a deity's personality) has a fixed value which remains unchanged whatever the context. Each is defined by, and acquires meaning through, its relationships with the other elements of the system to which it belongs: first, its relationships with the other elements which make up the nexus of which it is part (for example, the whole ritual, when the element under consideration is a ritual act or gesture; the pantheon, when the element considered is a deity); and second, each element is ascribed value through its relationships to the overall religious system of which element and nexus are part.[28] Another important characteristic of religion is that it interlocks and interacts with the other facets of the worshipping community's life. That is, a religious system and its component elements are also shaped and ascribed values through their relationships to the other systems (social, economic, political, ecological, and ideological other than religious) which make up the community's world-system. I should make clear that I am speaking of a complex and open world-system, in which are also inscribed the interactions with other systems, other societies. The notion that religion must not be studied in isolation, for it is one of the interacting systems that make up a society's world-system, is generally acceptable to all schools of social anthropology and social history.[29]

In these circumstances, it becomes clear that when one or more elements in the system change, all the other elements are affected.[30]

---

[27] On culture and its relationship to the social system cf. Boon 1982: 112–15, 138–41, 232–3; Sahlins 1976: p. vii. On religion as a cultural system cf. Geertz 1966: 1–46 (cf. esp. 4).

[28] The semiological principle just stated is now a generally accepted maxim, shared by all schools of thought concerned with symbolic, cultural or communication analyses (cf. Boon 1982: 249).

[29] See below, 'A Note on "Systems"'.

[30] Renfrew (1982: 10–1) rightly notes that many systems models in archaeology (of which the model of religious change proposed here can be said to be a generalized version of universal validity) are not clear-cut, not rigorously and precisely articulated, and depend on assumptions about systems behaviour. This is especially true here, where the model of religion and religious change is presented in the most generalized and vague terms. But this does not matter in our case. For I am not concerned with mapping out and explaining the

Thus, when the circumstances (and thus the other systems) of the worshipping group change, especially when they change significantly, as in the case under consideration, the religious system is affected in manifold ways and it changes[31] in response to new needs.[32] These changes, in their turn, generate new changes and adjustments, so that the religious system is in a state of flux before it reaches relative stabilization after the new realities and structures have become established in their main lines.[33] It should not be imagined that certain needs, such as the need for food and fertility of the earth, are so basic that they remain constant, and that the relevant religious representations and practices remain unchanged. For all needs, however basic, manifest themselves in culturally determined forms, are established and changed by social processes;[34] they are 'preferred choices within a cultural matrix'.[35] Even what seems to be simple survival is symbolic.[36] Since even basic needs manifest themselves in culturally determined forms, mediated by society, its systems of production, its institutions and representations—and it is, of course, in these mediated, culturally determined forms that they are involved in, and interact with, the

change—except in the most rudimentary and imprecise manner. My project is much less ambitious: I am trying to determine whether religious change is likely to have taken place in Crete between the Neopalatial and the historical Greek period; and if it did, what would its modalities have been in their very basic lines—for the purposes of proposing some very basic lines concerning the relationship between Minoan and historical Cretan religion.

[31] Renfrew (1972: 24) notes that the fact that different aspects of a culture are interrelated does not mean that changes in one subsystem (I prefer the term 'system') must necessarily produce changes in all the others. However, while this is true for minor changes whose effects can be overcome, it is not valid for major and sustained 'disturbances' causing drastic changes, of the type involved here (cf. op. cit. 25). Moreover, the intimate relationship between the religious and the other systems of society creates a special situation in which the religious system is particularly sensitive to changes elsewhere, and, I believe, is modified in response to new needs as it enters into play as an important part of the homeostatic controls preserving equilibrium. (Cf. e.g. the role of the Delphic oracle in the changing 8th-cent. and archaic Greek society.)

[32] For a definition of the concept of need in this context cf. Boon 1982: 85–7, 112–14; Hallpike 1979: 483; Hodder 1982b: 4. Cf. also Spiro 1966: 107–8.

[33] I have tried to show elsewhere (Sourvinou-Inwood 1991: 148–9) how the historical developments from the end of the Mycenaean period onwards affected esp. the shaping of Greek divine personalities in ways that created diversities between the panthea of the different cities.

[34] Cf. Hallpike 1979: 483.

[35] Cf. Hodder 1982b: 4.

[36] Cf. Boon 1982: 85–7, who mentions the wearing of coats, which is not determined by the survival need to preserve body heat *per se*: that need is culturally mediated and the wearing of coats is one particular culturally determined response to that need.

religious system—it follows that when the social and cultural system changes, so do the (forms of the) needs, and that includes the 'basic' needs, of the group. It would be equally misguided to claim that the fact that the physical environment was the same in Minoan, Dark Age, and historical Crete entails considerable continuity and stability in the human responses to the environment, and thus also in certain areas of the religious system. For the physical environment is not 'inert', it is not a stable unchanging reality independent of men; on the contrary, it is capable of being transformed by human action, and the collective representations in which it is implicated (including those implicated in the religious system), and the responses elicited by it, are dependent on the understanding and actions of men. It is not the case that the environment itself determines the representations.[37]

Since the different parts of the religious system are interdependent, and are defined through their relationships, we cannot have 'the same' element forming part of different religious systems. For if the context which defines it and ascribes it meaning has changed, the element is no longer 'the same'. Thus, we cannot have 'the same' deity belonging to different panthea, since a deity is neither a real person nor an 'essence' which remains unchanged; she is a construct, shaped by the societies which worship her and developing with those societies, and shaped also by her relationships of association and differentiation to the other deities of the pantheon to which she belongs.[38] Thus, changes in the circumstances of the community bring about changes in the deities' personalities. The same is true for all the elements of the religious system. Even if, for example, a particular cult practice appears superficially—and to the extent to which it is possible to judge in our circumstances of limited access—to have remained 'the same' through a period of change of the type referred to here, in fact it is not, and cannot be, the same. For its meanings and functions have inevitably changed as a result of the fact that it is now part of a different cultic—and generally religious—nexus, and is defined by different elements and serving changed needs in a different type of society. Still less does the presence of such an element prove that the whole nexus to which that element belongs had existed in this—or indeed in any

[37] Cf. e.g. Hallpike 1979: 482–3.
[38] Cf. Sourvinou-Inwood 1991: 147–88.

other—form in the Minoan period. That this is always the case, and that this fact has important methodological implications, will become clear when we consider the modality of religious change. I have spoken of the factors which stimulate and set in motion change in the religious system. They, and the motion towards change, represent one of the tendencies operating in the course of religious development. The other is conservatism, a force of inertia operating within all systems and within the religious system especially. Religious development is governed and shaped by the tension between these two tendencies.[39] The particular form which this tension takes, and its outcome, that is, the ways and directions in which they shape the developments, differ in the individual cases, depending on the particular circumstances. Thus, depending on the circumstances, new elements may be introduced—though modalities of introduction involving great complexity;[40] but the existing elements, the 'building blocks' of the system, are not (generally) discarded. They remain within that system, though they can be displaced, for example pushed to the periphery; but they are reshaped and/or reinterpreted; for they acquire new values in response to the new needs and realities—including the need for adjustments created by these ongoing changes within the religious system.[41] Religious change, then, takes place through a process of 'bricolage',[42] in which beliefs and practices (such as myths or parts of myths, rituals or fragments of rituals) that had belonged to the earlier system are, to a greater or lesser extent, displaced, reshaped, and reinterpreted.[43] This bricolage modality characterizes also the interaction between different religious systems, which is relevant to Minoan/Mycenaean interaction, especially in Crete after the Mycenaean conquest, and also to a series of subsequent interactions

[39] Cf. e.g. a contemporary example of continuity and change in a religious system in a period of dramatic political and social upheavals and also in interaction with another (the Christian) religious system: Duru 1983: 1–9.

[40] For the complexity of the modalities of introduction of new elements cf. e.g. Carless Hulin 1989: 90–6.

[41] For some historical Greek examples of such developments and changes illustrating these complex processes of graftings and reshapings of earlier religious material cf. the initiation rites of many Greek cities which became integrated in festive rituals forming part of divine cults and lost their profane significance in social organization (Brelich 1969: *passim*).

[42] On 'bricolage' cf. Lévi-Strauss, esp. Lévi-Strauss 1966: 16–36. Cf. also Douglas 1975: 170. Derrida discusses critically Lévi-Strauss's concept of bricolage and points out that all discourse is 'bricoleur' (1967: 418–21).

[43] Cf. also Brelich 1967: 11.

CONTENTS

PLATES

ABBREVIATIONS

ABL   C. H. Haspels, *Attic Black-Figure Lekythoi* (Paris 1936).
ABV   J. D. Beazley, *Attic Black-Figure Vase-Painters* (Oxford 1956).
ARV   J. D. Beazley, *Attic Red-Figure Vase-Painters*, 2nd edn. (Oxford 1963).
Add.   *Beazley Addenda. Additional References to ABV, ARV²* and *Paralipomena*, 2nd edn., compiled by T. H. Carpenter (Oxford 1989).
EGF   M. Davies (ed.), *Epicorum Graecorum Fragmenta* (Göttingen 1988).
GAAI   *Greek Art of the Aegean Islands* (The Metropolitan Museum of Art, New York, 1979).
GV   W. Peek, *Griechische Vers-Inschriften* I (Berlin 1955).
LSCG   F. Sokolowski, *Lois sacrées des cités grecques* (Paris 1969).
MusTar.   *Il Museo di Taranto. Cento anni di archeologia* (Taras 1988).
PEG   *Poetarum Epicorum Graecorum Testimonia et Fragmenta*, ed. A. Bernabe, Pars I (Leipzig 1987).
PMG   D. L. Page (ed.), *Poetae Melici Graeci* (Oxford 1962).
SEG   *Supplementum Epigraphicum Graecum*
SIG³   G. Dittenberger, *Sylloge Inscriptionum Graecarum³* (Leipzig 1915–24).
TrGF   i. B. Snell (ed.), *Tragicorum Graecorum Fragmenta*, vol. i. Didascaliae Tragicae, Catalogi Tragicorum et Tragoediarum Testimonia et Fragmenta Tragicorum Minorum (Göttingen 1971).
TrGF   ii. R. D. Kannicht and B. Snell (eds.), *Tragicorum Graecorum, Fragmenta*, vol. ii. Fragmenta Adespota. Testimonia volumini i. Addenda Indices ad volumina i et ii (Göttingen 1981).
TrGF   iii. S. Radt (ed.), *Tragicorum Graecorum Fragmenta*, vol. iii. Aeschylus (Göttingen 1985).
TrGF   iv. S. Radt (ed.), *Tragicorum Graecorum Fragmenta*, vol. iv. Sophocles (Göttingen 1977).

I.

Reading the Greek Discourse of Death.
Reading Ancient Texts

This book consists of a series of investigations into Greek collective attitudes and behaviour towards, and beliefs about, death and the dead, and also into images and texts pertaining to death. The investigations are independent of each other but also complementary; they contribute to the exploration of some important facets of the Greek death discourse. They are placed in a historical perspective and the question of change in the different facets of the death discourse in the course of time is neither *a priori* assumed nor rejected, it is investigated through as neutral a methodology as possible. Each investigation examines in depth the different types of data that can be brought to bear on each question in their own right (not one set as an appendix to the other), and according to the methodologies that are appropriate in each case. Indeed the methodologies for reading the Greek discourse of death, which involves the reading of texts, images, and archaeological evidence and also the interrelation of these readings, is another major focus of the book, as part of the wider Problematik pertaining to the reconstruction of a culture and its mentalities. I have discussed elsewhere[1] the Problematik of the 'reading' of Greek culture and its various cultural artefacts, and the methodologies capable of allowing us—in so far as this is possible—to read ancient texts through the eyes of their contemporary readers. Here I will elaborate a little on the reading of texts in order to provide the theoretical framework for the readings of the Homeric epics and of the epitaphs set out in Chapters II and III. Some aspects of this discussion will also highlight the process of making sense of data in general, and this

---

[1] Sourvinou-Inwood 1991: 3–23.

will also provide a background for the methodological discussion in the Appendix. In Chapter VI I shall set out three reading stories pertaining to the interpretation of a problematic inscription, which will, I hope, illustrate and confirm the validity of this framework. The intuitive ideal of reading ancient texts through ancient eyes underlies implicitly most classical scholarship. But it is only in recent years that the question of how our readings may differ from those of the texts' contemporaries has been explicitly debated, and the implications of the culturally determined nature of perception and understanding been focused upon, in the context of a wider concern with reading:[2] diverse studies in literary theory and semiotics have focused in different ways on reading and the reader, and the operations by means of which the latter receives, structures, and makes sense of, the text.[3] Many of the diverse approaches adopted by the various studies in reader-oriented literary criticism are not in conflict with one another but are complementary: 'The vitality of audience-oriented criticism depends precisely on the realization that various dimensions of analysis or interpretation are possible, and that a combination of approaches is not a negative eclecticism but a positive necessity', unless there are incompatibilities in the theoretical assumptions of the approaches involved.[4] I have argued elsewhere[5] that it is possible to construct methodologies capable of allowing us—within the limits of the possible—to read the ancient texts through the eyes, the perceptual filters, of their contemporary readers. The first step involves the reconstruction of the ancient filters through the systematic recovery of the relevant ancient assumptions. I will now consider briefly the process through which readers make sense of texts,[6] which will illustrate some of the modalities through which cultural assumptions determine reading.

A writer inscribes meanings through codes, which he shares with the audience he is addressing; the most fundamental of these is the basic dictionary. The reader activates these codes and extracts

---

[2] I have discussed these matters, with bibliog.: cf. Sourvinou-Inwood 1991: 3–23; also 1989a: 134–6; 1990a: 12–14.
[3] Cf. a survey in Suleiman 1980: 3–45; Culler 1981: *passim*, esp. 54, 121, cf. also 12; 1983: *passim*; Jauss (1974a: 23–4).
[4] Suleiman 1980: 7.
[5] Cf. above, n. 3.
[6] On text as communication, and on the processes by means of which readers read texts: Eco 1981: 3–43. For a model of the process of reading of a text cf. ibid. 14 fig. 0.3 (and cf. pp. 11–32). In the exposé of reading that follows I am following (substantially) Eco's account.

The bibliography is large because the book covers not only a variety of topics, but also different aspects of Greek death, and thus Greek culture in general, demanding detailed discussion of different types of evidence—literary, epigraphical, archaeological, iconographical. Given the very great pressures of space, the fact that the bibliography on some of the topics covered is colossal (e.g. on Ch. II) has meant that I have had to be highly selective in citing it. Except in the case of the more significant discussions of any given topic or problem (in the sense of discussions that are correct and/or interesting, informative and/or influential, or interestingly wrong, or that demand refutation), in the selection of 'informative references' directing the reader to further discussions of the topic in question, I give preference to the more recent studies, which also include the earlier bibliography.

For the illustrations I am very grateful to the following: for the photographs on Pls. 2, 4–7, and 9–10 to Mrs O. Tzachou-Alexandri, Director of the National Archaeological Museum, Athens, and to Dr K. Demakopoulou; for those on Pls. 3 and 8 to the German Archaeological Institute, Athens, and Mrs N. Lazaridou; for the photograph on Pl. 1 to Mrs Z. Karapa-Malizani and the Epigraphical Museum, Athens, and for that on Pl. 11 to Mr M. Vickers and the Visitors of the Ashmolean Museum, Oxford.

PREFACE

This book has been a long time in the writing. A first draft had been completed before the publication of Hansen (1983) even, let alone Hansen (1989) and the availability of *Ibycus*. In the course of these years many scholars have been kind enough to discuss various problems with me. I cannot record my gratitude to all, though some are mentioned in the appropriate places, so I shall single out Professor D. M. Lewis who has repeatedly discussed many questions with me and offered unstinting help. Dr P. A. Hansen has also kindly discussed epigrammatical questions with me, while Professor Ian Rutherford has discussed especially questions pertaining to *chairein*. I am especially grateful to Professor Anna Morpurgo Davies who not only discussed many problems pertaining to the Teithronion epigram with me, but also helped me with the composition and articulation of Chapter VI § ii.1e *'oude thanonta*: Readings and Meanings'. For the Appendix I am grateful to Professor R. Hägg who discussed at great length several relevant questions and read a draft of it, and to Professor I. Malkin who also read a draft and made useful suggestions. Dr C. B. R. Pelling kindly read a draft of some sections and made useful suggestions. To him and to Dr Robert Parker I am also very grateful for advice pertaining to structuring, as well as for many useful discussions. To Professor Martin Robertson I am very grateful for his long-standing and unfailing help and encouragement. I am also very grateful to Hilary O'Shea, Senior Classics Editor at Oxford University Press, for help far beyond the call of duty.

Shorter versions of some parts of the book formed the basis of several different lectures and papers delivered in Oxford, Cambridge, London, Paris, Tours, and Athens. A much-abridged and differently structured version of some parts of Chapter V § ii was published in French as an article entitled 'Images grecques de la mort: représentations, imaginaire, histoire', in *Archeologia e storia antica. Annali. Istituto Universitario Orientale. Napoli.* Dipartmento del mondo classico e del mediterraneo antico 9 (1987: 145–58).

To the memory of my mother
Ersi Vellianitou Sourvinou
and of my father
Spyridon Sourvinos

notion of a paradise exclusively for rulers would be only one option, and one that would not sit well with the notion of deification. Nilsson seems aware of this disjunction, for he tries to salvage his theory by separating the apotheosis of the rulers from the concept of paradise and having recourse to the notion of compatibility. He thought that the Minoan Land of the Dead was a 'Land of Bliss'[99] because the latter would be consistent with the belief in the apotheosis of rulers while it would be inconsistent with the Greek perceptions of Hades.[100]

In fact, all that the evidence allows us to determine about Minoan eschatology is that rulers probably had a differential, privileged, position in the afterlife. Also, the offering of cult of the dead and its pattern of development into a cult of the royal dead indicates that the nature of the shades was not felt to be incompatible with such offerings. The association of first cult of the dead and then cult of the royal dead with divine cult may confirm this by indicating that the nature of the afterlife was such that the protection of the appropriate deities was desirable. But this does not necessarily follow, as other explanations of this association are also possible.

One reason for the survival of the theory that Minoan rulers were deified and that this supports the view that Elysion originated in Minoan Crete is that it has been combined with another nexus of hypotheses which has been taken to provide further support for the Minoan origin of Elysion. The fact that model boats were found in a few Cretan graves has been taken to mean that they were offered to the dead to transport them to Elysion, a paradise beyond the sea.[101] This, it is claimed, is confirmed by the fact that a boat is offered to the deceased on the Haghia Triada sarcophagus.[102] As we saw, there are good reasons for thinking that the latter does not represent offerings to the deceased. But even if we were to accept that the man in front of the building was a dead person, it would

---

[99] Cf. Nilsson 1950: 625.

[100] I am leaving aside all discussion of possible Egyptian parallels. Even when such parallels are real, cultural interaction is a much more complex phenomenon than is assumed in discussions such as Nilsson's (1950: 625-7); the Minoans, we know, borrowed Egyptian forms and adapted them to fit their own systems, with radically changed meanings (cf. e.g. Sourvinou-Inwood 1973b: 149-58; 1989b: 97-100)—which fits the established modalities of religious interaction.

[101] Cf. e.g. Davaras 1984: 55-95, esp. 72-5, 92; on pp. 59-63 Davaras gives a list of all boat models known to him, but he includes Cypriot and other Aegean specimens and he does not distinguish them according to type or find context.

[102] On this image cf. e.g. Long 1974: pl. 19; fig. 52.

not be legitimate to assume that the boat is offered to him as a means of transport to a paradise beyond the sea. For even in that case the boat could have had other meanings; for example, the dead man may have been a shipowner, seafarer, or merchant, whose social persona was being articulated through this offering. As for the model boats found in graves, first, it is methodologically illegitimate to assume that grave offerings can only have been deposited to serve the deceased's needs in the afterlife—the implicit assumption on which the interpretation under discussion depends; it is now abundantly clear that the choice of grave goods is determined by a variety of motivational nexuses, and that interpretations of the kind discussed here reflect no more than the interpreters' own expectations. Moreover, besides being arbitrary and illegitimate, the assumption that the models of boats found in graves can only be interpreted as transport to the Land of the Dead does not fit the little evidence that is available, that is their pattern of appearance. As Pini pointed out, such boats would have been much more commonly found in graves if such an afterlife belief lay behind their presence.[103] Furthermore, we know that one important dimension in the nexus of the 'functions' of grave offerings is the articulation of the deceased's social persona. The hypothesis that the offering of a model boat related to the deceased's social persona, that he was a shipowner, or a seafarer, or a merchant who was one or both of the above, fits the scarce facts unproblematically. It would explain their pattern of distribution[104] and also the peculiar and peculiarly different types of boats involved; for example, besides the two Zapher Papoura pyxides,[105] the boat with a honeycomb inside it in the Mitsotakis Collection.[106] Finally, it would make them comparable to the other Minoan grave goods which, as far as we can see, pertain to the deceased's social persona. In these circumstances,

---

[103] Pini 1968: 74. Sakellarakis (1971: 188–233, esp. 221–2) is also unfavourably disposed towards the interpretation of such models as providing transport to a land of the dead over the sea; he excludes the possibility that the Zapher Papoura specimen (which was found in a tomb and which has been made much of in support of the theory here under discussion) could have had this function, for he argues that this model formed a pyxis.

[104] No models of boats have been found in the royal graves. The incomplete graffito of a boat engraved on a slab in the Temple Tomb (Evans 1935: 956 pl. 66*b*) cannot be described as adequate provision in the terms of the theory under consideration.

[105] Cf. Davaras 1984: 61–2 no. 19.

[106] Cf. Davaras 1984: 55–95. The peculiar shape of the boat can be explained in terms of the social persona of the deceased as a particular type of merchant without recourse to speculative projections and conflations of later Greek myths and beliefs.

the hypothesis that the Minoans gave models of boats to their dead as transport to Elysion, a paradise beyond the sea, seems to be as disprovable as anything can be, given the evidence and the problems involved of trying to reconstruct a system of beliefs on the basis of 'dumb' archaeological data.

Another monument that has been adduced as evidence in support of the hypothesis of a paradise beyond the sea is the Episkopi sarcophagus,[107] which depicts a chariot scene, hunting scenes, and animals. The human figures carry flowers, kylikes, and standards consisting of a disc on top of a stick. Vermeule thinks that the chariot is driven over sea waves represented by an octopus and that the three passengers on the chariot are dead; and that this is a 'grand ceremonial procession to an overseas haven like Elysion or the Isles of the Blest'.[108] Rutkowski[109] had also seen in the sarcophagus 'a reflection of the journey to the Island of the Blessed'. I cannot offer a systematic reading of the images on this sarcophagus here. I will only make a few remarks that will throw some doubt on these readings and the inadvisability of basing further theories on them. Given the syntax of Minoan iconography in general, and the little we know about sarcophagus iconography in particular, it is simply an assumption that the octopus in the corner is organically related to the chariot, that they are both elements of the same space that is coherently (if partly emblematically) articulated, and that they are not simply juxtaposed in an emblematic relationship. It is also simply an assumption that the octopus represents the sea, rather than itself, as, for example, for the sake of the argument, the sacred animal of a particular deity. But even if we were to accept all this as a working hypothesis, the fact is that the octopus is not shown under the whole of the chariot; the animal drawing the chariot is standing in front of, and next to, not over, the octopus, which would suggest that if the relationship is descriptive narrative and the octopus does indeed represent the sea, the most accurate reading of the relationship would be that the chariot is shown by the sea, on the beach, not over it. There are certainly other Minoan cultic scenes located by the sea. In my view, the chariot scene represents an image of the death ritual—I cannot set out the argument for this

---

[107] Cf. e.g. Vermeule 1979: 67 fig. 25, and pp. 67–8; 1965: 136; Rutkowski 1968: 226 n. 41.
[108] Vermeule 1979: 67–8.
[109] Rutkowski 1968: 226 n. 41.

view here, but as nothing further hangs on it this does not matter. Another argument against the Elysion reading is as follows. Of the three men on the chariot the driver is holding the reins, the other two are carrying disc-standards; they are all represented through the same iconographical schema as some of the men on the ground. The carrying of a disc-standard is also performed by one man on the ground, the large-scale human figure in the next panel, who is connected with the figures on the ground in the chariot panel through the fact that, like the latter, he is holding up a kylix in one hand, in a schema usually taken to depict a libation or toasting. The absence of differentiation between on the one hand the three men on the chariot, and on the other between these three men taken as a group and the people on the ground, makes it implausible that the scene represents the departure of the deceased and suggests that they were all participants in the same activity, perhaps a part of the death ritual.

Even if we were to suppose that this scene did represent the departure of the deceased for a Land of the Dead beyond the sea, far from supporting the nexus of notions that make up the 'Minoan origin of Elysion' theory, it would in fact expose some of the contradictions in the evidence that is implicitly assumed to be supporting it. For, first, here the journey takes place in a chariot that travels over the sea, not in a boat, as is demanded by the theory that the boat models found in graves prove the existence of the Minoan Elysion beyond the sea.[110] Another major contradiction with the nexus of hypotheses sustaining the Minoan Elysion theory, is this: since the Episkopi sarcophagus did not belong to a ruler, it does not support, but is in conflict with, the theory of paradise for Minoan rulers beyond the sea. For if this sarcophagus is relevant to eschatology, it would indicate, like the Haghia Triada sarcophagus and the boats (if they were relevant to eschatology), that there was a land of the dead *for all* beyond the sea—with no information as to its nature; not a paradise for the deified rulers only. It may well have been the case that the Minoan Land of the Dead was located

---

[110] It could be argued that both may have been perceived as possible means of transport to the afterlife. However, besides the implausibility of such a hypothesis, the juxtaposition of a boat and a chariot (with one occupant) on an as yet unpublished LMIIIB sarcophagus from Kalochorafitis (which, thanks to the generosity of Mrs A. Karetsou, will be published jointly by her and myself) makes this interpretation even less likely, and suggests that the boat in funerary contexts may have pertained to the social persona of the deceased—as did perhaps the chariot when it was not shown in operation during a funerary ritual.

beyond the sea. There is at present no way of knowing. What I have been trying to argue is that this is sheer speculation unsupported by any evidence; that there is no Minoan evidence to support this view, which can therefore be clearly seen to be entirely dependent on the assumption that the Homeric Elysion is of Minoan origin. Furthermore, even if we were to assume for the sake of the argument that there was a Land of the Dead beyond the sea, it would still not follow that it was a paradise. And even if we were to assume that it was a paradise, a paradise for all would be in conflict with the notion of the deification of the Minoan rulers which would be (on the theories under discussion) the belief reflected in the Homeric Elysion. Thus, even if we were to concede every argument put forward by the supporters of the Minoan origin of Elysion, there would still be the need to acknowledge that a radical change had taken place between what can be claimed—however unconvincingly—for the Minoan world and the Homeric Elysion. The fact that despite all this Nilsson believed that the Minoan Land of the Dead was a 'Land of Bliss'[111] because the latter would be consistent with the belief in the apotheosis of rulers while it would be inconsistent with the Greek perceptions of Hades shows that, ultimately, his whole case depends on culturally determined notions of what one would have expected to have been the case, while, as we shall see, the evidence points very strongly in the direction of Elysion being not a Minoan 'survival' but a recent development at the time of the final crystallization of the Homeric poems.

Elysion and Enelysioi. In these circumstances, even if the word 'Elysion' could be proved to be Minoan, it would not necessarily follow that it denoted a Land of the Dead; and even if it could be shown to have denoted a Land of the Dead, it would not necessarily follow that this Minoan Land of the Dead called Elysion was similar to the Homeric paradise for non-dead[112] called Elysion. But in any case, Elysion can now be proved to be a Greek word. No satisfactory Greek etymology had been suggested for *Elysion* before Burkert[113] put forward an attractive hypothesis of a Greek etymology, which has not, to my knowledge, been refuted and which has earned the

[111] Cf. Nilsson 1950: 625.
[112] Cf. Guthrie 1950: 291.
[113] Burkert 1961: 208–13.

approval of Heubeck[114] and West.[115] Burkert overcomes the obstacles which make a direct association of Elysion with *eleusomai* impossible, by concentrating on the words *enelysios*, 'struck by lightning', and *to enelysion*, 'the place struck by lightning', which can both easily be derived from *eleusomai*. Those who were killed by lightning, he says, were not believed to be dead like people who died from other causes; as cases like that of Semele and Asklepios suggest, they were thought to be transferred to a higher life. That is, he argues, the fate of the *enelysioi* would be equivalent to 'being in the Elysion'; and the place where lightning had struck would be an Elysion, with the word acquiring the significance of a place in the Other World where all the Blest were living only at a second stage. He admits that the name of the Fields of the Blest was always *Elysion*, not *Enelysion*, and suggests that the explanation of this discrepancy lies with a verbal misunderstanding, by which ἐνηλυσίῳ was understood as ἐν Ἠλυσίῳ, with the result that the second part of the misunderstood word became a new word, a frequently attested linguistic phenomenon. Such misunderstanding, could have originated in the recital of old epic poetry, for example with a hypothetical verse like

$$\star τῷ\ δ᾽\ ἄρ᾽\ ἐνηλυσίῳ\ βιοτὴ\ πέλει\ ἄφθιτος\ αἰεί.$$

He correctly remarks that behind this linguistic accident would lie an evolution in belief; but, because he accepts the Minoan origin of Elysion, he sees this development as resulting from the translation of pre-Greek beliefs into Greek through the use of the word for the Greek concept that was related to the relevant foreign one; in this case, the latter was that select people do not die, but go and live in Bliss on some secret islands in the Far West; the *enelysioi* also did not die, but led a higher life of Bliss; thus, the result of the synthesis was the belief that the *enelysioi* lived on in the Islands of the Blest; from *enelysios* was derived the name for the Fields of the Blest. However, Burkert's theory of linguistic misunderstanding works equally well if the notion of paradise was not a Minoan belief; as we saw, the notion that Elysion is Minoan is a modern construct extremely unlikely to be right. Indeed, it would, I believe, work better if the notion of paradise for select people who did not

[114] Heubeck 1972: 87–95.
[115] S. West 1988: 227 (*ad* 563 ff.).

die had not pre-dated, but had first been generated in interaction with, the notion that death by lightning conferred special status— came to be seen as a vehicle for transmission to a paradise—because it effected direct communication between Zeus and this world. The generation of this belief would have been facilitated by the existence of a belief that immersion in fire can lead to immortality; but we do not know when the latter first emerged in Greece. The date of the appearance of the concept of apotheosis by fire is unclear.[116] But a schema associating fire and immortality such as that of Thetis trying to make Achilles immortal by fire[117] certainly articulates the story of Demeter's attempt to make Demophon immortal by placing him in the fire in the *Homeric Hymn to Demeter*.[118] This is the earliest occurrence of the motif; we do not know whether it had pre-dated the association between immortality and death by lightning which was (on this hypothesis) pre-Homeric. Be that as it may, the *enelysioi* may have come to be seen as being *en elysio{i}* in the context of the development of the belief that they had a different destiny after 'death', in the wider context of the emergence of the notion that a chosen few did not die.

Certainly, the fact that the belief in a paradise for the select few has a very insignificant place in the Homeric epics but soon comes to acquire progressively greater importance best fits the notion of a recent development in response to pressures leading to changes within the eschatological system. Also, the fact that there were two early versions of paradise, Elysion and Isles of the Blest,[119] can best be explained if the concept of paradise was new in the eighth century, and if one of the strands that went into its creation was that pertaining to the *enelysioi*, which was soon overshadowed by the special heroes strand, as Elysion was overshadowed by the Isles of the Blest. It could also be argued that the generation of the belief

---

[116] Cf. Stinton 1987: 1–16.

[117] Cf. e.g. Apollod. 3. 13. 6 and Frazer ad loc.

[118] Hom.H.Dem. 239–45; cf. Richardson 1974: 231–42.

[119] Leuke, though a complex locus which cannot be discussed here, certainly had an Island of the Blest aspect. Achilles taken to Leuke by Thetis: Proclus, *Hypothesis* of *Aethiopis* (Davies *EGF* p. 47; cf. also Edwards 1985: 215–17) whose schematic views, which take no account of developments in eschatology and ideology, and depend on implicit assumptions about the relationship between text and belief that are, in my view, untenable, I do not share), where we are also told that in the *Aethiopis* Eos managed to persuade Zeus to give immortality to her son Memnon—thus illustrating the proliferation of the non-dead. On Leuke cf. also Burkert 1972: 152–3. Eventually Elysion became a field in the Isles of the Blest (cf. Lucian, *Jup. conf.* 17).

that death by lightning leads to immortality is more intelligible in a world in which cremation is the norm—and therefore not Minoan Crete or the Bronze Age in general. For in such a world lightning, which incinerated the victim, and was thought to effect direct communication with Zeus, could be seen, with the help of the schema 'death—burial/cremation—Hades', as a 'supernatural' sort of cremation in life that transferred the person to a paradise—while ordinary cremation integrated the dead into Hades. The dualism between a Land of the Blest and a Land of the Dead for the common dead would, of course, be inherent in the interpretation of *enelysios* as implying transference to a higher life instead of death, and thus *ex hypothesi* Greek, in whatever period this concept is taken to have arisen. Thus, the culturally determined notion of incompatibility of a Land of the Blest with Greek beliefs, which did so much to inspire and sustain the hypothesis of the Minoan origin of Elysion, is undermined further. I cannot discuss the Mycenaean evidence, though I shall say something about it below; I shall only say here that it is extremely unlikely that the dualism common dead/Hades *v.* select few/paradise had existed in Mycenaean times.[120]

The Emergence of Paradise: Conclusions. The emergence and development of hero cults from the eighth century onwards[121] is, in my view, the most closely fitting cultic correlative to these eschatological developments—with which the cults interacted. This supports further the thesis that the nexus Elysion was a recent construct when Homer composed the poems.

Instead of trying to reconstruct what was possible or impossible for the Greeks to have invented, on the basis of culturally determined perceptions of compatibility, we should try to focus on something which is (within certain parameters) more accessible: the epics' audience. Surely, the important point is that, if conflict

---

[120] This opinion of post-Mycenaean dualism cannot, in my view, be challenged by Heubeck's belief that *enelysios* must be a Mycenaean word because of the assibilation *thi/si*, as it is only based on the theory (Heubeck 1972: 93; on this assibilation cf. also Lejeune 1968: 733–43) that this assibilation is a peculiarity of the Mycenaean dialect which is absent from the Attic-Ionic and Arcado-Cypriot where it only appears as a Mycenaean relic. But even if this theory is correct, it does not prove that the 'Blest' concept was of Mycenaean date, because the word might only have meant 'struck by lightning', to which the belief that people killed in such circumstances went on to a higher life might have been subsequently superimposed.

[121] Cf. bibliog. n. 219 below.

was perceived to have existed between a paradise for the select few and the deeply rooted 'everyone must die' strand, the ultimate origin of each is irrelevant to the question of how the audience made sense of the conflict. In my view, the conflict would have been perceived as less sharp if it was reflecting contemporary eschatology, which had began to shift and include a challenge to the traditional 'everyone dies' strand; if the paradise concept was new and people were vague about it. The explanation given as to why Menelaos will be so privileged would have helped make sense of the differentiation. In the context of the epics it would have been understood to mean that everybody dies except Menelaos because of his relationship to Zeus. The question may then have arisen for the audience why Menelaos and not Herakles?—let alone anyone else. Perhaps this question was one of the factors that determined the elaboration concerning Herakles' fate and his presence and not-presence in Hades in *Odyssey* 11 which we shall discuss below. The presentation of Elysion would have enhanced uncertainty. As we saw, the prophecy that Menelaos will go to Elysion is contained in the embedded speech of the tertiary narrator/focalizer Proteus. The primary external narrator tells us on his own authority that Menelaos claims that all this happened and that Proteus had told him that he will go to Elysion, and (as far as the primary narrator authorizes) Proteus too may or may not have been speaking the truth at this point.[122] Later audiences would have perceived the 'conflict', and the differences between the Homeric image of the afterlife and the several different beliefs established in the archaic and classical period, in the conceptual space created by their distancing from the Homeric world (many of whose dramatis personae were heroes of 'present day' cult), in symbiosis with the concept of unknowability which was important in Greek religion.

Let us consider Menelaos' place in the *Odyssey*. The Trojan War heroes that come into play in the *Odyssey* belong to two groups: those who had already died at the narrative time of the epic and the much smaller group of those still alive, Odysseus, Nestor, and Menelaos. Of these three two come in contact with prophecy and are thus projected into the future, Odysseus through Teiresias' prophecy in 11. 100–37 and Menelaos through Proteus' prophecy.

---

[122] Presumably one can be *nemertes* and choose to lie. On the Proteus episode cf. also S. West 1988: 217–18 *ad* 384 ff.

Both prophecies are presented through a *prolepsis* in an embedded speech involving a tertiary narrator/focalizer able to prophesy the future. Odysseus' projection into the future goes up to the point of his death. Nothing is said about what is to happen afterwards; this would have been understood to imply that his afterlife fate was to be the same as that of the heroes that surround him while he is hearing this prophecy in Hades. Menelaos' projection into the future goes further; he learns of his fate after 'death'. It is in the context of this unusual prophecy that the concept crops up of Elysion, otherwise unknown and unhinted at in the epics, and in conflict with the deeply rooted ideology 'everyone dies' that permeates them. This suggests that the episode is a recent importation into the poems, the 'Proteus-to-Menelaos' prophecy being a modification and extension of the 'Teiresias-to-Odysseus' prophecy. This fits the fact that it is focused on Menelaos. For as one of the two major Trojan heroes (other than Odysseus) who was not yet dead, he would not have been associated in the epic tradition with Hades in a Nekyia; he could thus unproblematically become the focus of a new elaboration. His advantage over Nestor was that he had a connection with Zeus (albeit an indirect one) which allowed an explanation of why he and not any of the others would go to paradise. Odysseus, besides being the poem's main hero who was too important and deeply rooted to become the focus of such an elaboration, also did not have the divine connections conducive to the creation of an explanation for such a unique fate.

In these circumstances, I submit that the articulation of the belief in an immortality for a select few in the epics, as well as the post-Homeric pattern of the appearance of this belief, indicate very strongly that this was a new belief that was imported into the poems recently and reflected a new development, an eschatological strand that was to develop significantly in post-Homeric times and provide models of hope for the afterlife to ordinary mortals, correlatively with the development of eschatological trends promising a happy afterlife. As became clear above, developments in Crete in the Late Bronze Age and Dark Ages were somewhat different from those in the rest of the Greek world, as were the parameters of religious development, which involved greater complexity. We cannot exclude the possibility that the nexus of beliefs involving a paradise associated with King Rhadamanthys may have developed in Crete after the collapse of Minoan palatial society. What I am suggesting is that if so such a belief did not enter mainstream Greek eschatology until around the time of the final composition of the Homeric poems. That this is the case is suggested by the Homeric poems, by the subsequent pattern of appearance of the 'paradise' nexus in other texts, and by the fact that there is no archaeological situation before then that could be interpreted as a possible correlative to such an eschatology; such as, for example, a Minoan-type differentiation between some exceptional dead and the others, or the development of heroic cults.[123]

The convergence between on the one hand what Rhadamanthys and Minos have in common in the *Odyssey*, a differential, privileged, position in the afterlife, and on the other the conclusion derived from the consideration of the Minoan data, that Minoan rulers probably had a differential, privileged, position in the afterlife suggests strongly that the association of a Minoan ruler with a Land of the Dead and the differential privileged position of such ruler in the afterlife went back to the Minoan period; that these two themes, Rhadamanthys in Elysion and Minos with his sceptre in Hades, are later transformations of this element that developed separately out of a common nexus, according to the complex modalities of bricolage mentioned above.

In these circumstances, we conclude that the Homeric Elysion is a construct created not long before the Homeric poems took their final form, through the combination of elements of disparate origin into a nexus articulating a new concept, in response to what appears to have been a need to devise a fate worthy of the great heroes and generate models of hope for life after death. These elements are: the association of a Minoan ruler with a Land of the Dead and his differential privileged position; the 'need' just mentioned; the name Elysion and with it the notion of a privileged fate for a select few is yet another. Thus, three different strands of investigation (the Minoan data; the established modalities of religious development and of transmission of epic poetry; and the analyses of Homeric and post-Homeric patterns of appearance of this theme) lead independently to the conclusion that Elysion did not originate in Minoan Crete, but was created in the eighth century. Due to the quantity and nature of the available evidence, none of the three lead to totally conclusive results on their own. But

---

[123] The Lefkandi monument, on which cf. Ch. III §i.2, is something entirely different.

the fact that the conclusions of all three independent investigations coincide confirms, I submit, the validity of this conclusion.

3. DEATH AND THE JOURNEY TO HADES

Let us consider the *psyche*'s transition from life to death as it is represented in the Homeric poems. Death is first of all a separation. The *psyche* leaves the body and flies away; eventually it will enter Hades. In descriptions of the moment of death, for example in *Odyssey* 11. 221–2, the *thymos*[124] also leaves the body, never to be heard of again; presumably its existence is tied up with life, and eventually it dies. Elsewhere, when younger people are involved,[125] for example in *Iliad* 16. 453 and *Odyssey* 9. 523–4, it is the *aion*, the vital force, that is mentioned as leaving the body as the *psyche* does, but, unlike the *psyche*, and like the *thymos*, not to be heard of again. What remains is a decomposing corpse whose sinews have ceased to hold flesh and bones together.[126] It is senseless matter which will rot unless cremated.[127] The process of decomposition attracts no interest. Thus, only one of the elements that make up a living person survives death, the *psyche*,[128], which from the moment it leaves the body is also denoted by the word *eidolon*,[129] which stresses the *psyche*'s likeness to the living person. We must not assume that in the Greek perceptions the *psyche* that survived death was necessarily imagined as being identical with the *psyche* of the living person. It may have been thought to change when separated from the rest at death, as the other components of the self changed. The body that became corpse changed radically, through a process that ended in the destruction of the corpse's identity as part of the deceased, his spatio-temporal continuum, his body—either through rotting or through cremation, both of which reduced the body to inarticulate bits. The *thymos* also changed, since it died after the

---

[124] On the *thymos* cf. Garland 1981: 49–50; Padel 1992: 27–30.

[125] Cf. Bremmer 1983: 15–16.

[126] *Od.* 11. 217–22.

[127] *Il.* 24. 50–4.

[128] Cf. *Od.* 11. 219–22. On *psyche* cf. Bremmer 1983: 13–19, 66–89; Padel 1992: 30–2; cf. also Warden 1971: 95–103; Vermeule 1979: 2–9; Garland 1981: 48–9; Vernant 1991: 186–9; cf. also, esp. on the word *psyche*, Darcus 1979: 30–9.

[129] Bremmer 1983: 79–84; Burkert 1985: 195; cf. also Nilsson 1967: 194–5. On *eidola* in Homer and elsewhere cf. also Vernant 1991: 187–92. On *eidola* and their representation in Greek art cf. esp. Siebert 1981: 63–73; Peifer 1989: *passim*.

separation, as did the *aion*. This suggests that death involved both separation and change for each of the separated elements, and thus also for the *psyche*. It is certainly the case that a change took place in the sense that eventually the *psyche* became coterminous with the deceased's 'I'.

It is clear, both from the Homeric usage in the relevant passages, and from the beliefs articulated there, that until burial the 'I' of the deceased consists of the shade and the corpse; one or the other is identified with 'I', depending on the focus of the articulation.[130] The corpse also functions as the metonymic sign of the whole dead person during the death ritual.[131] At burial the corpse is handed over symbolically to the nether world; first, it is consumed by fire and then what remains is sealed away into the earth. What remains of the deceased in the world of the living is the sign marking his grave which, we shall see in Chapter III, was also the sign of the deceased and the focus of his memory in the world of the living. After burial the 'I' of the deceased—if we leave aside his survival in memory—is coterminous with his shade in Hades.

The word *psyche* is etymologically connected with *psycho*, breathe,[132] as the cessation of breathing is the simplest and most obvious sign of death. The image of a dying person's last breath being released into the air provided the model for the visualization and representation of the departure from the body at the moment of death of the person's surviving component.[133] This departure took place through the mouth,[134] paralleling the emission of the last breath, or—an image with a different symbolic focus—through a wound, the abnormal and disruptive opening of the body which was the cause of death.[135] Two significant and constant Homeric characteristics of a dead person's *psyche* are, first, that in substance it is breath-like, and second, that in form it has the exact appearance

---

[130] Cf. e.g. *Il.* 23. 71, and 72–3.

[131] Cf. Sourvinou-Inwood 1983: 38–9.

[132] On the etymological associations (and the meanings) of *psyche* cf. Frisk 1970: 1141–2 *s.v.*; Chantraine 1980: 1294 *s.v.*; cf. also Nilsson 1967: 41, 194; Burkert 1985: 195; Schnaufer 1970: 198.

[133] Cf. Nilsson 1967: 194; cf. also 41; Burkert 1985: 195; Schnaufer 1970: 204.

[134] *Il.* 9. 408–9.

[135] *Il.* 14. 518–19; 16. 505. *Ek retheon* in *Il.* 16. 856 and 22. 362 means 'from' not 'through' the limbs—i.e. at death the *psyche* left the limbs which it previously inhabited (cf. also Schol. B *Il.* 16. 856). On the meaning of *rhetheon* cf. Bremmer 1983: 17 and n. 10; Janko 1992: 420 *ad* 855–8; for a different view: Schnaufer 1970: 203 and n. 550; cf. also Schol. B *Il.* 16. 856.

of the dead person.[136] The *psyche*'s breath-like nature is, at least to some extent, implied in the images of the *psyche* leaving the body at the moment of death.[137] It also clearly underlies *Iliad* 23. 100–1 where the *psyche* (in movement) is compared to smoke: *psyche de kata chthonos eyte kapnos ocheto tetrigyia*. The simile *eyte kapnos*[138] undoubtedly connotes a gassy substance[139]—the whole passage describes a gassy substance in quick motion. This interpretation fits the immateriality of the *psyche* of the dead as illustrated in *Iliad* 23. 99–100 and *Odyssey* 11. 204–22. Finally, a breath-like substance is again implied in *Iliad* 22. 467, where Andromache *apo de psyche ekapysse* as she fainted—though in this case it is the *psyche* of a living person.[140]

The *psyche* moves at great speed, as is stated in *Iliad* 14. 518–19 and implied in Odysseus' question to the dead Elpenor in *Odyssey* 11. 57–8,[141] and also suggested by the simile 'like smoke' in *Iliad* 23. 100–1—for it could only have been selected in a context of a nexus of beliefs which included the notion of the *psyche*'s quick movement

---

[136] (*Il.* 23. 65–7, 106–7.) Hence it is called *eidolon*. The terminological distinction (cf. Vermeule 1979: 30–1) which ascribes the term *psyche* to the small-scale winged souls and *eidolon* to the larger representations of dead people resembling their living form can be misleading, for it does not correspond to the ancient usage. (Cf. e.g. *Od.* 11. 51, 84, 90, 467 for instances of *psyche* visualized as (which thus on this distinction should have been called) *eidola*; and *Od.* 11. 476, where *eidola* denotes a generic 'shades' pertaining to the ghosts referred to as *psyche* of so-and-so, and which in v. 564 are referred to as *psychai*). Most strikingly, in *Il.* 23 Patroklos' shade, which is described as looking exactly like Patroklos (vv. 65–7), is referred to as *psyche*; and Patroklos himself in v. 72 speaks of '*psychai, eidola kamonton*'. Like the words '*psyche*' and '*eidolon*' (which refer to the same thing by 'naming' different aspects of it) but not in correspondence with them, the small winged soul schema and the life-size schema are iconographical possibilities, particular articulations, selected to suit particular articulations, of the same semantic field 'shade, soul of the dead'. Cf. also Ch. V § ii.

[137] Cf. also Schol. *Il.* 16. 856; Schol B *Il.* 16. 856.

[138] On the similes used for the *psyche* cf. Schnaufer 1970: 66.

[139] Cf. Schol. *Il.* 23. 100; *Schol B Il.* 23. 100. Conceivably, the smoke-like manifestation here may have been perceived as a more condensed and visible version of the breath-like *psyche*.

[140] On the *psyche* during life cf. Bremmer 1983: 13–17.

[141] This passage is problematic (cf. Schol. *Od.* 11. 58 H.Q.). But whatever its exact meaning in the eyes of the Homeric audience, and the circumstances of its composition, what is important for us here is that in this context the use of *pezos* does not entail a belief that the shades went to Hades on foot. At one level Odysseus contrasts Elpenor's journey, which was unaided by technology, self-propelled, to his own on ship; and also his sea route to the 'land route', taken by the shades; at another perhaps the audience understood that Odysseus did not know, or was not sure, or wanted to confirm, that the shades flew to Hades. Heubeck (1989: 81 *ad* 57–8) comments 'the question is not so much an expression of surprise as an attempt to elicit information'.

through the air. Two passages are important for the nexus of beliefs about the *psyche*'s transition from life to death and Hades: *Iliad* 16. 856 and 23. 362, which describe the death of the two most important heroes to die in the *Iliad*, Patroklos and Hector. The same formula is used in both, *psyche d' ek retheon ptamene Aidosde bebekei*; this is a first indication that this formulaic description of the moment of death may reflect a belief which was deeply rooted in the epics. Indeed, the notion expressed here conforms, we shall see, with beliefs expressed throughout the epics, and does not conflict with any belief anywhere in them. This suggests that this belief had not changed throughout the period of the epics' formation. In this formula the *psyche* of Patroklos and Hector are described as flying to Hades. The same notion recurs in *Odyssey* 11. 222: *psyche . . . oneiros . . . apoptamene pepotetai*. This image of the shades flying to Hades expresses in concrete terms the notion of the extremely quick translation of an unseeable component of one's person to an unseeable realm. The image of flying offered an obvious model for expressing this notion, since the *psyche*'s departure from the body was visualized in terms of the last breath's release into the air.[142] This potential for quick motion through the air underlies the iconographical articulation in which the shade is represented as winged.[143] Thus the shades fly to Hades and reach it under their own steam, without the help of a psychopompic figure; nothing is said about the details of the journey. In the Homeric poems and in Hesiod's galaxy of divine beings there is no Charon, and Hermes Chthonios does not appear in the role of guide of the souls in Hades—except in the 'Continuation' of *Odyssey* 24 which I shall be discussing separately below. I shall be arguing there, and in Chapter V §iii, that the absence of Charon and of Hermes Chthonios as psychopompoi from Homer is not accidental, but an integral part of a nexus of representations in which they had no place.

It is unambiguously clear that Hades is under the earth.[144] What,

---

[142] As Nilsson (1967: 194) noted, *ptamene* expresses the sense perception that the last breath flies away into the air. *Petomai* denotes 'quick motion through the air'. On the movement of the *psyche* through the air see also Vernant 1965: 76.

[143] This articulation 'winged shades' has a long history; it is found both in the Mycenaean and the archaic and classical periods. For Mycenaean images cf. Vermeule 1979: 65; for archaic and classical ones cf. ibid. 8–9 and below Ch. V §ii.

[144] Cf. esp. *Il.* 20. 61–6; and e.g. *Il.* 23. 100–1; 7. 330; 14. 457; 6. 19; *Od.* 10. 560. Cf. also Arrigheti 1966: 35 ff.

then, of the notion expressed in *Odyssey* 10. 508–12 and 11. 13–22 that Hades lies beyond Okeanos and can be reached by sea? In *Odyssey* 10. 501–2 the notion that one can reach Hades by sea on a ship is presented as a new idea, revealed to Odysseus by Circe. For this is indicated by Odysseus' comment that no man has yet gone to Hades by ship. In this context, and given the assumptions set out above, the question who is going to guide the ship, for no man yet has reached Hades on ship, shows that the notion of reaching Hades by ship included the notion of reaching Hades alive; that is, the notion of reaching Hades by ship and alive, for which Odysseus assumed a guide was necessary,[145] is implicitly contrasted to 'normality', the shades flying to Hades unaided. This notion, which was presented as new information given by the supernatural witch, may have been a poetic creation rather than the reflection of established belief. Such an innovation was possible because Greek cosmography did allow such a perception: Hades was under the earth but it could also be reached by going west[146] and crossing Okeanos which encircled the earth and going over and under the edge—though the underlying articulation need not have been as specific as this.[147] Antikleia's statement in *Odyssey* 11. 155–9[148] confirms that in the constructed cosmology articulated in the Homeric *Odyssey* while the shades flew down to Hades the living could in theory reach the Land of the Dead by sailing west beyond Okeanos. For obvious reasons pertaining to the setting sun and its most obvious symbolic associations, the notion that the Land of the Dead lies in the west and/or that the west is associated with death, is found in several societies.[149] In the Greek world it is not exactly that the Land of the Dead lies in the west (it lies under the earth); but it can be reached either by going downwards or by going west. I shall be suggesting below that it was Homer who created this innovation, situating one entrance to the Underworld at the ends of the earth, which is encircled by Okeanos, so that the Land of

---

[145] *Od.* 10. 501; cf. 505.

[146] Cf. also N. Austin 1975: 95.

[147] On Homer's and Hesiod's cosmology, and on the journey to Hades involving a horizontal movement to the west, cf. Arrigheti 1966: 1–60, who, however, thinks that two different conceptions of the localization of Hades are involved in Homer and in Hesiod.

[148] These verses were rejected by Aristarchos; cf. Heubeck 1989: 87 ad loc. for bibliog. on the controversy.

[149] Cf. e.g. Rigby 1973: 269, 272–3; Evans-Pritchard 1973: 96.

the Dead was beyond Okeanos. I shall be suggesting a reason for this, connected with the poem's aims.

Throughout the epics a river separates Hades from the world of the living—or, rather, from a no-man's land between Hades and the upper world, which the shade haunts while in the between-and-betwixt stage between death and burial;[150] this river forms the frontier between the two worlds which, according to *Iliad* 23. 71–4, a shade is not allowed to cross; and thus enter Hades and become integrated in the world of the dead, until after burial.[151] The river is not named in *Iliad* 23. 71–4; it is simply called *potamos*. In *Iliad* 8. 369 the river dividing Hades from the world of the living is Styx. In *Odyssey* 10. 508–15[152] the rivers have multiplied: Okeanos comes in and so do Pyriphlegethon and Kokytos as well as Styx, and also Acheron, who is destined to become eventually *the* river-border separating Hades from the no-man's land which communicates with the upper world.[153] The appearance of Okeanos and the elaborated Underworld landscape are the result of the transfer of the entrance to the Underworld to the ends of the earth and the combination of that imaginary geography with elements from the Thesprotian landscape around the entrance to Hades, on which I shall say something more below.

The notion that a river divides (ultimately) the world of the living from that of the dead is, then, a consistent motif in the epics, though the identity of the river varies—not surprisingly, given the conflated nature of Homer's eschatology. This consistency suggests

---

[150] Cf. *Il.* 23. 70–101; *Od.* 11. 51–4. Cf. also Sourvinou-Inwood 1981: 27; 1983: 39.

[151] We cannot entirely exclude the possibility that the notion that the dead cannot enter Hades until after burial may have been a literary device, not a belief; but this is unlikely. First, in other societies the notion that the shade is not in the Land of the Dead while the corpse is above ground is a real belief (cf. e.g. Kruyt 1973: 79). Second, though the epics do not reflect a coherent system of beliefs, the nexus pertaining to death and burial is constant, and the connection between entering Hades and burial fits in this nexus; it is the eschatological equivalent of 'proper burial–good death'. Finally, there is, we shall see, a correlation between absence of psychopompoi and rule that the shades enter Hades after burial. Those who were not buried were not necessarily thought to be forever barred; their shades may have entered Hades—albeit not in the proper, honourable, manner—at a later stage, correlative with the state of their corpse; the most likely time would be at the decomposition of its flesh and reduction to bones, a significant symbolic stage in some societies, including, we shall see, the Minoan and Mycenaean.

[152] Cf. also 11. 155–9 and Schol. 157.

[153] Cf. Merry and Riddell (1886: 437 *ad Od.* 10. 513) who think that the Styx was the original Underworld river and that this passage is a later elaboration. I believe that the latter is correct, and that the Styx was the river separating Hades from the rest in the dominant strand in the Homeric poems.

that the river-border was a meaningful concept in Homer's time. The border-river most deeply rooted in the epics in that role is the Styx.[154] For it is in this way that we can make sense of the fact that it was by the waters of the Styx that the gods swore an oath.[155] The reason why this was a terrible oath was because the waters of the Styx, separating the world of the living from that of the dead, could be seen as standing for the articulation of the universe, the cosmic order which must not be violated, and whose guarantors the gods were. If a god whose role was to guarantee the cosmic order endangered it instead by forswearing himself on an oath sworn by the Styx, he is punished, Hesiod tells us,[156] through what amounts to a temporary lapse from divine status. First, through a spell of a polarized form of divinity lapse, a year of what amounts to quasi-death; and then through a longer period of penance, during which he is placed outside the divine community, cut off from the other gods. Gods who betray their role as guarantors of the cosmic order become temporarily non-gods.[157]

A river is an appropriate border between the two worlds, for it provides a definite and continuous division which can symbolize concretely the notions 'division' and 'border', and the crossing of which can be made to appear controlled. In her review of Terpening (1985), King[158] suggested that an interesting question to be asked is 'why is the boundary between worlds a river, rather than, for example, a chasm or a wall of fire?' She is right, though the attempt to answer it is vulnerable to cultural determination. The following strategy can minimize the danger. First we should determine what are the inalienable characteristics of the river as a boundary in contrast to those of other possible boundaries; and then assess whether those traits had formed the parameters of selection that had helped generate the representation of the river as the infernal

[154] Cf. also Furtwängler 1905: 199; Waser 1898: 9. On the Styx cf. M. L. West 1966 *ad* Hes. *Th.* 778–9, 784; and cf. Baladié 1980: 17–24 (who sees the relationship between reality and the 'imaginaire'—and the latter's refractions in literary texts—in more linear and less complex terms than I think is appropriate); Scalera McClintock 1989: 34, 67–9; Vernant 1991: 123–4, 132, 134.

[155] *Il.* 2. 755; 14. 271; 15. 36–8; *Od.* 5. 184–6; cf. also Hes. *Th.* 397–400, 775–806; M. L. West 1966: *ad* Hes. *Th.* 400, 778 ff. Cf. also *Hom.H.Dem.* 259.

[156] Hes. *Th.* 793–804.

[157] It is not important for our purposes whether this reflects established belief or Hesiod's elaboration; since a poet's creativity is determined by the parameters of collective belief, even poetic elaborations are determined by, and express, significant collective perceptions.

[158] King 1986b: 355.

boundary by considering how they relate to the society's funerary
ideology. If the two have common traits these are indeed likely to
have been relevant to the creation of the image of the river as
a boundary—though this assessment cannot itself escape cultural
determination. Besides the fact that a river provides a definite and
continuous division which can symbolize vividly 'division' and
'border', and the crossing of which can be made to appear controlled, the following traits distinguish a river from other possible
boundaries: it is a natural, frequently occurring, boundary of this
world; and it is not as dramatic as a chasm. These characteristics
make the transition between the two worlds undramatic; they also
make the boundary of the river, which is so fundamentally 'other'
from the boundaries between parts of this world, appear also in
some ways 'like' such common boundaries. Thus the division
between the upper world and Hades is definite but not dramatic.
This representation of the transition from life to Hades fits well,
seems to be a part of, the nexus of attitudes to death which, I have
argued elsewhere[159] and shall develop further in this book, was
dominant in Homer, involving an acceptance of death as a hateful,
but familiar, not frightening event; an inescapable evil, part of the
life-cycle in which the generations succeed each other and the
individual's discontinuity is contrasted with the continuity of the
family, the community, and humanity. The absence of psychopompoi is part of the same nexus of undramatic and unelab-
orated transition.

In Homer the shades, once they are in Hades, cannot cross again
and return to the upper world.[160] This seems constant in all the
strands of this conflated eschatology. Nor can anyone be allowed to
cross from the upper world to Hades, unless they were dead and
buried. Odysseus who was alive entered Hades thanks to Circe's
magical aid—for witchcraft was considered capable of changing the
natural order of things. Even so, as I shall be arguing in § ii.5 below,
the question of exactly how far he got into, whether he actually
entered, Hades proper is left open.

The notion that the shades, once in Hades, cannot return to the
upper world and that no one is allowed to cross from the upper
world to Hades unless they are dead and buried is articulated by the

[159] Cf. Sourvinou-Inwood 1981; 1983.
[160] *Il.* 23. 75–6.

shade of Patroklos who is visiting Achilles in *Iliad* 23. 65–101 in order to request burial. This, and the description of the circumstances of Patroklos' shade and its attempts to enter Hades which are unsuccessful, for the other shades prevent him from crossing the river because he is not buried, are given in a character text in which Patroklos is the secondary narrator/focalizer. Patroklos is a shade, albeit an unburied shade who could move about in the upper world, and we have it on the narrator's authority that he appeared to Achilles and said these things—as we have it in several places that people go to Hades. Thus, though the circumstances around the entrance of the Underworld are only given Patroklos' authority, the fact that he is capable of visiting the upper world is given the authority of the primary narrator. This, together with the consistency of this eschatological strand in the epic,[161] suggests very strongly that this was an established belief in Homer's time and had been an established belief throughout the centuries of the epics' transmission. I shall return to this. Let us now consider what else the primary narrator gives us on the afterlife on his own authority in this passage. First, the *psyche* of the dead person looks precisely as the living man had looked. Second, a living person cannot touch the *psyche* of a dead person. When Achilles tried to embrace Patroklos, his *psyche* disappeared like smoke and went under the earth. The question of the nature and faculties of the shades as articulated here will be considered below (p. 78). Now I shall return to the relationship between Hades and the world of the living.

The definite division between the two worlds and the controlled communication between them is also expressed through the image of the gates which are firmly attached to the Land of the Dead and to Hades the god in Homer, Hesiod, and other authors.[162] In Homer and Hesiod the gates reflect and symbolize the notion of controlled access in and out of the Land of the Dead, and especially the 'fact' that nobody is allowed to leave Hades. Cerberus articulates the same idea; according to Hesiod, *Theogony* 767–73, he is friendly to those who enter Hades, but devours anybody trying to get out of

---

[161] *Od.* 11. 51–2 Elpenor's shade came first, *ou gar po etethapto hypo chthonos* . . ., for he was not yet buried; cf. Heubeck 1989: 80–1 ad loc.

[162] Hom., *Il.* 5. 646; 8. 367; 13. 415; 23. 71; *Od.* 11. 277; 14. 156. Hes. *Th.* 773; cf. M. L. West 1966: 365. On other authors cf. M. L. West 1966: 364–5 (*ad Th.* 741). On Hades' gates cf. also Vermeule 1979: 35–6; 219 n. 62; Scalera McClintock 1989: 66–7.

the gates.[163] He is, then, a guardian of the gates, another instrument for the preservation of the division between the two worlds. In *Iliad* 23. 72–3 it is the shades themselves who safeguard the proper division between the two worlds in the other direction, by preventing the shade of someone who has not yet been buried from crossing the river and becoming integrated in Hades.[164] This definite division between the two worlds, naturally articulated and reinforced by the images of Cerberus and the gates, is a manifestation of an ordered and structured universe in which there are proper boundaries between life and death and the passage from one to the other is undramatic, but governed by fixed and strict rules which are an important part of the cosmic order.

There are, it will become clear below, significant divergences between the different strands of beliefs that make up Homeric eschatology, and these are particularly marked with regard to the nature of the shades in Hades. However, one element remains consistent throughout the epics, except in the Continuation of *Odyssey* 24 which shall be considered below: the transition of the shade of the dead person from life to death, the journey to Hades and the relationship between Hades and the world of the living. The absence of consistency in the other facets of Homeric eschatology and of the Homeric world in general makes this particular consistency strikingly significant, and suggests that it reflected a set of beliefs which had remained unchanged during the centuries of the epics' transmission. This hypothesis will gain further support through the consideration of the subsequent developments in this aspect of eschatology. In addition, this representation of the transition between life and death and between the world of the living and the world of the dead is, we saw, also in harmony with the other facets of the nexus of funerary attitudes that is dominant in the Homeric epics. Also (taking account of the fact that the surviving relevant Hesiodic passages are not describing narrative action, or dealing with a katabasis or with the journey of the shades to Hades, but are concerned with the divine beings associated with

---

[163] On Cerberus cf. also Hes. *Th.* 311. In Homer *Il.* 8. 367–8; *Od.* 11. 621–5 only mentions him en passant in the context of his abduction by Herakles. On Cerberus cf. also Rohde 1925: 237, 244 n. 6; Garland 1985: 54, 153–4; Brommer 1986: 43–6. The notion that he prevents the dead from leaving Hades continues also in the 5th cent.: cf. e.g. Eur. *Alc.* 361–2 where he is paired in that role with Charon.

[164] It cannot be excluded that this is Homer's articulation of the collective belief 'the shade only enters Hades at burial'.

the Underworld[165]) we can say that Hesiod presents the same image of this division between the two worlds as Homer.

4. THE DESTINY OF THE SHADES: COLLECTIVE *VERSUS* INDIVIDUAL

Another major eschatological question is whether all the shades have the same collective destiny, or there are differentiations such as rewards and punishments, depending on conduct in life. Besides beliefs that vary throughout the epics we have seen some, such as the transition between the world of the living and Hades, that are constant throughout; some others are constant but for a few, thinly scattered, new elements. A facet of Homeric eschatology that falls in the latter category is the collective destiny of the shades. The dominant picture in the epics is that there is no individual destiny for individual shades, no rewards or punishments for morally or otherwise reprehensible behaviour. It is in the following period that the concept of individual destiny and salvation develops. But the germs of this development can be found in Homer. The hierarchical differentiations associated with Achilles and Minos in *Odyssey* 11[166] could be seen as part of the erosion of the collective destiny, and in a way they are. But they do not involve a radically different fate depending on (ritual or moral) behaviour in life, and they do not

---

[165] Paus. 9. 31. 5 tells us that Hesiod wrote a katabasis of Theseus and Peirithous; cf. fr. 280 Merkelbach–West which is not informative for our purposes. On the articulation of the world, upper and lower, in Hesiod cf. M. L. West 1966: 358–9 (on Tartaros cf. also M. L. West 1971: 26; Scalera McClintock 1989: 64, 68–9). The three-storey universe (cf. M. L. West 1966: 358) described by Hesiod, which, as West notes, leaves out places like Hades and other parts of the world, for they do not belong to either Tartaros, Earth, or Heaven, is surely only the basic skeleton of a more complex nexus of articulations. Tartaros is the place where live divine beings antagonistic to 'the present' gods ruling the universe; Earth is the dwelling of human beings; the Heaven that of the gods ruling the universe. Given that Hades is under the Earth the space between Tartaros and the Earth contains Hades. Indeed Homer (*Il.* 8. 13–16) tells us that Tartaros is as far down underneath Hades as the Earth is from the Heavens. We are not told how that relates to the distance between the surface of the Earth and Hades, but everything suggests that this was meant to be very much smaller, a conclusion confirmed and reinforced by *Il.* 20. 61–6. So one possible articulation is to take the Earth and Hades as one composite unit, both parts of which contain human beings—while neither Heaven nor Tartaros do in these early Greek perceptions of the cosmos. If we take the Earth as a node, the lower part of the cosmos can also be thought of as articulated into three parts: Tartaros: gods' antagonists; Hades: dead men and chthonic gods; Earth: men. On the articulation of the cosmos and the possibilities of communication between Hades, Earth, and Heaven cf. also Bérard (1974: 25–6).

[166] Cf. Appendix.

involve rewards and punishments; they are a reflection of their position in life. However, the germs of that other development that does involve these traits are also present in the epics. They are not integrated in the eschatological survey of *Odyssey* 11, but are casually mentioned in the oath which invokes as witnesses—among others—the Erinyes who punish under the earth dead men who have sworn a false oath.[167] The Erinyes in Homer appear as upholders of justice and order, which was endangered by forswearing—for the oath played an important part in early Greek life. It was probably when life and social transactions became more complex and precarious, in the expanding communities and universe of the eighth century, that the oath acquired this eschatological underpinning in the context of a funerary ideology in which the inescapably collective destiny in Hades was under pressure.

The only people punished in Hades in *Odyssey* 11 are the three 'cosmic sinners' who offended against the gods and the cosmic order, Sisyphus, Tantalus, and Tityos (vv. 576–600). I have discussed their myth in detail elsewhere[168] and I shall say something more about their presence in *Odyssey* 11 below. Here I shall summarize some of my conclusions concerning the significance of their punishments. I argued that all three were perceived to have offended against the gods and the articulation of the cosmos; and that all three were punished in ways that are especially appropriate to, and reflect, their individual crime.

Tityos was punished for having tried to violate sexually the goddess Leto. He had thus offended against the gods and against the articulation of the universe by trying to force sexual intercourse on someone hierarchically superior to him. In Hades he was lying on the ground while two vultures tore at his liver; he was presumably immobile, since, as Odysseus remarks, he did not ward the birds off with his hands. Thus, his excessive sexual activity and aggression against a goddess's body was punished through immobility and painful erosion of his organ of sexual desire (his liver) through the savage continuous invasion of his body by vultures, a lower form of life to him, as he had been a lower form of life than the goddess

---

[167] *Il.* 3. 276–80; 19. 259–60. For the Erinyes in Homer cf. Lloyd-Jones 1971: 75; Padel 1992: 164–7.

[168] Sourvinou-Inwood 1986b: 37–58. For bibliog. see ibid. 37 n. 1 on all three sinners, 37 n. 3 for Tityos, 40 n. 17 on Tantalos, and 47 n. 52 on Sisyphos.

whose body he tried to invade. His punishment is based on a reversal of his transgressive behaviour. Tantalos was standing in water which receded every time he tried to assuage his thirst, and under trees with fruit which the wind moved out of his reach every time he tried to pick some to eat. His crime is not mentioned in *Odyssey* 11. I argued that there are strong reasons for thinking that his transgression would have been understood by the poet and the audience to have pertained to Tantalos' commensality with the gods, and to be related to the food and drink he shared with them. If so, there was perfect symmetry between crime and punishment. His violation of his privilege of commensality with the gods is punished through the reversal of this highest form of eating and drinking: hunger and thirst intensified by the immediate vicinity of food and drink. The symmetry is even stronger if, as I argued seems likely, his breaking of the alimentary code that helps articulate the cosmos was understood to have involved the cannibalistic banquet, which entailed an even more radical threat to the cosmic order and offence against the gods than the other versions of this transgression.

Sisyphos is pushing a large boulder up a hill, but the stone keeps rolling back, and he has to start again. In the dominant strand of the tradition Sisyphos' crime was that he tried to escape death, and he managed to escape from Hades. This story appears in different variants, but all ascribe to Sisyphos the same punishment as *Odyssey* 11. 593–600. I hope to have shown that the crime for which he was understood to be punished in the *Odyssey* was the attempt to escape death; this involved both an offence against Hades and Persephone and also against all the gods and the cosmic order, which he disturbed and threatened by disturbing the proper boundaries between life and death. I also hope to have shown that his punishment reflects his crime in a way comparable to the cases of Tityos and Tantalos. Sisyphos escaped into the upper world and was brought down again. Moving upwards and downwards again is the basic structure of his punishment, this is what his toiling to perform an unfinishable task involves. Since this up and down movement is the underlying structuring pattern, the central skeleton, of both his crime and his punishment, his punishment reproduces, and is structured by, the transgressive movement which constituted the crime—now endlessly repeated. In the Greek funerary representations 'up' stands for the upper world and 'down' for Hades.

The endless upwards and downwards movement of Sisyphos' punishment reproduces endlessly his crime, represents it through an image, and also symbolizes the impossibility of achieving what Sisyphos attempted, of escaping death. The futility of the toil he expended in his attempt to escape death corresponds to the futility of his physical toil in Hades.

These myths pertain also to the articulation of the human limits and of the perception that man must not overstep these limits. All three sinners in *Odyssey* 11 are punished for crimes which constituted offences against the cosmic order which they had endangered, as well as personal offences against the gods that were its guarantors. All three transgressions relate to, and help define, the limits of humanity; they articulate (among other things) the notion that there are proper boundaries between men and gods that must be respected. Tityos, Tantalos, and Sisyphos threatened that division with offences in the three most important areas of human experience pertaining to the most basic characteristics and needs of humanity: food (Tantalos); sex (Tityos) and death (Sisyphos). Men have to eat, copulate and reproduce themselves, and die. But these 'natural' areas—and the giving of death, killing—are governed by rules, ordered not only by natural laws but also by cultural edicts, perceived as being grounded in the cosmic order. Myths of transgression help define the normative. The eternal punishments of Tityos, Tantalos, and Sisyphos in *Odyssey* 11 help define the human limits and stress the boundaries between men and gods. This myth taken as a whole, then, pertains, above all, to the articulation of the cosmos. The eternal punishment of the cosmic sinners who transgressed against the gods and the cosmic order may not originally have been perceived as an eschatological myth; it may have originally belonged to a cosmic setting. If this is correct, the punishment may have been transferred to Hades in the context of the trend, observed, we saw, in other facets of Homeric eschatology, towards a gradual and very partial erosion of the conception of the collective and undifferentiated destiny of the shades, and the emergence of differentiations both in the positive and in the negative direction. In any case, whatever the theme's earlier history may have been (if any) the presence of the sinners in Hades in *Odyssey* 11 is one more element through which the collective destiny of the shades is eroded, one more element of eschatological differentiation. Certainly, this negative differentiation of mythological figures expanded in the archaic period, and the myth of the three sinners eventually inspired other myths of punishment in Hades, structured on the same pattern, such as that of Oknos, and the water-carriers.[169] Eventually, and in the context of further developments involving greater differentiation and the increasing movement towards a more individual destiny of the shades, in certain strands of belief the punishment of the mythological sinners furnished a paradigm on which was modelled the punishment in the afterlife of ordinary impious and unjust people.[170]

5. HADES AND THE SHADES OF THE DEAD[171]

(a) Odyssey 11: Its Place and its Composition

In order to reconstruct the ancient readings of, and thus also the beliefs articulated in, this book we must consider its position in the epic, its significance, and integrity. I cannot discuss the arguments put forward by the scholars who have expressed disquiet about the relationship of *Odyssey* 11 to the rest of the poem; but I submit that there cannot any longer be any doubt that *Odyssey* 11 and the rest of the narration at Phaeacia form a coherent and organic part of the *Odyssey* and were composed by Homer.[172] As we saw, this narration is a character-text, in which Odysseus is the secondary internal narrator and focalizer, a long external *analepsis*, a flash-back

---

[169] Cf. e.g. briefly Carpenter 1989: 79. On Oknos cf. esp. Graf 1974: 110–12, 188–94; on water-carriers: ibid. 112–19.

[170] Cf. e.g. Plato, *Rep.* 363c–d.

[171] An earlier version of some parts of this section made up a lecture delivered as a Kinchin Smith Memorial Lecture at the Institute of Education of the University of London in May 1977 and again at the École des Hautes Études in Paris in May 1979. Since books could be written on *Od.* 11, my discussion is very selective, as is my bibliography, which only includes the most 'necessary' references. On book 11 and its place in the *Odyssey* cf. Heubeck 1989: 3–11 with bibliog.; cf. also Commentary on book 11, *passim*; on the views put forward with regard to its origin and composition cf. esp. the brief critical discussion with bibliog. in Heubeck 1989: 75–7.

[172] Cf. e.g. Heubeck 1989: 4–11 with bibliog. (to which add Vidal-Naquet 1973: 269–92). Heubeck (1989: 8–11) discusses the 'unreal' world of the adventures in 9–12 and argues that these adventures are significantly related to the rest of poem and also that their order is significant in relation to the reduction of Odysseus from commander of a fleet to a pitiful lone seafarer and that there are subtle organic relationships between the different adventures. Cf. also below further aspects of the organic relationships between the Nekyia and the rest of the poem.

outside the time span of the primary fabula.[173] Let us consider the place of the Nekyia within this narration and within the epic as a whole.

It has been recognized[174] that Odysseus' adventures from the moment he leaves the land of the Kikones take place in an unreal, mythical world, a fairyland, which is opposed to the real world, of Ithaca especially and also of Pylos and Sparta; on the border of the two worlds stand the Phaeacians, who partake of both.[175] This fairyland is essentially non-human, at times super-human at others sub-human; Odysseus' journey is also the story of his return to normality and the human condition.[176] His journey nowhere cuts across Telemachos' journey in the real world.[177] There are only two points of contact between the two worlds: the borderline Phaeacians who, because they partake of both worlds are able to effect Odysseus' passage from one to the other; and, more indirectly, Proteus' revelation to Menelaos, repeated to Telemachos at Sparta, about Odysseus' being forcibly retained by Kalypso. This careful interaction indicates a unity of conception of the whole poem. In my view, the Nekyia relates very precisely and significantly to the rest of the fairyland. The visit to Hades forms the middle and highest point of the adventure sequence: there are seven encounters in Odysseus' narrative between leaving Troy and Hades: with the Kikones, the Lotus-eaters, the Cyclopes, Aiolos twice, the first encounter involving a helpful Aiolos, the second a hostile one, the Laestrygonians, Circe; and seven encounters between Odysseus' leaving Hades and his reaching Ithaca: Circe, the Sirens, Skylla and Charybdis (encounter with Skylla), the island of the Sun, Skylla and Charybdis again, this time encounter with Charybdis, Kalypso, the Phaeacians—not mentioned as an encounter but present as an audience. In my view, this central position corresponds to the special significance of the visit to Hades: in this fairyland of non-humanity, Hades provides a strong contact with humanity and

---

[173] A further refinement in the classification of this narrative pertains to content: in terms of its content it belongs to Genette's homodiegetical type, that is, it concerns the same characters as the primary narrator text; indeed this is the homodiegetical narrative through which Genette illustrates this type of character-text (though he does not use the latter term): 1969: 201; cf. 205.

[174] Cf. Heubeck 1989: 4–11 with bibliog.; to which add Vidal-Naquet 1973: 269–92.

[175] Cf. Segal 1962: 17–64.

[176] For the return of Odysseus to Ithaca as a return to humanity cf. also Segal 1962: 20.

[177] Cf. Vidal-Naquet 1973: 274–5.

normality. Hades belongs to the other world in so far as it lies beyond the limits of the experience of living beings; but it is also a part of the fate of humanity, of normality. It is the ultimate human experience. What is abnormal and part of the fairyland modality is that a living person should reach it. But by reaching it Odysseus regains a contact with humanity and normality in the middle of the non-human world. The Nekyia, then, relates to the humanity which he left behind and will ultimately regain at the end of the journey, a humanity that will eventually also bring death. The circumstances in Hades contribute to the awareness of this; Odysseus' encounter with his dead mother and comrades remind him of his own mortality, and Teiresias brings the point home by telling him how he will eventually die. This humanity aspect of the Nekyia is also brought out by the fact that Odysseus does not see, or come in contact with, the Underworld deities, as Herakles had done. Persephone causes things to happen; she is said to have sent forth the heroines' shades,[178] and Odysseus claims that he was afraid she might send him Gorgo's head.[179] But she is not a visible presence in *Odyssey* 11, she operates in a way comparable to that in which the other gods normally operate in the Upper World—though, of course, Athena is intensively present in the 'real' world of the *Odyssey*. But in Hades, unlike Herakles, Odysseus only sees the human experience after death.

The differentiation between the upper world and Hades is stressed through the contrast with the episodes that precede it and follow it, set in Circe's island. Darkness and lack of sun consistently characterize Hades.[180] Circe and her island have emphatic associations with light and the sun: she is the Sun's daughter and at her island 'are the dwellings and dancing floors' of Eos, the Dawn, and 'the rising places of the sun'.[181] This sharp contrast emphasizes the darkness and joylessness of Hades. These characteristics radiate into, and contaminate, its immediate surroundings: the land of the Kimmerians, at the *peirata Okeanoio* is dark, covered in mist and cloud and the sun does not shine on it.[182]

---

[178] *Od.* 11. 225; cf. also 385–6.
[179] *Od.* 11. 633–5.
[180] Helios in Hades, instead of shining on mortals and immortal gods, is a threat, of a reversed, disordered world: cf. *Od.* 12. 382–6.
[181] *Od.* 12. 3–4.
[182] *Od.* 11. 13–17. On the Kimmerians cf. Heubeck 1989: 77–9 with bibliog. Their association with darkness does not necessarily entail that the notion of the land of the

Hades relates both to the fairyland world and to the world of reality through oppositions:

Hades is normal humanity; the fairyland world is not.

Hades is associated with death, the fairyland world with life (including cases of immortality). This is articulated in physical terms: Hades is associated with darkness; the fairyland world with light.

Hades is human but different from normal human experience; the real world is the normal human experience.

Hades is connected with death; the real world is connected with (finite) life. This is articulated in physical terms through the opposition: Hades is dark, has no sun; the real world has light and sun.

Hades in the *Odyssey*, then, is a 'middle' place, conceptually located, and mediating, between fairyland and real world.

In these circumstances, it cannot be doubted that the Nekyia is an organic part of the *Odyssey*. But this does not mean that we should not consider its compositional prehistory, ask whether there are reasons for thinking that it may have redeployed and reshaped material from a Nekyia that had not belonged to the same position as *Odyssey* 11. It is necessary to abandon the perceptual cast derived from the dichotomy Unitarian *v.* Analytical, and go beyond the questions generated by one or the other approach. Hence, textual elements perceived by the analysts as inconsistencies that proved their thesis can help us see the epic in a wider perspective, if we consider them as possible products of the interactions between Homer's choices and the choices of his predecessors which he abandoned.

It has been noted[183] that though Circe sends Odysseus to Hades so that he can obtain Teiresias'[184] advice about his journey, he gets little advice on this point and Circe in book 12 repeats that advice and adds more; so there was no reason for this trip to the Under-

Kimmerians was invented for the purpose of making them neighbours of the Land of the Dead. For if the notion of a land in the dark west covered in mist and cloud (on which cf. Heubeck 1989: 79) had predated this articulation of the cosmos that allows one to reach Hades by travelling west, it may have helped its creation; the fact that it shared one of the characteristics of Hades may have been one of the factors that attracted Hades to the west.

[183] Cf. e.g. Page 1955: 28–47; Kirk 1962: 238.
[184] On Teiresias cf. Brisson 1976; cf. also Loraux 1989: 16–18.

world if it had been undertaken for the reasons given.[185] The advice that will not be duplicated and supplemented by Circe concerns Ithaca. Teiresias tells Odysseus about the Suitors, foretells his revenge, gives advice about what must be done after that, and finally prophesies Odysseus' death in happy old age. Thus he articulates closure; he prophesies not only the closure of Odysseus' journey, but also of his life, which will bring him full circle where he is standing now, in Hades, but this time as a shade, never to leave it. He tells Odysseus that, after he has killed the suitors, he must take an oar and travel inland until he finds people who know nothing about the sea. He will realize that he has reached such a place when he meets people who will mistake his oar for a winnowing fan. When this happens he must plant the oar in the earth and make a sacrifice to Poseidon of a ram, a bull, and a boar. Then he must return home and offer hecatombs to all the gods. This theme includes not only the motif of the appeasement of Poseidon, but also the motif of Odysseus reconnecting himself to the earth and settled life, of planting, fixing into the earth, the symbol of the sea, the wanderings, and the fairyland, as a sign of his formal acceptance of the stability, normality, and humanity associated with the cultivated earth. In the opposition between the oar, associated with the sea and the wanderings, and the winnowing fan, instrument of agriculture, a characteristic trait of normal, settled human life, it is the latter that is privileged and the former that is abandoned. Through being planted in the earth the oar is brought into the orbit of settled life, its original nature rejected. The sacrifice of the hecatomb to all the gods when he returns home sanctifies Odysseus' new beginning in settled life. The one advice, then, given to Odysseus by Teiresias that will not be duplicated by Circe involves strong closure, closure of the adventures and closure of Odysseus' life. In Homer's *Odyssey*—given Odysseus' plight at that moment of narrative time and the ostensible reason for his visit to Hades— this prophecy functions as a prefiguration of the adventure's happy ending and projects forward a closure beyond the text. One possible, alternative place for such a strong closure may have been the end of an earlier poem, in which the consultation of Teiresias was motivated by the desire to achieve precisely this closure and aus-

---

[185] Of course Page (1955: 28–47) faults the composition and integration of *Odyssey* 11 also for other reasons, mostly based on culturally determined judgements which he describes as 'common sense' (cf. 1955: 28). But common sense is culturally determined.

picious beginning. The juxtaposition of this closure to the less than happy Homeric motivation for the consultation suggests that this version of Teiresias' prophecy, and *Odyssey* 11, may have been created by Homer out of material inherited from a Nekyia which was part of a closure at the end of a poem in which Odysseus, after he settled his affairs in Ithaca, set out to ask Teiresias' advice either about how to reconcile himself with Poseidon, so that he would not be persecuted by divine anger in his new life, or generally about what he should do in order to obtain an auspicious beginning for his new life.[186]

Thus, it seems plausible that at least one pre-Homeric epic had a Nekyia at its end, functioning as a closure; and that Homer reshaped this Nekyia while transferring it to the middle of the fairyland adventures, as part of the choices that gave it the special significance and function in the fairyland mentioned above.[187] If so, the Hades which Odysseus had visited in the earlier epic would not have been reached through a journey to the ends of the earth, but descended down to through one of the entrances to the Underworld (which, it was believed, existed in various parts of Greece) in a place near Ithaca; this place can only have been Epirus, the geography of which is reflected in, provided material for the construction of, the geography of Hades, and in which was eventually situated the oracle of the dead.[188] If this is right, it would have been Homer who moved the entrance to the Underworld from Epirus to the ends of the earth in order to suit the new (geographical and conceptual)

---

[186] Since this prophecy takes its full significance only when situated at the end of Odysseus' adventures, the Nekyia on which Homer based his *Od.* book 11 was not, I submit, an independent poem, as has been suggested (cf. e.g. Page 1955: 28–47, esp. 46), but a Nekyia in the earlier poem situated at the end of Odysseus' adventures, after his return to Ithaca.

[187] The suggestion that this poem was pre-Homeric is based on the assumption that the Homeric *Odyssey* took shape over the years of oral performance during Homer's career into something closely resembling the poem as we have it, and also that other Homeric versions had not been radically different from the form in which we know it. As Dr C. B. R. Pelling has suggested to me, if we are to suppose that the Homeric *Odyssey* could have taken very different forms in the course of Homer's career, some of the epic material which I have been here attributing to an epic poem earlier than the *Odyssey* could have been part of an earlier alternative Homeric *Odyssey* which did not disappear when the *Odyssey* as we know it took its final form.

[188] The date of the beginning of the oracle of the dead cannot be determined precisely, nor the early modalities of its function—whether, for example, it had only involved chthonic deities, or chthonic heroes, or what. On the Nekyomanteion cf. Dakaris n.d.: *passim*; 1973: 139–49; Burkert 1985: 114–15; Vermeule 1979: 200–1, 252 n. 27 with further bibliog.; *Ergon* 1990: 73–7; 1991: 58–62.

location of the consultation. Pausanias[189] thought that Homer had used Thesprotian landscape elements to construct his Underworld, and this is much more plausible than the notion that the Thesprotian rivers were named after Homer, especially since the site of the Nekyomanteion, the oracle of the dead, does seem to be not entirely unrelated to the topography of the Underworld[190] in a way that suggests that the epic tradition had used real geographical Thesprotian features, because it was describing a real place, where an entrance to the Underworld was supposed to be situated. When Homer moved the Nekyia amid the fairyland adventures, he removed the entrance to the Underworld from the actual world of Greece and associated it with the fairyland. Thus, he placed his Hades at the ends of the earth, to be reached by ship, but retained the names of the geographical features of the earlier poem, which in that poem (on my hypothesis) had belonged to real life Thesprotia, while now they are in the Other World.

This notion of a Nekyia as a closing segment of an earlier epic drastically reshaped by Homer is simply a hypothesis, the validity of which does not affect the validity of my discussion of the afterlife. If correct, it would illuminate the parameters of Homer's compositional manipulation of the earlier material; it would also provide some help for the understanding of the circumstances of production of the Continuation of books 23. 297 ff. and 24, though again, as will become clear, the validity of the case for its inauthenticity is unaffected by the validity or otherwise of the hypothesis offered here.

(b) *Afterlife Beliefs in* Odyssey *11. 1–564 and Elsewhere*

In *Odyssey* 10. 493–5 Circe tells Odysseus that in Hades Teiresias' *phrenes*, his mind, his wits, are steadfast, *empedoi*, that Persephone has granted this privilege to him, to have *noon*, his mind, his wits, his capacity for intelligent thought, even in death, while the other dead dart about as shadows.[191] This concept is consistent with some articulations in the early part of *Odyssey* 11. Also, in *Odyssey* 11. 476 Achilles calls the dead *aphradees*, without intelligence. However,

[189] Pausanias 1. 17. 5.

[190] This is a deliberately minimalist statement, understating the case. Dakaris, the excavator of the Nekyomanteion, calls it a 'close correspondence' (Dakaris n.d.: 6).

[191] Cf. Heubeck 1989: 69 ad loc. On *phrenes* cf. Padel 1992: 19–25; on *noos*: ibid. 32–3; Bremmer 1983: 75–6; cf. 61–2 (on both).

to return to Circe's speech, then Circe goes on to tell Odysseus[192]
that when he reaches Hades he must make a chthonic libation to
the dead, supplicate them and vow that when he returns to Ithaca
he will sacrifice a barren heifer to them and separately a black ram
to Teiresias. After he has prayed to and supplicated the dead, he
must sacrifice a ram and a black ewe in a certain way; then his
companions must skin and burn the animals and offer prayers to
Hades and Persephone while he himself must ward off the shades
of the dead from the blood in the sacrificial trench—he must not
let them approach until after he has consulted Teiresias. Indeed this
is what Odysseus and his companions do in vv. 23 ff. But none of
these ritual acts that are addressed to the dead can easily be perceived
as capable of being addressed to the witless shadow-like shades
described in *Odyssey* 10. 493–5 that are only capable of the most
elementary mental activity after they have drunk blood that is
physically in front of them. For these ritual acts necessitate shades
able to register, and rejoice at, rites addressed to them by Odysseus
both in Hades and in Ithaca; they thus make sense in terms of, and
so can be seen as refracting, a funerary ideology in which ritual acts
were addressed to shades capable of registering, and rejoicing at,
them. It could be argued that they acquired that capacity after
drinking the blood of the sacrifice offered to them in the upper
world. But this will not do, for in *Odyssey* 11 they need physically
to go up individually to the sacrificial trench in front of them to
drink the blood. It is possible that this schema 'they drink the blood
of sacrifice' provided the conceptual space in which the Homeric
and later audience may have accommodated and made sense of the
'contradiction'; but, I submit, the belief in witless shades as articulated in *Odyssey* 11 could not have interacted with the ritual behaviour of libations and sacrifices to the dead.[193]

---

[192] *Od.* 10. 517–37.

[193] I am not alone in perceiving this to be the case, e.g. Rohde (1925: 38) also thinks that
these offerings are in contradiction with what he considers to be the strict Homeric view of
the shades; but he takes their inclusion to be an oversight of the poet's and to be the vestiges of
an ancient worship of the dead. I am arguing here (explicitly and implicitly) that notions such
as 'oversight' and 'vestiges' are not meaningful; and that we should try to understand the ways
in which the audience would have made sense of the poem in terms of what we know or can
reconstruct about their assumptions; and through this route try to gain some access to the
poet's selections, which are otherwise beyond the grasp of our culturally determined judgement which inevitably operates through logical schemata about what seems plausible to us, that
is through our own culturally determined assumptions. This is why I generally avoid the exercise of engaging with the different interpretations of the Nekyia that are based on such notions.

If this is right, if this segment of the text articulates an epically constructed eschatology made up of elements that had originally belonged to different belief systems and were conflated during the transmission of epic material, we must try to reconstruct how Homer's audience made sense of it. In my view, what seems to us a 'contradiction' would have been accommodated if for Homer and his audience offerings to the dead were common practice, and so part of their common assumptions; for in that case the audience would have seen the distanced witless shades of the inherited epic material in terms of their common assumptions pertaining to appropriate behaviour towards the dead, without questioning its suitability, or necessarily registering it as problematic. This attempted reading of their reading coincides, we shall see, with the results of the (independently conducted) investigation of funerary behaviour in the real world.

Let us consider the nature of the shades elsewhere in the poems and see how it relates to what we have seen so far. In *Iliad* 23. 103–7 Achilles expresses the view that there exists in Hades a *psyche* and an *eidolon atar phrenes ouk eni pampan*. This view is not given any special authority in the poem; it is presented as a surmise derived from his limited experience with the dead. But it is interesting that he expresses this view as though it followed from his encounter with Patroklos, while it does not. On the contrary, the shades who prevented Patroklos' shade from crossing the river and entering Hades (*Il*. 23. 71–3) do not belong together with the concept of witless shades. That is, the latter image was not articulated by a poet in whose assumptions the shades were witless. Thus, in this episode two different perceptions of the nature of the shades are juxtaposed. Would this have registered as a logical contradiction to the poet and his audience? Surely not; for otherwise this selection would not have been made. One context in which this can be made sense of is if we suppose that in the poet's and the audience's assumptions shades were 'lively', so that nothing problematic registers with regard to the shades' actions as reported by Patroklos, and Achilles' statement that the shades have no *phrenes* was perceived as one character's speculation.

In *Iliad* 24. 591–5 Achilles asks Patroklos, who has been buried and is in Hades, not to be angry with him, if he hears of the release of Hector's corpse. The notion that the dead in Hades can know what the living do[194] is not compatible with the perception of the

---

[194] Cf. Macleod 1982: 138 *ad* 592–4.

shades as witless. Most importantly, the 'witless shades' perception is incompatible with the belief (discussed in § ii.4 above) that the Erinyes punish under the earth dead men who have sworn a false oath.[195] In general, while a belief in the collective destiny of the shades is compatible both with witless and not-witless shades, the individual destiny of the shade is only compatible with the perception that the shades are not witless. Since the trend towards a more individualized destiny of the shades is the emerging and developing trend in the Homeric and post-Homeric world, we conclude that the belief in shades that were not witless is most likely to have corresponded to the beliefs of the culture in which the Homeric epics acquired their final form. Indeed, it will become clear that it is only through this hypothesis, which entails that the perceptual filters through which the epic material was perceived and manipulated by Homer and made sense of by his contemporary audience were shaped by a belief in 'lively' shades, that we can make sense of the fact that the divergence between the two strands of belief was not perceived by the poet and his audience as a logical contradiction of the type that blocks selections. The concept of the 'lively' shades articulates activities and beliefs in various parts of the epics, while the articulation of the belief in the witless shades is more circumscribed. Outside *Odyssey* 11 it only occurs in two statements, Circe's and Achilles', and even in *Odyssey* 11 it is confined to a very limited segment of the book. This suggests that the latter is an inherited concept that does not determine selections outside a very circumscribed context, in which the poet is deploying inherited material. Outside this context he does not stick to the constraints of the belief in witless shades; for to him (and to his audience), by whom the belief in the lively shades was taken for granted, the articulation of behaviour or belief involving the shades as lively did not register as other than 'natural'. Thus he (and they) attributed to the senseless ghosts of tradition behaviour-patterns that belonged with the more lively shades of their own belief system.

The idea that Achilles has great power among the dead in Hades also radically contradicts the concept of witless ghosts. In *Odyssey* 11. 485–6 Odysseus says to Achilles *nyn aute mega krateeis nekyessin enthad' eon*; this is taken up by Achilles in his famous reply at 489–

---

[195] *Il.* 3. 276–80; 19. 259–60. Cf. Scalera McClintock 1989: 75–6.

91, that he would prefer to be alive, even as the servant of a poor man, than to rule among all the dead, *e pasin nekyessi kataphthimenoisin anassein.* I have suggested[196] that, contrary to the generally held view,[197] this statement would not have indicated to Homer's contemporary audience that Achilles changed his mind about the choice he made to die a glorious death while young, that from the perspective of Hades things now look different. For the premise of Achilles' decision was that eventually we all have to die, and, given that, a glorious death, which ensures one's memory survival in song and the collective memory, is preferable. What is expressed through this image is not Achilles' regret for his earlier choice, but the early Greek love of life: any life is preferable to death, a wretched servant alive is better off than the king of the dead. It is clear, in a way that transcends the constraints of the cultural determination of our judgement, that notions such as *nyn aute mega krateeis nekyessin enthad' eon* and *pasin nekyessi kataphthimenoisin anassein* cannot have been generated in the same system as the belief in witless ghosts; for the idea of a witless ghost incapable of thought and recognition having power over other witless ghosts is self-contradictory. These notions, which involve the concept of an hierarchical articulation of the world of the dead, can only be sustained, and so generated, in a system in which the dead have faculties, values, and behaviour-patterns at least minimally comparable to those they had in life. If the belief in the witless ghosts without any faculties were held by the poet and his audience and had helped shape their perceptual filters, the notion of Achilles' status would have been literally inconceivable. But if, as I suggest, the filters of both poet and audience were shaped by a belief in a Hades which (whether or not it was explicitly hierarchically articulated) involved inhabitants with faculties, values, and behaviour-patterns at least minimally comparable to those they had in life, Achilles' superior status in Hades would have appeared 'only common sense', and so accepted unexamined; thus the fact that it was in conflict with the senseless ghosts concept articulated in *Odyssey* 11 would not have registered.[198]

---

[196] Sourvinou-Inwood 1981: 24.

[197] Cf. e.g. Heubeck 1989: 106 *ad* 488–503.

[198] It is not the case, as for example, Page believed (1955: 25–6) that there is on the one hand a normal Homeric conception of Hades which involves witless shades, and on the

Related to the question of the shades' faculties is the relationship between blood-drinking and the ability to have any intellectual activity of even the most elementary kind. Odysseus' mother Antikleia had not recognized her son until after she had drunk blood. Odysseus asked Teiresias (vv. 141–4) how he could make his mother recognize him and Teiresias told him that those shades whom he will allow to drink blood will speak to him, those whom he will turn away will leave. The implication is that unless a shade drinks blood (s)he cannot recognize Odysseus or speak to him. In the narrative that follows the heroines drink blood before they speak.[199] But later on in the poem, after Odysseus has resumed at v. 385 the narrative he had interrupted at v. 330—an interruption which involves a zooming to the narrative reality of Alkinoos' court[200]— the situation changes. Whether Agamemnon had drunk blood before he recognized, and spoke to, Odysseus, is a matter of controversy, depending on whether one thinks that *pien haima kelainon* in v. 390, found in many manuscripts, is Homeric or an ancient conjecture.[201] Certainly Achilles recognized and spoke to Odysseus immediately without anything being said about him having drunk blood. The notion that we are to supplement mentally the drinking of the blood every time is fallacious. Homer's intentions are inaccessible to us; what is less inaccessible is how would the audience have made sense of the narrative. Since one of the parameters determining their creation of meaning, one of the sets of assumptions through which they would have made sense of the poem, was the epic conventions and technique, which positively uses repetition, they would have taken the absence of repetition to entail that the action did not take place. Most significantly and unambiguously, in vv. 542–67 it is clear that Ajax does not need to drink blood to recover his faculties. For, still angry with Odysseus, Ajax stood apart and spurned him. So he had recognized him, and was feeling towards him the same emotion as he had when alive, anger; presumably he was also thought of as capable of hearing,

other the segment in vv. 568–627, which involves a different conception of the shades, with unimpaired faculties, and which is not Homeric.

[199] Cf. *Od.* 11. 225–34.

[200] On the so-called 'intermezzo' at the palace of Alkinoos, and its relationship to the Catalogue of heroines cf. Doherty 1991: 145–76. Doherty focuses on the presentation of women in book 11, in the internal audience that were the Phaeacians and in Odysseus' narration, and also on the relationship between the two.

[201] Cf. Heubeck 1989: 100–1 *ad* 390.

understanding and speaking, since Odysseus spoke to him and expected him to answer, which Ajax refused to do. Thus, Ajax was capable of doing all the things that we are elsewhere told shades could only do after they had drunk blood. Consequently, the connection between drinking blood and the ability to recognize, speak, and think is unstable and variable in the epics, indeed within *Odyssey* 11. 1–567.[202] This indicates that, whatever the nature and origin of this connection (whether it was a belief inherited in the epic material, or a device constructed by the poet), it was certainly not part of the beliefs, and thus of the perceptual filters, of Homer's own society. For otherwise the shades' ability to communicate without drinking blood would have registered, as a discrepancy, with both poet and audience. This indicates that the witless shades were inherited in the epic material, while in Homer's society shades were believed to have at least some faculties comparable to those of the living.

It has been suggested that the notion that drinking blood allows the shades to regain their faculties temporarily was probably not 'a genuine ancient belief' but an invention by the poet 'in order to make possible the various discourses which are in fact the main substance of the book.'[203] It is not implausible that the notion that drinking blood temporarily restores the shades' faculties was an epic invention. However, first, this would not obviate the need to make sense of the unstable pattern of its appearance; and second, the implicit assumption that the witless shades were constant, the only perception of the shades articulated in the epics, is mistaken. There was, clearly, some epic material involving witless shades, and it is for this material that the blood-drinking was necessary. The fact that the drinking of blood is clustered in the scene focused on Teiresias, and the non-drinking of blood is common in the encounters with his comrades and to the 'Minos section' may suggest that the Teiresias segment deployed earlier material pertaining both to a consultation of Teiresias and to witless shades. Thus, it may well be

---

[202] The implicit notion that such an inconsistency poses no problems because it can be accounted for in terms of poetic aims (cf. Heubeck 1989: 100 *ad* 387), besides being an arbitrary *a priori* belief about the poet's intentions, ignores the audience, and also ignores the fact that the poem–audience relationship was one of the parameters determining Homer's selections. Thus, we need to try to explain why it did not register as a discrepancy, how Homer's contemporary audience made sense of the fact that sometimes the shades needed to drink blood before they could recognize Odysseus and speak and sometimes not.

[203] The quotation is from Heubeck 1989: 86 *ad* 144–9.

that those scholars are right who think[204] that the blood-drinking was transferred to the Nekyia from the practice of oracular consultation of chthonic beings believed to be under the earth, and summonable by an offering of blood. The connection between blood and prophesying is preserved in the Nekyia: Teiresias has his wits about him, speaks and recognizes Odysseus on arrival, but only prophesies after he has drunk blood. On this view, the blood-drinking was then transferred to other shades in order to make it possible for them to communicate with Odysseus despite the fact that they are represented as being normally witless. The fact that the blood-drinking motif was not applied to all the shades suggests, we saw, that the poet(s) composing the Nekyia into more or less its present form did not share the belief in the witless shades. Thus it is possible to suggest tentatively that the 'Teiresias consultation + witless shades' segment went further back in the epic tradition behind the present Nekyia than the latter's other segments, and were elaborated over many generations. But this is only a hypothesis, and nothing hangs on it. What precedes and what follows are entirely independent of this hypothesis.

It is clear, then, that in *Odyssey* 11. 1–567, as in the rest of the epics, there are two strands of beliefs concerning the nature of the shades, and a tension between them, between the notion that shades are witless and devoid of faculties enabling intellectual activity of the most elementary kind, and one in which they have faculties to some extent comparable to those of the living.

Ambiguity and inconsistency of a different kind characterize the way in which the shades' materiality is handled. On the one hand, like Achilles with Patroklos' shade in *Iliad* 23. 99–100, Odysseus cannot clasp and embrace his mother's shade (11. 204–8), because it is immaterial, a point which she stresses in her reply. On the other, he keeps the shades away from the blood by threatening them with his sword, which implies some sort of corporeal nature, otherwise they would have walked through the sword, as ghosts do in our ghost-stories. Thus, we conclude that in the assumptions that shaped the parameters determining the poet's creativity there was probably some uncertainty and ambivalence as to the precise nature of the shades.

---

[204] Cf. e.g. Page 1955: 24–5, 48 n. 3 with bibliog. (chthonic heroes).

(c) Odyssey 11. 568–627

Several ancient and modern scholars have argued that these verses
are interpolated,[205] while others have defended their authenticity.[206]
Heubeck[207] argued that the overall structure of *Odyssey* 11 guarantees the authenticity of the disputed lines. I share this view. The
main support for the case for their authenticity will derive from the
demonstration that the important parts of the case against it are
mistaken.[208] The two most important arguments against authenticity
are of direct relevance to our concerns. The first maintains that the
nature of the shades in this passage is in sharp contrast to that in the
rest of *Odyssey* 11, because here the shades are not witless.[209] This
argument is fallacious. For it is based on the notion that except for
this passage there is a consistent set of beliefs about the nature of
the shades in the poems, within book 11, and elsewhere, which
contrast sharply with the beliefs in the disputed passage. In fact, as
we have seen, there are two strands of such beliefs in the epics: that
in which the shades are witless and that in which they have at least
some of their faculties. The first is more striking,[210] but it is the
second that is dominant—and there are good reasons for thinking
that this second strand corresponded to the beliefs of Homer and
his audience. The lively shades in vv. 568–627, then, are but one of
the several manifestations of this strand of belief, and do not provide
an argument against the authenticity of the passage.

[205] On the ancient discussions of this question cf. Petzl 1969: 6–43. Cf. briefly on the
question of their authenticity: Heubeck 1989: 110–11 *ad* 565–7 and esp. *ad* 567–627 with
bibliog. to which add also Schnaufer 1970: 99–107 with bibliog. S. West (1989: 143 n. 105)
mentions that she 'suspects' that the Continuator who wrote *Odyssey* 23. 297 ff. and 24
'made a significant contribution' to book 11; it is likely that it is the segment under
consideration that she has in mind.

[206] Cf. Heubeck 1989: 77 for bibliog. Eisenberger (1973: 183–91), who convincingly
defended the verses on stylistic and compositional grounds, approached, we shall see presently,
one of the problems raised by the opponents of authenticity with a subtlety that exposed the
crudity of some of those discussions.

[207] Heubeck 1989: 111 *ad* 567–627.

[208] I shall not say anything about the hypothesis (Von der Mühll 1938: 8 ff.) that this part
of the Nekyia is based on a katabasis of Herakles. It may well be right—though I doubt it—
but it is, in my view, based on *a priori* culturally determined judgements and assumptions.
Given the nature of the evidence it is possible to make a great variety of claims and
counterclaims based on what appears logical to our own culturally determined judgement.
Page (1955: 49 n. 7) also finds this view unconvincing.

[209] Cf. e.g. Page 1955: 25–6.

[210] The vividness of the Homeric image of the senseless ghosts is so strong and striking in
its starkness that it has coloured modern scholars' vision of this Hades; without doubt, it is
partly responsible for the monolithic interpretations put on it.

The second argument against authenticity that concerns us consists of the claim[211] that the passage is clumsily adapted to its surroundings. Odysseus was standing outside Hades, but here he is inside it, and yet when this passage ends, at 628, he says that he had not moved from his original position. I shall discuss this question in a moment. The other facet of what is considered to be the awkward integration of our passage concerns the verses that precede it, vv. 565–7, which have been condemned as 'drab', spoiling the sombre beauty of Ajax' sullen silent refusal to talk to Odysseus[212] with the claim that they might have spoken despite Ajax' wrath, but Odysseus was keen to see other shades. This is a crude reading; no attention is paid to the narratological context, and whatever does not fit the modern scholar's culturally determined expectations is rejected as unworthy of the poet. Eisenberger,[213] without using narratological terminology, took account of the fact that this is a character-text, and that it is Odysseus who is the narrator/focalizer; he noted that Ajax' reaction was a humiliation for Odysseus, who was not the man to report it without attempting to restore his self-esteem; through his comment in vv. 565–7 he appears to remain master of the situation. This is surely right; these verses are part of Odysseus' self-presentation, and thus of his characterization, part of the way in which Odysseus' persona was constructed. With regard to his location, the reading that takes the text as saying that he was first standing outside Hades, then he was inside—while at 628 he says that he had not moved from his original position—is not as certain as has often been thought. Heubeck[214] disagrees with the view that Odysseus is walking around within Hades in vv. 568–627 and thinks Odysseus is observing standing by the trench. Willcock[215] comments that Heubeck's 'contradiction of the common view . . . that up to the sight of Ajax Odysseus remains by the trench on the earth's surface, but from then on he is down in the world below . . .' is 'a surprise'. But Willcock's own formulation involves an assumption that may or may not be right: that the trench is on the earth's surface, clearly differentiated from the world below. In my view, it is left open and ambiguous whether the place of the

[211] Cf. e.g. Page 1955: 26–7.
[212] Page 1955: 26–7.
[213] Eisenberger 1973: 184.
[214] Heubeck 1989: 111 *ad* 568–627.
[215] Willcock 1990: 64.

sacrifice was part of the surface of the earth or already in some way part of Hades, or rather, of the 'no-man's land' between Hades and the world of the living which is already part of the 'other world'. It is in the conceptual space created by this ambiguity that is articulated the possibility that a living person goes to Hades (unlike Herakles without divine help) and the shades of the dead who cannot leave Hades come up to him. The same ambiguity may have governed Odysseus' position in vv. 568–627, and thus led to the jerky transitions. The question whether Odysseus had moved into Hades is only meaningful when it is defined in terms of how his position was visualized first, by Homer, and second, by his audience. The first is inaccessible to us except through the text, and since even to try to gain such access first involves trying to make sense of it through the ears of its contemporary audience, we come back to the second. In my view, the text did not impose one reading, and the audience may have visualized Odysseus' location either way; this ambiguity was correlative with the avoidance of articulating explicitly and precisely, even in a character-text, the notion that a living person entered Hades. If the audience assumed that one did not, unless they were explicitly told differently and given some sort of explanation, the perception that he did not enter Hades would have governed their reception, and they would have assumed that he had not, or at least left open the question whether he entered Hades.

What of vv. 602–4, in which Odysseus says that it was Herakles' *eidolon* that he saw in Hades, for the hero himself (*autos de*) was at Olympus with the immortals? The ancient commentators, who thought that they were a sixth-century interpolation,[216] were, in my view, right; these verses are post-Homeric, an interpolation inspired by the desire to reconcile Herakles' presence in Hades in this Nekyia with the fact that in the assumptions of the interpolator and his society his apotheosis was so well established as to raise problems in the reading of the Homeric text, which created a dissonance with the taken-for-granted world of the audience. The following considerations lead me to conclude that Herakles' apotheosis was a post-Homeric creation, and thus also that this explanation is post-Homeric rather than Homeric. First, the fact that the idea that Herakles dies and goes to Hades is so well rooted in the epics

---

[216] Cf. Petzl 1969: 28–41.

as to be a paradigm for the lot of the mortals.[217] Second, the trend towards a mythopoea of immortality is very circumscribed in the Homeric poems; and the gap between Elysion (itself an isolated *hapax* in conflict with the ideology most deeply rooted in the epics) and Olympus is greater than may appear to modern eyes. Third, the pattern of appearance of Herakles' apotheosis, which is not found before the sixth century,[218] when taken at face value coincides with the pattern of the emergence and development of the trend of the exceptional fate after death for a chosen few, which itself developed in interaction with the cultic phenomenon of the development of heroic cults in an ideological context pertaining to the emergence and crystallization of the polis.[219] This coincidence suggests that this pattern may indeed reflect historical reality, that Herakles' apotheosis was a concept that developed long after Homer gave the epics their final form.

Let us now consider vv. 568–627 in a little more detail. The presentation begins with Minos, son of Zeus, whom Odysseus describes as sitting holding a golden sceptre and giving judgements to the dead, settling the differences which these dead people have in Hades. Two important concepts are involved here. First, Minos is depicted as holding a symbol of authority and performing an important function. Second, the shades are not witless but lively, quarrelsome dead, whose faculties are at least up to a point comparable to those of the living. The latter concept, we saw, far from being limited to this part of *Odyssey* 11, is an important strand of belief throughout the epics. The notion that Minos has special status, an hierarchically superior position in Hades, denoted by the sceptre, and correlative to his exercising authority by giving judgements, is comparable to the notion in *Odyssey* 11. 485–6 (cf. 489–91) that Achilles has high status in Hades. Minos' position of authority is the second instance of a Minoan ruler's special association with a Land of the Dead/'Dead' in Homer; we found reasons for thinking that this motif may be what I called a 'later transformation' of a Minoan belief that the Minoan rulers retained their

[217] *Il.* 18. 117–19, cf. also M. W. Edwards 1991: 162 ad loc.
[218] Cf. M. L. West 1966: 416–17, *ad* 947–55; 1985: 130. On the cult of Herakles in Attica cf. Kearns 1989: 35–6, 166 with bibliog.; on Herakles' apotheosis cf. also Stinton 1987: 1–16, esp. 4–5.
[219] On the growth of heroic cults in the 8th cent. and their ideological context cf. Coldstream 1976: 8–17; Bérard 1982: 89–105; De Polignac 1984: 127–51; Whitley 1988: 173–82; Snodgrass 1988: 19–26; Hägg 1987: 93–9.

high status in the afterlife. After Minos Odysseus encounters Orion, who pursues in the afterlife the activity in which he had indulged when alive, hunting.[220] After Orion come the cosmic sinners. The latter form a thematic unit with distinct meanings; what of the Minos and Orion sequence?[221] Minos was a king, a son of Zeus, is represented with the symbol of authority and acts as judge and adjudicator of disputes. Orion is a giant hunter represented as associated with wild beasts and lonely mountains. This, then, is an opposition between man-made culture and civilization and wild nature. This opposition is relevant to Odysseus, who comes from civilization and will return to it, but in the meantime is at the mercy of the forces of nature, in a fairyland, away from humanity and man-made culture. Odysseus during his adventure stage ties up with Orion more specifically through the motif of hunting. Orion hunts in the Underworld, Odysseus hunted in the fairyland: on arrival at Circe's island he hunted and killed a great stag for him and his companions to eat.[222]

The punishment of the cosmic sinners was discussed in § ii.4 above. Its function in *Odyssey* 11 is to give a cosmic dimension to Hades, by including the punishment of the offenders against the gods and the cosmic order. This enlargement of vision accords well with the position of the Nekyia in the *Odyssey* as set out above. There is also a particular relevance in the sinners' inclusion. Because they are offenders against the gods, they are in a way comparable to Odysseus, whose great plight is that he incurred the wrath of Poseidon, and he, or rather his companions, will incur the wrath of Helios at 12. 260–402. However, unlike the cosmic sinners, Odysseus has not committed an offence against the gods involving also an offence against the cosmic order. Therefore, all will be well for him in the end, while the sinners will be punished forever. The special similarity in personality characteristics between Odysseus and Sisyphos, both of whom are both wise men and tricksters, hardly needs mentioning. Sisyphos went up to the world of the living while dead, Odysseus is visiting the world of the dead while still alive. But Sisyphos was trying to disturb the cosmic order by escaping the death that had come upon him, while Odysseus is

---

[220] On the figure of Orion as a hunter cf. Fontenrose 1981: 5–32.

[221] On the relationships between Minos, Orion, Herakles and the sinners in *Od.* 11 cf. also Scalera McClintock 1989: 76–8.

[222] *Od.* 10. 156–82.

using his tricks, and is visiting Hades, in an attempt to ensure that death does not come upon him. After the sinners, Odysseus observes Herakles, who is presented as a powerful, impressive hero; even the decoration of his baldric enhances this image: it depicts bears, wild boars, lions, massacres, and battles. Herakles recognizes Odysseus immediately, and proceeds to compare his own *kakon moron* with that of Odysseus and remind Odysseus that he also had had to visit Hades while still alive. Thus, Herakles, the powerful hero who triumphed against the forces of nature, wild beasts, and the evil force of men, prefigures the re-establishment of order and the return to normality which will be the ultimate fate of Odysseus. Herakles' successful return from the dead to the upper world of humanity, to which he draws attention, foreshadows Odysseus' final return, both from the dead and from the fairyland of non-humanity to the normal world of humanity and Ithaca.

All these thematic connections provide further support for the view that 11. 568–627 form an integral and significant part of the visit to Hades, and were composed by the poet of the *Odyssey*, who presented Odysseus presenting to the Phaeacians a narrative of Hades that was also a vision of the human condition. This vision of Hades served well the purpose to which the Visit to the Underworld was put, as a central point of Odysseus' adventures, partaking both of the other world and of humanity, a humanity alien to the rest of the fairyland and here placed into its cosmic context through the vision of death and the limits of humanity set by the cosmic order articulated through the cosmic sinners. As for the story, the Nekyia as narrated by Odysseus says through the mouth of Teiresias, and also hints in the ways suggested here, that the hero will return to Ithaca and normality, but with his humanity he will also take on his inevitable fate of death, for such is the destiny of man.

(d) *Homeric Beliefs about the Nature of the Shades*

We found strong reasons for thinking that the concept of the witless shades was not a belief of the poet's own time, but an inherited belief that had been perceived and handled, by Homer and his immediate predecessors, through filters shaped by the belief that shades were not witless. This argument stands on its own. But it is conceivable that some independent confirmation may be derived from another direction: an independent argument, based on a wholly different set of data, suggests that the notion that the shades are witless is the type of afterlife belief likely to have characterized Mycenaean eschatology. Though this argument is far from conclusive, the fact that its conclusions coincide with those of our main, independently conducted, analysis cannot, I submit, be considered to be entirely without significance.

As we saw, attempting to reconstruct belief systems on the basis of archaeological data is a highly complex and problematic enterprise. Given the purpose for which I am setting out this argument here (not in order to base a conclusion, or any further hypothesis, on it, but as an argument that may provide some tentative confirmation of results derived from our central, different, type of analysis) it is, I believe, legitimate to set out only the most basic lines of the case. If it is correct that cult of the dead was not practised in Mycenaean Greece,[223] its absence, when placed within the context of Mycenaean death-related behaviour, especially ritual behaviour pertaining to the rulers of the fully developed Mycenaean kingdoms,[224] may be capable of suggesting certain parameters for the reconstruction of (certain parameters of) the Mycenaean conceptions of the afterlife. In Mycenaean society, as in so many societies of various types,[225] the royal funerary ritual had an important ideological significance; this is seen in the very great amount of resources devoted to royal burials, and in the fact that the tholos was a type of ruler grave of impressive monumentality and increasingly elaborate decoration, that functioned as a physical manifestation of royal power.[226] Since the notion of continuity and legitimation through a relationship to one's ancestors is an important concept in royal ideology, and thus in the ideological manipulation of funerary ritual,[227] the practice of cult of the dead might have been expected to have been a preferred option in Mycenaean Greece—unless there was some serious reason that prevented it from being

---

[223] Cf. below, § ii.6.

[224] Without going into the question of Mycenaean state formation, which is not relevant to our present purposes.

[225] Cf. e.g. Cannadine and Price 1987: *passim*.

[226] Cf. e.g. Pelon 1990: 107–12; Wells 1990: 125–40, esp. 128. For a somewhat different conception of the ways in which tholoi were monumental expressions of power (of the top stratum of social groupings such as clans) cf. Wright 1987: 171–84 (answered by Pelon 1990: 110 f. and *passim*). For a different view on tholoi: Darcque 1987: 185–205.

[227] For the notion of legitimation of power through periodical contact with ancestors cf. e.g. Gilbert 1987: 326–7; Bloch 1987: 279, 280, 286.

practised; for it involved periodical offerings at the grave of one's ancestors, and this would offer the appropriate ritual matrix for periodically stressing dynastic continuity—especially desirable in unstable circumstances and generally when such a continuity was a fiction.

Not only does it appear to be the case that no cult of the dead was practised in Mycenaean Greece, but also the nature of Mycenaean tholos and chamber tomb burials makes it extremely likely that no other form of periodic contact with the dead had been practised or been considered desirable;[228] for the fact that the dead were sealed off behind sealed doors and filled-in dromoi suggests that the parameters of selection determining, and articulated in, the burial forms were governed by the notion of separation from, not periodic contact with, the dead—except during burials and secondary burials, for which the tombs were each time re-opened. It is not a matter of revulsion, or fear (for otherwise collective tombs, which involve periodic reopening, would not have been the preferred option) but of symbolic distancing.

Despite its vulnerability to cultural determination, this view, that, because of the ideological importance of royal burials, we would have expected the practice of cult of the royal dead to have been a preferred option unless there was some serious reason to exclude it, gains some support from the fact that the option to practise cult of the dead, and in particular cult of the royal dead, had become conceptually available to the Mycenaeans at least since they had come into contact with Minoan ideology and practice of cult offered to the royal dead. The fact that the Mycenaean rulers did not adopt this ideological ritual nexus from Crete despite the fact that it would have fulfilled identifiable Mycenaean ideological needs suggests that there was a serious obstacle that prevented such an adoption; in this context such an obstacle can only be located in the realm of eschatology. This is inevitably a culturally determined judgement. Nevertheless, I venture to suggest that the most likely explanation of this state of affairs is that Mycenaean afterlife beliefs were such that would have made such ritual meaningless. One (the

---

[228] Of course, we cannot exclude the possibility of some different form of contact with the ancestors, not situated at the grave. But this is a different matter. The possibility that there was contact at the grave of a type that did not leave archaeological traces is less likely; for the dominant burial forms articulate radical separation rather than contact between the dead and the living. Thus it is not only the absence of evidence for cult of the dead, but also the modality of the spatial articulation of the burial space that suggests absence of contact.

strongest) candidate for such a Mycenaean perception that would be incompatible with the practice of cult of the dead or periodic contact with the dead is the notion that, once fully integrated into Hades, the shades were witless ghosts to whom it was impossible to conceive of giving offerings or addressing periodic contact.

In these circumstances, it is legitimate to suggest as a very tentative conclusion that the Mycenaeans had perceived the nature of the shades in Hades to be incompatible with contact with, and offerings from, the living. This would be consistent with, and thus, I submit, offers a little, albeit tentative, confirmation to, the results of the investigation conducted above in this section, that the belief in the witless shades found in the Homeric epics was inherited in the epic tradition and was perceived and manipulated through the perceptual filters of successive generations of poets, which in Homer's own culture involved a belief in lively shades. Be that as it may, what, I submit, has been clearly demonstrated is that the Homeric epics are articulated by, and articulate, two very different strands of beliefs pertaining to the nature of the shades in Hades, that belonged to different eschatological systems. It has also been argued here that the coexistence of the two discrepant strands in the poems can be made sense of on the understanding that the nexus that shaped the perceptual filters of Homer and his audience was that involving the not-witless, 'lively', shades.

6. MARGINALIA ON CULT OF THE DEAD

The question whether cult of the dead had been practised in the Mycenaean world is extremely complex and cannot be adequately discussed here. This short note simply flashes a few signposts.

The view that no cult of the dead was practised in Mycenaean Greece, which is the generally accepted view on the matter, is periodically challenged, but not convincingly, especially since some of these challenges are based on culturally determined 'logical' judgements. Thus, for example, Protonotariou-Deilaki[229] thinks that the mere existence of a grave marker over a Mycenaean grave provides legitimate grounds for believing that cult of the dead was practised, a view that involves a serious misunderstanding of the complex function and significance of the grave marker, which will

[229] Protonotariou-Deilaki 1990: 82.

be discussed in Chapter III. Given this type of approach to what can be considered evidence for the practice of cult of the dead, I should add a note to attempt to forestall any future theory that may emerge as a result of a recent discovery. If it is right that the strange situation in the Kokla tholos (in which offerings but no human remains were found) is to be explained, as the excavator very plausibly suggested,[230] through the hypothesis that the human remains that had been buried in this tholos had been transferred somewhere else, and that this was done in the course of a ritual that involved the sacrifice of two animals in the dromos, and was concluded with the sealing of the tholos with the precious objects inside, probably with the intention of reusing it, an intention which was frustrated, perhaps because the roof collapsed, this would not offer support for the theory of cult of the dead. First, because the ritual in question is very distinct from the practice of cult of the dead. it is a one off rite, while cult of the dead consists of offerings made on fixed occasions for some years after burial. And second, since it would appear to pertain to a ritual associated with a practice of some sort of secondary burial,[231] and since it is at least arguable[232] that the Mycenaean dead may not have been considered to have been finally integrated in the community of the dead until after their remains had been reduced to disarticulated bones (whether or not these were reburied in a secondary burial), any ritual associated with that phase, whether addressed to the dead or only to the deities presiding over the dead, cannot be considered relevant to the behaviour towards, or the eschatology pertaining to the nature of, the shades after they were fully integrated into Hades. It is a very important characteristic of both Minoan and Mycenaean burial practices that there is a significant difference in behaviour towards on the one hand a corpse that still retained some flesh, and thus also its identity as one entity, a spatio-temporal continuum with the deceased, and on the other the disarticulated bones when all flesh had gone.[233] This is a complex matter that cannot be discussed here. I shall only mention, to support the point that what happens at a ceremony of secondary burial cannot be considered relevant to the

---

[230] Demakopoulou 1990: 113–23.

[231] On secondary burial in the Mycenaean world (not a universal Mycenaean practice) cf. Wells 1990: 135–6.

[232] Cf. Wells 1990: 135.

[233] Cf. e.g. Iakovidis 1969: ii. 76.

nature of the shades after they are in Hades, that, since cremation reduces the corpse to disarticulated bones, in some ways it is the secondary, not the primary, burial that can be considered the correlative of the Homeric burial.

The question of the practice of cult of the dead in the eighth century and its history is not unproblematic. The first appearance of a cult of the dead in the different areas is unclear. It is far from clear that, as is sometimes assumed, the Lefkandi monument[234] was more than a grand grave monument to the community leader and had involved cult of the dead—let alone, as some think, heroic cult. Nor is it clear when cult of the dead began to be practised in Athens; the ninth century has been suggested,[235] but this is far from certain, as it depends on interpreting the hole drilled in the base of (the upper part of) kraters functioning as grave markers as designed to allow liquid offerings to get into the earth, which is questionable.[236] And the exact significance of the ritual practices at Grotta in Naxos[237] is still the subject of debate. Nevertheless, it does appear that, to put it minimally, cult of the dead—as well as heroic cult—was practised in eighth-century Greece.[238]

iii. Odyssey 24: The Continuation

1. THE COMPOSITION

In this section I align myself with the widely held view that *Odyssey* 23. 296 ff. and 24, a section which has many oddities of style, is a later addition, a continuation of the *Odyssey* by someone else.[239] The scholia tell us that both Aristarchos and Aristophanes considered 23. 296 to be the end of the Odyssey; the interpretation and validity of

---

[234] On which cf. Ch. III § i.2.
[235] Cf. e.g. Whitley 1991: 116–17.
[236] Cf. Kurtz and Boardman 1971: 57–8.
[237] On which cf. Lambrinoudakis 1988: 235–46.
[238] Cf. Hägg 1983b: 193.
[239] The bibliog. is vast, but the recent publication of the Italian-Oxford Commentary makes it possible to curtail the bibliographical references radically: cf. Heubeck in: Russo, Fernandez-Galiano, and Heubeck 1992: 342–5, 346, 353–4 with bibliog. An important recent study is S. West 1989; cf. also Rutherford 1992: 14–16. For a discussion of the history of the question of the authenticity of *Od.* 23. 297 ff. and 24 in recent scholarship cf. also S. West 1989: 113–14; nn. 6–9.

this statement has been the subject of scholarly controversy.[240] Even if it cannot be proved that the Continuation as a whole is not Homeric, there can be little doubt that the section that primarily concerns us, the Deuteronekyia of Odyssey 24. 1–204 is the work of a later poet. Modern perception that it involves observable 'deviations from, or contraventions of, normal Homeric usage'[241] coincides with ancient opinion: Aristarchos athetized two long passages after 23. 296: 23. 310–43 and 24. 1–204. We shall consider below how this athetesis relates to his view that the Continuation was not Homeric; it will become clear that the two are not contradictory.

The views of critics who consider the Continuation inauthentic can be divided into two groups. One group considers the Homeric Odyssey to have ended at 23. 296 and the Continuation to have been added to this complete poem; the other group maintains that 'the epic as we know it represents the reworking of an older, shorter poem (or a conflation of several older poems) by a redactor usually termed "the B-poet"' to whom is to be attributed 'both the ending of the existing text and other passages (especially the so-called Telemachy, and some of the Phaeacis)'.[242] The arguments against Homeric authorship have been recently restated by S. West, who presented excellently the case against authenticity.[243] Her own position is that the Odyssey ended with Odysseus' household asleep at the end of their eventful day with the conflicts unresolved, and that it was when the Odyssey was officially included in the Panathenaia that the need for a self-contained narrative with a happy ending arose, as well as the need to provide a conclusion of restoring harmony for an audience that did not share the heroic spirit but was concerned about strife and the restoration of harmony in a community. The Continuator adapted and included epic material from elsewhere. Since West's statement of the case against authenticity Rutherford[244] has argued in favour of the view that the Odyssey did not end at 23. 296; he focused on the need for resolution of the public themes and argued that Odyssey 24 is thematically

[240] Cf. Schol. HMQ ad 296 (telos); M, V, Vind. 133 (perus); cf. on these scholia S. West 1989: 113, 118. On the ancient views on the Deuteronekyia of Odyssey 24 and the objections to its authenticity cf. Petzl 1969: 44–66.

[241] S. West 1989: 119; for a synthesis of these cf. ibid. 121–30.

[242] This summary (of an approach he does not share) is by Heubeck (1992: 353).

[243] Cf. S. West 1989.

[244] Rutherford 1992: 14–16.

integrated. My own position is that it is clear that the Continuation is not Homeric, but it is less easy to decide whether or not the Homeric *Odyssey* had ended at 23. 296. I think that it had probably not ended there. One reason for thinking that it did not is because a closure that included resolution of the major problems that would have been strongly perceived to have been generated at this part of the poem—most importantly the possibility of serious problems in Ithaca as a result of the Suitors' death—appears more satisfactory than one that did not. This may be a culturally determined judgement, but the following two considerations suggest, I submit, that it is not only that.

First, the closure in the *Iliad*[245] does involve the resolution of problems generated in the last segment (the last few books) of the poem. Taplin[246] is right that the end of the *Iliad* looks beyond the end to the future, when war and suffering will continue; but this is a different matter from leaving unresolved major problems generated in the previous section of the poem, as the possibility of serious problems in Ithaca as a result of the Suitors' death would have done. Second, as we saw, Teiresias' prophecy to Odysseus in 11. 100–37, like Proteus' prophecy to Menelaos in *Odyssey* 4, is a *prolepsis* presented in an embedded speech involving a tertiary narrator/focalizer able to prophesy the future. Odysseus' projection into the future goes up the point of his death. Thus this *prolepsis* carries the story beyond the end of the fabula and sets out a closure that goes beyond the closure of the *Odyssey* as we have it with or without the Continuation. The part of the *prolepsis* that involves events within the fabula ends at 11. 120 with the killing of the Suitors. The part that takes us beyond the end of the fabula begins with what Odysseus must do to appease Poseidon, which is presented in a seamless sequence from the killing of the Suitors. Thus the part of the *prolepsis* that involves events outside the fabula and sets out the projected closure involves a resolution to the last problem derived from Odysseus' adventures, the appeasement of Poseidon, while at the same time initiating and laying the foundations of Odysseus' new life, which is also included in the *prolepsis* which ends with his death. This articulation implies that all the problems in Ithaca have been resolved when Odysseus sets out to

---

[245] On the end of the *Iliad* and a discussion of the poem's closure cf. now Taplin 1992: 279–84.
[246] Ibid. 280–3.

appease Poseidon. But it does not tell us how, and the audience's expectations would have led them to want to hear how it happened. Also, the fact that the *prolepsis* is articulated by a trend towards resolution and closure (of the problems, and ultimately of Odysseus' life) suggests that, at whatever level of explicitness, the poem's closure was also defined by the trend towards resolution of problems and closure, and not hanging in the air and ambiguity; yet hanging in the air and ambiguity is precisely what we would have if the poem ended at 23. 296. To return to the arguments of those who defend the Continuation's authenticity, Heubeck[247] takes the view that the Continuation 'was always an integral part of the compositional plan of the author who created the *Odyssey* as we know it'; his main argument is thematic integration, 'the fact that the narrative of the last book is so carefully prepared for throughout the rest of the poem, and in such various ways, that a failure to fulfil the expectations aroused by both direct announcements and indirect indications would have been profoundly disappointing and irritating to the poet's audience'. This particular formulation is clearly vulnerable to culturally determined assumptions and expectations; but the basic point of thematic integration cannot be easily dismissed. Let us, then, unpack the different facets of this notion of thematic integration. The most significant from the point of view that concerns us here is the one pertaining to expectations and unresolved conflicts. The argument of the adequacy of closure is inevitably culturally determined, but, we saw, there are good reasons for thinking it unlikely that important problems would have been left unresolved. However, this is not an argument for the authenticity of our Continuation, only an argument in favour of the view that the Homeric *Odyssey* did not end at 23. 296, a view which I share. The notion that the Continuation picks up themes prepared for in the earlier parts of the poem is far less decisive. For an adequate Continuator would have done precisely that, would have interwoven his composition in precisely such a way into the main body of the *Odyssey*.

A theory that would both take account of this need for resolution and explain most satisfactorily what Aristarchos thought he was doing when he athetized two long passages after 23. 296 (23. 310–43 and 24. 1–204), despite the fact that he believed that the Homeric

---

[247] Heubeck 1992: 353–4.

Odyssey ended at 23. 296 and that the Continuation was not Homeric, would be the hypothesis that the Homeric *Odyssey* had had a different ending, which was replaced by the present Continuation, which incorporated material both from the original *Odyssey* ending and from elsewhere. West[248] suggested that the Alexandrians knew of some tradition about the Epilogue/ Continuation similar to that recorded in the Scholia about the Doloneia; that for Aristophanes and Aristarchos the Epilogue was not of a piece with the rest of the *Odyssey*. If this is right, the tradition may well have been that the present ending was not the original ending, but a rewriting of it, so that when athetizing the two long chunks, including the Deuteronekyia, Aristarchos was attempting to excise what he thought did not belong to the Homeric *Odyssey*. It cannot be excluded that the tradition may have included some more precise information, such as that the original Homeric *Odyssey* ending had not included a second Nekyia, but only the events in Ithaca. While the only valid argument in favour of authenticity, that the Continuation is thematically integrated with the rest of the *Odyssey*, is wholly compatible with the thesis that it is a later addition that deployed, among other things, some material from an original Homeric closure segment, the case for its inauthenticity is strong. Individual oddities may be capable of being 'explained away'; the high density of such oddities, of the various kinds of divergences from the Homeric usage, shows that the Continuation is not the work of the poet who gave the rest of the *Odyssey* its final form. This coincides with 'the eschatological incompatibility' of the Continuation with the epics, which will be discussed below.[249] My case for the inauthenticity of the Continuation does not depend on this eschatological incompatibility— and therefore my argument is not circular.

Besides these, the following problematic features in the Deuteronekyia are of special interest because they show, to my mind unambiguously, that it was stitched together from, first, earlier material deriving from an epic poem other than the *Odyssey* (that is, other than the hypothetical original ending of the *Odyssey* which

---

[248] West 1989: 120.

[249] I will not engage in an argument with the views of those defenders of the authenticity of the Continuation who have written on the subject of this eschatological incompatibility; Moulton (1974: 161) and Erbse (1972: 234–5) can illustrate the methodological shortcomings and the culturally determined nature of their approach to the discussion of afterlife beliefs.

I am postulating); and second, new material composed by the
Continuator to fit a second Nekyia at the end of the *Odyssey*,
stitching together something that made some sort of sense. Why
the Continuator should wish to add a Nekyia at this point is a
question I shall address in a moment.

The fact that in *Odyssey* 24. 1 ff. the descent of the shades to
Hades is presented by the external primary narrator is one of the
many ways in which this book is at odds with normal Homeric
usage; for normally the afterlife, Hades and its alternative Elysion,
is not presented by the external primary narrator but by a character
in the narrative, and is thus not given the authority of the primary
narrator. The Continuator would not have taken pains to imitate
the Homeric epics in this respect because, once the distinction lost
its importance,[250] it would not have registered as significant to the
Continuator or his audience. Furthermore, the following aspects of
faulty integration suggest an unsuccessful stitching together of the
theme 'Suitors and Hermes' with the episode 'the shades of Achilles,
Patroklos, Antilochos, Ajax, Agamemnon in Hades'; the form in
which the latter is articulated shows that in the organic version of
this episode, from which the Continuator took it over, the shades'
interlocutor had been Odysseus visiting Hades. First, the problem
centring on the identity of the subject of *euron de psychen* etc. at v.
15; Page notes that it cannot be Hermes and the Suitors, since they
do not arrive until 99–100.[251] Another reading[252] is that at v. 15
Hermes and the Suitors discovered the group and witnessed the
conversation, but Hermes did not bring them closer until v. 99. I
am not sure that this reading would have been open to the ancient
audience. If it was not, it would have registered as faulty integration
and strengthened the case for seeing this text as resulting from the
stitching together of disparate material, held in place by the device
of Hermes leading the Suitors' shades to Hades that makes a Nekyia
thematically possible at this point in the narrative. But whether
or not such a reading was open to the ancients, there is clearly
awkwardness here, a clumsy tension between the presence and the
absence of the Suitors; this suggests that it may be a not very
successful device aimed at accommodating the conflicting desires
on the one hand to integrate the Suitors into the narrative in order

[250] Cf. on this § i above.
[251] Cf. Page 1955: 119.
[252] Cf. Heubeck 1992: 361 *ad* 15–22.

to link the Deuteronekyia to what went on before,[253] and on the other not to involve them more than strictly necessary, in order to avoid rewriting earlier epic material and use it unaltered in large chunks, thus avoiding the risk of spoiling the Homeric style. There is no plausible reading that can in any way explain away the more serious difficulty involved in vv. 191–202. Agamemnon is supposed to be addressing Amphimedon; in fact he addresses Odysseus in the second person singular and praises Penelope's virtue and again compares his own case, having a treacherous wife, to that of Odysseus who was happy to have married such an excellent woman and faithful spouse. The use of the second person strongly suggests that this segment of the text had not been generated in the context in which we find it,[254] but was lifted from another context, in which Agamemnon had addressed Odysseus and had made precisely this comparison between himself and his interlocutor Odysseus who was visiting Hades. This hypothesis, that Agamemnon's speech in the Continuation is taken over from another poem in which it had been addressed to Odysseus, gains support from the consideration that it was singularly inappropriate to address admiring remarks about Odysseus' happiness to Odysseus' victim Amphimedon.[255] In addition, this speech about Odysseus' good luck relates to, and forms a coherent whole with, the earlier conversation between Agamemnon and Achilles in *Odyssey* 24. 24 ff, which included a comparison between Agamemnon's and Achilles' fate. Agamemnon envied Achilles his glorious death at Troy, which he compared to his own ignominious death at the hands of his wife and her lover. This comparison is extended further on, after the suitor Amphimedon had informed Agamemnon of the events surrounding Odysseus' return to Ithaca. The coherent whole formed by these three speeches compares the fate of the three great heroes of the Trojan War, Agamemnon, Achilles, and Odysseus, and estab-

[253] The fact that nothing of interest happens to the Suitors in Hades strengthens the view that they were a device deployed by the Continuator and not a part of the original Homeric composition.

[254] Even Heubeck who believes in the authenticity of *Odyssey* 24 acknowledges the difficulty (Heubeck 1992: 380 *ad* 24. 191), though he very much underplays it: 'the formulaic line is unusual here because it names Amphimedon (*ton*) as the listener to whom the speech is addressed, whereas in fact it introduces a speech directed to the absent son of Laertes'; nonsensical rather than unusual would have been a more apposite description. In addition, the address to the absent Odysseus is in itself not unproblematic, especially in this particular context.

[255] Cf. Petzl 1969: 65–6 where the relevant scholia are cited.

lishes a scale of comparative happiness for them—and thus also an evaluation of human life. Odysseus is the luckiest and happiest, Agamemnon his extreme opposite, miserable because of his wife's behaviour, while Odysseus had been lucky because of his wife's behaviour; between the two stands Achilles who died at Troy and whose life had been short, but who had a glorious death. This comparison, which can only take place in Hades if all three were to be present, is very appropriate to the end of Odysseus' adventures and contributes to the overall effect of his return.

If the hypothesis is to be sustained that the Deuteronekyia was put together from material deriving from an epic other than the *Odyssey* and new material composed by the Continuator, we need to explain its apparent thematic integration, its relationship to *Odyssey* 11 that has been seen as an argument for the authenticity of *Odyssey* 24. This is how this is set out by Rutherford.[256] 'As in book 11 the poet stresses the contrast between Odysseus' successful return and, on the one hand the death of Achilles at Troy in glorious battle, and on the other, the humiliating murder of Agamemnon by his wife and her lover. But whereas in book 11 Agamemnon had spoken bitterly of womankind in general, and had warned Odysseus not to be too open with Penelope, here he retracts his earlier suspicions, and gives Penelope her due tribute (11. 440–56, 24. 192–202). Odysseus' triumph is acknowledged and respected by his dead comrades ... '. An easy answer to this argument would be that the Continuator simply took up those themes he found in *Odyssey* 11 and reworked them from the viewpoint of the end of the *Odyssey*. But it could be argued that this cannot be the whole story; that this comparison belongs, and thus would more naturally be expected to have been generated, at the end of the poem, not its middle, and thus that the *Odyssey* 11 version should be considered secondary to a version taking place during a Nekyia situated at the end of the poem. This may be right, but again, it would be compatible with the hypothesis put forward here, that the Continuation incorporated epic material both from the original *Odyssey* ending and from a different epic which had preceded the *Odyssey*, in which the Nekyia had been situated at the end of the poem. If this hypothesis is right, the comparison of the fate of the three heroes would have been part of this pre-*Odyssey* poem(s). When,

[256] Rutherford 1992: 14.

on my hypothesis, Homer transferred the Nekyia to the middle of the fairyland adventures he took up this contrast and modified it by skilfully altering the perspective to fit the context of *Odyssey* 11, where, despite his mother's reassurances concerning Penelope,[257] Odysseus cannot be certain that all will be well with his marriage by the time he returns; thus he cannot be certain that Agamemnon may not be right when he warns him that, despite Penelope's virtues, he should not trust her.[258] This creates a tension for Odysseus, while the external narratee, the audience of the *Odyssey*, would have evaluated this advice by contrasting it with Penelope's 'real' behaviour; what the Continuation does is to take this contrast up again and make it explicit, stress it by putting it in the mouth of the earlier doubter. In the previous section we found reasons for thinking that a consultation of the dead Teiresias had been located at the end of a poem earlier than the *Odyssey*[259] that were entirely independent of any consideration of the Continuation. My case against the authenticity of the Continuation does not depend on the validity of this hypothesis; but, I submit, the mere possibility that the hypothesis may be right robs the case for authenticity of any vestigial support it might have been thought to have had.

The reasons for the composition of the Continuation are beyond our grasp. Perhaps the taste of the archaic age found the earlier poem's closure more satisfactory; perhaps the archaic taste for more katabasis literature led to the desire to add a second Nekyia at the end. This addition would have transformed what, on my hypothesis, would have been a closure in Ithaca in Homer's *Odyssey* into a wider closure framework that included the descent of the souls of the Suitors to Hades and a scene in Hades. It may well be that, as West suggested,[260] it was in the context of the *Odyssey*'s inclusion at the Panathenaia that the Continuation was composed to meet the expectations created by changed tastes and perhaps also the

---

[257] Whether Antikleia is referring to the situation at the time of her death or gives an up-to-date account (cf. on this Heubeck 1989: 88 *ad* 181–203).

[258] *Od.* 11. 441 and 454–6 (for the defence of the authenticity of the latter cf. Heubeck 1989: 104 *ad loc.*).

[259] In theory, that consultation could have been above ground; it need not have involved a katabasis. But the convergence of the two independent arguments makes this unlikely. In addition, if my central thesis is right, the Continuator, who would have been following the earlier poem, would not have been inspired to add a Nekyia here if at the end of that poem there had only been a consultation of Teiresias, which was now in book 11.

[260] S. West 1989: 132.

desire for a poem of a certain length—with an ending longer than the original ending of the Homeric *Odyssey* would have been on the hypothesis put forward here.

2. THE JOURNEY TO HADES

Once the inauthenticity of the Continuation is acknowledged it becomes clear that its representations of the fate of the shades are chronologically intermediate between those in Homer and the fifth-century nexus that will be described in Chapter V. They are also intermediate between those two nexuses with regard to their content. Formally, the variant in *Odyssey* 24 is much more elaborate than that in Homer, and less elaborate than that of the fifth century. It has no Charon, but it does have one divine psychopompos, Hermes, who leads the souls of the Suitors to Hades; the shades enter Hades before they are buried. Thus, the journey to Hades in *Odyssey* 24 is in conflict with the representation of the same journey which is constant throughout the epics; the absence of consistency in the other facets of Homeric eschatology and of the Homeric world in general makes this particular consistency very significant, and indicates that it reflected beliefs which had remained unchanged throughout the centuries of the epics' transmission.[261] When viewed through the perceptual filters of that eschatology, the conflict with the representations in *Odyssey* 24 is very strong. The latter clash with beliefs concerning the journey to Hades otherwise consistently found in the epics in the following ways.

First, the Suitors enter Hades though they have not been buried. In my view, this belief could not have been tolerated by Homer himself, for whom the idea that you cannot enter the Underworld before burial was apparently part of the natural order of things; but it would not have jarred on the Continuator if he did not himself hold that belief. For in that case, he would not have perceived it as incompatible with the rest—which it is, for the ancient commentators who submitted the Homeric text to analysis,[262] for us, as historians of religion, but also for those who shared in that Homeric funerary ideology, to whom such a thing would be literally incon-

---

[261] Thus, it could not have been Homer who did not share these beliefs and left his traces in *Od.* 24; otherwise there would not be consistency everywhere except in a section suspect also on many other grounds.

[262] Cf. Schol. *Od.* 24. 1; also 187.

ceivable. Second, the shades do not reach Hades under their own steam: they are guided by Hermes, designated with the epithet Kyllenios.[263] The geography of the journey to Hades in *Odyssey* 24 has been elaborated in a poetic way, with unexpected associations, like the community of dreams and the gates of the Sun,[264] which give this passage a surrealistic flavour. Of the other landscape elements through which the souls' journey to Hades under Hermes' guidance is articulated, some, such as Okeanos, are derived from the Nekyia in *Odyssey* 11;[265] *Leukada petren* in v. 11[266] is derived from the landscape encountered on the way to the Nekyomanteion: a visitor who came from Southern Greece went past the Leukatas promontory on the southern tip of Leukas to reach the mouth of Acheron.[267] This geographical element belonging to the Nekyomanteion nexus may perhaps provide some support for the view suggested above that the Hades which Odysseus had visited in the earlier poem which inspired the Continuator was reached through the entrance to the Underworld located in the area of the Nekyomanteion.

Since the probable date of the composition of *Odyssey* 24 is the late seventh or more probably the first half of the sixth century, this is the first known instance in which Hermes appears in the role of conductor of the shades to Hades—and this is associated with an elaboration of the journey from the upper world to Hades, especially through the spelling out of particular landscape elements. This role of Hermes as guide of the souls to Hades is an extension and development of the god's overall persona as crosser of borders in

---

[263] If, as suggested by Balladié (1980: 17–24; cf. also the brief discussion of the problem in M. L. West 1966, *ad* 778–9), Styx had geographical associations with Arcadia, and in particular with the vicinity of Kyllene, it is possible that at the early stages of the creation of Hermes' role as guide of the souls this association of part of the infernal landscape and transition to Hades with the Kyllene area determined the selection of the epithet Kyllenios (cf. the scholiast's comment on this epithet: Schol. *Od.* 24. 1) to characterize Hermes whose mythological and religious connection with Kyllene were very strong, in his role as *psychopompos*. If that is correct, the fact that, it would seem, Kyllenios soon ceased to characterize Hermes in his psychopompic function would be correlative with the submersion of the Arcadian dimension in conjunction with the fact that the epithet *Chthonios* pertained more directly to Hermes' psychopompic function and thus also involved a symbolic separation between this, funerary, aspect of the god and the other facets of his persona, concerned with the upper world.

[264] Cf. D'Agostino 1982: 44.
[265] Compare *Od.* 24. 11 to 11. 21. On Okeanos cf. also Nagy 1973: 149–52.
[266] On which cf. Page 1955: 117–18; Nagy 1973: 137–77.
[267] Cf. Dakaris n.d.: 22. On Leukas and Leukatas cf. Strabo 10. 2. 8.

general,[268] and in particular of his role as crosser of the border separating Hades from the upper world.[269] The kernel out of which his psychopompic function can be seen to have developed is present in Homer, and also in the *Homeric Hymn to Demeter*. In *Odyssey* 11. 625–6 Hermes appears in a related but different role: he is said to have guided Herakles when the hero went to Hades to fetch Cerberus; this is different from his function as psychopompos, since Herakles was alive and Hermes was acting as a divine helper of Zeus' son. Nevertheless, this role of Hermes as guide in the transition between the upper world and Hades and vice versa, in the case of Herakles and also of Persephone in the *Homeric Hymn*, and of messenger between the gods of the two realms, pertains to the same aspect of his persona as his role of guide of the souls, which appears as its development. Rudhardt[270] argues, in my view correctly, that the *Homeric Hymn to Demeter* shows that Hermes the god of passages is the only god of the upper world who can cross the infernal frontier.[271] Thus, Hermes' role as guide of the shades in their transition from the upper world to Hades is closely related to, and can be seen as a development of, his role of crosser of the infernal frontier as seen in the stories of Herakles and Persephone. The wand which Hermes uses in *Odyssey* 24. 1–5, with which he can *thelgein* the eyes of men if he so wishes, and awake those who are asleep, and through which he summons the Suitors' shades to lead them to Hades, is a development of the wand which he has in *Iliad* 24. 339–45 and *Odyssey* 5. 43–9, with which again he can *thelgein* the eyes of men if he so wishes, and awake those who are asleep[272]—the same expression is used in *Odyssey* 24 as in *Iliad* 24 and *Odyssey* 5; the difference is that in *Odyssey* 24 another function

[268] Cf. Burkert 1985: 157–8; Kahn 1978: 177–80, and *passim*.

[269] Cf. also Bérard 1974: 25–6.

[270] Rudhardt 1978: 8–9.

[271] Admittedly, *Od*. 11. 626, esp. when taken in conjunction with *Il*. 8. 366–9, may present difficulties, unless we consider Athena's help, which would have included advice, to have been located in the upper world, and Hermes to have guided Herakles into and out of Hades. Athena's presence in representations of Cerberus' capture is not informative in that respect, not even with regard to later beliefs and perceptions. For it does not necessarily indicate that she was believed to have been present in Hades: she may be an 'emblematic' element, indicating her role as Herakles' helper in this and the other labours. (The earliest known representation of Cerberus' capture by Herakles (cf. Boardman 1975: 7, and nn. 1–2 with bibliog.) is Corinthian, of *c*.590–80 and includes both Athena and Hermes as do most of the later 6th-cent. representations of Cerberus' capture (on these scenes cf. also Brommer 1986: 43–6).)

[272] On Hermes and *thelgein* cf. also Kahn 1978: 136–42, 193.

has been added to those performed by the wand in the other two passages: Hermes moves it and the souls follow him into Hades.[273] Thus, the relationship between Hermes' wand in the main epics and Hermes' wand in *Odyssey* 24 is similar and homologous to the relationship between Hermes' role as Herakles' guide to Hades in the epics and his role as psychopompos in *Odyssey* 24. This strengthens the view that the whole nexus of Hermes as guide of the souls in *Odyssey* 24 developed[274] out of the nexus 'Hermes' reflected in the epics, his role as crosser of borders, and especially of the infernal border, of guide of mythological characters in and out of Hades, and his wand. The fact that, as will become clear in Chapter V, the representations pertaining to the fate of the shades in *Odyssey* 24, which are intermediate chronologically between the Homeric and the fifth-century ones, are also intermediate in terms of content provides some confirmation for the pattern of development suggested here. Indeed, the overall case in favour of the eschatological development proposed here provides further support for the thesis that *Odyssey* 24 was a Continuation written in the archaic period.

iv. *Conclusions: Homeric Eschatologies*

Let me sum up the conclusions of these analyses. The following beliefs are deeply rooted, and consistently articulated, in the epics: at death the shades flew down to Hades, a dark place under the earth, on their own without any assistance from psychopompoi; they could not enter Hades until after their corpse had been buried; once a shade entered Hades it could never return to the upper world. In *Odyssey* 24, which was an archaic Continuation of the Homeric *Odyssey*, the journey to Hades has begun to be elaborated and the first psychopompic figure, Hermes, has appeared; the shades of the dead can enter Hades before burial.

Also deeply rooted in the epics, but already eroded somewhat by the appearance of a different set of beliefs, are the following two beliefs. First, the belief that everyone dies, which has begun to be

---

[273] This type of reuse and transformation of a Homeric motif to express different ideas is found in the Epic Cycle (Griffin 1977: 44). On the wand cf. De Waele 1927: *passim*; Bremmer 1983: 50.

[274] In circumstances that will be discussed in Ch. V.

eroded through the emergence (still very timid and limited) of the notion that some exceptional people do not die, but gain immortality. The most notable instance of this belief is that involving Menelaos and Elysion. It has been argued here that Elysion, far from being a Minoan concept, was a new belief, which had emerged not long before the Homeric poems had taken their final form, and had been constructed, under the impetus of the new trend involving the notion that some exceptional people had an exceptional fate after death, out of stuff that had included one element, the association of a Minoan king with a Land of the Dead/Land of the 'Dead', that may have originated in the Minoan world, but had been reshaped and radically modified to fit its new position and function. The second belief that is deeply rooted in the epics, but already eroded somewhat by the appearance of a different set of beliefs, is not unconnected with the first; it is the belief in the collective destiny of the shades, which is eroded through the appearance of notions that challenge and modify it, such as the notion that men who swear false oaths were punished in Hades.

As far as the nature of the shades and of existence in Hades is concerned, there are two major strands of belief in the Homeric epics. The first is the belief in the witless ghosts with all that entails about life in Hades; the second perceives the shades as not-witless, lively, living an existence in Hades that involved some awareness and activity and also some hierarchy, and appreciative of offerings made to them by the living. I argued that the first belief, which is unstable in the epics, was inherited in the epic material and was perceived and manipulated through the filters of the second, which corresponded to the beliefs of Homer's own time, probably also to those of his immediate predecessors, who had perceived and manipulated the epic material through the filters of their own eschatology.

III.

Signs of the Dead:
The Grave Monument in Homer
and the Archaic Age

i. The Grave Monument in Homer

1. GENERAL

The study of the grave monument[1] in the Homeric poems is important in itself and also necessary for the proper study of the archaic grave monument, since earlier perceptions contributed to the latter's making. Also, the Homeric terminology was inherited by the archaic epitaph-writers, who adapted it to their own needs. We must determine what had been inherited, and how this inherited stock was deployed in the archaic age.

As we saw was the case with other aspects of the Homeric world, Homeric burial customs do not have correlatives in a real society;[2] they are a construct, a conflation of elements that had originated in different periods and places. I am not concerned here with real-life burial customs in themselves—though, as we shall see, they do impinge on the argument. I shall investigate the Homeric references to graves and grave monuments, and attempt to establish the exact meaning of the relevant terms, the ideas associated with them, and thus also the perceptions of the grave monument in the Homeric poems. In investigating the precise semantic content of the various terms I will confine myself to the Homeric evidence alone. For later usages can be misleading, since slight semantic shifts in the

---

[1] I use the term 'grave monument' to denote all grave-markers, the visible sign above the burial space marking the burial.

[2] Cf. Snodgrass 1971: 391.

course of time cannot be excluded, especially when, as here, there are developments in the nature and function of the objects themselves.

2. THE GRAVE MONUMENT IN THE HOMERIC DEATH-RITUAL: MEANINGS AND FUNCTION

I begin with the significance of the grave monument in Homer as it can be reconstructed through the consideration of its position and function within the burial ceremony.[3] These conclusions will be confirmed, extended, and refined through the study of the references to the grave monument.

The heaping of the burial mound or erection of any other form of grave monument is the last act in the manipulation of the deceased's remains during the last stage of the burial ceremony, which marked the end of the period of abnormality that followed a death and the restoration of normality and order.[4] The closure of the grave, completed and sealed with the erection of the mound, marks the final stage in the separation of the deceased from the world of the living and the community: now his shade is incorporated into Hades and his body/bones into the earth, both beyond boundaries: the shade beyond the infernal river, the corpse beyond the mound of earth or other less emphatic physical boundary of the burial space. Since in the burial ceremony the remains also played the role of metonymic sign for the whole persona of the deceased, the act marking the remains' exclusion from this world, the erection of the grave monument, marked also, and symbolized, the final separation of the deceased, all parts of his persona, from the world of the living. It is thus clear that the first important function of the grave monument is to seal and mark the burial space, to complete and mark its closure as well as its position, and so testify to the separation of the deceased's remains, shade, and social persona, from the world of the living. Thus its erection was inextricably connected with this separation. Multiple burials will be considered below. In Homer, apart from the common *tymbos* erected for the war-dead after the

---

[3] I analysed the death-ritual in Sourvinou-Inwood 1983: 37–43; cf. also 1981: 25–31.
[4] Cf. Sourvinou-Inwood 1983: 39–42.

funerals of *Iliad* 7 (*Il.* 7. 336–7, 435–6) a grave monument is erected regularly over simple burials.[5]

Iliad 23. 45–6 confirms that the *sema* was perceived as completing the burial ceremony of which it was an indispensable part and conveying the idea of the final separation of the deceased from the world of the living. Achilles offers a synopsis of the burial ceremony when he expresses and articulates the concept 'bury Patroklos' by means of references to three acts, which must, therefore, be presumed to be crucial to this ceremony. First he mentions the cremation of the corpse. Second the erection of the *sema*. And third the cutting off of the mourners'—in this case his own—hair; this ritual gesture represents symbolically, among other things, the mourners' separation from the deceased, and is a sign of this separation, and also of the status of mourners following the burial ceremony when they are reintegrated into the social group.[6] Cremation, which transforms the corpse, entails its separation from its former state and so also from the observable aspects of his persona as a living being. In inhumation the transformation/separation follows, and is symbolically subsumed into, the act of burial, sealed by the erection of the *sema*. On the hypothesis put forward here, the erection of the *sema* also signifies separation: it seals the act by which the remains of the deceased are shut out of the world of the living while at the same time the shade crosses into Hades. My interpretation of the symbolic significance of the act of the erection of the *sema*, then, fits the context of this passage perfectly. First, because the ascription of the value of separation to this act would enrich the passage by giving it enhanced thematic symmetry and density of signification. Thematic symmetry, it should be noted, was not a notion alien to the composition of *Iliad* 23. 45–6 and imported from

---

[5] Snodgrass (1974: 123) remarks on this and notes 'historically the tumulus almost always contains a multiple burial'; he suggests that perhaps this erection of a tumulus over a simple cremation was due to the requirements of the plot. But it is possible that here plot requirements and practice coincide, insofar as a mound—however small—was probably erected over the remains after each burial, sealing them and marking their separation and that of the deceased from the world of the living; this mound would have been dismantled—or partly dismantled—to accommodate subsequent burials. Something like this will happen when the modest mound erected for Patroklos (though not, in this case, covering his bones) is replaced by the permanent mound after Achilles' death, which will be the common *tymbos* for both. This practice of temporary sealing off can be paralleled in the Mycenaean tholoi and chamber tombs which housed multiple burials: after each burial their door was blocked, and the dromos filled with earth—to be reopened for the next burial.

[6] Sourvinou-Inwood 1983: 41.

the outside. This is shown by the way in which the condensation of the burial is articulated through three acts of ritual behaviour which—whatever significance we ascribe to them—belong one in each of the three stages of the burial ceremony: the cutting of the hair belongs to the first stage, the cremation of the corpse to the second, the erection of the *sema* to the third. Secondly, a more complex point. The choice to signify burial through these acts which, if I am right, bring about and symbolize the separation of the deceased (of his corpse/remains and of his shade) from the persona of his living self, from the community, and from the mourners, corresponds to the fact that separation emerges, on my analysis, as one of the fundamental values and attitudes expressed during burial—the last stage of the death-ritual.[7] If this is correct, then *Iliad* 23. 45–6 did not convey to the contemporary audience simply the notion of burial, or of the three acts *per se*, or just the performance of one's duty to the dead; it also conveyed very strongly the notion of separation from the deceased, and this would enrich the emotional content and strengthen the impact of the passage very considerably. Clearly here the emotional element, Achilles' grief for Patroklos, reposes on, and is articulated by means of, ritual behaviour and symbolism which increase its intensity and enrich its scope. Achilles is refusing to wash (v. 44) until after he has buried Patroklos.[8] This is a narrative transformation—serving to stress Achilles' distress—of the ritual behaviour pertaining to the death-ritual before the burial ceremony which involves deliberately taking on pollution as part of the process of embracing death; this embracing of pollution and death entails also a partial identification with the deceased and it is acted out in the pre-burial part of the death-ritual.[9] On my hypothesis, this nexus of ideas and emotional attitudes contrasts sharply with, and is counterpointed by, the notions of separation from Patroklos and return to normality and reintegration with the social group which, if I am right, were strongly conveyed by the acts into which the concept 'bury Patroklos' was articulated. In this way, and through this contrast, Achilles' grief is presented in a deeper and more tragic light. This complex and significant condensation of the notion 'bury Patroklos' here contrasts with the matter of fact summing-up of the concept of

[7] Ibid. 41–2.
[8] On Achilles and food cf. also Lloyd-Jones 1981: 22–3.
[9] Sourvinou-Inwood 1981: 27–8; 1983: 38–9.

burial in *Odyssey* 3. 285 which does not convey such rich subtext connotations: *ophr' hetaron thaptoi kai epi kterea kteriseien*. In the minds of the contemporary audience, this nexus of ideas placed Achilles' grief in the framework of the unsolvable and truly tragic conflict between, on the one hand the desire to 'stay with' the dead, refuse to let them go and in a way identify with them, and on the other the necessity, social need and even desire to let them go, separate ourselves from them, and carry on living.

In these circumstances, it is clear that, because the first function of the *sema* was to seal off the grave and so seal and mark the separation of the deceased from the world of the living, the idea of this separation between the living and the dead became symbolically attached to the act of the erection of the grave monument; and the grave monument for a person X marked not only the burial place of his remains but also the fact of his separation from the living, of his death[10] and so also of his life; thus it became the mark which X left in the world of the living, a mark of his passage through that world, the 'sign', the *sema* of X. For after the completion of the burial and of the separation no part of the deceased's persona is left in the world of the living. His remains have been sealed off and excluded from this world, his shade has crossed into Hades and will never return to the upper world and his social persona has been separated from the survivors and the community, prior to the social group's regrouping and restructuring itself without him. Only two 'entities' pertaining to the deceased remain in the world of the living, after the separation has been completed, two new entities that emerged from the 'rite de passage' which is the death-ritual and are the 'successors' to the deceased's physical and social persona. One is abstract and results from the transformation of his social persona: the memory of the deceased in the community. The other is concrete and physical, the grave monument set up over the burial space of his remains. The two became inevitably connected;[11] we shall now consider how.

The word which denotes the grave monument in its function as grave monument is *sema*, the basic meaning of which is 'sign'. I shall investigate below this and the other words used for the grave monument in Homer. Here I will consider to what extent what

---

we have reconstructed with regard to the grave monument on the basis of its place in the death-ritual can help make sense of it as the sign of the deceased. Let us consider which, if any, categories pertaining to signs and their function apply to the Homeric grave monument as *sema* of the dead.[12] The perception of the sign and of signification varies, depending on the 'ideological' perspective.[13] My 'ideological perspective' is a very idiosyncratic post-structuralist one. But here I am not concerned with the more complex aspects of signs. I am only interested in some of the basic categories which organize signs and determine their nature and function. There is no standard classification of signs, and no standard terminology, or definition of notions such as 'index', 'symbol', 'icon', 'signal'.[14] But the diversity, in the ways in which the categories which organize the signs have been clustered to create sign-types in the work of different scholars, is not methodologically very significant, provided the system being used is clearly and unambiguously defined. For example, the recognition of the major referential categories here labelled 'indexical' and 'symbolic' is much more important for the investigation of the significance and modes of operation of individual signs than the names we ascribe to these referential categories, or the sign-classifications we derive from them. I will say something very briefly about some of these categories, which will help us understand more clearly the function of the Homeric and later grave monument. Signs are organized by two major categories of reference, which can be called 'indexical' and 'symbolic'. In the indexical type the sign indicates the presence of something; in the symbolic it stands for, represents, something else. These two categories of reference can collaborate; for example, an indexical sign can function as a (metonymically based) symbol. As we shall see, these distinctions will be partly deconstructed; but it is important to recognize the content that goes into the making of the categories, the channels through which signs function, even if subsequently the categories themselves blend with, and replace, each other. An

[12] The bibliography on the notion of sign and on signification is vast. Cf. e.g. Eco 1976: 48 ff., 178, and *passim*, Culler 1975: 16 20; Boon 1982: 116 ff.; Derrida 1974, 1976: 3–73; 1967: 293–340; 1972: 29–46, 105–30; Giovannangeli 1979: 26–156; Lyons 1981: 13–14; Martinet 1973: 49 55; Leach 1976: 12, 23–4.

[13] Cf. e.g. for an attack on the structuralist notion of the sign in post-structuralist writings: Harari 1979: 29–31.

[14] On the diversity in the terminology and the classification of signs cf. e.g. Leach 1976: 10; Barthes 1967: 35–8; Lyons 1977: 95–109; Culler 1976: 96–103; Elam 1980: 19–21.

indexical reference is one in which 'there is a known or assumed connection' between the something perceived and that which it signifies, so that the occurrence of the former is taken to indicate the presence or existence of that which it signifies, when it is also the case that the signifier, the perceived 'sign', gives, at the same time, information about its source which lies in that which it signifies.[15] The classic example of an indexical relationship is that of smoke with fire. In symbolic reference something perceived stands for something else, either through arbitrary convention, or because the two are somehow connected. The latter, a motivated symbolic reference, can be based on metonymy, a relationship of contiguity, or be metaphorical, based on perceived resemblance.[16] The distinctions on which these categories are based have now been questioned; the distinction between metaphor[17] and metonymy has been deconstructed[18]—as has that between the literal and the metaphorical.[19]

The following referential relationships can be seen to obtain between the grave monument and the dead person in Homer. First, the grave monument indicates the presence of the buried remains of a given person X. It is therefore (1) an index testifying to the presence of a burial; and (2) an index testifying to the fact that a given person's, X's, remains are buried there. The first indexical reference will last for as long as the grave monument lasts and is recognized as a grave monument.[20] This indexical reference is

[15] Cf. Lyons 1977: 106–7. This definition is based on the one proposed by Peirce (1931–3: ii. paras. 92, 247–8, 283–91, 305–6); cf. also Peirce 1958: 391. Some semiologists exclude from the category 'index' signs which are produced with the intention of communicating; cf. Martinet 1973: 49–53, 55–9, 99–102. On indices in general cf. also Culler 1975: 17–18; Leach 1976: 10, 12, 23–4, 29–30, 39, 52; Elam 1980: 21–2.

[16] On symbols cf. esp. Martinet 1973: 69–72; Lyons 1977: 100–2, 105. In Peirce's terminology 'symbol' is only applied to purely arbitrary signs: Peirce 1958: 391; 1931–3: ii. paras. 292–300. Leach (1976: 10, 12–13) also reserves the term 'symbol' for unmotivated symbols and confusingly calls the motivated ones signs. On motivated signs, and metaphorical and metonymic analogy and substitution cf. Guiraud 1975: 25–7; Elam 1980: 28–9. On icons cf. Martinet 1973: 59–69; Elam 1980: 21–7; Culler 1975: 16–17; Leach 1976: 12; Lyons 1977: 102–5; Peirce 1931–3: ii. paras. 276–82. On metonymic symbols cf. Leach 1976: 12–15, 21–2, 29–31, 39, 43, 70. Arbitrary and motivated in linguistics: Barthes 1967: 50–1; in semiology: ibid. 51–4.

[17] The bibliog. on metaphors is vast; cf. Shibles (1971) for a list and summaries of items published before its completion; cf. also Miall (1982) with later bibliog.

[18] Cf. Culler 1981: 197–202, 206–7.

[19] Cf. Culler 1983: 147–50; 1981: 202–7.

[20] Cf. *Il.* 23. 326–32 for an example of uncertainty as to whether something was a grave monument of a person long dead.

related to the natural indices (the state of a refilled newly dug grave)[21] indicating the presence of a burial. It thus can be seen as presenting the grave monument as a fixed, longer-lasting, and more conspicuous extension of such indices, which helps seal, or stress the sealing of, the grave more firmly. One function of the grave monument at this first level of indexical reference is that it informs that someone is buried there, and that his remains have been scaled off, and he has been separated from the world of the living.

Dark-Age and eighth-century grave monuments took various forms; the common types were vases, grave-mounds of earth with or without a stele (an elongated stone block) or other additional grave-marker and heaps of stones with or without a stele; a stele and a vase were sometimes combined.[22] They operated at the first level of indexical reference in informing that someone is buried there, but sometimes they conveyed a little more information about the type of person this someone was, by articulating some aspects of his social persona. Sometimes they were gender-differentiated;[23] sometimes they indicated status.[24] In the eighth century the position and groupings of grave-markers could indicate family affiliation.[25] The oar over Elpenor's mound (*Od.* 11. 77–8) gives the information that the deceased was an oarsman. The grand grave monument at Lefkandi[26] belongs to a special category; it indicated the exceptional status of the dead leader for whom it was erected. It is a grand building, dated to the early tenth century BC, not later than *c*.950;[27] it was covered by a tumulus very soon after its erection. There are various problems associated with this building, and controversy concerning the exact circumstances and purpose of its erection.

---

[21] On this category of natural index cf. Martinet 1973: 58.

[22] On Dark-Age and 8th-cent. grave monuments cf. Andronikos 1961/2: 177–206; cf. also: Kurtz and Boardman 1971: 56–8, 219, cf. also 38, and 35; Andronikos 1968: W118–19; Whitley 1991: 18–19, 116–17, 132, 135–8, 156–7, 159–62; Lambrinoudakis 1988: 238; N. Yalouris, *Ergon* (1963), 117–18; Desborough 1972: 76; Popham, Sackett, and Themelis 1979: 215; Vokotopoulou 1986: 329, 336; Kübler 1954; 17–18, 33–6; Snodgrass 1971: 142, 156–9, 160–3, 171–3, 175, 190, 194–5; Andronikos 1968, W110–14, and esp. 111–14; Kraiker and Kübler 1939: 6, 9, 95, 181; Coldstream 1977: 135–7.

[23] On gender differentiation through grave-markers cf. Kurtz and Boardman 1971: 58; Boardman 1988: 171–9; Whitley 1991: 132.

[24] Grave-markers signalling status: cf. Coldstream 1977: 137; Whitley 1991: 18–19, 135–6, 159, 160–1.

[25] On 'family plots' in 8th-cent. burials see below.

[26] Cf. Kalligas 1981: 29–36; Popham, Touloupa and Sackett 1982: 169–74; Catling and Lemos 1990; cf. also Bérard 1985: 274–5; Blome (1984: 9–22).

[27] Catling and Lemos 1990: 91–5, cf. esp. 95.

The excavator, Mr Mervyn Popham, will be setting out all the evidence on which an interpretation can be based in the final publication of the building. Thus any detailed argumentation concerning those issues must be postponed until then. I will only present here my own understanding of the building, which is that it is a grave monument, built in what clearly seems to be a cemetery area on the model of a leader's 'palace'. This impressive version of a grave monument involves, in my view, a quantitative rather than qualitative leap, a colossal increase in the scale of the *sema* commemorating the deceased, but not a different mentality,[28] except in so far as the scale itself lifts an element to the 'abnormal' by making it exceptional within the category 'Dark-Age community leaders'. The man in whose honour it was erected was clearly an exceptional leader, and his grave monument mirrored, in scale, importance and distinctiveness, this exceptionality, the memory of which it symbolized. Dark-Age and eighth-century grave monuments then, when they gave more information than just the indication that someone was buried there, indicated, at most, aspects of the social persona of the deceased, the type of person whose remains were marked, his place in the group and role in varying degrees of specification.[29] Not all Dark-Age and eighth-century graves have grave-markers that survived. This must not be taken to entail that sometimes the grave was not marked when the burial was sealed. For we know that some of the grave-markers in use at that time were of a type that becomes archaeologically invisible; this was the case, for example, with Elpenor's oar, and indeed with the small mound of earth.[30] This, and also the implausibility of the notion that the parameters of variation in the attitudes to the dead in these communities were so wide as to allow some graves to be marked and others to become invisible the moment they were sealed, make the view that some graves were not given any marker highly unlikely. If this is right, we should think of the variations in the visibility of the grave monument in terms of high and low visibility, with differences in emphasis, one pole being a grave monument of high visibility with an emphatic articulation of the

---

[28] For the death-ritual of community leaders cf. Sourvinou-Inwood 1981: 30 n. 53; 1983: 42 n. 55; Toher 1991: 171–4.

[29] Cf. now also Whitley (1991: 135–6, 159–61) on the ways in which the grave-marker articulated the deceased's social persona in the Dark Ages and the 8th cent.

[30] Cf. e.g. Popham, Sackett, and Themelis 1979: 215.

deceased's persona in monumental ways, and the other low visibility and no such articulation, a restriction of the grave monument to its first level of indexical reference. It is not a question of presence versus absence of the grave monument.[31] The information conveyed by grave monuments could be understood for as long as the code through which it was conveyed was understood. At one extreme, all the information articulated in it is decoded. At the other, the identity itself of the grave monument as grave monument over a burial can be in doubt. The basic features of the code necessary to understand the information that is conveyed at this first level of indexical reference seem to have remained unchanged for centuries and to have been widespread in Dark-Age and eighth-century Greece.

The second indexical reference conveys the information that a given individual's remains are buried there. But this reference depends on factors external to the grave monument. It depends on the community, or certain individuals in it, remembering that X was buried there, that this was the grave monument of X. In other words, it depends on the preservation of factual information of a specific kind pertaining to the particular grave monument, and not simply on shared communicative competence; for at this time grave monuments (unlike the inscribed archaic grave monuments) did not carry information which identified them as marking the remains of a particular individual. Thus this second indexical reference had a much shorter life-span than the first. It only lasted for as long as

---

[31] Whitley (1991: 159–61) contrasts certain 8th-cent. graves with monumental grave-markers and thus high visibility after burial with others which he says had no grave-markers—and were also differentiated from those of the first group in other ways; elsewhere (Whitley 1991: 163) he contrasts the period before and after c.740, with the latter involving decreased visibility; the graves in the latter period, he claims, become invisible after the sealing of the tomb. But in fact, while he has brought out an important difference in the emphasis put on the role of the grave monument, the notion that one pole is high visibility of the grave monument after burial and the other invisibility of the grave is not legitimate, and the correct antithesis is between on the one hand high visibility of the grave monument and on the other low visibility and the restriction of the grave monument to its first level of indexical reference. It is unfortunate that Whitley's intelligent, interesting, and potentially important book is marred by its acceptance of Morris's (1987) thesis that large sections of the population were excluded from burial for long periods during which burial was limited to the élite. It is beyond my scope to discuss this thesis, which I consider to be a culturally determined construct which is methodologically radically flawed and involves factual errors. An excellent brief discussion by Humphreys (1990: 263–8) sets out admirably important objections, methodological flaws, and errors. In the Appendix I am dismantling another Morris construct (Morris 1989), which is directly related to the concerns of this book.

the memory of the deceased lived on in the memory of the local community, and included the knowledge that this *sema* marked the burial of X, was X's grave monument. Naturally, the more important the deceased had been, the longer his memory survived. In the epics we also find the idea that important men who had won glory in fighting were celebrated, and thus commemorated, through song across many communities and areas.[32] This kind of long-term memory-survival depended on excellence and was limited to the élite. At this second level of indexical reference, then, the grave monument conveyed information about the location of X's remains, and indeed, that X was dead and that he had had the proper and complete death ritual performed for him; for as long as the deceased's memory lived on in the community, and the grave monument was identified as the index of his burial, its physical presence inevitably activated the memory of the deceased, in those who perceived it, and in this way it also fed the memory and contributed to its preservation. A grand and distinctive grave monument such as that at Lefkandi would play a more active role in the preservation of the person's memory. The dead man had to have been extraordinary, so that his memory would have lived long in the community, as that of a hero,[33] probably also celebrated and commemorated through song. The impressiveness of the grave monument, in interaction with this special man's memory, would have strengthened that memory; the memory of the great man and the grandeur of his grave monument interacted and undoubtedly resulted in the man's achievement of *kleos aphthiton.*

Because the grave monument was an index for X's burial, (indicating on the one hand the location of X's remains and on the other that X had received the death-ritual and his remains had been sealed off), it was obviously also an index for X's death and absence, and so also an index of his (terminated) life, of his past presence, indicating his passage through life. Thus, it was also as an index for X himself, in his persona as deceased, that it referred contemporary viewers indexically to the deceased X. First, it marked the physical location of the only part of the deceased X's persona which, though shut out from the world of the living had a physical, material presence and so a location in space. Second, it was evidence that X

---

[32] Cf. *Il.* 9. 410–13; 18. 121; *Od.* 8. 73–82. On the *kleos* of exceptional men cf. Ch. VI § i.4.

[33] A comparable example in the epics: Ilos' *sema* (cf. below).

had existed, the token of his passage through this world, the 'mark-ing' he left on this world which testifies that he has been here, and thus triggers off, in those who see it, remembrance of the deceased and feeds his memory in the memory of the community.

These distinctions may appear tedious, but they are important for understanding the Greek perception of the grave monument. Failure to make them, and to investigate systematically the notion of the sign, has led to misconceptions. One such, we shall see, is the confusion between symbolic representation and identification, which led some people to mistake the relationship between grave monument and deceased and think that it involved an identification of the former with the latter, especially in the case of archaic and classical stelai and grave statues. Equally, in the absence of analyses which bring out the ways in which the grave monument functioned as a sign, it is not always understood that its function as a symbol for the deceased does not depend on its similarity to the human form, and that the grave monument provided a concrete material form for this persona which functioned as a focus for his memory and, when appropriate, as for example when offerings are made, a material object that lent itself to symbolic manipulation.[34]

As we saw, according to Homeric belief, when someone dies his shade goes (eventually) to Hades and his corpse or, rather, his burnt remains, are buried; 'in the place of' both all that is left is the grave monument set up at the moment when the corpse and shade were finally separated from the world of the living. In the course of the death-ritual, the corpse/bones functioned also as a metonymic

[34] Cf. below 141 and n. 107. Another, much more sophisticated, view which, I submit, also includes a misconception of a comparable kind is the notion (Day 1989: 16–28, esp. 23) that the significance of the *sema*, and its importance in archaic epitaphs, depends on its relationship to the funeral, that the grave monument served as a memorial of the funeral. This theory, which, I suggest, implicitly relies on a faulty understanding of the operation of the metaphor in Pi. *I.* 8. 59–65, is not wholly wrong (in so far as the *sema* does signify the sealing off of the remains at the conclusion of the funeral); but it elides the important difference between on the one hand the funeral, which is still part of the death ritual and of the abnormal time before the final separation of the deceased from the world of the living, and on the other the world of the living and normality, in which the *sema* is the symbol and 'representative' of the deceased. Equally, even when scenes from the death ritual decorate the grave monument, it must not be assumed that they were simply perceived, and had been placed there as, simply commemorations of the funeral; looked at from the viewpoint that obtained after the deceased was separated from the world of the living, they were also, like other grave monuments, especially most relief stelai, helping articulate the deceased's social persona, in this case by representing aspects of his death ritual which articulated that persona. I shall consider the images represented on grave monuments below.

symbol for the deceased as a whole, including, that is, his shade and his social persona. The sealing-off of the remains represented the final exclusion of all parts of the deceased's persona from the world of the living. But the deceased did not evaporate from the world of the living: a new form, successor to his living persona, remained behind, his memory. When the remains of the deceased were sealed off and he ceased to exist in the world of the living their role as metonymic symbol for the deceased was terminated. All that remained in the world of the living was a reference to them, their index, that is the grave monument. Consequently, it was inevitably to the grave monument that was transferred all 'reference' to the deceased which had previously been associated with the corpse/bones; and, after the separation of the deceased from the world of the living, this meant the reference to his new persona, and especially his memory, the remembrance of his living persona. It follows that, when the burial was sealed off, and the grave monument erected, this became the (metonymically derived) symbol for the deceased's new persona, and most emphatically for that part of his new persona which existed in the world of the living, that is, his memory, the continued existence of his persona in the memory of the living.

A *sema* was erected for Patroklos despite the fact that his bones were temporarily stored elsewhere, in the world of the living, until Achilles' death. This, though a plot-element, is like all compositional selections, inevitably determined by, and reflects, the assumptions, knowledge, and attitudes through which the poet operated. It shows that the grave monument's function was not perceived to be simply—or even primarily—to mark the grave, thus confirming the conclusions reached above concerning the symbolic function of the grave monument. The fact that Achilles drags Hector's corpse around Patroklos' *sema*[35] though Patroklos' bones are not buried there (and he does not drag it around the hut in which the bones are kept) shows that, as suggested above, at the completion of the burial the deceased's physical remains (normally sealed off inside the earth) were symbolically neutralized and the function of symbol for the deceased—in his new persona as deceased—was invested in the grave monument which was what 'stood for' the deceased in the world of the living, the 'sign of' the

[35] *Il.* 24. 16, 51–2, 416–17, 754–6.

deceased. It is for this reason that the *sema* is presented (in an hypothetical case) as the focus of jeering by one's enemies after one's death (*Il.* 4. 174–7). The case of Patroklos, then, shows that the grave monument performs that symbolic function even without the indexical relationship with the deceased's physical remains. That this was indeed the case in the nexus of attitudes reflected in the Homeric poems is confirmed by the custom of erecting a *sema*-cenotaph,[36] which functions as a grave monument simply by virtue of the fact that it had been erected for that purpose, without any indexical relationship to the deceased's remains.[37]

I shall now consider how the existence of a single grave monument over multiple burials fits into our analysis. How does the idea that the grave monument is, among other things, an index for the deceased and a (metonymic) symbol for his memory fit the case of multiple burials? For both types of burial are in use during the period we are considering. Once it is clear that neither of these entails identification with the deceased, it become obvious that a grave monument over a collective burial functions as a sign in comparable ways to those in which it functions when it marks a single burial. For example, if the collective burials are those of a group, buried at the same time, as is the case in *Iliad* 7. 336–7, 435–6, the grave monument is an index and a symbol and preserves the memory of the dead, as a group, for example, those fallen at the battle of Y; and the indexical and symbolic reference to, and the remembrance of the, individual members of the group *qua* individuals (rather than *qua* members of the group) is at low intensity. If it is the burial of a family over successive generations, the predominant reference and memory would be associated with the more recent burials each time, and moreover, there would also be a family memory dimension in the associations of the grave monument, an awareness and memory of past generations of the family *qua* generations of the family, long after the memory of them as individuals had disappeared.

The place of the grave monument in the death-ritual, then, and

---

[36] Cf. *Od.* 1. 289–91; cf. *Od.* 4. 584; cf. Snodgrass 1971: 391; cf. also Kurtz and Boardman 1971: 66, 99–100, 257–9.

[37] Of course, such abnormal cases feed off the normal situation in which the symbolic reference is derived from the indexical one of marking the bones. But what interests us here is that the symbolic reference could function on its own and even generate a custom (the cenotaph) in which this symbolic reference was the sole function of the grave monument.

its function with reference to the deceased's remains and to his memory show that it was indeed a 'sign' of the deceased, as is indicated by the fact that it is called *sema*. Despite the specialization of its meaning to 'grave monument', the *sema* of A. meant not only 'the grave monument', but also 'the sign' of A. This conclusion will be confirmed by the analyses that follow.

3. *SEMA, TYMBOS, CHYTE GAIA, ERION:* WORDS AND MEANINGS

When Homer refers to the grave he uses words which denote the grave monument above the burial space. He does not speak of 'the grave of A', but of the 'grave monument' of A. The burial space itself is only spoken of once, in the context of the disposal of Hector's bones in the description of his burial, in *Iliad* 24. 797. This is the only reference to anything pertaining to the grave complex other than the grave monument. The word used for the burial space in *Iliad* 24. 797 is *kapetos*, which means 'trench'.[38] The fact that only the *sema* is referred to after the burial has been completed—and not, for example, something more generic in which the burial space itself would be more distinctly 'heard'—is correlative with the fact that it is the only part of the grave complex that belongs to the world of the living; its erection sealed off, and marked the exclusion of, the remains of the deceased and their burial space from 'our world'.

I will begin the consideration of the Homeric terms referring to the grave monument with the expression *chyte . . . gaia*, which is used in *Odyssey* 3. 258, *Iliad* 6. 464; 23. 256, and also in *Iliad* 14. 114, a verse rejected by Aristophanes and Zenodotos. In order to determine the precise semantic content of this expression, and its relationship to terms such as *tymbos* and *sema*, and the differences between them, if any, in the epic, it is necessary to embark on a somewhat detailed analysis of the usage of *chyte . . . gaia* expressions in the contexts in which they occur. In the process, we will gain an incidental glimpse of a few more instances of the subtlety of Homer's compositional technique.[39]

---

[38] Cf. *Il.* 15. 356; 18. 564.

[39] By reconstructing the assumptions through which Homer operated, I am, of course, attempting to make explicit the implicit knowledge which enabled Homer to produce certain literary effects for audiences who shared his assumptions.

The expression *chyten epi gaian echeuan* occurs in *Odyssey* 3. 258 and *Iliad* 23. 256, both times at the end of the line. It is a formula. The variant *chyte kata gaia kalyptoi* in *Iliad* 6. 464, again at the end of the line (and, if it is Homeric, *chyte kata gaia kalyptei* in *Iliad* 14. 114) is a modified version of this same formula. The first variant, which we can be certain had crystallized in this form, since we have two good instances of it, refers to the act of burial, the second, of which we have one certain and one doubtful instance, refers to the situation after the grave was completed, when the mound of earth is said to be covering someone. Let us consider the contexts in detail. In *Iliad* 23. 256 the context is straightforwardly descriptive; this is the most detailed description of the construction of a grave monument, that for Patroklos, in its first, temporary form, before the death of Achilles. The expression *chyten epi gaian echeuan* describes one—the most important and final—of the concrete physical activities which make up the concept 'erection of the grave monument'. In *Odyssey* 3. 256–61 Nestor is saying that if Menelaos had found Aigisthos alive the latter would not have received burial, but would have been eaten by dogs and birds on the plain away from the city, and unmourned (cf. esp. vv. 258–9). The context here is again unambiguously one of burial—though of course the theme and circumstances are different from those in *Iliad* 23. 256. The choice of the expression *chyten epi gaian echeuan* to give voice to the concept of burial stresses the actual physical act of entombment by analysing part of its action plot. In this way, the audience is directed to the plane of concrete physical reality of burial, and thus at the same time also of its opposite, that to which burial is here contrasted: the horrifying image of burial withheld and the corpse being eaten by dogs and birds. It is possible that this choice of expression may have reinforced the gruesome image to which it is contrasted. I suggested elsewhere[40] that this 'dogs-and-birds' image, which represents nature at its most savage disposing of the body, contains a series of concepts which contrast with those involved in the 'normal'—and, of course, desirable—situation of burial in the following significant ways: BURIAL: Culture: men: fire and/or constructed grave v. NON-BURIAL/DOGS-AND-BIRDS: Nature: animals: eating raw; the concepts of non-construction, non-involvement of *techne* are also implied. Clearly, some of these notions

---

[40] Sourvinou-Inwood 1981: 31–2; cf. 1983: 43.

are explicitly mentioned in *Odyssey* 3. 258–61, and they supplement and enhance the main part of the dogs-and-birds image; he would have lain in a plain away from the city, that is, outside the community, in nature, unmourned by the women of the community. It seems possible that *chyten epi gaian echeuan* contributed to this building up and sharpening of the contrasts—and so also to the vividness of the central image; for it brought to mind not only the agency of men (and so one aspect of the community's involvement in the death ritual) and the "culture' element of marking the grave, but also, more specifically, the act of construction, and thus the element of *techne*, which is a *par excellence* feature of culture. These suggestions and the ones that follow imply great (though, of course, not necessarily conscious) compositional subtlety in the choice of words and expressions to enhance the dramatic effect.

Iliad 6. 464 does not refer to burial, but to the time after the burial has been completed. Hector is envisaging his own death, indeed, he is wishing for it, as preferable to the agony of being a witness to the misery that the fall of Troy, which he perceives as inescapable, will bring upon his wife: *alla me tethneota chyte kata gaia kalyptoi, prin* . . . The equivalent expression in English would be 'let me be dead and buried, before I hear . . .'. The choice of words is significant and once again reinforces the image. The expression *me tethneota chyte kata gaia kalyptoi*, by naming explicitly the physical mass covering the remains of the dead person, draws attention to two things. The physical remains of the deceased themselves, which are the focus of the expression, while in the overwhelmingly more frequent expressions involving *sema* or the like only the visible grave monument comes into play, and the remains which it marks are shut out from the mental image. Also, partly because of this focus, this expression conveys the notion of the separation of the dead from this world. First through the imagery, for the mound of earth covering Hector's remains and separating them from the world of the living is a visual articulation of the notion of distancing, which, we shall see, is the central concept here. Then, and more strikingly for Homer's contemporaries, the notion of this separation is inextricably connected with the heaping of the funeral mound.[41] For this mound was the final stage in this separation of the dead from the living, of his remains, and in the eschatological plane of the

[41] On *Il.* 6. 459–65 cf. also Redfield 1975: 175.

shade; thus, the funeral mound, when perceived primarily not as a completed *sema*, but as a heap of earth in the process of being piled up on the grave during burial, would inevitably evoke this separation of the dead and the cessation of the self's existence in the world of the living—other than as a memory. This idea was expressed through the word-group *chyten epi gaian echeuan* in contexts where the focus is the burial ceremony itself; *chyte kata gaia kalyptoi*, used when the viewpoint was situated after the completion of the burial, is a modification of the previous formula. Because it is based on the word-group expressing the piling-up of the mound, and it includes the words *chyte . . . gaia echeuan*, it evokes the material reality of the mound and the physical act of its erection, and directs the mind to the same notion of separation of the dead and cessation of the self's existence in this world. *Sema* and *tymbos*, by contrast, denote, we shall see, the completed grave monument which belongs to the world of normality and of the living. This analysis of *chyte gaia* expressions in general, and *chyte kata gaia kalyptoi* in particular, gains some confirmation from the fact that this idea of separation from the world of the living and cessation of the self's existence in this world, fits excellently the context of *Iliad* 6. 464. Hector's wish is not to know about Andromache's future misfortunes; terrible things are going to happen but he doesn't want to witness them.[42]

As for *Iliad* 14. 114, it may well be that Aristophanes and Zenodotos were right that the verse is not Homeric. The expression *chyte kata gaia kalyptei* here is a periphrasis to say that a person is dead (and buried): . . . *Tydeos, hon Thebesi chyte kata gaia kalyptei*. In one way, this is a way of saying 'he has a grave monument', and thus 'he is dead'. But the particular expression chosen for referring to the grave monument, rather unusually for Homer, is one that is not exclusively focused on the monument itself, but brings into play more directly also the physical remains of the deceased.

Of the other Homeric terms used to refer to the grave monu-

---

[42] The fact that, as we saw in Ch. II § ii.5*b*, in one of the strands of Homeric eschatology the dead are interested in, and able to find out about, the fate of their loved ones is irrelevant for the understanding of this passage. What we are talking about here is imagery which, given certain connotations attached to the terms that come into play, functions effectively. For whether or not Hector could have found out about Andromache's troubles in Hades, what he is saying is, 'I don't want to be there when it happens' in the polarized form 'I want to be dead'; and he expresses this through a word-combination which contributes very significantly to the build-up of the notion of distancing in the extreme form of death, separation from, and the cessation of the self's existence in, the world of the living.

ment, *erion* occurs only once. *Erion* is generally translated as 'mound, barrow, tomb'.[43] The notion that *erion* means primarily 'mound' is based on a particular decoding of this word in *Iliad* 23. 126, which itself rests on uncertain foundations, on an oversimplification of the terms of the problem. The meaning 'mound' cannot be excluded, but a detailed examination of what little data are available suggests that its correct meaning is very much more likely to be 'grave monument' in the sense of *sema*, the visible sign above, and marking, the grave, which had certain functions and certain characteristics— rather than 'mound', which is a particular type of grave monument. The fact that the grave monument spoken of as *erion* in *Iliad* 23. 126 (that is, the projected permanent monument of the burials of Patroklos and Achilles) was actually a mound, and is referred to as *tymbos* in *Iliad* 23. 245–8 does not entail that the two terms are identical; it simply means that both are applicable to this monument. Normally, we would not be expecting any kind of consistency in Homer's description of any one thing over several passages. Here, however, the proximity of the passages involved, and the fact that the focus is on Patroklos' burial over the whole of this part of book 23, would lead us to expect that the poet would have had a mental image of one particular type of grave monument, while he was applying different terms to it. The following are the terms involved. First, *tymbos*, in *Iliad* 23. 245–8, which denotes the grave monument's physical type; this passage makes clear that the temporary monument for Patroklos and the projected permanent one for Patroklos and Achilles were envisaged as exactly the same, except in size, the latter being a bigger and more impressive version of the former. Given this, it is legitimate to claim that the term *sema* was also applied to the grave monument in question, in so far as it was applied to the temporary monument for Patroklos.[44] *Sema* denotes the grave monument in terms of its function and position, independently from its physical type. Finally, there is *erion*, the term which we wish to elucidate and assign to one or the other of these two semantic categories pertaining to this grave monument. The expression used in *Iliad* 23. 126 is *phrassato Patrokloi mega erion ede hoi autoi*. A consideration of the pattern of usage of *phrazomai* in this sense[45] makes clear that its object denotes the ultimate purpose,

[43] Thus Liddell and Scott, s.v.; Immerwahr (1967: 262): 'mound, tomb'.
[44] *Il.* 23. 255, 257; also 24. 16, 51, 417, 755–6.
[45] Cf. *Il.* 12. 212; *Od.* 2. 367; 3. 242; 4. 444; 12. 212; 13. 373; cf. also 1. 205.

and so tends to be an abstract concept rather than a material object. It could thus be argued that we should expect the word denoting the grave monument in *Iliad* 23. 126 to be a term in which the semantic emphasis lay not on the mound perceived as a physical object, but on the grave monument as a concept involving a certain function and certain other characteristics, independently of its precise physical form.

This tentative conclusion might gain a little support from the passage in the *Athenaion Politeia* (55. 2–3), which tells us that every Athenian was asked, before taking office, *eria ei estin kai pou tauta*. For *erion* cannot, clearly, mean 'mound' here since not all Athenian grave monuments had a mound.[46] The general idea here is,[47] 'tombs', family tombs. If we are looking for greater precision we should gravitate towards the concept 'grave monument'. For the term normally used, by the orators, for these family tombs is *mnemata*. And *mnemata* leads us again to the same semantic area of grave monument/memorial which, I am suggesting, was central in the word *erion*. Thus, if we can deduce anything relevant to the archaic usage of the word from the passage in the *Athenaion Politeia*, it would seem to confirm rather than invalidate the suggestion made here. If *erion* had indeed originally meant 'grave monument', it eventually ceased to have that specialized meaning, and came to cover the whole concept of 'tomb'.[48] When the distinctions cease

---

[46] Nor can it mean 'family-plot' as Immerwahr believes (1967: 262–4), since there is no evidence whatsoever to support the idea that '*erion* was an old Attic word for the family plots of Athenian citizens' (op. cit. 262)—other than Immerwahr's interpretation of the *Ath.Pol.* passage. For the recent discovery of the family grave plot of the orator Lykourgos cf. Matthaiou 1987: 31–44; cf. also Vassilopoulou 1987: 149–52.

[47] As Humphreys noted (1983: 121).

[48] Cf. *Etym Magn.* s.v. *eria*; Harpokration s.v. *eria*. Whether or not *erion* is the word to be read in the gold tablet from Hipponion (cf. esp. Pugliese-Carratelli 1974a: 108–26; Burkert 1975: 81–104; Zuntz 1976: 129–51; Cole 1980: with bibliog. in p. 223 n. 3) is a matter of controversy, which is beyond my scope to review here (on this problem cf. esp. Zuntz 1976: 134; also Lloyd Jones 1985: 271). It is certainly true that the expression is unmetrical and that the substitution of the word *doron* for *erion* would restore the metre. If *erion* were the correct word, the meaning 'grave monument' which I am proposing as its primary and original meaning would make better sense than 'the grave of Mnemosyne' (Zuntz 1976: 134). Mnemosyne is very important in these gold tablets (Pugliese-Carratelli 1974a: 117–18; 1974b: 139–40). Since she is the goddess that assures the permanence of the vital piece of the knowledge that liberates the initiate from the common lot of mortals, the gold tablet carrying the 'instructions' for the successful transition to blessedness (cf. Pugliese-Carratelli 1974a: 124, 126) might have been capable of being represented as the sign and memorial of Mnemosyne, who governed memory, and to whom the initiate had special access; it might have been capable of being perceived as the sign and memorial of the initiate's special access

to be significant, they become blurred and eventually may vanish altogether.

Tymbos denotes the mound of earth over the grave—though it can also be erected as a cenotaph (*Odyssey* 4. 584.) In the epics it is mentioned on its own or in combination with a stele; once it is combined with an oar as additional grave-marker (*Odyssey* 11. 77) and once it is combined with both oar and grave stele (*Odyssey* 12. 14–15). The word *tymbos* appears on its own in twelve passages.[49] *Tymbos* is combined with a stele in five passages.[50] All instances of *tymbos*-and-stele grave monuments are erected over an individual burial. The simile involving a *tymbos* and stele in *Iliad* 17. 434–5 may suggest that this is what was perceived to be normal—at least by the composer of the simile: a stele standing on the *tymbos* erected over a simple burial. Of the twelve instances of *tymbos* on its own, one refers to the erection of a *tymbos* as a cenotaph—situated outside the community. Of the remaining eleven most referred to a *tymbos* erected over a single burial.[51] The others refer to *tymboi* over double, triple, or multiple burials. In *Iliad* 7. 336–7 and 435–6 a communal *tymbos* is erected for the war-dead.[52] In *Iliad* 23. 245–8 a *tymbos* will be erected over the double burial of Achilles and Patroklos;[53] and in *Odyssey* 24. 80–1 a *tymbos* is said to have been erected over the triple burial of Achilles, Patroklos, and Antilochos.

The references to *tymbos* on its own can be grouped into the

to the functions controlled by Mnemosyne, and to her protection; so that the tablet would be the memorial and sign of the deceased's memory as an initiate, of the possession, and the memory, of the knowledge, which will eventually lead to the 'sacred way' which leads to blessedness.

[49] *Il.* 2. 604, 793; 4. 177, 435; 23. 245–8; 24. 667; *Od.* 1. 239 = 14. 369; 4. 584; 24. 32, 80.

[50] *Il.* 11. 371; 16. 457 = 675; 17. 434; and also *Od.* 12. 14–15 where, we just saw, an extra marker, the oar, is fixed on the *tymbos*.

[51] *Il.* 2. 603–4, 792–3; 4. 174–7; 24. 667; *Od.* 1. 239; 14. 369; 24. 32.

[52] As Aristarchos noted, vv. 334–5 are interpolated. They clash with Homeric practice throughout, and are contradicted by the passage describing the execution of the suggestions (vv. 433–6) which describes primary cremation. This contradiction is significant, for the latter passage is dependent on the former and in very close proximity to it. The passage is discussed (with bibliog.) by Andronikos (1968: W31–2); in my view, his conclusions are arguable, for some of the premises on which they are based are doubtful. For the epics, with their conflated burial customs, contain instances of both primary and secondary cremation, and the temporary placing of Patroklos' bones in a receptacle in Achilles' tent does not testify to a practice of carrying bones back home; it is based on, it is an 'abnormal' version of, the practices involved in secondary cremations such as that of Hector in *Il.* 24. 792–9—here combined with a *tymbos* erected around the funeral pyre. On *Il.* 7. 334–5 cf. Pritchett 1985: 100–1.

[53] Cf. also *Il.* 23. 126 where, we saw, the word *erion* is used.

following semantic categories: (1) Reference to, or description of, the erection of a *tymbos*.[54] Among references in this category *Odyssey* 4. 584 (*cheu' Agamemnoni tymbon, hin' asbeston kleos eie*) deserves special mention because it contains a word-group which articulates one of the fundamental concepts associated with the grave monument in the epics: *tymbon, hin' asbeston kleos eie*. (2) Reference to the *tymbos* of a person long dead as a landmark and/or focus of activity (*Iliad* 2. 604 (of Aipytos); 793 (of Aisyetes)). (3) *Iliad* 4. 174–7 belongs to a special *ad hoc* category: the (hypothetical) *tymbos* of a recently dead person becomes the focus of hostile activity and jeering. The references to *tymbos* in combination with a stele can be grouped into the following semantic categories. (1) Reference to, or description of, the erection of a *tymbos* with a stele.[55] (2) Reference to the *tymbos* with stele of a person long dead as a focus of activity.[56] (3) The stele on the *tymbos* is used in a simile (*Iliad* 17. 434–5).

If we leave aside on the one hand the special reference to Menelaos' hypothetical *tymbos* in *Iliad* 4. 174–7, and on the other the *tymbos*-and-stele simile, the same two major semantic categories are involved in the *tymbos*-and-stele references as in those of *tymbos* on its own—though in each of them the former are far less numerous than the latter. It is not the case that every reference to *tymbos* is to be understood as (was 'meant' by the poet and taken by the audience to mean) *tymbos* and stele.[57] This view is (explicitly or implicitly) based on the following arguments. First, the fact that in *Iliad* 16. 457 (= 675) the *tymbos*-and-stele grave monument is said to be *geras thanonton*. And second, the fact that in some cases the *sema* consists of a *tymbos* and stele.[58] However, first, it is not this particular form of grave monument that is considered *geras thanonton*, and thus normal; what is *geras thanonton* is proper burial. For in

---

[54] There are three groups of references in this category. (a) *Il.* 7. 435; 24. 667; *Od.* 1. 239; 14. 369; 24. 32, in all of which the verb *poio* is used. (b) *Il.* 7. 336; *Od.* 4. 584; 24. 80–1, in all of which *cheuo* is used. (c) *Il.* 23. 245–8, where *poneesthai* is used in v. 245 and *tithemenai* in v. 247. In *Il.* 21. 323 the activity of erecting a *tymbos* is called *tymbochoe*.

[55] (a) *Od.* 12. 14–15 describes the erection of a *tymbos* with a stele and an oar (cf. *Od.* 11. 77: request for the erection of a *tymbos* with an oar only as a marker). (b) *Il.* 16. 456–7 = 674–5: the focus of the expression here is the act of burial.

[56] *Il.* 11. 371–2: the *tymbos* and stele of Ilos. There are also three references to the *sema* of Ilos: *Il.* 10. 415; 11. 166; 24. 349.

[57] As implied by Andronikos 1968: W33; Mylonas 1962: 485, 486.

[58] Ilos' *sema*: *sema*: *Il.* 10. 415; 11. 166; 24. 349; *tymbos* with stele: *Il.* 11. 372; and Elpenor's *sema*: *Od.* 11. 75–8; 12. 14).

Homer it is not only the burial involving the erection of a *tymbos*-and-stele that is said to be the due of the dead, but also mourning and weeping for them.[59] In other words, any part or aspect of the prescriptive death-ritual can be called *geras thanonton*, for what was 'the due of the dead' was the whole of that death-ritual, proper burial, mourning and lament, the *sine qua non* of a good death.[60] As for the second argument, given the nature of Homeric diction, it is illegitimate to assume consistency, to postulate that every *tymbos* reference was understood to convey, by *synecdoche*, the notion *tymbos* and stele, especially since mounds without stelai were one of the types of real grave monument which helped shape the audience's perceptual filters through which they made sense of the epics.

Throughout the centuries of the poems' composition, real-life burial customs impinged on the epics in two major ways. First, they provided raw material for their composition and reshaping. And second, they functioned as perceptual models, matrices, by means of which each generation of audiences perceived and understood the burial customs described in the inherited material and each generation of poets both made sense of, and reshaped that material. As we saw, Dark-Age and eighth-century grave monuments took various forms, including grave-mounds with or without a stele or other additional grave-marker. These real-life 'common' frames, and the expectations aroused by the conventions of the genre, shaped the poet's and his contemporary audience's perceptual filters,[61] in a way that would not be conducive to understanding '*tymbos*' as always conveying the meaning '*tymbos* and stele'. Given the conflated nature of Homeric objects and institutions, neither common nor intertextual frames could compellingly convey the mental image of a particular type of object beyond the characteristics that are present in the verbal description (and, of course, those common to all objects of that class, such as that a helmet is always worn on the head). Some elements of the Homeric burial customs were derived from the audience's contemporary reality. But even

---

[59] *Il.* 23. 9–10; *Od.* 4. 195–8—cf. also 24. 189–90, 296.

[60] Cf. Sourvinou-Inwood 1981: 31–2. A brief discussion of *geras thanonton* in Homer and the archaic epitaphs in Hausle 1979: 123–5, with bibliog. On *geras thanonton* in Homer cf. also Schnaufer 1970: 160; Garland 1982: 69–80. The *sema* is said to be *geras thanontos* in an archaic epitaph (Hansen 1983: 40; *GV* 156).

[61] On common frames cf. Eco 1981: 20–1. On the expectations aroused by the conventions of the genre in which a 'text' belongs cf. Culler 1975: 145–8; also 1981: 117.

they appeared different, both because they were combined with other features, of different origin, and because they differed from the real-life models in such aspects as the pattern of usage: cremation, for example, was not universally practised in the eighth century, not even in Ionia, as it is in the epics. Of course, Homer's audience was not aware of the conflated nature of the Homeric world, which was perceived by them simply as different from everyday reality because pertaining to the distanced heroic world of the past, in which (their perception would be) even familiar objects took unfamiliar forms. In other words, the conflation (which had naturally taken place over the generations) became one of the nexus of characteristics by means of which the distancing of the epic world from that of everyday experiences was effected.[62] Because of this distancing, the dimension of unfamiliarity even in the apparently familiar, and the fluidity and diversity in the descriptions of objects and practices in the epics, the audience was conditioned towards not making—and thus the poets towards not requiring—assumptions of the kind that the *synecdoche* discussed here would involve. Finally, another expectation aroused by the genre provides more support for this conclusion: repetition, the cumulation of detail, is a characteristic of the Homeric epics, and of oral poetry in general.[63] This would work against the readings (by the audience) of *tymbos* as meaning '*tymbos* and stele'. Consequently, it is not legitimate to believe that the numerous *tymbos* references in the epic activated not the frame 'mound as grave monument' but the much rarer textual frame '*tymbos* and stele', with the audience mentally complementing '*tymbos*' with 'stele'. I submit that *tymbos* conveyed the notion 'grave-mound', and that only the combination of stele with *tymbos* conveyed the concept 'mound crowned by a stele'.

Sema in the sense of grave monument occurs twenty-one times in the epics.[64] These twenty-one references can be separated into four semantic groups. (1) References to, or description of, the

---

[62] The distancing operated, of course, on many levels, and by means of many factors and devices.

[63] Cf. on the Homeric epics Hainsworth 1970: 97. On oral poetry in general cf. the critical discussion in Finnegan 1977: 127–33.

[64] Here the 24th book of the *Odyssey* is included: *Il.* 2. 814; 6. 419; 7. 86, 89; 10. 415; 11. 166; 21. 323; 23. 45, 255, 257, 331; 24. 16, 51, 349, 417, 755, 799, 801; *Od.* 1. 291; 2. 222; 11. 75.

setting up of a *sema*.[65] (2) Reference to the *sema* of a person long
dead as a landmark and/or a focus of activity. These references fall
into different categories, (*a*) reference to activities around the *sema*
of Ilos,[66] (*b*) reference to other *semata*. This category can be divided
into two subcategories, (i) *sema* of a named individual,[67] (ii)
unnamed and uncertain *sema*.[68] (3) Reference to Hector's corpse
being dragged around Patroklos' *sema*.[69] (4) A special category,
represented by one instance (*Iliad* 7. 89) involves a hypothetical
description of a hypothetical *sema* by a (hypothetical) man of the
future. The following expressions are associated with the erection
of a *sema*: the phrase *cheuantes de to sema palin kion autar* (*Iliad* 23.
257; 24. 801.) which connects the completion of the burial with
whatever comes after it. It contains a form of a very frequent word-
group involving *sema, sema cheein/cheuein*.[70] The fact that *cheuein* is
associated with *sema* does not entail that *sema* in Homer means
'grave-mound'[71]—as opposed to 'grave monument', a word stressing its function rather than its appearance. When this is specified,
it is usually a grave-mound, sometimes with stele, or has a physical
appearance not otherwise specified. *De facto* Homeric grave monuments consisted of, or contained, a mound; the *tymbos* on its own
is the most frequently mentioned grave monument. This explains
the context of the expression *cheo sema*. In a context in which the
canonical form of the *sema* is the grave-mound, *cheo chyten gaian*
describes the physical activity, *cheo tymbon* describes the result of the
action, refers to the physical object produced by the action, while

---

[65] Eleven instances: *Il.* 6. 419; 7. 86; 21. 322; 23. 45, 255, 257, 24. 799, 801; *Od.* 1. 291;
2. 222; 11. 75. *Od.* 1. 291 and 2. 222 refer to the erection of a cenotaph-*sema*, not one over
a grave.
[66] References to activities around the *sema* of Ilos (which in *Il.* 11. 371–2 is described as
a *tymbos* with a stele): *Il.* 10. 415; 11. 166; 24. 349.
[67] *Il.* 2. 811–14 (*sema* of Myrine). A *tymbos* is also referred to as a landmark and/or focus
of activity elsewhere in the epic: not only Ilos' but also that of Aipytos (*Il.* 2. 792).
[68] *Il.* 23. 326.
[69] *Il.* 24. 16, 51–2, 416–17, 754–6.
[70] Other forms: *Il.* 6. 419; 24. 799; 23. 45; 7. 86; *Od.* 1. 291; 2. 222; 11. 75. Other
expressions: *Il.* 21. 322 (*s. teteuxetai*, in an oxymoron (that began in v. 318; on the oxymoron
cf. vv. 318–20: McLeod 1982: 157 *ad* 796); for the meaning in 321–3 surely is: 'I will put so
much mud over him, that a *sema* will be made for him there, and there will be no need for
the Achaeans to pour a mound when they honour him with funeral rights.' It is an oxymoron
because the mud would be concealing the place where Achilles' remains would be lying
unburied, while a *sema* marks the place where the deceased's remains are buried.) In *Il.* 23.
255 *tornosanto de sema* describes one stage in the construction.
[71] As is thought by some scholars (cf. e.g. Andronikos 1968: W33 and Eichler 1914: 138).

cheo sema describes the action in terms of its ultimate aim, refers to the end product in terms of its function, for which the operation was undertaken, and is a type of *synecdoche*.[72] The mound is only one of the types of *sema* known to the poet and his audience. There is no argument in favour of the view that *sema* means 'grave-mound' rather than 'grave monument' and there are several arguments against it. In *Iliad* 23. 326–32 what is described as a possible *sema brotoio palai katatethneotos* (it is either a grave monument or the turning post for a race) is an object consisting of a stump of wood against which are set two stones, one on each side.[73] This shows unequivocally that here at least *sema* refers to the function of the grave monument and does not mean grave-mound. All the evidence suggests that this is the case everywhere. Thus, whenever the meaning is 'grave-mound and stele' the term used is always *tymbos*; there is no combination of *sema* and stele. This absence suggests that *sema* did not refer to the grave-mound as a physical object, as *tymbos* did.

This argument on its own would be considered an *argumentum ex silentio*, but in fact it is part of a much wider pattern of differential usage of *sema* and *tymbos*, which consistently and strongly supports the view of their differential meaning suggested here, as I shall show in a moment. But in any case, I believe that the limitations of *argumenta ex silentio* must not be overstressed; for in this way what masquerades as rigour may in fact militate against precision. Absences of certain combinations are as significant as presences, and if we ignore the evidence of absences because it involves an *argumentum ex silentio* we are often leaving out important aspects of the evidence, and thus (since meanings are relational) not simply leaving the picture incomplete, but corrupting the discourse. The undervaluing of the evidential value of absences is one version of a wider implicit strategy in which the inevitable limitations of our access to the ancient world are used, like the *argumentum ex silentio* criticism, to protect the *status quo* of opinion. This strategy will perhaps be deployed against the case I am presenting here concerning the differential meanings of *sema* and *tymbos*. It would be claimed that my case involves an over-refinement of meaning which cannot be conclusively proved; and thus (by implication or

---

[72] Cf. Culler (1975: 180–1) on this type.
[73] On this passage cf. Andronikos 1968: W33.

explicitly) it will be claimed that the orthodox interpretation must stand. However, in cases where, as here, all the indications point very strongly in one direction, the fact that our limitations of access prevent that view from being proved correct must not (explicitly or implicitly) be taken to entail that the opposite view, against which all the evidence points, is right. Such an approach, when made explicit—which usually it is not: it functions as a filter weighting scholarly reception in one direction rather than another—can be seen to be untenable. It relies implicitly on the unexamined unconscious notion 'a negative approach is more rigorous; it is more rigorous to take the view that something cannot be proved'. This maxim is a methodological virtue in some cases, but not when (as would be the case here) it is implicitly taken to allow the proposition 'all the indications point towards *x*' to slide into '*x* cannot be conclusively proved, therefore *y* must be correct'. Nor is it less fallacious to under-refine the meaning of a word than to over-refine it. On the contrary, over-refining is easier to test and invalidate and less pernicious in its consequences.[74]

To return to the differential usage of *sema* and *tymbos*, there is a correlation between a context in which the emphasis is on the grave monument in its function as grave monument and the selection of the word *sema*;[75] and between a context in which the emphasis is on the physical object mound and the selection of the word *tymbos*.[76] Of course, in many cases the emphasis is on both.[77] The same correlations can be seen in the references to one grave monument, that of Ilos: in *Iliad* 10. 415; 11. 166; 24. 349, where Ilos' grave monument is referred to as the monument of a long-dead hero which serves both as a landmark and a symbolic focus for his memory and for the community,[78] *sema* is used; in *Iliad* 11. 372, where the physical object is being spoken of, we hear of the stele on the *tymbos* of Ilos. The problem with this argument is that the

---

[74] Thus, under-definition can lead to the blurring of important distinctions and the creation of interpretative constructs which do not correspond to the ancient realities. The corresponding over-definition would be likely to be empirically falsified.

[75] Cf. e.g. *Il*. 7. 89; 23. 331; the oxymoron in *Il*. 21. 321–3; *Od*. 11. 75; *Il*. 23. 45; *Il*. 2. 811–14; 7. 84–91; *Od*. 1. 289–92.

[76] *Od*. 12. 14–15; 11. 78; *Il*. 24. 667 (on the 11th day: the physical process of erecting a monument is stressed); *Il*. 2. 792–3; 7. 336, 435; 23. 245–8; 4. 174–7.

[77] Cf. e.g. *Il*. 23. 255–7; 24. 15–16, 799–801 (*sema* is used); or *Od*. 1. 239; 4. 584 (*tymbos* is used).

[78] Cf. Bérard (1982: 92–3).

assessment as to where the emphasis of meaning is in any particular context cannot escape subjectivity and cultural determination. Nevertheless, at least some of the above specimens can function as supportive arguments to the main case, which thus acquires considerable cumulative weight.

Another argument in favour of the thesis presented here, again involving an *argumentum ex silentio*, may be provided by the fact that *sema* is only ever used in the epics to denote the grave of a single individual. The communal mound in *Iliad* 7. 336 and 435 is referred to as *tymbos* and the permanent grave monument to be erected over the double burial of Achilles and Patroklos is called *erion* in *Iliad* 23. 126 and *tymbos* in *Iliad* 23. 245–8, while Patroklos' temporary monument is *tymbos* in this latter passage (v. 245) and *soma* in vv. 255 and 257. Also in *Odyssey* 24. 80–1 it is a *tymbos* that is erected over the triple burial of Achilles, Patroklos, and Antilochos. Since the sample of non-individual grave monuments is so small, it cannot be shown that *sema* was an inappropriate term for such monuments. But I feel that the choice of the word *erion* in *Iliad* 23. 126, which is unique, should perhaps be given some weight. Conceivably, it may indicate that the apparently obvious choice *sema* was not necessarily semantically suitable; for the metrical suitability of *erion* is obviously not the answer, or at least not the whole answer, especially when we consider that this is a unique usage: a basic concept and term like *sema* is one of the factors that would have helped shape the verse; if *sema* had been desired, the poet would have devised some other form for the verse. In my view, this supports the interpretation of *sema* suggested here. For if *sema* meant 'grave-mound' we would have expected the word to be used to refer to the grave monument over multiple burials as well. But *sema* would not be selected in the case of multiple burials if the poet's selections were determined by the assumption that *sema* meant 'grave monument in its function as grave monument' and included the meaning 'sign of', normally associated with the function of being the sign of a single individual.

In these circumstances, I submit that *sema* names the grave monument in terms of its function, not, like *tymbos*, in terms of the physical object that constitutes it. Of course, in a world in which the canonical grave monument is, or includes, a mound, both words carry both connotations. But this is not what is at issue here. We are concerned with the precise meaning, the definition of the

semantic field, of *sema* in relation to the other Homeric terms for
the grave monument; I will now pursue this further.

4. OTHER *SEMATA:* THE HOMERIC USAGE

I shall now consider the different usages of the word *sema* in
the epics to denote things other than grave monuments.[79] My
classifications of the meanings covered by *sema* in Homer is very
different from those adopted by Ebeling in the *Homeric Lexicon* and
by Liddell and Scott. I am ignoring the type of object or thing
involved, and concentrating on function and mechanics; that is, I
consider how each *sema* is a *sema*, what types of function are involved
when something is said to be a *sema*, in order to determine what
we can learn about Homeric notions concerning the grave monument from the fact that it is called *sema*.

We observe the following main categories of meaning of *sema* in
the epics.[80] (1) *Sema* is something set up intentionally to mark a
location one wants to recognize at a later time.[81] A variant of this is
the *sema* which is the intentional marking made to recognize an
object again.[82] The reference is indexical: the *sema* indicates past
activity (the marking) and in this way allows identification. (2) In
Iliad 23. 326 *sema* is something which was not set up with the
intention of marking a location, but which does, in fact, allow one
to identify a certain place. Its presence indicates that this is the place
one wishes to identify, and of which the *sema* is part. The reference
is indexical.[83] A variant of this is a *sema*, a bodily mark, which allows
the identification of a person, either evidence of past activity, like a
scar made by a boar,[84] or a natural bodily peculiarity.[85] Related to
this is the use of *sema* to denote the identifying characteristics of an
object which had been given those characteristics as a result of past
human activity, and which made it distinctive.[86] (3) *Sema* is the

---

[79] I will not include *Od.* 24 here, to avoid the risk of contaminating my analysis with later
usages which, in theory, may be different. On *sema* in Homer cf. also Andronikos 1961/2:
208; cf. also 208–10 on Homeric grave monuments.
[80] On the usage and meaning of *sema* in Homer cf. also Nagy 1983: 35–55; 1990: 208–
12.
[81] *Il.* 10. 466; 23. 843; *Od.* 8. 192, 195.
[82] *Il.* 7. 189 (cf. 7. 175).
[83] On this *sema* cf. also Nagy 1983: 46–51.
[84] *Od.* 21. 217; 23. 73.
[85] *Il.* 23. 455, an animal rather than human, body.
[86] *Od.* 23. 202.

revelation of knowledge which identifies a person, either as being a particular individual[87] or as belonging to a category, possessing some particular knowledge.[88] The reference is indexical: the *sema* indicates the presence of a whole (a particular individual, possession of particular knowledge and thus member of a particular category) of which it is part. A similar indexical reference obtains in the case of another type of sema: (4) The *sema* is a certain type of behaviour, which by its presence indicates a certain state of affairs.[89] (5) In *Iliad* 22. 29–30 the thing which is a (*kakon*) *sema* is a phenomenon (the Dog of Orion) which brings—according to Homer—another phenomenon: fever.[90] The *sema* here indicates the forthcoming presence of the other part of the whole of which (according to this mentality) the thing that functions as a *sema* is a part. The reference is indexical. (6) The *sema* is a certain type of behaviour/set of events which, it is prearranged, will function as a signal to trigger off a certain action.[91] The reference here is both indexical and symbolic; indexical because it indicates (by conventional arrangement) the presence of the conditions considered appropriate for the initiation of a certain action; and symbolic because, in virtue of this indexical reference it stands for the command 'begin action *a*'. This case helps us see that the distinction between 'indexical' and 'symbolic' reference should be deconstructed. For what is here clear, that the indexical reference slides into, and can be represented as, symbolic, pertains also to the other instances of *sema*, as can be seen if the same substitution is applied to the other uses of *semata* mentioned, in which the reference appears *prima facie* to be unambiguously indexical. This is of special interest to our investigation of the ways in which the grave monument related to the deceased. It shows, for example, that any notion that it functioned only as a grave-marker (that is, only an index of his remains) and focus for his memory without any symbolic reference would be the product of rationalizing distinctions that do not correspond to the modes of operation of signs—in ritual symbolism and elsewhere. (7) In *Iliad* 6. 168–78 there is a series of references to *sema* and *semata* which refer to different aspects of the same message, the message from

---

[87] *Od.* 23. 202, 206 (cf. 23. 110).
[88] *Od.* 19. 250: knowledge of Odysseus.
[89] *Odyssey* 11. 126; 23. 273.
[90] On similar notions of *post-hoc* reasoning cf. Hallpike 1979: 443.
[91] *Od.* 21. 231.

Proitos carried to the king of Lycia by Bellerophon. In v. 176 *sema* means 'token', evidence indicating through indexical reference comparable to (1) above, that he came from the person he claimed he was coming from, and, at the same time, it contains the notion 'message'. For in vv. 168–9 Proitos *poren . . . semata lygra, grapsas en pinaki thymophthora polla.* Here *semata* are intentionally produced signs which convey a message. They are, then, symbols; they are letters representing sounds which make up a message.[92] The dominant reference is symbolic. In v. 178 the word *sema* (*sema kakon paredexato gambrou*), like *sema* in v. 176, includes the meanings 'token' and 'message', though here *kakon* gives greater emphasis to the notion 'message', and to symbolic reference. (8) A specialized use of *sema* is its denotation of a particular type of sign, omens. As is the case with the grave monument, through being applied to one particular category of signs, *sema* acquired the extra specialized meaning 'omen'.[93] *Sema* is used to denote an omen in many Homeric passages.[94] It is beyond my scope here to discuss the mentality pertaining to omens.[95] I will simply note that, however we understand this mentality about and mode of operation of omens, we can distinguish the following elements pertaining to their function as signs. Omens indicate by their presence a certain state of affairs (favourable or unfavourable conditions), approval/encouragement or disapproval/discouragement by the gods (in Homer it is always Zeus who sends *semata*). Because of this, they also stand for, represent, a message, stand for approval or disapproval.[96] The message is sometimes something specific, for example, the siege and eventual fall of Troy indicated and symbolized by an omen interpreted by Kalchas in *Iliad* 2.308–20. In omens indexical and symbolic reference blend into each other. They

---

[92] On this passage and the question of writing cf. Jeffery 1990: 19; Tritsch 1968a: 124–37; 1968b: 1223–30. The use of the word *semata* refers to the role of the characters making up the message as signs, and need not, therefore, imply anything about the nature of the script. That is (*pace* Tritsch 1968a: 132) it does not need to be taken as suggesting a non-alphabetical script. Our own alphabetical characters are signs with a symbolic reference (see Martinet 1973: 70).

[93] Another word denoting similar kinds of omen as *sema* is *tera*, *terata*. *Sema*, of course, puts the emphasis (cf. Nilsson 1967: 166) on the sign-role of the omens. *Teras* clearly pertains to the nature of the manifestations—or some of them.

[94] *Il.* 2. 308–20, 350–3; 4. 380–1; 8. 170–1; 9. 236–7; 13. 241–4; *Od.* 20. 111; 21. 413.

[95] On this art cf. Burkert 1985: 113; Nilsson 1967: 56, 166–9. On Homeric *semata* as omens cf. Schnapp-Gourbeillon 1981: 179–85.

[96] The representation operates by means of a code which does not concern us here.

are indications of a certain disposition of the gods[97] intentionally produced by the gods, and they are also symbols representing messages, the message that this is what the disposition of the gods is.

To sum up. The primary type of reference in the signs referred to as *sema* is indexical; but the indexical reference slides into a symbolic one which is more pronounced in some types of *semata* and less so in others.

5. THE SIGN OF THE DECEASED AND MEMORY-SURVIVAL

These conclusions regarding the use of the word *sema* coincide with the conclusions of our earlier analyses: the semantic categories and sign-functions ascribed to the grave monument as a result of those analyses are indeed the same as those which Homer and his audience bring to bear on a thing called *sema*. This coincidence offers some confirmation for the validity of those analyses. It confirms that an expression such as *sema Ilou* was felt to include the meaning 'sign of Ilos' as well as 'grave monument of Ilos'; and that the notion of the grave monument as a 'sign of the dead person' was strongly present in Homeric perceptions, in which the grave monument stood for the dead person in the world of the living; for as long as the community remembered the deceased, the grave monument functioned as the focus of that memory. In the case of Ilos' *sema*, the community had preserved the memory of a long-dead hero and a particular monument was identified as his *sema*; that *sema* was a symbolically important focus for the community.[98] Thus, a person's posthumous memory is focused on, and activated or reinforced by, the grave monument.[99] The idea is that the deceased's memory will survive within the community, and the grave monument will keep it alive longer by activating it and serving as a focus for it. Dark-Age and eighth-century grave markers gave little information about

[97] On omens as indices cf. Martinet 1973: 57.
[98] Cf. Bérard 1982: 92–3.
[99] Cf. e.g. *Il.* 11. 371–2; *Od.* 11. 71–8 (cf. Heubeck 1989: 82 ad loc.). In a more complex variant, in *Il.* 7. 85–90, one's victim's grave monument is expected to preserve one's own memory (on this passage cf. also Kirk 1990: 245–6 ad loc.).

the deceased[100] and could not by themselves preserve his memory, by recording the fact of his life and death, like the archaic and classical monuments. But they did focus it and activate it.[101]

ii. *The Grave Monument in the Archaic Age*

1. NAME, NATURE, FUNCTION, PERCEPTIONS

In this section I shall consider the nature, meanings, and function of the grave monument in the archaic period and attempt to determine what, if any, changes have taken place as compared to the earlier periods reflected in Homer and how these relate to the archaic funerary ideology and practice. I begin with its name, for which grave inscriptions are a rich source of information. I shall be discussing the relevant formulations in Section 2a. Here I shall summarize the facts and compare them to the Homeric usage. In the archaic period the word *sema* continued to be commonly used for the grave monument; this was the word most commonly used for the grave monument on grave inscriptions. The most striking development in terminology pertains to the word *mnema*: in the archaic period *mnema* is often used to denote the grave monument, while in Homer *mnema* never refers to the grave monument. Whatever view is taken of its precise semantic field and relationship to *sema*,[102] *mnema* undoubtedly pertains to memory, and to things that preserve memory; thus this development is itself sufficient to suggest that in the archaic period there was a greater emphasis on the role

---

[100] The notion (cf. e.g. Skiadas 1972: 61–7; Häusle 1979: 79 and n. 131) that *Iliad* 7. 84–91 implies an inscribed grave monument—otherwise unattested in the archaeological record or in literature—arises from a misunderstanding of the way in which the grave monument functions in the Homeric epics, from a reading through the filters of later assumptions. In the Homeric epics the grave monument is the focus for the community memory, and thus does not rely on inscribed information.

[101] Cf. Lambrinoudakis (1988: 238) for a case in which an important grave-marker ('a huge prismatic stone 1.35 m. high') over a Late Protogeometric grave is associated with significant ritual activity by subsequent generations.

[102] When both words are used the specific meanings of each can drift away from their common semantic core which refers to the grave monument, in different directions; one modality of differentiation (cf. e.g. Hansen 1983: 139) is for *mnema* to emphasize the memorial aspect, while *sema* evokes the physical creation of the grave monument; another is that seen e.g. in Hansen (1983: 32). In other cases the differentiation, if it was heard at all, is more subtle (cf. e.g. Hansen 1983: 42). See n. 143 below for bibliog. on their relationship.

of the grave monument in the survival of the deceased's memory.[103] Indeed, the pattern of usage of *sema* and *mnema* in this period can be seen as a representation of the roles and meanings of the grave monument in the archaic age, of the fact that the *sema* function remains fundamental, the grave monument as the metonymic sign, the 'presence', of the deceased in the world of the living,[104] while its function as a 'memorial' that activates as well as focuses the deceased's memory is radically expanded. As was the case before, when a *sema* marks more than one burial, whether or not it had originally been the *sema* of one person,[105] it functioned as the sign of a group, for example, the descendants of X.[106] The grave monument as the sign of the deceased provided a concrete material form for the deceased's persona which functioned not only as a focus for his memory but also as a material object that lent itself to symbolic manipulation, that could, for example, receive offerings and other ritual attentions 'on behalf of' the deceased.[107]

[103] As will become clear in the course of this section, several other reasons also indicate a shift involving greater concern for memory survival focused on the grave monument.

[104] Cf. also Vernant 1991: 161–2. Vernant 1965: 72–8 related the symbolic relationship between the deceased and the grave monument in stone to the affinity and symbolic relationship which he perceives between the dead and stone, esp. the stone grave monument because of its immobility. But grave monuments not made of stone had a similar symbolic function: e.g., in Homer, grave-mounds without a stele also had that function, and vases, we saw, were used as grave-markers in the same cultural horizon as stone markers (cf. e.g. Kurtz and Boardman 1971: 56–7).

[105] Cf. e.g. Humphreys 1983: 95–101.

[106] A recently discovered mound covering many burials at Anavyssos is to be added to those already known in Attica: Kakavoyanni 1989. 43–5.

[107] One such example of symbolic manipulation involving more than offerings was the washing and anointing the stelai of the Plataia dead: Plut. *Arist.* 21. 4–5. On such practices cf. also Hägg 1992: 169–76. The misconceptions concerning the significance of such manipulations, and the claims made with regard to the identification of grave monument and deceased are exactly of the type described (in another context, of course) by De Man (1979a: 123): 'the possibility of unwarranted substitutions leading to ontological claims based on misinterpreted systems of relationship (such as, for example, substituting identity for signification)'. In the absence of analyses of the kind conducted here, which bring out the ways in which the grave monument functioned as a sign, it has not always been clear to everyone that the function of the grave monument as a symbol for the deceased does not depend on the monument's similarity to the human form. Thus Kurtz and Boardman (1971: 218–19) suggest that the stele's function 'as a form of surrogate or symbol of the dead ... is easiest argued when the stele approximates to human form, carries the representation of a human figure, or is replaced by a statue'. They go on to say that it is not likely, 'to judge from the early evidence', that such a function of the stele was the stele's prime function, which was more practical. However, first, the 'practical' use of the stele and the grave monument in general has implications for its function as a sign. And, second, the only thing that can be considered early evidence against the 'symbolic' function of the grave monument is the fact that its early forms did not approximate the human form. But this is only an

It is, of course, this primary function of the *sema* as the metonymic sign for the deceased in the world of the living that generated its function as a memorial;[108] for it made the grave monument the focus and (for all those not celebrated in song or folk memory) the vehicle, for the preservation and activation of the deceased's memory. Its function of 'memorial' that activates as well as focuses the deceased's memory is very significantly expanded and the modalities of its operation extended in the archaic period. As we shall see, some grave monuments, of different types, bear a grave inscription that 'names' the grave monument or burial. Obviously, the emergence of the grave inscription brought about a major extension of the role of the grave monument in preserving the deceased's memory; for the inscribed archaic grave monument can itself preserve the deceased's memory by recording and preserving a record of their life and death. The notion that the grave monument will preserve the deceased's memory is explicitly articulated in the alleged epitaph for Midas which was attributed to Kleoboulos of Rhodes and in Simonides fr. 581 *PMG*, where the same mentality as that expressed in the alleged epitaph for Midas is ascribed to Kleoboulos, the belief that the grave monument will last forever and proclaim that 'here lies' the deceased;[109] this belief in the durability of the grave monument is derided by Simonides.

Grave monuments take many different forms in the archaic period: they can take the form of a vase,[110] a mound (often crowned by an additional grave-marker, a vase or a stele),[111] a built tomb,[112] an unworked stone,[113] or a stele proper, with or without sculpted

argument against its symbolic function if it is assumed that approximation to human form was a necessary condition which, it is surely clear by now, is a wrong assumption. The investigation of the Homeric evidence, especially the investigation of the meanings of the word *sema*, demonstrated and clarified the function of the grave monument as the metonymic sign of the deceased.

[108] On the role of the archaic grave monument as a vehicle for the deceased's memory cf. also Lausberg 1982: 102–5.

[109] *GV* 1171; Pfohl 1967a: 24; cf. Jeffery 1976: 198.

[110] Cf. M. Robertson 1975: 27–9, 45, 50–154; Andronikos 1961/2: 184–6; Christou 1964a: *passim*, esp. 136, 153–5 with bibliog.; 1964b: *passim*, esp. 193–6; Simantoni-Bournia 1984: 54–5, 165 n. 63, and *passim*.

[111] Cf. e.g. Knigge 1988: 27–9; cf. also n. 10.

[112] On mounds and built tombs cf. Kurtz and Boardman 1971: 79–84, 244–6; on built tombs cf. also Lebessi 1976: 68–70. For the pattern of appearance and popularity of these types in archaic Athens cf. Humphreys 1983: 90, 95–101.

[113] Cf. e.g. a 7th-cent. elongated unworked stone marker, 0.52 m. high above the original surface, from Sellada in Thera (Zapheiropoulos 1977: 402).

decoration, over a grave not covered by a mound,[114] with or without a sphinx supported on a capital crowning the stele,[115] a statue,[116] sometimes supported by a column, or a column supporting some other object;[117] a 'trapeza' (or block marker);[118] or a grave structure.[119] Some of these grave monuments carried inscriptions, some carried images, and some both. I shall be discussing archaic grave inscriptions later on in this chapter, and I shall also be considering the images that appear on, and make up, archaic grave monuments, and the ways in which they reflect, and can help us further reconstruct, the functions of these monuments and the perceptions articulated in them. But first I shall consider some of the perceptions associated with the erection of the grave monument that do not depend on the reading of the images.

Without discussing the precise meanings of grave statues, we know that a statue was perceived to be, among other things, a beautiful thing, an *agalma*, an *agalma* for the deity when presented as a votive offering.[120] In so far as it was perceived to be beautiful, the statue did not cease to be perceived as an *agalma* when it was erected not as an offering to the gods but as a grave monument.[121] Indeed, the beauty of the grave monument is one of the themes articulated in archaic funerary epigrams.[122] This notion of the beauty of the grave monument was not confined to grave statues; it was also perceived to obtain in the case of grave stelai.[123] This beauty of the grave monument which was the metonymic sign of the deceased could represent metaphorically the now perished beauty of the deceased[124] and it generally enhanced and coloured positively the memory of that deceased. Thus, it can hardly be doubted that the notion of the grave monument as an *agalma* which helped the

[114] Cf. Kurtz and Boardman 1971: 81.
[115] Cf. below; on Attic stelai cf. esp. Richter 1961.
[116] Cf. e.g. Ridgway 1977: 149–62. Cf. below.
[117] Cf. Kurtz and Boardman 1971: 240–1.
[118] Cf. ibid. 235–6. It is not impossible that at Thera a form of trapeza may have functioned as a *sema* already in the 8th cent. (cf. Andronikos 1961/2: 191–2).
[119] Cf. Lebessi 1976: 68–70.
[120] On the use of the word *agalma* in dedicatory inscriptions cf. Lazzarini 1976: 95–8.
[121] Cf. Karouzos 1961: 28–30.
[122] On the theme of the beauty of the grave monument cf. Hansen 1983: 18 (the grave monument was a kore), 26, 161, 165. On this theme cf. also Karouzos 1972: 99–101, cf. also 150–1; Skiadas 1967: 21–5.
[123] Cf. e.g. the epitaph for Learete (Hansen 1983: 161).
[124] Cf. also Vernant 1991: 162–3.

positive presentation of the deceased's social persona was perceived to be inherent in many archaic grave monuments, perhaps in all those perceived to be a *kalon sema*.

I shall now define further this notion of the grave monument as an *agalma* and delve more deeply into the perceptions associated with the erection of the archaic grave monument, by examining a hypothesis that ascribes a votive function to the grave monument comparable to that of votive offerings to the gods. In her important 1982 essay on funerary kouroi and korai in Attica[125] D'Onofrio, in my view, overstresses the notion of the votive facet of the grave monument and underestimates the differences between votive offerings to the gods on the one hand and the erection of a grave monument on the other.[126] A significant part of her argument is based on the important observation that in some cases in which this is possible to determine, the statue was not directly above the grave but in a votive area;[127] she believes this to be an expression of the statue's nature as *anathema*.[128] In her 1988 article she shifted the emphasis of the explanation of this phenomenon in what is, in my view, the right direction: she emphasized[129] the increase in the importance of the grave monument as a 'form of social communication' pertaining to the preservation of the deceased's memory within the community, and connected its location with the resulting desire of greater visibility. I agree with this view; it is part of my own argument that the *mnema* aspect of the grave monument increased dramatically in the course of the archaic period, in conjunction with an increase in the concern for memory survival. However, I also want to stress that what we are dealing with is a shift in the emphasis of the meanings of the grave monument, not a change of function. The indexical function of the *sema* has not disappeared or diminished; it is only that the modalities of its functioning became subordinated to, and shaped by, the *mnema* function which has now significantly expanded. Furthermore, I

[125] D'Onofrio 1982: 148–50.
[126] Cf. ibid. 162.
[127] Cf. also on this D'Onofrio 1988: 85–8.
[128] 'la sua natura di *geras*, estrema prestazione fornita dal gruppo al defunto' (D'Onofrio 1982: 150).
[129] Cf. esp. D'Onofrio 1988: 84, 94–5. Of course the commemorative function was also mentioned in the earlier paper, the fact that the grave monument guarantees the memory of the deceased within the group (cf. D'Onofrio 1982: 162). But in that paper it was the votive dimension that had been emphasized.

.

believe that, given the complex interplay between family burial area and individual *sema*, especially in the case of a tumulus covering more than one burial, the location of individual stelai or statues other than exactly above the burial space is one of the options available from the purely indexical point of view. This would have been especially the case where 'the family burial space' was a more important perception than 'the individual burial space'; for this would have strengthened even further the tendency of the element 'individual' to drift to the individual *sema*, the vehicle of the individual's memory survival, and away from the burial space and its associated collective *sema*. Thus it is not necessary to imagine a significant change in the indexical function of the grave monument, especially since the placing of a *sema* in a place other than over the burial space may not have been entirely unrelated to the place of the *sema* in the death-ritual. For when we are dealing with a tumulus covering more than one burial, placing the *sema* over an offering ditch—if, as is extremely likely, offering ditches represent offerings made at the conclusion of the burial ceremony[130]—may have been perceived as placing it over the most individualized surface area pertaining to the deceased's remains; the tumulus functioned as the *sema* of the family group, while the individual *sema* was placed over the area which, while being associated with the sealing of the deceased's remains, was more individual, and also a stage further removed from the actual burial act and its associated space, and closer to the world of the living in which the *sema* stands for the deceased in his persona as deceased. If this reconstruction is correct, once the practice was established, and so also the perception that this was one possible position for the *sema*, it would have been unproblematically applied also where the situation that had originally generated it did not pertain, where there was no tumulus covering more than one burial; for that position would simply have been seen as one appropriate space for the grave monument. Also, once the direct vertical connection between burial space and *sema* had ceased to be perceived as indispensable, other options became open, and may have been taken in response to desires such as that for greater visibility, generated by the expanded significance of the grave monument's *mnema* function.

D'Onofrio's case in support of her votive interpretation of the

---

[130] Cf. Sourvinou-Inwood 1983: 47.

grave statues includes, besides the above considered thesis pertaining
to the placing of a *sema*, also the following arguments. In her view,[131]
the statues found carefully buried like Phrasikleia[132] were not buried
in order to protect them but because they were damaged; on this,
at best unproven, contention[133] she based a further argument: she
argued that the fact that damaged statues were not destroyed but
buried, separately from their bases thus breaking the funerary monument, confirms the votive function of funerary statues. I cannot see
how this argument can be valid; for I do not see how, even if her
interpretation of the buried statues were right, this would support
the votive interpretation, since it is equally plausible that the same
behaviour can be explained by the belief (which is in fact attested)[134]
that the *sema* of the deceased in the world of the living—of whatever
type—should be treated with respect, a belief the extent of which
could vary according to individuals and circumstances. Indeed, this
explanation makes best sense of the fact that in the ancient realities
what happened to the grave monument when removed from function varied widely: the spectrum went from their use by the polis
in the Themistoklean wall in the case limit of perceived national
crisis[135] to the reverent burial (presumably by members of later
generations of the deceased's family) of some kouroi and korai
statues. The statues and stelai ceased to be *semata* proper by being
separated from their bases as well as moved from their original place.

Of course, in so far as a grave statue is also an *agalma* set up to be
the sign of the deceased, to perform a function on their behalf, and
thus in some way offered 'to' them, it is possible to call it an
'*anathema* to' the deceased; but this would implicitly understress
important distinctions and create false similarities with deities,[136]
which would be a serious mistake. For differences have a fundamental role in the creation of meaning, and they are perceived
much more strongly by the members of the cultural community

---

[131] D'Onofrio 1982: 151–2.

[132] I shall discuss this statue in § ii.4c below.

[133] On a more plausible context for the burial of statues cf. Hornblower 1991: 210 *ad* 1.
126. 12 with bibliog.

[134] Cf. below.

[135] Cf. Thuc. 1. 93. 2; Hornblower 1991: 137–8 ad loc.

[136] Indeed the similarity is explicitly suggested in D'Onofrio (1982: 162), that the relationship constructed between living and dead through the erection of the funerary monument
'appare strutturalment vicino a quello che lega il fedele alla divinità e che si esprime attraverso
l'offerta votiva.'

that generated the perceptions that are being investigated than by
the observer; subsuming different phenomena into broad categories
is a move especially vulnerable to cultural determination, and often
leads to the creation of constructs which distort the ancient realities.

2. THE EPITAPHS

(a) *The 'Naming' of the Grave Monument*

All archaic funerary epigrams known to have been inscribed above
a grave include at least one reference to the grave monument, or,
more rarely, to burial;[137] prose grave inscriptions also include such
a reference. I will now try to prove the truth of this opening
statement, by examining apparent exceptions; I will also explore further these references, which, it will become clear after the
archaic grave monument has been considered as a whole, had an
important function, and were not simply reflecting unmotivated
tradition.

Most references to the grave monument in archaic funerary
epigrams are direct. They take forms such as 'This is the *sema* of A.'
There are also references of a somewhat less direct form, such as
'*Stethi kai oiktiron Kroiso para sema . . .*'. In extremely rare cases the
reference to the grave monument could be indirect, without the
actual word being used, but it is nevertheless unambiguous. Thus,
in the epitaph for Tettichos,[138] the grave monument, though not
mentioned by 'name', is the focus of the epitaph, the tangible spatial
point of reference for, and focus of, the action represented in, and
invited by, the epigram, and thus the focus of its reading. Thus the
absence of the word presents itself as a play, a trope of interplay
between concealment and enunciation.[139] This epitaph combines
two themes: invitation to passers-by to feel pity for the deceased as
they go past his grave monument, and invitation to passers-by to

---

[137] Such as 'here lies A' or 'B laid A here'. Gragg (1910: 16–17; cf. 19) had already noted
that in archaic sepulchral epigrams there is 'always some word meaning "tomb" '—except
for the Tettichos epigram (cf. below); and cf. Gentili 1968: 61.

[138] Hansen 1983: 13; *GV* 1226; Pfohl 1967: 55; Jeffery 1962: 133 no. 34; 1990: 77 no. 19,
401 pl. 3. Cf. also Lausberg 1982: 116.

[139] It is not impossible that at this early stage in the history of Attic funerary epigrams
such 'experimentation' (which did not, however, run counter to the mentality behind, and
the function of, the grave monument in archaic society) was less uncommon than when the
conventions had become more crystallized.

lament for the deceased at his grave monument. It reads as follows:

> [εἴτε ἀστό]ς τις ἀνὲρ εἴτε χσένος [ς ἅλοθεν ἐλθὸν :
> Τέτιχον οἰκτίρα|ς ἄνδρ' ἀγαθὸν παρίτο, :
> ἐν πολέμοι|φθίμενον, νεαρὰν ἥβεν ὀλέσαν | τα. :
> ταῦτ' ἀποδυράμενοι νε͂σθε ἐπ|ὶ πρᾶγμ' ἀγαθόν.

This is the furthest that any archaic funerary epigram ever gets from a direct reference to the grave monument or burial.[140]

There are, broadly speaking, three main types of reference to the grave monument/burial[141] in archaic funerary epigrams.[142]

The first type, which includes the majority of archaic epigrams, refers to the grave monument and/or its erection and sometimes its manufacture. The most frequent term in this category is sema, followed in frequency by *mnema*;[143] we also find *tymbos*,[144] *stele*[145] and, rarely, some other word.[146] Two epigrams contain the expressions *se ch[yte k]ata gaian ekalyphsen*[147] and *ton kata gai' ekalyphsen*.[148] These expressions denote the grave-mound and so belong

---

[140] Later in this section I shall be discussing another apparent exception, the epigram for Pleistias, and also the non-metrical *oimoi* inscriptions from Selinous, which, we shall see, far from invalidating the thesis put forward here, reinforce its strength and demonstrate its importance.

[141] When I refer to the grave monument I mean any part of the grave above and outside the burial space, mound, stele or any other type of gravestone such as trapeza, statue, column, and any other kind of superstructure which covered the burial such as a built tomb. When I refer to the grave I include the burial, the burial space and the grave monument.

[142] I am not attempting to classify the funerary epigrams here, only the types of references to the grave, irrespective of their formal position within the epigrams, and of whether or not they are combined with other themes.

[143] On the two terms cf. Karouzos (1961: 93 n. 85), who notes that *sema* is the more generic term, while *mnema* is one function of the *sema*; cf. also Eichler 1914; 138–43; Pfohl 1953: 96–119; Wenz 1913: 17 ff.; Pircher 1979: 20; Simondon 1982: 81–94.

[144] Cf. Hansen 1983: 144, 146.

[145] Cf. e.g. the fragmentary epigram on a slab from Cyrene (Hansen 1983: 164; SEG 20. 745). For *stele epi tymbo*: cf. Hansen 1983: 146; *GV* 67 (*stala epi tymoi*), on which cf. also Guarducci 1967: 178–80. We find stele on the lower part of the stele for Archias and Phile (Hansen 1983: 26; *GV* 74; Jeffery 1962: 139–40 no. 48; 1990: 74, 78 no. 31, 401 pl. 4) and on the epigram on the little pyramid from Sinope (Hansen 1983: 174).

[146] Cf. e.g.: *oi⸢⸣on* in the epigram for Deidamas (Hansen 1983; 152; *GV* 1413; *IG* xii. 7. 442; Pfohl 1967: 1). For other rarely used terms referring to grave monuments cf. Guarducci 1974: 142–6.

[147] Hansen 1983: 69; Willemsen 1963: 145–7 no. 12; Pfohl 1967: 36 inscribed on a marble block which (Willemsen 1963: 146) belonged to a larger monument.

[148] Hansen 1983: 76; *GV* 320; Peek 1960: 35; Jeffery 1990: 86, 88 no. 14; *IG* xii. 9. 287 Suppl. p. 186; Pfohl 1967: 126.

to this category, though the concept of 'burial' is also conjured up. More than one of these words can be used together, which may indicate concern with these notions.[149] References to the grave monument that belong to this type appear in several variants, two major and some minor, each of which appears in more than one subvariant. The first two variants account for most of the epigrams belonging to this first category of references.

Variant I: I am/This is the *sema/mnema* of A.[150]
Variant II: B put up this *sema/mnema* for A.[151]

The other[152] variants are here grouped together in the composite category.

Variant III(*a*) 'C made it (i.e. the monument)'. This appears in combination with some other reference to the grave or monument.[153]

III(*b*) References involving seeing, and looking at the *sema*.[154]

---

[149] Cf. e.g. *mnama* and *sama* in the gravestone of Androkles from Methana (Hansen 1983: 137; GV 158; Jeffery 1990: 181 no. 1, 406 pl. 32); Praxiteles' epigram on a stone pillar from Troizen (Hansen 1983: 139; GV 165; Jeffery 1990: 176 f., 182 no. 3, 406 pl. 32); Neilonides' epigram (Hansen 1983: 42; GV 72; Jeffery 1962: 127 no. 19); on the base of the grave monument for the two children of Kylon (Hansen 1983: 32, GV 147; Jeffery 1990: 73, 77 no. 22; Jeffery 1962: 136 no. 41); and on the base for Philoitios and Ktesias (Hansen 1983: 70; GV 74a). *Tymbos* and *stele* (*stala*) in the epitaph for Xenares (Hansen 1983, 146; GV 52; IG ix. 1. 869) and restored in the epitaph on the grave stele of Polynoe (Hansen 1983: 144; GV 67; Jeffery 1990: 232–3, 234 no. 8, 409 pl. 40).

[150] Cf. e.g. the epigram of Arniadas (Hansen 1983: 145; GV 73; IG ix. 1. 868; Jeffery 1990: 233, 234 no. 11, 409 pl. 46).

[151] Cf. e.g. Hansen 1983: 25 (GV 148; Jeffery 1962: 146–7 no. 63); Hansen 1983: 38 (GV 144; Jeffery 1962: 121 no. 12); Hansen 1983: 161 (GV 164. On the epigram for Androkles, from Methana, which belongs here, there is a combination of *sama* and *mnama* (Hansen 1983: 137 (GV 158; Jeffery 1990: 181 no. 1; 406 pl. 32)).

[152] For a kind of conflation of (I) and (II) cf. Hansen 1983: 42 (GV 72; Pfohl 1967: 42; cf. comm. Friedländer and Hoffleit 1948: 77).

[153] For a combination with variant I: cf. e.g. Hansen 1983: 42 (GV 72; Jeffery 1962: 127 no. 19), and Hansen 1983: 14 (GV 159; Jeffery 1962: 118 no. 2). Combined with the simple genitive of the dead person's name which stands for 'A's [*sema eimi*]' (cf. below) inscribed separately: on Aristion's stele, where, under the figure's feet we read *Ergon Aristocleos* and on the base *Aristionos* (Guarducci 1961; 170 no. 67, figs. 155–6; Jeffery 1962: 141 no. 52). For a combination with variant II: cf. e.g. Hansen 1983: 18 (GV 155; Jeffery 1962: 120 no. 8) and cf. below in IIIb. A combination of variants I–III is found in the epigram for Archias and his sister (Hansen 1983: 26; GV 74; Jeffery 1962: 139–40, no. 48. On the interpretation cf. Peek 1942: 87; Jeffery, op. cit). Finally, variant III is also combined with themes here classified in category 2 (cf. infra): cf. e.g. the epigram for Lampito (Hansen 1983: 66; GV 286; Jeffery 1962: 130 no. 24).

[154] Cf. Hansen 1983: 19 (GV 1488); Hansen 1983: 28 (GV 1225); Hansen 1983: 68 (GV 1223), and cf. the new epigram from Nikaia (Matthaiou 1986: 31–4; Lewis 1987: 188).

This type can also be combined with other variants.[155]
III(*c*) References mentioning adjacency to the *sema*.[156]
III(*d*) References of the *kata gai' ekalyphsen* type.[157]

The second type refers to the burial rather than the grave monument—though the two types can be combined in one epigram.
There are two basic variants in this category.

Variant I: 'Here lies A.'[158]
Variant II: 'B laid A here.'[159]

The *third* and minor *type* of reference includes miscellaneous references to the grave/grave monument.[160] The expressions articulating the two main types of reference often appear in an

[155] In the epigram Hansen 1983: 150 (Jeffery 1990: 304 no. 12, 412 pl. 55) it is combined
with variant IIIa. It can be combined also with variant II (cf. e.g. Hansen 1983: 46).

[156] Cf. Hansen 1983: 27 (*GV* 1224); Hansen 1983: 34 (*GV* 1227).

[157] Cf. *supra*.

[158] Cf. the stele for Lysanias: (Hansen 1983: 85; *GV* 323; *IG* 12, 1018; Pfohl 1967: 111);
Philon's stele (Hansen 1983: 76; *GV* 320; Jeffery 1989: 86, 88 no. 14; Pfohl 1967: 126. The
relief stele of Deines (Hansen 1983: 172; *GV* 326; Jeffery 1990: 326, 372 no. 54, 416 pl. 72;
Pfohl 1967: 188; cf. also Daux 1972: 521–2). Cf. the restoration of Phanes' stele: Hansen
1983: 112; *GV* 321; Pfohl 1967: no. 134. Cf. also the variant, on clay, *andros ap[ophthim]enoio
rak[os] ka[k]on enthade keima[i]* (Karouzos 1961: 33–4; no. 62). Hansen (1983: 438) writes
'*andros ap[ophthim]enoio kaṛe ka[l]on enthade keima[i]*' (cf. comm. ad loc.). Cf. also the variant
in the epigram of Xanthippe transmitted through the literary tradition (*AP* xiii. 26) which
may conceivably fall within our period (*GV* 1187; Pfohl 1967: 195). The epigram on
the stele of Idagygos (Hansen 1983: 170) which belongs to this type is just outside our
period.

[159] Cf. the epigram for Lampito (Hansen 1983: 66; *GV* 286; Jeffery 1962: 130 no. 24;
Jeffery 1990: 78 no. 40, 401 pl. 4; Pircher 1979: 15–18 no. 1; Pfohl 1967: 53 (*katetheke*,
combined with a reference of the type 1.IIIa)); the epigram on the capital from the grave of
Hysematas (Hansen 1983: 136; *GV* no. 305; Jeffery 1990: 154, 159, 168 no. 15; Pfohl 1967:
156 (*thapsa*)). Cf. also the epigram on the stele of Jakleitos (Hansen 1983: 134; *GV* 2068;
Jeffery 1990: 135–6, 137 no. 3, 404 pl. 22; Pfohl 1967: 153). In the epigram for Choro and
Elos or Atelos from Comiso in Sicily, the precise date of which is uncertain, and may fall
just outside the archaic period (cf. Jeffery 1990: 268–9, 276 no. 17), variants I and II (type 2)
are combined: *teide ... kei(n)tai ... -ethapse*: Hansen 1983: 147; *GV* 322; Jeffery 1990: 268–
9, 276 no. 17, 411 pl. 51; Pfohl 1967: 173. On the marble disc of Gnathon we find both the
formula 'This is the *sema* of A.' (1.I.) and 'B buried him/A.' (2.II): Hansen 1983: 37; *GV*
58; Jeffery 1962: 147 no. 64. On the grave stele of Leoxos (Hansen 1983: 173; *GV* 1172;
Jeffery 1990: 368, 372 no. 60, 416 pl. 72) the epigram has been restored to read *tele pole[os]
... kei]tai Leoxos ho Molpagoṛe[o]*, while a prose inscription on the back adds 'I am the *mnema*
of Leoxos son of Molpagoras'.

[160] Cf. e.g. the epigram for Tettichos cited above; its content is focused on the grave
monument, which however is not mentioned by name; all its themes are closely paralleled
among those regularly found in the two main types of reference, 1 and 2.

abbreviated form (e.g. *Sema Phrasikleias*).[161] As we shall see, abbreviations are extremely frequent in prose inscriptions.

I shall now discuss apparent exceptions to the rule set out here, that all archaic funerary epigrams contain a reference to the grave monument or to burial. The consideration of one apparent exception, the epitaph for Pleistias,[162] must be postponed until after the discussion of a particular category of prose inscriptions, which will set in place the wider framework necessary for the proper consideration of this epigram.

The epigram GV 914, transmitted through the literary tradition, which does not contain references to the grave monument, is unlikely to have been a grave inscription, or indeed to have been archaic in date.[163] The epigram Hansen 1983: 455 inscribed on rock is not funerary.[164] The epigrams Hansen 1983: 67 and 158 are too fragmentary to allow us to reach any conclusions.[165] I am aware that it could be argued that if we exclude from the corpus of funerary epigrams all specimens which may appear to be possible exceptions to what is claimed to be a norm, the argument becomes circular, and the 'rule' self-validating. However, this is not the case here, for the following (independent, but mutually reinforcing) reasons. First, because the number of possible exceptions involved is truly minuscule, and not a single one of the comparatively large sample of epigrams which were indisputably funerary, and also inscribed above a grave falls into this category of possible exceptions. Second, because the consideration of funerary inscriptions in prose, both complex and simple, will reveal that these references to the grave and grave monument are the fundamental core of all archaic grave inscriptions, whatever their genre. Finally, it will become clear in

---

[161] Hansen 1983: 24; GV 68.
[162] From Eretria, c.500–475? (Hansen 1983: 77; GV 862; Jeffery 1990: 86, 88 no. 17, 402 pl. 6 no. 17; Pfohl 1967: 127; IG xii. 9. 286; IG xii. Suppl. p. 186). Cf. also Pfohl (1967b, 11–12 no. 1).
[163] On this epigram cf. Page 1981: 296–7 ('Simonides' lxxvii); Pfohl 1967: 194; AP vii. 302; cf. Gentili 1968: 61 n. 4.
[164] Cf. L. H. Jeffery, Review of GV, JHS 78 (1958), 145; cf. also Pfohl 1967: 2 and Jeffery 1990: 304 no. 16. Indeed Hansen has classified it under 'Tituli Varii' (no. 455).
[165] If the epigram for Aristophon and Megatimos which has been transmitted through the literary tradition (Pfohl 1967: 175; cf. Friedländer and Hoffleit 1948: 67; AP vii. 441), and which may conceivably have been of archaic date (Friedländer and Hoffleit 1948: 67) was indeed archaic and had ever been inscribed over a grave, it would have been conceived (and perceived) as a variation on the formula *enthade kei(n)tai*, probably under the influence of the formula *kata gai' ekalyphsen* (1.IIId.).

§ ii.6 that these references express a fundamental aspect of the archaic Greek mentality pertaining to the grave monument. Thus the empirical observation that such references form the core of archaic funerary inscriptions will be validated by the independent conclusion that they express a fundamental aspect of the relevant mentality.

I will now consider a group of non-metrical[166] inscriptions which provide the one and only exception to the thesis put forward here that all archaic funerary epigrams and prose grave inscriptions contain a reference to the grave monument or burial. We shall see that, far from invalidating this thesis, these inscriptions will on the contrary confirm and reinforce it. The inscriptions in question are the *oimoi* inscriptions from Selinous. There are nine archaic *oimoi* inscriptions from Selinous,[167] one from Hybla Heraia, also in Sicily,[168] and two (with a third one possible, relying on restoration), from Mainland Greece, in which, however, the type has been modified so that the 'rule' enunciated here is not breached. The inscriptions from Selinous take the form *oimoi o* and the name of the deceased in the vocative: cf. *oimoi o Gorge;*[169] *oi]moi o phile Sel[ini] ho Iasoida;*[170] *o Id[mon]ida oimoi.*[171] The inscription from Hybla Heraia reads *oim[oi] Epaly.[d]o to Sanϙo.* So, *oimoi* is here combined with the name in the genitive.

The two certain *oimoi* inscriptions from Mainland Greece are the following. First, the epitaph for the Selinountian Archedamos found at Delphi:[172]

οἴ μοι ὀρχέδαμε ho Πυθέᾳ Σελινόντιος

on the back:

ερίον.

Here we find the Selinountian formula *oimoi o* and the name of the deceased in the vocative. But something has been added which, we

---

[166] Cf. Wallace 1970: 95–6.

[167] On the archaic *oimoi* inscriptions from Selinous cf. Guarducci 1966: 179–99; 1967: 320–1. Wallace 1970: 95–6 (and nn. 4–6 with bibliog.); Manni Piraino 1963; 1964; 1966.

[168] From a Sikel grave: P. Orsi, *NSc* (1899), 410 ff.; Jeffery 1990: 269, 276 no. 21, 411 pl. 52 no. 21; cf. 1962: 142 on no. 54.

[169] Guarducci 1966: 180, correcting the reading in Manni Piraino 1963: 138–41 no. 2; cf. 1964: 484.

[170] Guarducci 1966: 185–6.

[171] Manni Piraino 1963: 142–3 no. 5; Guarducci 1966. 181.

[172] *GV* 1670; Pfohl 1967: no. 169; Jeffery 1990: 271, 277 no. 33, 411 pl. 52 no. 33; Bousquet 1964: 380–2.

shall see, changes the state of affairs in one important respect. The other certain example of an *oimoi* inscription found on the Greek Mainland comes from Attica.[173]

οἴμοι Πεδιάρχο το 'Ενπεδίονος.
Πεδίαρχος ἄρχει τὸ⟨ν⟩ σεμάτον

Here we find the form of the formula which is not—as far as we know—found in the inscriptions of Selinous itself: *oimoi* with the name of the deceased in the genitive.[174] A third instance of an *oimoi* formulation on the Greek Mainland might possibly have been included in the epitaph for Myrrhine, also from Attica, which Jeffery[175] suggested should be restored *[?oi]moi thanoses eimi sema Myrrhines*—and not *[loi]moi*.[176] Jeffery[177] interpreted this formulation as follows: 'In Myrrhine's epitaph we should then have a conflation of two stock formulas: *oimoi Myrrhines (k.t.l.)* and *Myrrhines eimi sema (k.t.l.)*.' The formula consisting of *oimoi* + genitive of the deceased's name which occurs in the inscription from Hybla Heraia and in the epitaph for Pediarchos, she interpreted as a causal genitive, 'a construction like the English "Alas for ..."'. This is undoubtedly correct. But I think we can go further, basing ourselves on Jeffery's two observations, and suggest that the formulation *oimoi* + genitive of the name may have involved a conflation in all cases, and not only in the case of Myrrhine's epitaph where the word *sema* is actually mentioned.[178] For, given the associations attached to the genitive of the deceased's name inscribed on the grave monument, and thus the expectations through which such a genitive was read, the archaic reader may have read such a formulation as including the word *sema*. This reading may have been inescapable in the case of the epitaph for Pediarchos, given the fact that *sematon* in the

[173] *GV* 1671; Jeffery 1962: 136 no. 42; Peek 1942: 88–9; *SEG* iii. 56; *IG* i³. 1267; Humphreys 1983: 94.
[174] Neither of these two inscriptions is metrical; cf. Bousquet 1964: 380–2; Wallace 1970: 95–6.
[175] Jeffery 1962: 142 no. 54.
[176] Epitaph for Myrrhine: Jeffery 1962: 142 no. 54; 1990: 269 n. 3; Hansen 1983: 49; *GV* 65. The restoration proposed by Jeffery has been accepted by Bousquet 1964: 382, Hansen s.v., and Immerwahr 1967: 258 n. 9. It has been unconvincingly argued against by Calder 1965: 263 n. 10.
[177] Jeffery 1962: loc. cit. above, n. 175.
[178] This hypothesis is independent from and not affected by whether the restoration *oi]moi* is right in Myrrhine's epitaph—though if it is, since the word *sema* is explicitly mentioned in it, we would have an actual example of the conflation spelt out.

second line brought the word *sema*, which was regularly associated with the deceased's name in the genitive in Attica, to the forefront of the reader's mind, thus compelling the intertextual frame *sema* + genitive of the deceased's name on to the formulation *oimoi Pediarcho*. Because of the strength of the presence of this intertextual frame in the set of expectations through which archaic epitaphs were read, it is almost certain that *Pediarcho tode sema* was read into the formulation.[179] Since the genitive of the deceased's name carried its associations with it also during the process of composition, it would have presented itself in the writer's mind as the focus of the intertextual frame (*sema*) *Pediarcho* (*tod' estin*); and therefore it would inevitably have been used by the epitaph writer as an inseparable part of this whole intertextual frame which is conjured up by its presence. This, of course, is only true in those areas in which this intertextual frame was established, in which such formulations involving the name of the deceased in the genitive were common. This was the case in Attica. In the Attic archaic grave inscriptions we find all variations of the intertextual frame *sema tod' estin* (or *mnema eimi*)[180] + name of the deceased in the genitive, from the complete formulation[181] to the simple name of the deceased in the genitive,[182] passing through versions such as *Dechsandrido eimi*[183] in which the word *sema* is mentally supplemented, and *Bylo to sema toutelionido*,[184] in which it is the verb that is omitted and mentally added. The fact that the intertextual frame '*sema tod' esti* (or *mnema eimi*) + the name of the deceased in the genitive', was articulated in this variety of versions in the Attic funerary inscriptions confirms that the frame was very well established, an important part of the horizon of expectations by means of which Attic archaic epitaphs were written and read; and that, therefore, it would have compelled itself upon any formulation consisting of, or including, the name

---

[179] The way this was done was probably variable, whether they read (1) *oimoi Pediarcho (Pediarcho) to Enpedionos (tode sema)*. *Pediarchos archei ton sematon*—or: *oimoi Pediarcho (sema Pediarcho) to Enpedionos* etc. or (2) *oimoi. Pediarcho to Enpedionos (tode sema)* etc.—or: *oimoi (sema) Pediarcho to Enpedionos* etc.

[180] The usual formulations are either *sema tod' esti tou deina* or *tou deina eimi mnema* (cf. Jeffery 1962: 134 *ad* no. 36).

[181] Cf. e.g. Jeffery 1962: 119 no. 6; 146 no. 62, and the epigrams Hansen 1983: 42 (*GV* 72; Jeffery 1962: 127 no. 19; Pfohl 1967: 42); Hansen 1983: 72 (*GV* 64, Pfohl 1967: 115; Jeffery 1962: 134 no. 36).

[182] Cf. e.g. Jeffery 1962: 131 no. 29; 135 nos. 38 and 39; 145 no. 59.

[183] Jeffery 1962, 133–4 no. 35; cf. 128–9 no. 21.

[184] Jeffery 1962, 134–5 no. 37; cf. also 126–7 no. 18.

of the deceased in the genitive inscribed on the grave monument.
There is some reason for thinking that the epitaph from Hybla
Heraia would also have been read in a similar way. Either *oimoi
Epalydo. [Epalydo] to Sanꟼo [sama tode]* or: *oimoi. Epalydo to Sanꟼo
[sama tode]*. For the only other archaic grave inscription known to
me from Hybla Heraia[185] reads *ꟼostiꟼo*, the name of the deceased in
the genitive, mentally supplemented *ꟼostiꟼo [sama eimi]*. This suggests that there was also in this non-Greek city, an intertextual frame
'*sama eimi* + name of the deceased in the genitive', which could not
be divorced from, and therefore was called up by, the name of the
deceased in the genitive inscribed on the grave monument. There
are, then, two types of formulation involving *oimoi*. The first consists
of *oimoi o* and the name of the deceased in the vocative; it is only
found at Selinous and in the epitaph of Archedamos who is explicitly
identified as a Selinountian. The second formulation consists of
oimoi and the name of the deceased in the genitive. It is not found
in Selinous itself, but it occurs in the inscription from Hybla Heraia
and in the Attic inscription for Pediarchos—and also for Myrrhine
if Myrrhine's epitaph was indeed an *oimoi* inscription.

I argued that in the latter case the concept '*sema*' was implicitly
included in the formulation. That this is the case, and that this
is significant, will be confirmed when we consider the epitaph
for Selinountian Archedamos found at Delphi. First I must make
clear that whether or not my interpretation of the formula
oimoi + genitive of the deceased's name is correct, the indisputable
fact is that the two Attic inscriptions (Pediarchos' and the uncertain
one for Myrrhine) do, in any case, include a reference to the grave
monument, and thus conform to the rule that such references are
indispensable in archaic epitaphs. The epitaph for Myrrhine contains the formula *eimi [se]ma Myrines*; that for Pediarchos refers to
the grave monument by means of the statement, in its second part,
that he, his grave monument, begins the *semata*, 'begins a new set
of tombs in which his own will serve as the focus round which that
of other family members ... will be grouped'.[186] This state of

---

[185] Orsi, *NSc* (1899), 410 ff.; Jeffery 1990: 269, 276 no. 22, 411 pl. 52.

[186] Humphreys 1983: 94. The only inscription that hangs on the validity of my interpretation for its inclusion in the normal category of archaic epitaphs containing a reference to
the grave monuments is the one from a Sikel grave from the non-Greek city of Hybla Heraia,
for a man whose name and patronymic sound Sikel rather than Greek (cf. Jeffery 1989: 269).
I think I am right, and the word *sema* was mentally supplemented in this epitaph. But even

affairs suggests that, in non-Selinountine epitaphs, the original Selinountine formula was modified to fit the normal Greek expectations that an epitaph should include a reference to the grave monument. The epitaph for Archedamos belongs to the category of *oimoi* inscriptions which is otherwise found only in Selinous, involving *oimoi o* + the name of the deceased in the vocative. It reminds us especially of the Selinous inscriptions *oi]moi o phile Sel[ini] ho lasoida*[187] and[188] of the fifth-century one *oimoi o Euryphon ho Archinida*.[189] The fact that the epitaph belongs to a purely Selinountine type is not surprising: this is a Selinountine inscription for a man who had probably died while he was in some embassy at Delphi.[190] In this it differs from the other *oimoi* inscription found on the Greek Mainland (or inscriptions, counting Myrrhine's). For even if Calder is right that Pediarchos is a Selinountine[191] but not an Attic name, the man, whatever his origin, had obviously been settled in Attica, since he was beginning a new set of family *semata*. But it differs from the *oimoi o* + vocative inscriptions found at Selinous in one respect which has generally been disregarded as of little importance but which, in my opinion, in this context, reveals itself to be of great significance. Archedamos' epitaph has an additional element: the word *erion* inscribed on the back of the stele. I discussed the precise meaning of the word *erion* in § i.3 above, and concluded that the basic, primary, meaning of *erion* is 'grave monument', independently of its precise physical form. Thus Dittenberger was on the right lines when he commented[192] that *erion* here means 'cippus sepulcralis' rather than 'tumulus'.[193] The word *erion* inscribed at the back of Archedamos' stele, then, designates, 'names' the stele as a grave monument. This is extremely significant. For why should

---

if I am wrong, an aberrant formulation would not be surprising here and would not affect my overall case.

[187] Guarducci 1966: 185–6.
[188] Bousquet 1964: 380.
[189] Cf. Bovio Marconi 1961: 109–12. On the combination of vocative and nominative cf. Friedländer and Hoffleit 1948: 161.
[190] Cf. Jeffery 1990: 271; Friedländer and Hoffleit 1948: 175.
[191] Calder 1965: 264 pointed out that the name Pediarchos occurs in an archaic Selinountian inscription from the precinct of Zeus Meilichios (Jeffery 1989: 270, 277 no. 31).
[192] Dittenberger *SIG*³ 11 *ad* 11.
[193] Immerwahr (1967: 263 n. 19) suggests that on the stele of Archedamos the word refers to the funerary plot. This unwarranted suggestion depends on the untenable hypothesis that *eria* means family plots in *Ath. Pol.* 55. 3.

this be necessary? It must have been obvious that this was a grave-stele, so why bother to say so on the back? This designation is unparalleled among Greek funerary monuments; for the inscription of the type *ech ton erion eini*,[194] and *ek to erio*,[195] attested on three marble discs that formed part of grave monuments[196] and meant to ensure that these discs were not stolen to be used for some other purpose (given that, as Jeffery remarked, they were useful and portable objects),[197] are entirely different. First, because there is a fundamental difference in the form of the expression: in the case of Archedamos' stele it is the stele itself that is designated as 'grave monument'.[198] And second, because the idea of protection from theft is not applicable here—or no more than it is for any other grave-stele. In any case, since the epitaph itself marked the function of the stele, and would have prevented its reuse for other purposes, the inscription *erion* was redundant. Jeffery also saw that the designation *erion* on the Archedamos stele had a different function from the inscriptions on the discs; for she suggested[199] not, as she did for the discs, that it was meant to prevent theft, but that *erion* had been added 'perhaps to remind those wayfarers who came upon it from the rear that this stone was sacred'. Yes, but why did this only happen for this stele and no other? My answer is, that only in this case was it felt necessary to add a word that designated the stele as a grave monument. And that this was because this is the only epitaph leaving aside the ones in Selinous—which did not include, or, at least, was not understood in Mainland Greece as including, a reference to the grave monument or burial. So the

---

[194] Cf. Jeffery 1962: 145 no. 59a.

[195] Ibid. 147 no. 64.

[196] Cf. Jeffery 1962: 147 on no. 64. On marble discs and their functions and their inscriptions cf. also Jacobsthal 1933: 17 ff.; and Immerwahr 1967: 262–5. An alternative interpretation, suggested by Jacobsthal (cf. discussion and bibliog. in Immerwahr 1967: 263–5 and nn. 21–2) is 'from the mounds', i e. the funeral games. This interpretation is untenable—though if it were right it would have strengthened my hypothesis more, by isolating the inscription at the back of Archedamos' stele even more sharply. As Jeffery rightly notes (1962: 147 on no. 64) 'out of the grave-mound(s)' is an odd expression for 'from the funeral games' and indeed 'out of the grave monuments' which we should now decode it as, is, if anything, even odder. (Cf. the brief discussion in Ridgway 1977: 168–9; Kurtz and Boardman 1971: 88.)

[197] Jeffery 1962: 147 on no. 64.

[198] Perhaps the choice of the word *erion* to designate the grave monument here derives from the formula used on the discs to protect them from theft, taken over and modified, to fit its different function on Archedamos' stele.

[199] Jeffery 1990: 271 (cf. 277 no. 33).

designation 'grave monument' was added at the back to remedy this absence. The fact that the designation *erion* was added uniquely, in this epitaph, provides confirmation for my thesis that a reference to the grave monument was strongly felt to be an indispensable part of archaic Greek epitaphs—at least outside Selinous.

Let us now consider the inscriptions from Selinous itself. They may be an exception to the general rule formulated here. Even if this is indeed the case, my main thesis would not be affected; on the contrary, this thesis is strengthened by the fact that outside Selinous the formula is modified, and other elements added with the purpose of including the reference to the grave monument which was perceived to be lacking from the Selinountine formulations. And, of course, Selinous, the outpost of Greek civilization in Western Sicily, can hardly be considered a typical Greek city—a point to which I will return below. But it is possible that such references to the grave monument/burial might not have been perceived as lacking from the epitaphs by the Selinountians themselves. Given that there was a tradition, in Selinous, of one-word funerary inscriptions consisting of the name of the deceased in the nominative,[200] mentally supplemented with *enthade keitai*, it cannot be excluded that at least formulations combining vocative and nominative, such as *oi]moi o phile Sel[ini] ho lasoida*[201] may have been mentally supplemented in comparable ways; that is, as follows: *oi]moi o phile Sel[ini]; (Selinis) ho lasoida (enthade keitai)*. Similar associations may also have been carried by the simpler formulations *oimoi o* + vocative. But this is speculation—especially since the earliest *oimoi* inscription known to me, *oimoi o Gorge*, from the end of the seventh century,[202] belongs to the simple vocative type, and it is doubtful whether the intertextual frame including the nominative (which would have been more naturally complemented with *enthade keitai*) had been established by then. The important point is that it is clear that these epitaphs were a purely local fashion in a very idiosyncratic cultural environment, with conditions that did not pertain to any part of metropolitan Greece. It is, of course, methodologically incorrect to explain away as due to 'indigenous influ-

---

[200] Cf. Manni Piraino 1963: 142 no. 3; Guarducci 1966, 181; Manni Piraino 1963: 142 no. 4; 137 no. 1.

[201] Guarducci 1966: 185–6; cf. Archedamos' epitaph.

[202] Guarducci 1966: 180, correcting the reading in Manni Piraino 1963: 138–41 no. 2; cf. 1964: 484.

ence' any feature of Greek colonial culture that does not fit our preconceived ideas of Greek attitudes, religion, and so on. But it is legitimate to consider the possibility that such influences may have been exerted if (*a*) we are faced with a phenomenon that appears to be significantly unique in the Greek world; (*b*) this phenomenon is of a kind that might legitimately be considered open to such influences; and (*c*) the conditions of interaction can be seen to have existed. I think that all three conditions are fulfilled in the Selinous epitaphs. We have seen that (*a*) is certainly the case. As regards (*b*), attitudes towards death, which are reflected in the grave monument, are affected by the whole cultural system of a society and its circumstances. Thus, it is possible that the special historical and cultural circumstances pertaining to Selinous, that outpost of Greek civilization in Western Sicily, may have brought about—whether or not as a result of indigenous influences—slight changes in these death-related attitudes, sufficient to create small divergences in the perception of the inscribed grave monument that were reflected in the form of the epitaphs; that these epitaphs came to place a greater emphasis on the element of lament than on that facet of the mentality pertaining to memory-survival which made naming the grave monuments so important. It is, of course, emphasis that is at issue here. As we shall see in § 2*b*, non-Selinountine epitaphs often included lament; and the Selinountine epitaphs did preserve the memory of the deceased. It is the explicit focusing on the grave monuments as sign and vehicle for the memory of the deceased that appears to have been abandoned at Selinous.[203] As regards (*c*), first the indigenous influences need not be direct, but might have helped to bring about the circumstances that motivated the changes. Second, the fact that indigenous names appear among the *oimoi* inscriptions suggests that there was some interaction between Greeks and non-Greeks in the funerary sphere—even though the influence is seen to flow from the Greek to the non-Greek. It might perhaps be further argued tentatively that the presence of non-Greek names in the *oimoi* epitaphs may indicate that those epitaphs expressed attitudes which those non-Greeks found suitable for themselves; for we cannot necessarily assume that they took over Greek customs uncritically, in this most deeply felt facet of life that

---

[203] The early (end of the 7th cent.) inscription *sa]ma eimi Mysϙo to Menepto[lemo]* (Guarducci 1967: 318) conforms to the usual Greek type.

was the epitaph, the expression of one's attitudes towards one's dead. In these circumstances, the notion that the special conditions in Selinous may have created circumstances that motivated a small shift in attitudes reflected in a change of emphasis in the perception of the grave monument and epitaph reflected in the *oimoi* inscriptions is a distinct possibility. However, the validity of this hypothesis does not affect my case. For the versions of *oimoi* epitaphs found on the Greek Mainland show that the lack of references to the grave monument or burial which was tolerated in Selinous was not tolerated on the Greek Mainland.

To recapitulate. The archaic funerary epigrams inscribed on grave monuments always contained at least one reference to the grave monument or burial. Their most immediate function is to name and identify. References of type 1 identify the grave monument as being that of this particular deceased—and those of type 1 variant II also identify the person who set up the monument. References of type 2 identify the grave, name the deceased who was buried there—and those of type 2 variant II also name the person responsible for the burial.

Grave inscriptions in prose contain the same kind of references to the grave, grave monument, or burial, as the funerary epigrams. There is, for example, a very early prose version of our type 1 variant I of the epigrams.[204] Variant II of our type 1 also finds parallels in prose inscriptions.[205] Also prose variations corresponding

---

[204] The stele of Keramo: Jeffery 1962: 129 no. 22; 1990: 67–8, 71, 76 no. 8, 401 pl. 2; and a few 6th-cent. examples, one from Attica (Jeffery 1962: 119 no. 6), one from Halone (Jeffery 1990: 372 no. 52; 416 pl. 72), and one from Samos (Buschor 1933: 24–5, no. 3). The formula is also contained in the long and complex grave inscription of Phanodikos (on which cf. Guarducci 1961: 165–8 no. 53 with bibliog.; cf. also Jeffery 1990: 366–7, 371 nos. 43–4, 416 pl. 71).

[205] Cf. the grave stele of Xenokrite from Arkesine, Amorgos (*IG* xii. 7. 139; Jeffery 1990: 304, no. 19); that of Stesimachos from Arkesine, Amorgos (*IG* xii. 7. 140; Jeffery 1990: 304 no. 18); of Alexo from Arkesine, Amorgos (*IG* xii. 7. 142; Jeffery 1990: 293, 304 no. 20, 412 pl. 56); that of Antigenes, from Attica (Guarducci 1961: 169–70 no. 61; Jeffery 1990: 78 no. 34, 401 pl. 4). Cf. also '*Ankylion . . . epoie*' on an early (early 7th cent.?) gravestone from Anaphe (*IG* xii. 3. 255; Jeffery 1990: 322, 324 no. 26, 413 pl. 62) in which *epoie* undoubtedly means 'set up' rather than 'made' (on this meaning of the word *poio* in funerary inscriptions cf. Peek 1942: 87; cf. also Skiadas 1967: 22 n. 1, 23). It should be noted that only Ankylion who erected the gravestone is named here; the name of the deceased is omitted—though it is possible that it may have been inscribed as a different part of the grave monument; this is a very early example, and our knowledge of the period is too faulty to allow us to speculate profitably on this matter. The grave stele of Praxilas from Thera (*IG* xii. 3. 763; Jeffery 1990: 323 no. 4) (end of 7th cent.?) also belongs to this category, the prose equivalent to the epigram reference variant II of type 1.

to epigram references of type I are the expressions *mnema [mnama]*
(or *sema [sama]*) *epi A* (with the name of the deceased in the
dative).[206] A prose variation on the theme 'here lies' can be found
in the non-metrical funerary inscription of Lenos from Kyme.[207]
The shorter and simpler grave inscriptions, often consisting of only
one word, the name of the deceased, are abbreviated forms of the
expressions found in the more complex epitaphs. In inscriptions
such as that on the grave trapeza from Krommyon *Patrokleos e⟨i⟩mi*[208]
or on the base of the grave monument (kouros) of Nausistratos,
Nausistrato eimi to Euthymacho[209] or on the Samian grave-stele of
Konche[210] the word *sema/mnema* is obviously meant to be mentally
supplemented.[211] In other inscriptions[212] the verb *eimi/esti* is
omitted, as it is often omitted also in the epigrams. Finally, the same
formula 'I am the *sema* of A' underlies the very common grave
inscriptions which consist simply of the dead person's name in the
genitive,[213] in which the words '*sema/mnema eimi*' or '*tode sema [esti]*'
are meant to be mentally supplemented.[214] Some epitaphs give a
fuller formula for the name in the genitive.[215] Another category of
prose inscriptions is that in which the formulation consists of *mnema*
epi and the dative of the name. The formulation *mnema epi* and the
dative of the name also occurs as part of funerary epigrams.[216]
Another category of prose inscriptions consists of simply *epi* and

[206] Cf. the non-metrical inscription from Thespiai 1890 (*GV* 59; Guarducci 1961: 170–1
no. 731 Pfohl 1909: 131, Jeffery 1990: 91 no. 741 409 pl. 8), or for a prose combination of 'I
am the *sema/mnema* of A' and 'B. put me up' (Prose versions of 1.I and 1.II) cf. the gravestone
of Timo (Jeffery 1990: 314, 316 no. 20, 413 pl. 60). And cf. the 7th-cent. non-metrical
funerary inscription from Thasos on Glaukos' memorial (*GV* p. 677 (51a); Jeffery 1990: 300–
1, 307 no. 61, 412 pl. 58; Pfohl 1967: 15).
[207] *IG* xiv. 871; Jeffery 1990: 240 no. 7, 409 pl. 47.
[208] Peek 1934: 44–5; Jeffery 1990: 128, 131 no. 23, 404 pl. 20.
[209] Karouzos 1961: 65 no. A26.
[210] Buschor 1933: 25 no. 5; Jeffery 1990: 342 no. 14.
[211] Cf. also e.g. the inscription from Megara Hyblaea (Orsi 1892: 786–7; Jeffery 1990: 276
no. 26, 411 pl. 52); from Samos (Buschor 1933: 25 no. 5). Cf. also the stele of Menephron
from Eretria (*IG* xii. 9. 297; Jeffery 1990: 88 no. 13, 402 pl. 6): *epi Menephroni eimi*.
[212] Cf. e.g. the stele of Keramo mentioned already (cf. n. 204); cf. also *IG* iv. 48;
Friedländer and Hoffleit 1948: 163A, 163B.
[213] Cf. e.g. a 7th-cent. (?) gravestone from Vari (Jeffery 1962: 135 no. 139); a grave
inscription from Hybla Heraia (Jeffery 1990: 269, 276 no. 22, 411 pl. 52); some gravestones
from Opountian Locris (Jeffery 1990: 107, 108 nos. 12–16; *IG* ix. 1. 291–5).
[214] Karouzos (1961: 35).
[215] Cf. e.g. the inscription for Aischros (Karouzos 1961: 65 A 27); cf. also the inscription
on the kouros which had stood over the grave of Somrotidas which will be discussed in
§ ii.4c.
[216] Cf. e.g. Hansen 1983: 113.

the dative of the name.[217] There can be no doubt that these inscriptions were read to mean *mnema epi* X. Sometimes the grave inscription consists only of the name in the dative.[218] The name appears in the dative also in some epigrams, in formulations of the type *Lyseai . . . sema . . . pater . . . epetheken*[219] and the like. As with the inscriptions consisting of *epi* + the dative, the archaic reader of the grave inscription consisting of the name of the dative supplemented words involving the notion '*mnema*'—or *sema*.

Thus, of the short grave inscriptions consisting only of the dead person's name[220] both those in which the name is in the genitive and those in which it is in the dative were read as fragments of the fuller formulations found in epigrams and prose inscriptions that involved the notions of *sema/mnema*. I now turn to the grave inscriptions in which the name is in the nominative, which I shall consider in a little more detail. For their interpretation is still controversial. A case has been made[221] in favour of the view that I consider to be the correct one, but it has not become generally accepted.

Some of these inscriptions have the simple form of the name, consisting of one word.[222] In others the name in the nominative consists of the name in the nominative and the patronymic in the genitive.[223] In yet another type the name in the nominative consists

---

[217] This formulation was e.g. not uncommon in a series of grave stelai from Phokikon in Phokis (French 1984: 92, 93, 95; Vanderpool 1964: 84–5 no. 2), common in neighbouring Boeotia (French 1984: 92; Keramopoullos 1920: 28; cf. Fraser and Rönne 1957: 92, 98 (and n. 52) who discuss the appearance of *epi* + dative in Boeotia and elsewhere) and it is also found in neighbouring Doris (Rousset 1990: 459, 460). Other forms of short prose inscriptions are also found in Phokis (cf. *mnama Chionos* (Jeffery 1990: 103 no. 3, 403 pl. 12)).

[218] On grave inscriptions in which the name of the deceased is in the dative cf. Häusle 1979: 116–17; Guarducci 1974: 147–8.

[219] Hansen 1983: 53.

[220] On inscriptions of this type cf. also Häusle 1979: 106–31.

[221] Cf. Karouzos 1961: 35–7; Guarducci 1974: 147.

[222] Cf. e.g. the gravestone of Philotima from Thera (*IG* xii. 3. 805; Jeffery 1990: 323 no. 11); also several other examples from Thera: flat gravestones and tables from the Sellada (Jeffery 1990: 323 no. 12, 413 pl. 61; *IG* xii. 3. 785, 772, 779, 776–7, 780, 789, 807); gravestone with the names of two children (Jeffery 1990: 318, 323 no. 6, 413 pl. 61; *IG* xii. 3. Suppl. 1609); gravestone of Phexanor and others (Jeffery 1990: 317–18, 323 no. 5, 413 pl. 61; *IG* xii. 3. 762; *IG* xii Suppl. pp. 89, 762). The name of the deceased in the nominative was sometimes written on the rock: cf. the grave of Hyperas in the Mesavouno cemetery, Thera (Jeffery 1990: 318, 322 no. 8; *IG* xii. 3 Suppl. 1610; Pfuhl 1903: 87–8). Gravestone of Syko from Akrai (*IG* xiv. 228; Jeffery 1990: 276 no. 14, 411 pl. 51).

[223] Cf. e.g.: fragments from two gravestones from Palairos, Acarnania (*IG* ix. 1. 458; Jeffery 1990: 229 no. 3b and *IG* ix. 1. 459; Jeffery 1990: 229 no. 3a); the gravestone of (L)ysis from Akrai (*IG* xiv. 227; Jeffery 1990: 275 no. 13, 411 pl. 51).

of the name proper, and then, the father's name in the genitive and/or some other qualification.[224] There are clear local preferences as to the case in which the deceased's name will be when this constitutes the whole inscription.[225] Fashions in a wider sense can also be distinguished, in the type of grave inscription, epigram, prose, type of prose and so on.[226] We note, for example, in Arkesine on Amorgos, the popularity of the prose inscriptions of the type 2.II. Inscriptions consisting of the name of the deceased in the nominative are popular at Phokikon in Phokis.[227] But, we shall see, there are certain aspects of the grave inscriptions which always remain constant, irrespective of local fashion; fashion only operates within the parameters of these constant traits. Let us now try to reconstruct the ways in which the contemporary viewers read those inscriptions. I submit that any attempt to suggest an answer must take account of, and explain, the following sets of circumstances.

(1) Inscriptions consisting of the deceased's name in the nominative, like inscriptions with the name of the deceased in the genitive, are found in a variety of grave monuments, including flat gravestones and grave tables and grave pillars.[228] A grave inscription consisting of the deceased's name in the nominative can also be written not on a grave monument, but on a rock.[229] In the late sixth and fifth century chamber tombs at Aigina, the name(s) of the dead, in the nominative or the genitive, were inscribed on the stone coping or 'lid' of the shaft, or on the rock wall of the chamber,

---

[224] Cf. e.g. the funeral stele of Philistides (*NSc* 1900: 281; Jeffery 1990: 278 no. 54), which could belong just outside our period (the indication of Philistides' profession follows the name and the father's name); the gravestone of Charopinos and Aristodemos from Messenia, in which the title *hiaros* which tells us that they were officials of the Mysteries, precedes each name (*IG* v. 1. 1356; Jeffery 1990: 203, 206 no. 6., 407 pl. 39).

[225] This is clear even from the very small sample cited here; cf. also on this Karouzos 1961: 35 7; Häusle 1979: 114 17.

[226] Cf. Wallace 1970: 97.

[227] Cf. French and Vanderpool 1963: 223 no. 6; Vanderpool 1964: 84 no. 1; French 1984: 92; 93; 94. They also occur elsewhere in Phokis (cf. Jeffery 1990: 103 no. 2, 403 pl. 12).

[228] Cf. the case of Pleistias that will be discussed below, where the name of the deceased in the nominative complements an epigram. (On grave pillars and grave columns cf. Kontoleon 1970: 48 with bibliog.; Kurtz and Boardman 1971: 240.) Cf. also the names in the nominative in the lead strips encircling the top of a funerary column from Karystos in Euboea (*IG* xii. 9. 41; Jeffery 1990: 89 no. 30), which may fall outside our period.

[229] An example carved on a rock combining more than one formulation is seen in the late 6th- or early 5th-cent. set of inscriptions on a rock at Sounion: the first reads *Posthonos mnema*, and upside down to this *Posthon* in the nominative; there is also a third, fragmentary instance of the name; in addition the outline of a left foot is carved on the rock (Langdon 1985: 145–8).

or on the side of the sarcophagus.[230] This coincidence of context between the two types suggests that the inscriptions consisting of the deceased's name in the nominative are not likely to have a meaning radically different from those consisting of the name in the genitive. (2) The relationship between the inscriptions consisting of the name in the genitive and the prose inscriptions (themselves corresponding to more complex expressions in the epigrams) of which the name-in-the-genitive inscriptions are abbreviations should lead us to expect as an *optimum* in any interpretation some comparable relationship between name-in-the-nominative inscriptions and longer prose inscriptions and epigrams. Thus an interpretation which involves such a relationship is more likely to be correct than one that does not. This argument is strengthened by the fact that the inscriptions with the deceased's name in the dative conform to the same pattern, shorter formulations which are abbreviations of, and mentally supplemented on the basis of, the full prose formulation, which itself also occurs as part of funerary epigrams. The interpretation which fits all these conditions, and which is semantically equivalent to 'this is the sema of A' of the inscriptions consisting of the name of the deceased in the genitive,[231] is that the name of the deceased in the nominative was understood as saying 'A *enthade keitai*'.

The alternative interpretation[232] is that it indicates an identification between the grave monument and the deceased. Even leaving aside the *a priori* implausibility of such a notion, which relies on discredited notions of 'primitive' thinking, and the further implausibility that such identification would have obtained for some grave monuments, but not for all the other very similar ones that are said to be the *sema* or *mnema* of the deceased, a variety of reasons, including the fallacy of the arguments on which it rests, make this hypothesis untenable. It is true that on the very-high-relief grave stele of Dermys and Kitylos[233] the names 'Dermys' and 'Kitylos', inscribed each on the side of one of the figures and

---

[230] Cf. Jeffery 1974: 75–9, esp. 77; cf. also 1990: 113 no. 10; 439.

[231] Which in its turn makes good sense of the fact that the two types sometimes coexist (cf. Karouzos 1961: 35–6, 91 n. 73; cf. also Jeffery 1974: 76–9).

[232] On which cf. Häusle 1979: 110–31 with bibliog. Cf. also Schmaltz 1983: 177–9. For a case against cf. Karouzos 1961: 36–7. On the alleged identity between stele and deceased cf. esp. Thimme 1964: 24–5; cf. also Schiering 1974: 652–3.

[233] Richter 1960: 48–98 no. 11, figs. 76–7; Guarducci 1961: 155–6 no. 9; *GV* 137; Pfohl 1967: 129.

separate from the epigram, which is inscribed on the base, 'name' and 'identify' each figure. But let us not confuse what is involved here. The names identify *representations* of the deceased, each of which is *part* of a grave monument which consists of much more than simply the two figures added together;[234] the inscriptions name each of the two represented males with the name of one of the two deceased whose grave monument this is, as we learn from the epigram that is inscribed on the rather massive base on which the two figures stand, and which makes clear that the grave monument is not to be identified with Dermys and Kitylos: *Amphalkes estas' epi Kityloi ed' epi Dermyi*.[235] This cannot conceivably validate the notion that inscriptions in the nominative ascribe the name of the deceased to the grave monument and identify the two; important distinctions are involved which must not be blurred. The fact that the one grave statue that is as near the individual human form as a kouros can get, the grave statue that stood over the grave of Aristodikos,[236] is inscribed not '*Aristodikos*' but '*Aristodiko*', '[I am/this is the grave monument] of *Aristodikos*', surely makes it clear that the notion that the grave monument and the deceased were identified is incorrect even in cases where in our culturally determined assumptions such identifications may appear obvious, grave monuments the major part of which consist of a representation of the deceased. This can be strengthened by further arguments. First, there is no inscription on a funerary kouros or kore that says 'I am A',[237] as one might have expected if there had been such an identification. On the contrary, a kouros or kore is often said through an inscription to be the *sema/mnema* of someone, rather than that someone.[238] Nor are there any examples in which the grave monument consists of a statue and the inscription consists of the name of the deceased in the nominative. These are not simply *argumenta ex silentio*, for their combination suggests a pattern of differentiation and distancing: where the form of the grave monument approximates most the deceased's form the formulation that would have left open the possibility of identifying that statue as

[234] Cf. the illustrations in Richter 1961: figs. 31–3, 192–5.
[235] Hansen 1983: 109.
[236] Cf. Richter 1960: 139 no. 165, figs. 489, 492–3.
[237] Cf. Kontoleon 1970: 53.
[238] Cf. e.g. the inscription on the kouros standing over the grave of Somrotidas cited in Ch. VI §i.5; or the epigram for Phrasikleia (Hansen 1983: 24).

'being' in some way the deceased is not chosen. This suggests that in the assumptions that formed the parameters of selection for the creation of the inscribed grave monument the possibility of identifying the deceased with the grave monument was excluded. The same attitude governs the selection to erect a statue of the wrong sex over a grave;[239] for this fits the notion of this statue being the *sema* of someone, but not that of identification with the deceased. The fact that in the overwhelming majority of cases the name in the nominative is inscribed on undecorated stelai, flat gravestones and especially grave tables and tomb walls and rocks, constitutes another important argument against the thesis criticized here. For it entails that that thesis would need to ascribe radically different meanings to the same phenomenon, the name in the nominative, in different grave monuments. Thus it relies on special pleading and cannot account for the overwhelming majority of cases in which the inscribed name is in the nominative. As we saw, there are no grave monuments for which it can account; not that of Dermys and Kitylos—unless we accept the fallacious blurring of distinctions between the representation of the deceased which is part of the grave monument and the grave monument as a whole. In some cases, this identification can be unambiguously proved to be fallacious, as, for example, in the case of the gravestone of Kalliades.[240] This is a low square gravestone inscribed *Kaliades Thotimido hyios* and decorated on one face with a running Gorgon in relief; this may conceivably have been cut off from the bottom of a more complex monument rather than be an independent grave monument of its own. In either case, the name of the deceased in the nominative is most closely associated with either the grave monument itself, or the representation of a Gorgon, or both, not with a representation of the deceased, even if we assume that one had originally been part of the grave monument.

A more sophisticated variant of this theory, which does try to take account of some, albeit not all, these difficulties[241] attempts to manipulate the notion of the name 'being' somehow the deceased, and the notion that the inscribed name of the deceased in the nominative is somehow an 'image' of the deceased. This hypothesis,

---

[239] Cf. *GV* 1171; Pfohl 1967: 24; cf. Jeffery 1976: 198; Ridgeway 1977: 56 n. 14.

[240] Cf. Ridgway 1977: 169; cf. also Karouzos 1961: 91 n. 76.

[241] Häusle 1979: 110–31. But he does not deny the possibility that the name in the nominative is to be understood as an abbreviated form of *enthade keitai* or the like (p. 121).

which again involves implicit notions of 'primitive' mentality, would still not account for all the objections set out here, and would not explain why significantly different perceptions would have been involved in the different grave inscriptions—on the one hand those consisting of the name in the nominative and on the other all the others; it does not account for the fact that the former would be the only ones to be conjuring up this image of the deceased while all the others relate to the *sema* of the deceased. I shall be returning to this subject in § ii.4c. To sum up at this point. All grave monuments have the primary function of being a *sema*. Some grave monuments either primarily consist of, or include, a (schematic) representation of the deceased. It is fallacious to imagine that any grave monument is to be identified with the deceased, it is modern confusion of ancient categories that gave rise to animistic beliefs in connection with the archaic grave monument.

To return to the meanings of the inscriptions consisting of the name of the deceased in the nominative. It is clear that the hypothesis that fits all the known facts, and corresponds to the situation pertaining to the inscriptions consisting of the name of the deceased in the genitive, is that which understands the grave inscriptions that consist of the name of the deceased in the nominative to be abbreviated forms of, and to be read by the contemporary viewers as '*X [enthade keitai]*'. To put it differently. If all we had was the knowledge that some grave inscriptions consisted of the name of the deceased in the nominative, and did not know, first, the type of grave monuments on which they were inscribed and second, that there were also one-word archaic grave inscriptions consisting of the name of the deceased in the genitive and in the dative, and we did not know that these are situated at one end of a spectrum at the other end of which are full formulations of the type 'This is the sema of X' and 'X put up this grave monument over Y' with other shorter versions in-between, it could have been conceivable to believe, on the basis of a culturally determined reading, that the inscriptions that consist of the name of the deceased in the nominative may have implied some sort of identification of the grave monument with the deceased or, more generally, could have meant to their contemporaries something other than '*X [enthade keitai]*'. However, all the above provide the context within which the grave inscriptions consisting of the name of the deceased in the nominative must be made sense of. In these circumstances, it is clear that these inscriptions were read with the help of the formula *enthade keitai* which was mentally supplemented in the course of the reading. Consequently, all the inscriptions consisting of the name of the deceased also fit into this same pattern of 'naming' the grave monument.

Let us now discuss the one apparent exception to the 'rule' that all grave epigrams contain a reference to the grave monument or to burial; this apparent exception, the consideration of which was postponed until after the discussion of the prose inscriptions, is the epitaph for Pleistias,[242] an Attic epigram from Eretria:

(i, in abaco pilae)
Πλειστίας.
(ii, in pila, deorsum incisus)
Σπάρτα μὲν πατρίς ἐστιν, ἐν εὐρυχ|όροισι ⟨δ'⟩ Ἀθάναις
ἐθράφθε, θανάτο | δὲ ἐνθάδε μοῖρ' ἔχιχε.

It is inscribed on the shaft of a grave pillar, the capital of which bears the inscribed name 'Pleistias'. This epigram, which belongs to the very end of our period, and may conceivably fall just outside it, shows signs of the incipient disintegration of the pattern of reference to the grave monument; but this pattern is still present. For, as was the case with the one-word inscriptions with the name in the nominative, *Pleistias* here was mentally supplemented by the contemporary readers into *Pleistias enthade keitai*. That this is how the Pleistias epigram was read by its contemporary audience is difficult to doubt. For not only was there the wider intertextual frame established by the grave inscriptions consisting of the name of the deceased in the nominative, but also, and more importantly, in the years *c.*500–475 to which this epigram belongs, there was, within the genre of the funerary epigram, an established intertextual frame—commonly appearing in that (approximate) quarter of a century—consisting of the name of the deceased in the nominative plus *enthade keitai*.[243]

242 From Eretria, *c.*500–475? (Hansen 1983: 77; *GV* 862; Jeffery 1990: 86, 88 no. 17, 402 pl. 6 no. 17; *IG* xii. 9. 286; *IG* xii. Suppl. p. 186). Cf. also Pfohl 1967*b*, 11–12 no. 1.

243 Cf. the following examples: Hansen 1983: 76 (*GV* 320; Jeffery 1990: 86, 88 no. 14, of *c.*500–480 and like the Pleistias epigram, from Eretria); Hansen 1983: 172 (*GV* 326; Jeffery 1990: 368, 372 no. 54, 416 pl. 72 no. 54; Clairmont 1970: no. 8; cf. Daux 1972: 521–2; *SEG* xv. 430; Mihailov 1970: no. 405; *c.*500–475); cf. (restored): Hansen 1983: 112 (*GV* 321; *IG* vii. 2247; cf. *SEG* xv. 327); Hansen 1983: 170 (*GV* 324; Jeffery 1990: 353, 358 no. 41, 415 pl. 69 no. 41; *c.*475). Cf. also Karouzos 1961: 33–4; 90 n. 62.

In these circumstances, the name of the deceased in the nominative in a prominent place just above the funerary epigram would have conjured up the intertextual frame 'name of deceased in the nominative + *enthade keitai*'. Thus, in the contemporaries' readings, the funerary epigram was preceded by the formula referring to the burial. It is possible that this activation of the intertextual frame may have been further reinforced in the Pleistias epitaph—not that such reinforcement was necessary for the frame to operate. For it could be argued that the word *enthade* in the last line, though covering a wider concept than *enthade* does in the formula *enthade keitai*, nevertheless evoked that formula, thus reinforcing the mental supplementation effected by the activation of the intertextual frames. The spatial arrangement of the epigram,[244] which associated visually the word *enthade* with the name *Pleistias* written at a right angle above it, with only *de* separating the two, is likely to have reinforced the association for the reader—whether or not that association had actually motivated the spatial arrangement in the first place. It is indeed quite possible that this 'reference-to-be-constructed' represents a stage in the development of the funerary epigram (albeit not a necessary or linear one), during which, in a context of a certain loosening of the bond between grave inscription and reference to the grave monument, one available selection was to play about with, but not abandon, this reference to the grave monument. Thus, this epigram does not invalidate the rule that throughout the archaic period every epitaph names the grave monument or burial. A second apparent exception to this rule, an epigram from Teithronion in Phokis, will be discussed in great detail in Chapter VI where it will be shown that, for a variety of independent reasons, it cannot have been an epitaph. The mention of the grave monument, or the burial, refers, and draws attention to, the physical remains of the deceased, and/or the monument which marks them; even when the reference is to the burial, and not to the monument, the fact that it is inscribed on the grave monument spells out the fact that the latter marks the deceased's remains. The 'naming' of the grave monument, then, formed the core of all archaic epitaphs. This does not change until approximately two decades after the Persian Wars. I shall return to this question in § ii.6.

---

[244] Cf. Jeffery 1990: pl. 6 no. 17.

(b) *Attitudes and 'Ideology': The Themes of Praise and of Pity and Lament*

Besides their common core of reference to the grave monument or burial, there is more generally a definite degree of conformity in archaic funerary epigrams,[245] certainly more considerable than will be the case later, as will become clear after we have considered some later epitaphs in the following section. In terms of ideology archaic epitaphs reflect the established attitudes of the community, and in particular of the social group which commissioned inscribed grave monuments in the archaic Greek period, that is, the élite section of society: their ideological bias is that of the archaic aristocracy.[246] Their ideological structures are those derived from the established, collective attitudes of that group; there is no place in the epitaphs for individual ideological deviations; all articulations are situated within certain parameters determined by the group's ideology. That the archaic epitaphs reflect aristocratic ideology becomes clear when we consider one of the important themes in archaic epitaphs, the praise of the dead.[247] The praise formulations in archaic funerary epigrams reflect the values of the archaic aristocracy. They are as follows.[248]

The valour of the deceased is praised though various expressions.[249] Sometimes he is said to have died fighting among the *promachoi*.[250] The deceased is described as *agathos*[251] or, sometimes,

---

[245] Cf. e.g. Gragg 1910: 16–17.

[246] Cf. Stupperich 1977: 67; cf. also, on a related aspect, Labarbe 1968: 353.

[247] On praise in archaic epitaphs cf: Pircher 1979; Wallace 1970: 100–1; North 1966: 13–15; Skiadas 1967: 18; Clairmont 1970: 10; Stecher 1963; 1981. On praise in Greek epitaphs in general: cf. Lattimore 1962: 290–300; in classical epitaphs: Clairmont 1970: 51–2. On praise in grave epigrams (in general), Stecher 1981: 7, 16–24, 25. Of warriors: Stecher 1981: 20–3, 25–47 (both polyandria and individual dead). On praise of warriors and athletes, Stecher 1981. On praise in prose epitaphs of different periods cf. Tod 1951: 182–90. Day (1989: *passim*, cf. esp. 16–20) argued that the fundamental message of archaic verse epitaphs was praise of the deceased, expressed in forms characteristic of praise poetry. There is conformity in the forms of praise in the epitaphs in the different periods, and in the development of these forms of praise through time; the praise of the deceased in the epitaphs changes in the course of time as the society's cultural assumptions change (cf. Stecher 1981: 17).

[248] I am only including those which are not so fragmentary as to make the precise meaning ambiguous.

[249] Cf. e.g.: *anorean echsochos helikias*: Hansen 1983: 31.

[250] Hansen 1983: 27; killed *arissteuon en promachois*: 1983: 112, cf. also 145.

[251] Cf. e.g.: *andr' agathon* (Hansen 1983: 13); *agathon paida* (ibid. 14).

agathos and *sophron*.²⁵² The terms *sophrosyne* and *arete* are also found
in combination.²⁵³ Once he is described as *kalos*.²⁵⁴ Elsewhere the
deceased is described as *gennaios aner*.²⁵⁵ Some epigrams apply to the
deceased a whole series of positive epithets. In one²⁵⁶ the deceased
is described as *sophron, euchsynetos, chsenikos, pi[ny]tos, ta kal' [eido]s*.
In another²⁵⁷ he is said to be *eudochsos, sophron*, and *pinytos* and to
have *pasan areten*. In yet another²⁵⁸ the deceased is said to have been
agathos, sophron, ae⟨th⟩lophoros and *sophos halikiai*. Another epigram
claims the deceased was *dokimotatos aston* and also that he died
amometos.²⁵⁹ In one epigram²⁶⁰ the deceased is said to be *philos* to
the citizens and the *xenoi*—as well to have been killed *arissteuon en
promachois*, and in another²⁶¹ to have been *potheinos damoi*. The
potheinos theme is related to the *philos* theme.²⁶² It refers to the
attitudes towards the deceased after his death and emphasizes the
longing and desire which the living feel for the deceased.²⁶³ In this
theme, which is a variant of the grief/lament theme, the praise is
constructed out of the lament, on the basis of the large number of
people said to have been distressed by the death. Praise and lament
are related.²⁶⁴ One of the virtues claimed for the deceased in some
epigrams is that he was hospitable.²⁶⁵ One epigram claims that the
deceased was skilful *[sophos]* in *xenia* and *hipposyne*.²⁶⁶ A woman is
described as *aidoia*.²⁶⁷ The funerary epigram for a doctor calls itself

²⁵² Hansen 1983: 34, 36. On *agathos* and *sophron* cf. also Stecher 1981: 18–19, 23; cf. also
64 n. 26 on some aspects of the meanings of *agathos* and *arete*.
²⁵³ Cf Hansen 1983: 41, 58.
²⁵⁴ Ibid. 68.
²⁵⁵ Ibid. 52.
²⁵⁶ Ibid. 67.
²⁵⁷ Ibid. 69. On the forms of praise in this epigram cf. also below in this chapter.
²⁵⁸ Hansen 1983: 136.
²⁵⁹ Ibid. 172.
²⁶⁰ Ibid. 112.
²⁶¹ Ibid. 128.
²⁶² Cf. Stecher 1981: 22; 68 n. 60. On the *philos* theme cf. also ibid. 24. Cf. also the 5th-cent. (3rd quarter) epigram for Gastron (Hansen 1983: 123; GV 77): *hoss mala pollo[is] astois kai xeinois doke thanon anian*.
²⁶³ On the longing and desire which the living feel for the deceased cf. Vernant 1990: 41–50.
²⁶⁴ Cf. Lausberg 1982: 106, cf. 117–18; Day 1989: 17–20, who privileges the praise element and understresses that of lament.
²⁶⁵ Philoxenos: Hansen 1983: 140; xenikos: ibid. 67.
²⁶⁶ Hansen 1983: 111.
²⁶⁷ Ibid. 66. On this praise cf. also Stecher 1981, 18.

a *mnema* . . . *Aineo sophias iatro aristo.*[268] The epigram Hansen 1983:
43 describes the deceased as an Olympic victor; this, of course, is a
factual statement which communicates high achievement and thus
creates high praise. It is not dissimilar to *ae⟨th⟩lophoros* in the epigram
Hansen 1983: 136. Thus these praise formulations ascribe to the deceased certain
types of social virtues. One category pertains to valour or involves
terms, like *agathos* and *arete*, which cover both generic excellence
and valour; *agathos*, like *gennaios*, denotes qualities of character,
associated[269] with noble birth. Another category pertains to athletic
sporting prowess and success. Another important group of formulations praises qualities of the mind and character, among which
sophron is the most common. *Arete* is often combined with *sophrosyne*
and *agathos* with *sophron*. Another virtue praised is hospitality.
Another category of formulations states that the deceased was held
in high social esteem,[270] or that he had been dear to the citizens and
foreigners alike, or that he was missed by the demos. All these
positive traits pertain to the aristocratic social persona. A woman
described as *aidoia*, worthy of regard, fitted the established perceptions of a good, virtuous woman. The memory of deceased is
always presented in a positive light in our epitaphs. The praise aims
at creating, or contributing to the creation of, his good memory.
In one theme this process is taken further: a (positive) statement is
made about the deceased's reputation, not only in life and at the
moment of his death, but also after his death. The theme is
extremely rare in archaic epitaphs. I know of only two instances.
In the epigram for Alkimachos, from Athens,[271] the deceased is told
eudochson se ch[yte k]ata gai' ekalyphsen—and then follow other, more
usual epithets of praise. In the epigram for Deines, from Apollonia
on the Black Sea,[272] we find *[d]okimotatos astoy*, followed by *ke⟨i⟩tai
amometos̩ t̩erma la[ch]on thanato*.

Many archaic epitaphs do not contain a praise formulation. This
suggests that the praise of the deceased, though very important, was
not perceived as indispensable in an archaic epitaph, and thus was

[268] Ibid. 62. The forms of praise in doctors' epitaphs will be discussed in more detail in
Ch. VI § i.4, for reasons that will become apparent there.
[269] In their meanings and in the archaic Greek attitudes.
[270] Cf. the most approved of all citizens in Hansen 1983: 172.
[271] Hansen 1983: 69; Willemsen 1963: 145–7 no. 12 pl. 61.
[272] Hansen 1983: 172; *GV* 326; Jeffery 1990: 368, 372 no. 54, 416 pl. 72 no. 54; Friedländer
and Hoffleit 1948: 78; Clairmont 1970: no. 8; Daux 1972: 521–2; Mihailov 1970: 405.

not felt to constitute its primary purpose. I shall return to this point.[273]

The ideology reflected in the archaic epitaphs is complex and multifaceted. One important aspect is that it presents death as sad and the condition of being dead as pitiful. There is no deviation from this, notwithstanding the fact that the spectrum of eschatological beliefs current in the archaic period includes some which, when viewed through modern assumptions and expectations, might have been expected to have led to a less negative perception of death. For in the archaic period, besides the mainstream eschatology and collective representations, there took place also other developments, outside the mainstream: new beliefs appear, promising individual salvation and a happy afterlife gained through moral behaviour and/or individual initiations to Mysteries or sects, and a judgement of the dead, followed by rewards and punishments in Hades for one's conduct in life.[274] The influence of intellectual/philosophical thought on this type of eschatology is strong. However, there is not the slightest hint of a reflection of any of these beliefs in any archaic epitaph anywhere in the Greek world. The first known mysteric funerary inscription dates from c.450 and comes from Kyme;[275] it is not an actual epitaph and explicitly sets itself apart. It is beyond my scope here to discuss the relationship between the eschatology of the Eleusinian Mysteries and archaic Athenian attitudes towards death. Suffice to say that the attitudes reflected in the archaic Attic epitaphs give no hint of an influence of mysteric beliefs in a happy afterlife. This is not necessarily surprising. For the archaic inscribed grave monument reflects, we shall see, a nexus of attitudes in which the maximum preoccupation is with the survival of the memory of the deceased's social persona. This is not incompatible with Eleusinian, and, generally, mysteric funerary ideology and the same individuals may be concerned with both. But it appears that at this time each nexus of attitudes expresses different concerns in different vehicles and circumstances, and the prevailing publicly articulated ethos of the aristocratic circles in which the model for the inscribed archaic grave monument had

<hr/>

[273] I shall also be discussing some special types of praise formulations in certain archaic epitaphs in Ch. VI.

[274] On these developments and eschatologies cf. Graf 1974: 79–126; Burkert 1985: 285–301; 1987: *passim*, cf. esp. 4–5, 21–4.

[275] Jeffery 1990: 240 no. 12.

first been established stressed a heightened concern for memory-survival. This model remained valid throughout the archaic period. So that, even when individuals who subscribed to mysteric beliefs involving a happy afterlife had inscribed grave monuments erected for them, their epitaphs did not reflect these beliefs but expressed the established, socially sanctioned concerns with memory-survival and associated attitudes, which included the sadness of death. This sadness at the loss of life need not be contradictory with the belief in a happy afterlife. For it is not necessarily the case that, at this time at least, the happier afterlife promised by the Eleusinian Mysteries was considered to be preferable to life itself. Sadness at the loss of life may have been incompatible with a belief in heroization/deification, but in the archaic period such beliefs do not apply to the ordinary dead, but only to very exceptional people.[276]

Among the themes that commonly appear in addition to the core recording the deceased's name there is a nexus of related themes which illustrate vividly the perceptions of the dead reflected in these epitaphs. They are the following:

A1. Invitation to passers-by to feel pity for the deceased.[277]

---

[276] Cf. Bérard 1982: 89–105.

[277] This theme is included in the following epigrams. (1) Epigram for Kroisos (Hansen 1983: 27). (2) Epigram for Kleoites (Hansen 1983: 68). (3) Epigram for Thrason (Hansen 1983: 28. I give the text below in § ii.3*l*). (4) Epigram for Diokleas (Hansen 1983: 117). (5) Epigram for Tettichos (Hansen 1983: 13). (6) An invitation to feel pity is also included in the epigram for the little Carian girl Parthenia (in ll. 2 and 6) (Hansen 1983: 174; *GV* 1960a (p. 689); cf. L. Robert, *Gnomon* 31 (1959), 4). (7) To the first half of the 5th cent. belongs a fragmentary epigram from Selinous which includes the word *oiktire* (Hansen 1983: 148; Manni-Piraino 1966: 202–4). On this theme cf. also Willemsen 1963: 119–21. Day (1989: 17–20), in discussing epitaphs such as that of Tettichos, understresses the importance of the themes 'invitation to passers-by to feel pity for the deceased' and 'invitation to passers-by to lament for the deceased' and privileges that of praise. In my view, despite his claims (Day 1989: 17–18), this hierarchization is culturally determined, and dependent on his central hypothesis (Day 1989: *passim*) that the fundamental message of archaic funerary epigrams was praise for the deceased in forms characteristic of praise poetry, and that both funerary epigrams and praise poetry were dependent on funerary ritual, which, he argues, epigram and grave monument had the common goal of memorializing. I take the view that the situation was more complex than this, and that the persona and relationship of the living with the deceased during the funeral was different from that after the sealing of the grave and the erection of the grave monument. Praise was indeed a very important aspect of the latter relationship, but the wide way in which Day appears to be implicitly defining this concept includes dangers of cultural determination and the elision of important distinctions; for in the archaic Greek world even what could be loosely called 'the praise facet' of the themes of lament and pity is very important in culturally specific ways: these themes

A2. Invitation to passers-by to lament for the deceased.[278]
B. A nameless 'I' expresses feelings of sorrow or pity while looking at the grave monument.[279] It is each passer-by that becomes the 'I' of the epigram. Thus category B is equivalent to the fulfilment, as it were, of the invitations issued in epigrams of category A.
C. Various formulations expressing grief and sorrow at the death of the deceased.[280]

The combined incidence of these three related themes within the corpus of archaic epitaphs is high, and they are the only themes in this corpus to be dealing explicitly with emotions pertaining to the death.[281] They express most poignantly the view that for the

articulated in a modality appropriate to the (perceived as) pitiful status of being dead the importance of his social persona in the world of the living.

[278] This theme is included in the following epigrams. (1) For Telephanes of Thasos (Hansen 1983: 159). (2) For Antilochos (Hansen 1983: 34). (3) For Tettichos (Hansen 1983: 13).

[279] This category includes the following epigrams. (1) For Autokleides (Matthaiou 1986: 31–4; Lewis 1987: 188; *SEG* 36 (1986) no. 51). (2) For Smikythos (Willemsen 1963: 118–22 no. 4; Hansen 1983, 51. For the fact that *oiktiro* in l. 1 must not be emended, and that therefore the epigram belongs to this category cf. Lewis 1987: 188). For *AP* vii. 511 cf. ibid.

[280] (i) Grief and sorrow felt by relatives and friends: (1) epigram for Xenophantos (Hansen 1983: 50; Willemsen 1963: 136–9 no. 8), by the father; (2) epigram for Chairedemos (Hansen 1983: 14), by the father; (3) probably also, though it is fragmentary: the epigram for an Olympic victor (Hansen 1983: 43, Willemsen 1963, 116–17 no. 2); (4) epigram for Diokleus (see above A5), ll. 1–2 by mother; (5) perhaps the epigram for Polynoe (Hansen 1983: 144; Jeffery 1990: 232–3; 234 no. 8), by the son (but cf. also the different type of restoration and different reading, proposed in Wallace 1970: 98); (6) cf. the fragmentary epigram Hansen 1983: 59. Related to this is the formulation in the epigram for Smikythos (see above B (2) l. 2. On *elp'* cf. Willemsen 1963: 119 and n. 50). Cf. also the epigram for Praxiteles (Hansen 1983: 139). (7) Epigram for Oligeidas (Hansen 1983: 113). The father. (ii) Other formulations: (1) epigram for Anaxilas (Hansen 1983: 58; Willemsen 1963: 141–5 no. 11). Cf. also the epigram for King Midas transmitted through the literary tradition *GV* 1171; Peek 1960: 29; Pfohl 1967: no. 24 l. 5. (iii) Unclear (fragmentary): epigram for Anaxipolis (?) (Hansen 1983: 158; Jeffery 1990: 301, 307 no. 66).

[281] In a few, extremely rare, cases an echo of a sentiment pertaining to the death may be expressed which does not fit totally into these categories, but is always thematically related to these three themes and attitudes. Thus, if *thanato[s dakry]oes* is correctly restored in Hansen 1983: 46, we have here an adjective characterizing death which fits into the Homeric cluster of epithets for death. In Homer it is *polemos* that is *dakryoeis* (*Il.* 5. 737), but *thanatos dakryoeis* belongs together with the Homeric expressions *thanatos dyseleges* (*Od.* 22. 325) and *taneleges thanatos* (which is a formula, and part of a longer formula: *Il.* 8. 70; 22. 210; *Od.* 11. 171). Homeric influence has been recognized in several epigrams, of course. (Cf. Friedländer and Hoffleit 1948: 7–8; Peek 1960: 9; Raubitschek 1968: 1–26, esp. 25–6, and cf. discussion 27–36; cf. also Loraux 1981: 55. Cf. a discussion of literary influences on epigrams, with bibliog. Häusle 1979: 79–85. On the relationship between grave epigrams and elegy cf. Lausberg 1982: 106 and bibliog. at 533 nn. 18–20; Lewis 1987: 188 (on the relationship between lament and early elegy cf. E. L. Bowie 1986: 22–7; Lewis 1987: 188).) But, independently of the controversy about the extent, manner, etc. of this influence, the composers of archaic

deceased and those close to him death is tragic, and nothing but tragic, and that a dead person arouses feelings of pity and compassion. Theme A1, which invites the passers-by to feel pity for the deceased, is related to, but not identical with, theme A2. *Oiktiron* is often translated as 'weep',[282] 'Klage' or 'erhebe die Klage'. This is an approximate translation, based on the (implicit) assumption that the choice of words is not significant; for it obscures an important distinction, a difference in emphasis as between A1 and A2. We should assign to *oiktiro* its proper meaning, 'feel pity for', and preserve the distinctions made by the epigrams' writers.[283]

In the discussion that follows, the number in parentheses refers to the epitaphs cited in nn. 277–80. The first implication of the requests *stethi kai oiktiron para sema* (A1 (1)); *stethi kai oiktiron sema* ... *idon* (A1 (3))[284] and *mnem' esoron oiktir'* (A1 (2)) and their variations is that the passer-by should stop and look at the grave monument and think of the deceased, activate his memory. The same intimate connection between looking at the grave monument and feelings of pity and sorrow is observed in the theme B, in the statements *sema* ... *prosoron aniomai* (B1) and *oiktiro prosoron* ... *sema* (B2). This spells out the function of the grave monument as a vehicle for the preservation of the deceased's memory. The fact that this invitation to activate the memory of the deceased takes the form 'have pity for him', shows that pity is the appropriate sentiment when thinking of a dead person. This is confirmed by the fact that theme A1 provides one of the only two explicit exhortations in archaic epitaphs requesting the passer-by to think of the deceased— the other being the invitation to lament for him (theme A2). Theme A1, then, shows that the epitaphs perceive the dead as arousing pity. The epigram for Tettichos (A1 (5) and A2 (3)) shows that *oiktirein* in this context, took—or could take—the form of lamentation. The two themes, and the two exhortations, are very closely related. Their differences are differences of emphasis; A1 emphasizes the aspect 'think of X', activate his memory, while A2 focuses on the

epitaphs (like all writers operating within the parameters of a genre with a particular social role relating it to the established attitudes) only used Homeric elements when these suited the mentality and aims of archaic epitaphs, or could be adapted to do so. On literary echoes and influences in Attic epigrams cf. also Pfohl 1953: 241–53. So, thematically Hansen 1983: 46 echoes weakly the themes under discussion.

[282] Cf. Friedländer and Hoffleit 1948: 85–8.
[283] Humphreys (1983: 91–2) translates *oiktiron* correctly as 'pity' and 'feel pity'.
[284] Cf. also A1 (6).

concrete activity of lamentation. Like A1, theme A2[285] activates the
deceased's memory in terms of sorrow. Lament is an established
pattern of ritual behaviour towards the dead, echoing the ritual
activities at the time of the death and burial. But this does not mean
that the epitaphs could have requested the passers-by to lament for
the deceased if lamentation was not appropriate to the present
situation. On the contrary, precisely because lament is not a spontaneous show of emotion, but a regulated symbol into which
emotions of grief and sorrow are channelled when these are felt, or
through which they are created when not, the invitation to lament
in the epigrams shows that grief and sorrow were the appropriate
emotions to be generated in connection with the activation of a
dead person's memory.

Through the lamentation at the death-ritual people expressed
not just sorrow, but also their involvement with the deceased, and
their participation in his death. Lament was one of the ways through
which the deceased's social persona was articulated and given value,
and his importance stressed.[286] The invited lamentation at the grave
was to some extent an echo of that occasion, a kind of re-enactment
of the ritual behaviour which had helped confer value on the
deceased at the moment of his separation from the world of the
living, confer value on his life. The epigram for Telephanes (A2
(1)) explicitly relates the invitation to the passers-by to lament for
him with the moment of his *ekphora*; it represents the requested
lament at his grave as a substitute for their non-participation in his
funeral. But the lamentation at the grave requested by the epitaphs
is different; the distance of time and the deceased's separation from
the world of the living have changed its focus and function: it is
now the memory of the deceased to which value is being conferred
rather than his social persona before its final separation from the
living. Thus the epitaphs brought about the survival and validation
of the deceased's memory with all those who saw the grave monument.[287] The *oimoi* epitaphs, we saw, involve a formulation com-

[285] On the theme 'invitation to lament' cf. also Gentili 1968: 54–5; Friedländer and
Hoffleit 1948: 85–9; Skiadas 1967: 27–38; Peek 1960: 16–17; Lausberg 1982: 115–18, cf
118–19.
[286] On these aspects of lament: cf. Huntington and Metcalf 1979: 24–33; cf. Sourvinou-
Inwood 1981, 27–9. On lament in Greece cf. also Alexiou 1974: 12–14, 102–3; Vermeule
1979: 14–17.
[287] This invitation to lament, and, less explicitly, the invitation to feel pity for the deceased,
may appear to be in some apparent conflict with the spirit of the funerary legislation

posed of either *oimoi o* plus the name of the deceased in the vocative, or of *oimoi* plus the name of the deceased in the genitive. In the first the deceased is addressed in terms of *oimoi*, which, like theme A1, reflects the feeling that sorrow, grief, and pity are the appropriate emotions with which the dead are to be thought of. Both could be seen as a response, permanently recorded—and thus ensuring continuous actualization by a series of readers—to the request of theme A1 to stand by the grave and feel pity for the deceased. The genitive combined with the *oimoi* in the second group is a causal genitive; so this version explicitly states that the deceased arouses feelings of pity and sorrow: 'Alas for Pediarchos!'[288] Expressions of grief and sorrow at the death of the deceased preserved lastingly in stone (theme C) reflect the notion of lasting grief at the loss of the irreplaceable other. The fact that such emotions were articulated in public in a permanent form shows that they are part of the established funerary ideology,[289] which represents the death of the (important) other as arousing emotions of great intensity and lasting nature. At the same time, theme C also reflects strong concern for memory-survival. For the sorrow and grief caused by the deceased's death was also part of his social persona, it validated his life and importance, by pointing out the gap he left; the recording of these emotions also entailed the recording of this validation. Like the invitation to lament, then, this theme reactivates the validation of the deceased that took place after his death with

attributed to Solon ([Dem.] 43. 62; Plut. *Sol.* 12. 21; Cic. *De leg.* 2. 59 ff.) which, among other things forbade lamentations for earlier dead at another's funeral, and visits to the graves of non-kin except for funerals. I have discussed archaic funerary legislation elsewhere and will return to it in Ch. VI; I argued that these and the other archaic funerary laws had aimed at restricting death's encroachment on community life by limiting the disruption and lowering the emotional tone of the death-ritual and generally forcing a low visibility on death-related ritual activities. Snodgrass noted (1980: 146) that in Athens these restrictions in the death-ritual coincided with a great increase in expenditure on grave monuments and suggested that this type of commemoration, clearly not included within the scope of the law, may have been stimulated by the wish to compensate for the restrictions in ritual death-related behaviour. It is possible that something comparable may have happened here: that the restrictions on more regular lamentations at the grave may have generated the notion of incorporating, as it were, the potential for renewed lament, an activating switch, into the grave monument and thus giving it permanent form. As I mentioned, the reading of the epigram activated the deceased's memory through mental images of the activity. The reason why the passers-by should fulfil the request is spelt out in A2 (2): for they too will die.

[288] Cf. Jeffery 1962: 142.

[289] Whether or not these emotions were genuinely felt in each case. It is a general characteristic of epitaphs that they reproduced the ideal rather than the reality. Cf. Lattimore 1962: 275; Pircher 1979: 11.

the changed time perspective adding the dimension of lasting grief and sorrow. The expression of grief and sorrow at the deceased's death was a record of his importance, so the theme can be considered as part of the broad category of praise.[290] It certainly contributes to the enhancement of the deceased's memory.

(c) *Other Themes*

Other minor themes found in a few epitaphs that are not associated with the major thematic categories discussed above[291] include: first, themes pertaining to the circumstances of the person's death;[292] such themes, found alone or in combination are: (s)he died young; he died at war; she died unmarried; (s)he died abroad; he died at sea. Some of these are associated, or overlap, with another thematic category, the themes that give a few biographical details,[293] which sometimes pertained to the relationship of the deceased to the person who erected the grave monument.[294] Then, there were two themes that referred to the high visibility of the *sema*: the common theme 'near the road'[295] and, a theme attested only once, 'near the hippodrome'[296]—that is, an especially prominent place. Thus, these themes pertain, first, to the social persona of deceased—which includes their status when they died, including the fact that they died young or unmarried; second, to the manner and/or circumstances of their death, especially when it took place abroad, or at sea; and third, to the high visibility of the *sema*, which entails that more people will see it and thus activate and preserve the deceased's memory. Consequently, they pertain to the larger category 'articulation of the deceased's social persona and preservation

---

[290] Cf. also Lausberg 1982: 106 and cf. also pp. 117–18 on the fact that praise and lament are related. On theme C in Attic epitaphs cf. Pfohl 1953: 161–6.

[291] As e.g. 'X erected this grave monument' or 'X made this grave monument' are associated, with the theme 'reference to the grave monument'; *to gar geras esti thanonto[s]* (Hansen 1983: 40), 'looking at the grave monument', and the like were also referred to as part of the 'reference to the grave monument'; they are both themes in their own right in that they express some specific meanings and they also belong to a version of 'reference to the grave monument'; *to gar geras esti thanonto[s]*, for example, is also an elaboration of the theme 'X erected this grave monument'.

[292] Cf. below and nn. 166–9 and cf. Appendix.

[293] Cf. e.g. Hansen 1983: 77, 76.

[294] Cf. e.g. Hansen 1983: 37 (*helithion noselesausa*), which can also be classified as pertaining to the manner of the deceased's death.

[295] Cf. e.g. Hansen 1983: 16, 39, 74; and cf. on this theme Humphreys 1983: 91–2; Stecher 1981: 60 n. 13.

[296] Hansen 1983: 136.

of his memory through the grave monument'. I shall return to the themes pertaining to the circumstances of the death in section ii.6 below.

(d) *Some Conclusions*

To sum up: all archaic epitaphs contained a common thematic core 'naming' the grave monument, which belongs to the larger thematic category 'articulation of the deceased's social persona and preservation of his memory through the grave monument', to which also belong the praise themes (which, though important, were not indispensable), and also the rarer themes. The combined incidence of the themes involving expressions of grief and lament and invitation to lament, and/or feel pity for, the deceased is high. They express the view that for the deceased and those close to him death is tragic and the dead person arouses feelings of pity; they activate, and so help preserve, the deceased's memory. Thus, the parameters that shaped the composition of archaic funerary epigrams were a strong concern for memory-survival and a poignant perception of death. The fact that in these epitaphs death is associated with grief and sorrow and the dead are objects of pity may seem natural to us, but it was in fact not a universal but a culturally determined, phenomenon; as we shall see in the next section, at other times other Greeks wrote different things on their epitaphs.

3. Absence and Difference: *Chaire* in Epitaphs and Elsewhere

(a) *Introduction*

This section has several functions. First, to show that an element that has been assumed to be present in archaic epitaphs as it was in later ones, *chaire* addressed to the dead, is in fact absent; and that this absence is correlative with important aspects of the archaic epitaphs. Second, to investigate in depth this use of *chaire* and in the process discuss several other aspects of post-archaic funerary ideology and behaviour. Finally, the classical and Hellenistic epitaphs that will come into play will function as a model of difference, illustrate the other choices made in other periods, and the attitudes reflected in them; this will place the archaic epitaphs in a wider perspective, allow us to see them in their proper ideological context.

In later periods epitaphs did address *chaire* to the dead, and the investigation of this usage and the mentality it reflects will illustrate the fact that the choice of the archaic epitaphs to stress grief and sorrow and represent the dead as objects of pity, which seems 'natural' to us, was in fact a culturally determined phenomenon; at other times other Greeks made different choices on their epitaphs.

If we leave aside one epigram from Teithronion,[297] which will be discussed in detail in Chapter VI, and which, we shall see, could not have been an epitaph (for a series of independent reasons of which the use of *chaire* is only one), in no archaic epitaph, whether epigram or prose inscription, is *chaire* ever addressed to the deceased.[298] I will argue that this absence is not due to accident (either of find or of composition); that, given their ideological uniformity, archaic epitaphs could not have addressed *chaire* to the deceased. With two possible, but highly doubtful, exceptions that may conceivably belong to the end of the fifth century, there is no *chaire* or *chairete* addressed to the deceased in fifth-century BC private epitaphs either. This already reduces the plausibility of the notion that the absence of *chaire* addressed to the deceased from archaic epitaphs could be accidental—even independently of all the other arguments which will suggest that this absence was strongly motivated. There is one *chairete* addressed to the dead in a fifth-century Athenian public collective epitaph. Because such epitaphs reflected different attitudes towards the dead from those of private epitaphs, this occurrence in fact strengthens our case. Leaving aside the two doubtful specimens, the earliest instances in which the deceased is addressed with *chaire* in a private epitaph come from the fourth century BC. This address begins to become common in the third century BC, both in funerary epigrams and in prose grave inscriptions.[299]

I will argue that this pattern of usage corresponds to certain attitudes towards death which can be seen to motivate both absence and presence of *chaire* addressed to the deceased. There is a correspondence between its absence and the presence of a nexus of

---

[297] Ibid. 127.

[298] There is no *chaire* or *chairete* at all addressed to anyone in archaic epitaphs, though there is one instance of *chairete* addressed to the passer-by in a related epigram, not a grave inscription, but a memorial to a dead person inscribed on the blocks of a tower in Thasos (Hansen 1983: 162; cf. below § ii.3*l*).

[299] Cf. Pouilloux 1960: 160; Couilloud 1974: 486.

attitudes that would seem to preclude it; and between its presence and the presence of a nexus of attitudes which appears to tolerate it or even invite it. Thus, even though there might still remain some uncertainty (due to insufficient evidence) as regards certain aspects of the reconstruction of each of these two patterns (of *chaire*-usage, and of attitudes) when taken on their own, the correspondence between them will provide confirmation of their validity. For the analyses are kept separate, and thus the argument is not circular. The investigation is divided into two parts. In the first (*b–j*) I argue that the pattern of appearance of *chaire* addressed to the dead shows that this usage was originally associated with a special category of attitudes which is not only different from, but actually contrasted to, the nexus of attitudes reflected in archaic (and fifth-century private) epitaphs. And that *chaire* began to be addressed to the dead in private epitaphs only when changes in the attitudes that were reflected in the epitaphs made those special attitudes suitable for the ordinary dead. In the second part (*k–l*) I try to show that, given the connotations carried by the word *chaire*, the attitudes towards death and the dead reflected in the archaic epitaphs precluded that *chaire* could have been used to address the deceased. The conclusions of the two parts confirm and complement each other.[300]

(b) *The Homeric Usage*

Chaire is addressed to a dead person twice in Homer: in *Iliad* 23. 19–20 during one of the ritual laments for Patroklos, and in *Iliad* 23. 179–80, in the course of Patroklos' burial, during the preparation of the funeral pyre. In both cases Achilles is addressing Patroklos with the same verses

χαῖρέ μοι, ὦ Πάτροκλε, καὶ εἰν Ἀΐδαο δόμοισι·
πάντα γὰρ ἤδη τοι τελέω τὰ πάροιθεν ὑπέστην,

and then he goes on to detail the promises in slightly different terms

---

[300] Though the reconstruction of the attitudes towards death and the dead relates to both parts of the investigation, this does not invalidate the claim that the two parts are independent from each other. First, because only one segment of these attitudes is relevant to both parts, and that segment involves attitudes explicitly expressed in the epitaphs. And second, because while this common segment is a fundamental element of the case in the second part, in the first it functions only as an explanatory background to certain unambiguously observed phenomena, so that the validity of the main argument does not depend on the validity of the reconstruction of these attitudes. Though, of course, the fact that the attitudes in question can explain and motivate the observed pattern of usage reinforces its validity and strength.

in each case. This usage of *chaire* is different from any possible usage of *chaire* addressed to the deceased in an epitaph in a number of ways. One, immediately apparent, significant difference between the two lies in the different nature of the two utterances. In Homer *chaire* is addressed to a dead person in the course of a time-bound speech-act. After it has been uttered, the effect of the salutation disappears. It does not remain permanently attached to Patroklos, nor will it characterize him for ever, define him in his condition as a dead person. While statements contained in epitaphs are permanent, they are forever associated with the deceased, characterizing him in his condition as deceased. In fact, in Homer the utterance of *chaire* takes place in a narrative situation which stresses its impermanence, the *ad hoc* nature of the salutation. Patroklos is urged *chairein* on a specific occasion for a specific, very special, reason, which reinforces the exceptionality; while the emblematic character of epitaphs stresses the permanence, the eternal application of its elements to the deceased. These are important differences. If it is right that, as I shall argue, *chaire* could not be used to address the dead in archaic epitaphs because it clashed with fundamental aspects of the attitudes reflected in these epitaphs, this conflict need not have prevented a momentary use in a passing moment of narrative if there were good reasons for it; but it could not have tolerated the permanent characterization of the deceased through a term the connotations of which clashed violently with the perception of his condition as deceased. Thus, the ideological structures of a writer who shared in these attitudes would have prevented him from thinking up such a usage, or sanctioning its inclusion in an epitaph (which functioned in terms of the socially established attitudes) if, *per impossibile* he had thought it up. Another difference between Patroklos as addressee of *chaire* and the dead addressed in the epitaphs, which may be of some marginal importance, is that in *Iliad* 23. 19 Patroklos was not yet buried when he was addressed with *chaire*, and was thus not in Hades but 'betwixt and between', between Hades and the upper world, as he stated in *Iliad* 23. 64–76. He was still in this liminal condition in v. 179, since his cremation had not yet begun. It could be argued that, though *chaire* is not appropriate for addressing the dead, its use might have been tolerated (in special circumstances) when the dead thus addressed were not yet buried and had not entered Hades, because symbolically they had not yet acquired the full status of dead, and had not fully shed all characteristics pertaining to the living—which included certain oppositions to those defining the dead, of which, I will argue, being addressed with *chaire* is one. The expression *kai ein Aidao domoisi*, which follows *chaire moi o Patrokle*, is a formula, also occurring in *Il*. 22. 52 and 23. 103–4. It is not to be understood literally; it conveys the concept 'being dead'.[301] That is why it is used here, though Patroklos is not yet inside Hades.[302]

An important difference between the Homeric passages and the epitaphs is that in Homer the use of *chaire* is explicitly motivated: a very strong reason is given why Achilles is urging Patroklos *chairein* (*kai ein Aidao domoisi*). The exceptionality of this reason and of the circumstances matches the exceptionality of the use of *chaire* to address the dead—even though only within a narrative, time-bound situation in which this is a momentary act. The exceptional character of the use of *chaire* to address the dead person in *Iliad* 23. 19 and 179 becomes clear when we consider the wider context. I need hardly stress that the death and burial of Patroklos are exceptional. They provide the main focus of this part of the poem, mirroring motivating, and opposing the other focus, the death of Hector, the act of withholding burial from his corpse and the ultimate granting of it. Achilles is the pivot between the two; the grief, rage, and guilt he feels for the first, motivating his behaviour with reference to the second, is marked off as excessive; his behaviour, involving acts of revenge for Patroklos' death, is disapproved of, and marked as abnormal (*Iliad* 24. 44–54). It is in this context of excess and abnormality that the exhortation *chaire moi o Patrokle* belongs. For it is those acts of revenge, the humiliation of Hector's corpse and the slaughter of the twelve Trojan youths, that Achilles had promised to Patroklos and is now fulfilling, and it is for these acts that he exhorts Patroklos *chairein*.[303] This context, then,

---

[301] For a similar usage of a related nexus of formulas denoting the concept 'to die' and involving expressions such as *domon Aidos* cf. *JHS* 92 (1972), 221–2.

[302] Though, as we saw, we cannot expect consistency in Homer, it would be to misunderstand the nature of the Homeric poems to suppose, as one would have to, that Homer could tell us that Patroklos was inside Hades in 23. 19, then 51 verses later go on about how Patroklos could not enter Hades until after his burial, and then again tell us that Patroklos was inside Hades 103 verses further on, when what is at issue here is a fundamental eschatological belief, touching upon a matter, the post-mortem state of Patroklos, which is of crucial importance throughout book 23 (as well as earlier), and would thus be at the forefront of the poet's—as well as the audience's—mind.

[303] Schnapp-Gourbeillon (1982: 81) rightly remarks that Patroklos' funeral is characterized by excess. Though I also agree with the view that Patroklos' funeral had 'abnormal' elements,

inevitably ascribes the colouring of abnormality also to Achilles' address to Patroklos through *chaire*. I suggest that it is precisely because Achilles' whole behaviour is abnormal that he addresses a dead person with *chaire*; that the latter, which (in the eyes of Homer and his contemporaries) is abnormal, is part, and a sign, of Achilles' abnormal behaviour of excessive grief, wrath, and revenge. If this is correct, it would reinforce our hypothesis about the absence of *chaire* from the archaic epitaphs. But even if it is not correct, or cannot be proved to be so, the abnormality of the context certainly marks off this use of *chaire* as abnormal or at least exceptional.

The assumption motivating Achilles' behaviour and utterances is that his acts of revenge will give satisfaction to Patroklos' shade. The viewpoint which presents Achilles as assuaging his own guilt and thirst for revenge while projecting his needs on to the dead Patroklos, which is given hierarchical priority by the fact that it underlies Apollo's statement about Achilles' behaviour and grief in *Iliad* 24. 44–54, also comes into play here; both perspectives generate perceptions that differentiate significantly the address to the dead Patroklos from the context of the archaic epitaphs. Achilles believes that the facts which constitute the reason for the *chairein* (and for the exhortation *chairein*) will affect positively the permanent condition of the dead Patroklos: it will give him the satisfaction that his death has been avenged. This may make his addressing Patroklos with *chaire* appropriate on this one occasion, to mark the achievement of this positive condition, the shade satisfied that he has been avenged, before he takes on his full status in Hades after his burial. Then, the dead Patroklos is also a reflection of Achilles who is alive but will soon die;[304] in the context of the revenge he is the mirror upon which Achilles projects his own motivation, needs and desires. Thus, at one level the *chaire* addressed to Patroklos by Achilles

these are directly related to Achilles' abnormal behaviour of revenge, and, in my view, it is a little misguided to believe that elements of sacrifice have been introduced into the funerary ritual. That some connotations of sacrificial practice may have been attracted to this ritual cannot be excluded. But that Patroklos is perceived as a perfectly normal deceased, with no 'divine' elements whatsoever, indeed, that such elements would be in violent conflict with the perception of Patroklos' death and funeral and with the attitudes to death and the dead articulated in the epic, is abundantly clear. Patroklos' funeral may be abnormal in the direction of excess but it is governed by two parameters: the ritual/ideological structures of the actual death-ritual and the narrative parameter of Achilles' excessive grief wrath and revenge which introduce abnormality.

[304] Cf. Loraux 1982: 30.

was perceived as in a way addressed to, refracted towards, himself; it was, again, the reflection of his own emotions projected on to his dead friend. This may have helped motivate and sanction this use of *chaire*. Given these significant divergences between the use of *chaire* to address Patroklos in Homer and its alleged use to address the dead in archaic epitaphs the former cannot legitimately be used to support the existence of the latter. This conclusion is not affected by the question of the precise meanings of *chaire* and *kai ein Aidao domoisi*. But these expressions may in fact provide further support for our conclusion. As Latacz argued,[305] *chaire* in Homer is not a worn-out conventional salutation without specific meaning, but a wish through which people wished each other a physical and spiritual well-being. Even if this view is challenged, it cannot be denied that *chaire*'s connotations 'rejoice/be well' would have compelled themselves upon the audience in the particular context under consideration. For a word's exact meaning in any utterance is determined by the context,[306] and in this case the selections[307] made by the audience would inevitably have pulled *chaire* strongly towards the 'rejoice' pole of its semantic field. For the motivation *panta gar* etc. which follows, especially when taken within the wider context of Achilles' acts of revenge and his belief that he is performing them for the sake of Patroklos, demands a stronger, more emphatic element to relate to, and motivate, than a neutral salutation,[308] and would thus have pushed the meaning of *chaire* towards 'rejoice'.[309] Given the Homeric perception of death as black and joyless, if *chaire* meant 'rejoice/be well', the *kai* in *kai ein Aidao domoisi* would inevitably be understood as introducing an antithesis, and thus meaning 'even though', 'even though you are dead'; for since in these perceptions the concepts 'being well/rejoicing' and 'being dead' are antithetical, *kai* could only be understood as expressing that antithesis. The force of the concepts 'rejoice because

---

[305] On *chaire* in Homer cf. Latacz 1966: 45–52.

[306] On context in linguistics cf. Lyons 1977: 570–635; 1981: 195–219.

[307] Eco 1981: 19.

[308] Dr Oliver Taplin and Dr Oswyn Murray have kindly let me know that, in their view, the fact that *gar* is strongly explanatory in Homer constitutes a strong argument in favour of my interpretation.

[309] Even in an oral performance audiences react to and perceive nexuses of meanings—at least within a comparatively short span; the to-and-fro process of perception and crystallization of meanings is not confined to reading, especially since Homer's audiences were alive to small nuances which we are here laboriously trying to reconstruct in their crude outlines. This, or rather, its mirror-image, is also valid for oral composition.

I am avenging you' is increased by the qualification 'even though you are dead', which on my interpretation is added to 'rejoice'.[310] These expressions, then, suggest that a contrast was felt to exist between *chaire* and the condition of being dead, which helps support the view that saying *chaire* to the dead was exceptional and abnormal. In these circumstances, the investigation of the Homeric use of *chaire* to address the dead Patroklos leads us to conclude that this use cannot support the view that *chaire* could be addressed to the dead in archaic epitaphs—or that there was a practice of addressing the deceased with *chaire* in the course of the death-ritual. On the contrary, this Homeric use is exceptional and abnormal, involving circumstances that can never pertain to the archaic epitaphs.[311] We also found evidence which appears to suggest that it is indeed perceived to be abnormal to address *chaire* to the dead, and that in Homer *chaire* is contrasted to the condition of being dead.

(c) *Greeting the Deceased: Prothesis and the Grave*

Another crutch supporting the view that *chaire* can be addressed to the dead in archaic epitaphs is the belief[312] that people addressed the deceased with *chaire* when they came to view the corpse and pay their respects during the prothesis[313] and also—or alternatively – the belief that passers-by addressed the deceased with *chaire* as they stepped up to the tomb.[314] There is no evidence whatsoever for the first belief, and only very much later evidence for the second. I will try to show that the first belief is mistaken, and, most importantly, that even if it were not, it could not provide support for the notion that *chaire* could be addressed to the deceased in archaic epitaphs. I will consider the second belief first, and try to show that it is mistakenly applied to the archaic period. There is no archaic evi-

---

[310] The passage in which Achilles had made his promise to the dead Patroklos (during an earlier part of the lament: *Il*. 18. 324–42) and which is therefore closely related to *Il*. 23. 19 ff and 179 ff, begins with *o popoi*.

[311] On the salutation, *chaire, kan Haidou domois eu soi genoito*, in Eur. *Alc*. 626–7, cf. below Ch. III § ii.3*g*.

[312] Cf. Peek 1960: 14.

[313] On prothesis cf. Vermeule 1979: 12–18; Kurtz and Boardman 1971: 58–61; 77–8; 143–4; cf. also some further bibliog. in Sourvinou-Inwood 1983: 39 n. 35. Cf. on the prothesis as part of the early Greek death ritual Sourvinou-Inwood 1981: 27 and 1983: 39.

[314] Peek 1960: 14; Friedländer and Hoffleit 1948: p. 89. In the analysis of these arguments which follows I am trying to articulate explicitly and coherently notions that are only implicit in the discussions cited. For the notion that *chaire* was addressed to dead people in archaic epitaphs has never been challenged before, so it was in no need of defending.

dence for the view that people said *chaire* to the deceased as they passed by a tomb. There is the same serious objection against this hypothesis as there is against the notion that *chaire* could be addressed to the deceased in archaic epitaphs: the connotations conveyed by the word *chaire* clash with the archaic perception of the condition of being dead. The case rests implicitly on a circular argument: the notion that *chaire* in the Teithronion epigram cited above (to be discussed in Chapter VI) is addressed to a dead man is not questioned because of the alleged practice of saying *chaire* to the deceased when approaching a tomb. And the case for the existence of this practice rests entirely on fourth-century and later epitaphs, the testimony of which is thought to be relevant to the archaic period precisely and only because it is alleged that *chaire* is addressed to a dead man in the Teithronion epigram; or else this hypothesis rests entirely on the fundamental methodological fallacy that chronological distinctions do not matter, and that what was valid for the fourth century or later was necessarily also valid for the archaic period.[315] The evidence which explicitly testifies to a practice of greeting the deceased with *chaire* when passing by a grave comes from a much later period,[316] in which the use of *chaire* to address the dead in epitaphs had already been established. Thus it is not possible to decide whether the appearance of *chaire* addressed to the deceased in the epitaphs reflected a (new) practice of greeting the deceased with *chaire* when passing by a grave, or, on the contrary, whether the latter practice—if it is not a literary invention—reflected the introduction of *chaire* in the epitaph and resulted from the reading out of the salutation *chaire* addressed to the deceased inscribed in the epitaph. For, we shall see, the *chaire* addressed to the deceased in epitaphs has an independent function and significance, and does not need to reflect a practice of addressing the dead with *chaire* when passing by a grave.

The expression *o chaire, patros mnem'* uttered by Theoklymenos in Euripides' *Helen* 1165 (produced in 412) cannot be used to support the view that in the fifth century people addressed the dead with *chaire* when passing by a grave. For Theoklymenos' father Proteus was not an ordinary dead person, and his grave was not an

---

[315] The assertion (Peek 1960: 14) that the earliest examples of *chaire* go up to the early 6th cent. is unsupported by evidence—it is presumably based on inference, itself based on the notion that when the passer-by stepped up to the tomb he greeted the deceased with *chaire*.

[316] Cf. Peek 1960: 145; *GV* 1312, 698; cf. *GV* 1214, 1221.

ordinary grave: Proteus had superhuman status and his grave received cult and functioned as a sanctuary for Helen.[317] As we shall see, this correlation between a dead person's higher than normal status after death and the use of *chaire* to address him is also found elsewhere and is very significant. Despite Proteus' special status, Theoklymenos addresses his father's grave monument, not the dead father himself. Perhaps this betrays a certain reluctance to address a dead person with *chaire*, even though that person had superhuman status—at least when the salutation takes place in circumstances in which that superhuman status is not especially stressed.[318] Consequently, the notion that *chaire* was addressed to the deceased in archaic epitaphs can gain no support from the alleged practice of saying *chaire* to the deceased when passing a grave, which is later and cannot be legitimately projected back to the archaic period.

The belief that people greeted the deceased with *chaire* when they came to view the corpse and pay their respects during the prothesis is also adduced in support of the view that *chaire* could be addressed to the deceased in archaic epitaphs. But there is no evidence to support the hypothesis that such a salutation took place. On the contrary, the only example known to me of an exclamation inscribed on the representation of a prothesis on a funerary plaque (which was fastened to a grave monument)[319] is *oimoi*, on a black-figure plaque, Paris, Louvre MNB 905.[320] This is in harmony with the attitudes towards death and the dead in the archaic period. In fact, we saw, *oimoi* is also found in a series of epitaphs, as part of an address to the deceased. There is, therefore, a correspondence

---

[317] On Proteus' superhuman status: cf. Hom. *Od.* 4. 384–6 and esp., more directly comparable, Hdt. 2. 112–17. On the status of Proteus' tomb in the play cf. Kannicht 1969: *ad* 800–1; on the cult offered to Proteus cf. ibid. *ad* 547. On *Hel.* 1165 cf. Kannicht 1969: ad loc. who, however, despite the fact that he has commented extensively on the special status of Proteus' tomb, relates this *chaire* to the alleged custom of addressing the dead with *chaire*; he believes that grave epigrams show that from the 6th cent. onwards the dead were addressed with *chaire* by passers-by, basing himself on discussions the circularity of which I am here trying to demonstrate (he cites the discussion of the Teithronion epigram in Friedländer and Hoffleit 1948). Of the examples he quotes the only one earlier than the 4th cent. is this epigram. It is precisely because the address of Proteus' tomb with *chaire* is dependent on the tomb's special status (stressed by Kannicht himself (1969: *ad* 800–1)) that, as Dale remarks (1967: *ad* 1165) the greeting to the tomb 'takes the place' of the greeting to the *theoi patrooi* elsewhere.

[318] On the expression *chaire taphos Melites* in Hansen 1989: no. 530 (Peek 1960: 101) of *c.*365–40 BC, cf. Ch. III § ii.3*j*.

[319] On funerary plaques cf. the brief discussion in Kurtz and Boardman 1971: 83.

[320] Cf. Boardman 1955: 62 no. 28; 1974: fig. 265.

between the only attested exclamation at a prothesis and the address to the dead in archaic epitaphs, and both belong to the context of grief and express the negative approach towards death attested in the mainstream collective attitudes reflected in all archaic epitaphs.[321]

In these circumstances, it is clear that the hypothesis that *chaire* was addressed to the deceased during the prothesis is unwarranted; the little evidence available to us argues against it. In any case, even if it could be proved that the deceased was addressed with *chaire* during the prothesis, this would still not support the notion that *chaire* could have been addressed to the deceased on archaic epitaphs. For, while the expression of grief and lament through *oimoi* fits and has a comparable role in both contexts, since *chaire* does not pertain to this unchanged dimension of grief, pity, and lament, the hypothetical act of saying *chaire* to the dead in the prothesis would differ from the addressing of *chaire* to the deceased in epitaphs in significant ways. First, as in the Homeric instances, the act of addressing *chaire* to the deceased in the course of the prothesis would have been a momentary, time-bound act, while addressing *chaire* to the deceased in epitaphs would be attaching the word to him in a permanent way, and characterizing him forever by means of this word. Secondly, again as in the Homeric passages, the shade of the deceased during the prothesis is in the betwixt-and-between state, and could conceivably be still capable of being characterized by some elements pertaining to the living and not to the fully-dead. Finally, the high intensity collective ritual activity within which such a *chaire*-address

---

[321] I suspect that the notion that people said *chaire* to the dead when taking leave of him at the prothesis may have stemmed (implicitly and unconsciously) from an arbitrary decoding of the gestures (the raised arms and open mouths) of the men in prothesis representations (Cf. esp. the plaque Paris, Louvre MNB 905 just mentioned: cf. also the funerary plaque by Lydos in Athens, Vlasto Collection (*ABV* 113, 84; *Add.* 32)) combined with the expectation that they are saying something like 'farewell', which is implicitly translated as *chaire*, possibly under the influence of the Homeric passages discussed above—which in fact, we have seen, cannot support such an inference; and possibly also because in tragedy the dying often say *chaire/chairete* when taking leave of the world of the living (cf. e.g. Soph. *Aj.* 859–63; *Trach.* 920–2). In reality the two contexts are entirely different; the context 'the dying are saying farewell to the world of the living' is symbolically contrasted to 'the living are saying farewell to the dying/dead'; the former is symbolically related to the epitaphs in which the deceased addresses the passers-by with *chairete*—which is also symbolically contrasted to the living saying farewell to the dying/dead. (On these contrasts see below III.ii.3l.) The decoding of the gestures is also arbitrary and culturally determined. In reality, to judge by what we know about the tone of the prothesis, combined with the one inscribed *oimoi* on the Louvre plaque, they are much more likely to be exclaiming *oimoi* or *oimoi [o] Phrasikleia* (for example) or something related to it.

would be placed, characterized by mourning, sadness, and lament, would have had the power of directing the perception of the word *chaire*—assuming that it could be used in such circumstances—strongly towards the pole of its 'farewell' meaning and pushing away the meanings 'be well/rejoice' which were incompatible with the established attitudes towards the dead. Whereas these circumstances did not pertain to the inscription of the epitaph, to its composition as a permanent memorial of the deceased, or to its reading by the passer-by. In these circumstances, I submit that *chaire* could not have been selected for addressing the deceased in an archaic epitaph even if it could be shown to have been addressed to the dead during the prothesis—which, we saw, is very far from being the case.[322]

(d) *Fifth-century Athenian Public Epitaphs for the War Dead*

The only fifth-century example of *chaire/chairete* addressed to the dead is found in an Athenian public epitaph, probably the epigram for the Athenians who died in the battle of Tanagra, which begins *chairete aristees*.[323] I will now discuss briefly the attitudes associated with the Athenian war dead in the fifth century, which are reflected in, and shaped, the public collective epitaphs.[324] These attitudes contrast with those associated with the dead (including those who died in battle) in the archaic epitaphs. Thus, the occurrence of this *chairete* addressed to the dead in a fifth-century public collective epitaph cannot be used to support a claim that *chaire* could be addressed to the deceased in the archaic period. On the contrary, this occurrence argues against that claim. For the presence of an element in one type of funerary ideology does not support, but militates against, the assumption that the same element could be present in texts reflecting the opposite ideology. The attitudes towards the war dead reflected in these Athenian public epitaphs are the opposite of those of the archaic epitaphs. For in the official rhetoric reflected in them the death of these Athenian war dead is presented as inviting a positive response and excluding grief and lament. This places the *chairete* of the epitaph in the context of a

---

[322] Dr Oliver Taplin has kindly told me that in his view the fact that *chaire* does not occur in *threnoi* or similar contexts from the relevant period constitutes a strong *argumentum ex silentio* in favour of my thesis.

[323] Hansen 1983: 4; *GV* 14; Pritchett 1985: no. 25, pp. 180–1; Clairmont 1983: 138–9.

[324] I will not take the 4th cent. into account, because there appear to be certain differences in the mentality (cf. Loraux 1981: 114), and the matter is outside my present scope.

positive evaluation of the death of the people to whom it is addressed—in contrast to the negative perception of the death of the individuals commemorated in the archaic epitaphs. Moreover, and most importantly, in the fifth century the war dead were associated with three different kinds of immortality; thus the *chairete* of this epitaph is addressed to dead people of a special status.

The Athenian public collective epitaphs, like the concept and practice of public burial of the war dead, the *epitaphios logos*, and the sacrifices and other cult acts performed annually in honour of the war dead, are facets of a nexus of civic funerary ideology and behaviour (attributed by Thucydides (2. 34) to a *patrios nomos*[325]) which[326] was the product of Athenian democracy and crystallized into the form known to us probably in the early to middle 460s.[327] It goes further than simply glorifying death in the service of the polis: it excludes from the official rhetoric grief and lament for the war dead in favour of praise.[328] This is in striking contrast to archaic epitaphs, including the (private) epitaphs of men killed in war, which do include, indeed, are sometimes dominated by, grief and lament. The positive content of death in the service of one's country is not new, but now it is part of a nexus of attitudes in which the focus of the epitaph, and of the memory of the dead, has shifted from the individual to the polis. This changed the emphasis in the concept of death in battle, so that it became transformed, in the official rhetoric, into an entirely positive event, and was coupled with the important notion of the heroization of the war dead. In the archaic private epitaphs death is presented as an individual tragedy; the aim of the epitaph is to record this perception and preserve the memory of the individual. In the fifth-century Athenian public collective epitaphs[329]—as in the *epitaphioi logoi*—the

[325] Cf. also Thuc. 2. 34–6 on this nexus.

[326] On this ideology and behaviour cf. Loraux 1981: esp. 43–56, 100–5. On the ideology of good death in the service of the city cf. also Loraux 1982: 27–43; Vernant 1982: 45–76; 1990: 52–8. On the burial of the Greek war dead cf. Pritchett 1985: 94–259. On public burial in Athens cf. also: Stupperich 1977: *passim*, esp. 4–56, 62–70, 200–50; Clairmont 1983: *passim*; Jacoby 1956: 260–315. On polyandria cf. Stupperich 1977: *passim*, and esp. 26–31, 64–70; Kurtz and Boardman 1971: 108–21, 245–57, cf. also 198–9, cf. also Skiadas 1967: 49–61.

[327] On the date cf. esp. Pritchett 1985, 112–16; cf. also 117–21, and esp. 122–4; cf. also: Loraux 1981: 28–31; Stupperich 1977: 200–38; Wallace 1970: 102–3; cf. also Jacoby 1956: 284–7.

[328] Cf. Loraux 1981: 44–51, 54–6, 372 n. 193; Stupperich 1977: 14.

[329] On polyandria epitaphs cf. Pritchett 1985: 153 ff.; Lausberg 1982: 126–36, 434; Stup-

point of reference and ideological focus is the polis, rather than the individual dead men.[330] Thus, death in battle is a glorious event which elevates the war dead as a collectivity to a higher status, for it happens in the service of the city which validates the lives of the individuals; it does not invite grief and lament, but praise and glorification[331] of the dead, and through them of death in the service of the polis, which contributes to the glorification of the polis itself.[332] An expression such as *andras . . . polis hede pothei*[333] of the epitaph for those fallen at Poteidaia[334] is the nearest fifth-century Athenian public collective epitaphs ever came to an expression of regret at the men's death.[335] The private epitaphs of the fifth century, Athenian and other, continue to express grief and sorrow at the death of the person they commemorate.[336]

In the ideology reflected in these public epitaphs, the *epitaphioi*

perich 1977: 12–14, 67–70, 206–14; Peek 1960: 18–28; Loraux 1981: 54–60; Clairmont 1983: 87–91, 97–8, 105, 124–48, 165–77.

[330] Cf. Loraux 1981: 47.

[331] The epitaph which contains the word *chairete* (Hansen 1983: 4) appears as the epitome of this mentality, with a very dense clustering of elements of praise/glorification in its four lines: apart from *chairete*, there are also *aristees, polemo mega kydos echontes,* and *echsochoi hipposynai; cf. also pleistois Hellanon antia marnamenoi.*

[332] Cf. Loraux 1981: 43–56, cf. esp. 47. This change and its ideology have not always been clearly understood, and there is sometimes some confusion as to what changes took place and when in the expression of grief for the fallen in battle (cf. Skiadas 1967: 31; followed by Lorenz 1976: 43–4). In Skiadas (1967: 61) it is implied that the mentality behind polyandria epigrams was the same as that underlying individual epitaphs. This, of course, as is clear from even the short discussion included here, is manifestly erroneous (cf. esp. Loraux 1981: *passim*).

[333] On this notion cf. Vernant 1990: 41–50.

[334] Hansen 1983: 10; *GV* 20.

[335] Cf. also Stupperich 1977: 14 and n. 4; 13 nn., n. 4. The public epitaph Hansen 1983: 135 (*GV* 15; Meiggs and Lewis 1988: no. 35; a different restoration was proposed by Peek 1978: 18–19) where the word *penthos* is mentioned, is an Argive, not an Athenian, epitaph, for the Argives who fell in the battle at Tanagra. In the epitaph Hansen 1983: 5 (*GV* 17; Peek 1960: 10; Pfohl 1967: 90; Pritchett 1985: no. 28; cf. also Skiadas 1967: 53–61) the word *tlemones* is addressed to the dead, and there is some disagreement about its meaning. (Cf. the bibliog. on the controversy in Skiadas 1967: 55–6, though Skiadas' own view is erroneous (cf. n. 332 above, on a basic fallacy underlying his treatment of polyandria epitaphs).) Loraux, who does not discuss the matter, takes it to mean 'malheureux' (1981: 56 and n. 212). Stecher (1981: 33 and 77 n. 105) also translates 'ihr Armen' or 'ihr Unglücklichen'. Peek opted for 'Dulder ihr' (1960: 10). But Bowra (1938: 80–1) has argued convincingly that *tlemones* here must mean 'enduring ones'. And this interpretation is also adopted by Liddell and Scott (s.v.). This, well-established meaning of *tlemon* = 'patient, steadfast, stout-hearted' appears to be by far the most plausible one in *GV* 17—though the connotations of unhappiness probably also allowed the creation of an ambiguous resonance of (private) pity and of the sadness of the individual deaths.

[336] This is also true for at least some non-Athenian private epitaphs for warriors: cf. the epitaph from Kopai Boeotia (Hansen 1983: 114).

and the official nexus of behaviour towards the war dead, death in war elevates the dead to a higher status, confers on them different types of immortality. First, civic immortality through glory.[337] Second, heroization.[338] The problem of the heroization of the fifth-century war dead is complex; but there can be no doubt[339] that fifth-century Athens did confer heroization upon the men killed in battle. In the epitaph for the Athenians fallen in the battle of Poteidaia[340] (1, 5) the dead are associated with yet another type of immortality, celestial immortality,[341] a concept which originated in philosophical thought.[342] These associations of the war dead with immortality, especially of the first two types, which are firmly established in fifth-century Athenian ideology and funerary behaviour, give us the context in which *chairete* appears in a fifth-century public epitaph. Thus, as with Theoklymenos' salutation to his father's grave, there is a correlation between the use of *chaire* to address the deceased and the possession of a heroic/divine status by the deceased thus addressed. Consequently, far from supporting the view that *chaire* could have been used to address the deceased in archaic epitaphs, the use of *chairete* in this epitaph helps to show that such a usage would have been inappropriate and incongruous. I have not yet proved the correlation between the use of *chaire* to address the dead and the heroic or divine status of the dead thus addressed, but it is already clear that the funerary ideology reflected in the Athenian public epitaphs is antithetical to that of the archaic epitaphs, in which death brings only grief and sorrow and the dead

---

[337] Cf. Loraux 1981: 116.

[338] On the heroization of the war dead cf. esp. Loraux 1981: 28–30, 38–42. Cf. also: Stupperich 1977: 65–6 and 77 n., 65 nn. 6–7, 66 n. 1); Amandry 1971: 612–14, 620–5; Jacoby 1956: 265, 303; cf. also Boardman 1977: 43–5. On the definition of the concept of heroization of the war dead cf. Loraux 1981: 39–42. On the connection between heroization and the ideology of the Greek polis cf. Bérard 1982: 89–105.

[339] Cf. esp. Loraux 1981: 28–30 and 38–42.

[340] Hansen 1983: 10; *GV* 20; Peek 1960: 12; Pfohl 1967: 94; Pritchett 1985: 186 no. 31; Clairmont 1983: 174–7 no. 41.

[341] Cf. the comparable formulations in tragedy: Eur. fr. 971 N²; Eur., *Erechtheus* fr. 65. 71–4 (C. Austin 1968).

[342] On the celestial immortality of the war dead cf. Loraux 1981: 117; Dover 1974: 265. On immortality in the *aither* cf. also Eur. *Erechtheus* fr. 65. 71–4 Austin; and cf. Eur. fr. 971 N². On the concept of celestial immortality cf. Burkert 1972: 357–68; Nilsson 1967: 702–3; Garland 1985: 75, 159–60. Cf. also Cumont 1922: 91–109 *passim*. On celestial immortality on private epitaphs of different periods (from the 4th cent. BC onwards) cf. Lattimore 1962: 31–6; cf. also Peek 1941: 68–9.

arc to be pitied, and which reflect no belief in the achievement of a higher status after death.

(e) *An Orphic Tablet*

That the connection between *chaire* addressed to the deceased and the latter's achievement of immortality/heroization is not coincidental is suggested by the fact that a comparable correlation is also found in what may conceivably be[343] the second earliest text to address the deceased by means of *chaire*, one of the 'Orphic' tablets from Thurii.[344] It is the tablet A4 in Zuntz's classification[345] the text of which, like that of A1,[346] holds out the striking promise of actual deification; lines 3–6· (A4):

χαῖρε παθὼν τὸ πάθημα τὸ δ' οὔπω πρόσθ' ἐπεπόνθεις
θεὸς ἐγένου ἐξ ἀνθρώπου· ἔριφος ἐς γάλα ἔπετες.
χαῖρ⟨ε⟩ χαῖρε· δεξιὰν ὁδειπόρ⟨ει⟩
λειμῶνάς τε ἱερούς καὶ ἄλσεα Περσεφονείας.

This promise goes beyond anything else we know about Mysteric thought and belief in the classical period. It is an exceptional case which subverts the traditional system of Greek religion; it is paralleled in Empedokles' thought.[347]

(f) *Chaire Addressed to the Heroized/Deified Dead*

These two documents, the public epitaph and the Thurn tablet, contain what may be two of the earliest instances of *chaire/chairete* addressed to dead people; the epitaph is certainly the earliest. The fact that both show the use of *chaire* addressed to the deceased in

---

[343] Depending on the precise date of the text (cf. the next note) and on the date of two other inscriptions, both of which, in my view, are early 4th cent. at the earliest, but for which a claim of a late 5th-cent. date has been made.

[344] Among the extensive bibliog. on the tablets and mysteric and sectarian eschatology cf. esp. Nilsson 1974: 235–49; Zuntz 1971: 277–393; Burkert 1985: 290–304; 1975: 81–104; Zuntz 1976: 129–51, cf. esp. pp. 166–7 on promises of deification or heroization in the tablets; Graf 1982: 25–6; Lloyd-Jones 1990: 80–109. Tsantsanoglou and Parassoglou (1987: 3–17) have published two new gold leaves from Thessaly (on which cf. Lloyd-Jones 1990: 105–9). On the problem of the date of the tablet under consideration (possibly end of the 5th cent. BC, possibly middle of the 4th) cf. Burkert 1975: 104.

[345] Zuntz 1971: 328–33, 335–43.

[346] Cf. the comparison in Zuntz 1971: 335–43.

[347] VS 31B 146; 112. Burkert (1975: 101–4) suggested that the grave which contained A4, in which one person only was buried and which received cult, may have been the tomb of Lampon. On deification/heroization in the tablets cf. also Zuntz 1976: 146–8.

connection with the achievement of immortality/heroization/ deification for the deceased in question should not be too easily dismissed as a coincidence—especially since it is in harmony with certain uses of *chaire* in tragedy which I shall consider in a moment. Moreover, the two documents are the products of two entirely different environments,[348] and differ from each other with regard to the nature of the text, its function and content, in fact in everything except in their expression of a positive perception of death and in the fact that they reflect an ideology in which the dead are promised immortality/heroization in the one case, and immortality/deification in the other. This difference in their contexts of production reduces very considerably the plausibility of the hypothesis that the connection between immortality and *chaire* addressed to dead people is due to coincidence. And even this implausible hypothesis cannot account for the fact that, as we shall see, the use of *chaire* in tragedy conforms exactly to the same pattern. Furthermore, the implausibility of the coincidence hypothesis is greatly increased when we consider the meaning of the word *chaire* in the two documents. It is not possible to demonstrate conclusively that in the epitaph the greeting included a 'rejoice' element, but in the case of the Thurii tablet the 'rejoice' meaning is unambiguous, and fits the context of immortality.[349] *Chaire* in A4 is an acclamation which both precedes and follows the statement 'you have become a god', and which corresponds to *olbie kai makariste* in A1.[350] Zuntz suggested[351] that the acclamation is a ritual formula which attributes the status of god to the deceased—he believes the tablets 'contain main items . . . of a Pythagorean *Missa pro defunctis* celebrated at the burial of those who took the tablets with them to the other world'.[352] Whether or not the tablets reflected a ritual, of whatever 'denomination', the validity of Zuntz's central suggestion appears incontrovertible. The acclamation by means of *chaire* undoubtedly makes sense in this context if it is interpreted as the acclamation of deification, like that by means of *olbie kai makariste* in A1.[353] In the

---

[348] One expressing the official ideology of the Athenian polis, the other reflecting Mysteric beliefs, which, as it happens, appear to be connected with Eleusis (cf. Burkert 1975: 100–4).

[349] Cf. esp. Burkert's trans. (1975: 96; 1985: 295).

[350] Cf. Zuntz 1971: 331.

[351] Ibid. 343.

[352] Ibid. But cf. on these tablets Burkert 1975: 93–104.

[353] On *olbie kai makariste* and *makarismos* in general: cf. Snell 1966: 84–5; Richardson 1974: 313–14 *ad* 480; cf. also Seaford 1981: 260; on *olbios* cf. also Leveque 1982: 113–26.

new tablets from Thessaly, which have definite similarities with both A1 and A4,[354] *trisolbic* follows the formulation *nyn ethanes* and *nyn egenou* with which the text begins.

It is interesting that there is another case, in a very different context, in which *chairein* is part of an announcement that will eventually lead to heroization. In Pindar, *Pythian* 4. 60–3, Battos is addressed by the Pythia at Delphi, who announces to him that he will be the oecist and king of Cyrene, a destiny and status that will lead to his future heroization after his death: *ha se chairein estris audasaisa pepromenon basile' amphanen Kyranai*. The view that *chaire* is not appropriate for addressing the ordinary dead before some time in the fourth century, and that before that time it is only the dead who attained a heroic or divine status after death who were so addressed, is confirmed by the use of *chaire* to address the dead or dying in tragedy, to which we now turn.

(g) The Tragic Use

We saw that the only grave monument addressed with *chaire* in tragedy was that of Proteus, who had attained a heroic/divine status after his death, which the play makes clear. We shall now see that this usage is part of a wider pattern: the only dead or dying people to be addressed with *chaire* in tragedy are those who, the play tells us, attain special status after death. *Chaire* is never addressed to anyone either about to die or dead to whom such special status is not assigned. It is not even addressed to Herakles in Sophocles' *Trachiniai*, which is correlative with the fact that his apotheosis is 'bracketed', not signalled, in the world of the play—though the audience's knowledge of it placed the action on the stage in its wider, cosmic, framework that deconstructed—though it did not neutralize—Herakles' suffering.

In Euripides' *Alcestis* 997–1005 the chorus address Alcestis and ascribe her divine status, in a context that reminds us of a deification acclamation; in v. 1004 she is addressed with *chaire – chair' o potni—* at the conclusion of the second antistrophe, which is reminiscent of the tablet acclamation through which divine status was attributed to the deceased (vv. 994–1005).

---

[354] Cf. Tsantsanoglou and Parassoglou 1987: 5, 1–3.

μηδὲ νεκρῶν ὡς φθιμένων χῶμα νομιζέσθω
τύμβος σᾶς ἀλόχου, θεοῖσι δ᾽ ὁμοίως
τιμάσθω, σέβας ἐμπόρων.
καί τις δοχμίαν κέλευθον
ἐμβαίνων τόδ᾽ ἐρεῖ·
αὗτα ποτὲ προὔθαν᾽ ἀνδρός,
νῦν δ᾽ ἐστὶ μάκαιρα δαίμων·
χαῖρ᾽, ὦ πότνι᾽, εὖ δὲ δοίης.
τοῖαί νιν προσεροῦσι φᾶμαι.

It is in the light of this deification explicitly ascribed to Alcestis by
the chorus eventually that we must perceive the *chaire* the chorus
addressed to the dead Alcestis at v. 743,[355] and by Pheres at vv. 626–
7. The latter salutation, *chaire, kan Haidou domois eu soi genoito*, is a
transformation of the Homeric formulation discussed above, here
used for a dead woman of exceptional status. In Euripides, *Orestes*
1673–4, we observe a similar address through *chaire* to one newly
'dead'—or rather not-dead (see 1631–8)—and deified, Menelaos'
address to Helen who has appeared in epiphany with Apollo:

ὦ Ζηνὸς Ἑλένη χαῖρε παῖ· ζηλῶ δέ σε
θεῶν κατοικήσασαν ὄλβιον δόμον.

In Euripides, *Hippolytos* 1437, Artemis uses *chaire* when taking
her leave of the dying Hippolytos,[356] after she has announced that
he will receive cult after his death (1423–30). So here also, in the
mouth of a deity, we find a correlation between *chaire* and heroization. In Euripides, *Erechtheus* fr. 53.33 and *Heraclids* 600, *kai chaire*
is addressed to a girl who is about to be sacrificed to Persephone.
Erechtheus' daughter will be deified. For Makaria also a pattern of
exceptionality pertains: in vv. 600–1 the *chaire* address is placed
firmly in the context of Makaria's consecration:

καὶ χαῖρε· δυσφημεῖν γὰρ ἄζομαι θεάν,
ᾗ σὸν κατῆρκται σῶμα, Δήμητρος κόρην

Iolaos is saying 'I say *chaire* and not, as I normally would, words of
pity and lamentation, for I stand in awe of the goddess to whom
your body is consecrated, so I do not want to speak words of ill
omen, that is, the words of lamentation that are appropriate since

---

[355] Cf. also *chairousa* in v. 436.
[356] The fact that *chaire* is used here primarily in the sense of 'farewell' does not alter the
fact that, on the argument put forward here, it could not be used unless it were appropriate.

you are going to die'.[357] This passage also confirms that one did not address the dying or dead with *chaire*, except when they had attained or were about to attain, heroic or divine status, in which case *chaire* was appropriate, indeed it was part of the vocabulary through which that higher status was proclaimed; another, not unrelated exception was that of a person about to die consecrated to a deity.

(i) Chaire *and the Attainment of a Higher Status after Death*

The view that until some time in the fourth century *chaire* was not appropriate for the common dead, but only for the exceptional ones, is strengthened by the fact that one of the main uses of *chaire* was to address deities and other supernatural beings in invocations, salutations and the like. This use is too well established to need discussion.[358] Thus the observed pattern of addressing *chaire* only to those dead people who had achieved heroic or divine status in afterlife makes perfect sense in terms of the word's established usage: it is one particular application of the common usage of addressing divine and heroic beings with *chaire*. This harmony between the observed pattern of *chaire* addressed to the dead (and dying) an an established major use of *chaire* provides some confirmation for the validity of that pattern. I submit, therefore, that *chaire* was first addressed to the heroized/deified dead, and that its use was later

---

[357] *Dysphemein* here does not mean 'speak ill of' (as in LSJ) or 'curse' (as in the Loeb trans.); for in that case the *gar* does not make sense. It means 'use words of ill omen', as lamentation would be, the same as in Aesch. *Ag.* 1078–9, which in fact expresses a notion which, in one of its facets, is very close to the meaning I am proposing for *Heracl.* 600–1.

[358] It is commonly used in the Homeric Hymns: cf. e.g. *Hom.H.Apollo* 14; *Hom.H.Hermes* 579 (cf. *Hom.H.* 18. 10); *Hom.H.Aphr.* 292; *Hom.H.* 6. 19; 7. 58; 9. 7; 11. 5; 13. 3; 14. 6; 16. 5; 17. 5; 19. 48. Cf. a brief discussion of the use of *chaire* in the Homeric Hymns: Miller 1979: 176–8, and cf. 186 n. 44 on the use of *chairete* in Pi. *I.* 1. 32; Bundy 1972: 49–54; Race 1982: 8–9. It is also, of course, used elsewhere: cf. e.g. Alcaeus fr. 308B (L.-P.); Pind. fr. 33c Snell–Maehler; cf. *PMG* fr. 885. Epigraphically it appears also in a 6th-cent. BC dedication to Herakles in Lucania, inscribed on a clay pillar: Hansen 1983: 396; *IG* xiv. 652; Friedländer and Hoffleit 1948: no. 111 (and see p. 107). *Chaire* is also used to address the Underworld divinities in tragedy: cf. Aesch. *TrGF* iii. F 228. On *chaire Charon* addressed to the infernal ferryman cf. Ch. VI. The formulation *chaire, o hiereu* which concludes the dedicatory inscription on a bronze bull-head rhyton of Oriental origin from the Heraion of Samos (of *c*.600, on which a Greek inscription was incised late in the first quarter or early in the second quarter of the 6th cent. (Homann-Wedeking 1966: 159 and fig. 2; 1969: 553–4; Kyrieleis 1983: 20 fig. 8)) though it does not belong to the category '*chaire* addressed to divine and heroic beings', is semantically connected with that usage by the fact that it is used in a dedicatory inscription to address a priest; it can be seen as a transformation of that usage, its application to humans with a special connection to the gods.

extended to other dead people, when the concept of heroization in the afterlife was extended and eventually became a somewhat routine notion. In these circumstances, the view that *chaire* could be addressed to the pitiful dead of the archaic epitaphs who are not associated with an ideology involving heroization or deification is extremely implausible. This can be strongly illustrated by the Thurii tablet, in which *chaire* was part of an acclamation attributing divine status to the deceased, and thus differentiated him from the ordinary dead, and assimilated him to divine beings. A formulation that had that role could not have been addressed to the pitiful dead of the archaic epitaphs who were not associated with heroization or deification. *Chaire* as understood here could naturally perform these functions.

(j) *Fourth-century and Later Epitaphs and the Use of* Chaire *Addressed to the Dead*

I will begin with the two texts for which a fifth-century date has been suggested. First, an inscription on a limestone grave stele, from Macedonia,[359] reads as follows: *hye Chionos chaire Chionide, enthade kef.* Its date is not certain. J. and L. Robert considered it to be a 'fragment d'épitaphe tardive'.[360] Bingen[361] dated it to the end of the fifth/early fourth century and Sacco[362] considers it to be not later than the beginning of the fourth century; Hansen[363] gives 'saec. IV in.?'. Professor David Lewis kindly tells me that he considers its most likely date to be the early fourth century. In any case, the fact that Macedonia had still at this time a somewhat marginal position in the Greek world entails that we should not assume that its funerary attitudes and practices were necessarily identical to those of the rest in every particular, and therefore that we should not necessarily expect exact chronological correspondence in all developments. The second problematic inscription is *IG* ii/iii². 3. 2. 12837 (Epigraphical Museum, Athens 8864; here Pl. 1), on a stele with a pediment, and it reads: *chaire Hyla.* This inscription is normally dated to the fifth century, but there are serious objections against such a date. The stele is reused. Dr C.

[359] Hansen 1989: 719; *SEG* 27 (1977), 296.
[360] Robert and Robert 1978: no. 294.
[361] *SEG* 27 (1977), 296.
[362] Sacco 1978: 76.
[363] Hansen 719.

Dallas has kindly let me know that in his view the original stele of which the *chaire Hyla* stele is a reused part would have to have been of a type that belongs at the earliest in the fourth century. This gives us a *terminus post quem* for the reuse of the stele and the inscription. Professor David Lewis has kindly told me that he does not believe that the letters need to be fifth century, and that they could have been produced later. In these circumstances, the fifth-century date appears highly implausible. Given that the myth of the hero Hylas was well known in classical Athens,[364] and given that he was one of the youths whose abduction by supernatural females was a metaphor for the death of a young person, the inscription may have marked the grave of a youth called Hylas and have functioned as a means of metaphorical identification of the dead youth with the hero. *Chaire Hyla* could have been read as a salutation to the hero, appropriate for the grave of a youth called Hylas, which blurred imperceptibly into a salutation to the dead youth, thus expressing allusively the hope of the latter's potential (or fantasized) elevation to a higher status. All this would fit extremely well with the types of attitude that, as will become clear, appear in fourth-century epitaphs. The first definitely dated appearances of *chaire* addressed to the deceased in a private epitaph are in two epitaphs of the middle of the fourth century BC, the epitaphs for Epinike[365] and for Philokydis.[366] I will consider them briefly after I have said something about fourth-century BC epitaphs in general and thus placed the appearance of *chaire* in the two epigrams in its proper framework.

Fourth-century BC private epitaphs show less uniformity in the attitudes they reflect than earlier epitaphs. For example, some express grief explicitly and strongly;[367] others contain more restrained expressions of regret.[368] A more positive view of death in youth than was traditionally the case in epitaphs is presented in the

---

[364] Cf. e.g. the Mysian lament for Hylas referred to in Aesch. *Pers.* 1055 (cf. Hesych. s.v. *epiboa to Mysion*); the fruitless search for Hylas is probably referred to in Ar. *Ploutos* 1127 (cf. Schol. Ar. *Ploutos* 1127; cf. also Apost. 8. 34).

[365] Hansen 1989: 655; GV 1385; Peck 1941: 66–7 no. 14.

[366] Hansen 1989: 522; Clairmont 1970: Appendix ii, 169–70; Daux 1972: 565. The authenticity of this stele has been doubted (by H. Hiller, in her review of Clairmont (1970), in *Gnomon* 47 (1975), 592, citing also H. Möbius); but the grounds for this do not appear convincing (cf. also Hansen op. cit.).

[367] Cf. e.g. Hansen 1989: 515, 518, 695.

[368] Cf. e.g. Hansen 1989: 511, 564, 501.

epitaph Hansen 1989: 489.[369] This contrasts with the very negative perception of the deceased's death (possibly in youth and unmarried[370]) in the epitaph Hansen 1989: 495. More importantly for our purposes, some fourth century private epitaphs contain (sometimes veiled) expressions of hope for the afterlife.[371] There are even expectations of immortality on Olympos,[372] and of celestial immortality; the latter is promised on the epitaph Hansen 1989: 535, which is to be compared with the collective epitaph Hansen 1983: 10 which, we saw above, promises celestial immortality to the Athenians fallen at Poteidaia.[373] The epitaph Hansen 1989: 535 runs as follows:

Εὐρυμάχου ψυχὴν καὶ ὑπερφιάλος διανοίας
αἰθὴρ ὑγρὸς ἔχει, σῶμα δὲ τύνβος ὅδε

Compare the public epitaph (Hansen 1983: 10):

αἰθὲρ μὲμ φσυχὰς ὑπεδέχσατο, σόμ[ατα δὲ χθὸν

Thus what was reserved for the heroized war dead of the public epitaphs in the fifth century is now extended to ordinary ones, as, on my argument, is the case with *chaire* addressed to the dead. A comparable contrast between the material remains of the deceased

---

[369] And compare Menander, fr. 125 Edmonds. For a more positive perception of death in old age cf. Hansen 1989: 601 (a traditional perception of 'good death'); the epitaph Hansen 1989: 477 from Aigaleo (Attica).

[370] Cf. Clairmont 1970: 141–2 on no. 63 for the argument in favour of this view.

[371] Cf. e.g. Hansen 1989: 603, 571, 575. Clairmont (1970: 140–1) believes that the epigram Hansen 1989: 575 dated to the second half of the 4th cent., 'flatly ... contradicts ... the often expressed thesis that heroization or deification played a substantial part in the cult of the dead during the fourth century'. But this view (which shows that Clairmont has not taken account of the diversity of 4th-cent. epitaphs) is mistaken and somewhat simplistic. What the epitaph shows is awareness of the existence of the notion of deification for mortals, a notion which we know in any case had been in existence in mysteric environments by that time; and a reticence to apply such notions to this particular deceased, other than in a very indirect way. For a 4th-cent. Greek when reading the lines *ei themis en, thneten enarithmion hagneuousan athanatais nomisai* would conjure up the frame 'deification for mortals' and thus obliquely think of the deceased in those terms. The mirror image of this is valid for the epitaph's composition. In any case, even if one were to accept, for a moment, Clairmont's misguided hypothesis of rejection, this rejection would be very limited. First, it would be only a rejection of deification, not of heroization. The two notions are related but distinct, and must not be confused. And second, it would be a rejection in this particular case, by the particular people involved with this epitaph, and could have told us nothing about the notions held by other circles of people whose beliefs are reflected in 4th-cent. epitaphs.

[372] Cf. Hansen 1989: 558. Cf. Dover 1974: 265.

[373] Hansen 1989: 535 is the epitaph for Eurymachos, from before the middle of the 4th cent. On this epitaph cf. Dover 1974: 265. On the Poteidaia epigram cf. § ii.3d above.

and his *psyche* is also found in other fourth century epitaphs, for example the epitaph Hansen (1989: 545):

ὀστέα μὲν καὶ σάρκας ἔ{ι}χει χθὼν παῖδα τὸν ἡδύν,
ψυχὴ δὲ εὐσεβέων οἴχεται εἰς θάλαμον

A different type of contrast is seen in Chrysanthe's epitaph,[374] in which *soma men entos ge katechei* is not contrasted to *psyche de*, but to *ten sophrosynen de . . . ten sen* (which *ou katekrypse taphos*): the fate of the body is contrasted not to that of the soul, but to the survival of the deceased's (good) memory.[375] There is even the rather strange (for classical Greece) formulation *ek gaias blaston gaia palin gegona*,[376] a concept which in an epitaph of the third century BC[377] (which begins with *chaire* addressed to the deceased) is associated with what seem to be oblique references to immortality/ deification.[378]

Fourth-century epitaphs also display greater variety of content, form and formulations than had hitherto been the case; this is connected with the fourth-century enlargement of their themes and motifs.[379] The literary development of the genre is only one of the reasons for this diversity. Changes in the social and ideological conditions and norms also affected the composition of epitaphs. One of the factors that are correlative with this shift is the change in the composition of the group which commissioned grave monuments: now a much greater number of people, from a wider spectrum of society than before, had grave monuments. Another may be the increase in the impact on the Greek collective representations of eschatological beliefs of mysteric and sectarian origin. Finally, the shift of emphasis in the grave monuments of the fourth century

---

[374] Hansen 1989: 479.
[375] The same contrast of the fate of the body to the survival of the deceased's memory is found in Hansen 1989: 611 (cf. Daux: 1972: 544 on no. 37; 554 on no. 54). Cf. also the related type, Hansen 1989: 549.
[376] Hansen 1989: 482.
[377] GV 1126; Peek 1960: 220.
[378] Cf. also the much later epitaph GV 1941 (Peek 1960: 451).
[379] Cf. Gentili 1968: 54; cf. also Alexiou 1974: 106. Gragg 1910: 301; 38 remarks on the individualistic tone of the 4th-cent. epitaphs. Some of the changes mentioned here first appear in the late 5th cent.; but the shift does not come to full fruition and crystallization until the 4th cent. Daux 1973/4: 242 remarks that while in the archaic period the funerary epigrams are short, and do not philosophize, in the 4th cent. they reflect more learned beliefs and distinguish between benevolent and cruel divinities; before long they will be chattering and holding forth. On the shifts in the late 5th and 4th cents. see also Lausberg 1982: 137.

(starting at the end of the fifth and most clearly observed in Athens) away from the public sphere and values, and towards the family, and family values which are now stressed[380] would have entailed that the different funerary attitudes of the different families (belonging to different circles and subscribing to different funerary ideologies) came to be reflected in these epitaphs. Thus, some fourth-century funerary epigrams expressed beliefs and representations of death that diverged from those of the earlier epitaphs which expressed the established ideology of the significant group, in the archaic period the dominant ethos of the aristocracy.[381] Let us consider the two mid-fourth-century epitaphs in which the deceased is addressed with *chaire*. The epitaph for Epinike[382] reads as follows:

χαῖρε 'Επινίκη
Φίλτωνος θύγατερ Με|νδαίου καὶ Θεοτίμης,
οὓς ἀπέλειπες | ἄπαιδας ἐν οἰκτροῖς πένθεσι γήρως.

The emphasis is on family relationships, which is in harmony with the spirit of fourth-century grave monuments. The formulations are part of the normal epigrammatic repertory.[383] The epitaph of Philokydis[384] reads as follows:

Τιμαγόρας θύγατερ καὶ 'Αριστοκλέους Φιλοκυδί, |
χαῖρε· ποθεῖ σε Εὔκλεια ἥν ἔλιπες προγόνοις.

The emphasis is again on the family. The word *pothei* which we found in the fifth century in a public epitaph,[385] in the formulation *andras . . . polis pothei* applied to the war dead, is here used to refer

---

[380] Cf. Humphreys 1983: 104–18.

[381] With very rare exceptions in the 5th cent., explicitly setting themselves apart, such as the Kyme funerary inscription of *c*.450 (?) which is not in fact an actual epitaph (Jeffery 1990: 240 no. 12, 409 pl. 48 no. 12).

[382] Hansen 1989: 655.

[383] The expression *hous apeleipes apaidas en oiktrois penthesi geros*, is very clearly an adaptation of the formulation, frequently found in epitaphs, expressing the concept that the dead person 'left grief' to the survivors, usually the parents: cf. e.g. the 5th-cent. epitaph for Mnesagora and Nikochares (Hansen 1983: 84), 1.3: *patri philoi kai metri liponte amphoim mega penthos*. Cf. *penthos oiktron*, as in our epitaph, in the epitaph for Pausimache (first quarter of the 4th cent.) (Hansen 1989: 518). Cf. *penthos* in: e.g. Hansen 1989: 513 (early 4th cent.); Hansen 1989: 529 (*c*.360–50, cf. Daux 1972: 549); cf. also Hansen 1989: 593 (*GV* 1889). This is a variant of an expression already found in Homer: cf. *Il.* 17. 37 *tokeusi goon kai penthos ethekas*; cf. also, e.g. Hansen 1983: 113 and Hansen 1983: 50 (Willemsen 1963: 136–9 no. 8).

[384] Hansen 1989: 522; Clairmont 1970: Appendix ii. 169–70; Daux 1972: 565.

[385] Hansen 1983: 10. 10.

to the feelings of the deceased's daughter Eukleia.[386] There is nothing in either epitaph to show that the deceased belonged to a sect which promised immortality—heroization or deification—to its members.[387] This does not necessarily mean that there are no elements in the epitaphs which would have signalled such an adherence to a fourth-century reader. If I am right about the link between addressing *chaire* to the deceased and immortality/ heroization/deification, this *chaire* addressed to the deceased may have reflected that adherence, and thus allowed the epitaph's contemporaries to 'place' it within that particular eschatological context. If this is right, the belief that the deceased achieved immortality may have been expressed in the epitaphs of Epinike and of Philokydis, and perhaps also in the fragmentary epitaph for Chionides, in a manner opaque to the modern eye. If Epinike, Philokydis, and Chionides had been members of a sect promising heroization or deification, their being addressed with *chaire* in their epitaphs would be an extension in the use of the deification formula of the tablets, and presumably the ritual, which recorded in a permanent form and advertised the deceased's new status, by inscribing it on the grave monument which represents the deceased in the world of the living and is the focus of his memory. Certainly, as we saw, other fourth-century funerary epigrams did record on the grave monument the notion that the deceased has achieved immortality/heroization.

Chaire addressed to the dead becomes common in private epitaphs from the third century BC onwards.[388] Notions of immortality/heroization applied to the ordinary dead made their first appearance in fourth-century epitaphs but only became fre-

---

[386] On the appearance of the motif of *pothos* in the context of grief cf. Vernant 1990: 41–50.

[387] It cannot be excluded that the fact that the deceased's daughter bears the name Eukleia may hint at Philokydis' adherence to one of the sects in which Eukles was one of the main deities, as is seen in the 'Orphic' tablets mentioned above, where Eukles is one of the divine triad (on Eukles: Zuntz 1971: 310). Eukleia is also an epithet of Artemis, and she is also an independent figure (on Eukleia and Artemis Eukleia: cf. Nilsson 1967: 493–4; Braund 1980: 184–5; on Eukleia cf. also Andronikos 1984: 24, 49–51). But since normally theophoric names involve a modified form of the theonym, rather than the theonym itself, she is more likely to have been named after Eukles than after Eukleia. However, we cannot exclude that her name was simply based on the common noun *eukleia* without reference to any theonym.

[388] Cf. Pouilloux 1960: 160; Klaffenbach 1966: 58–9; Couilloud 1974: 486; Kaloyeropoulou 1974: 290–1; cf. Pircher 1979: 74 no. 6.

quent from the third century BC onwards.[389] Thus the pattern of
appearance of immortality/heroization for the ordinary dead in
private epitaphs coincides exactly with the pattern of appearance
of the word *chaire* addressed to the deceased in such epitaphs. This
adds further support to the thesis proposed here.

Once the use of
chaire addressed to the deceased was established in the context of
the funerary ideology of immortality/heroization, which became
increasingly a routine one, the direct link between such beliefs and
the use of *chaire* to address the dead eventually lapsed.[390] When
notions of immortality/heroization became common, *chaire* was
addressed to dead people often enough for it to become a *topos*;
after that it was probably used generally, not only when a particular
deceased person subscribed to beliefs promising immortality.
Explicit references to immortality/heroization together with *chaire*
addressed to the deceased are sometimes found in later epitaphs,[391]
but as both had become common by this time this need not be
significant. It is likely that the link had lapsed at least by the third
century BC. It cannot be excluded that the connection between
chaire addressed to the dead and immortality had lapsed already in
the fourth century or, at least, was not necessarily present in every
epitaph in which *chaire* was addressed to the dead; the fact that beliefs

---

[389] On immortality/heroization in general, and in the 4th cent. BC, Hellenistic and
Graeco-Roman in particular cf. Nilsson 1967: 715–19; 1974: 115–17, 137–45, 232–3; Rohde
1925: 542–3; Nock 1972: 842–3; Lattimore 1962: 31–6, 48–54; cf. 97–9, 342. Cf. also
100–1 on deification. Cf. Plato, *Laws* 927a; Arist., fr. 44. And cf. some examples: *GV* 1128,
842, 1157, 1822, 1755; IG ii². 8870. The distinction must be stressed between promises
for a happy afterlife such as that found in *Hom.H.Dem.* vv. 480–2 and promises of
immortality/heroization/deification. It is only in the latter contexts that we find the earlier
use of *chaire* addressed to dead people. For a discussion of the controversy on 4th cent.
heroization with bibliog. cf. Clairmont 1970: 64–71. In discussing heroization in, or rather
as he sees it, the absence of references to heroization from, Attic epitaphs (though he does
not deny that there was (p. 69): 'a general tendency towards heroization in Attica during the
fourth century') Clairmont leaves out the consideration of the related beliefs in immortality
(e.g. celestial immortality) for which there is definite evidence from 4th-cent. Attica. Also,
he disregards veiled references to hope for a more elevated status in afterlife and thinks, as
others do, that if references to heroization/deification are not as explicit as they are in later
times they are not there at all. This approach disregards the possibility that reticences (truly
felt or rhetorical) may have been attendant on stating publicly and permanently, with
reference to oneself/one's 'other' (i.e. ordinary mortals), notions previously only expressed
in the epitaphs of the exceptional dead.

[390] In later epitaphs sometimes the *chaire* addressed to the dead is combined with
heroization/immortality (cf. e.g. *GV* 699, 1334) and sometimes it is found in epitaphs which
appear to exclude such beliefs (cf. e.g. *GV* 847).

[391] Cf. previous note and cf. the epitaph for Myrto (3rd/2nd cent. BC: *GV* 1390; Peek
1960: 221); cf. also the epitaph for Diogenes (3rd cent. BC: *GV* 1126; Peek 1960: 220).

in immortality/heroization for the ordinary dead were reflected in these epitaphs may have sanctioned a more general use of *chaire* addressed to the dead which, on my thesis, had been associated with such beliefs. But the epitaph for Melite,[392] dated *c.*365–40 BC, suggests otherwise. This epitaph which begins *chaire, taphos Melites,* does not address the deceased herself with *chaire.* It is closer to Theoklymenos' salutation to his father's grave monument. This addressing of *chaire* to the grave, the shift from the address to the grave to the address to the deceased, and the fact that the deceased replies to the latter with *kai sy chaire, philtat' andron,* as though the initial *chaire* had been addressed to her rather than to her grave, suggest, I believe, a reticence, a holding back from addressing *chaire* directly to the deceased. Thus this epitaph appears to show awareness of a type of epitaph which addressed the deceased by means of *chaire,* but to have modified that type, perhaps under the influence of a model such as Theoklymenos' salutation, precisely in order to avoid using *chaire* to address the deceased. In my view, at this time, the deceased was addressed with *chaire* when (s)he was believed to have attained immortality/heroization, while the modification seen in Melite's epitaph was probably used in epitaphs which did not reflect such beliefs.

(k) *Words and Meanings*

If *chaire* was not a salutation empty of specific meaning, but was felt to include the wish 'be well/rejoice' it would make perfect sense, and thus confirm the validity of the empirically observed pattern of its usage, that it should not be addressed to dead people except when they are believed to have attained immortality. For in that case *chaire* would have been appropriate to the living, to the gods and to the heroized dead, but not to the ordinary dead, since in Greek mentality death is a pitiful condition[393] antithetical to joy and well-being. Whether or not the meanings 'I wish you/be well and/or rejoice'[394] were always felt they certainly could be activated by the context, as is made clear by several literary passages. Two such examples, to which I will return, are Eur. *Or.* 1083–4:

---

[392] Hansen 1989: 530; *GV* 1387; Pircher 1979: 39–41 no. 12; Clairmont 1970: no. 39; cf. Daux 1972: 545.
[393] More or less pitiful; from the archaic period on it depends on the particular version of eschatology involved in each case.
[394] Cf. Latacz 1966: 47–52.

χαῖρ᾽· οὐ γὰρ ἡμῖν ἔστι τοῦτο, σοί γε μήν·
οἱ γὰρ θανόντες χαρμάτων τητώμεθα.

and Astydamas II, TrGF F5:

χαῖρ᾽, εἰ τὸ χαίρειν ἔστι τοῖς κάτω χθονός·
δοκῶ δ᾽ ὅτῳ γὰρ μὴ ἔστι λυπεῖσθαι βίῳ,
ἔστιν τὸ χαίρειν τῶν κακῶν λελησμένῳ.

The following considerations suggest that the meanings 'I wish you be well and/or rejoice' were felt and heard in the salutations *chaire/chairete*.[395] As we saw, *chaire* does include the meaning 'be well/rejoice' in Homer; at the other end of the chronological spectrum, Lucian's *De lapsu* indicates that, while by his time the use of *chaire* was restricted to certain set times and occasions, it was felt to include the connotation 'rejoice'.[396] Moreover, *chaire/chairete* does include the meaning 'rejoice/take pleasure' when addressed to deities in hymns,[397] one of the salutation's major usages. As Bundy stressed,[398] there are passages in literature which make it unambiguously clear that *chaire/chairete* includes the connotation 'rejoice' even when used as a normal salutation (as opposed to a hymnal one). But it is not possible to be certain that this meaning has not been simply activated by the context; that it was implicit, though not necessarily always heard, irrespective of context. However, it is in any case likely that in the archaic epitaphs these connotations would indeed have been activated by the context. It is possible to argue that, given the influence of the epics on epitaphs, the Homeric usage of *chaire* addressed to the dead Patroklos may have established an intertextual frame which interposed itself between the epitaph writers (and readers) and any possible use of

[395] The meaning of *chaire* is 'be well/rejoice' (cf. Latacz 1966: 47–52; Bundy 1972: 49–54; cf. Laks 1982: 214–20, esp. on *chairon ithi* and the like). It is also used in contexts in which it performs the function, and takes on the meaning, of certain other English words. Thus (I am following here the categories recognized in LSJ s.v.), on meeting someone, *chaire* performs the function of 'hail', 'welcome'; at leave-taking, 'farewell' (cf. Bond 1963: 126 on *kai chaire* as an ending to Euripides' farewell speeches); and on other occasions, 'be of good cheer, good luck/farewell' (cf. also Lloyd-Jones 1973: 123) and the like. The fact that *chaire* performs these functions does not entail that in those contexts it has lost the meaning 'rejoice', but that this semantic nucleus 'rejoice' performs certain specific functions in which the context of the exhortation as well as its content is of importance and in this way it acquires specialized meanings.

[396] Cf. Lucian, *De lapsu* esp. 5, 6, 12.

[397] Cf. Bundy 1972: 49–54; cf. also Race 1982: 8–9.

[398] Bundy 1972: 50.

chaire to address the dead in epitaphs, connecting any such potential use with the meaning 'rejoice', qualified by 'even though you are dead'. If this is right, it would reinforce my argument that the element 'rejoice' would have been present in any use of *chaire* to address the dead; and that this made *chaire* inappropriate for addressing the dead in the archaic epitaphs because it clashed with the attitudes reflected in them. This Homeric intertextual frame would have further blocked the possibility of any such usage being thought up by an archaic epitaph-writer also for another reason: because in it the use of *chaire* to address the dead is characterized as exceptional. It could be argued, incidentally, that, given the epic influence on archaic funerary epigrams, we might have expected them to have made frequent use of these Homeric verses, or of some part or variation of them, unless there was some strong reason that prevented such usage; for, on the face of it, and if we ignore the case I have been building up here, they sound suitable material for epitaphs. In fact, these verses, adaptations and segments of them, do appear in much later (Hellenistic and later) funerary epigrams, after it had become common to address the deceased with *chaire*.[399] Therefore, the fact that no such example has survived from the archaic period may perhaps be taken to provide tentative support for the thesis that there was some strong reason that prevented the dead of the archaic epitaphs from being addressed with *chaire*.

The presence and strength of the semantic core 'rejoice' in *chaire* was reinforced by the fact that *chairein* was a common Greek word, which meant that the identity of *chaire* as a form of the verb 'rejoice' formed an important parameter in its perception, selection and reception. To put it minimally, even if we were to suppose that the connotation 'rejoice' was not necessarily consciously felt, the word was nevertheless placed within the semantic field of rejoicing.[400] This would explain why it was not activated in a semantic area (the world of the dead) which, as presented in the archaic epitaphs, was characterized by the diametrically opposed state.[401]

---

[399] Cf. *GV* 1396, 1388; cf. also *GV* 1389, 1397 (l. 2), 1405.

[400] As a native (modern) Greek speaker I am incapable of saying whether or not the common modern Greek salutation *chairete* is always felt to be containing the connotation 'rejoice', though my suspicion is that at some level it does.

[401] Pfohl (1953: 69) suggests that *chaire* addressed to the dead is a 'Segenswunsch' of the living for a happy fate for the dead. So his actual decoding of the word converges with mine. But, we saw, such a happy fate is not open to the dead of the archaic epitaphs as it is to those of later periods.

To sum up. The hypothesis that *chaire* was felt to include the wish 'be well/rejoice', if correct, would explain why the dead were not addressed with that salutation until the fourth century: the pitiful dead of the representations reflected in the archaic epitaphs could never again be well and rejoice. This would add confirmation to my thesis that *chaire* not only was not, but could not have been, addressed to the deceased in an archaic epitaph.

(l) *Life and Death: The Dead and the Dying say* Chaire/Chairete

If these remarks about the meaning of *chaire* are correct, they motivate, and thus explain, the fact that, as I will now try to show, in the fifth-century representations being addressed with *chaire* was perceived as something characterizing the living and contrasted to the condition of being dead. Let us look at two passages quoted above. Euripides, *Orestes* 1083–4, shows not only that *chaire* was understood to include the wish 'rejoice', but also that rejoicing characterized the living but not the dead, and that this is why Orestes (who thinks he is about to die) addresses *chaire* to Pylades. The fragment from the *Nauplios* by one of the Astydamantes belongs to the fourth century—when, as we have seen, attitudes had changed, at least in some circles—but still reflects a certain reticence in addressing *chaire* to a dead person; for it argues that *chaire* and rejoicing *are* appropriate to the dead, which suggests that the established or at least earlier view was, as the Euripidean passage shows, that they were thought to be inappropriate. The passage from the *Orestes* also provides the right context in which to make sense of the fact that, while *chaire* is never addressed to the (ordinary) dead or the (ordinary) dying in tragedy, the dead, and the characters who are about die, themselves frequently address the survivors, or the landscape, with *chaire/chairete*.[402] In fact, in Euripides' *Hippolytos* v. 357 *chaire/chairete* is one of the modes of speech through which the nurse expresses the notion 'I cannot stand this . . . Let me die . . . I am dying . . . '. It is because *chaire* characterizes the world of the living in contrast to that of the dead that the characters adopt this mode of addressing not only the survivors but also the landscape; it adds poignancy to their death. Euripides, *Orestes* 1083–4, makes

---

[402] *Chaire* by the dead: Dareios' ghost in Aesch. *Pers.* 840. A few examples of *chaire* by people about to die: S. *Aj.* 859–63; *Trach.* 920–2; Eur. *Ph.* 1453; *Heracl.* 574; *IT* 708; *IA* 1450, 1509; *HF* 512.

PLATE I.   Stele, Epigraphical Museum, Athens 8864 (IG II/III² 3.2.12837).

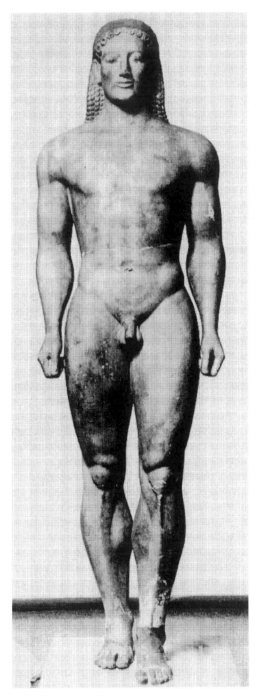

PLATE 2. The grave
monument of Kroisos,
Athens, NM 3851.

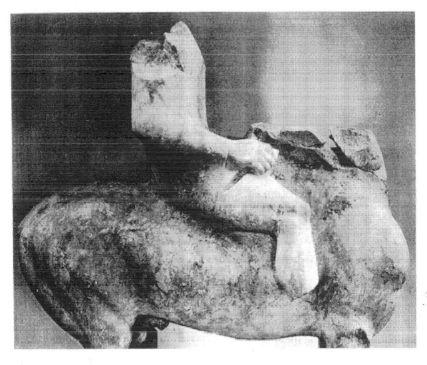

PLATE 3. The grave monument of Xerophantos, Athens, Kerameikos 2709. Photo DAI Athens.

PLATE 4. The grave monument of Aristion, Athens, NM 29.

PLATES 5–7.   The three sides of the base, Athens, NM 3476.

PLATE 8. Sphinx on a cavetto capital (that had crowned a grave stele), Athens, Kerameikos 8124. Photo DAI Athens.

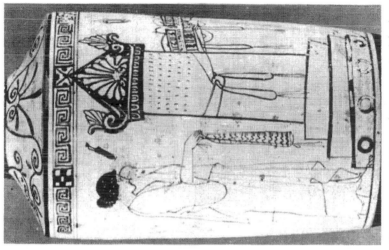

PLATE 10. Attic white-ground lekythos, Athens, NM 1958 (CC 1690).

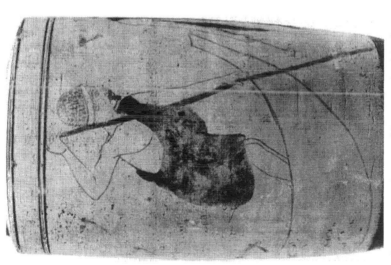

PLATE 9. Attic white-ground lekythos, Athens, NM 1926 (CC 1668).

PLATE II. Attic white-ground lekythos, Oxford,
Ashmolean Museum G 258 (547). (Courtesy of the Visitors
of the Ashmolean Museum, Oxford).

explicit what in the other cases in which characters about to die say *chaire/chairete* is implicit, but was read into, or activated by the context in, the salutation by the audience who shared in those assumptions. This contrast is also articulated in three funerary epigrams in which either the grave monument or the deceased address the passers by with *chairete*. The first, from the end of the archaic period, is not a grave inscription, but a memorial to a dead man inscribed on the blocks of an ancient tower at the north-east end of the Potamia bay in Thasos.[403] It is the *mnema* which speaks.

['Α]κηράτο ε[ἰ]μὶ μνῆμα τὸ Φ[ρασ]ιηρίδο,
κεῖμαι δ' ἐπ' [ἄ]κρο ναυσ[τ]ά | [ϑ]μο σωτήριον
νηυσίν τε κα[ὶ] ναύτηισιν ἀλλὰ χαίρετ[ε].

Here there is no explicit contrast between the deceased and the living who are addressed with *chairete*. The salutation is comparable to those salutations in tragedy by the dying and the dead. The other two are epitaphs from about the middle of the fifth century; one is from Aegina, for the Athenian Antistates:[404]

(i) χαίρετε οἱ παριό | ντες ' ἐγὸ δὲ 'Αντιστά | τες hυὸς 'Ατάρβο
κεῖμαι | ιεῖδε θανὸν πατρίδα | γῆν προλιπόν.

(ii) 'Αντιστάτες | 'Αθεναῖος.

The second is from Eretria, for the Aeginetan Mnesitheos:[405]

χαίρετε τοὶ παριό | ντες, · ἐγὸ δὲ θανὸν | κατάκειμαι.:
δεῦρ | ο ἰὸν ἀνάνεμαι, ἀν | ἐρ τίς τἔδε τέθαπ | πται ·:
ξἔνος ἀπ' Αἰγ | ίνες, Μνεσίθεος δ' ὄν | υμα ·
καί μοι μνἔμ' ἐπέ | θεκε · φίλε μέτερ Τιμ | αρέτε
τύμοι ἐπ' ἄκροτ | άτοι στέλεν ἀκάματον, |
hάτις ἐρεῖ παριῶσι δια | μερὲς ἄματα πάντα
Τ | ιμαρέτε μ' ἔσστεσε φίλ | οι ἐπὶ παιδὶ θανόντι.

In both it is the deceased who is speaking. Although the two are in other respects quite different, there are very marked similarities in the formulations involving, and following, *chairete*. In both the

[403] Hansen 1983: 162; Jeffery 1990: 301–2, 307 no. 67; Pfohl 1967: no. 21. Cf. Jeffery 1958: 145; Friedländer and Hoffleit 1948: 156 n. 6.
[404] Hansen 1983: 80; GV 1209; Jeffery 1990: 112, 113 no. 19, IG iv. 50; Pfohl 1967: 151; Friedländer and Hoffleit 1948: 76.
[405] Hansen 1983: 108; GV 1210; Jeffery 1990: 86, 88 no. 21; Pfohl 1967: 128; Friedländer and Hoffleit 1948: 140; IG xii. 9. 285; xii. Suppl. p. 186.

emphatic *ego*[406] follows *chairete hoi/toi pariontes*, to which it is related by means of *de*. *Ego de* is followed by, in one case *keimai teide thanon*, and in the other *thanon katakeimai*. Thus the basic schema underlying both is *chairete hoi pariontes, ego de thanon keimai*. Given that *chairete/chaire, ego de* . . . is elsewhere a general formula of transition[407] are we entitled to take *de* here to be adversative? In my view we are indeed, for the following reasons. First, if it is correct that *chaire* includes the wish 'rejoice', it follows that its meaning contrasts with what follows: the perception of death as sad conforms with the attitudes in the fifth-century private epitaphs and death is presented as sad in these two epitaphs: in both *ego de thanon keimai* is followed by a motif which (in the Greek attitudes) made death even sadder and more poignant, the theme 'I/he died away from home'.[408] This theme, then, confirms for us and intensified for the fifth-century reader the sadness of *ego de thanon keimai*—which was thus felt to contrast with the *chairete* to the passers-by. The epitaph for Kallimachos from the beginning of the fourth century BC (Hansen 1989: 492), which belongs to this same type, states explicitly this aspect of the epitaph which is only suggested here:

Καλλίμαχος.
Καλλιμάχου μνημεῖον ἐν ἀνθρώποισι τόδ᾽ ἔσται·
χαίρετε δ᾽ οἱ παριόντες ἐ⟨γ⟩ὼ δὲ λιπὼν πατρίδα ἐνθάδε κεῖμαι
δύσμορος, οὐδὲ φίλους γονέας ἐπιδών.

The view that the salutation *chairete hoi pariontes* involves the wish 'rejoice' also gains support from the fact that in the hymns, which are a primary context for the formula *chaire/chairete, ego de* . . ., *chairete* includes the meaning 'rejoice'. It also gains support from the epitaph Hansen 1983: 110, where a comparable wish is expressed through a comparable formulation:

Καλλία Αἰγίθοιο · τὺ δ᾽ εὖ πρᾶσ᾽, [ὅ] παροδõτα

If *Kallia* is a nominative,[409] the epitaph would be mentally sup-

---

[406] Cf. on this Gentili 1968: 66–7.
[407] Cf. Pi. *I*. 1. 33. On *chaire/chairete, ego de* (and on *chaire/chairete autar ego*): cf. Miller 1979: 177.
[408] Griffin 1980: 108–9; cf. Sourvinou-Inwood 1981: 31; Lattimore 1962: 200–1. In the archaic period and the 5th cent. BC death away from home was one of the circumstances of death (like death in youth) which warranted the erection of an inscribed grave monument (cf. Wallace 1970: 98; cf. below § ii.6).
[409] Cf. Friedländer and Hoffleit 1948: 14.

plemented in the minds of its contemporary readers with *enthade keimai/keitai*.[410] If it is a genitive it would be supplemented by *sama/mnama*. In either case, but especially in the former, the semantic pattern of this epitaph is the same as that proposed for those of Antistates and Mnesitheos, and similar to that of Akeratos' memorial, with an unambiguous positive wish element included in the greeting in Kallia's epitaph.

Another reason why, in my view, *de* is adversative here is because for archaic and fifth-century epitaphs the passer-by is not only a person whose co-operation is desired in order to activate and preserve the memory of the deceased but also a point of reference, a standard of comparison, of identification or of contrast, that serves to point out the poignancy of the deceased's death and so also of the prospective death of the passer-by. The identification with the deceased also has the effect of prompting his co-operation, and this can be formulated explicitly:[411] [δάκρυ κ]άταρ[χ]σον, ἐπεὶ καὶ σὲ μένει θάνατος. The epitaph for Tettichos[412] also articulates (differently) the contrast between the pitiful condition of the dead and the active and positive one of the living as represented by the passers-by (1.4): ταῦτ' ἀποδυράμενοι νέσθε ἐπὶ πρᾶγ' ἀγαθού.[413] The epitaph for Thrason[414] expresses the contrast between the normality of everyday life represented by the passers-by and the tragedy of death:

ἄνθροπε hὸστείχε[ι]ς : καθ'ὁδὸ | ν : φρασὶν:ἄλα μενοινὸν, : στέθι | καὶ οἴκτιρον : σέμα Θράσονος : ἰδόν.

This role of the passer-by as point of reference is the context in which the epitaphs beginning with *chairete hoi pariontes* should be placed. Thus we would expect these epitaphs to present the relationship between deceased and passer-by not neutrally, but either in terms of similarity/identification[415] ('you will find yourself where I am now') or of contrast, as in the other epitaphs which contrast the condition of the living with that of the

[410] Cf. Guarducci 1974: 147.
[411] Epitaph Hansen 1983: 34; *GV* 1227, l. 2.
[412] Hansen 1983: 13.
[413] Cf. Peek 1960: 17; Friedländer and Hoffleit 1948: 125.
[414] Hansen 1983: 28; *GV* 1225.
[415] As in the epitaph Hansen 1983: 34.

dead.[416] This is precisely the contrast that emerges when we take account of the 'rejoice' content of *chaire* and read *de* as adversative, which, I submit, the ancient reader, given his assumptions, could not fail to do. If this is right, the formulations involving *chairete hoi pariontes* in these epitaphs express the contrast between the normality and positive condition of the living and the pitiful state of the dead. They give voice to this contrast by means of the antithesis *chairete* . . . *ego de thanon keimai*, in which *chairete* is opposed to the condition of being dead and used to characterize the living.

The third argument in favour of the view that *de* was read as adversative and the epitaphs expressed this contrast is that later writers of funerary epigrams who made use of these same formulations read them in this contrastive manner. Though themes and *topoi* become reinterpreted in the course of time, it is legitimate to use this argument as confirmation here. For I have not projected the later readings on to the mid-fifth-century epigrams; I am only using the perceptions of the later epitaph-writers to cross-check the results of a wholly independent analysis. And the possibility that this analysis erred in exactly the direction taken by the later epigram-writers is remote. The later epitaphs beginning with *chairete hoi pariontes* show that the entire for-mulation *chairete hoi pariontes, ego de* . . . persisted beyond the fifth century. In the fourth century it includes some more explicit negative statement pertaining to the deceased's condition of being dead which is contrasted to the exhortation *chairete hoi pariontes*, for example,[417] *chairete de hoi pariontes: ⟨e⟩go de philos kataleipo*. We have already seen the epigram for Kallimachos from the beginning of the fourth century with its explicit variant of the fifth-century formulations. These later usages show first, that the formulation *chairete hoi pariontes, ego de* . . . became a topos; and second, for this is what is suggested by the explicit versions of the contrast,

---

[416] The epitaph Hansen 1989: 487 (*GV* 1653), from the Piraeus, of the beginning of the 4th cent., in which it is the grave monument which speaks, begins with 'death is the common lot of humanity' and ends with *chairete hoi pariontes*:

πάντων ἀνθρώπων νόμος ἐστὶ κοινὸς τὸ ἀποθανὲν.
ἐνθάδε κεῖται Θεοίτης παῖς Τελέσωνος Τεγεάτας Τεγεάτο
καὶ μητρὸς Νικαρέτης χρηστῆς γε γυναικός.
χαίρετε οἱ παρι⟨ό⟩ντες, ἐγὼ δὲ τἀμὰ φυ⟨λά⟩ττω

[417] Epitaph Hansen 1989: 677; cf. also 520. 4–5 (*o philoi* . . . *chairete*).

that it was understood by the writers of these later epigrams to involve the contrast suggested here between the *chairete* addressed to the passers-by and the pitiful condition of the deceased. In fact, this is probably the reason why this formulation became a topos in the epitaphs, because it offered a satisfactory—and flexible—set pattern for expressing the poignancy of death, by stressing the contrast between life and death, between the deceased buried there whom the epitaph commemorates, and the passers-by. A similar contrast between the living (characterized by the exchange of greetings) and the dead (*nyni de ⟨ph⟩th⟨i⟩menoi keimetha ges aphaneis*) is also expressed in an epitaph[418] of *c.*360 BC, where the deceased says *o philoi emeteroi . . . chairete*, a greeting comparable to those we encountered in tragedy.[419]

Consequently, it is clear that in these epitaphs the formulation *chairete, ego de . . .* of the hymns was adapted to perform a different function, in an expression which contrasts the salutation *chaire*, which pertains to the living, to the condition of being dead. This presents the deceased's death in a more poignant light and compels the co-operation of the passer-by in remembering and feeling pity for him. As De Man remarked,[420] the epitaph fiction of addressing the passer-by includes a 'sinister' facet; not only the prefiguration of one's own mortality, but also an entry 'into the frozen world of the dead'. The use of *chairete* through which the living are contrasted to the dead distances the passer-by from this world of the dead, 'protects' him symbolically in his fictional entry in that world, and signals his allegiance to the world of the living. But this contrast is in fact only temporary, for the passer-by too will die, as some epitaphs state explicitly, thus deconstructing the contrast between living and dead articulated through the *chairete* by placing it in the long-term perspective, in which we will all, all successive generations of passers-by, be dead.

---

[418] Hansen 1989: 520. 9 (*GV* 1211).

[419] Cf. also the very much later epitaph *GV* 1219 of the 2nd/3rd cent. AD, which expresses sentiments not dissimilar from those expressed in Aesch. *Pers.* 839–42 in which Dareios' ghost addresses the chorus with *chairete*. On the contrast between life and death in classical epitaphs cf. Clairmont 1970: 55. The motif *chairete* to the passers-by persisted for a long time. The following is a list of epitaphs containing such an expression and which are not mentioned in the text: *GV* 3/4, 1216, 1218, 1220, 1221, 2003.17, 1853; cf. also 1217. In one 3rd-cent. BC epitaph (*GV* 1213), we find the variant wish *o parion, hygiaine, dikaiosynen te phylat⟨t⟩e*.

[420] De Man 1979b: 927–8.

If it is right that being addressed with *chaire* characterized the living in contrast to the dead,[421] the view that *chaire* could not be addressed to the dead in archaic epitaphs gains further support, since the perception of the dead on which this contrast is based was the same as that of the archaic epitaphs. Since this contrast between *chaire/chairete* and the condition of being dead was one of the conceptual schemata through which epitaph-writers operated, it was impossible for them to use *chaire* to address the deceased in an epitaph. The conclusion that *chaire/chairete* was contrasted to the condition of being dead also provides further support for the thesis that *chaire* began to be addressed to the deceased in the context of heroization/deification beliefs. If *chaire* is indeed incompatible with the condition of being dead, it follows that when it is addressed to the dead there is some radical difference in the perception of the condition of being dead which makes it compatible. The beliefs involving immortality offer such a radically different perception, one in which being dead is coterminous with the condition of the higher beings who are appropriately addressed with *chaire*.

(m) *The Use of* Chaire*: A Summary of the Conclusions*

Chaire began to be addressed to special, heroized/deified, dead, and dying people as an extension, and adaptation, of the salutation addressed to gods and heroes. Before the fourth century[422] *chaire* was not associated with the ordinary dead; for it characterized life and the living in contrast to the dead. The use of *chaire* to address the dead became more widespread when heroization/deification became more widespread. Both eventually became routine. The absence of *chaire* addressed to the dead from the archaic epitaphs is correlative with the attitudes reflected in these epitaphs, which, like their choice of themes, were culturally determined and differed from those of other periods.

---

[421] If this is correct, we can see a special aptness in Pheres' words when he is justifying his decision not to give up his life in order to save his son to Admetos in Eur. *Alc.* 691: *chaireis horon phos; patera d' ou chairein dokeis?*

[422] Before the end of the 5th cent. if we accept the earliest conceivable dates (however unlikely) for the Hylas and Chionides epitaphs.

4. THE IMAGES

(a) *Images on Early Greek* Semata: *An Introduction*

In the archaic period images are represented on, or make up part of, several types of grave monument. I shall discuss these images and attempt to reconstruct their meanings after I have said something about some earlier representations, those on the large vases with figure decoration that stood over some eighth-century graves.[423] For the comparison of the two sets of images will be informative.

The following major categories of images are represented on the eighth-century vases which served as grave-markers.[424] First, images of the death-ritual, scenes of *prothesis* and *ekphora*,[425] second, apparently depicted on vases marking men's graves, images of warriors, battles, and sea-battles; and finally, a continuous frieze of chariots.[426] Exactly how these scenes were perceived by their contemporaries, as specific mythological scenes or 'idealized' representations based on the heroic past, or as depicting contemporary life, is unclear to us, and thus a matter of controversy (cf. n. 1). What, in my view, cannot be doubted is that, whatever their meanings were perceived to be in the first instance, there was a level of signification in which death images standing over the grave were seen as relating to the deceased whose *sema* the vase carrying the images was. They related to the deceased either directly (if they were seen as representing everyday reality) or indirectly (if they were perceived as mythological or as idealized representations based on the heroic past). But in any case they were public images of death, involving a group activity that pertains to, and represents the articulation of, the deceased's social persona. Thus the scenes of *prothesis* and *ekphora* represent death through the public rituals by means of which the community as well as the family reacted to the death and dispatched the shade to Hades. This articulates the deceased's social persona

---

[423] For reasons that will become clear in the course of this discussion the remarks that follow are independent from the controversy concerning the precise nature of these scenes, whether they depict contemporary life, mythological scenes, or 'idealized' representations based on the heroic past. (For a recent summary of this controversy with bibliog. cf. Sparkes 1991: 65–6; cf. also the discussion in Whitley 1991: 48–53.)

[424] On these images cf. also Andronikos 1961/2: 199–203.

[425] Cf. Ahlberg 1971a; M. Robertson 1975: 19; Kurtz and Boardman 1971: 58–61; R. Osborne 1988: 5; Whitley 1991: 52, 139–42.

[426] Cf. Ahlberg 1971b; Whitley 1991: 52–3, 141–2.

218   *Signs of the Dead*

iconographically through the representation of the death ritual at which that persona was articulated ritually; by representing the mourning triggered off by the death it valorized the deceased. The images of war and warriors again relate to the deceased's social persona. They represent war activities as relevant to him, in a modality that is not entirely clear to us; they probably represent the deceased as a warrior. The chariot scenes may pertain to the deceased's athletic activities or they may have been perceived to be referring to chariot races as part (real or ideal, a Homeric paradigm) of the death-ritual,[427] or both. I shall return to these images below, to compare them to the images of death represented on archaic grave monuments.

(b) *Painted Plaques and Representations on Vases-Semata*

One category of images decorating archaic grave monuments is plaques on built tombs. Built tombs were decorated with painted plaques representing (non-mythological) scenes from the death-ritual, especially the *prothesis* and various scenes of mourning and lamentation.[428] There are two types of plaques, those that were part of a series, which articulated various scenes from the death ritual, and the much smaller 'single' plaques each of which is complete in itself. The series plaques were earlier, from the late seventh century to *c.*530, while the single plaques come mostly from the end of the sixth century. The single plaque New York Metropolitan Museum 54.11.15[429] had a predella below the main (*prothesis*) scene depicting a chariot race. Thus, here a chariot race is represented as a part of the death-ritual. This, almost certainly, did not reflect a ritual reality, but an ideal image, an image presenting a death-ritual—inevitably perceived as relating to the deceased whose *sema* this was—that included an element modelled on the Homeric paradigm.[430] This

---

[427] Cf. e.g. Andronikos 1961/2: 200.

[428] Boardman 1955: 51–66; Richter 1942–3: 80–92; Kurtz and Boardman 1971: 83; Cordano 1980: 186–97, cf. esp. 188–94, 195; Shapiro 1991: 633–9; cf. also Schmaltz 1983: 180.

[429] Shapiro 1991: 638 fig. 11.

[430] Shapiro (1991: 632–42) argues that this is an expression of a heroizing intent, in the sense of representing the dead as 'likened to the heroes whose *arete* was celebrated in the Homeric poems' (p. 632), which he detects also elsewhere in archaic grave monuments, esp., in its strongest form, in grave statues and grave stelai. It will become clear in this chapter that while I do not consider this type of view to be exactly wrong, I believe that the situation is more complex and varied; and that it is preferable to begin by considering the specificity of each phenomenon and its differences from others and not to assume implicitly that a

image articulated the notion of a high valorization of the deceased at the death-ritual through group activity. Because of the Homeric paradigm, this sprinkled the social persona of the deceased with a connotation of metaphorically heroic colouring, but in a very specific, group-oriented, and limited way. Built tombs may also have been decorated with marble plaques in relief; it is likely that some late archaic marble slabs with representations of Hermes Chthonios and the deceased had decorated such a tomb.[431]

Images, either painted or in relief, were also carried on vases that functioned as grave-markers.[432] Archaic vases used as *semata* depict representations of various kinds.[433] One major category is mythological scenes. I shall not discuss these images here; for a whole book would be needed for the proper investigation of their meanings and their relationships to death and the deceased. Another category of representation on such vases is divinities in some form of epi-

variety of phenomena can be subsumed into broad categories, through which they are then inevitably viewed. In this case the idealization of the social persona of the deceased is articulated in terms of his place in the social group. His valorization is articulated through the representation of a group activity at the death-ritual that is modelled on the Homeric paradigm. Of course, this image ascribes a small element of a heroic persona to the social persona of the deceased, but in a very specific and limited way. A comparandum to illustrate one of the modalities of the specificity would be provided by the different forms of praise we find, between epigrams in which the deceased is described as *agathos* (e.g. Hansen 1983: 16) and epigrams in which it said that he is *demoi potheinos* (cf. e.g. Hansen 1983: 28 (*andri potheinoi damoi*)). It is the latter that would be in this respect nearer the iconographical modality here under discussion.

[431] Cf. Karusu 1961: 91–106; Kurtz and Boardman 1971: 83–4; Ridgway 1977: 168, 181; Willemsen 1970: 30–4; cf. also Noack 1907: 543–5 and pl. xxii.1.

[432] That the images when present were indeed important is shown by the fact that only one side was decorated, the main side, and that when the vase was set on the ground horizontally it was the decorated side that was set upwards, so that it would be visible (cf. Christou 1964a: 153; cf. 283, Eng. summary), though in this case it is not clear for how long the vase and its scene would have remained visible; it functioned as a *sema* for a group of graves in combination with a mound of ashes and animal bones with a low retaining wall (cf. also Simantoni-Bournia 1984: 55).

[433] The fact that many of the relevant vases have not been found *in situ* means that we cannot be certain which of the vases belonging to one of the types which we know was used as a grave monument had in fact been put to that use; even when such vases are known to have come from a cemetery we cannot be certain as to whether they were used as a *sema* or as a burial urn. It seems that some vases may have been first used as a *sema* and then as the recipient of the deceased's remains (cf. M. Robertson 1975: 50; Christou 1964a: 153–5). There are, then, some uncertainties as to whether some subjects did indeed appear on vases that served as *semata*. However, as we shall see, some subjects can be certainly identified as images thought to be appropriate to appear on grave monuments, either because they are represented on a vase found *in situ* or because they appear on other types of grave monument.

phany.[434] Another is sphinxes;[435] other monsters and fantastical beings form another category;[436] yet another is that of representations of animals, including, but not limited to, lions.[437] Hunt scenes involving lions and other animals also occur.[438] Other images depicted on vases functioning as grave monuments represent warriors, horsemen and/or chariots.[439] The Laconian relief amphorae serving as *semata* appear to have had a relatively systematic and more or less standardized organization of decoration,[440] involving chariots on the shoulder, and on the neck (when the neck is decorated) either hunt scenes or warrior scenes, or sphinxes, or lions or winged horses. The hunt and warrior scenes[441] are clearly iconographical articulations of the social persona of the deceased. The chariot scenes are differentiated from those represented on the eighth-century grave vases (and also some other subgeometric and postgeometric vases):[442] it is not a continuous frieze or procession of chariots that is depicted on the Laconian amphorae; the frieze is divided into a series of groups consisting of a chariot with a charioteer and a warrior following on foot.[443] They thus resemble the scenes representing a chariot, a charioteer, and a warrior on some archaic Attic grave monuments, on the subsidiary zone of a relief stele,[444] or on the base of the grave statue of a young male.[445] The warrior mounting a chariot is probably a 'heroic' image of war, and may also have evoked the deceased's connection with

---

[434] Cf. Themelis 1976: 90–3; Schäfer 1957: 34–6, 79–82.

[435] Cf. Simantoni-Bournia 1984, 64–5; Schäfer 1957: 31–3; Christou 1964*b*: 194 and n. 67.

[436] Cf. e.g. the sirens that are combined with horsemen on an early black figure vase which almost certainly crowned a grave-mound in the Kerameikos: Knigge 1988: 28 fig. 22; cf. also Schäfer 1957: 33–4, 37, 79 for examples of such beings on vases with relief decoration, many of which functioned as *semata*.

[437] On animals on relief pithoi functioning as grave monuments (cf. Simantoni-Bournia 1984: 54–5): Schäfer 1957: 27–31, 54, 77–9; Christou 1964*b*: 172–3, 194 and n. 68; Simantoni-Bournia 1984: 57–63, 66–83 (lion representations).

[438] Cf. Christou 1964*b*: 189.

[439] Cf. Simantoni-Bournia 1984: 84–113; Schäfer 1957: 36–7, 55; Christou 1964*b*: 173–4.

[440] Christou 1964*b*: 191–265, cf. esp. 193–7.

[441] They are described by Christou as a reference to the life of the deceased; he sees no problem in the fact that the amphora found in situ was the *sema* of a group of graves (Christou 1964*a*); as he sees it it would be referring either to the whole family's pursuits or to those of its head (Christou 1964*b*: 197).

[442] Cf. Christou 1964*b*: 235.

[443] Christou 1964*b*: 234–5; cf. also fig. 5.

[444] Cf. e.g. Richter 1961: no. 45 fig. 126.

[445] Cf. e.g. D'Onofrio 1986: pl. 55. 2–3; cf. below.

chariot-racing.[446] Such images, then, almost certainly pertain to the deceased's social persona. I shall return to the chariots representations and I discuss the significance of the lion, the sphinx and of divinities on grave monuments later on in this section. First I shall consider two other types of grave monument involving images, grave statues and decorated stelai.

(c) Grave Stelai, Kouroi, Korai and Other Grave Statues

The most common funerary statues in this period were korai (standing, draped, young women) and especially kouroi (standing, naked, young men);[447] other types were standing, draped males, one of whom is holding a snake,[448] horsemen,[449] seated figures, both male and female,[450] and animals and monsters, lions,[451] sphinxes,[452] rarely gorgons,[453] and conceivably also sirens.[454]

In this period[455] many of the stelai standing over the grave had

[446] They are less likely to refer to (really performed or ideally wished for) rites at the grave as Christou assumed (1964b: 195, 237, 248). For, first, they are separated into individual groups and resemble the stelai scenes which focus on one individual chariot. And second, the man who is sometimes mounting, sometimes about to mount the chariot is a warrior; this makes these scenes very similar to those on the Attic grave monuments, which pertain to the deceased's social persona. By contrast, on the two archaic Attic chariot scenes in a funerary context that are most likely to be representing such (really performed or ideally wished for) chariot races at the grave, the predella underneath the *prothesis* of the plaque New York Metropolitan Museum 54.11.15 (cf. n. 429 above) and the frieze with a chariot race on the black-figure loutrophoros Athens NM 450 (ABL 229 no. 59; cf. also Shapiro 1991: 640 figs. 12–13), all the other scenes on which are representations of parts of the death ritual, only a man dressed as a charioteer is shown on the chariot and a continuous frieze of chariots depicts a race in the descriptive narrative mode.

[447] Cf. Pl. 2. On the pattern of the appearance of kouroi and korai as *semata* in the different regions cf. Ridgway 1977: 149–50. On their meanings cf. esp. D'Onofrio 1982: 135–70; 1988: 83–96; Stewart 1986: 54–70; R. Osborne 1988: 1–16; cf. below.

[448] For this interpretation of the draped figure from a cemetery near Tanagra cf. Ridgway 1977: 150; on this figure cf. Pharaklas 1969: 66–73; cf. also Ridgway 1977: 75 n. 32; 86. On the base of this statue there is the inscription *IMA R Q U*. On standing draped males as grave statues cf. Ridgway 1977: 75. Cf. below.

[449] Cf. Pl. 3; cf. Ridway 1977: 151; cf. also 140–1; cf. also below.

[450] Cf. Ridgway 1977: 151; cf. also 129, 135–7; Boardman 1978: 86. The archaic seated female figure is discussed (with special reference to its votive use) in Tuchelt 1970: 217–19.

[451] Cf. Ridway 1977: 152–6.

[452] Possibly also directly on the grave, and not only crowning the stele (cf. Ridgway 1977: 156–60; cf. esp. 159).

[453] Cf. Ridgway 1977: 162.

[454] Cf. ibid. 160–62.

[455] It is not clear whether any earlier funerary stelai were decorated. Two decorated stelai which may be funerary have been dated to the late eighth century, a stele from Kymisala in Rhodes (Andronikos 1961/2: 192–4 and pl. 88) and a stele from Kimolos (Kurtz and Boardman 1971: 220 and fig. 45b; Andronikos 1961/2, 194; Ridgway 1977: 163). The latter

relief decoration.[456] The overwhelming majority of archaic stelai with representational relief decoration depict the deceased through an iconographical schema sculpted on the shaft which articulates the type of social persona to which (s)he belonged, which would best define him or her. The commonest schemata through which the deceased are depicted on these archaic stelai are 'youth', including 'youth as athlete'; 'young warrior'; and 'bearded mature man as warrior'. The schema 'beardless youth as athlete' appears in different types, including that in which the youth is characterized as an athlete through an aryballos,[457] and others in which he is characterized as an athlete in a particular sport, for example, as a discus-thrower, in the image of a youth holding a discus.[458] Another schema involving a beardless youth is the schema 'beardless youth as warrior with a

was found near a Late Geometric cemetery; it is a limestone block whose upper part is carved in the shape of a (now headless) female torso with one arm on her breast and the other across her waist. It has been compared to the stelai from Neandria which are said to recall a human figure in that they have a centre–top projection like a head (cf. Kurtz and Boardman 1971: 220). Its date and use are uncertain. The Kymisala stele consists of a disc on top of a wide 'neck' which had originally been fastened on some base; the disc is surmounted by a rectangular element resembling somewhat the abacus of a Doric capital on which an additional element had originally been fastened; on the front side of the disc six birds are rendered in low relief, on the back a rosette is incised. Andronikos (1961/2: 192–4) considers it to be funerary and of 8th-cent. date. Kurtz and Boardman (1971: 219) claim that 'It does not look more Geometric than Byzantine.' But the early date may gain a little support from the fact that, in my view, there are some similarities between this stele and a type of composite terracotta figurine that was fastened on the top of some Mycenaean sarcophagi from Tanagra (Spyropoulos 1970: 190 fig. 8, cf. p. 188); these Mycenaean figurines consist of a disc with painted decoration on a rather wide 'neck' that comes out of a base in the form of horns of consecration; on top of the disc there was a bird. (The figurines, incidentally, are similar to a type of bronze pendants that does not appear before the 8th cent., cf. e.g. Kilian 1975: pl. 3.4.) If the missing upper element of the Kymisala stele were a bird the similarity would be extremely close; as it is the combination of the disc on a neck with the birds is in a different modality in the two cases. The similarity may be coincidental; if it is not it would add some support to the view that this is an early funerary stele; its form would have ultimately originated in a Mycenaean funerary element, and the missing links in the development may have been rare and/or in perishable material.

[456] Cf. Pl. 4. On archaic relief stelai with sculpted decoration cf. Richter 1961; M. Robertson 1975: 108–12; Ridgway 1977: 163–77; Boardman 1978: 162–5; Stewart 1990: 50, 120; D'Onofrio 1988: 89–91.

[457] Cf. e.g. Richter 1961: no. 28, where the youth is also wearing a wreath and holding two pomegranates to denote his persona as deceased (on the polysemic nature of the pomegranates and the way the funerary context stresses their association with the Underworld and its deities cf. below the discussion of the funerary korai); Richter 1961: no. 37, the brother and sister stele, where the youth is holding a pomegranate and has an aryballos hanging from his wrist, while the girl is holding a flower (on which cf. below the discussion of the korai).

[458] Cf. Richter 1961: nos. 25, 26.

spear'.[459] The schema 'bearded young man as a warrior' appears both in the type in which the young man is depicted naked with a spear and sword[460] and that in which he is dressed as a hoplite and holding a spear.[461] Less common schemata include 'seated woman', including 'mother and child';[462] 'young girl';[463] 'mature man with dog';[464] 'mature man as boxer';[465] 'horseman' on the main field;[466] 'brother and sister (youth and girl)',[467] 'seated mature man as a doctor',[468] and some other schemata with two figures.[469] The bearded male on the stele of Lyseas[470] who is wearing a long chiton and himation may be representing the schema 'symposiast' which is also found on some grave statues. I shall discuss this schema while considering those statues. The kantharos Lyseas is holding either refers directly to the symposion, or alludes to it through its association with Dionysos, or both. On the panel below the main image a horseman on a galloping horse may be a jockey.[471]

Two categories of warriors are shown on the stelai. The first is the beardless youth. The schema 'bearded male warrior' as, for example, seen in Aristion's *sema*, also appears to be representing a young male warrior, in which case there would appear to be two types, and age bands of young males represented on the stelai. However, can we be sure this is not a culturally determined impression? In my view it is not. I cannot discuss the question of the date of the introduction of the Athenian ephebeia, though I have no doubt that an institution closely related to what we know as the later ephebeia was practised in the sixth century. But even if

[459] Cf. ibid. no. 27. That it is a spear and not a staff becomes apparent when it is compared to the spear held by the man with spear and sword on the stele Richter 1961: no. 23. In some cases only the lower part of the shaft is preserved, and we cannot be totally sure it is a youth (cf. e.g. Richter 1961: no. 33, where it is classified as a youth). Cf. also the stele from Cyrene in Ridgway 1977: fig. 56 (discussed in Richter 1961: 53).

[460] Cf. e.g. Richter 1961: no. 23.

[461] Cf. e.g. the stele of Aristion (Richter 1961: no. 67).

[462] Cf. Ridgway 1977: 165–6.

[463] Cf. Boardman 1978: fig. 246.

[464] Cf. ibid. 164.

[465] Richter 1961: no. 27.

[466] Cf. Ridgway 1977: fig. 54.

[467] Cf. Richter 1961, no. 37, cf. pp. 27–9 and figs. 96–109 and 159–65 (= Guarducci 1961: 159–65) (Hansen 1983: 25).

[468] Berger 1970: 49–59; Ridgway 1977: 175, 182.

[469] Cf. Ridgway 1977: 167–8; Boardman 1978: 164.

[470] Richter 1961: no. 70; Hansen 1983: 53.

[471] Cf. for a summary of the discussions of this representation, with bibliography: Richter 1961: p. 48.

we only limit ourselves to the age categories articulating Greek life and institutions, I hope that it is uncontroversial that, first, pre-hoplite age-and-status youths old enough to be in some way involved with military training and the like formed a distinct cat-egory; and second, that within the category 'adult citizen/adult warrior' there was a category 'young full citizen/young adult war-rior' which went up to the age of 30, when a male became, for example, qualified for membership of the boule and the dikasteria in Athens after the Kleisthenic reforms[472] and in Sparta he was admitted to the assembly.[473] In these circumstances, I suggest that the two iconographical types of warrior in the stelai correspond to the two age bands covered by the category 'young warrior' in Greek life and thought, the 'ephebic' type warrior[474] and the young warrior under 30. There would be nothing problematic about the resulting overwhelming predominance of young people represented on the stelai. As will become clear in the next section, we should not expect the majority of images on archaic grave monuments to be representing mature/elderly men. The epigrams make clear that a large proportion of inscribed grave monuments were erected for people who died young—for reasons that will become apparent. Among those erected for older people many would not necessarily have been *semata* involving a human representation; of those that were, we would expect that most would be grave statues of the type that we know that in Greek images articulates iconographically the mature/elderly/high-status man: a male seated statue. A further argument in favour of the view that the warriors under discussion are indeed 'young males' in the sense defined here is provided by the fact that the same male type (albeit in a different persona) can be seen to be representing a young male on the painted stele of Lyseas, who, I suggested, is depicted as a symposiast. For Lyseas belonged to the category 'young' at least in the cultural sense, since his *sema* was erected by his father.[475]

The representations on the main field are sometimes associated with chariots and/or horses in a subsidiary frieze[476] and/or base,[477]

---

[472] Cf. e.g. Hignett 1952: 224.
[473] Cf. e.g. Forrest 1980: 52.
[474] On this type of warrior cf. Lissarague 1990.
[475] On this category cf. below Ch. III § ii.6.
[476] Cf. Ridgway 1977: 169–70.
[477] Cf. e.g. Boardman 1978: fig. 240.

while on other stelai the predella may be decorated with an apotropaic figure such as a Gorgon.[478] Thus the images on the stelai articulated iconographically the deceased's social persona, mostly in the emblematic mode on the main field: a young man is shown with a sword and a spear, or wearing armour and holding a spear, or with the implements of an athlete; that is, the deceased's persona is articulated through a schema corresponding to its defining aspect, 'warrior' or 'athlete'. More rarely the main scene on the shaft is in the descriptive narrative idiom, but the scene functions emblematically. For example, a man is shown holding a spear or javelin in his raised right and about to throw it. Also, on the stele Ny Carlsberg Glyptothek, Copenhagen, IN 2787[479] the representation on the shaft, two men in an ambush, is in the descriptive narrative idiom; but the scene functions emblematically in that through it the deceased is represented as a warrior. Another comparable scene is that on the doctor's stele in Basle depicting a seated man facing a young attendant with medical equipment hanging in the background, which represents the deceased as a doctor.[480] Some other such scenes with comparable mixtures of the descriptive narrative and the emblematic involve women.[481] On some stelai the main representation on the shaft is in the emblematic mode, for example the deceased as warrior, and there is also a scene in a subsidiary zone in the descriptive narrative idiom, for example a warrior mounting a chariot, which defines further his social persona.[482] The warrior mounting a chariot is probably a 'heroic' image of war, which may also have evoked a connection with chariot racing. This interpretation is, I believe, confirmed by the appearance on a base of the same group, of charioteer in a chariot into which a warrior is mounting, together with figures of warriors on foot.[483] For this cannot fit the notion of funeral games,[484] but does fit the notion of an image of war, elevated to a more distanced,

---

[478] Cf. Ridgway 1977: 169–70.

[479] Richter 1961: no. 77 (pp. 50–1, fig. 172).

[480] Berger 1970: 49–59; Ridgway 1977: 175, 182.

[481] Cf. e.g. the 'mother and child' representation on the fragmentary stele from Anavyssos (Richter 1961: no. 59, pp. 42–3, figs. 151–3).

[482] The example cited, the warrior on the shaft with a warrior mounting a chariot in the subsidiary zone, is from the stele New York, Metropolitan Museum 36.11.13, Fletcher Fund, 1938 (Richter 1961: no. 45, pp. 32–3, figs. 126–8).

[483] Cf. the base Athens National Museum 3477 (cf. Boardman 1978: fig. 241) which shall be discussed below in this section.

[484] Cf. also above n. 446 and below.

heroic plane through the representation of the chariot which was no longer in use in real war, and which inevitably also conjured up its other semantic facet, the real-life situation in which it was used, chariot-racing, which was a preserve of the aristocratic élite and thus denoted status as well as athletic interests and prowess. All these scenes, though in the descriptive narrative idiom, function emblematically, to represent the deceased's social persona in the same way as the comparable scenes (such as that of ambush) on the shaft. On other stelai in the subsidiary zone there may be an emblematic representation of one figure, a protective Gorgon,[485] or a figure like that of the boar on the stele from Syme[486] which represents emblematically an aspect of the deceased's social persona; for the boar was an image of valour but valour in defeat, and thus appropriate for signifying the dead warrior.[487] In the subsidiary zones the deceased's social persona is sometimes articulated through the representation of a human figure other than the deceased. Thus on two sides of the cavetto capital from Lamptrai, Athens NM no. 41,[488] are shown mourners, male and female, with arms raised to their heads, while on the front the horseman leading a second horse and with two spears is the squire of the deceased.[489] The mourners would have been seen either as fragments of the death ritual, valorizing the deceased's persona through the representation of that ritual and of the grief caused by his death; or as emblematic representations depicting the grief in a permanent form, comparable to the expression of grief in the epitaphs; or, more plausibly, as both. The squire or jockey on a horse indicating the deceased's association with horsemanship also appears on subsidiary zones in other stelai.[490] On the base of the kouros over the grave of Neilonides, son of Neilon,[491] the painted figure of a seated bearded male is framed between the two inscriptions, the vertical statement that Endoios made it, and the horizontal epitaph, and relates directly to the latter. It was thus undoubtedly a representation of the father

---

[485] Cf. e.g. Boardman 1978: fig. 231; the significance of the Gorgon on funerary monuments will be discussed below in this section.

[486] Cf. Ridgway 1977: 175, 182; Boardman 1978: fig. 245.

[487] On the significance of the boar cf. Vermeule 1979: 88–91.

[488] Richter 1961: no. 20, figs. 66–9.

[489] Cf. Richter 1961: pp. 18, 19.

[490] Cf. Richter 1961: nos. 64, 70, 71, cf. pp. 46, 48–9.

[491] Hansen 1983: 42 with refs. to illustrations.

who set up the monument, like an iconographical articulation of the (unstated) subject of the second verse.

The prevailing scholarly opinion is that there is a dichotomy between the representations of the social persona of the deceased on the one hand on stelai and on the other through grave statues. I will argue that this perception of a dichotomy is not quite correct, and that the picture is much more complicated.

From around 570 the stele with relief decoration was much the most popular form of grave monument in Attica.[492] Stelai of this type, articulating the social persona of the deceased, were not limited to Attica.[493] In my view the Prinias stelai[494] should be included among the non-Attic specimens of this type of grave monument (though in this case the stelai were not free-standing, they were embedded in standing masonry),[495] despite the doubts expressed as to their funerary function,[496] which I find far from compelling. The case made by Lebessi[497] is overwhelming. The iconographical schemata represented on these stelai are 'the warrior',[498] 'the woman with distaff',[499] 'female figure with bird and wreath'[500] and one 'seated (probably male) figure with sceptre'.[501] These schemata correspond to the following types of social persona: 'male citizen (presumed to perform his duty as a warrior, this being a very important aspect of his citizen persona)'; 'married woman, *gyne*, shown in her persona as spinner, that is, performing a domestic task, symbolic of the desired virtues of the ideal Greek woman'; 'parthenos'; and 'high-status mature person, possibly magistrate, community leader'.

---

[492] Cf. Stewart 1990: 120.
[493] On the question of regional and chronological differences cf. esp. Ridgway 1977: 171–3, 177, cf. 173–7. In my view, though there are regional preferences, and though some trends are greatly increased in the later archaic period, the basic parameters are the same throughout, and we must resist attempts to tidy up the complex picture by forcing the data into schemata that distort the fluid complex and polysemic ancient realities. It should also be remembered with regard to Attica that circumstances have been favourable to both preservation and recovery of archaic grave monuments; to give but one example of a favourable factor, several have been found in the Themistoklean Wall.
[494] On the Prinias stelai cf. Lebessi 1976.
[495] Cf. Lebessi 1976: pl. 1a.
[496] Cf. a short discussion in Ridgway 1977: 164, 180; Boardman 1978: 165.
[497] In Lebessi 1976: *passim*.
[498] Ibid. 71–83.
[499] Ibid. 86–90.
[500] Ibid. 90–1.
[501] Ibid. 83–6.

We saw that the notion that the Greeks identified the grave monument with the deceased is based on a misconception. We have also seen that, while all *semata* were metonymic signs of the deceased, only some either primarily consisted of, or included, a (schematic) representation of the social persona of the deceased. Grave stelai with relief decoration belong to the former category and grave statues can belong to the latter, as we shall now see. It may appear obvious to us that a statue representing a human being standing over a grave must have represented the deceased. But this obviousness is a culturally determined perception, that may or may not have corresponded to the ancient perceptions which we need to reconstruct. Certainly, not all human statues standing over a grave could have represented the deceased, since, we saw, it seems that a kore could stand over a man's grave. Moreover, if statues standing over a grave were perceived to be representing the deceased, it would have been in a very particular way that needs to be defined. For otherwise we could not explain the fact that, as we saw, no grave statue is identified as the deceased by an inscription, but always as the *sema* of the deceased, a state of affairs that contrasts sharply with that of the votive statues, among which some do bear an inscription identifying them with the dedicator, such as the inscription on the seated statue of Chares from Didyma, *Chares eimi o Klesios Teichioses archos; agalma to Apollonos;*[502] or the name in the nominative inscribed on statues, such as the inscriptions that name Ornithe and Philippe in the Geneleos group dedication.[503] The contrast with, for example, the statue inscribed *Aristodiko*, (the *sema*) of Aristodikos, is most striking. This suggests very strongly that while the statue of a votary could be identified with the dedicator or a member of the dedicator's family, the grave statue could never be identified with the deceased. This fits our reconstruction of the perceptions associated with the early Greek *sema*. The fact that the *sema* is a metonymic sign of the deceased symbolizing his social persona as a memory in the world of the living entails that when it consisted of a statue (with its base and inscription), it would have been perceived to be representing that persona iconographically, when, for example, a kore marked the grave of a maiden. For the statue's full meanings were created in context; and the statue of a

---

[502] Tuchelt 1970: K 47, pp. 78–80 pls. 43–6, cf. also pp. 144, 215, 218; Jeffery 1990: 414 pl. 64.29; Lazzarini 1976: 96, 315.

[503] Richter 1968: nos. 67, 68; Freyer-Schauenburg 1974: nos. 61 and 62.

maiden standing over the grave, and functioning as the metonymic sign, of a maiden would have been inevitably perceived by its contemporaries—whom we know to have been attuned to the representation of the social persona of the deceased at least from the stelai—as a sign of the deceased that in some way represented the social persona of the deceased, the persona that was also articulated in the grave epigram. Thus the *sema* would be representing the deceased's social persona without being perceived as 'representing the actual deceased', let alone being identified with him or her.

A *sema* can be the metonymic sign of the deceased symbolizing his social persona as a memory after death without representing that persona iconographically; such iconographical representation is only one of the options for the grave monument; and when that option was taken further options were open as to the greater or lesser definition of that persona. The perceived (by the ancient viewers) relationship between the *sema* and the dead person was variable within wide parameters. The fact that there were different types of grave monuments, indeed of grave statues, including animals and monsters as well as different human types, shows that this relationship was not fixed and unchanging even within the category 'grave statues', though most of the members of this category involved a relationship to the deceased's persona closer than simply the one that all grave monuments have to that persona as metonymic signs of the deceased. Clearly, this cannot obtain except in the most indirect way in the case of a kore standing over a male grave, which would not have been understood as belonging to the category of *sema* that involved a schematic representation of the deceased. The selection of the statue of a kore as a *sema* for a male grave can be made sense of in terms of the Greek mentality associated with such statues. For, we saw in § ii.2, a grave statue was, among other things, a beautiful thing, an *agalma*, that enhanced and coloured positively the memory of that deceased. The beautiful statue of a beautiful maiden makes an especially beautiful *agalma*, given the close symbolic association between beauty and the marriageable parthenos; for this, we shall see, is what the kore statue represents, the schema 'marriageable parthenos'. Thus the archaic grave monuments that include an image involved a polysemic spectrum of meanings centred around the core function of the grave monument as the metonymic sign of the deceased and involving varying combinations of the (varying) representation of the social persona of the deceased, the dimension of signification of the '*agalma* type', and the dimension of protection which I shall discuss below in this section. I shall now consider the different types of grave statues representing human beings, beginning with the less common types. First, seated statues. If they do not all represent divinities,[504] if some functioned as schematic representations of, or somehow referred to, the deceased, they are denoting maturity and high status; for the seated position is associated with higher status and/or maturity in Greek iconography. The fact that seated votive statues could represent the dedicator lends support to the view that at least some seated statues that functioned as *semata* also referred to the deceased's social persona, articulated it iconographically through a schema denoting (high) status. The view that seated statues represent some aspects of the social persona of a certain category of dead people gains support from the fact that on the stelai the seated position is indeed used to indicate an aspect of the social persona of the deceased pertaining to status and/or age, as in the stelai involving women as matrons, or in the doctor's stele.

Now let us consider the grave statues representing riders. The defining feature of the representation, association with horses, is, as we saw, also found elsewhere on grave monuments, as part of the definition of the social persona of the deceased: on grave vases, on the scenes on some of the stelai with relief decoration which include representations involving chariots and/or horses in a subsidiary frieze or the base, and also, we shall see, on some bases of kouroi. Moreover, as we saw in § ii.2, some epitaphs included praise of the deceased's horsemanship, which is thus shown to be a socially important quality. The epitaph for Xenophantos, which was inscribed on the base of an equestrian statue the head of which is missing (Pl. 3),[505] tells us that the *sema* was put up by the deceased's father which suggests that Xenophantos died young.[506] Horsemanship is not mentioned in this epigram, instead the stress is on the father's grief at the loss of his son; what is elsewhere articulated in the epitaph is here represented through the equestrian statue. Horsemanship did not only pertain to sporting prowess. Ownership

---

[504] For statues of divinities in cemeteries cf. below.
[505] Athens Kerameikos 2709 (Hansen 1983: 50; Ridgway 1977: 140, 147, figs. 40–1).
[506] Cf. also below Ch. III § ii.6.

of a horse in archaic Athens involved belonging to a wealthy group; though Solon's reforms gave the name *hippeis* to his second class, the associations of the horse remained élite and aristocratic. In Xenophantos' *sema* the rider is wearing a Thracian cloak, which in fifth-century iconography has been shown to characterize the young Athenian knight.[507] The second Attic equestrian statue known to have functioned as a *sema* comes from Vari;[508] the rider wears a short chiton. It is clear, then, that the equestrian statue is part of the articulation of the deceased's social persona, which it represents through the schema of the rider.

There are three categories of statues of standing youths and maidens: kouroi (naked, standing, young males), korai (draped, standing, young females), and standing, draped youths. All three functioned as *semata* over the grave as well as as votive offerings. In order to reconstruct the meanings of these statues when they functioned as *semata* it is necessary to consider first the meanings of the general schemata 'kouros', 'kore', 'young draped male'. Some important recent studies[509] have advanced and refined our understanding of some of these schemata and their meanings, but I shall attempt to reconsider this question from a somewhat different perspective, partly as a result of the overall framework pertaining to the grave monument as has been set out here, and partly in other ways that will now become clear. I begin with the young draped males.[510] The overwhelming majority of draped youths wear a long chiton with a himation, like most korai; but they wear it differently, in the reverse schema from the usual schema seen in the korai, looped below the right arm, leaving it free for action.[511] This difference is clearly correlative with the perception of males as above all active, and females as above all, and symbolically, passive. The same correlative difference is observed in the stance. These draped youths mostly stand in the same position as the kouroi; that is, like the kouroi, some are shown striding, with one foot and leg significantly and decisively in front of the other,[512] others have one

[507] Lissarague 1990: 191–231; cf. esp. 213, 215–16.
[508] Cf. Loeschke 1879: 302–5 and pl. 3; cf. also Jeffery 1962: 136 no. 1.
[509] D'Onofrio 1982: 135–70; D'Onofrio 1988: 83–96; Stewart 1986: 54–70; cf. also (R.) Osborne 1988: 1–16.
[510] Cf. e.g. the statues discussed in Tuchelt 1970: nos. K21–K33; Freyer-Schauenburg 1974: nos. 73–5.
[511] Cf. Ridgway 1977: 76.
[512] Cf. e.g. the statue Didyma DiS 17 (Tuchelt 1970: K21, pp. 61–2, pl. 23).

foot only slightly forward.[513] The korai, we shall see, are shown either standing statically, with feet close to each other, or sometimes 'walking', with one foot in front of the other. While draped males are at least sometimes shown striding, korai are not.[514] Most young draped males have their arms by their sides, fists clenched. But some touch the edge of their mantle with the right, in a gesture reminiscent of the korai pulling their skirt.[515] Thus we see that the statues of young draped males are in some respects in-between the kouroi and the korai, though their most important characteristic, the iconographical articulation of an active nature, is a male one. Some standing draped males were votive, but at least two were certainly found in cemeteries. The first is datable to *c.*630–620 and comes from a cemetery near Tanagra;[516] it is the statue of a youth wearing a long chiton and a himation and holding a snake.[517] On its base there is the inscription *I M A R O U*. The second is the statue from Pitane at Bergama Museum.[518] The youth from Tanagra, whose lower part is missing, appears to have been standing in a static position. The statue from Pitane appears[519] to have one foot slightly in front of the other, but the general impression is not that the statue is walking—let alone striding—but that it is static, that it is standing with one foot slightly in front of the other. The fact that the hands are not pulling at the garment helps reinforce that impression. Though the sample is too small for us to be certain that this is significant, it is interesting that both these statues that are certain to have functioned as *semata* appear to be static. The notion that this may be significant is strengthened by the fact that, as we shall see, the korai functioning as *semata* also stand in a static position, indeed in an even more emphatically static position than the draped males—though the two series coincide in their degree of 'staticity' in so far as it seems that this stance is as static as standing draped young males ever get. As we shall see, the kouroi do not conform

[513] Cf. e.g. the statue from Pitane at Bergama Museum (Akurgal 1961, figs. 195–7; Boehringer 1959: 167–8 figs. 34–5).

[514] Tuchelt 1970: 61.

[515] Cf. e.g. for standing draped males gathering up their garment with their right: Tuchelt 1970: K29, pp. 64–5, pls. 30–1; K31, p. 65, pl. 32; cf. also Ridgway 1977: 75–6.

[516] Cf. Pharaklas 1969: 66–73; cf. also Ridgway 1977: 75 n. 32, 86.

[517] For this interpretation of the figure cf. Ridgway 1977: 150.

[518] Boehringer 1959: 167–8 figs. 34–5; Akurgal 1961: figs. 195–7, cf. p. 229.

[519] On the basis of the published illustrations (Akurgal 1961: figs. 195–7; Boehringer 1959: 167–8 figs. 34–5).

to this pattern of consistent selection of a static (or 'more static') stance for the *semata* statues. But it must not be assumed that this shows that the pattern seen in the other two series is illusory; for there may be very good reasons why a static stance should be appropriate for korai and draped youths but not for kouroi. I will be suggesting that this is indeed the case, and that the differences reflect important differences in the perceptions articulated in the three series.

Given the fragmentary state of our evidence, and the uncertainty surrounding both the context and the precise schema of so many grave statues, it might be thought more prudent to refrain from attempting to determine any patterns of appearance, and correlations between context and use on the one hand and precise iconographical schema on the other. Such restraint appears superficially more rigorous; for it is perceived through, and coloured by, the mental schema 'we cannot be certain, thus we should not try to go beyond what the evidence allows us by trying to determine correlations', which, at this moment in the history of scholarship still convinces (unconsciously) more readily than 'what evidence there is suggests there were certain correlations, and we should thus take the possibility that there were such correlations seriously and attempt to reconstruct its significance.' However, this appearance of rigour is a construct of reception, generated by the implicit and unconscious presumption of rigour when what is asserted has a negative, apparently sceptical, form. In reality, such agnosticism about correlations far from being neutral is methodologically dangerous; for it slides unconsciously into the implicit assumption that there were no significant correlations, and this assumption then implicitly and unquestioningly informs the attempt to make sense of archaic grave statues; and this, if incorrect (as, I submit, all the available evidence suggests is the case here), inevitably distorts very significantly the attempt to reconstruct the meanings of these *semata*.

With regard to the interpretation of standing, draped, male statues, one suggestion has been that they represent important people who, however, did not rank high enough for a seated statue, another that they are shown in everyday attire in contrast to the heroic nakedness of the kouroi.[520] But the long chiton and himation

[520] Cf. Ridgway 1977: 75.

are not everyday male attire. There is one context in which they are characteristic male attire, in a particular type of statue, statuette, and figurine, representing figures in a particular context: reclining figures, representing males as symposiasts. Thus, for example, in the Geneleos dedication at the Samian Heraion, that is a cultural milieu in which young draped males were popular, the male dedicator, whose name was -*arches*, is represented in a reclining position and wearing a long chiton[521] and himation;[522] the object he is holding in his hand is damaged and cannot be identified. Another reclining male with a long chiton and himation, also from the Samian Heraion, is holding a rhyton in his hand,[523] and can thus be securely interpreted as a symposiast.[524] The long chiton and himation is also seen in other reclining figures, especially statuettes and figurines.[525] The long chiton and himation is also sometimes worn by some men in symposium scenes on vases.[526] In these circumstances, I would like to suggest that the long chiton and himation worn by the draped young males characterizes them as symposiasts, that is members of the aristocratic sympotic group. They are not depicted in the reclining schema that corresponds to the symposiastic position and in which other, and certainly mature, males are shown. They combine elements of the kouros and of the reclining symposiast figures. I suggest that the striding and walking stance (which characterizes all archaic statues of young males, that is, both kouroi and young draped males, in opposition to the korai, who are shown either standing statically or walking, never striding, and represents a male characteristic, the active nature of the young male),[527] is combined in these statues with an iconographical element signifying the symposion, the long chiton and himation, to create a variation on the kouros, which stresses the social persona of symposiast, member of the sympotic group. To understand this choice we must remember that the symposion was a central institution in the archaic city, in which the ruling group of aristocratic males defined itself

---

[521] On this type of chiton cf. Freyer-Schauenburg 1974: 117, 120–1.

[522] Freyer-Schauenburg 1974: no. 63, pp. 116–23 pls. 51–3.

[523] Ibid. no. 70A/B, pp. 148–9 pl. 58.

[524] Cf. ibid. 149.

[525] Cf. ibid. 120–1 for a list.

[526] Cf. e.g. the black-figure cup Berlin 4516 (*ABV* 52.27; *Add.* 13).

[527] Boardman (1978: 22) sets out various practical and aesthetic advantages in having one leg advanced but also acknowledges that this stance 'enhances the impression of energy and movement', and it is this that is relevant here.

and expressed its identity.[528] That the life of the symposion was positively coloured in archaic Greece hardly needs mentioning. What should be stressed is that the softness and luxuriousness that are arguably conveyed by the draped males and their gestures, which is often associated with Ionia, were seen as positive rather than negative traits even in the democratic Athens of the second half of the fifth century.[529]

The long chiton and himation is an alternative to the nudity of the kouroi, often referred to as 'heroic nudity'. I shall consider briefly the meanings of this iconographical element, which is important for the reconstruction of the meanings of the kouroi, but also of those statues, like the draped young males, who did not select it. I begin by stating my own view. Though I accept that the nudity of many archaic and classical males is symbolic, that it was invested with certain values and signified certain things, I am not convinced that there is a secure basis for thinking that it represented man in an ideal or archetypal or generalizing way. In my view, the association between *gymnos*, *gymnasion*, and *gymnazo*[530] makes it clear that in Greek mentality the primary association of nudity was with the world of the *gymnasion* and its educational and social values. In so far as an element of 'ideal' came in, it was a very culturally specific ideal referring to membership of a particular social and age group, in the archaic period young aristocrats; of course, beauty and *arete* were associated with it, but both were firmly located in, and defined through the world and values of, the *gymnasion*. The representations of naked males articulated this notion and also expressed relationships between membership of that group and the exercise of its activities and the represented context. (Though it cannot be excluded that the schema then spread to other contexts as a marker denoting higher status whether or not it was appropriate.) Thus, for example, a representation of a naked warrior expressed, among other things, the relationship between the world of the *gymnasion* and its values and activities on the one hand and war on the other. The fact that there was a close relationship between athletics and warfare is well known; there was also a symbolic relationship, a homology, between warfare between the

---

[528] Cf. Murray 1983: 195–9; cf. also Schmitt-Pantel 1990: 15 with bibliog., 24–6.
[529] Cf. e.g. Edmunds 1987: 43–6.
[530] On the meanings of *gymnos* cf. also McDonnell 1991: 183 and nn. 3–4 with bibliog.

poleis and the *agones*,[531] especially the Panhellenic *agones*, in which the athletes competed as members of their poleis. In the archaic period athletic *agones*, especially the Panhellenic ones, were also a privileged locus for the complex interaction of the international aristocracy, on the one hand competitive and agonistic (like war) and on the other co-operative and integrative (like intermarriages and the institution of *xenia*), and thus also of the definition of the international aristocracy as a group. Consequently, the athletic persona that, on my interpretation, is articulated in the kouros, inevitably also conveyed this aspect of the social persona of the deceased, 'member of the international aristocracy and possibly victor, perhaps simply competitor, or potential competitor in the Panhellenic Games'. One epigram mentions the deceased's identity as Olympic victor;[532] another says he was *aethlophoros*.[533] It may not be without significance that neither grave monument involved a kouros, which (on my reading) would have been representing the same persona in a more general and less triumphant form than the epigrams, which told not simply of participation, but of victory, in the *agones*. To represent the deceased's persona through a kouros was a particular choice, that stressed a particular facet of that persona; not everyone made that choice. These differential choices are intelligible if the three types, the naked kouros, the draped young rider, and the draped young symposiast, were symmetrical, less so if one represented an idealized young man and the others not. As we shall see, a similar comparability obtains between the choice between a kouros statue and a stele, despite claims to the contrary that will be considered below.

Let me now consider the alternative interpretation of heroic nudity by focusing on a most perceptive and important, if brief, discussion of this question by Stewart. In a recent discussion Stewart[534] interprets heroic nudity as representing 'man in an "ideal", or rather archetypal and generalizing way', signifying beauty and *arete* and 'affirming the superiority of men over women, and soon, of Greeks over barbarians'.[535] His objection to interpreting nudity in Greek art in connection with athletic

[531] Cf. Vernant 1974: 45.
[532] Cf. Hansen 1983: 43.
[533] Cf. ibid. 136.
[534] Stewart 1990: 105–6.
[535] Ibid. 106.

nudity is, first, that he takes athletic nudity to be later than the general appearance of male nudity in Greek art, which he dates *c.*750;[536] for according to the eighth-century tradition, the first athlete to run naked did so by accident at 720 BC, and this fits with the fact that in Homer boxers, wrestlers, and others still wear loincloths or even cloaks. But, he adds, even if the victor lists are wrong and Homer anachronistic, the 'Olympic' theory of athletic nudity still would not explain the nudity of the early (from the tenth century onwards) 'Zeus' and 'Hera' figurines. In my view, this case is not compelling. First, there is no reason to believe that the tradition that places this change at *c.*720 (and the others that do so at 724 or 652)[537] has any historicity, and that nudity had not in fact been a feature in the Olympic Games straight from the very beginning.[538] Second, the argument depends on the assumption that all nudity is exactly the same, independently of context, and that this significance does not change in the course of time; and that therefore a single explanation must cover both the early figurines and all subsequent phenomena. This assumption is semiologically unsafe, and its validity is shown to be especially questionable in this case because the very fact of the introduction of athletic nudity, whenever that had happened, on Stewart's own view after heroic nudity had been established, inevitably changed the assumptions pertaining to nudity and thus also the meanings ascribed to it. Third, in any case, if nudity did not reflect the reality of athletics in the eighth century or indeed later, it does not follow that it was perceived to be archetypal, generalized and ideal. In the conceptual art of *c.*750 the likelihood is that the schemata 'naked male', 'draped female' were the iconographical articulation of contemporary perceptions of men and women, a choice to stress their different natures, in this case in symmetrical iconographical articulations. If this is correct, though nudity would have been a gender characteristic at that time, there is no reason to think that it was more 'ideal' and more heroic that the equivalent women's 'clothedness'. In

---

[536] It has recently been argued that 'nude exercising was generally practised by the mid-sixth century at Athens and probably earlier in Sparta and at the Olympic Games' (McDonnell 1991: 182–93; the quotation is from p. 193).

[537] On these traditions cf. McDonnell 1991: 183 and n. 2.

[538] Whenever that may have been, but this is another complex story that I cannot discuss here.

addition, when athletic nudity became the norm, which on this theory it was at a subsequent stage, its significance would inevitably have changed, for the connection with the world of the *gymnasion* and the *agon* would inevitably have invested this element with a specialized athletic reference. A serious objection against the view that heroic nudity was 'ideal', is that while the resulting asymmetry of female statues could be explained as an articulation of the ideological superiority of the male over the female, as Stewart suggests, this explanation cannot meet the case of equestrian statues, especially not those standing over the grave which we know were somehow related to the deceased's social persona; for the rider is draped in both the Attic[539] equestrian statues functioning as *semata* known to me. Indeed one of them, we saw, represented a draped youth wearing a garment that at least in the fifth century came to characterize the élite group of knights. For, as we saw, the equestrian statue pertains to a person of high status, and the fact that they were dressed would be inexplicable if it had indeed been a sign of inferiority to nudity's sign of superiority. But the choice makes perfect sense if we assume that nudity was one particular schema pertaining to the athletic realm and the world of the *gymnasion*, while at the same time it evoked through the trope of metonymy the whole nexus 'young member of the aristocratic élite' of which the world of the *gymnasion* was part; exactly like the equestrian statues with the articulation of the 'horseman' persona, and, if my interpretation is right, the standing young draped male with the symposiastic dress, all evoking metonymically the whole nexus of young member of the élite, educated in the *gymnasion*, and member of the sympotic group, with all the attached social values. This does indeed correspond to Stewart's view that the kouros represents male upper-class *arete* which includes beauty and nobility, *kalokagathia*;[540] but in my view this is done not through a generic and idealized schema, but through the articulation of a specific social persona, which calls up the whole nexus of that social persona, alternative articulations of which were the equestrian statue and the standing young draped male. This picture is not invalidated by the fact that in some equestrian

---

[539] And thus both directly comparable to a significant part of the grave monuments under discussion and capable of being situated in the social realities of which they were part.

[540] Stewart 1986: 60–1.

statues from the Athenian Acropolis the rider is naked.[541] On the contrary, the equestrian statue from the Athenian Acropolis known as the Rampin horseman,[542] which is one of those in which the rider is naked, shows us that the nakedness of the votive equestrian statues offers another argument in favour of the interpretation proposed here. For if his nudity is interpreted in the way suggested here, the statue would be representing the social persona of an individual male in terms of both horsemanship and athletics, the world of the *gymnasion*, and more widely sport and agonistic competition; and this reading coincides with, and is thus confirmed by, that imposed by another element of the statue: the rider is wearing a wreath of wild celery, the prize in the Isthmian and Nemean Games, which defined him as an athlete, a victorious agonistic competitor.

Another argument against the view that nudity is 'heroic' and characterizes the ideal, and generic, is provided by the fact that nudity was not limited to the kouroi, but is also found on the stelai, which Stewart and others consider to be at the opposite end of the spectrum from the generic kouroi and korai.[543] I shall discuss the relationship between the two types of grave monument below. What is relevant here is that if Stewart's perceptions and differentiation were right, heroic nudity should not have appeared in the non-generic stelai images; but it does. In the case of athletes this may be taken as simply a reflection of reality, but it is also found on some warriors,[544] while others are shown wearing armour.[545] This suggests that both options were open; that both articulations reflected perceptions pertaining to the representation of a warrior's social persona on a stele, with the 'heroic nudity' (on my interpretation) referring to the world of the *gymnasion* that trained the aristocratic young not only for the agonistic competitions in which the archaic international aristocracy was involved, but also in preparation for their transformation into (aristocratic) citizens/warriors.[546] If the so-called Marathon runner

---

[541] Cf. e.g. Broneer 1938: 246 fig. 74; Schuchhardt 1939: no. 317, pls. 142–3.

[542] Cf. Ridgway 1977: 141, 147 with bibliog.; cf. also Boardman 1978: fig. 114; Stewart 1990: 120 and figs. 125, 127–8.

[543] Cf. Stewart 1990: 50; cf. also R. Osborne 1988: 8.

[544] Cf. e.g. Boardman 1978: figs. 230, 236.

[545] Cf. e.g. Boardman 1978: fig. 235.

[546] This situation obtains irrespectively of whether it is correct that the nudity of warriors is an earlier phenomenon (cf. e.g. Boardman 1978: caption to fig. 230), a view dependent

stele[547] represents a runner in *hoplitodromos*, with the helmet signifying the hoplite gear and the running schema the running, which seems the most plausible interpretation of this image,[548] it would follow that the schema selected is the one with the greatest proportion of 'heroic nudity' among those available in the iconographical repertory of Athenian artists to represent an armed runner, and would again, if I am right, be stressing, by evoking in a more general (not simply competition-specific) way, the world of the *gymnasion* and athletic competition, and its connection with warfare.[549] Whether this stele was free-standing or had decorated a built grave,[550] this would confirm that nudity was one of the options in the stelai, the chosen option in kouroi, but only one of the options in male grave statues taken as a whole. My conclusions on 'heroic nudity' will gain further support through some considerations pertaining to kouros statues that will be set out below.[551]

Let us now return to the male draped statues functioning as *semata*, to add something about the one statue of this type known to have included an additional iconographical element, the statue of a youth holding a snake from a cemetery near Tanagra. In the eyes of its contemporaries this element characterized the *sema*

on interpreting Copenhagen, Ny Carlsberg IN 2787 (Richter 1961: 50–1 no. 77) as non-funerary (but cf. now Ridgway 1977: 166). If this view is right, it means that in the later period this selection became dominant.

[547] Cf. Ridgway 1977: 166 and n. 23 with bibliog.; Boardman 1978: fig. 239. In my view the notion that it could have been votive was generated by a misreading of the representation.

[548] On this stele cf. also D'Onofrio 1988: 89 and n. 38.

[549] For Attic representations of *hoplitodromos* on red-figure vases involving helmet, shield, and greaves: cf. e.g. amphora Louvre G 214 (*ARV* 203.96; *Add.* 193); cf. also Olivova 1984: ill. on p. 103. Cf. the bronze statuette of an armed runner at Tübingen, Universitätssammlung: Stewart 1990: fig. 183. A different type is illustrated by a bronze statuette of Peloponnesian workmanship from Dodona (Ioannina Museum 4913) which shows the man wearing full hoplite armour and shown running: Vokotopoulou 1973: 68, pl. 25 and colour pl. III. In some red-figure images the figure has only a shield in addition to the helmet, and in some only the helmet, in the same schema as that on the stele under discussion; cf. examples for both the latter schemata on the cup in Munich illustrated in Drees 1968: figs. 40*a/b* (Museum no. not given), where the emblematic figure on the tondo has a helmet and shield as does the emblem on his shield.

[550] Cf. Ridgway 1977: 166 and n. 23.

[551] The fact that the nakedness of the kouroi was one choice that eventually imposed itself, after a short-lived experimentation with a belt that indicated clothing in an abbreviated way, by the Naxian school between 640 and 600 (cf. Stewart 1986: 57–9), itself, I submit, lends a little further support to the conclusion reached here. For it suggests that, contrary to what is necessitated by the 'generic ideal' theory, nudity was not an inseparable part of the nexus 'standing young male' articulated in the kouros, but simply became the preferred choice for this type of statue.

further, in ways similar to those in which korai holding objects were characterized. If the object is indeed a snake, an animal with strong chthonic connections, it may be signifying one or both of the following. It may be stressing its own nature as the *sema* of a person who now belongs to the nether world and the nether gods; or it may be representing the deceased's involvement with a chthonic cult, through, for example, holding a priestly office. If the latter, the statue, in articulating the deceased's social persona, would be stressing an aspect that is important to the shade in afterlife as well as to his memory in the world of the living. If the deceased had had no such involvement, it would be representing him as a devotee, as well as subject, of the nether gods, in a schema comparable to that of korai statues in sanctuaries holding objects, such as a dove, associated with that cult. As we shall see, some grave korai held objects that were closely associated with Persephone.

I now turn to the main series of grave statues, the kouroi and korai. Both series included types without any additional elements and also types with some additional elements. Such elements, and the gestures of the figures, and/or their context defined some statues as representing, for example, a deity, or a worshipper. There can be no doubt that kouroi and korai were statues of young people, and not generic 'male' and 'female' types. This is unambiguous in the case of the kouroi: for, in contrast to our culture, in Greek iconography beardlessness was a specific sign; it meant 'youth'; it did not denote the 'generically male'. I shall return to this question below. As we shall now see, in the case of korai also there were elements which created the meaning 'maiden', rather than simply 'female'.

A kore is a statue of a standing, draped, young female who either has both arms by her side, or holds objects, or has one hand on her breast, and/or pulls at her drapery. She is richly dressed and bejewelled. Korai statues were both dedicated in sanctuaries and functioned as *semata* over graves. They are sometimes shown standing statically, with feet close to each other, sometimes 'walking' with one foot in front of the other. Sometimes the kore is shown pulling at her skirt. Though it is not the case that only the korai shown walking are pulling at their skirt,[552] it certainly does seem to

---

[552] Phrasikleia, for example (on which cf. below n. 603), and kore Richter 1968: no. 55

be the case that it is only when the kore is shown walking that we find the schema in which a lot of the skirt is pulled, so that the whole arrangement of the drapery is radically altered as a result of the gesture. The fact that there is a correlation between the gesture of pulling a lot of skirt and the 'walking' arrangement of their legs and feet suggests that the schema in such korai is one of action. Some of the korai holding objects are holding them in an offering position, and it is possible to argue that they are in fact shown in the action of offering, holding out an object.[553] This would still be representing the kore as an *offerans* emblematically, but through the representation of an action, and thus in a somewhat different mode than is the case in a static kore who is holding an object connected with the relevant cult against her chest and/or in a lowered hand,[554] where the mode is purely emblematic. Thus some korai are shown static, in 'being', as it were, though a 'being' that may be emblematically characterized through the addition of certain objects, while others are shown in 'action'. Some votive korai are static, with their feet close together,[555] while other votive korai are 'walking' while pulling their skirt.[556] The situation appears to be different in the case of the korai that functioned as *semata*. Of the ones certain to have had this function both those whose lower body and/or feet are preserved, Phrasikleia,[557] and the statue of which the base with the feet and the epigram is preserved,[558] are static, with feet close together. Of the three statues that probably but not provenly had that function the so-called Berlin Goddess[559] is static with feet close together, as are the New York Metropolitan Museum 07.286.110 Rogers Fund and Piraeus Archaeological Museum 2530. Thus, in so far as we are able to ascertain, funerary korai are always shown in the static position. This contrasts both with the fact that some votive korai are shown in a static stance while others are shown 'walking', and also with the fact that kouroi functioning as *semata* are, like

---

are static, but are lightly pulling their skirt. The same is also observable in bronze statuettes (cf. Richter 1968: no. 101).

[553] Cf. e.g. Richter 1968: no. 122.
[554] Cf. e.g. ibid. no. 43.
[555] Cf. e.g. Freyer-Schauenburg 1974: nos. 7, 12.
[556] Cf. ibid. nos. 16, 20, 22, 25.
[557] Cf. below n. 603.
[558] Richter 1968: no. 91; Hansen 1983: 18.
[559] On this and the other statues mentioned here cf. below nn. 587–92, 603.

votive kouroi, shown striding or (usually emphatically) walking. The korai hold objects in one or both hands. Both votive and funerary korai can be shown with or without objects. In many cases we do not know whether they had held objects, and what these were; the arms of most korai are missing, and in other cases the arm is preserved but the object is missing. We have the following information for each of the categories distinguished here, korai functioning as *semata*, korai from votive contexts, and korai from unclear contexts. The objects held by the funerary korai are first, a flower; and second, a pomegranate. As for objects held by korai found in votive contexts, first, the following korai from the Athenian Acropolis, that is, the same cultural and ritual milieu as all the korai known to have functioned as *semata*, are holding the following objects. (1) Kore Acropolis Museum no. 593[560] is holding a wreath and a pomegranate (she is also wearing a necklace similar to that of the Berlin Goddess).[561] (2) Kore Acropolis Museum no. 677 is holding a pomegranate in her left;[562] we do not know what, if anything, she may have held in her right. (3) Kore Acropolis Museum no. 680[563] is holding out an apple or pomegranate with her right. (4) Kore Lyons Museum and Acropolis Museum 269 + 163 + 164,[564] who is wearing a polos, is holding a dove. (5) Kore Acropolis Museum no. 683[565] is holding a bird. Second, korai found in other votive contexts—which in reality comes down to the Samian Heraion — are holding the following objects. (1) Kore Berlin, Staatliche Museen Inv. 1750 from the Heraion at Samos[566] is holding a hare. (2) A kore at Vathy Museum, Samos, from the Heraion[567] is holding a bird. (3) A kore found east of the Samian Heraion[568] is also holding a bird. Finally, the following objects are held by korai that come from unclear contexts. (1) A dove is held by the kore Berlin, Staatliche Museen, Inv. 1791 from Miletos.[569] (2) A bird is held by the following korai: Berlin, Staatliche Museen

[560] Richter 1968: no. 43.
[561] On which cf. n. 592 below.
[562] Richter 1968: no. 59.
[563] Ibid. no. 122.
[564] Ibid. no. 89.
[565] Ibid. no. 120.
[566] Ibid. no. 56.
[567] Freyer-Schauenburg 1974: no. 20.
[568] Ibid. no. 21A/B.
[569] Richter 1968: no. 57.

Inv. 1577;[570] Paris, Louvre 3380, found near Klazomenai;[571] London, British Museum B319.[572]

There thus appear to be different patterns in the objects held by the korai in the different areas and sanctuaries, with the bird appearing to be especially popular in East Greece, and perhaps somewhat less so in Athens.[573] The evidence is very fragmentary, and we cannot base any secure conclusions on it. But the late archaic terracottas from the Acropolis of a standing female figure with the left leg slightly forward, wearing chiton and himation, holding in her right, which is bent and brought against her breast (clearly echoing the korai and representing young votaries) a flower or a fruit[574] confirm that such objects were appropriate for this particular ritual context. Some korai, at least one from a votive context[575] and at least one funerary,[576] have one hand on the breast. The hand on breast gesture combined with the other arm being lowered along the body, which, we shall see, is found in a kore that functioned as a *sema*, is also found on female statuettes, most notably the Auxerre one.[577] It is also found on small-size marble kouroi from votive contexts (sanctuaries) at Naukratis.[578] It is considered to be a gesture of worship, a 'submissive, humble salutation', underlying prayer when mortals address gods.[579] Thus, it characterized emblematically the statue or statuette as a worshipper in a state of prayer.

Korai statues represent young maidens. In the absence of any age signs comparable to the beardlessness of the males, we are relying on the following considerations. First, the korai look young. But this may be a culturally determined impression, that may not be taking account of undiscovered (by us) conventions and assumptions through which their contemporaries perceived those statues.[580]

---

[570] Ibid. no. 161.

[571] Ibid. no. 163.

[572] Ibid. no. 167.

[573] It is possible that, besides the korai mentioned above, the kore Athens Acropolis Museum 656 (Brouskari 1974: 96–7, fig. 179) may also have held a bird.

[574] Cf. Brouskari 1974: 35–6, figs. 35–40.

[575] Cf. Freyer-Schauenburg 1974: no. 3A, pp. 16–18, pl. 2. Cf. also Richter 1968: no. 73, which comes from an unclear context and is wearing a polos.

[576] Cf. below on this.

[577] Richter 1968: no. 18.

[578] Ibid. nos. 59 and 60.

[579] Cf. Brandt 1965: 109–11.

[580] Cf. on such conventions pertaining to the representation of female age on vases Sourvinou-Inwood 1988: *passim*.

Second, given that in the stelai, and in male statues, it is the seated position that corresponds to the representation of higher status and/or maturity, both of which characterize the *gyne* in opposition to the *parthenos*, it is extremely likely that statues of seated women represented *gynaikes*, and korai represented maidens. If this is right, the great numerical superiority of the latter over the former can be understood in the context of the statues' both votive and funerary use. With regard to the latter, it would simply correspond to the fact that, as we shall see, most archaic grave monuments were erected for young people. With regard to the former, it makes sense in the following context. In my view, votive korai represent young female worshippers, but are not always representations of the dedicator, which is why males can dedicate korai statues.[581] To present an image of oneself as a votary was clearly one choice open to those dedicating votive statues. To present an image of a beautiful *parthenos* as a votary was clearly another option open to a male, perhaps even if he did not have a daughter whose image this statue could be deemed to be, in a sense correlatively with the roles played by the daughter in the ritual of the *oikos* under the headship of the father. For the symbolic (as well as often real) association between beauty and the marriageable *parthenos* made the image of a beautiful girl a particularly appropriate *agalma* to offer a deity—perhaps especially a female deity. The korai, then, represented young maidens of the marriageable *parthenos* age, an important social category in ancient Greece;[582] the richness of their dress and jewellery corresponds to, and articulates iconographically, the fact that in Greek mentality the marriageable *parthenos* was symbolically associated with beauty and beautification.[583] Sometimes the statues represented the girls as votaries, bringing offerings to a deity or making a gesture of worship. The schema of the kore in its various versions corresponds exactly to, and thus makes perfect sense as the iconographical articulation of, the social persona of the *parthenos* in the Greek world, which, in contrast to that of the young male, was very restricted. The focal aspect of a woman's social persona was her status as a woman, her status of either *parthenos* or *gyne*; the only social role either could perform outside the *oikos* was in the religious

---

[581] Cf. e.g. the kore Acropolis Museum 686 + 609 (Richter 1968: no. 180).
[582] On this category and its iconographical representations cf. Sourvinou-Inwood 1988: 28–30, 51–7.
[583] Cf. Calame 1977: 447.

sphere. Thus, the social persona of the *parthenos* consisted entirely of, first, the status 'marriageable girl', capable of, and about to enter into, marriage, the ultimate goal and fulfilment of a Greek woman's life, for which she was ascribed symbolic beauty whatever her individual physical reality may have been; and second her participation and role in religion, in cult activities in the *oikos* and in the polis and its subdivisions. The cultic office most closely connected with the age and social category 'marriageable *parthenos*' is that of *kanephoros*.[584] Thus the kore statue articulates the two aspects of the marriageable *parthenos*' social persona, with various versions emphasizing different aspects in different ways.

Given the gender asymmetry between males and females (and, if this is right, given that the korai articulate sometimes one sometimes both aspects of the marriageable *parthenos*' social persona), we should expect statues of young men to be articulating the much greater range and many facets of the social persona of the young male (aristocrat), either in combination or as alternatives. This is exactly what would be the case on my interpretation: the young male was represented either as an athlete (evoking the whole nexus of young aristocratic male *arete*), or as a symposiast (also evoking further aspects of the persona of the young aristocrat) or as a horseman (with a comparable evocation of more general connotations). But on the orthodox interpretation of the kouros as a generic young male there is no such asymmetrical homology; instead, while the young female's 'marriageable *parthenos*' social persona was represented, for the young male it would be a matter of a choice between a schema representing a generic youth, or a specific one (horseman) and what on the hitherto proposed interpretations would be a more or less generic one (draped youth). I submit that the fact that on my interpretation the patterns in the images correspond to the configurations of the social persona within each gender and between the asymmetrical genders as these are known from other sources offers another argument in favour of the interpretations proposed here, which, though not in itself conclusive, helps strengthen further what is a very strong case.

As is the case with the votive korai, some of which hold no objects while others hold one or more objects,[585] among the korai

[584] Cf. Sourvinou-Inwood 1988: 54, 94 n. 253.
[585] Cf. e.g.: without objects Richter 1968: nos. 67, 68, 69; Freyer-Schauenburg 1974: no. 16; with objects: Richter 1968: nos. 43, 89, 120, 122.

functioning as *semata* some are holding objects, others are not. Phrasikleia is holding a flower, the so-called Berlin Goddess is holding a pomegranate, as is New York Metropolitan Museum 07.286.110 Rogers Fund. The headless kore Piraeus Archaeological Museum 2530, has her right arm lowered and connected to her body and the left bent with her hand on her breast. All these korai, some of which are certain to have been grave statues and the others likely to have been so, come from Attica. The ones certain to have functioned as *semata* are the following.[586] Phrasikleia; the kore Athens, NM 81, that is the statue that functioned as a *sema* of which the base with the feet and epigram is preserved;[587] and the kore from Moschato, Athens NM 3859.[588] The following statues almost certainly functioned as *semata*, but cannot be proved to have done so. First, the so-called Berlin Goddess; second, the kore, New York Metropolitan Museum 07.286.110 Rogers Fund;[589] and third, the kore, Piraeus Archaeological Museum 2530.[590] The head of a kore from Myrrhinous,[591] a surface find from a necropolis, is almost certainly funerary, but hardly informative for our purposes. All of the above korai whose lower part survives and thus allows us to determine the position of their legs and feet (that is, all except the kore from Moschato) are static, with their feet closely together. The sample is not large, but it is not insignificant either; in addition, the fact that, as we saw, the two statues of young draped males known to have certainly come from cemeteries, are either static or almost static makes it not implausible that this choice is significant. This goes together with the fact that when objects are held by korai functioning as *semata* they are held against the body, not held out in the action of offering. Those of these korai who are holding part of their drapery, Phrasikleia and the kore, New York Metropolitan Museum 07.286.110 Rogers Fund, are doing so in a slight, emblematic manner, not in the strong pulling of the drapery that goes together with the 'walking' korai and can be seen as part of the schema of the 'walking kore', the kore in action. The gesture 'hand on breast' made by the kore, Piraeus Archaeological Museum 2530

[586] Cf. D'Onofrio 1982: 142, 144–5.
[587] Richter 1968: no. 91; Hansen 1983: 18.
[588] Richter 1968: no. 40.
[589] Ibid. no. 138, figs. 441–4.
[590] Lazaridis 1968: 34 and fig. 3.
[591] Daux 1962: 664, 669 fig. 28.

and, in a slightly modified form, by the 'Berlin Goddess', was, we saw, a gesture of worship which characterized emblematically a figure as a worshipper. It would appear, then, that it was appropriate for the korai functioning as *semata* to be represented not in action, but in being, as emblematic images. In other respects, different choices were made in the individual statues functioning as *semata*, such as, for example, association with certain objects.

The 'Berlin Goddess'[592] is wearing a peplos and an epiblema, a polos with incised and painted decoration of maeander and lotus, a spiral bracelet, and also a necklace and earrings with pendants of the same design which may be representing pomegranates. She is certainly holding a pomegranate in her right hand. It may be argued that this statue of a young female wearing rich jewellery and holding a pomegranate, is 'simply' an especially rich and beautiful *agalma*. But the significant question is 'how did its contemporary viewers make sense of these iconographical elements, and thus of the statue as a whole?' To start with the most marginal element, the decoration on her polos, it has been suggested that the lotus flower is, among other things, an erotic symbol.[593] The exact significance, if any, of the polos is unclear.[594] It has been suggested[595] that it was associated with the non-human sphere, and that when it was worn by humans it denoted some symbolic association with the divine, for example that the woman wearing it was a priestess; and that the fact that it is worn by some korai that were grave statues is to be explained either in terms of an alleged heroic significance of the funerary statues or as being modelled on that of a goddess because of some special connection of the deceased with that goddess. Simon[596] argued that it was associated with marriage and with Hera as a marriage goddess and that people who died unmarried were given it in the grave; and that the 'Berlin Goddess' is the grave statue of a girl who died unmarried. It is certainly true that not all korai wear a polos, and not all korai carry or wear pomegranates. It is worth noting that the busts of an Underworld goddess, who may be Persephone, some with an aniconic face, that stood over graves

[592] Cf. Richter 1968: no. 42, pp. 39–40, figs. 139–46; M. Robertson 1975: 99–100.
[593] Cf. Koch-Harnack 1989: 72–89.
[594] Cf. on this Simon 1972: 205–20; Ridgway 1977: 108–10; Boardman 1978: 11–12.
[595] Cf. previous note.
[596] Simon 1972: 214.

at Cyrene were wearing a polos.[597] Persephone, especially in her persona as bride of Hades, was closely associated with the pomegranate in Panhellenic myth,[598] though she was not the only goddess associated with this fruit.[599] Nor is it the case that only korai that are *semata* are holding a pomegranate; some votive korai are also holding it, including korai from the Athenian Acropolis. This corresponds to the fact that in the eighth century and the archaic period terracotta pomegranates were both placed in graves and dedicated in sanctuaries.[600] But meanings are created in context; here the funerary context would have strongly foregrounded the pomegranate's association with Persephone. A pomegranate and a lotus flower, the same combination as in this statue, appears in connection with the worship of the Underworld deities in another ritual milieu: the female votary in front of the seated Underworld deities (undoubtedly Hades and Persephone) on the Laconian relief Berlin Staatliche Museen Inv. 731[601] is holding a pomegranate and a lotus flower.[602]

Phrasikleia,[603] like the 'Berlin Goddess', is wearing jewellery and a polos with highly elaborate rich relief decoration of lotus flowers and buds; her necklace is surely made of pomegranates. Her left arm is against her chest, holding a flower, her right is lightly pulling her skirt. The schema 'young girl with flower' is common in Greek iconography. This does not mean that it carried no specific connotations; on the contrary, the ancient viewers could not but make sense of it through their assumptions concerning the association 'girls and flowers'. Flowers and flower-gathering was associated with the *parthenos*, prenuptial rites and marriage, and also Persephone.[604] If it is correct that her necklace is made of pomegranates this is another connection with Persephone, especially in her persona as bride of Hades. Thus these two statues have elements

[597] On these busts cf. below and n. 681.
[598] Cf. Sourvinou-Inwood 1991: 160 and cf. 183–4 n. 60.
[599] Cf. Simon 1972: 208–10; Sourvinou-Inwood 1991: 183–4 n. 60; Kourou 1987: 105–6, 107, 109, 111, 116 n. 106. Cf. also Muthmann 1982: 52, 67, 64, 39; cf. also L. Burn, Review Muthmann 1982, *JHS* 104 (1984), 268–9.
[600] Cf. Kourou 1987: 101 and *passim* with bibliog.
[601] On these reliefs cf. Andronikos 1956: 253–314; cf. esp. 305.
[602] Cf. Richter 1968: no. 92 fig. 288.
[603] On the statue that was the *sema* of Phrasikleia cf. Mastrokostas 1972; cf. esp. M. Robertson 1975: 100–1; Stewart 1990: 119–20. (For bibliog. cf. Ridgway 1977: 116, 109 n. 32, 302.)
[604] Cf. Sourvinou-Inwood 1991: 65, 90 n. 36, 108–10, 161.

associated with, which in this funerary context could not but evoke, Persephone, especially in her persona as bride of Hades. This persona had generated a paradigmatic relationship between the goddess and marriageable girls and brides;[605] this relationship had generated, among other things, the metaphor 'bride of Hades',[606] which expresses the notion 'instead of marriage she got death', which, in the Greek representations meant also 'she died unfulfilled'. For in Greek mentality marriage is a woman's fulfilment, and dying unmarried means dying unfulfilled; the 'bride of Hades' metaphor articulates this perception. Thus the 'Berlin Goddess' and Phrasikleia may be seen as iconographical articulations of the metaphor that eventually crystallized into the 'bride of Hades' metaphor, through the *iconographical* partial assimilation of the two statues to Persephone, the real bride of Hades; this expressed iconographically the notion that the statue was the *sema* of a girl who died unmarried. This reading of the images is confirmed by Phrasikleia's epigram,[607] *kore keklesomai aei, anti gamo para theon touto lachousa onoma,* which characterizes her as, above all, a girl who died unmarried.[608] The 'Berlin Goddess' and Phrasikleia, then, are *semata* that articulate a particular social persona, which in Phrasikleia's case coincides with that ascribed to her by the epigram.

All other korai certain to have functioned as grave statues[609] consist of fragments that are not very informative. The only one of which something can be said, the kore, Athens NM 3859, which consists of a torso from neck to waist, has the left forearm against the front of her body, with her hand at and just below the breasts, and with the right arm 'presumably lowered'.[610] It seems that she held an object in her left, but what this object was is unclear. Of the probables, besides the 'Berlin Goddess', one, New York Metropolitan Museum 07.286.110 Rogers Fund, whose head and left arm are the results of an ancient repair, has her right arm at the

---

[605] Cf. Sourvinou-Inwood 1973a: 12–20; Jenkins 1983: 142; Sourvinou-Inwood 1991: 67–8, 92 n. 56, 150–80. This relationship was stronger in some cities than in others.

[606] On the 'bride of Hades' theme in tragedy cf. Rose 1925a: 238–42 (cf. also Rose 1925b: 147–50); Guépin 1968: 141–2; Kamerbeek 1978: 146–9; Loraux 1985: 68–74.

[607] Hansen 1983: 24.

[608] This does *not* entail theological assimilation to Persephone or heroized status as has been suggested by some scholars on the basis of the formulation of the epigram: cf. Daux 1973/4: 239–42 for an unanswerable case against such interpretations.

[609] Cf. above; cf. also the lists in D'Onofrio 1982: 142, 144–5.

[610] Richter 1968: p. 39 no. 40.

chest holding a pomegranate, while the left had originally been lowered and held a fold of the drapery.[611] On my interpretation this is part of the schema through which the maiden standing over the grave, and functioning as the sign, of an unmarried girl is shown as a metaphorical Persephone. The headless kore, Piraeus Archaeological Museum 2530,[612] has her right arm lowered and connected to her body and the left bent with her hand on her breast. It is not totally clear from the illustration whether she had originally held an object, but it would appear that she did not, since Lazaridis states that the arrangement of her arms and hands is reminiscent of that of the Auxerre statuette. As we saw, the gesture of the hand on the breast is also found on other korai, including at least one from a votive context, and the hand on the breast combined with the other arm shown lowered, along the body, is also found on female statuettes, and on small-size marble kouroi from votive contexts at Naukratis. It is a gesture of worship and characterized the figure (through an action that functioned emblematically) as a worshipper in a state of prayer.

I set out above the reasons why, in my view, the kore represents a *parthenos*. Given that the statue over the grave often represented the social persona of the deceased, and that (contrary to our culturally determined assumptions) the state of *parthenos* was *not* the perfect moment in a woman's life, but an unfulfilled state leading on to what was perceived to be the goal of every female's life, I suggest that among women only girls who died unmarried had a kore as a *sema*—though, of course, not all girls who died unmarried did have such a *sema*. If I am right that the status of *parthenos* was iconographically articulated in the funerary korai with additional elements relating to the bride of Hades metaphor, this would add further support to the hypothesis that a kore was only erected as a *sema* for girls who died unmarried. If this is right, the *parthenos* status of the deceased would have been apparent by the mere presence of a kore as a *sema*. The iconographical articulation relating to the bride of Hades metaphor would have stressed the pathos of the death of the unmarried girl.[613] At the same time, the lotus

[611] Ibid. no. 138, figs. 441–4.

[612] Lazaridis 1968: 34 and fig. 3.

[613] D'Onofrio (1982: 166) thinks that the kore is above all a splendid image whose beauty is underlined by the rich drapery and jewels that adorn her; the kore statue thus expresses the typical function of women in archaic society, that of 'bene di prestigio, centro e impulso

and the pomegranate also helped represent the girl as a votary of Persephone, as they characterized the girl votary on the Laconian relief; thus the monument was perhaps also seen as placing the deceased under Persephone's protection. I shall be discussing images of protection on archaic grave monuments below.

What counts as a kouros is a matter of definition. It could be confined to the commonest type of such statues, the naked young male 'striding' or 'walking', one leg in front of the other, with arms at his sides and not holding anything. Normally the category includes at least some kouroi who are not in this canonical stance, but either hold sacrificial animals, or attributes, or vary somewhat · in their stance. Kouroi belonging to these types are the following. First, bearers of sacrificial animals. An example of this type is the so-called Thasos kriophoros,[614] who holds a ram in his left, in front of his body, and has his right by his side. In every respect except the ram he looks exactly like a kouros.[615] Monumental statues of youths carrying sacrificial animals are so far only known from the Ionian world.[616] Some kouroi are shown holding objects. Thus, the kouros Geneva Museum no. 19175[617] held an object in his right hand pressed against his thigh; a kouros from Paros in Copenhagen has his right resting on his hip and possibly carrying an object,

degli scambi che intorno ad essa si organizzano, strumento essenziale per la riproduzione e la proiezione del gruppo verso l'esterno'. This definition of the role of women is not wrong, but it is, I feel, one-sided and not wholly adequate. First, it leaves out the role of woman as actor (e.g. in religion) which is reflected in the statues. Second, it does not recognize the particularity of the *parthenos* and the perceptions pertaining to her in contrast with the *gyne*. Finally, it brackets and elides the fact that archaic women were also individuals who functioned as the important other whose death caused sadness, as stressed in many epigrams; this whole nexus of perceptions and attitudes, we shall see, was not insignificant in the context of the erection of archaic grave monuments, and thus must not be left out from the discussion of the perceptions articulated in the grave statues.

[614] Richter 1960: no. 14.

[615] Other specimens: an over-life-size naked male from Didyma, in every other respect a kouros, is carrying a sacrificial victim (Tuchelt 1970: K16, p. 59, pls. 18–19), as is another from Didyma, close to life-size, of which a fragment survives (Tuchelt 1970: K17 pp. 59–60, pl. 20.2), and another from Claros (ibid. pp. 59–130). Other Kouroi holding offerings are the Samian kouros Inv. III P 8 + II S 242 (Freyer-Schauenburg 1974: no. 45 pp. 84–8, pls. 28–9), which only differs from the kouros schema through the position of his arms, which carried a sacrificial victim, and the unfinished Samian kouros formerly Tigani Museum Inv. 72 (Freyer-Schauenburg 1974: no. 46 pp. 87–8, pl. 31).

[616] There are some regional preferences in the pattern of appearance of archaic statues of human figures. For example, draped young males were common in Ionian Asia Minor and Samos. But these were preferred choices within common parameters, as can be seen from the widespread pattern of distribution of the different types fulfilling the same functions.

[617] Richter 1960: no. 90.

while his left appears to have been carved against his chest.[618] The statue dedicated by the Naxians to Apollo on Delos[619] wore a belt and once held a cylindrical metal object, presumably a bow, in his left, representing Apollo;[620] the Piraeus bronze[621] the head of which is lowered, arms strongly bent (as they are in other kouroi of this stylistic group) and holding what seem to be the remains of a phiale and bow, also represents Apollo. A very rare category is the male standing statues shown in a different stance from the normal kouros one. A mid-sixth-century kouros from Grotta in Naxos[622] has the elbows bent at right angles and the forearms and hands set horizontally on the flanks on either side of the *rectus abdominis*. The excavator, Kontoleon, considers it to be unique and compares it to the small sized stone kouroi with one hand on the breast; he thinks that the statue is represented in action like the stelai and bronze statuettes. The only other directly comparable figures are the two alabaster statuettes from Naukratis cited above.[623] Kontoleon tentatively suggested that this may be the representation of a runner; and that it would be reasonable to expect this kouros to have been the *sema* of a grave (it was not found *in situ*, but in a fill).

Kouroi are not static; they are striding, one leg in front of the other, with arms at the sides (cf. Pl. 2). In some cases the leg and foot are less emphatically in front, and we should define the action as 'walking'. The kouros, then, is shown in a particular form of action; it can be seen as either a statue in action, the action of striding, or as an 'emblematic' statue, emblematically characterized by the action of striding. There is no significant difference between the two possibilities; it was surely both. That striding was perceived as characterizing the kouroi cannot be doubted. Korai do not stride, though some are shown walking, while others are standing in a static position. But statues of draped males can be shown striding,[624] which suggests that striding characterizes males but not females. It clearly represents energetic, quick, vigorous walking. The fact that

---

[618] The hand on the chest gesture was discussed above; Ridgway (1977: 73–4) compares the gesture of the Copenhagen kouros to the Naukratis kouroi and the Ionic korai.

[619] Richter 1960: no. 15.

[620] Cf. Stewart 1986: 57.

[621] Richter 1960: no. 159 *bis*; cf. esp. Stewart 1986: 57.

[622] Kontoleon 1972: 144 pls. 124–5; *Ergon* (1972), 97–8 and fig. 92.

[623] Richter 1960: no. 59 (found in the temenos of Aphrodite); no. 60 (from the temenos of Apollo).

[624] Tuchelt 1970: 61.

this characterized males in opposition to females suggests the possibility that this action may have metonymically signified young male vigour in general and the active nature of the (ideal) young male. The fact that later kouroi, such as Aristodikos' *sema*[625] often combine the walking/striding position of the lower part of the body with arms held away from the body and bent at the elbow, which adds further animation to the stance, at a time when the relationship of the kouros statue to the male body becomes closer, with the former acquiring a deceptively 'almost naturalistic' surface look, means that the representation of the facet 'action' increased (albeit in a schematic, not naturalistic manner) when the relationship between statue and male body became closer; which in its turn perhaps suggests that the facet 'action' characterizing the kouroi emblematically was an important facet of that representation. The fact that all the korai that functioned as *semata* are static, with their feet closely together, and that the two statues of young draped males known to have certainly come from cemeteries, are either static or almost static, while the kouroi functioning as *semata* are not static, but are shown either striding or walking, suggests that the action of striding/walking emblematically characterized the kouroi, and to a much lesser extent the draped youths, but not the korai. This contrast between kouroi and korai corresponds to Greek perceptions of male as active and female as passive. As for the less significant difference between the draped males and the kouroi, it makes sense in the framework of the interpretations of both that have been offered here, according to which the kouros articulates above all the young man as athlete—and through it the whole nexus of young male aristocratic virtues—while the draped statues articulate the young man as a symposiast—and through this the same nexus, but with a different emphasis. This convergence, I submit, offers support to these interpretations.

The fact that meaning is created in context entails that the objects added to the schema 'kouros' determine the meaning of the overall image. Therefore, the fact that the addition of certain objects turns the kouros into Apollo does not mean, as Stewart believes, that 'the basic type' was generic, that 'the very fact' that the kouros 'has to be furnished with attributes to depict specific personalities like offering bearers, athletes, or Apollo, indicates that no particular

---

[625] Richter 1960: no. 165.

personality can be attached to the basic type.'[626] This deduction, which is based on general semiological principles, is confirmed by further arguments. The modality of signification operating when objects are added to a kore or a draped young male statue is different from the one postulated by Stewart for the kouroi. Certainly, if the interpretations set out here are correct, the korai represent the social persona *'parthenos'* and the draped young males the social persona 'symposiast', whether or not they are holding objects, which thus further define or stress certain aspects of the social persona. The modality postulated in my interpretation is well established in Greek iconography, where, for example, the schema 'Dionysos' sometimes includes and sometimes omits the kantharos or the drinking horn. On my interpretation the offering-bearing kouroi operate on this modality: the representation of an athlete becomes the representation of an athlete as a worshipper. This is a common modality of representation in Greek votive statues and figurines. But what, it may be asked, of the particular example of Apollo, which, on the interpretation suggested here, would involve a change of meaning from something specific, namely a young athlete, to something else specific, namely a young god? I see no problems with such a change, since there are examples in Greek iconography in general and archaic sculptural iconography in particular where the addition of an element changes the meaning from something specific, to something else with the same degree of specificity. This is precisely what happens when the beard is added to a male statue: from representing a young male it comes to represent an older male. At a greater degree of specificity, the addition of a dolphin changes a representation of Theseus erotically pursuing a girl to one of Peleus erotically pursuing Thetis.[627]

The stelai often had descriptive narrative scenes on their subsidiary zones and bases;[628] kouroi sometimes also had bases decorated with descriptive narrative scenes,[629] some on three sides. The base Athens NM 3476 depicts a *gymnasion* scene on the front, involving a jumper, wrestlers, and a youth with a javelin, a ball game on

[626] Stewart 1986: 60.

[627] Cf. Sourvinou-Inwood 1991: 61–3 and 88 n. 21.

[628] For a stele base with a scene similar to those of grave statues cf. the base Kerameikos Museum P 1001 that represents four horsemen (cf. e.g. Boardman 1978: fig. 240).

[629] On kouros bases cf. esp. D'Onofrio 1986: 175–93.

one side,[630] and youths setting up a cat and dog fight on the other.[631] The base Athens NM 3477 also has descriptive narrative scenes on all three sides: a scene of 'hockey' playing is depicted on the front, and on each of the sides a chariot with a charioteer in it and a warrior shown in the act of mounting, with two hoplite warriors walking in line behind.[632] With regard to this last scene, D'Onofrio,[633] who discussed the base recently, rejected the interpretation that it represents a funerary procession, and suggested that it is an agonistic image, though the context cannot be shown to have been the *apobates*.[634] There are, we saw, similarities between these images on kouroi bases, those on the subsidiary zone of stelai, and the chariot scenes on the Laconian relief amphorae that functioned as *semata*. I argued against the funerary interpretation for the latter, and the presently discussed scenes can, in my view, also be most plausibly interpreted as 'heroic' images of war, especially in view of the two hoplites walking behind the chariot; I would not exclude that the image may also have evoked the deceased's connection with chariot-racing; if so, it is the *apobates* contest that would surely be most strongly evoked, an event that was important in Athens, but rare elsewhere.[635] In any case, these images clearly articulate the deceased's social persona in the descriptive narrative idiom, through schemata involving many-figured compositions representing social interaction. Another type of scene found on a kouros base is emblematic: on one side of the base Kerameikos Museum P 1002 are represented a lion and a boar;[636] on the front there is a ball game and on the other side horsemen, two scenes that articulate the deceased's social persona in the descriptive narrative mode. The emblematic representation through the lion and the boar image[637] operates in a similar mode as that of the boar on the subsidiary zone of the stele mentioned above; the lion and the

---

[630] On the ball-game and its place in the gymnasium, and thus in proper Athenian civic education, cf. D'Onofrio 1986: 178–9.

[631] D'Onofrio 1986: pl. 54 figs. 1–3; cf. also Boardman: 1978: fig. 242. For a discussion of this base cf. D'Onofrio 1986: 183–5; she argues that the cat and dog scene creates a homoerotic atmosphere and is indirectly connected to courtship scenes.

[632] D'Onofrio 1986: pl. 55 figs. 1–3. She discusses this base at pp. 185–8.

[633] Ibid.

[634] On the *apobates* cf. most recently Crowther 1991: 174–6.

[635] Cf. ibid. 174–5.

[636] Cf. D'Onofrio 1986: 177 and pl. 53 figs. 1–3; (she discusses this base in detail, pp. 178–83); cf. also Boardman 1978: fig. 243.

[637] On which cf. esp. D'Onofrio 1986: 179–82.

boar confronting each other on a funerary monument represent a complex interplay in which the valour of the deceased is represented by both animals, the lion representing valour triumphant and the boar valour in defeat;[638] the lion represented on the grave monument may also have functioned as a protective figure, a function which we shall discuss below.[639] The representation of horsemen undoubtedly referred to horsemanship and equestrian competition,[640] and may conceivably also have evoked war; it helped define the deceased's persona in the descriptive narrative mode. One side represented, and signified his involvement with, and perhaps prowess in, a sporting activity perceived to be of significance in civic education, the other did the same with horsemanship, while the representation of the lion fighting the boar represents the deceased's valour in defeat, either because he was killed in battle, or simply because he is dead. D'Onofrio takes[641] all the scenes in these three bases to be agonistic and to celebrate Athenian (aristocratic) education, with NM 3477 introducing also the *telos* of male education, the citizen as warrior, by alluding to war through a collective image. In my view this interpretation is somewhat restrictive. Undoubtedly, sporting activities played an important part in Athenian education, and it was part of the way aristocratic youths were prepared to be citizens/warriors. But those activities were also perceived to be important in themselves, and defined the youths as aristocratic young men, some no doubt with special prowess in particular sports. In my view the images represent all these aspects of the social identity. This fits excellently the combination of scenes in the three bases. Thus on the base Kerameikos P 1002 one image represents a ball game, the other, the riders, involves sport but may conceivably also evoke war, while the third is above all an image of valour in defeat, probably an image of death at war. Similarly, the base Athens NM 3477 represents another ball game on one side and a heroic image of war on the two others. In contrast, the base Athens NM

---

[638] On the significance of the lion and boar cf. Vermeule 1979: 90–1; Schnapp-Gourbeillon 1981: 46; D'Onofrio 1986: 180–2; cf. also Markoe 1989: 110–15 on the attacking lion as a metaphor for death in battle.

[639] The protective function of the lion would not have been eliminated by the fact that in these images lion and boar are combined and fighting. If the lion over a grave was perceived as protective, the representation of a lion triumphant over a grave would inevitably have been read through assumptions that included its perception as protector of the grave.

[640] Cf. the discussion in D'Onofrio 1986: 182–3.

[641] Ibid. 190–2.

3476 involves scenes from the leisurely life of an aristocratic young man, sport and the cat and dog scene. Any evocation of war is entirely absent, and this young man probably died in his bed.

All three bases, the only ones known to me to belong to, and thus further define, a kouros statue, either consist of or include one or more images of athletic activity. Most significantly, whatever there is on the sides, the central scene in all three is an athletic one, pertaining to the world of the *gymnasion* and agonistic competition. Athens NM 3476 has in the prominent frontal position a *gymnasion* scene and on the sides a ball game and the 'cat and dog scene'. Athens NM 3477 has a ball game, a 'hockey' scene, at the centre and chariots and warriors on the two sides. Kerameikos P 1002 has a ball game at the front and on the sides horsemen and the lion and boar. This emphasis on the representation of the social persona of the deceased as above all an athlete on these bases, and the fact that on all three it is his athlete's persona that is articulated on the principal side of the grave monument, leave no doubt as to the central importance in these grave monuments of the articulation of the deceased's persona as an athlete; and this provides some confirmation for my interpretation of the kouros as (not a generic image, but) a representation of the deceased's persona as athlete which by metonymy signified his whole persona, the whole nexus of the young male aristocrat with its associated notions of *kalokagathia*. On my interpretation, when the viewer was looking at the grave monument's principal side he would be perceiving two different representations of the deceased as an athlete: first the dominant one in the emblematic mode, an image of the deceased which strongly evoked the whole nexus of the young male aristocratic persona *kalos kagathos*; and then through a scene articulating that persona through the descriptive narrative idiom portraying a particular sporting activity through an image of the social group of which he was part and which defined him. The scenes on the base, like the epitaphs, helped shape the way the grave statue and the deceased's social persona was perceived. The statue, the context, the base and the epitaph were all parts of one system, each acquiring its meanings also through its interaction with the others.[642] No

---

[642] R. Osborne (1988: 6–7) notes, with reference to the grave of Kroisos, that while the epigram (Hansen 1983: 27) tells the viewer that this is the tomb of a warrior the statue (Richter 1960: no. 136) makes no reference to military prowess or the fact that he died in battle; this figure, he says 'neither positively identifies itself with Kroisos nor positively

funerary kouros holds an object, in contrast to the funerary korai and the draped young males some of which did hold objects. If my interpretation of the kouros as an image of the young man as an athlete, evoking the whole nexus of the young *kalos kagathos* persona, is right, no additional objects can be conceived that would supplement this persona without restricting it (to, for example, an athlete in a particular sport). The objects held by kouroi in votive contexts are either attributes identifying the statue as the image of a god, or a sacrificial animal. The addition of the latter generates the image of the young aristocratic *kalos kagathos* athlete in the role of sacrificer. This is an appropriate image for a votive offering; but since the cultic role was not especially characteristic of young male aristocrats (in contrast to females, whose cultic role was a most important aspect of their restricted persona), we should not expect it to be represented in a *sema* kouros. When placed in the interpretative framework proposed here, the Grotta kouros, if it was indeed a *sema*,[643] fits well into the series without forcing us to postulate a radical break. If it is correct that the kouroi represented the young aristocratic male as above all an athlete, and that it was through this persona that the whole *kalos kagathos* nexus was evoked, with the striding/walking stance being part of the articulation of this schema, the Grotta kouros can be seen as a particular version of the schema, albeit not one that was a preferred choice: his running stance is a further development of the striding/walking stance of the kouroi, but it is still an action articulating a young male as an athlete, though in this case the action represents a particular type of athlete. This latter trait can also be seen as a unique version of a

differentiates itself from the viewer. The *kouros* represents the viewer *and* Kroisos to the viewer. In coming face to face with this *kouros* the viewer comes face to face with his own death.' Death, he alleges, 'removes all that is specific; death freezes and erases the possibility of differentiation by action.' That the *sema* reminds the passer-by of his or her own mortality is generally accepted; but this does not depend on the kouros being generic. For the fact that not all viewers were male, and [if one thinks that the male was the only significant viewer in Greek culture] not all grave statues were male, and also the fact that the kouros certainly represents a *young* male, throws serious doubt on the notion that it does not positively differentiate itself from the viewer. Obviously, the kouros and the kore standing over a grave were more or less differentiated from the different viewers depending on the latters' gender and social persona; but this is true as much for the equestrian and seated grave statues (and for the stelai) as it is for the kouroi and korai. On my interpretation, there is nothing surprising about the epigram and the statue complementing each other by articulating different (complementary) aspects of the deceased's social persona.

[643] And if it does represent a runner: but this, or a similar athletic stance, is by far the most likely.

phenomenon which elsewhere in the series is articulated in a different modality: the differential specificity of grave monuments involving kouroi, some of which have bases with relief scenes articulating a more specific athletic and other social persona for the deceased, as, on this interpretation, the Grotta kouros is doing.

An important question that remains to be discussed is who received a kouros as a grave monument; was it only young men, or also older men, as is believed by some scholars?[644] We found very strong reasons for concluding that among female graves only those of a young *parthenos* could have a kore as a *sema* and also for thinking that the kouros, far from being a generic male represented a particular persona of a young male member of the élite, through which the whole nexus of the persona 'young *kalos kagathos*' aristocrat was evoked. But does this mean that only the graves of such young men could have had a kouros as a *sema*? As we saw, not all human images on *semata* are images of the social persona of the deceased. Thus, one possibility is that a male grave may have had a kouros *sema* as an *agalma*, in the way it could, we saw, have a kore. Given the asymmetry of the two genders we cannot assume that this was so, but that the kouros statue could have that function is a theoretical possibility. However, there is an important difference. Given that one of the main modalities in which the archaic grave monument with images functioned involved the representation of the social persona of the deceased, a male statue over a male grave would inevitably have been made sense of also in those terms; unlike the kore over the male grave it could not function exclusively as an *agalma*, but would inevitably have been seen as representing the deceased's persona. So the first possibility collapses into the

---

[644] Cf. e.g. Stewart (1990: 109) who thinks that the deceased's age seems irrelevant. D'Onofrio (1982: 163–4) takes the youth of the kouroi to be a 'historical' category according to a classification in which the body of active men consists of *kouroi* and *gerontes*. In this system, D'Onofrio argues, youth is the prerogative of the warrior, and death in war brings *kleos aphthiton* which in return for the life of a man in his prime gives him the status of *ageraos* in the memory of the group. The kouros statue represents this active citizen and expresses the highest level of the human condition. I assume that if she were right, it would then follow that the kouros would be set over the grave of any man that fitted that social category 'kouros'. In my view, this reading is mistaken. I find the notion of the division into these two categories in the epics, or in the mentality of the archaic Greeks ultimately unconvincing. Of course all age categories are socially constructed, but there is no evidence to suggest that those under consideration differed from the age categories known to us from the Greek world and roughly corresponding to the main biological bands.

second: is it possible that any male (member of the élite) could have been in some way signified through the ideal male type of the perfectly formed young man? If it was not, the choice to set up a kouros as the *sema* of an older man was not conceivable, and if conceived, its function as a *sema* (which depended on the collaboration of the community and strangers passing by) would have been problematic—which is not what one wants from a *sema*. Thus that choice would not have been made; the parameters determining selection would have excluded it. The central question then is, was it possible for the social persona of any male (member of the élite) to have been represented metaphorically through the ideal male type of the perfectly formed young man? It is impossible to answer this question with certainty. But, in my view, in so far as it possible to judge, the available evidence suggests that kouroi stood only over the graves of young males, while seated statues represented the social persona of the deceased in the *semata* of older men. Whenever it is possible to check, the deceased whose grave monument involves a kouros is a young male. Thus, the three kouroi which had bases decorated with relief representations articulate the social persona of a young athlete, and therefore (since it is generally accepted, indeed it is postulated by the theories which assume that the kouros is a generic representation, that scenes in this idiom, also found on the stelai, do not represent an idealized generic deceased, but express his social persona through narrative) this representation indicates that the deceased in these cases was indeed a young man. In addition, the epitaphs of some other grave monuments involving kouroi have been preserved, and they state that the grave monument was erected by the deceased's father;[645] and this, as we shall see in more detail below, places the deceased, probably biologically, and certainly symbolically, into the category 'male who died young/before his time'.[646]

Let us then try to define more clearly what exactly is meant by 'young' in this context. In the stelai, we saw, there are two categories of young males, beardless youths corresponding to what we may

[645] Cf. Hansen 1983: 41, 42; conceivably also Hansen 1983: 14.

[646] Cf. below §ii.6 and Annex. The painted figure of the seated male on the base of the kouros over the grave of Neilonides, son of Neilon (Hansen 1983: 42 with refs. to illustrations), framed between the two inscriptions, the vertical statement that Endoios made it, and the horizontal epitaph, and compositionally relating directly to the latter, was a representation of the father who set up the monument, like an iconographical articulation of the unstated subject of the second verse.

conventionally call 'pre-ephebic and ephebic' age, and young men whom we found reason to believe belonged to the age band that went from the 'post-ephebic' age to the age of 30. Given that no element has a fixed meaning, and meaning is determined in interaction with the context and the element's alternatives that might have been chosen in its place but were not, though 'beardless' means 'young' in Greek iconography, we must not assume that it means the same type of 'young' in the kouroi as on the stelai. There are good reasons for thinking that kouroi represented the social persona of both bands of young male through one iconographical type. First, they clearly were not limited to representing the social persona of males in the pre-ephebic and ephebic age, as is clear from some of the epitaphs. Xenokles', for example,[647] describes him as an *aichmetes aner*; and if Kroisos' epigram[648] is not presenting a grossly misleading version of his death, he died fighting *eni pro-machois*, which also indicates that he was not an ephebe, but a young man of our second 'young' band. Second, the grave statue named by the inscription on its leg as the *sema* of Sombrotidas the doctor[649] appears to be that of a young man—though the head is missing and this impression may be misleading. Clearly Sombrotidas could not have been of 'pre-ephebic' or 'ephebic' age; but he could have died while a very young *iatros*.[650]

In these circumstances, it is clear that all the evidence points strongly in favour of the conclusion that the kouros represented the social persona of the two age bands represented through separate types on the stelai, the 'pre-ephebic' and 'ephebic' age band on the one hand, and the 'post-ephebic' up to the age of 30 on the other. If this is correct, it indicates an articulation reflecting the attitude that the important distinction was between those who died young in the sense of 'too young', before their time, on the one hand, and the others on the other. As we shall see, there was indeed a special,

---

[647] Hansen 1983: 19.

[648] Ibid. 27.

[649] Cf. Richter 1960: 112 no. 134; Bernabò Brea 1950: 59–66; cf. Jeffery 1990: 270, 276 no. 25; 411 pl. 52 no. 25; Berger 1970: 154–5, 191 n. 392; Guarducci 1967: 314; cf. also Krug 1985: 27.

[650] The possibility that Sombrotidas was in fact older, despite the fact that his *sema* was that of a youth, cannot be totally excluded. There is no reason to think it is right, and there are strong reasons for thinking that older men did not have a kouros as sema, but the possibility cannot be *proved* wrong. But it is naive to think that because it cannot be *proved* wrong it is more rigorous to assume that it is right, even though a whole series of reasons point independently in the opposite direction.

tragic, significance, attached to those who died too young, before their time, without progeny, before their parents. I shall return to this. As will become clear, a large proportion of archaic grave monuments were erected for such people. The fact that the whole age band is represented through the characteristics of one of its poles, the beardlessness, which as an iconographical sign characterizes the 'pre-ephebic' and 'ephebic' age band (and biologically only the younger segment of the pre-ephebic one) corresponds to a modality of age representation also observable elsewhere in Greek iconography. For I hope to have shown[651] that in Attic iconography first, age bands did not represent 'pure' biological reality but biological reality mediated by social perceptions, reflecting socio-culturally significant divisions and transitions, which were them-selves reflecting biological reality socioculturally mediated. Second, that the iconographical types representing particular age bands were characterized by particular age-signs, iconographical signs (such as, for example, full breasts or 'budding' breasts) based on, but not reproducing faithfully, biological reality: biological reality was mediated and rendered through perceptual filters shaped both by sociocultural perceptions and by artistic conventions. The fact that the whole 'pre-ephebic' and 'ephebic' male age band is icon-ographically characterized by beardlessness is a result of this modality, and of the resulting conventionality of age representation. Thirdly, I hope to have also shown that figures belonging to a particular age band were represented through the age-signs charac-terizing either the younger or the older pole of the band. Again, the fact that the whole 'pre-ephebic' and 'ephebic' male age band is iconographically characterized by beardlessness is a result of this modality. The kouroi, on the thesis put forward here, represent the whole age band 'young male up to 30 years old', reflecting an age articulation significant in the perceptions of, and attitudes to, death rather than the actual social articulation; for it includes three of the bands of the latter, as the 'beardless youth' on the stelai includes two such categories, 'pre-ephebic' and 'ephebic'. The choice of the younger age type for the representation of the whole band is correlative with, and was surely determined by, the fact that the resulting stress on the deceased's youth increased the pathos of the perception of his death generated by the grave monument with a

---

[651] Cf. Sourvinou-Inwood 1988: 51–62, cf. 33–9.

kouros, in which the representation of the social persona of the deceased was visually dominant. Thus the differences in the articulation of the social persona of the deceased in the stelai and through kouroi are correlative with the differences in the parameters of selection for the two types of monument (as these have been reconstructed here), the parameters that shaped the choices to articulate and stress particular aspects of the social persona of the deceased in interaction with the medium in which the image was articulated.

Since in a 'set' such as that of the archaic grave statues the meanings of each element were also determined by its relationships to its alternatives that were not chosen,[652] the fact that seated figures functioned as funerary representations of the deceased, denoting maturity and high status, may be taken as a further indication in favour of the conclusion that kouroi were only appropriate for the grave of young men (those for whom an equestrian or draped statue was not preferred). The rarity of the seated statues would correspond to the relative rarity of epitaphs for people who can be identified as mature men. The conclusion that kouroi stood only over the grave of young men and articulated iconographically aspects of the social persona of the deceased in the ways suggested here would restore a relationship of homology between kouroi and korai and also between kouroi and equestrian (on my reading also draped) and seated statues which stood as *semata* over the grave and signalled specific aspects of the deceased's social persona. This, I submit, constitutes a further argument in favour of the readings proposed here.

Let us now consider the relationship between images on stelai and grave statues, especially kouroi. The prevailing scholarly opinion is that there is a dichotomy between the representations of the social persona of the deceased on stelai on the one hand and through kouroi and korai on the other. One difference between stelai and kouroi that does *prima facie* appear important, and seems to support the above view, is that on the stelai the figures are associated with characterizing objects, while the funerary kouroi are not. This does not mean that the stelai are narrative and the kouroi are not. For on most of the stelai the schema is an emblematic representation of a figure with an object characterizing it, such as a spear, the same

---

[652] Cf. Sourvinou-Inwood 1991: 11.

as that of the korai and the draped and the offering males. When action is shown on the stelai it is mostly when the persona represented can best be articulated through the representation of action, as, for example, is the case with the javelin-thrower.[653] It is in rare scenes like the 'ambush'[654] that the narrative mode is, unusually, deployed, and even there the image articulated through the narrative mode functions emblematically. Truly narrative scenes representing many figured action are mostly in subsidiary zones and bases. Equally, we saw, the emblematic representation of the grave statues incorporates elements of narrative: striding or walking, and in the case of korai also making a gesture of worship, carrying something, pulling at the skirt. With regard to their relationship to characterizing objects, the differentiation is not between stelai on the one hand and grave (and votive) statues on the other; for korai, and to a lesser extent draped youths, are similar to the stelai, not to the kouroi. Indeed there are striking similarities between the characterizing objects held by, and thus the schemata through which are depicted, some figures represented on stelai on the one hand and those of some korai on the other. Compare on the one hand grave statues like the 'Berlin Goddess' and the kore New York Metropolitan Museum 07.286.110 Rogers Fund, both holding a pomegranate, and more strikingly, a votive kore like Athens Acropolis Museum no. 593,[655] who is holding a wreath and a pomegranate, and the youth represented on the stele Boston Museum of Fine Arts 08.288,[656] who is wearing a wreath and holding a stem with two pomegranates and an aryballos, on the other. The youth on the 'brother and sister' stele[657] is holding up a pomegranate (with an aryballos hanging from his wrist) while the girl is holding a flower like the kore that was Phrasikleia's *sema* and also the youth on the stele Louvre MND 1863.[658] Since context is central in meaning creation, the similarity with the votive statues must not be assumed to be significant. We saw that the pomegranate was associated with Persephone's persona as Hades' bride and that the schema 'kore with pomegranate' stressed the dead girl's unmarried status.

---

[653] Stele Athens NM 1772 (Richter 1961: no. 48).

[654] Stele Ny Carlsberg Glyptothek, Copenhagen IN 2787 (Richter 1961: no. 77).

[655] Richter 1968: no. 43.

[656] Richter 1961: no. 28.

[657] Metropolitan Museum, New York 11.185. Hewitt Fund, 1911, Munsey Fund, 1936, 1938, and Anonymous Gift, 1951. Staatliche Museen, Berlin, A7 (Richter 1961: no. 37).

[658] Richter 1961: no. 57.

Perhaps this schema was eventually extended to youths, so that 'young person with pomegranate' became appropriate for the representation of the social persona of dead youths as well as maidens.

To return to the relationships between grave statues and stelai, the similarities just noted and the fact that at least one grave statue representing a draped youth was holding an object suggest that the difference is not between on the one hand stelai and on the other grave statues, nor on the one hand stelai and on the other male grave statues, but on the one hand stelai and grave statues of maidens and draped youths and on the other kouroi. The traditional answer to this has been that the kouros is generic. However, besides the arguments set out against this view above, this solution also involves an asymmetry not only between the representation of male and female but also between the representation of naked and draped standing young male, of naked standing and of equestrian young male, of naked standing male and of seated male, and finally also of naked male over a grave and a naked male functioning as a votive, while the interpretation offered here would make the kouros symmetrical with all these types of statue, asymmetrically symmetrical when appropriate, corresponding to the relationships between the types of social persona involved. If we read the kouros as an athlete evoking the whole nexus of the *kalos kagathos* persona, the absence of characterizing objects would be correlative with the desire to represent 'young man as athlete', not an athlete in a particular field of sport, like the discobolos characterized by the discus. It would be semantically correlative to the aryballos as a generic athletic sign, which was not necessary in the kouros because while youths on the stelai were also shown as other than athletes, characterized by other objects, such as the spear or the flower, kouroi (on this view) represented athletes. The fact that the schemata involving characterizing objects drifted, and preferentially crystallized, to the images of the stelai is probably not unrelated to the observation that in these relief images a richer and more varied schema makes for a more satisfactory representation and overall decoration; this may have been one of the parameters determining selection when the iconographical schemata of the stelai were being created.

I shall complete my investigation of the relationship between stelai and kouroi by considering some recent discussions.

D'Onofrio[659] is one of the scholars who perceive a dichotomy between kouroi and stelai. In the latter she sees a reflection of the age articulations of the contemporary civic group, each represented by the social figure most appropriate to it, while the former would be reflecting an alleged epic dichotomy between kouroi and *gerontes*. The kouros, she thinks, lacking all attribute evoking the assumption of any specific role in the social group, expresses a distancing from the citizen model in which the individual takes on roles appropriate to his age. This view depends on a series of assumptions. First, that the kouroi reflect an epic bipartite division of the male group into kouroi and elders, which is not convincing either for the epics, or, we saw, for the kouroi statues. We found strong reasons for thinking that the latter represent the two age bands that make up the concept 'young' in ancient Greek society and mentality, the pre-ephebic and ephebic, and the post-ephebic up to the age of 30; and that this grouping together of these two age bands reflects the significance of the concept 'dying young, dying unmarried without progeny' in the Greek collective attitudes. Second, D'Onofrio's thesis depends on the assumption that the kouroi do not evoke any particular role; we found good reasons for considering this view mistaken, but in any case it cannot be denied that it is at the very least arguable; it is thus methodologically dangerous to base a thesis on the assumption that it is valid. Finally, the meanings of a kouros standing as a *sema* over a grave were determined also by the context, which included the epitaph; and in the epitaph—as well as, in a few cases, in the decorated base—it is precisely the citizen model allegedly repudiated in the image that is articulated. In addition, the distinction made by D'Onofrio between ethical and political value, the former being those expressed in the kouros in contrast to the latter,[660] is shown to be mistaken by the fact that, we saw, the two are inextricably intertwined in the epigrams. Furthermore, in the cases in which it is possible to determine this, the contents and articulations of the archaic epigrams belonging to grave monuments involving a stele are similar to those belonging to grave monuments involving a kouros; while if the theory under discussion were right we would most plausibly expect them to betray a similar dichotomy. Moreover, some kouroi bases have relief decoration articulating

---

[659] D'Onofrio 1982: 167; cf. 1988: 89–90.
[660] D'Onofrio 1982: 167.

aspects of the deceased's social persona in modalities similar to those on the stelai, which again if the theory under discussion were correct we would most plausibly expect not to find. Osborne[661] also sees a dichotomy in attitudes, with a stele such as that of Aristion[662] remembering the deceased 'in death for his status in the community' and avoiding 'contemplating death as such, preferring to recuperate life', an attitude he considers 'incompatible with that displayed by the *kouros* . . .' which 'brings one face to face with death, asserting that for all an individual's particular achievements all a man can in the end lay claim to is humanity. The kouros thus focusses on man's potential, not on any specific personal or social achievement.' However, even if we disregard the fact that, we saw, there are good reasons for thinking that the latter view is incorrect, what is certainly not correct is that the stelai as a category of grave monument avoided contemplating death as such. First, because all representations on the grave monument show the social persona of the deceased *as deceased* by virtue of their context as parts of the grave monument; the context, which included the base and the epitaph, and the image on the stele or the statue were all parts of one system, each acquiring its meanings also through its interaction with the others. Thus the stelai do not represent the deceased in life, but articulate his type of social persona through scenes representing the activities associated with that social persona in life. The two are close but not identical; their context ascribes to the scenes under consideration the meaning 'emblematic representation of the social persona of a dead person'. Since the descriptive narrative scenes on the kouros bases represented the deceased's social persona in the same modality and idiom as the stelai we cannot even speak of a dichotomy in the idiom and modality of the representation of the deceased's social persona as between the stelai and the kouroi; it is a spectrum that straddles genres of funerary sculpture. Second, and very importantly, the early grave stelai were crowned by a sphinx, who was, we shall see, a death demon whose presence, among other things, stressed the funerary frame of the images on the stelai. On some stelai this funerary frame was further stressed through the representation on the subsidiary zone, just under the representation of the social persona of the deceased, of a

---

[661] R. Osborne 1988: 8.
[662] Richter 1961: no. 67.

Gorgon, an infernal being whose meaning we shall discuss below. Stewart[663] sees the situation as follows: 'Funerary kouroi and korai presumably allude to life's "jewelled springtime" and compliment the dead by presenting them with a gift (*geras*) that recalls the splendor of Homer's heroes and heroines, while the stelai show them integrated into the social fabric, as typical members of the polis community: the men are warriors, athletes, horsemen, and so on, the rare females are nubile girls or dutiful mothers ... These two basic modes of representing the dead, which one might call the "symbolic" and the "factual", or (from the client's point of view) the "prospective" and "restrospective", continue throughout ancient funerary art ...'. The assumption is that the dead who had kouroi and korai as their *semata* were not necessarily young. However, we found strong reasons for thinking that this is wrong, and also first, that the kouroi, let alone the korai, were not generic, and second, that both types of images are both 'symbolic' and 'factual', both 'prospective' and 'restrospective'. Of course, the *agalma* dimension of signification was also present. Among the grave statues representing humans there was a spectrum of meanings, a multidimensional spectrum, one dimension of which pertains to the representation of the social persona of the deceased. In the different grave monuments involving a human figure this persona is usually, but not always, articulated; when it is, it is articulated with lesser or greater specificity along a spectrum of greater or lesser specificity—not in a way that sharply contrasts two particular types of grave monuments. For example, while a kore over a man's grave does not represent the deceased's persona at all, a kouros does, and a kouros with a base with relief representations does so with much greater specificity than one without such a base.

Consequently, there is no dichotomy and contrast between kouroi and grave stelai; there is a multidimensional spectrum of possible choices, of perceptions articulated in the different images on archaic *semata*, with common parameters of selection but the possibility of divergences in the preferred options. Archaic grave monuments with images were polysemic; at their core is the fact that they are the metonymic sign of the deceased; this is related to their *mnema* function; the different grave monuments are located at different points along a spectrum of meanings involving varying

combinations of the dimension of signification 'representation of
the deceased's social persona', the notion of the monument as an
agalma which enhances and colours positively the memory of the
deceased, and the dimension of protection which shall be discussed
in a moment; there were also different modalities of representation.
The articulation of the deceased's persona through image and
epigram affected, of course, the modality of the grave monument's
function as the metonymic sign of the deceased and its operation
as a *mnema*, the vehicle for the preservation of his memory. For the
function of the *sema* as the metonymic sign of the deceased did not
operate in exactly the same way in all grave monuments, whatever
their form; it depended on the nature of those monuments, for
example, on whether they represented iconographically the
deceased's persona. At one pole of this spectrum, that of the
maximum '*agalma*' dimension and the minimum social persona
definition, is the kore standing over a male grave; at the other the
inscribed stele with relief decoration on the shaft, on a main and a
subsidiary zone, and on the base, all articulating the deceased's
persona. Within this spectrum there are variations in the representation of the deceased's social persona in the greater or lesser
degree of its definition: on the kouros end there is the kouros with
descriptive narrative scenes on its base, the kouros or kore without
descriptive narrative scenes on its base; and at the stele end of the
spectrum we also have variations, stelai with only the emblematic
representation on the shaft and stelai with the emblematic representation on the shaft and descriptive narrative scenes on a subsidiary zone and/or its base.

The iconographical representation of the social persona of the
deceased gives permanent form to, and thus ensures, the memory
survival of that persona. Grave inscriptions name the grave monument, and thus ensure the survival of the memory of the deceased,
in varying degrees of specificity; at one end they are limited to just
their name, at the other they articulate significant aspects of their
social persona. At one end of the spectrum stands the minimalist
grave monument, which only records the name, the fact of the
person's life and death; one of the monuments at the other end of
this spectrum is the Attic grave stele from the last years of the
seventh century until *c.*530 which consisted of a tall shaft set on a
base crowned by a capital which was surmounted by a sphinx (cf.
e.g. Pl. 8). For this type of grave monument includes the *agalma*

dimension which pertains to the whole grave monument, and two important facets of the archaic grave monument focused on two different parts of the monument. The image on the shaft represented the deceased's social persona, while the Sphinx articulated the notion of protection which is another major facet of the *sema* in the archaic period. Funerary behaviour seeking to ensure the infernal powers' protection for the deceased is well-established in archaic Greece.[664] In the archaic grave monuments the idea of protection was expressed through representations of sphinxes, lions, gorgons, and deities.

The Sphinx is a chthonic being who is represented over a grave as a figure of protection.[665] As she is also a death bringer, an agent of death,[666] this is also, at another level, an image of death.[667] In some cases a sphinx may have stood directly on the grave;[668] normally, she formed the upper part of the grave monument; sphinxes formed the upper part of Attic stelai from the late seventh century until *c.*530 when these stelai were replaced by a simpler type. The sphinx stelai consisted of a tall shaft set on a base, crowned by a capital surmounted by a sphinx.[669] An epigram of *c.*450 inscribed on the base for a column which had originally carried a sphinx, from Demetrias in Thessaly,[670] spells out the guardian role of the sphinx over a grave:[671]

---

[664] Ridgway (1977: 163) believes that protection was one of the two main concepts stressed by grave-markers in the round in the archaic period, the other being status (what here is subsumed in the wider notion of the social persona of the deceased). I don't agree with all her relevant interpretations, but the protective nature of some images is incontrovertible.

[665] On the sphinx as protector of the grave cf. Lacroix 1982: 77–8; Ridgway 1977: 156, 160; *contra*: Demisch 1977: 85–8. On the Sphinx as a chthonic creature cf. also Peifer 1989: 280–92; Demisch 1977: 83–5. On the meanings of the Sphinx in archaic and classical Greece cf. also Moret 1984: 9–29, and esp. 20–2. Moret (1984: 22) ascribes to the Sphinx, among others, the function of guarantor of the cosmic order. On the appearance and early history of the sphinx in the Greek world in the first millennium cf. now Kourou 1991: 112–15, 119–21, 122.

[666] Cf. Eur. *Phoen.* 806–11, 1019–42. Cf. Vermeule 1979: 69, 171–3.

[667] Cf. M. Robertson 1975: 108; cf. also Vermeule 1979: 173.

[668] Cf. Ridgway 1977: 156–60, esp. 159.

[669] Cf. Richter 1961: 1–36; M. Robertson 1975: 87, 108–10, fig. 29*a*; Boardman 1978: 162–3; Ridgway 1977: 156–7, fig. 52; Kontoleon 1970: 47–8. On the funerary use of sphinxes outside Attica cf. Ridgway 1977: 156, 157 9.

[670] Hansen 1983: 120; *GV* 1831; Pfohl 1967: 140; Jeffery 1990: 97–8, 99 no. 8, 402 pl. 11 no. 8; *SEG* xv. 381; Friedländer and Hoffleit 1948: 139A, pp. 129–30; Lorenz 1976: 97 no. 11.

[671] Cf. the restorations in: Jeffery 1990: op. cit.; Pfohl 1967: op. cit.; and (slightly different ones) *GV*; Lorenz 1976: op. cit.

σφίξ, haίδ[α]ο κύον, τίν' ε[...] | οπιν[...(.) φυ]λάσεις :
hεμέν[α .] | ρο[.....]δο[.] ἀπο⟨φ⟩θιμ[ένο]; |
ξεῖ[ν(ε) (◡◡)-◡῀◡-◡ ἀπο] | φθ[ιμένο(ιο) (◡)◡--:]
[-◡◡-|◡◡--◡◡-◡◡-].

The sphinx is guarding the *sema*, not the grave. This is articulated clearly in the Attic stelai in which the sphinx is sitting on top of the stele with capital. In the Demetrias *sema* she sat on top of the column. This is correlative with the fact that in archaic Greek mentality, as we have seen, it is the *sema* that is dominant, not the grave itself.

Concern for the preservation of the grave monument fits the archaic attitudes towards death as they are reconstructed here: it is concern for the preservation of the only part of the deceased left in the world of the living, his metonymic sign, and through this also of his memory of which the *sema* is the vehicle and focus. This makes sense of the complex, composite form of the sphinx stelai, especially the Attic ones, which gave almost equal weight to the elements of protection and commemoration, within the framework of the grave monument which, as a whole, was a *mnema*. Given that the grave monument was the metonymic sign of the deceased, the representation of the sphinx guarding it articulated the conceptual image 'the chthonic monster guarding and protecting the deceased'. Through protecting his metonymic sign and perhaps also (the protection may have been perceived to have included) his physical remains in the liminal space that was his grave proper, the burial space, which did not symbolically belong to the upper world of the living, but in the realm of the nether gods, the chthonic monster itself would be protecting (the representation articulated the wish that she should be protecting) the deceased's shade in Hades. To put this differently: the sphinx monument depicting the monster as guarding the *sema* brought into being, by establishing symbolically (as an image) a relationship of benevolence and protection between the sphinx and the deceased. This expressed the wish to bring about in 'reality' such a relationship of protection between the chthonic monster—both in itself, and as a symbol of the infernal powers of the Underworld—and the deceased. By representing this relationship as already established, the monument also expressed the hope that this was indeed so and made it true at the level of symbolism. This conveyed messages: of reassurance about the deceased, and about oneself, the spectator as a prospective deceased; and of propitiation and placation to the infernal powers.

The symbolic representation of the desired relationship was part of the attempt to achieve it, and at one level its representation did in fact bring that relationship into being.

Another demonic figure sometimes represented on the grave monument in relief, sometimes standing over the grave as a statue in the round, is the Gorgon,[672] also an infernal being who was represented as a protector of the grave monument.[673] The concept of protection is expressed in these grave monuments also through the figure of the lion standing over the grave.[674] This role of guardianship[675] was related to the lion's central persona: it was associated with, and thus symbolized and articulated iconographically, might, power, success in hunting and over its enemies, and related concepts.[676] Thus, a lion standing over a grave represented also strength, which would have been seen (given the perceptions of the grave monument) as pertaining to the deceased's social persona, and thus representing also the deceased's strength and spirit.[677] Since, we saw, valour and high birth were associated in archaic mentality, and since the lion was associated with heroes and had itself high status, it may have also have functioned as a sign of the deceased's high status.[678] Thus, the lion represented also an aspect of the deceased's persona through a trope, the precise nature of which is difficult to reconstruct; if it is right that the relationship between the *sema* and the deceased was perceived to be variable within wide parameters, depending on the perceived relationship between the two, it could have been seen as functioning through a simile, that he was like the lion that made up his *sema*, or a metaphor, if the *sema* was taken to be in some complex way a representation of the deceased's social persona.

The lion belongs to the world of reality, and it is the only creature from this world to be represented as the protector of a *sema*; the other figures shown in this role belong to the supernatural world.

---

[672] Cf. Ridgway 1977: 162, 180, 169; Boardman 1978: 164, 162.

[673] Cf. Woysch-Méautis 1982: 81–3 with bibliog.; Lacroix 1982: 78. On the figure of the Gorgon in general cf. esp. Vernant 1991: 111–38; cf. also Frontisi-Ducroux 1988: 27–40; Scalera McClintock 1989: 60–1, 85.

[674] On lions over graves cf. Ridgway 1977: 152–6; Kurtz and Boardman 1971: 84, 176, 238–9, cf. 135–6; Markoe 1989: 109–10.

[675] Cf. Vermeule 1979: 87–8 (and cf. 233 n. 7 for further bibliog. on lions as grave monuments); Woysch-Méautis 1982: 74–7; Müller 1978: IV.6/7; Boardman 1986: 93–4.

[676] Cf. also Vermeule 1979: 85–91; Markoe 1989: 110–11.

[677] Cf. GV 1173.

[678] Cf. also Stähler 1967: 20.

Besides the chthonic monsters divinities are also sometimes (albeit rather rarely) represented over the grave, or in the cemetery.[679] Ridgway notes that some Greeks, in some areas, such as Kyme and Cyrene, stressed in their grave monuments the idea of divine protection rather than of commemoration.[680] Busts of an Underworld goddess wearing a polos, some with an aniconic face, stood over graves at Cyrene.[681] From Aeolic Kyme there is at least one statue of Cybele that was erected in a cemetery.[682] There is also a Kourotrophos found over a subterranean grave in the cemetery of Megara Hyblaia.[683] A statue of Dionysos was found in a cemetery area in Athens.[684] It is not unlikely that the group of two (naked) fragmentary horsemen from a cemetery at Megara Hyblaia, which apparently stood against a background, perhaps of a naiskos, represented the Dioskouroi.[685] It has also been suggested that the female figure represented in three grave stelai (from Paros, Kimolos, and Malessina) is not the deceased but a funerary goddess.[686] Even if we leave aside the uncertain examples, and also those from the borders of the Greek world,[687] it is clear that the attempt to ensure divine protection for the dead by erecting on the grave, and possibly also elsewhere in the cemetery, representations of Underworld deities, was a practice which, though not common, was certainly present in archaic funerary mentality and behaviour. More generally, the notion of ensuring the protection of the Underworld powers for the dead by setting up images of these powers and images of the desired relationship of benevolence and protection between these powers and the dead, is well established in archaic Greece. The phenomenon of shrines within cemeteries[688] may also be related to this desire to ensure protection

---

[679] Cf. also on this Lebessi 1976: 92–106; 177; Woysch-Méautis 1982: 77.

[680] Ridgway 1977: 151.

[681] Cf. Beschi 1969/70: 208–17, 315–20, 324–9, 335–6, and *passim*; cf. also Ridgway 1977: 151.

[682] Ridgway 1977: 56, 131, 151; Lebessi 1976: 105.

[683] *NSc* (1954), 99–104; cf. Ridgway 1977: 135.

[684] Cf. Boardman 1978: 86.

[685] On this group cf. *NSc* (1954), 109–10; cf. also Ridgway 1977: 140.

[686] Cf. Kontoleon 1970: 49–51; cf. also Lebessi 1976: 105–6, 177.

[687] Cf. e.g. the Dorylaion stele, Istanbul Museum 680 (cf. Ridgway 1977: 174, 182; Woysch-Méautis 1982: 24, 77, 105–6).

[688] Cf. e.g. Themelis 1973–4: 109–10; Andronikos 1961/2: 178; Coldstream 1977: 102; Zaphiropoulou 1983: 1–4; Lauter 1985: 162 ff.; Knigge 1988: 103–4. The fact that at least some of these are known to be shrines of deities or established heroes, such as that to the Tritopatres in the Kerameikos (Knigge 1988: 103–4) shows that it should not be assumed

for the dead. As we saw, even some of the korai may be representing the persona of the deceased as a votary of Persephone, and may thus also have been seen as representing a relationship that placed the deceased under Persephone's protection—or so it was hoped.

(d) *Images on Archaic* Semata: *Conclusions*

It is clear that some themes, deities, sphinxes, lions, and chariot scenes (and perhaps sirens), are represented on more than one type of grave monument. The common meanings of deities, sphinxes, and lions pertain to protection, though the different images created different meanings within these common parameters. All three themes are, of course, polysemic. Sphinxes were also death-bringers, and thus created particular images of death; the lion also referred to the deceased's social persona through a metaphor; and the representations of deities associated with death above the grave also created meanings pertaining to the unseeable realm of death and its divine denizens. Chariot representations referred to the social persona of the deceased on the stelai and probably also on some of the vases; it cannot be excluded that when more than one chariot is shown on some vases the schema 'funeral games' and thus 'death-ritual' may also have been evoked.

Among the images on archaic grave monuments it is the ones representing the deceased's social persona that become dominant and widespread. The way this persona was represented in these preferred archaic images differs from that in which it was represented on the eighth-century vases, while another series of archaic images can be considered as being located somewhere between the two. The images that became dominant and widespread are those in which the deceased's persona is represented as the constructed essence of an individual, through an iconographical schema involving a human being of the same gender and age group as the deceased and either associated with things that denote a particular status or activity, or in a schema (for example, seated) which denoted a particular type of social persona. Such images appear on the main field of most decorated stelai and also as grave statues. On the eighth-century vases the images of death were 'public'. They represented the deceased's social persona through first, images of the

that shrines in cemeteries pertained to an alleged cult offered to the allegedly heroized dead buried in that cemetery.

death-ritual, the public ritual by means of which the community dealt with the death and valorized the deceased; and second, through images of war; but always through public images involving group activity. Such images do not disappear from the grave monuments in the archaic period, but their relative importance is diminished; they are no longer dominant and they are often modified. Mostly they are in a subordinate position; the bases of some stelai and statues are decorated with images that articulate the deceased's social persona through the representation of a group activity, for example an athletic pursuit which characterizes the deceased as an athlete. Elsewhere group activity images are modified, as on the Laconian amphorae, where the chariot frieze is divided into a series of groups consisting of a chariot with a charioteer and a warrior following on foot, resembling the representations on some subsidiary zones on the stelai. In the plaques decorating built tombs, which represented the death-ritual, a shift appears eventually to have taken place, which distanced it from the eighth-century representations; in the later sixth century the series plaques were replaced by the much smaller single plaques, which depicted a smaller scale representation involving the deceased's family, and thus represented a less public, less community involved and more family-centred, death-ritual. The images of group activity other than the death-ritual in the archaic period are no longer limited to images of war; the social persona articulated in such images is now not only, as was the case in the eighth century, that of a warrior, which is of central importance to the community, but also others, among which most prominent is the persona 'athlete'. This persona also had a dominant position in the images involving a schema articulating the 'essence' of a social persona on the stelai and (on my thesis) in the grave statues. This persona 'athlete' which evoked the whole nexus 'kalos kagathos young member of the international aristocracy' is one valued primarily by the self (and the self's family)—though benefits to the community were also involved, skills useful in war and honour through victory in the Panhellenic Games. The persona 'girl who died unmarried' is also 'self-centred', though the notion that she had not lived to give sons to the community could also have come into play.

Thus it appears that the dominant images of death in the archaic period articulate the deceased's persona as perceived above all from the deceased's own, not simply the community's, viewpoint. This general trend for the preferred images of death represented on the grave monuments to shift somewhat, and for the more self-oriented images of the deceased and of death to become dominant, is perhaps an expression of a shift from public to more self-oriented images on the *sema*. In the eighth century the public images of death articulated perceptions in which the public dimension predominated: death was above all a public event, and each death was represented on the grave monument in social terms, through the death ritual which treated each death as a (tragic but inevitable) manifestation of the individual discontinuity necessary for the life-cycle of the community and the species, which alone validated the individual existence. Now the social persona of the deceased is articulated through images of self with an emphasis on, and gradual progression towards preference for, the more self-oriented images of self. The images of protection involved in archaic *semata* also articulate 'self-centred' rather than public perceptions; by setting up relationships of protection (and thus reassurance) they articulate perceptions of need, indicating an anxiety about death which was not detectable on eighth-century grave monuments. I shall return to both these points below.

The fact that the same types of images with the same sets of meanings appear on grave monuments of different types confirms that common parameters of function and perceptions of the grave monument determined all choices of grave monument in the archaic period. This is comparable to the fact that grave inscriptions of the same types are inscribed on different types of grave monument, which indicates that the same mentality, within the same parameters, was associated with different types of grave monument. In addition, there is a significant coincidence between the meanings created by the different images on the different archaic grave monuments and those in the epitaphs.

(e) *Epitaphs and Images*

The articulation of the deceased's social persona and the grief and sadness at his death are articulated both in the epitaphs and in the images. The thematic category of protection is represented in the images but not in the epitaphs. This was not because the protection facet was desired on different grave monuments from those which were inscribed, since for a long time all Attic grave stelai were crowned by the protective figure of the sphinx. Perhaps there was a preference for expressing that aspect iconographically rather than verbally, and the verbal articulation was a choice that it was preferred not to make, or at least not to make often enough for any specimens of it to have survived.

5. The Archaic Grave Monument: Diversity and Common Parameters

There were, we saw, significant differences in form, and thus in modalities of operation, between the different grave monuments in the archaic age, but all were dependent on a common mentality, a mentality operating within the same parameters. The central difference between inscribed and uninscribed monuments is that the former recorded, reactivated, and thus preserved, the memory of the deceased on their own, while the latter did not. The uninscribed grave monuments were—at least for a time—identifiable as *semata*, some even as *semata* of a particular type of person; but it is only through the co-operation of the community that they could preserve their identity as the *sema* of a particular dead person and thus contribute to the preservation of his memory. There was a wide spectrum of variation pertaining to most aspects of the archaic grave monument. First, in visibility: their visibility ranges from the very high visibility of a sculpted monument near the street to the low visibility of, for example, the Laconian vases. The same is true of permanence; the marble monument scores high on permanence, vases on their own score low. There is also a spectrum of variation in specificity, in the ways in which the different types of grave monument do or do not in some way represent the social persona of the deceased, and in what degree of specificity. Sculpted monuments tend to be on the high end of the spectrum, though not all are equally high on the specificity of the representation of the social persona, and thus of the individualization of the grave monument. Mounds of earth without an additional grave-marker on top score low on specificity. Clearly, then, the inscribed, sculpted grave monument with images scores very high on all these aspects.

The following important and widespread developments and changes took place in the course of the long period we call 'the archaic age'. First, the use of vases as grave monuments declined radically. Second the inscribed grave monument, especially with sculpted images, becomes progressively more common, a trend that reaches its climax in the later archaic period. The fact that this type of monument can preserve the deceased's memory on its own and also scores very high on visibility, permanence and individualization suggests that this was the reason for the increase in its popularity, that in the course of the archaic period these things were sought after more by more people. But what seems to us a reasonable conclusion may be culturally determined and fallacious; we must therefore approach the problem from another angle, consider the aspects of the archaic inscribed grave monument that have not yet been investigated and then pull all the strands together, try to reconstruct the mentality associated with the inscribed archaic grave monument and see how that picture relates to the conclusion proposed here.

6. The Inscribed Archaic Grave Monument: Voices, Pattern of Appearance, Mentality, and Perceptions

Inscriptions, we saw, appear on grave monuments of different types, and an inscription naming the deceased was sometimes inscribed not on a grave monument, but on the walls of the grave chamber, or on the side of the sarcophagus. Funerary epigrams were also inscribed on different types of grave monument, including grave pillars[689] and mud brick tombs,[690] but their commonest occurrence is on the bases of stelai and statues.[691] All archaic epitaphs name the grave monument. Let us now consider who it is who does this naming, invites the passer-by to lament, and praises the deceased; whose voice speaks in the epitaphs. There are two different speaking voices in the earliest epitaphs, and these continue to be the most frequent types of voices even when other types also emerge. Of these

[689] Cf. e.g. Hansen 1983: 77, 138.
[690] Cf. ibid. 29.
[691] A minimalist inscribed grave monument was the inscription of the name of the deceased on the entrance slabs at the lip of the vertical shaft of a chamber tomb, or on the chamber walls, or the like (cf. e.g. Kurtz and Boardman 1971: 182, and above). I shall be focusing on non-minimalist grave monuments, those which consisted of a separate above-ground element, instead of those, in particular geographical areas, in which that part was subsumed into the burial area itself. For the latter which, given the importance of the grave monument in the archaic period, are clearly dependent on the former, and the ensuing complex ways in which they functioned, is more elusive.

early and common voices, one belongs to the grave monument. 'I
am the *sema* of X' with or without some additional statement. The
other is in free indirect speech: 'Of X *tode sema*' with or without
some additional statement. Additional statements in the two formulations take, for example, the form 'Y set me up', or 'he died in
war', or 'her son is mourning her' and the like. In almost all these
epitaphs the addressee is the passer-by; in most cases this is implicit,
sometimes the passer-by is addressed directly, and urged to do
something, usually lament or pity the deceased; for example, *stethi
kai oiktiron Kroiso para sema thanontos.*[692] Sometimes, rarely, the
epitaph is addressed to the deceased.[693] The latter case is an apostrophe. The apostrophe makes the objects of the universe potentially
responsive, sentient forces, turns objects into subject with which it
attempts to establish a harmonious relationship. Apostrophes address
the addressee as a potential presence; they create a discursive time
and space, a now in which absent objects or beings are present
subjects in the discourse.

The epitaphs in which the speaking voice is that of the grave
monument do not present problems. Funerary inscriptions of the
type 'I am the *sema* of X' are directly comparable to votive inscriptions of the type 'X dedicated me to Apollo', and both are directly
comparable to the eighth-century ownership inscriptions, such as
Nestoros eimi eupoton poterion etc.[694] The fact that the speaking voice
is that of the object is correlative with the nature of the inscription:
it articulates in a permanent form aspects of the object's identity, it
is an explication and articulation of its being. (This is also true of
the votive dedications, since the fact that they were dedicated to,
say, Apollo, by X was the most important aspect of their identity.)
The voice is that of the grave monument, the viewpoint that of the
dedicator of the monument. In some epitaphs it is the deceased
who speaks; we saw some fifth-century examples above, in the
epitaphs in which the deceased contrasts himself to the passer-by
(*Chairete hoi pariontes; ego de thanon keimai* etc.). But the deceased
can also appear as the speaking 'I' in some archaic epitaphs, though
this only happens rarely. In some of these the identity of the speaking
'I' may appear ambiguous, in that it is not made explicit whether it

[692] Hansen 1983: 27; cf. also the forms of address in Hansen 1983: 28 and 13; cf. also Day
1989: 18–20.
[693] Cf. Hansen 1983: 19, 69, 50.
[694] On 'speaking objects' in Greek inscriptions cf. Svenbro 1988: 37–8 with bibliog.

is the deceased or the grave monument who speaks. Thus Svenbro[695] thinks that in the epigram of Phrasikleia *kore keklesomai aiei, anti gamo para theon touto lachos' onoma* refers to the grave monument. However, there can be no doubt whatsoever that in some epigrams, such as that of Telephanes, the speaking voice is that of the deceased:

[ὅ]στις μὴ παρ[ε | τ]ύνχαν᾽ ὅτ᾽ ἐ[χο] | ἐφερόν με θαν | ὁντα,
νῦν μ᾽ ὁ[λο] | φυράσθω · μν[ῆμ] | α δὲ Τηλεφ[άνε] | ος.

The last words, clearly, are spoken by a different voice. The same switch happens also in the grave inscription of Phrasikleia, which begins with *Sema Phrasikleias*, continues *kore keklesomai aiei* etc. and concludes *[Aris]tion Pari[os ep]o[ie]se*. In my view, the ancient reader would have understood *Sema Phrasikleias* to be a separate segment of the epigram, in a different voice from the rest, the same voice as that who speaks in the additional last sentence. First, because whatever one may think of *kore keklesomai aiei*, the formulation *anti gamo para theon touto lachos' onoma* does not make sense when applied to the monument, notwithstanding its nature as the part of the deceased's persona that remains in the world of the living. And second, because the same schema as the one that would pertain if this interpretation is right appears in the epigram for Telephanes. This other speaking voice is clearly the same as that in the epitaphs of the second type mentioned above, to which we now turn.

Inscriptions of the type 'Of X *tode sema*' are normally taken to be short versions of 'Of X *tode sema esti*'.[696] Free indirect speech can be seen as a rhetorical device to give authority to the statement. The viewpoint is that of the person who set up the grave monument, but who is the speaker, whose voice would the ancient reader understand this to be (whether or not such 'understanding' was articulated at the conscious level)? The common formulations of the type '*X*

---

[695] Svenbro 1988: 23.

[696] Only Svenbro (1988: 38–45) thinks that until *c.*550 in these cases also it is the grave monument that speaks, and we are to understand *sema tode eimi*, not *esti*. He admits that in some later archaic monuments the speaking voice is not that of the monument, which is clearly referred to in the third person, but he thinks that a change took place at *c.*550 and from then on in some epitaphs the voice is that of the monument, in others that of the family. In my view this interpretation is wrong, in interesting ways: it is both overcomplicated and too simplistic. Given that there can be no doubt, as is indeed acknowledged by Svenbro, that in some archaic epitaphs it is indeed *esti* that complements *sema tode*, given that free indirect speech does appear in some of the earliest epitaphs which do not include these formulations (cf. Hansen 1983: 13), it is illegitimate to postulate a change without any shred of supporting evidence.

tode sema estese' show that the erector of the monument is not the
narrator. So whose voice is it? The addressee is obviously the passer-
by who, as always, will also lend his voice to articulate the text and
thus also assume the role of narrator. In the first modality the
monument voiced its own identity; in this second modality the
identity of the monument is given from the outside, by another
party. In the case of non-inscribed grave monuments the distributor
of such information to a passer-by would have been the community,
represented by any one of its members. The knowledge 'This is the
sema of X' was preserved by the collective memory of the community, or of a section of it (such as the deceased's family), and
could be communicated to a passer-by by any of its members that
happened to be around. I suggest that the epitaphs in free indirect
speech reproduce, in writing, that situation; that it was the community that was perceived to be the speaking voice in these epitaphs
(at whatever level of, and at whatever point in the conscious/
unconscious spectrum in the process of reading that perception
came into play). This lent authority to the statement, and gave
a wider framework to the sadness at, and the importance of, the
deceased's death expressed in the epitaph, and to the preservation of his memory.[697] The person who erected the grave monument can also, albeit rarely, be the narrator, the speaking 'I'.[698] A
recent find has made clear that[699] there is also another category, in
which a first person says '*aniaomai* or *oiktiro* when I look at the grave
monument of X.' I suggest that the identity of the speaking voice
here is ambiguous, the speaking 'I' shifts between on the one hand
the 'voice of the community' discussed above as being the narrator
in epitaphs in free indirect speech,[700] and on the other a vague
anyone looking at the grave monument, which is then focused and
incarnated in any passer-by who reads the epitaph, and who here

---

[697] Svenbro's answer is that the 'we' behind the free indirect speech is the family and the
passers-by (1988: 43). This view is based on an *a priori* common sense approach. The family's
viewpoint would have been presumed to be represented through that of the erector of the
grave monument, but though the family may have been subsumed into the voice of the
narrator, it must not be assumed to have been identical with it. While the passer-by assumed
the role of narrator as well as addressee in the act of reading the epitaph and activating the
deceased's memory.

[698] Cf. e.g. Hansen 1983: 136.

[699] Cf. Lewis 1987: 188.

[700] This voice may perhaps sometimes have been seen as focusing primarily on the person
who erected the grave monument, thus sliding towards the category in which the speaking
'I' is the erector of the monument.

fits the speaking voice more closely than in any other category, and thus also adopts the narrator's focalization of the presentation of the deceased's death even more strongly. The *oimoi* inscriptions can also be seen as versions of this type of speaking voice.

Svenbro is right[701] that in all epitaphs it is the passer-by that lends his voice to the text's narrator. But there is a varying distance in the different epitaphs between the epitaph's speaking 'I' and the passer-by who incarnates it. The most radically distanced are the epitaphs in which the speaking 'I' is the deceased. As we saw, in the fifth-century epitaphs in which the speaking 'I' is that of the deceased the latter contrasts himself to the passer-by (*Chairete hoi pariontes; ego de thanon keimai* etc.), thus underlining and stressing the distance. Also distanced is the relationship in the epitaphs where the speaking 'I' is the person who erected the grave monument. The epitaphs in which a first person says *aniaomai* or *oiktiro* offer a close fit between the epitaph's 'I' and the passer-by who incarnates it. The mid-fifth-century Thessalian epitaph[702] cited in § ii.4 sets in place a dialogue between the passer-by and the sphinx who was a part of the monument, and thus a total identification between the passer-by and one of the voices. Between these two distances there is the spectrum covered by the various epitaphs in free indirect speech. In epitaphs of the 'this is the *sema* of X' type the passer-by lends his voice to, and so incarnates, the narrator at the same time as he is functioning as the implicit addressee. In epitaphs involving expressions like *stethi kai oiktiron*, whether or not they also include a direct explicit address to the passer-by,[703] the latter is the text's explicit addressee addressed by the text's narrator whom he incarnates.

The fact that in all early epigrams and prose epitaphs the two speaking voices involved are that of the grave monument, in the common modality of the speaking object, and the free indirect speech, here identified as the voice of the community, is the result, and expression, of the function of the grave inscription: these two speaking voices represent the available modalities for articulating in a permanent form the memory of the community as to the identity of the *sema* and the social persona of the deceased. As we saw, in the archaic period the inscribed monument became the vehicle

[701] Svenbro 1988: 55.
[702] Hansen 1983: 120.
[703] Like that in Hansen 1983: 28 for example.

for the preservation of the deceased's memory, which it made independent of the collective memory of the community by giving a permanent and independent form to the 'naming' of the grave monument. Hence the importance of this naming, which performed the most fundamental function ascribed to the archaic inscribed grave monument, and for this reason formed the indispensable core of all archaic grave inscriptions. It was not until approximately two decades after the Persian Wars that this naming ceased to be indispensable, became subsumed, as it were, in the inscribed grave monument itself. This may perhaps have happened as a result of the development of the genre of the funerary epigram, especially under the influence of the public collective epitaphs of the Persian Wars and the following decades, some of which at least had been written by major poets. For these public epitaphs (several of which have been handed down in the literary tradition) do not normally include references to the grave monument or burial.[704]
But, in so far as it is possible to ascertain, references to the grave monument or burial do not cease to be an indispensable part of the private funerary epigram until a decade or so before the middle of the fifth century. The mentality associated with public collective epitaphs is, we saw, different from that of individual epitaphs. One difference explains why the naming of the grave was not indispensable in public collective epitaphs. In official ideology death for one's country is presented as automatically ensuring glory and the preservation of one's memory within the community. Thus the grave epigram, though a vehicle and a focus for that memory, is presented as secondary, not as the only means for the preservation of the memory but as another record of it. Consequently, the naming which was associated with the notion that the grave monument is the chief vehicle for the preservation of the deceased's memory, a substitute as well as a permanent version of the community's remembrance of the fact that 'this is the *sema* of A', was ideologically redundant in the polyandria, and thus was not one of the parameters determining selections in the composition of public collective epitaphs.

Let us now consider the circumstances of the emergence, and the pattern of appearance, of the inscribed grave monument. First,

[704] Cf. e.g. Hansen 1983: 4, 5; *GV* 7, 8, 12, 3, 5, 6, 9, 11. Some of those which are attested epigraphically contain some oblique and generalized references to burial (cf. e.g. Hansen 1983: 1.ii.1; 131.2).

its emergence. Obviously the invention, and thus the new availability, of writing was crucial. But it must not be assumed that the
inscribed grave monument was the automatic result of the fact that
writing was available. This is wrong first, on *a priori* grounds,
because such a view depends on a simplistic perception of the
relationship between availability and need. Second, and most
importantly, because there was a considerable interval between the
invention of writing, for which the mid-eighth century is the
terminus ante quem,[705] and the earliest epitaphs, the earliest of which
belong to the mid-seventh century.[706] Their pattern of appearance
during the next few decades—it is only in the late seventh, and
especially in the sixth that they cease to be extremely rare—invali-
dates any notion that this interval can be explained through the
accident of survival, as does the fact that we possess very considerable
numbers of graves dating to the second half of the eighth century
none of which have an epitaph.[707] The marking of ownership
seems to have been the main determinable use of the earliest
inscriptions.[708] Thus the naming of the inscribed object, 'I am (or
this is) the *poterion* of X' was a fundamental use of writing, and
writing and naming would have been intimately connected in early
Greek mentality.[709] This makes it all the more remarkable that it
was not used for the purpose of naming the grave monument
earlier. The fact that it was not shows that the naming of the
grave monument was not the automatic result of the availability of
writing, but only came about when circumstances obtained that
made this naming especially desirable, so that a need was created.
What happened to bring this about?

We must begin by considering another aspect of the pattern of
appearance of the archaic inscribed grave monument, the question
'who received what was the most individualized, permanent and
visible type of grave monument, an inscribed monument that could
by itself preserve the deceased's memory? and why? and what does

[705] Cf. Johnston 1990: 425.
[706] Jeffery 1990: 61. On the emergence and early pattern of appearance of epigrams
inscribed on the grave cf. also Wallace 1984: 304–5, 315.
[707] Thus Svenbro's suggestion (1988: 14) that perhaps the main reason for the adoption of
the alphabet was in order to commemorate the dead is wrong.
[708] Cf. Johnston 1983: 67.
[709] Svenbro 1988: 75 is right in saying 'dès son arrivée en Grèce l'écriture a été mise au
service du nom propre'. On the place of writing in Greek thought and practice in general
cf. Detienne 1988a: 7–26; 1988b: 29–81; Thomas 1989: *passim*.

this tell us about the mentality associated with the grave monument in general and the inscribed grave monument in particular?' As has been often noted,[710] many archaic grave monuments were erected for young people. By my calculations[711] about half of the epitaphs that are not so fragmentary as to be impossible to determine, were for young people, including young men who died at war; such epitaphs often state that the grave monument was set up by the young person's parent(s).[712] Many do not give any indication of age or other special circumstances. A few are for people who perished at sea or who died and were buried abroad.[713] Some others, many but not all very late archaic, from 510–500 onwards, do not belong to any of these categories. I must stress that the numbers must remain approximate; for the evidence on the basis of which we can attempt to ascribe epigrams in one or the other category is far from unambiguous. For example, are we to assume that all those whose grave monuments were erected by their parents were young people? The likelihood is that they were, at least in the majority of cases. In some epitaphs the motif 'the grave monument has been erected by the parent(s)' is combined with a statement about the deceased's youth. In other epitaphs that state that the grave monument was erected by the parent(s) we have other reasons for thinking that the deceased were young. Thus, when a grave monument is erected not for one child, but for two siblings, it is likely that the two died, either together or consecutively,[714] at a young age. When the grave monument has been erected for a daughter her husband would have been expected to have been at least associated if she had been married; and her sons if she had any would have been the ones to have buried her if they were of appropriate age; since the fact of dying unmarried is a most important facet of death in youth, one that, we shall see, is of special relevance in this context, it is likely that even if the daughter were not very young she may have been deemed to have died a death symbolically correlative to that in young age. We cannot be sure that all the dead whose grave monuments were erected by their parent(s) were young, since it is

---

[710] Cf. e.g. Wallace 1970: 98; Humphreys 1983: 93; Schmaltz 1979: 34–7.

[711] Cf. the Annex to this section for my calculations of the numbers in each of these categories and the references to the epigrams in the different categories; here I am only giving a very small illustrative sample of references.

[712] Monuments for young people: cf. Hansen 1983: 13, 18, 25, 26.

[713] Cf. e.g. Guarducci 1961: no. 53 (165–8); no. 78 (171); cf. also Wallace 1970: 98.

[714] Cf. also D'Onofrio 1988: 88.

perfectly possible that a middle-aged man may have been buried by his old father. But we can be certain that the erection of a grave monument by the parent to the child reversed what was perceived to be the natural order:[715] the parent is burying the child instead of the child burying the parent, a state of affairs presented as *par excellence* tragic.[716] And, we shall see, this is of special significance in this context. Thus, even if we could not be certain that all those whose grave monument was erected by their parent(s) were young and unmarried, the category a 'grave monument erected by the parent(s)' in itself had comparable negative connotations in that it involved a reversal of the normal pattern of generations. I shall return to this. The archaic grave monuments that articulate iconographically the social persona of the deceased in ways that allow us to reconstruct its main traits confirm this picture. Even if we confine ourselves to the stelai to avoid relying on my own conclusions concerning grave statues, and thus avoid any conceivable hint of circularity in my case, the pattern suggested by the epitaphs, in which young people predominate, coincides with that seen in the stelai as a whole, in which many representations are of young people.[717]

In these circumstances, the pattern of appearance of the grave monument inscribed with a funerary epigram suggests that, even if there are uncertainties, and we cannot hope to explain all the inscribed archaic grave monuments, we can reconstruct, at least partly, some of the parameters that determined the selection to erect such a grave monument. This will give us certain general directions concerning the mentality associated with the grave monument. It is clear that in the early period at least a very significant proportion was erected for people who died young and a smaller one for people who died at sea; at a later period also a not insignificant proportion for people who died abroad. In the later archaic period grave monuments for people who do not belong to any of these categories become more common than they were in the early period. These three categories of dead people, which

---

[715] Cf. on this Griessmair 1966: 44–7.

[716] Cf. e.g. Hom. *Il.* 5. 152–8 and Kirk 1990: 74 ad loc. On parents putting up a grave monument to their children cf. Schmaltz 1979: 34–7; cf. also Skiadas 1972: 79–84.

[717] There is, of course, some overlap between the two categories, epitaphs and decorated stelai, so that some grave monuments are counted twice, once in each group, but this is unavoidable and does not affect the overall picture.

cover a considerable proportion of archaic epitaphs, have one
important thing in common, something that pertains to the perception of the death, to the manner and location or to the moment
of the death. In Greek mentality all these deaths had a negative
connotation: they involved either a bad death or at least an unfulfilled life which involves at least one facet of bad death. Those who
died young[718] had an unfulfilled life, especially girls who died
unmarried and did not fulfil their ideal role of wife and mother.
We saw that Phrasikleia's epitaph and the statue standing over her
grave stress the fact that she died unmarried. But young men who
died young also led unfulfilled lives, especially if they did not live
long enough to have progeny and thus plug themselves into the
biological stream of continuity through the generations.[719] Though
we cannot be certain that all those whose grave monument was
erected by their parent(s) were young and unmarried, the category
'grave monument erected by the parent(s)' in itself, we saw, has
negative connotations in that it involves a reversal of the normal
pattern of generations and the natural order. There was a certain
dimension of good death in the death of those killed in war, but
this did not diminish the tragedy of their early death. The mentality
reflected in the epitaphs of those killed in war in the archaic period
is radically different from that associated with the public epitaphs
of fifth-century Athenian polyandria, where the death is presented
as positive, for which lament is not appropriate. In the archaic
epitaphs death at war is tragic and invites lament. The notion
that death at sea is bad death is common in the Greek collective
representations;[720] it is a lonely death, away from one's community
and without the proper death-ritual which, among other things,
reflects, and symbolically represents, the perception of the death as
a moment in the history of the community whose continuity gives
meaning to individual discontinuity. The theme of dying abroad
has some elements of that, but in a less severe form.[721]

Thus, a common factor in these categories is something unfulfilled, especially with reference to one's 'continuity' in the world

---

[718] On dying young cf. Griessmair 1966; cf. Skiadas 1967: 82–9.

[719] On dying without children cf. Griessmair 1966: 75–7.

[720] On death at sea being a bad death cf. Sourvinou-Inwood 1981: 31; 1983: 43; and
Georgoudi 1988: 53–61, who discusses death at sea in Greek epitaphs in general.

[721] Cf. Sourvinou-Inwood 1981: 31; 1983: 43; Griffin 1980: 108–9; Lattimore 1962:
200–1.

of the living after death. Consequently, a large proportion of archaic inscribed grave monuments, especially until about 510, was associated with dead people whose death involved an especially negative aspect, was felt to be not only especially tragic, but also, and above all, deficient in continuity in the world of the living after death. It is as though the grave monument was compensating for, making up, this deficiency in memory survival. This in its turn suggests that the mentality associated with, and motivating, the erection of the grave monument pertains primarily to the sphere of attitudes to death and should not be seen simply in terms of élite competition. There can be no doubt that the grave monument was put to the service of the self advertisement of the wealth and importance of individual members and families of the élite. In Athens after the first wave of funerary legislation which regulated the death ritual including funerals,[722] there was another which regulated grave monuments. Some time after that first wave[723] a further law[724] ordained that no grave monument was to be more elaborate than the work of ten men would accomplish in ten days, that tombs were not to be adorned with *opus tectorium* nor to have 'herms' erected on them. 'Herms' seems to be a general term for any standing stone grave-marker.[725] *Opus tectorium* may refer to the painted plaques decorating built tombs discussed above. Humphreys convincingly suggested that the ordination that no grave monument should be more elaborate than the work ten men would accomplish in ten days referred to grave mounds, since sculpted monuments were covered by the prohibition of herms, and since 'it is scarcely credible that their ostentation could have been thought of in terms of the labour time involved in making them.'[726] I would only add that it is likely that built tombs would also have been included in this category. Undoubtedly, this law curbed excessive ostentation by the élite who were using the grave as a locus of self-advertisement. All this meets precisely modern expectations in which the sociopolitical and the dimension of ideological manipulation are privileged. But this is not the whole story, which is more

[722] Cf. Appendix; cf. also Sourvinou-Inwood 1983: 47–8.

[723] *post aliquanto*: Cic. *De leg.* 2. 64.

[724] On this legislation cf. also Garland 1989: 5–7.

[725] Humphreys 1983: 89. Kurtz and Boardman (1971: 122) suggest that it was stelai with figure decoration in relief that were forbidden.

[726] Humphreys 1983: 90.

complex. For the inscribed grave monument does not fit the simple picture that privileges politico-ideological manipulation and underprivileges attitudes to death and funerary ideology; and the fact that it is the grave monument which gives us more explicit access to its function and the mentality associated with it, the grave monument which, as it were, speaks to us about itself through the epitaph that does not fit the simpler picture, and does not meet modern expectations, should be a warning. As we saw, it is dead people who, in Greek eyes, suffered from a deficiency in memory survival that appear to have been the focal group to get inscribed grave monuments, out of which the practice expanded to others; their getting the grave monument that can remedy that deficiency appears to be a form of compensation. To put it simply, a large proportion of archaic grave monuments are for young people (of aristocratic families) because their parents were concerned to mark their children's passage through life, to set up a *sema* of their life (and death) that will preserve their memory since they would have left no descendants.

Given that absences are as important as differences and that what has not been chosen helps determine the significance of what has been chosen, we must also note that the people whom we might have expected to have this type of grave monument as a permanent record of their achievements and importance do not appear to get them. On the basis of our expectations of political use and self-advertisement we would have expected most inscribed grave monuments to have been erected for the most important leading and politically, militarily, or religiously active members of the aristocracy and to be advertising such achievements. Surely, if political use and self-advertisement were the determining factors, we would have expected many if not most epitaphs to say things like:

Here lies Stesagoras, son of Kimon, Philaid, who led the army of the polis and won great glory when he defeated the might of the Megarians, and who offered great sacrifices to the gods when he was *archon basileus*, thus making the city beloved to the gods and himself beloved to the demos.

Of course we have no archaic epitaphs of this kind.[727] It is possible

[727] The nearest that an archaic epitaph comes to this type of thing involves a motivated recording: the stele for Phanodikos, son of Hermokrates from Prokonnesos (Guarducci 1961: 165–8 no. 53), who was buried at Sigeion, records his donation to the citizens of a mixing bowl with a stand and strainer for the prytaneion before enjoining them to care for the monument, as an incentive to grant this request because they owed him a *charis*.

that one factor behind this absence may have been that such leaders were deemed to be remembered by the community because they were great men; their *sema* would not have been forgotten, it would have become the focus for the activation of their memory that remained alive. It could be argued that it may have been a point of honour that such people did not need inscribed grave monuments in order to be remembered. However, this assumes that the possibility that such grave monuments might have been erected to such people had arisen and been thought about; and if that were the case we might have expected at least some members of that élite to have found ways to maintain the fiction while gaining the self-advertisement *via* the advertisement of their fathers' or grandfathers' achievements the positive presentation of which in a permanent form would undoubtedly have been *de facto* advantageous. But in any case, whatever the ideological nexus behind that absence, the fact remains that the presence, the erection of the inscribed grave monument, which was the one type of monument that could become the vehicle for the permanent memory survival of the deceased, was determined by factors pertaining to funerary ideology.[728] The pattern of the first appearance of the inscribed grave monument leads us in the same direction. It fits neither the primarily politically ideological explanation nor the notion that it followed 'naturally' from the invention of writing.[729] Either of those two factors, or both in combination, would have led to the emergence and widespread popularity of the inscribed grave monument at least in the late eighth century. We must therefore ask why it did not and what had led to that emergence. What (if anything) had changed? Dying young and dying at sea were aspects of bad death already in Homer, so it is not the emergence of attitudes associated with these special circumstances of dying that can provide the explanation.

Before considering this question let us place in perspective our

[728] Another aspect of archaic epitaphs that creates difficulties for the view that privileges sociopolitical manipulation by aristocratic families is that, as Thomas (1989: 105) noted, archaic epitaphs present the deceased 'as a heroic type, detached from his family and the period in which he lived'.

[729] The first appearance of the 'individualized' grave monument, through first a statue and then a decorated stele, is either at the same time as, or a little later than, that of the inscribed grave monument. Monumental sculpture begins at *c*.650. We cannot be certain as to whether the use of funerary statues relating to the social persona of the deceased began straightaway.

conclusion that the uses of the archaic grave monument were not
the political and manipulative ones which our cultural assumptions
tend to privilege and which appear to modern eyes to be rational
and logical—often in symbiosis with implicit or explicit universalist
notions of timeless grief and unchanging familial piety. The privileging of the sociopolitical at the expense of the more generally
ideological, which includes attitudes towards death and eschatology,
is *a priori* simplistic because it starts with the fallacious presupposition
that one subsystem of the interactive social system is totally dependent on, and subordinated to, another, the sociopolitical, instead of
interacting with it. For the fact that a community's social structure
articulates, and is articulated in, the death-ritual does not entail that
the latter can be collapsed into, or is entirely determined by, the
former. Anthropology confirms that the privileging of the sociopolitical is culturally determined, and shows that factors other than
the sociopolitical affect aspects of burial customs such as differential
treatment, that *prima facie* might have appeared to be directly connected with social structure.[730] Studies of nineteenth-and twentieth-
century mortuary practices also show that attitudes towards death
and the dead are a major determinant of such practices, as regards
both the death-ritual and the grave monument.[731] Of course,
'rational' political aims were indeed articulated in archaic cemeteries, and the grave monument did play a role in this. But this
was far from being its only, or indeed its primary, function.

I shall now try to determine whether the emergence and pattern
of appearance of the inscribed grave monument can be explained
in terms of funerary ideology. Let us focus on what we know about
this monument. It is a vehicle for the preservation of the deceased's
memory; it has expanded radically the grave monument's function
pertaining to memory survival. Epitaphs, like many of the images
on the grave monuments, articulated aspects of, and coloured
positively, the deceased's social persona, thus ensuring his memory
survival. Another important semantic dimension of the funerary
epigrams is the expression of sadness and lamentation for the
deceased and the perception that the death has caused grief and
the dead are to be pitied. Other images articulate the notion of
supernatural protection.

---

[730] Cf. e.g. Humphreys 1983: 173–4; Hodder 1982a: 141–4.
[731] Cf. e.g. Parker Pearson 1982: 99–113, cf. esp. 110–12.

The function of a grave monument as a grave monument is dependent on the knowledge that it is the grave monument of a certain individual. The inscribed grave monument gives permanent form to that information and makes it independent of the community. Given the gap between the availability of writing and the emergence of the inscribed grave monument, this emergence is likely to have been correlative with a perception that the community memory was no longer able adequately to perform the role of preserving that knowledge; this change in perceptions would have taken place either because the community had changed, or because the desire for memory survival had changed, had become stronger and generated the desire for assured and long memory survival (at least in some circles), or because both sets of circumstances obtained, interacted, and were correlative. Since what inscribed grave monuments did was to preserve the memory of the deceased in a uniquely strong way, and since a significant proportion of such monuments, especially in the earlier period, were erected for people who were perceived to be in some ways deficient in memory survival, it would be reasonable to conclude that (besides, and in interaction with, the complex changes in the communities brought about by the emergence of the polis)[732] the creation of the inscribed grave monument resulted from an increased concern for memory survival, which was often associated, and may conceivably have begun in connection with, but was not limited to, negative case limits which were perceived to be in special need to compensate for deficiency. But is this conclusion that appears reasonable to us correct, or is it culturally determined? The following considerations suggest that it is indeed a correct reconstruction of ancient mentality.

First, we saw, there are other reasons for thinking that there was an increased concern for memory survival in the archaic period. The fact that in the archaic period *mnema* is often used to denote the grave monument, a use absent from the Homeric poems, suggests that in that period there was a greater emphasis on the role of the grave monument in the survival of the deceased's memory. Second, a greater concern for memory survival is expressed in literature also.[733] In these circumstances, the archaic inscribed grave monument can be seen as correlative with, and thus can be inter-

---

[732] Cf. Ch. IV.
[733] Cf. Sourvinou-Inwood 1983: 45 and n. 74.

preted as being a manifestation of, a greater anxiety about memory survival and a more acute sadness about death that have gravitated above all to the deaths of those (members of the élite) who are deficient in memory survival. This interpretation gains further support from the fact that, we saw, there were some shifts in the preferred images of death, which point in the same direction. First, a new type of image emerges which articulates the notion of supernatural protection. Second, the preferred images on the grave monuments that pertain to the social persona of the deceased also shift: there is a trend for these preferred images and certainly for those that were dominant in the archaic period, to change somewhat, and for the more self-oriented images of the deceased and of death to become dominant.

In these circumstances, I submit that the emergence of the inscribed grave monument was a manifestation of a nexus of funerary attitudes which involved a greater concern for the survival of one's memory and a more anxious and emotionally intense perception of one's own death, and of the death of the important other. In the following chapter I will be suggesting that the nexus of attitudes manifested in the emergence and pattern of use of the inscribed grave monument and in the shift in the preferred images of death was part of a more general (albeit partial) shift in the collective attitudes towards death that had taken place in certain circles in the archaic period. I must stress that my analysis of the archaic grave monument is entirely independent of that thesis concerning the shift in attitudes. The latter can provide an explanatory model for the conclusions of the former, but these conclusions were based entirely on analyses of the evidence pertaining to the grave monument, which (in contrast to the model testing strategies that will be criticized in the Appendix) was not structured through questions derived from a prior explanatory framework.

Annex to § ii.6. I have considered two sets of epitaphs, one much smaller than the other. The two sets overlap, but this, of course, does not affect the sample of proportions each provides. The first set consists of the epitaphs discussed by Guarducci (1961), that is all inscriptions of all types on archaic Attic grave stelai with relief decoration known at that time. The overall number of epitaphs included in the set was 18. These fall into the following categories: (1) Epitaphs for young people, whether or not the grave monuments state they have been erected by the parent(s): 5 specimens. (2) People who died and were buried abroad: 2 specimens, and perhaps also a third if *to Delio* on no. 79 means 'the Delian' rather than 'the son of Delios'. (3) No indication, simply, 'this is the grave monument of X', with or without 'Y put me up' and/or Z 'made me': 4 specimens. (4) Only the name of the deceased: 3 specimens. (5) The name of the deceased + 'Y put me up' or 'I am the work of Z': 2 specimens. (6) Too fragmentary to be clear: 1 specimen. Some of the epitaphs that do not say that the deceased was young or that the grave monument was erected by the parent(s) may also have belonged to grave monuments for young persons. One of the epitaphs here classified under category 3, that for Dermys and Kittylos,[734] is inscribed on a grave monument which represents Dermys and Kittylos as two youths.[735] This suggests that among the epitaphs now separated from their images some may have commemorated young persons, whose youth was represented in the image, despite the fact that the epitaph does not say anything to that effect. Thus, the funerary epigram Hansen 1983: 26, sounds as though it could be reflecting, and accompanying, an iconographical schema such as that on the stele Metropolitan Museum New York 11.185 and Staatliche Museen, Berlin, A7,[736] which is accompanied by the epigram Hansen 1983: 25. We know, then, that one of the epitaphs which do not appear in the young persons' category as listed above was indeed the monument to young people. We also suspect that the same may have been the case with a second one. Thus of the 17 inscribed grave monuments under consideration (leaving aside the one that was so fragmentary as to be impossible to consider), 6 are certainly, 7 possibly, grave monuments erected for young persons and 2 certainly, 3 probably grave monuments erected for people who died and were buried abroad.

The second, and much larger, set of archaic epitaphs I have considered is the archaic funerary epigrams published in Hansen (1983). The overall number of archaic epitaphs included is 95.[737] They fall into the following categories: (1) Epitaphs for young

---

[734] Guarducci 1961: no. 9 p. 155.

[735] Richter 1961: no. 9 p. 13 figs. 31–3.

[736] Richter 1961: no. 37 pp. 27–9, cf. also 159–65 (Guarducci 1961).

[737] I am not counting no. 47 as a grave inscription nor the Teithronion epigram that will be discussed in Ch. VI.

people: 32 specimens, with 3 more possibles.[738] (2) People who died and were buried abroad: 5 specimens,[739] all from the late archaic period. (3) People who died at sea: 2 specimens,[740] both early. (4) No indication, simply, 'this is the grave monument of X', with or without 'Y put me up' and/or 'Z made me' or some other comparable formulation with or without other themes such as lament themes: 14 specimens.[741] (5) None of these: 13 specimens.[742] (6) Too fragmentary to be clear: 25 specimens. The category 'epitaphs for people who died young' is made of epitaphs ascribed to it for the following reasons. The deceased's youth is mentioned.[743] It is stated that the grave monument has been erected by the parent(s).[744] Either some other information is given which conveys the same idea, or the accompanying representation shows the deceased's youth, or both.[745] I have classified three as likely to be monuments for young people for the following reasons: no. 19 because it was inscribed on the base of what could only have been a kouros;[746] no. 26 because of its similarities to no. 25 mentioned above in the discussion of the first set of epitaphs; 31 because the formulation *hapases . . . echsochos helikias* suggests, I believe, youth. A certain number of those who died young died in war.[747] Very rarely someone is said to have died at war, but his age not stated.[748]

[738] The possibles are nos. 19, 26, 31.
[739] Nos. 52, 58, 66, 77, 173.
[740] Nos. 132, 143 (public epitaph).
[741] Nos. 28, 37, 38, 49, 40, 54, 70, 72, 110, 139, 140, 146, 159, 164.
[742] Nos. 34, 36, 57, 61, 62 (doctor) (perhaps also 64 and 144 in that the epitaph states that the deceased are buried by their son, but they are too fragmentary, esp. 144, to be sure they did not include for example, the information that they died at sea, or died abroad), 67, 69, 74, 76, 111, 112, 172.
[743] In nos. 13, 43, 45, 51, 68, 75, 76, 136, 160, 163.
[744] Cf. on this category above in the text; they are nos. 14, 18, 20, 25, 32, 35, 41, 42, 43, 46, 50, 53 (this monument, which belonged together with a stele representing a bearded male, was not for a youth, since in that case the figure would have been beardless; but, we saw, the category 'young' was not limited to beardless youths), 55, 71, 113, 137, 138, 152, 157, 161, 169.
[745] Cf. no. 24 (Phrasikleia), 27 (Kroisos (on the view that kouroi and korai stood over the grave of young men and maidens rather than mature individuals cf. above)), 109 (Dermys and Kitylos: the representations).
[746] And is thus comparable to Kroisos.
[747] Cf. e.g. 13, 27, 136.
[748] Such is the case of Kroisos, whose youth we deduce from the statue that was his *sema*. Another is no. 145, the epitaph of Arniadas. We cannot exclude that he at least may not have been very young, and that there was a distinct category of people who died at war which largely overlaps, but is not identical, with, the 'died at war very young', category, and which includes people who died at war not very young, and who also got inscribed grave

If we leave aside those epitaphs that are too fragmentary to be clear we are left with 70, of which we know that 32, probably 35, that is half or almost half, were for young people, a fact which in almost all these cases is explicitly stated or otherwise conveyed. 14 further epitaphs do not give any indication of age or other special circumstances, but the fact that, we saw, some epigrams do not mention the deceased's youth, which was only articulated through the accompanying representation which we happen to have (e.g. no. 27), shows that not all epigrams mentioned the deceased's youth even indirectly, that many allowed it to be shown by the representation, so that we are probably seriously underestimating the number and proportion of inscribed grave monuments erected for young people. Two were for people who died at sea. Of the remaining epitaphs 5, all, as it happens, from the late archaic period, were for people who died and were buried abroad. 12 epitaphs do not belong to any of these categories. Two more do not belong to the category 'epitaph on the grave monument of a young person' but are too fragmentary for us to be sure that they did not belong to the 'died at sea', or 'died abroad' category. 10 of the 12 are from the very late archaic period, from 510–500 onwards. It thus appears that while the grave monuments for young people are more or less evenly distributed throughout the archaic period, starting very early, the category involving people who did not belong to any of these 'special' categories tends to be more common in the later part of the archaic period.

monuments. In Sparta Lycurgan legislation only allowed the inscription of the name of the deceased on the grave monument of men who died at war (cf. Toher 1991: 171), and of a particular category of woman, though which particular category was so excepted is controversial (cf. Toher 1991: 170 and n. 45; on Spartan funerary legislation cf. also Garland 1989: 13–14).

IV.

Coping with Death:
Shifting Attitudes in a Changing
World

We saw in Chapter III that the circumstances of the emergence, and the pattern of usage, of the inscribed grave monument, especially of the most individualized permanent and highly visible type, the sculpted monument with images and epigram, and also the content of the grave inscriptions, indicate an increasingly stronger concern for the lasting survival of one's memory after death; and that the epitaphs stress very strongly a poignantly sad perception of death, while the preferred images of death indicate an increasingly individual, self-centred representation of the deceased's social persona.

In Chapter II we saw that in two facets of Homeric eschatology a deeply rooted nexus of beliefs coexisted with a very rarely expressed and not eschatologically integrated different type of belief, which represented a seminal manifestation of developments that accelerated and crystallized in the archaic period. First, the dominant picture concerning the destiny of the shades is that there is no individual destiny, no rewards or punishments, for individual shades; but we also found the seeds of a concept of individual destiny, a notion that will develop significantly in the archaic period and come to include the possibility of a happy afterlife. Second, the belief that everyone dies and goes to Hades is dominant; but there is also a very thin layer of belief according to which a few select people gain immortality. This strand developed significantly in post-Homeric times and provided models of hope for the afterlife to common mortals, correlatively with the development of eschatologies promising a happy afterlife.

I have argued elsewhere[1] that these developments were part, and one of the many manifestations, of a general (but very partial) shift in the collective attitudes towards death, which involved increased anxiety about death and the preservation of one's memory, and a more individual perception of death. I had also suggested, without investigating the grave monument, that the appearance of the individualized grave monument in the archaic age may also be seen as a manifestation of this shift. The detailed investigation of the grave monument, the circumstances of its emergence, its pattern of appearance, its forms, its epitaphs and images conducted above provides, I submit, strong support for this thesis, the main aspects of which I will now summarize very briefly as part of the building up of the image of the early Greek death discourse articulated in this book. I had argued that the funerary attitudes and behaviour characterizing the Dark Ages and still dominant in the Homeric epics involved familiarity with death, which was hateful but not frightening, and was accepted as an inescapable evil, part of the life-cycle in which the generations succeed each other and the individual's discontinuity contrasts with the continuity of the family, the community and the human species, an attitude expressed strikingly in *Iliad* 6. 145–9.

Already in the eighth century a certain shift in these attitudes had begun to take place, which accelerated and crystallized in the archaic age, when a partial shift in attitudes can be identified; in certain circles (aristocratic and intellectual circles in the more advanced societies) a set of attitudes and behaviour appears which is different from and sometimes in conflict with the earlier nexus, and involves a certain loss of familiarity with and recession in the acceptance of death, and also the desire to push it away; for it now generates greater fear and even revulsion. There is a more individual and anxious approach to one's death, now perceived as above all the end of one's (now more strongly felt) personal identity, a personal tragedy—rather than primarily as an unavoidable (if sad) episode in the species' life-cycle and the community's history. It is accepted with greater reluctance, and there is more anxiety about it, and a greater concern for the survival of one's memory, and also, in certain circles, for a happy afterlife. The death of the important other is articulated more strongly, poignantly, and lastingly. This

[1] Sourvinou-Inwood 1983: 33–48; 1981: 15–39.

was a partial shift, not a radical transformation. When collective representations change—which they only do slowly—stratifications take place so that old attitudes live on side by side with new ones. In this case, the earlier attitudes of acceptance of, and familiarity with, death survived during the archaic period in some circles, while in others they were modified, and lived on in this modified form.

This thesis has been challenged, and I shall answer that challenge in detail in the Appendix: first, in order to show that this critique of my argument is invalid; second, because that discussion will bring up some aspects of funerary behaviour and ideology, such as the disappearance of intramural burial and the archaic funerary legislation, and the spectrum of attitudes towards death articulated in archaic literature, which I have discussed elsewhere and do not wish simply to repeat here, but which are deployed, expanded, some of their complexities elucidated, and put into their proper context, in the framework of this 'critique of a critique' that allows me to round off my discourse on the early Greek death discourse. Finally, and not least importantly, this critique of a critique gives me the opportunity to discuss some important methodological issues. For the methodology that had governed those investigations has been misunderstood and I shall discuss this misunderstanding in the Appendix, not simply in self-defence, but because it raises important methodological questions. Here I will set out briefly the methodology on which the conclusions I have just summarized were based—and which has also governed the attempted reading of the Greek discourse of death in this book.

A fundamental principle is that the relevant grids of evidence must be studied separately and independently of each other. First, in order to prevent the various parts of the argument from being dependent on, and so 'contaminated' by, the others, and thus avoid self-validation and hidden circularity; and second, because this strategy allows us to cross-check the results: the convergence of the conclusions of the independently conducted analyses provides some confirmation for their validity. I submit that such convergence and confirmation was indeed achieved in those studies.

The analysis and interpretation of the evidence, the drawing of inferences, is itself vulnerable to the dangers of subjectivity and above all cultural determination; for the notion of 'common sense', of what 'is reasonable to conclude' is not neutral, but depends on the investigator's cultural assumptions. It is for this reason that I made use of comparative evidence of various kinds. First, as eye-openers, possibilities, correctives to implicit presuppositions derived from our own cultural assumptions, that may otherwise implicitly inform the discourse. Then also as analogies, which allow some kind of check, as, for example, in the comparison of my conclusions to the proposed basic models of attitudes to death derived from other societies.[2] This can show whether certain types of behaviour and attitudes which have been grouped together in the reconstruction proposed are known to belong together in other societies; if, as in this case, they do, one's conclusions can be seen not to be simply one's own artificial culturally determined construct, and this provides some confirmation for their validity.

Thus, the fact that an individualization of the grave monument comparable to that of the archaic age took place in comparable circumstances of largely comparable shifting attitudes to death in the European Late Middle Ages[3] indicates that the proposed interpretation of this ancient phenomenon is not just a culturally determined modern construct. Another way in which I tried to explore problematic evidence while attempting to guard as far as possible against cultural determination, was by taking account, first, of some modal tendencies which, it has been proposed, can be revealed behind the variability of funerary data, patterns of correlation between archaeological data and categories of thought;[4] and second, of certain observations concerning the basic modalities of funerary behaviour which empirical research by social anthropologists suggests have universal validity; for example, that weeping and self-aggression in the death ritual are not spontaneous manifestations of emotion, but a regulated symbol channelling grief when this is experienced, generating it when not, and in any case amplifying it as part of a release-mechanism leading to adjustment; and that what is acceptable and/or prescriptive emotion at death-rituals varies greatly from one society to another.[5]

It is useful to use the cross-cultural perspectives as eye-openers to help make clear what is culturally determined in our own assumptions; but it is wrong to use them as explanatory models.

[2] Sourvinou-Inwood 1983: 33.
[3] Ariès 1977: 205–13.
[4] Cf. Sourvinou-Inwood 1983: 33.
[5] Cf. ibid. 34.

For the strategy of model-building and model-testing is seriously flawed, as I will be arguing in the Appendix, where I discuss how the methodology I described here has been misunderstood and in the process address some important methodological issues that are implicated in the study of things funerary.

V.

Charon, Hermes, and the Journey
of Death

i. Charon and the Journey to Hades in the Fifth Century

Charon[1] is first attested in the epic Minyas,[2] which the ancients
attributed to Prodikos of Phocaea,[3] where he is described as the old
ferryman who ferries the souls of the dead in his boat.

> ἔνθ᾽ ἤτοι νέα μὲν νεκυάμβατον ἦν ὁ γεραιός
> πορθμεὺς ἦγε Χάρων, οὐκ ἔλλαβον ἔνδοθεν ὅρμου

The date of the Minyas, like most things about it, is impossible to
determine. Some time in the late seventh, or more plausibly perhaps
in the sixth, century is all that it is possible to say.[4] Charon's earliest
known images are two black-figure scenes of c.500, which show
him ferrying the winged shades in his boat.[5] They tell us that at
c.500 Charon's role as ferryman of the dead was sufficiently well
known to be represented on vases. The corpus of Charon scenes
on white-ground lekythoi begins late in the second quarter of the

---

[1] On Charon cf. Von Duhn 1885: 2–23; Rocco 1897: passim; Furtwängler 1905: 191–
202; Waser 1898: passim; Wilamowitz 1899: 227–30; Papaspyridi 1923: 134–9; Brommer
1969: 167–71; Alexiou 1978: 221–36; Garland 1985: 23, 54–6; Terpening 1985: 11–123 (and
cf. also the review by King 1986b: 355–6); Sourvinou-Inwood 1986a: 210–25; Hoffmann
1984: 65–9; 1986: 173–204; Peifer 1989: 116–19, 147–55; cf. also Kurtz and Boardman 1971:
166, 204, 211. Cf. also some further refs. in Sourvinou-Inwood 1986a: 212.
[2] Minyas EGF fr. 1 (= Kinkel fr. 1 p. 215; = Paus. x.28.2); cf. PEG 137–42; cf. 219.
[3] Cf. EGF p. 145 F 5 (Minyas). Cf. also Bowra 1952: 123; Lloyd-Jones 1967: 227–8.
[4] Cf. on the date of the epic cycle: Lesky 1971: 104; Griffin 1977: 39 and n. 9; cf. also
Davies 1989a: 3–5.
[5] The eschara Frankfurt, Liebighaus 560 (CVA Frankfurt am Main 2 pl. 46. 5–6; Eckstein
and Legher 1969: no. 65 pl. 65; Sourvinou-Inwood 1986a: no. 1) and the fragment of a
phormiskos, Tübingen, Archaeological Institute S/10 1507 (Mommsen 1982: 205–12 fig. 2
and pl. 43. 1–2; Sourvinou-Inwood 1986a: no. 1a).

fifth century; also in the second quarter of the fifth century belongs the representation of Charon in the Nekyia painted by Polygnotos in the Lesche of the Knidians at Delphi, of which only a literary description has survived.[6] As we saw in Chapter II §§ ii.3 and iii, in the Homeric poems (and in Hesiod's galaxy of divine beings) there is no Charon, and Hermes does not guide the shades to Hades, except in the later Continuation of *Odyssey* 24.[7] I argued there that Charon did not exist, nor was Hermes a guide of the shades, until the archaic period; the study of the subsequent developments in the myths pertaining to the shade's transition from life to Hades that will be conducted in this section will confirm this thesis.[8] Let us consider how the journey to Hades was imagined in the fifth century. While in Homer the transition between life and death is brief and condensed and not explicitly articulated, in the fifth century it is elaborated into a journey involving more than one stage and the help of Charon and Hermes Chthonios.[9] Hermes' function is twofold. He leads the shades from the upper to the lower world[10] and he controls their access to the upper world.[11] That is,

---

[6] On the Nekyia cf. C. Robert 1892; Weizsäcker 1895: 37–68; M. Robertson 1975: 248, 266–70; Felten 1975: 65–88; Touchefeu-Meynier 1968: 133–4; Kebric 1983: 3–13; Pollitt 1990: 133–40; Stansbury-O'Donnell 1990: 213–35.

[7] Eustath. *ad* Hom. *Od.* 10.502 notes that Charon's appearance is post-Homeric; Diod. 1. 92. 2–3 implies that he was invented by Orpheus. We know that a *katabasis* ascribed to Orpheus (Kern Orph.F. 296 (= Serv. Aen. vi. 392; cf. Myth.Vat. 2. 149–50)) told the only 'myth' associated with the ferryman of the dead (see Lloyd-Jones 1967: 222); on the myth see below.

[8] I shall discuss and criticize the different views on Charon held by different scholars in Ch. V § iv below.

[9] On this function of Hermes: Nilsson 1967: 509; Farnell 1909: 12–15; Eitrem 1909: *passim*; Simon 1985: 302–3, 313; Burkert 1985: 157–8; Zanker 1965: 104–11; Bérard 1974: 25–7, 129–31, 141–5, cf. also 86–7; Karusu 1976: 91–106; Kahn 1978: 179; Herter 1976: 217–18; Vermeule 1979: 25–6 and 207 with further bibliog.; Garvie 1986: 48–9; Garland 1985: 54–5, 154; Rudhardt 1958: 115; Lebessi 1985: 177–8. The epithet *psychopompos* to describe this function of Hermes is later (cf. on this Herter 1976: 217 and n. 88; Simon 1985: 302). In an expression such as *chthonion th' Hermen pompon phthimenon* (Aesch. *Psychagogoi, TrGF* iii. F 273a v. 8) the epithet is *chthonion*, while *pompon* describes Hermes' role. It is probably from expressions like this in combinations with articulations speaking of him leading, or receiving, the *psychai* (cf. e.g. Socrates of Argos *FGrH* 310 F 5a) that eventually the epithet *psychopompos* was inspired.

[10] Soph. *Aj.* 831–4; Eur. *Alc.* 743–4. Cf. also Socrates of Argos *FGrH* 310 F 5a. Cf. esp. some representations of Hermes as guide of the dead discussed below.

[11] Cf. Herter 1976: 218. In Aesch. *Pers.* 628–30: three *chthonioi daimones hagnoi* are asked to send up a soul from the lower world to the upper: Ge, Hades, and Hermes. (Cf. also vv. 640–51; cf. also 688–90. Cf. also Aesch. *Psychagogoi TrGF* iii. F 273a vv. 7–10). This is probably also the notion reflected in, and articulating, the white-ground lekythos Jena 338

he controls the proper traffic between the upper world and Hades. This is also illustrated by his role in one of the versions of the Sisyphos myth,[12] according to which, when Sisyphos had returned to the world of the living and refused to go back to Hades, Hermes took him back down against his will; that is, he policed and enforced the proper division and separation between the two worlds and ensured that there was no unauthorized mixing. Hermes played a similar role also in the story of Protesilaos in Euripides' *Protesilaos*, accompanying Protesilaos on his anabasis and ensuring his return to Hades.[13] He also acted as a general middleman between the two worlds;[14] thus he performed the function of a *keryx*, summoning up the denizens of the lower world to listen to the messages sent them by the living.[15] I should mention that the notion that in certain circumstances the dead could come up from Hades into the upper world[16] was a genuine belief in archaic and classical times, as

(*ARV* 760.41; *Para.* 414; *Add.* 286; to which add Peifer 1989: 119–21), where Hermes appears to be directing the movement of small winged souls who are coming out of a jar set in the ground, probably from the Underworld to the upper world. The precise meaning of the scene is destined to elude us. But this is one possible articulation of Hermes' role concerning the souls of the dead, shaped by and reflecting underlying belief; it does not necessarily entail an established belief that a jar is involved in the movement of the souls from Hades to the upper world, but a possible expression of this movement. For a jar in the ground provides one possible iconographical articulation of the notion of controlled access from Hades to the upper world; it provides a kind of symbolic tunnel, an access tunnel for the souls moving between Hades and the upper world, expressing the notion of controlled communication presided over by Hermes. Perhaps this image articulates the notion that Hermes allows the souls to come up to the upper world to enjoy offerings made to them. The upper part of the jar set in the ground resembles the (considerably earlier) bottomless vase from Kameiros which Nilsson (1967: 177, cf. pl. 52.4) interpreted as a vase set on a grave through which libation offerings were poured. (On the function of the black-figure eschara which Nilsson used as one of the arguments in favour of his interpretation see Mommsen 1982: 209 n. 16.) A vase of this (general) type may have helped inspire the schema represented on the Jena lekythos. Hermes' role in directing/controlling the movement is consistent with what we know from other sources of different types, and thus clearly reflects belief. The association with the Anthesteria (see e.g. Siebert 1981: 68) is problematic; on the notion that the souls came up to the upper world during the Anthesteria cf. Deubner 1969: 111–14; Parke 1977: 116–17; Burkert 1983: 226–9; 1985: 238; Bremmer 1983: 108–20.

[12] Schol. Pi. *Ol.* i. 97. On this myth cf. Ch. II §ii.4; cf. also Sourvinou-Inwood 1986b: 47–58.

[13] Eur. *Protesilaos* fr. 646a, 647–57 N2, cf. N2 p 563. Cf. Jouan 1966: 317–36; for Hermes' role cf. Jouan 1966: 324, 325. On Eur. *Protesilaos* cf. esp. on what can be said about the plot, and on the relationship between the surviving fragments which can be identified as coming from this play, Haslam 1977: 20–1; Oranje 1980: 169–72; cf. also Seaford 1990: 165.

[14] See e.g. Herter 1976: 217.

[15] Cf. e.g. Aesch. *Cho.* 124 ff.; cf. also *Cho.* 1 and Garvie 1986: ad loc. (pp. 48–9).

[16] As e.g. in Soph. *Polyxena, TrGF* iv. F 523; Eur. *Hec.* 37–41, 93–5, 108–14, 389–90 (on Polydoros' ghost in Eur. *Hec.* see also below in this section); Eur. *Protesilaos* fr. 646a, 647–57

is confirmed by the existence of the Nekyomanteion, which involved the apparition of the shades of the dead—at least in the fifth century.[17] I shall return to this. In the classical period Hermes does not lead the dead right into Hades. He takes them from the upper world through the symbolic no-man's land to the shore of the infernal water where he hands them over to Charon who ferries them over into the Land of the Dead proper. This division of the task of leading the souls to Hades[18] is reflected on the white-ground lekythoi which show Hermes standing on the shore with a dead person and Charon in his boat, at, or poling to, the shore, about to receive the shade.[19] In fifth-century eschatology, then, the separation from life is presided over by Hermes. The transition could be articulated in more detail, and include Thanatos, the agent of death, who would hand over the shade to Hermes—with Charon again involved in the final stage. These are the roles of the three figures in Euripides' *Alcestis*.[20] The same representation (Thanatos is the

N2; Eur. fr. 912 N2, ll. 9–13; cf. also Eur. *Alc.* 1128; Pi. *P.* iv. 159–61. On the apparition and evocation of the dead in tragedy, and its relationship to religious beliefs and magical practices see Jouan 1981: 403–21 with discussion of earlier views.

[17] Cf. Hdt. 5. 92. On the Nekyomanteion cf. Dakaris n.d.: *passim*; 1973: 139–49; Burkert 1985: 114–15; Vermeule 1979: 200–1, 252 n. 27; *Ergon* (1990), 73–7; *Ergon* (1991), 58–62. On the evocation of the dead cf. also Burkert 1962: 40–9; on *psychagogoi* cf. also *TrGF* iii. 370–1, *ad* Aeschylus, *Psychagogoi*.

[18] This division is not invalidated by Timokles, *Heroes* fr. 13a Edmonds: first, this belongs to the later 4th cent., by which time many perceptions pertaining to the dead had changed, and second, the formulation does not necessarily imply that Hermes helped Charon to row (*pace* Edmonds' translation).

[19] Cf. e.g. Sourvinou-Inwood 1986a: nos. 5, 6, 7a + 7b; 10, 12, 22. Much later Lucian articulates his own representations of the collaboration and division of labour between Hermes and Charon: cf. e.g. *Cat. passim*; *Nec.* 10; *DMort.* 10; *DMort.* 4. In Ar. *Ranae* Herakles and Dionysos, who were not dead, did not need the services of Hermes to reach the lake over which Charon ferries the dead.

[20] The notion that Thanatos is the same as Hades in the Alcestis (cf. discussion in Garland 1985: 58) is, in my view, based on a misunderstanding of poetic language. Surely, *pterotos Haidas* in v. 262 is a metaphorical way of describing Thanatos, and in 268 *plesion Haidas* refers both to this metaphorical reference and to the notion that she is near dying and going to Hades. De Ruyt (1932: 64) claims that in *Alcestis* Thanatos fulfils the function of Hermes 'psychopompos'; and that this 'confusion' continues in the following centuries. This is wrong; for *Alc.* 741–4 makes clear that Hermes will be receiving Alcestis; thus he does play a role in her transition to Hades. Simply, in the other parts of the play there is no occasion to mention Hermes. (As for De Ruyt's notion of 'confusion', the ambiguity and ambivalence of the collective representations, and their complex relationships with the texts in which we catch their reflection, must not be mistaken for confusion and contradiction.) Alcestis' vision of Charon awaiting her and calling her (252–7) does not entail that she was to pass from Thanatos' hands directly to Charon's boat. It is an image through which she expresses the imminence of her death by means of the dominant metaphor of death as the final crossing

agent of death, then Hermes takes over and guides the shade) seems to underlie the scene on the lekythos Louvre CA 1264[21] which shows Thanatos pursuing a woman in the presence of Hermes and a tomb.[22] To reach Hades proper the shades must cross a stretch of water in Charon's ferry. This water is sometimes said to be a river, normally Acheron,[23] and sometimes a lake, Acherousia, though it is not always named.[24] Sometimes it is not clear whether a river or a lake is meant. Porphyry[25] concludes from Sophocles' *Polyxena TrGF* iv. F 523, concerning the anabasis of Achilles' ghost, that the stream Acheron and the lake Acherousia were the same, but the conclusion appears unwarranted from the text; what is suggested is rather a connection between the two, as in the case of the river Acheron by the Nekyomanteion which formed the lake Acherousia. In Plato, *Phaidon* 112e–113a, the river Acheron flows into the lake Acherousia as in real-life Thesprotia.[26] The Styx, we saw, was the river separating Hades from the no-man's land communicating with the land of the living which was most deeply rooted in Homer,

into Hades in Charon's boat. (Charon is called the ferryman of the dead (v. 253) and the conductor of the dead (v. 361: *psychopompos*; v. 441: *nekropompos*).) Elsewhere the requirements of the plot entail an emphasis on Thanatos who is the agent of death; thus, a figure who is not normally in the centre of the collective representations, is here at the forefront. On Thanatos cf. also Garland 1985: 56–9; Vermeule 1979: 145–51; Alexiou 1978: 222–3; Peifer 1989: 212–66; Vernant 1991: 95–7, 101.

[21] *ARV* 1384.19; *Add.* 372.

[22] It is interesting that attempts to escape from death's clutches (such as Sisyphos', and Herakles' liberation of Alcestis) only take place at either end, in the upper world or in Hades proper, and involve either Thanatos (who can be defeated by force in the upper world) or the Underworld divinities in Hades, who can be persuaded to release someone, as they did with Sisyphos and Eurydice, and as Herakles was visualizing as a possibility if he failed to catch up with Thanatos (Eur. *Alc.* 851). The alternative to defeating Thanatos by violence is persuading the nether gods in *Alc.* 847–53; 1140–2. The two are combined in a particular version of the myth of Sisyphos, in Pherekydes *FGrH* 3 F 19. No such attempt is located in the marginal border area presided over by Hermes Chthonios and Charon. Thus it would appear that, once the shades began the journey under Hermes' guidance, they could not interrupt it until they reached Hades.

[23] Aesch. *Sept.* 856; Theocr. 17. 47; *AP* 7. 67. 68; cf. Melanippides fr. 3 Page; Bacchylides V.64 (Kokytos); Apul. *Met.* 6. 18 (flumen), and Eust. *ad* Hom. *Od.* 10. 513 (Kokytos, Acheron, and Pyriphlegethon). Cf. Polygnotos' Nekyia (n. 4 supra): Paus. 10. 28. 4.

[24] Eur. *Alc.* 252–3, 443, 900–2 (cf. also Kokytos in 458–9); Eur. fr. 868 N2; Ar. *Ranae* 181–3, 193. Cf. Soph. *El.* 137–8; Hermesianax, *Leontion* fr. 7; Lib. 3, 1–6 Powell p. 98; *AP* 7. 365; Lucian, *DMort.* 20.1; *Nec.* 10; *Cont.* 7; *Luct.* 3; *Etym.m.* s.v. *danakes*.

[25] In Stob. *Ecl.* i. 49, 50 p. 419, 4.

[26] Thuc. 1. 46. In Verg. *Aen.* 298–304 Charon crosses the Stygian marsh at the confluence of Acheron and Kokytos (cf. Clark 1970: 251 n. 21) in Tib. 1. 10. 36 Charon is called the sailor of Styx.

while in *Odyssey* 10. 508–15 the rivers, now multiplied, include Styx and Acheron. The latter's establishment in the role of river-frontier (in alternation or combination with lake Acherousia) may be the result of the influence of the Nekyomanteion by Acheron and Acherousia—a landscape which, we saw, had probably already contributed to the creation of the Homeric infernal landscape.[27] The crossing of the water is the last and definitive step that integrates the shade into the Land of the Dead; in Homer it could only take place after the body was buried and the deceased thus definitely separated from the living. This is why this crossing became a metaphor for dying, and why Charon, as we shall see, became a metaphor for death. Charon's ferrying is a kind of 'introduction'; he 'guarantees' the shades' transition and integration. This elaborated form of the death journey has a structure similar to that of rites of passage: first separation, then marginality and finally the reintegration into the new status.

Charon almost entirely lacks genealogical connections[28] and he is only associated with one myth,[29] told in a katabasis ascribed to Orpheus:[30] Charon, out of fear, had ferried Herakles into Hades when the hero had come to fetch Cerberus, and was punished for this dereliction of duty by spending a year in fetters. The story is echoed in Vergil, *Aeneid* 6. 384–94,[31] where Charon affirms, in an aggressive manner, that the living are not allowed to cross in his ferry, and that it was with reluctance that he had accepted Herakles, Theseus, and Peirithous, despite their heroic status and divine parentage.[32] The same story probably also lies behind Charon's anger mentioned in Achaios *TrGF* i. 20 F 11. As we shall now see, the 'presence' of this myth, and the 'absence' of any others, is directly related to the infernal ferryman's nature and functions. These included the control of the movement in and out of Hades. Euripides, *Alcestis* 357–62, reflects the notion that Charon and

---

[27] For a different view of the history of the development of the infernal rivers: Vermeule 1979: 211 n. 6.

[28] Cf. Waser 1898: 17–18. The only genealogical reference concerning Charon (Hesych. s.v. Akmonides), that he was a son of Akmon, is of dubious validity; it is not certain that it is not the result of textual corruption (cf. *RE* i. 1. 1173–4 s.v. Akmon 1 and Akmonides 2). Cf. also § iv below.

[29] Cf. Waser 1898: 20.

[30] Cf. Servius *ad* Ver. *Aen.* 6. 392.

[31] Cf. Norden 1970: 237.

[32] Cf. also Sen. *Herc. Fur.* 770–7; cf. Terpening 1985: 98.

Cerberus are guardians of Hades' exit, prevent the shades from leaving Hades. Charon's one myth involves dereliction of his duty and punishment, and reflects the same idea, Charon's role as a guardian of the proper traffic between Hades and the upper world and guarantor of the border between the two worlds and of their proper separation; for he is punished because he failed in that duty: the norm is also defined through its transgression. If this story of Charon's punishment does indeed lie behind Charon's anger in Achaios *TrGF* i. 20 F 11,[33] we would have a *terminus ante quo* for this myth,[34] which would thus have been an early part of the Charon nexus. The fact that Charon has almost no genealogical connections and only one myth, which articulates his role of guarantor of the separation between the world of the living and that of the dead, is correlative with his nature, with the fact that he is coterminous with his function of infernal ferryman and belongs to the margins between two worlds.

Let us compare these fifth-century representations with those articulating the Homeric poems.[35] In the fifth century the transition between life and Hades, and the separation between Hades and the upper world, rely on entities of a higher status than in the Homeric poems, where the proper separation between the two worlds and the passage from one to the other was safeguarded—under the supreme jurisdiction of Hades and Persephone, as was also the case later—by the shades themselves, who prevented the unburied from crossing the river, and by the gates and Cerberus; in the fifth century the transition is effected under the guidance of a god and a divine/demonic ferryman, with Cerberus still controlling the exit out of Hades, but now in conjunction with Charon.[36] Thus the borders between the two worlds and their separation are now symbolically upgraded and more secure.[37] Another difference

[33] On Charon's anger cf. also Norden 1970: 237.

[34] This would involve a pre-Achaios, very possibly a 6th-cent., *katabasis* containing this story and ascribed to Orpheus. On epic *katabaseis* and the *katabasis* of Orpheus: Lloyd-Jones 1967; Graf 1974: 139–50; M. L. West 1983: 6, 9–10, 12–13. On epic *katabaseis* cf. Ettig 1891: 278; Ganschinietz 1919: 2401–2 and *passim* (cols. 2359–449).

[35] Leaving aside, for the moment, the transitional stage represented by *Od.* 24.

[36] See Eur. *Alc.* 357–62; cf. Rohde 1925: 237; and of course, with the gates playing the same role. On the gates cf. Theogn. 709–10.

[37] Pi. *Ol.* 9. 33–5, which speaks of Hades' wand by means of which *brotea somath'* . . . *katagei koilan pros agyian*, is surely an image based on the established representations (such as Hermes' wand; Farnell (1932: *ad* Pi. *Ol.* 9. 32) also takes this wand of Hades to have been a Pindaric creation based on the wand of Hermes) through which Pindar represented Hades'

between the Homeric and the fifth-century eschatological nexus is that in the latter (but not in the former) the dead can enter Hades even before they are buried: though presumably they would only be considered to be properly and honourably integrated into the community of the dead after they had undergone the final stage of the appropriate *rite de passage*, that is, been buried. The following arguments, in my view, show that in the fifth century the dead were thought to be able to enter Hades even before burial. To begin with, there are pre- and post-fifth-century instances in which it is stated explicitly or virtually explicitly that the shades can enter Hades unburied. This, we saw, is the case with *Odyssey* 24. After the fifth century, the views expressed by Teles[38] make clear that, at that time, there was no collective belief that lack of burial affected the fate of the soul and its ability to reach Hades. These earlier and later formulations create a *prima facie* case for thinking that in the fifth century the Homeric 'rule' that one could not enter Hades until after burial did not pertain. This hypothesis is confirmed by the consideration of fifth-century evidence.

First, in all the tragedies where burial is an issue, the argument that the unburied person's shade would not be able to enter Hades is never mentioned, though it would have been a matter of serious concern.[39] Second, in my view, Polydoros' words in Euripides, *Hecuba* 49–50,[40] entail that he has already entered Hades; for he has negotiated with the nether gods and been allowed to appear to the living with the authority of those gods in order to obtain burial and thus remedy his 'bad death'.[41] Polydoros thus differs from Patroklos in *Iliad* 23. 71–6 who is in a genuinely betwixt and between stage.

ultimate control and authority over human beings from the moment of their death (control and authority also expressed—from a different viewpoint and with a different reference—in S. *Ant.* 1070–3).

[38] Teles pp. 29–31 Hense.

[39] I have discussed Sophocles' *Antigone* elsewhere (cf. esp. Sourvinou-Inwood 1989*a*; 1990). That the ability of Polyneikes' soul to enter Hades is not affected by the fate of his body has been noted by T. von Wilamowitz-Moellendorf 1917: 26–38, esp. 37 and others (cf. Hester 1971: 21–2; Kitto 1961: 126; 1956: 147–50). The notion that this absence cannot be taken as evidence of collective attitudes, a notion based on the assumption that beliefs can be 'suppressed' by authors for literary purposes, belongs to an age when the ways audiences created meanings, and the role of assumptions shared by the author and his contemporary audience in the creation of meaning, were not properly understood, and should have no place in contemporary discourse.

[40] 'I begged the sovereigns of the dead' etc.

[41] On the notion of bad death and its relationship to lack of burial see Sourvinou-Inwood 1981: 31–2; 1983: 43.

Third, the imagery of death in certain tragic passages such as Aeschylus, *Septem* 854–60,[42] and Euripides, *Alcestis* 252–7, suggests that these reflect, and are shaped by, perceptions of the transition between life and Hades in which the shade can enter Hades at death and not only after burial. A further argument involves some uncertainty. The myth of Sisyphos shows that the shade could enter Hades without the corpse being buried, at least in the version in which Sisyphos instructed his wife not to bury him;[43] in another version, in Pherekydes,[44] he instructed her not to send the *nenomismena* to Hades. We cannot be certain of the date of the different versions, though as I have argued elsewhere,[45] there are good reasons for thinking that Pherekydes' version is the earliest, and that the variant in which Sisyphos enters Hades although he is not buried was created in the archaic period.[46]

Thus we have two major differences between the Homeric and the fifth-century representations concerning the fate of the shade from the moment of death until its integration in Hades: in the latter Charon and Hermes act as psychopompoi and the shade can enter Hades before its corpse is buried. The representations reflected in *Odyssey* 24, which we saw to be chronologically intermediate between the fifth-century nexus described here and Homer, are also intermediate between those two nexuses with regard to content. Formally, *Odyssey* 24 appears to reflect a less elaborate, less developed, variant of the fifth-century representations; a variant in which there is no Charon but in which one divine psychopompos, Hermes, leads the souls of the Suitors to Hades; and in which the shades enter Hades before they were buried. In the fifth-century myth Hermes has been joined by a superhuman being who has a

[42] On which Hutchinson 1985: ad loc. (pp. 187–90).

[43] Cf. Schol. Pi. *Ol.* i. 97 Boeck; cf. n. 10 above.

[44] Pherekydes *FGrH* 3 F 119.

[45] Sourvinou-Inwood 1986b: 47–51.

[46] The incident in Ar. *Ran.* 170–2, in which Dionysos wants to hire a dead man who is carried (*ekpheromenos*) on the stage to carry some stuff for him to Hades, in which the concept 'dead man' slides ambiguously between corpse and shade, does not entail the belief that the shade went to Hades only at burial; it is a joke determined on the one hand by the parameters of established belief and on the other by the natural images thrown up as a result of the interaction of the concepts Hades—luggage-carrier—dead man—and so, given the theatrical need for materiality—corpse; the incident would not have been funny if Dionysos had been negotiating with the dead man's shade rather than his corpse; the corpse has to be carried on to the stage, so the natural image is the *ekphora*; and the joke depends on his being about to go to Hades. This is not in conflict with the beliefs set out here, which simply entail the possibility of going to Hades without being buried.

similar function to his, and who effects the final transition over the
infernal frontier proper. Charon is a wholly marginal person; he
has no other existence or history outside his role of infernal ferryman, and he never leaves that frontier.[47] He is not in the archaic
or classical period called a god, at least not explicitly; he is probably
thought of as a divine/demonic being. Because he was located in
Hades, he may have been modelled[48] on, imagined in terms of,
other supernatural beings who are somehow inferior and confined
to the nether regions: the 'older gods', divine beings who live in
Tartaros, such as the Titans, but also and especially the Hekatoncheires, who were sons of Gaia and Ouranos and fought on
the side of Zeus and the Olympians against the Titans.[49] West[50] does
not accept that they act as prison-guards,[51] but says that they live
there because that is where their home is, and there was no place
for them on Olympos. However, myths are complex and polysemic,
and the fact that this was their home does not exclude that the
Hekatoncheires may have been perceived to be acting as guards:
this would have appeared to be giving a good reason for the
confinement of these allies of Zeus' in the nether world. In any
case, they could be seen as offering a model for Charon—a very
close one if they were indeed guards.[52]

Hermes' chronological priority as psychopompos over Charon,
suggested by the pattern of their appearance in the surviving
sources,[53] is supported by the consideration that, as we have seen,
the raw material for the creation of Hermes' psychopompic role
was part of the god's established persona, ready for interaction with
the mythological imagination elaborating the journey between life
and Hades, in circumstances, and in response to needs, that will

---

[47] The scenes on white-ground lekythoi in which Charon is approaching a grave monument in his boat (cf. e.g. Athens NM 1758 (CC 1660) (*ARV* 1241.1; Sourvinou-Inwood
1986: no. 28)) do not represent the ferryman coming up in the cemetery to collect the
shade. For the idiom in these scenes is not descriptive narrative, but emblematic. The
iconographical schema involves the conflation of two common schemata 'Charon in his
boat' and 'visit to the tomb' which we shall discuss in § ii.2.
[48] When he was created in circumstances that will be considered below in § iii.
[49] Cf. Hes. *Th.* 734–5.
[50] M. L. West 1966: 363 *ad Th.* 734–5.
[51] As was understood by Tz. *Th.* 277.
[52] This is probably the reason behind, and the meaning of, Charon's epithet Akmonides
(Hesych. s.v. Akmonides), if Akmon refers to Ouranos or a Ouranos-like figure (e.g.
Ouranos' father). But, we saw, the ascription of the designation Akmonides to Charon is
not absolutely certain (see *RE* i. 1. 1173–4 s.v. Akmon 1).
[53] Cf. also § iv below.

be discussed below. This interaction led to the creation of his psychopompic function out of his role as mediator and crosser of frontiers par excellence. Charon's creation involved a more complex interaction, which included models borrowed from abroad, in order to fill 'spaces' created by local needs. Hermes who crosses borders is the appropriate deity for guiding the souls through the infernal frontier. But when the journey was elaborated Charon took over the actual crossing of that frontier, while Hermes led the shades up to it: given the opportunity of further articulation, even the god of the margins avoids the regular crossing of the infernal frontier. The addition of Charon gave a more mundane and trivial colouring to the journey of death: now one crossed the river in a ferry poled by an old ferryman to whom one paid the fare. How, then, did Charon the ferryman of the dead emerge? The river separating Hades from the marginal no-man's land bordering on the upper world was deeply rooted in Greek belief; in the context of the elaboration of the journey to Hades the 'space' 'divine guide of the dead' had been created and filled by Hermes. Given Charon's similarity to the Sumerian ferryman of the river of death,[54] his emergence can be seen as the result of the interaction between local elements and needs (to which I shall return) and an Oriental model that helped elaborate further the journey to Hades.

To sum up. In the earliest attested representations of the journey to Hades there are no psychopompoi, and the shades only enter Hades after burial; at the other end of our spectrum, the fifth century, there are two psychopompoi and the shades can enter Hades even before they are buried. In the representations which are chronologically intermediate there is one psychopompos, and the shades enter Hades before they are buried. In these circumstances, and given that the relationship between *Odyssey* 24 and the fifth-century representations confirms the tendency towards greater elaboration, the presumption must be strongly in favour of the view that this chronological pattern of appearance of the psychopompoi corresponds to the true development of the Greek collective representations. This view is further supported by other arguments, as I shall try to show. The implications of this thesis is that some time before the composition of the Continuation, which

---

[54] Cf. Kirk (1970: 100), who suggested (cf. also p. 224) that the Sumerian ferryman is Charon's 'prototype'.

may have taken place in the first half of the sixth century, the journey to Hades had begun to be elaborated, and Hermes had become a psychopompos; at a subsequent stage, and before 500 BC at the latest, Charon took over the function of taking the shades over the infernal water-frontier into Hades proper. This elaboration may have taken place in the context of epic poetry, perhaps in the (relatively) popular archaic *katabasis* literature, which, like the elaboration of the shade's journey to Hades, involves the articulation of the unseeable and frightening realm in concrete terms.[55] But I would not exclude that Hermes Chthonios, and perhaps Charon, may have emerged in connection with a particular sanctuary and cult, such as, for example, that associated with the Nekyomanteion. The hypothesis involving the Nekyomanteion might explain why Acheron and Acherousia became the dominant stretch of water over which Charon ferried the dead.

I shall now set out a further series of arguments in support of the view that the chronological pattern of the appearance of Charon and Hermes Chthonios reflects the true historical development of these mythological representations. First, the pattern of emergence proposed here provides a context within which the two other major eschatological changes can be satisfactorily made sense of: that burial is not a necessary precondition for entering Hades; and that once in Hades, the shades are, under certain circumstances, able to leave it and temporarily return to the upper world. For both can be seen to be correlative with the emergence of the two psychopompoi. In the Homeric system proper access to Hades and the ordered communication between the two worlds depended only on these rules; the shade's transition to Hades was effected through the death-ritual of which burial was the culminating point integrating the deceased to the community of the dead. But in a system in which divine psychopompoi effect the transition and control access to Hades and the communication with the upper world the importance of the rules and behaviour patterns which had previously fulfilled that function is diminished, and eventually, because no longer 'necessary', the burial rule lapses. The correlation between these two changes is shown by the fact that Charon is supposed to ensure that no unauthorized person entered Hades—

---

[55] On *katabaseis* cf. n. 34 above. On the role of archaic *katabaseis* in the articulation and elaboration of the journey to Hades see also Rohde 1925: 236–7.

as the myth of his transgression and punishment shows. The same is true of communication in the other direction, hence the rule that once properly in Hades the shades cannot leave it also lapses. The existence of divine supervising beings safeguards and guarantees the correct preservation of the frontiers, and the strict rules which had been previously necessary became redundant and eventually lapsed. That the two sets of beliefs are correlative is further confirmed by the fact that the shades' return to the upper world takes place under the supervision of Hermes. Also, Charon is specifically mentioned as someone who, with Cerberus, prevents the shades' unauthorized exit from Hades.[56] The fate of the river is comparable. For as long as the river formed an important border separating Hades from the no-man's land communicating with the upper world it remained a river, since a river is a most appropriate and effective border, which can stop (with the help of the shades on the 'landing' side as in *Iliad* 23. 71–3) improper entry into the world of the dead and vice versa. But by the fifth century the function of this water as keeping the two worlds apart had to some extent lapsed. Since the borders between the different worlds are presided over by divine beings who guarantee the safe separation between worlds and controlled access from one to the other, the spatial border of the river became to some extent redundant in all but its symbolic significance. What *is not* redundant is the crossing of the water as a potent image of the final transition to the Land of the Dead. What *is* redundant is the notion that the water should form an actual real border which necessitates that it should be continuous. The infernal ferryman's role cannot be satisfactorily accounted for at the level of everyday 'utilitarian' logic, that he simply provides a travelling service. First, because the souls were conceived as winged. In fact, one of the earliest representations of Charon[57] shows some winged souls sitting or standing in Charon's boat and others flying around it; the other early representation is fragmentary: only Charon and one winged soul standing in the boat remain.[58] Thus, at the level of everyday logic, the shades should have been able to fly over the water and into Hades, even if not all were able to swim. And when the water is conceived as a lake, the souls could have walked

[56] Eur. *Alc.* 358–62; see also Rohde 1925: 237.
[57] Cf. the eschara cited in n. 5 above.
[58] Cf. the fragment of a phormiskos cited in n. 5 above.

around it, as Xanthias did in Aristophanes' *Ranae.*[59] This last example illustrates the point that crossing in Charon's boat was not perceived to be physically necessary so much as symbolically desirable.[60] Aristophanes in *Ranae* represents Charon on the model of a very mundane ferryman.[61] This joke has the serious effect of demystifying the infernal ferryman, and thus also the whole process of death. One aspect of this trivialization which is probably older than Aristophanes is manifest in the notion of the obols, Charon's fee; Aristophanes' joke[62] is that it was Theseus who introduced them, a play on Theseus' persona as the Athenian civilizing hero par excellence, who introduced into Hades an unpleasant aspect of human culture. Trivialization is clearly semantically contrasted to the awesomeness of the representation, the journey to Hades, and thus, to some extent, neutralizes that awesomeness. Trivializing and making jokes about the infernal world renders thinkable, and copable in the constructed world of the joke, what is in fact awesomely frightening, and so this frightening unthinkable becomes easier to come to terms with.[63] Thus Charon, the old ferryman whom one had to pay in order to be taken into Hades, is part of a mythological elaboration that makes the journey to Hades less frightening by articulating it explicitly and trivializing it. The elaborated version of the journey to Hades is itself a reassuring representation. For the absence of details concerning the transition from life to death enhances the anxiety generated by the prospect of one's own death: what is mysterious is more frightening than that which is explicitly articulated. The articulation of that awesome transition by means

---

[59] Ar. *Ran.* 190–3; cf. also 271–5.

[60] I do not believe that this notion, that one could, or in certain circumstances had to, go round the lake, necessarily reflects a belief; it is a joke based on the showing up of the illogicality, the 'absurdity' (when examined from a rationalist viewpoint), of the representation 'crossing into Hades on Charon's boat'; through the manipulation of that representation other jokes are forged. But whether Xanthias' circumvention of the lake reflected an established belief or was (as I believe) a manipulation of belief to create a joke, it shows that crossing the water in Charon's boat was not felt to be the only conceivable means of access to Hades, just the best.

[61] A similar treatment, in a much more elaborate and detailed form, building on an already existing tradition, is also found much later in Lucian (cf. e.g. *DMort.* 4, 10, 22; *Cat.* 19, 21, and *passim*; cf. also Sourvinou-Inwood 1986a: 211).

[62] *Ran.* 141–2. On Charon's fee cf. now Stevens 1991: 215–29.

[63] On the notion of laughing at the frightening in ancient Greece cf. also Moret 1984: 148 and n. 4. The same result is achieved by the jokes about nuclear disasters and their aftermath (cf. e.g. the British television series 'Who dares wins').

of familiar, concrete, and so reassuring, activities, removes some of the anxiety and terror attached to the moment of death. The fact that the shades no longer have to face the journey to Hades alone as they do in Homer, but are guided by Hermes and Charon, is an especially reassuring element. That Hermes Chthonios and Charon are reassuring images in so far as they guide, and thus can be seen as providing some support to, the shades may appear obvious. But such a judgement is in danger of being culturally determined, therefore I will now present a systematic and detailed argument in support of this view. I will concentrate on Charon.[64]

First, that the two psychopompoi were benevolent protective and reassuring is suggested by the fact that Hermes had that benevolent and protective, and thus reassuring, role in the stories of Herakles and Persephone, which were the mythological prototypes of his role as psychopompos. Second, the benevolent protective and reassuring role of both psychopompoi is clear in two passages of Euripides' *Alcestis*; in verses 436–44 the chorus is offering a 'recommendation' to Hades and Charon on behalf of Alcestis.[65] Inherent in this recommendation of Alcestis' virtues is the request for the protection and benevolence of these divine beings. In verses 741–4 there is a semantic equivalent of this recommendation, involving Hades and Hermes Chthonios; this takes the form of a wish, which is at the same time an (oblique) request, for Hades' and Hermes Chthonios' benevolence towards Alcestis.[66] In both cases Hades, in whose supreme jurisdiction the dead belong, and one psychopompos are invoked. In the *Anthologia Palatina* we find[67] propitiatiory invocations of Charon (Charon ferryman receive me). The later date and the genre make it necessary to use caution in considering this evidence.[68] But the existence of the fifth-century

---

[64] That Hermes the guide of the shades is represented as a figure of reassurance in the white-ground lekythoi (on which cf. § ii below) is also suggested by Bérard 1984: 101. Bérard (1988: 166, citing Sourvinou-Inwood 1987) agrees that with regard to death 'les rituels, les textes et les images travaillent précisement à transmettre un savoir rassurant'.

[65] On this passage cf. also Dale 1954: ad loc.

[66] *prophron se chthonios th' Hermes Haides te dechoito,*

[67] *AP* vii. 63, 67, 68, 365; cf. 66.

[68] This evidence is admissible as a supporting argument because the epigrams invoke Charon as a ferryman, and they refer to death through the metaphor centred on Charon's boat; that is, they do not refer to him in his later character of generic death-god (Waser 1898: 23) in which he acquired some of the functions which had earlier belonged to Thanatos (cf. Alexiou 1978: 224 and some examples from the Anthology in 232 n. 37; but Alexiou oversimplifies the process and conflates 5th-cent. metaphor and considerably later belief; cf.

'recommendation' of Alcestis to Charon, and certain comparable meanings in the representations on the fifth-century white-ground lekythoi which will be considered below, make it legitimate to mention these invocations as supporting evidence. I have consistently tried to keep the two sets of analyses, of texts and of images, separate for methodological reasons;[69] I do not feel that this principle is impaired if I mention here that the validity of this use of the epigrams (which is of very marginal importance) is strengthened somewhat by the fact that it not only reflects comparable situations in earlier texts but is also very close to the representation of the relevant theme in earlier images. In *Anthologia Palatina* vii. 365, attributed to Diodorus Zonas, Charon is asked to stretch out his hand to help a boy board his boat and receive him, and is thus clearly presented as potentially a supportive figure of reassurance, whose benevolence is requested for a particular dead person. A fifth-century representation on a white-ground lekythos, Athens NM 1814 (CC 1662),[70] is an approximate iconographical equivalent of this epigram: Charon is standing in his boat leaning on the pole, and stretching his right hand out to a naked child who is sitting on a high rock on the shore. The child turns towards Charon and stretches out his hand towards him. Behind the child is a woman holding a bird and on the ground a chest. As we shall see below, the iconographical analysis of this and the other Charonian images shows that in the white-ground lekythoi Charon was represented as a benevolent reassuring figure. Thus the resemblance between fifth-century image and later epigram cannot be dismissed as accidental or its recognition culturally determined.[71] Indeed, passing to my final argument, the fact that the independently conducted iconographical analyses of the fifth-century representations of Charon, which are set out below, lead to the conclusion that these images depict Charon as a benevolent and reassuring figure provides a separate strong argument in favour of the view that Charon and Hermes were protective figures of reassurance.

In Homer the metaphor 'to enter/fly to Hades' for 'to die' is

also § iv below) in which case their representations would not necessarily have been relevant to the 5th-cent. ferryman.

[69] Cf. also Sourvinou-Inwood 1991: 7.

[70] Riezler 1914: 135 pl. 79; Fairbanks 1914: 85 no. 8.

[71] In a very different cultural context, on a 4th-cent. Campanian tomb, a winged Charon also stretches out his hand to assist a woman into his boat (*ArchRep*) 1969/70, 34.

common; it is articulated through several formulas,[72] which shows that this metaphorical way of speaking of death was deeply rooted in the epics. As with all metaphors, the two ways of expressing the concept do not convey identical meanings. This metaphor was at the same time a statement about what death was perceived to be, since it did not refer to the knowable cessation of life, but expressed the belief/hope that part of the dead person survives and travels to an unknowable realm.[73] In the archaic age, when the transition to Hades was elaborated and transformed through the introduction of the two psychopompoi in whom became invested the forces that ensured the transition, Charon, who effected the passage into the land of the dead, became the favourite focus of the metaphor in which the transition to Hades stands for death. In Euripides' *Alcestis* vv. 252–7, the vision of Alcestis' imminent death is articulated through her vision of Charon waiting for her in his boat; through this vision she contemplates her imminent death, sees herself in her own death. Because the metaphor 'crossing in Charon's ferry' was a way of saying 'to die', the version 'Charon is waiting' came to express the notion 'imminent death', became an image of death. This theme 'Charon is waiting' for 'imminent death', in various versions, is not uncommon in literature.[74] Other themes also use Charon and his boat as an image of death.[75] In Pindar fragment 143 Snell–Maehler the image 'escaping Acheron's ferry' expresses immortality; Theocritus 17. 46–50 uses a similar image to express apotheosis. From the notion of Charon waiting, and not allowing you to linger,[76] a further development is generated, first attested in Antiphanes, *Diplasioi*,[77] where Charon is the agent of death, a metaphor for the 'force' that causes death. This type of metaphor, that is, generated its own force so that, through it, Charon came to be perceived as having the characteristics of the agent of death, a role which initially he had only been ascribed metaphorically. This ascription of the role of agent of death to Charon eventually escaped the context of the particular metaphors in which it had emerged

---

[72] Cf. e.g. the selection cited in *JHS* 92 (1972) 221.

[73] There are obvious euphemistic equivalents for 'dying' in our own society.

[74] Cf. Eur. *Herc.* 430–4; Timotheos, *Niobe* fr. 10 (Page *PMG* fr. 786; cf. Machon, *Vita* Edmonds = Athenaeus 8. 314c); cf. also Ar. *Lys.* 605–7 and *Plut.* 277–8.

[75] Cf. e.g. that in Theocr. 16. 40–1.

[76] Cf. Timotheos, *Niobe* fr. 10 (Page *PMG* fr. 786; cf. Machon, *Vita* Edmonds = Athenaeus 8. 314c).

[77] *CAF* II fr. 86.

and became general, so that, finally, Charon himself is identified with death and/or Thanatos.[78] It is a case of a metaphor being taken literally and generating a new reality.[79]

The image in which Charon stood for death involves a metaphor based on metonymy:[80] a part of the (imagined) process of death, the crossing of the water into Hades in Charon's boat, stands for the whole process, death; and Charon, who effects that passage, eventually comes to stand for the force and event which removes people from life and sends them to Hades. The metaphorical relationship between Charon and this force and event articulates, and is articulated by, a perception of death as a transition to another space and to another state. It was part of the representations of death as a journey, of dying as embarking on, and effecting, the journey to Hades. This nexus of imagery, in which metaphor and metonymy are closely intertwined and interacting, acquired great symbolic weight, so that the event of death, especially one's own death, came to be seen primarily in terms of that journey.[81] This metonymically derived metaphor focused on Charon reflects the concept of the personal experience of death as a journey to Hades; it lays the stress on death as experienced by the individual, the death of the self. Thus, every time it is articulated in an image or text, it contains the possibility of being perceived by the viewer/reader as the prefiguration of everyone's death, including their own. This metaphor also allows a symbolic manipulation which helps people cope with the experience of death. For it creates a different reality, in which death can be invoked and propitiated in the person of Charon. This is what happens when the chorus 'recommends' Alcestis to Charon, Hermes, and Hades in Euripides, *Alcestis* vv. 436–44; 741–4. Thus the notion 'propitiating death', wishing for, and requesting an easy death—which is itself a mode of channelling the fear of death itself—can be condensed symbolically in the notion of propitiating Charon. As for the relationship between Charon and Thanatos and its development, it is clear that in the fifth century Charon had not yet acquired any of Thanatos' characteristics,

[78] Cf. Suda s.v. *Charon. ho thanatos.*

[79] Cf. on this process Moretti 1982: 83.

[80] On metonymically derived metaphors, and the relationship between metonymy and metaphor cf. Genette 1972: 42–3, 50, 55–8; De Man 1979a; 14, 15, 18, 60–72; Culler 1983: 188–209, esp. 189–202; cf. also Eco 1981: 67–89; 1976: 279–83.

[81] Cf. e.g. Anacreon fr. 395 Page *PMG*; and cf. the white-ground lekythoi which will be discussed in § ii.

as he did later; on the contrary, the distinction between Charon and Thanatos is unequivocal in Euripides' *Alcestis* and in iconography.[82]

In these circumstances, we may conclude that the representations of death which included Charon and Hermes Chthonios differ from those in which these figures do not appear in significant ways. First, the former offer a more reassuring version of the journey to Hades. Second, because the crossing of the border between the upper world and Hades now takes place under the guidance and supervision of divine beings who thus become its guardians and guarantors, this border becomes symbolically upgraded, and the separation between the world of the living and that of the dead becomes sharper and firmer and more secure. At the same time, and because of this, it is possible for the shades to leave Hades temporarily and visit the upper world. The circumstances in which these developments took place shall be considered below in § iii. First I shall consider another series of articulations of the journey to Hades and Charon's role, in images representing Charon on a series of fifth-century Athenian vases used for funerary purposes and decorated with funerary scenes, the white-ground lekythoi.

ii. *Images of Charon on White-Ground Lekythoi: Reassurance and 'Propitiation'*[83]

1. SCENES WITH CHARON: A TYPOLOGY

The representations of Charon on white-ground lekythoi[84] begin late in the second quarter of the fifth century and stop at the end

---

[82] See below *passim* and § iv. Alexiou (1978: 224) has misunderstood the meaning and function within the play of Alcestis' vision of Charon in vv. 252–7 and of the metaphorical reference to Thanatos (see above n. 20 on *pterotos Haidas*) in vv. 261–4. The two are not the same; the movement from the vision of Charon to the proximity of the violent and frightening Thanatos expresses the progressive approach of the awful moment of death. It is a movement from the relatively reassuring vision of the final passage into Hades, through which death is presented in terms of a benign image, to the violent and anxious image of being seized by Thanatos, prefiguring in reverse order the real events of her death: her death, envisaged as a grabbing by Thanatos, followed by her passage into Hades, here articulated though the recommendation of the chorus to Hades and Charon.

[83] A short version of some parts of this chapter was delivered as a paper to the Colloque Eidos 86 at Tours and subsequently published in French in *AION Arch. st. ant.* 9 (1987), 145–58 (= Sourvinou-Inwood 1987).

[84] Cf. Pls. 9 and 11. On white-ground lekythoi: Pottier 1883; Fairbanks 1907; 1914

of the century. Here I shall try to reconstruct the meanings which these images had in the eyes of the fifth-century Athenians,[85] and thus also the perceptions pertaining to Charon that articulated, and were articulated, in them.

Images of Charon on white-ground lekythoi appear in different variants. The most common (variant A), itself found in different versions, depicts Charon in his boat, facing, and about to receive, a shade who is standing on the shore alone or accompanied by Hermes and sometimes by another human being, either in addition to Hermes or in his stead.[86] The second variant (variant B), the first appearance of which occurs slightly later, involves a conflation between the first variant and another funerary theme, represented on its own on other white-ground lekythoi.[87] Most of the shades shown with Charon are women, with a few adolescent youths and a few rare children.[88] Fully adult males are never shown with Charon on these images.[89] Images of Charon not conflated with other themes can be divided into different types.[90] In type 1, one or more shades are shown with Charon. This type is divided into three subtypes: (*a*) one shade is facing Charon alone; (*b*) one shade and a companion figure are facing Charon; (*c*) a woman is seated in Charon's boat and on the shore there is another woman and a

(cf. esp. 216–41); Riezler 1914; Kurtz 1975; Beazley 1938; M. Robertson 1959: 140–53; 1975: 324–6; Kurtz and Boardman 1971: 102–4; Kurtz 1985: 321–8; Clairmont 1983: 74 ff. On the iconography of Charon cf. also Sourvinou-Inwood 1986*a*; Felten 1975: 86–90; Fairbanks 1914: 218–23; Kurtz 1975: 63; 1985: 325; Hoffman 1984: 65–9; 1986: 173–204.

[85] I have discussed the methodology which is, in my view, appropriate for this purpose in Sourvinou-Inwood 1991: 3–15.

[86] Cf. e.g.: Charon and one shade: lekythos Athens NM 1946 (CC 1666) *ARV* 1168. 129; Sourvinou-Inwood 1986*a*: no. 14. Charon, Hermes and shade: cf. e.g. lekythos Athens NM 1926 (CC 1668) *ARV* 846. 193; *Para.* 423; *Add.* 145; Sourvinou-Inwood 1986*a*: no. 5; Pl. 9. Charon, shade, and companion: cf. e.g. white-ground lekythos Brussels Mus.Roy. A 903 (*ARV* 1237.14; *CVA* 1 pl. 4.1; Sourvinou-Inwood 1986*a*: no. 25).

[87] Cf. e.g. lekythoi Athens NM 1758 (CC 1660) (*ARV* 1241.1; Sourvinou-Inwood 1986*a*: no. 28); Hamburg Mus. KG 1917.817 (*ARV* 1381.111; *Add.* 186; Sourvinou-Inwood 1986*a*: no. 40).

[88] Adolescents: cf. e.g. the lekythos Oxford, AM 1889.827 (V 264) (Sourvinou-Inwood 1986*a*: no. 19); children cf. e.g. Athens NM 1814 (CC 1662): (Sourvinou-Inwood 1986*a*: no. 23).

[89] Cf. also Kurtz 1985: 325.

[90] On the typology of the Charon scenes and references to images belonging to the different types and subtypes cf. Sourvinou-Inwood 1986*a*: 219–20. From this point on, to avoid overloading the footnotes I shall be referring to the lekythoi through their numbers in the LIMC Catalogue (= Sourvinou-Inwood 1986*a*).

youth. In type 2, one or more shades are facing Charon in the company of Hermes. This variant also occurs in three subtypes: (*a*) one shade accompanied by Hermes is facing Charon; (*b*) one shade and a companion figure, accompanied by Hermes, are facing Charon; (*c*) a woman is seated in Charon's boat, and on the shore a second woman is standing behind Hermes. Thus the subtypes in the type which includes Hermes are the same as those in the type without him. Scenes of type 2 with Hermes are far less frequent than those of type 1. Most representations of type 1 depict one shade alone. This subtype 1*a* is the commonest version of all the 'Charon and shades' scenes. Most of the shades shown alone are women, the other few are youths. In type 1*b* the companions are a maid, and a woman accompanying a child. Among type 2 scenes also, type 2*a* (representations with one shade alone) is the most frequent. In 2*b* the second figure is a small servant accompanying a woman or a woman accompanying a boy of about 14. Thus the details pertaining to the subtypes of the two versions are also closely related.

Variant B involves the conflation of a Charonian scene with another funerary theme, which on other lekythoi is represented on its own. Type 1 is a conflation between variant A and the theme 'visit to the tomb'.[91] In scenes of this type Charon in his boat is shown on one side and next to him a grave stele, that is a grave monument, with one or two figures sitting on and/or standing by it. This type contains two subtypes: (*a*) represents Charon in his boat, a grave stele and two figures. On some[92] a youth is standing in front of, or sitting on, the grave, and a girl or woman is bringing offerings to the grave (fillets, or fillets and a cup); on others a woman is sitting on the steps of the grave, and a man or a woman[93] are standing on the other side of the grave; or[94] a woman with offerings is standing in front of the stele, and a youth is standing on its other side. Subtype (*b*) represents Charon in his boat, a grave stele and one figure: Charon is shown on one side of the stele, and either a woman with offerings[95] or a young man with spears[96]

[91] Cf. e.g. Sourvinou-Inwood 1986*a*: nos. 28, 40.
[92] Ibid. nos. 27–9.
[93] Cf. Ibid. nos. 40, 43.
[94] Ibid. no. 42.
[95] Ibid. nos. 30, 41.
[96] Ibid. no. 39.

is standing on the other side. Type 2 of variant B involves a conflation between variant A and the theme 'Hypnos and Thanatos carrying a dead body'. Only one specimen of this type survives,[97] and in it the body which Hypnos and Thanatos are carrying is a woman's and Hermes is present. For reasons that will become apparent I will discuss the two themes which are conflated with Charonian scenes before I attempt to recover the meanings which the Charonian images had in the eyes of their contemporaries.

2. 'Visit to the Tomb': The Death of the Other

The theme 'visit to the tomb' (Pl. 10)[98] occurs in many variants; it depicts the visit to the tomb by the deceased's relatives and the presentation of offerings at the grave. The deceased is sometimes represented at the tomb.[99] This theme then, is centred on the actions

---

[97] Ibid. no. 31.

[98] White-ground lekythos Athens NM 1958 (CC 1690) (*ARV* 748.2; *Add.* 284). On the theme 'visit to the tomb' cf. Kurtz 1975: 36–7, 61–3, 64, 66–7, 202; 1984: 327–8; Baldasarre 1988: 107–15; Kurtz and Boardman 1971: 104–5; M. Robertson 1975: 325; Siebert 1981: 68–9; Bazant 1986: 37–44 (and Siebert's remarks, pp 43–4); Shapiro 1991: 651–3.

[99] Whether or not one of the figures shown in visit to the tomb scenes represents the dead person is a well-known problem (cf. Kurtz and Boardman 1971: 104–5; M. Robertson 1975: 325; Siebert 1981: 68–9; Bazant 1986 (and Siebert's remarks in Bazant 1986); Baldasarre 1988: 115. I believe that in the representations in which a visit to the tomb is conflated with a Charon scene at least, and at least in in subtype (*a*), the deceased is represented. The iconographical idiom of the scene is synoptical, and the motif of Charon stretching out his hand towards one of the figures in the grave scene, a motif found also in the Charon scenes of variant A, is a compositional device for connecting the two constituent elements. Though the outstretched hand is also found in the abbreviated variants where the deceased is apparently omitted (Sourvinou-Inwood 1986*a*: nos. 30, 41), the initial selection of this element as a connecting device presupposes the representation of the deceased as a pivot between the two themes, and suggests that the figure sitting on, or standing in front, of the grave, represented the deceased (except in Sourvinou-Inwood 1986*a*: no. 42 where the positions of dead and living seems reversed). This question is of no particular importance for our argument. With reference to the general problem of the representation of the deceased on the lekythoi, I will only add the observation that in some cases the coincidence between the persona of the deceased as denoted by the objects associated with the stele and one of the figures, the one who is a candidate to be the figure of the dead on other grounds, leaves little room to doubt that the deceased is indeed represented by his stele. (Cf. e.g. the lekythos Boston, Museum of Fine Arts O1.8080; Kurtz 1975: pl. 31.1 and p. 210; *ARV* 1231; *Add.* 352) in which a youth is shown simply standing by the tomb heavily wrapped up in a cloak and gazing ahead (in contrast to the man shown in a very unusual, undoubtedly ritual pose (cf. Kurtz 1975: 210) on the other side of the stele), which would suggest that he is the deceased in this representation, and this coincides with the fact that a series of other elements also shows that the deceased of the representation was an ephebe: on the grave monument two statues of a youth are shown as acroteria, one with a strigil and a spear/javelin, the statue

of the dead person's relatives, their grief, and their ritual practices. It thus articulates the importance of that death for the deceased's family and so 'evaluates' and valorizes the deceased, marks his/her place in life. Since in fifth-century Athens bringing offerings to the tomb was the duty of the immediate family,[100] the theme 'visit to the tomb' emphasizes the relationship between the dead and their family, and slants the articulation of the death primarily in terms of the death of the other (the near and dear). It represents the death as, above all, a family affair, involving certain duties and practices as well as emotional responses. The offering of these images of familial piety was also a prefiguration of the offering family's future fulfilment of the proper practices of visit and offerings due to the dead. The 'visit to the tomb' was by far the most frequent funerary subject on the white-ground lekythoi,[101] which is not surprising, since it was the family who purchased these funerary lekythoi.

of an athlete and the other with a spear, perhaps characterizing the youth whose grave monument they adorned in the representation as an ephebe (for the association between ephebes and the spear: cf. Sourvinou-Inwood 1991: 63, 89 n. 25) as well as an athlete. The characterization of the deceased as an athlete is (cf. Kurtz 1975: 210) also indicated through the athletic scene on the painted grave monument's pediment, and also through the diskos which is represented in the field on the same side as the athlete's statue; on the other side, next to what I would be inclined to consider as the ephebe's statue, there is a lyre in the field, which alludes to the ephebe's musical education and thus is, I think, part of the characterization of the deceased as an ephebe. Such a rich articulation of the deceased's social persona is unusual, and it is for this reason that so often there is not enough evidence to allow us to read the image in this way. But the fact that there are at least some cases in which the deceased is shown as 'ideally' present in 'visit to the tomb' scenes suggests that they may have been present also in other scenes where this is less clear to our own culturally determined eye. This representation of the deceased in 'visit to the tomb' scenes as he/she had been in life was, of course ambivalent, ambiguous, and polysemic. It represented the deceased whose tomb is being visited and for whom the offerings and practices take place, that is, denoting (through a generic type such as 'athlete') that it is this particular deceased who is being honoured; it helped articulate the notion that the dead person was present in the memory of his family, who visualized him as he had been in life, and thus also stressed the relationship between the dead and the living; it articulated the belief that the deceased was aware of the fact that his tomb was visited and offerings presented; finally, it may conceivably also have been expressing the belief/hope that, at least on some occasions, the shade was invisibly present. Sometimes a small-scale winged shade is represented hovering in the air (cf. e.g. lekythos Berlin 2459 (*ARV* 1374); lekythos Athens 1762 (CC 1680; *ARV* 1241.1)). We shall find the same parallel representation of full-scale shade and small winged *eidola* in some Charon scenes, and I will discuss this question there.

[100] On the practices and duty cf. e.g. Garland 1985: 104–20; Humphreys 1983: 83–8; cf. also Baldasarre 1988: 111.

[101] Kurtz and Boardman 1971: 104; Kurtz 1985: 327.

3. 'GOOD DEATH': HYPNOS AND THANATOS

The theme of Hypnos and Thanatos carrying a dead body, usually of a warrior,[102] is modelled on the story and representations of Sarpedon.[103] In Homer Hypnos and Thanatos transported Sarpedon's corpse home to Lycia from Troy, after his heroic 'good death', as an expression of exceptional honour and a sign of exceptional divine favour.[104] The lekythoi scenes are iconographically modelled on, and call up, this Homeric episode and its representations; thus they evoke the concept of the heroic 'good death' centred on 'good burial'. Proper burial was a preoccupation of paramount importance for the Greeks, and formed an important part of their concept of good death. The symbolic importance of burial was strongly reinforced in fifth-century Athens in the context of the ideology which glorified death in battle, and made the public burial of the war dead, brought home from the battlefield, into an important focus of polis ideology. It is in the context of this ideology that we find the semantic field that corresponds to the representation of Hypnos and Thanatos carrying a dead body home from the battlefield, that is, to the heroic good death connected with glorious burial at home. The 'good death' articulated in these images of Hypnos and Thanatos corresponds to the 'good death' of the Athenian citizens killed in battle, transported home and buried with a public funeral. This was subsequently extended and came to express and articulate the concept 'good death' in general, as can be deduced from the fact that Hypnos and Thanatos are sometimes carrying the dead body of non-heroic people, of a woman or a child or an adolescent.[105] Consequently, we may conclude that these images, which are a version of the representation of a mythological 'good death in battle and glorious burial', originally referred to the 'good death' of the Athenian war dead buried gloriously by the polis; eventually they acquired a more generic meaning of (socially) 'good death' connected to good burial and thus they came also to

---

[102] On this theme: Kurtz and Boardman 1971: 103–4; Kurtz 1985: 325; M. Robertson 1975: 326; Brommer 1969: 164–7; Bérard 1988: 167–8. On Hypnos and Thanatos cf. also Vermeule 1979: 145–56.

[103] On this theme cf. v. Bothmer 1981: 63–80.

[104] *Il.* 16. 450–61, 667–83.

[105] Woman: Athens NM 1928 (CC 1655) (*ARV* 1237.3; *CVA* 1 pl. 11.8); child: Athens NM 17294 (*ARV* 750; *CVA* 2 pl. 20.1.) Combined with Charon, woman's body: Sourvinou-Inwood 1986a: no. 31.

be used for women and adolescents. Such a development can be easily understood in the context of fifth-century attitudes. For in the official ideology death in battle with public burial by the polis was the good death *par excellence*, which therefore would be naturally extended so as to express, through a metaphor based on metonymy, the general concept 'good death'. Thus the images in which this 'good death' is articulated, the representation of Hypnos and Thanatos carrying a dead body, came to represent all good (social) death. This suggests a significant internalization of the official ideology of good death, a phenomenon we will encounter again, in a different form, in the Charonian images.

4. IMAGES OF CHARON: THE DEATH OF THE SELF

(a) *General*

The Charonian scenes[106] are different from all other themes on white-ground lekythoi because they are centred on the shade. They represent an imaginary reality, the articulation of an ideality according to which the souls survive the death of the body and, guided by Hermes, reach the infernal water where they are received by Charon who will ferry them to Hades. Since this journey also functioned as a metaphor for death in general, these images represented also death as a whole, and not only one episode in the journey to Hades. That is, they represented death in terms of the shade's reception by Charon and the passage into Hades. The visit to the tomb[107] is situated in the world of the living and represents death in terms of the death of the other.[108] Other lekythoi represent scenes from life set in a funerary context represented by the stele, or with funerary connotations;[109] they are thus also centred on the

---

[106] I will only consider variant A here; for variant B cf. below.

[107] And the rare scenes of prothesis: on this theme cf. Kurtz 1985: 324; Shapiro 1991: 648–50.

[108] The emblematic representation of the deceased in some scenes, esp. the winged *eidola* that sometimes hover in the air, introduce an element of the other world, and may have alluded (in Athenian eyes) to the viewpoint of the shade observing the practices in its honour; but the centre of the image is the world of the living and death as death of the other. Elements move from one sphere to the other so that some scenes involve conflations between the two spheres; major conflations like Variant B (1) and (2) are at one end of the spectrum, 'pure' versions at the other; many are situated in-between. I am trying to show how each theme's 'centre' relate to those of the others.

[109] Cf. below n. 112.

world of the living, on the past life of the deceased, whose death is only hinted at and not dwelt on, on the memory of the deceased's social persona, also represented by the stele. The scenes with Hypnos and Thanatos are centred on the corpse and on burial, on socially good death associated with burial. By contrast, the scenes representing Charon with a shade are images of the deceased's own experience in the other world, of the death of the self from the viewpoint of its surviving part. Of course, in the eyes of the survivors these images of the death of the self appear as images of the death of the other: it is other people who are dead, and whose shades are shown with Charon. But this dead other is also—at a certain level of perception—a prefiguration of oneself in (eventual) death, and the images a prefiguration of the death of the self.

(b) The Shades: Iconographical Analyses

All but two of the shades received by Charon are shown as full-scale 'normal' human figures, as they were represented in life. In the two earliest known representations of Charon on white-ground lekythoi, both by the Tymbos Painter, the shade is a winged *eidolon*,[110] smaller than the *eidola* in the black-figure Charonian scenes, but rather larger than the winged *eidola* shown hovering in the air in other scenes on lekythoi,[111] well formed and wearing a long dress. The earliest representations of Charon on white-ground lekythoi, then, follow the iconographical tradition of the black-figure Charonian scenes. This iconographical option was later abandoned. The shades may be accompanied by one of two types of figure: a small servant, who accompanies a woman, and a woman who accompanies a small child or a boy. To reconstruct the meanings of these companion figures we must recover the significance of these combinations of figures in other scenes in which their meanings may be clearer, or which can help us chart the types of contexts in which they appear. The schemata under consideration are found also on other white-ground lekythoi and on contemporary and near-contemporary grave reliefs. The 'mistress and maid' schemata, often with the maid carrying, as in the Charon scenes, a small chest, a perfume vase, or basket, appear also in scenes on white-ground

---

[110] Sourvinou-Inwood 1986a: nos. 2 and 3.
[111] In visits to the tomb, for example, and in Charon scenes in which the shade is a full-scale normal figure and winged *eidola* are also depicted (cf. below).

lekythoi (situated in a constructed iconic space) whose reference is
the real world, the women's quarters; these scenes present themselves as 'scenes from life', but they often have connotations of
death; some of the women are clearly mourners, preparing to visit
the grave.[112] The 'mistress and maid' schema also appears on red-
figure vases with scenes from women's life.[113] These schemata
then represent aspects of the women's everyday life. Through the
representation of such facets of the deceased's life these images
signal the latter's status, role, emotional attachments and everyday
concerns, thus defining her social persona. That these schemata and
the images they belong to do indeed function in this way is shown
by fact that the same and comparable schemata appear on some
grave reliefs,[114] where that function is clear.[115] Such reliefs, we saw,
articulate the deceased's social persona. These classical grave reliefs
represent that persona through a defining activity which characterized his life, through a generic type such as 'youth', in his persona
as athlete or warrior.[116] The 'mistress and maid' schema represents
the dead woman through an image of her life which condenses and
defines her social persona. An Athenian woman's persona included
her role as mourner, and this was also represented on some lekythoi;
the representation of this role evoked the funerary sphere to which
these lekythoi belonged. Thus the images representing mistress and
maid as mourners in the women's quarters were both images of
familial piety towards the death, like the visits to the tomb which
represents the next stage in the procedure, and also images of the
social persona of women which included their role as mourners.

The schema 'woman with a child' is also found on white-ground

[112] Cf. e.g. lekythos now in Munich, formerly Lugano, Schoen 79 (*ARV* 997.154; *Add.*
312) with mistress and a maid holding a trinket chest; and many others by the Achilles
Painter: cf. *ARV* 995–1001 *passim*, some clearly localized in the women's quarters (cf. e.g.
ARV 995.122 in which the stool and the heron especially help localize the scene in the
women's quarters while the basket with the fillets connotes the funerary dimension). On
'maid and mistress' schemata and the question of their funerary connotations cf. M. Robertson 1975: 325; Kurtz 1988: 141–9; Fairbanks 1914: 217, 239; Shapiro 1991: 651; cf. also
Reilly 1989: 411–44.

[113] Cf. e.g. the red-figure lekythos Athens 1645 (*ARV* 652.34).

[114] On the relationship between the iconography of these lekythoi and that of grave reliefs
cf. Shapiro 1991: 653–4.

[115] Cf. e.g. the grave relief of Hegeso, in which a woman is depicted taking jewellery out
of a box offered by a maid (M. Robertson 1975: pl. 121*d* and p. 367).

[116] Cf. Ch. III §ii.4*c*. On an archaic representation of a woman and maid see Willemsen
1970: 39, who also remarks (p. 38) that the sitting position was the natural expression of a
woman's married status.

lekythoi and on grave reliefs.[117] Among the former[118] the scene on the lekythos Munich 7619[119] is especially interesting for us: it represents a child crawling on the steps of a tomb, and a woman extending her arms towards it. Beazley[120] remarks that the scene shows the mother teaching the child to walk, a scene from everyday life, with the tomb saying that one of them is dead. In my view, the intimate iconographical association of the child with the tomb suggests that it is the child who is dead, and this fits with the fact that it is characterized through a scene from everyday life that summarizes virtually all there was to say about a small child: its age and place (just learning to walk) and the social tie with the mother. Thus this image articulates the concept 'death of a small child'. In the Charon scenes also, the small child, if he is the only one who is dead, is defined through his mother's presence; for the tie with the mother is the main social tie that will be severed by the death of a very small child. The schema of the woman accompanying the boy who is between 13 and 14 is based on that of woman and small child; this extension is probably motivated by the fact that in Athenian mentality a boy belonged symbolically to the world of women until the beginning of his ephebeia.

That companions were perceived as 'ideally', emblematically, rather than 'narratively', present is clear; for even if we were to think that the children had died at the same time as their mother, only the hypothesis of an emblematic presence can explain the representation of the servants accompanying their mistress. These scenes, which depict aspects of the shade's social persona, can also be considered to be conflations combining the 'reception by Charon' with elements of 'scenes from life/definition of social persona'. There is not always a clear distinction between conflated scenes and scenes made up by the weaving together of emblematic elements in a 'constructed' iconic space. The conclusion that the shades' companions are emblematically represented will be reinforced by the consideration of the objects held by both companions and shades; for these, we shall now see, are also emblematic

---

[117] Cf. e.g. the examples listed in Rühfel 1974: 44, 46–7.
[118] Cf. for another scene at the tomb Munich 2170 (Fairbanks 1907: pl. 14.2). A mother, child, and maid schema is shown on the white-ground lekythos Athens 1947 (CC 1841) (*ARV* 1168.133).
[119] *ARV* 1233.18; Beazley 1938: pl. 6.2.
[120] Beazley 1938: 22.

elements that help characterize the deceased and the context. Some
of the shades arriving in front of Charon are associated with various
objects; sometimes the shade is holding one or more objects,
sometimes the accompanying figure is holding them, more rarely
one or more objects are shown in the field or on the ground or on
other landscape elements. The following objects are held by the
shade. First, in two of the scenes in which the shade about to be
received by Charon is that of a youth the youth is holding two
spears.[121] Second, a small child's shade is once shown holding a toy
cart.[122] Third, a woman's shade sometimes holds one of the following objects or combinations of objects: a small chest;[123] a small
chest and a perfume vase;[124] an alabastron;[125] an aryballos;[126] one or
two baskets with fillets;[127] a rectangular object, probably a writing
tablet.[128] The maid accompanying her mistress is sometimes shown
holding a small chest and an alabastron;[129] a small chest and a
basket,[130] or a perfume vase.[131] The woman accompanying the small
child in one of the two Charon with child scenes is holding a bird,
almost certainly a goose.[132] The woman accompanying a youth in
one scene is holding a basket.[133] The following objects are shown
in the field, or on the ground, or on other landscape elements. A
sakkos is shown in the field in one scene in which a woman is
accompanied by her maid.[134] In the scene in which the woman
accompanying the small child is holding a goose there is a small
chest on the ground. Finally, in some scenes a fillet is hanging on
the reeds which populate the Charonian landscape.[135]

I will now consider the significance of these objects, beginning
with the contexts in which they occur in other scenes; the relationships (of combination and substitution) between the objects them-

[121] Sourvinou-Inwood 1986a: nos. 38 and 39.
[122] Ibid. no. 13.
[123] Ibid. nos. 14, 16, 34b.
[124] Ibid. no. 21.
[125] Ibid. no. 15.
[126] Ibid. no. 36.
[127] Ibid. no. 18: one; 37: two, one with fillets.
[128] Ibid. no. 33.
[129] Ibid. no. 9.
[130] Ibid. no. 32.
[131] Ibid. no. 25.
[132] Ibid. no. 23.
[133] Ibid. no. 26.
[134] Ibid. no. 25.
[135] Ibid. nos. 35, 36, 38.

selves in these Charonian scenes and between the objects and the figures with which they are associated will also help us recover the meanings of these objects in our scenes.[136] The small chest was used as a container for jewellery, small textiles and writing materials.[137] It is primarily associated with the world of women, and has a special connection with weddings;[138] it also appears in scenes representing visits to the tomb,[139] as a crowning of a tomb (again on white-ground lekythoi and also in the round)[140] and on grave reliefs.[141] Because it was closely associated with women's life and pursuits, it could represent metonymically all that life and those pursuits,[142] their social persona, and thus could function as their sign in death.[143] The alabastron[144] was used as a perfume container and was associated with the world of women and especially with weddings.[145] It sometimes also appears in visits to the tomb.[146] The elaborate perfume vase whose ancient name is not known with certainty[147] is found in wedding contexts[148] and generally in connection with the life of

---

[136]   See Sourvinou-Inwood 1991: 11.

[137]   On the uses of chests in ancient Greece: Brümmer 1985: 94–119.

[138]   Small chests in wedding representations: ibid. 138–51.

[139]   Cf. for examples and discussion ibid. 154–8.

[140]   Ibid. 154–8; see esp. figs. 38a (in the round, combined with a kalathos); 39a on a white-ground lekythos combined with a lyre.

[141]   Ibid. 97 n. 423.

[142]   For it functioned in many areas of women's lives, from beautification to (the larger chests) domestic duties.

[143]   Other objects associated with the life of women shown crowning, and thus marking, the grave on white-ground lekythoi are the stool (New York, MMA 12.229.10 (Kurtz 1975: pl. 33.1; *ARV* 1229.26; *Add.* 351)), and the stool combined with the kalathos (Vienna, Kunsth. Mus. 3746 (Kurtz 1975: pl. 33.2; *ARV* 998.164; *Add.* 313)); the kalathos is combined with a chest in the grave monument in the round mentioned above. The small chest and the kalathos can also be shown in combination (e.g. held by the same person) in wedding scenes; see e.g. the hydria New York MMA 17.230.15 (*ARV* 1104.16; *Add.* 329). That the objects crowning the grave on some lekythoi are signs of the persona of the deceased can be seen on London D 58 (Kurtz 1975: pl. 32.4; *ARV* 1228.12; *Add.* 351) in which the deceased whose corpse is carried by Hypnos and Thanatos is a young warrior and his stele has a warrior's helmet on it.

[144]   On which cf. Angermeier 1936: Wehgartner 1983: 112.

[145]   Cf. Angermeier 1936: 37–8, 39–41, cf. also 44. Cf. e.g. *ARV* 99.7–101.30; 624.88–625.94; 661.78–81; 726.1–727.22. Cf. also Wehgartner 1983: 128–34; Sourvinou-Inwood 1991: 106–18.

[146]   Cf. e.g. Athens NM 1956 (Kurtz 1975: pl. 44.1); Oxford 1896.41 (V 545) (*ARV* 998.165; *Add.* 313; Kurtz 1975: pl. 36.2).

[147]   For perfume vases of this type: CVA Oxford 2 pl. 65 nos. 29–30 and Beazley's comm. ad loc. with bibliog.

[148]   Loutrophoros Oxford 1927.4066 (CVA Oxford 2 pl. 59.1–2); loutrophoros Oxford 1927.4067 (CVA Oxford 2 pl. 59.3–4); hydria New York MMA 17.230.15 (*ARV* 1104.16; *Add.* 329).

women[149] and also very frequently in visit to the tomb scenes, as one of the objects held by the participants.[150] The basket is also connected both with weddings[151] and with the death ritual.[152] The basket with wreaths and/or fillets such as those held by the female figures in the Charonian scenes appears often in visits to the tomb and is clearly closely connected with the funerary ritual.[153] The baskets with fillets in the representation of the shade's reception by Charon probably connote offerings to the grave, and thus introduce another facet of death in these scenes, mourning and funerary rites. They can be seen as conflating elements of the theme 'visit to the tomb' with Charon scenes, to connect the latter more closely with the mourning ritual. The sakkos[154] is associated with women's scenes, including weddings,[155] and is also sometimes found in a funerary context, in visits to the tomb.[156] The aryballos is, like the lekythos, an oil bottle; as a toilet vase it was associated with women, as well as with athletes. The identity of the rectangular object held by the woman on the lekythos Athens NM 1759[157] is not certain; it may be a writing tablet. It is not certain that writing tablets are represented in other lekythoi scenes.[158] If the object is a writing tablet it should not be assumed that it has a mysteric significance, that it is similar to the tablets with sectarian texts pertaining to the afterlife found in graves. Given that, as we shall see, all its equivalent iconographical elements refer to the deceased's life and characterize their social persona, if the object is a writing tablet it is much more likely to be a sign that the deceased was literate, or versed in cultural matters.[159] The two spears held by the youth on two Charonian scenes are also associated with the dead person's usual pursuits in

---

[149] Cup Compiègne, Musée Vivenel 1090 (*ARV* 922.1; *Add.* 305).

[150] Cf. Lekythos Athens NM 1821 (*ARV* 998. 168; *Add.* 313).

[151] Cf. e.g. loutrophoros Copenhagen NM 9080 (*ARV* 841.75; *Add.* 296).

[152] Cf. e.g. Athens NM 1938 (Kurtz 1975: pl. 36.3).

[153] Cf. e.g. Cassel T 379 (*ARV* 1234.14; *Add.* 352); Boston 94.127 (*ARV* 1230.40); Louvre CA 1640 (Kurtz 1975: pl. 20.1); Boston FA 1970.428 (Kurtz 1975: pl. 20.2).

[154] Cf. Jenkins 1986, 26; Jenkins and Williams 1985: 413–16.

[155] Cf. e.g. the loutrophoros Oxford 1927.4067 (*ARV* 1179).

[156] Lekythos Madrid 19497 (*ARV* 748.1; *Add.* 284).

[157] *ARV* 1376; Sourvinou-Inwood 1986a: no. 33a.

[158] It is possible that one was represented on the lekythos Boston 00.359 (*ARV* 1229.23; *Add.* 351) where the iconographical schema is different from ours. On the objects in the lekythoi illustrated in Fairbanks 1914: pl. 22.2 and 23.2 being rolled ribbons rather than writing tablets cf. Kurtz 1975: 221.

[159] On women being literate and pursuing cultural interests: Bérard 1984: 86.

life, such as hunting. Spears are closely connected with ephebes,[160] in whose training and activities they played an important part; they were part of the iconographical scheme which represented the ephebe in Attic iconography. Thus the spears probably define the dead youths as ephebes. As for the child's toy cart, toy carts of this type are common in representations of children on choes.[161] They represent the small child's pursuits, and thus characterize them as children. The goose was a household pet[162] with a similar relationship to small children who are again represented in the company of a goose on some choes;[163] the goose is also associated with funerary contexts: it is sometimes held by a woman in visits to the tomb.[164] In some places it is associated with the Underworld deities.[165] The small chest, shown on the ground in connection with the small child, is, we saw, closely associated with women; the association between the child and the chest may be due to the fact that children belonged to the world of women; alternatively, or in addition, the small chest was perceived as the child's toy box. Fillets hang in the field in wedding scenes[166] and frequently hang on the stele in visit to the tomb scenes.[167] Because of the common funerary context it is the latter that are evoked by the fillets on the reeds in the Charonian scenes, which thus connote mourning, and evoke the death ritual of the living (and its representations) in the midst of the infernal landscape; they connect the shade's experience with the funerary ritual, and bring the Charonian landscape symbolically closer to the world of the living.[168] The schemata in which shades are holding baskets with fillets create funerary meanings and also represent an aspect of the shades' social persona, their role of mourners for the family, which was part of a woman's social persona. This is confirmed by the fact that only female shades are shown with baskets in Charon scenes, as only female shades carry

[160] Cf. Sourvinou-Inwood 1991: 40–1.

[161] Cf. Van Hoorn 1951: 44 on toy carts on choes.

[162] Cf. Van Hoorn 1951: 48.

[163] Chous Würzburg H 4220 (Van Hoorn 1951: fig. 219), where a toy roller is also shown; chous Munich 2462 (Van Hoorn 1951: fig. 294).

[164] Cf. Karlsruhe B 2689 (*ARV* 1386.20; *Add.* 372).

[165] Cf. Sourvinou-Inwood 1991: 157–8, 160.

[166] Cf. refs. in Sourvinou-Inwood 1991: 80.

[167] Cf. e.g. Kurtz 1975: pls. 26.2, 40.3, 41.1, 41.3. For the appearance of fillets in funerary contexts, including grave reliefs cf. Berger 1990: 41–53.

[168] The connection between the funerary ritual and the Charonian landscape is expanded and intensified in variant B.1.

baskets in 'visit to the tomb' and other funerary scenes. Many of the objects connected with the life of women, we saw, also had a place in the funerary ritual. In the Charon scenes the context emphasizes their funerary aspect, but they also signal the deceased's life and social persona, especially since the association of such elements, and of the 'mistress and maid' schema, with the representation of the deceased's social persona in grave reliefs reinforces this semantic dimension.

Thus, all the iconographical elements associated with the shades in Charonian scenes[169] represent aspects of, and help evoke, the shades' life and social persona, their status, role, emotional attachments, and everyday concerns: the child's toys and pets and the tie with the mother, the youth's hunting and role as ephebe, the world of women and the role of young matron. No old women are shown with Charon. This is probably because these are not representations of the social persona of the individual deceased as the images on grave monuments are;[170] they are images of the death of the self through the representation of the meeting between Charon and a shade representing the social persona *pertaining to* the deceased for whom the lekythos was bought—if it was always desired to match the deceased's persona and these images, which is uncertain.[171] An image of Charon with a young matron, who was the idealized type of female social persona, would have been one option for old women, and this, clearly, was the option chosen.

Thus, the representation of the shades in the Charonian scenes is, up to a point, individualized: through generic types of social persona. This is, to a certain extent, comparable to the representations of the dead on grave monuments, which are fully individualized through the naming inscription. This articulation of the deceased's persona helps define the 'gap' created by the death, stresses (especially in cases like the child's) the poignancy of the death, and so helps valorize it. In any case, the juxtaposition of the deceased's life evoked by these elements to the fact of their death also creates an effect of poignancy. The fact that in these scenes which represent the world of the dead the shade is depicted through the schema which represents the deceased's social persona in the

---

[169] The fillets hanging on the reeds are not an exception, since, we saw, they are equivalent to the fillets on stelai and characterize the landscape and context and not the shade itself.

[170] On older women on Attic grave monuments cf. Pfisterer-Haas 1990: 179–96.

[171] We lack the find-contexts that would have allowed us to determine this.

world of the living involves an understressing of the distance between the person in life and the shade in death, and helps diminish (in that particular representation) the perceived distance between the world of the living and that of the dead, between life and death, and between the person in life and his shade in death. These individualized shades contrast with the undifferentiated shades of the black-figure Charon scenes and with the two representations on white-ground lekythoi in which the shade received by Charon is a winged small-scale *eidolon*.[172] The representation of the shades with Charon as largish *eidola* was completely abandoned very soon after the beginning of the vogue of Charon images on white-ground lekythoi; within the individualized shade schema there is a spectrum of greater or lesser individualization, but all versions show the full-scale human being. This suggests that the meanings produced by the full-scale shades suited the artists' and viewers' conception of the scenes very much better than those of the small winged *eidola*. The latter schema represents the shade as an undifferentiated generic soul, which looks very different from its living self; it thus stresses the discontinuity between life and death and the otherness of death and of the dead. The full-scale human shade and the small winged *eidolon* are two different ways of articulating the notion 'the surviving part of a dead person'.[173] There is no fixed essence 'shade', evoked unchanged whether what is shown is a small winged soul or a human being. The different iconographical schemata emphasize different aspects of the semantic field 'deceased' and 'death'. The small winged *eidola* emphasize the otherness of death and the dead, the full-scale shades the continuity between the shade and the living person (and the memory of that person) and so also the shade's individuality. The pattern of appearance of the two schemata suggests that the individualized representation of the shade that was similar to the living person best represented the meanings felt to be most appropriate. Consequently, the iconography of the shades in the Charon scenes, and especially the change to the (conventionally) individualized full-scale human figure suggest that these scenes represent death as an individual experience, rather than a generic and undifferentiated one. In the two black-figure scenes the encounter with Charon (death) was

[172] Sourvinou-Inwood 1986a: nos. 2 and 3. (See pl. 11.)
[173] On the representation of shades cf. Siebert 1981: 63–73, esp. 68–9.

shown as a collective experience, involving several generic and undifferentiated shades. In the Tymbos Painter's two scenes the encounter involves a one-to-one relationship between Charon and the shade, but the shade is represented as generic and undifferentiated. In the crystallized white-ground Charonian imagery that became the preferred option the experience is individual and the representation of the shade individualized.

This representation, which understresses the distance between the person in life and the shade in death, is not the only perception of the shade that is articulated in all scenes. In some Charonian scenes there is multivocality, the dominant perception being deconstructed by another, which is itself coloured by its relationship to the dominant meanings. This is what happens in some Charon images in which small *eidola* are flying about,[174] either one[175] or two[176] or several.[177] These *eidola* evoke the shade's distancing from life, the otherness of death. Of course, these winged *eidola* are polysemic. They are also part of the landscape, they help denote the localization of the scene in the Underworld; and they also participate in the shade's reception, help articulate her introduction in the community of the dead, especially in a scene such as Athens NM 1926[178] in which many *eidola* are represented, the majority shown coming from the direction of Hades on the other side of the water, like a reception committee. Winged *eidola* in the Charon scenes often make mourning gestures. These are obviously appropriate for a funerary context of this kind; they also reflect, and evoke, the mourning gestures of the living. Thus these members of the community of the dead which the shade is joining mirror the community of the living from whom the shade has been separated. And this to some extent deconstructs, reduces somewhat, the distanced nature of the winged *eidola*, and thus to some extent deconstructs the element which deconstructed the dominant representation of the shade in these Charonian scenes as 'like in life'. This complexity of conflicting discourses reflects the ambivalence, ambiguity and complexity of the Greek collective representations pertaining to death.

---

[174] On winged *eidola* in Charon scenes see also Fairbanks 1907: 192.
[175] Cf. e.g. Sourvinou-Inwood 1986a: nos. 8, 19.
[176] Cf. e.g. ibid. no. 4.
[177] Cf. e.g. ibid. no. 5.
[178] Ibid. no. 5.

(c) *Death as an Individual Experience*

The representation of small undifferentiated *eidola* does not alter the central one-to-one relationship between Charon and the shade he is receiving,[179] a schema that suggests that the centre of these images is the perception and articulation of death as an individual experience. These representations, in which a shade looking like the living is facing the ferryman, represent death through an individual's reception by Charon for the final crossing. Thus, the Charon scenes are images of death from the viewpoint of the dead person, images of the death of the self. Though they are, of course, seen through the mirror of the representation of the death of another, in these articulations one can also see oneself in that other, see oneself in death, one's own death. That the encounter with Charon is an image of the death of the self perceived as an individual experience is confirmed by Euripides' *Alcestis*, vv. 252–7, where, we saw, the vision of Alcestis' imminent death is articulated through the vision of Charon waiting for her in his boat; through this vision she contemplates her imminent death, sees herself in death.

5. BENEVOLENT CHARON

(a) *The Argument*

I will now argue that on the lekythoi Charon is benevolent and death is represented in reassuring terms; and that these images are propitiatory, seek Charon's benevolence by depicting the shade being received benevolently by him. My case is based on a series of different arguments; the convergence of their conclusions provides confirmation for its validity.

The combination of subject-matter and circumstances of production, physical context, and use creates a strong presumption in favour of the view that the Charonian scenes are positive images of death and present the unseeable reality of the afterlife in positive,

---

[179] For, we saw, in almost every scene the companions are only 'ideally' emblematically, present. The exceptions, that involve the reception of more than one shade by Charon, are Sourvinou-Inwood 1986a: nos. 12 and 26, in both of which a woman is seated in Charon's boat, while on 12 a second woman is standing on the shore behind Hermes, and on 26 a woman and a youth are standing on the shore.

hopeful, colours.[180] As we saw, the Charonian scenes, alone among
the major themes on the white-ground lekythoi, focus on the
shade.[181] Since these images were painted on vases that were first
displayed at the burial and then buried, the presumption must be
that in the eyes of the participants in the funeral their dominant
meanings were positive; that the representation of the shades' reception by Charon was a positive image of death. In fact, we saw in
the previous section, the 'recommendation' of Alcestis to Charon
and Hades in Euripides' *Alcestis* shows that in fifth-century Athens
Charon was indeed perceived as (at least potentially) a supportive
figure, whose benevolence could be solicited on behalf of a dead
person; but I do not want to use non-iconographical arguments
here, in order to keep the two sets of analyses separate. As we shall
now see, the strongest argument in favour of the interpretation put
forward here is that Charon's gestures towards the shade and the
shade's gestures towards Charon show that the relationship between
them was represented as friendly, and that Charon was depicted,
and thus also perceived, as benevolent and protective.

In order to read these images through fifth-century perceptual
filters we need to compare Charon's gestures and the gestures of the
shades to the repertory represented in the white-ground lekythoi,
especially in scenes where the context and the relationship between
the figures is clearer.[182] The gestures made by Charon towards the
shade and by the shade towards Charon are elsewhere exchanged
between figures whose relationships we know to have been friendly
and even affectionate. In some scenes the gestures relating Charon
and the shade are very similar to those elsewhere relating a small

---

[180] That Hermes is represented as a figure of reassurance in the white-ground lekythoi is
also suggested by Bérard 1984: 101. Bérard (1988: 166) accepts the suggestion I made in the
summary version of parts of this chapter (in Sourvinou-Inwood 1987) that these images on
white-ground lekythoi articulate reassurance.

[181] A few scenes with Hermes without Charon also do so (e.g. lekythos Athens NM 1940
(*ARV* 1004.41; *Add.* 313)) but they do not constitute a major theme.

[182] I am not trying to determine the gestures' exact significance, for, given the paucity of
our evidence, such an enterprise would be very vulnerable to cultural determination; only
the contexts in which they appear, especially in this series of funerary scenes. I am focusing
on this series because this is safer methodologically. Gestures are polysemic, and we cannot
assume that they have the same significance in our series where meanings are determined by
the funerary context, as elsewhere, nor that they necessarily had a precise real-life reference,
or indeed any existence at all outside the system of iconographical conventions of this series
(however likely this assumption may be). However, given the (relative) numerical limitations
of our series, I will also take account of red-figure scenes, provided that the context is closely
similar.

child and its parent, normally the mother. This shows that the relationship between Charon and the shade was thought of as similar to that between the mother and the small child, which involves also the former protecting the latter. This similarity is especially clear in one of the cases in which the shade is a small child—which would have been perceived as the most vulnerable and frightened type of shade to come in the presence of Charon. I shall discuss this in a moment; first I shall consider the two early lekythoi in which the shade is a small winged *eidolon*.

On the lekythos Oxford Ashmolean Museum G 258 (Pl. 11)[183] Charon holds the pole in his right, and his left is bent at the elbow, his forearm and hand stretched towards the shade, palm upwards. The shade is flying with both arms extended towards him, a gesture elsewhere made by a small child towards its parent, often its mother, sometimes an elder sister;[184] that is, towards someone who performs a parental or quasi-parental, certainly a benevolent and protective, role.[185] Charon's gesture, the arm bent at the elbow, forearm and hand extended, palm upwards, also found, we shall see, in other Charonian scenes, occurs in the following contexts on white-

---

[183] Sourvinou-Inwood 1986a: no. 3.

[184] The child extending both arms to its parent or parent-like figure (in different variations, upwards, sideways, and so on) is a common gesture in Greek iconography, and there are many examples in different media; I will only mention a very few. Cf. e.g. the fragmentary white-ground lekythos London BM 1905.7-10.10 fr. (*ARV* 1227.10; *Add*. 350); in a scene located in the women' quarter on the hydria London BM E 219 (*ARV* 1258; *Add*. 355) the child's arms are extended sideways to the mother; on the red-figure lekythos Oxford 322 (*CVA* pl. 37.1-2) the child's arms are extended sideways to the father (Herakles); on a grave relief of the second quarter of the 5th cent., Xanthippos' relief (Cook 1976: fig. 84) the small child on the right stretches both arms upwards towards her seated father; on the grave relief of Mnesagora and Nikochares (cf. e.g. Garland 1985: 85 fig. 19) the latter's arms are extended upwards to his elder sister.

[185] In 5th-cent. iconography the gesture of extending both arms towards another figure, in a somewhat different form, is a common gesture of supplication in scenes representing aggression, (cf. e.g. Neumann 1965: 72). Since meaning is created in context, the fact that the context is different from that involving the shades entails that the extended arms cannot have had the same meanings in the two cases. But it cannot be excluded that this gesture, the meaning of which as a gesture of supplication was well established, may have evoked the notion of supplication and helped colour the perception of the relationship between Charon and the shade in the image. It cannot be excluded that the relationship between Charon and the shade, which was represented above all as comparable to that between parent and small child, may also have acquired a colouring of supplication; a supplication to Charon to receive the shade with benevolence, like a parent. The different versions of the different gestures in the different images create different (albeit, given the spectrum involved, clearly not significantly different) meanings.

ground lekythoi. First, in generic friendly contexts.[186] Second, in scenes at the tomb, where such gestures are directed towards the stele and/or other figures represented there.[187] Third, it is made by a parent or surrogate parent preparing to receive a small child or baby[188] or by a figure preparing to receive an object.[189] The same gesture also occurs in a representation which combines the notion of receiving a child and of holding something, and which resembles iconographically our Oxford lekythos: on the lekythos Boston 03.801[190] a small winged child, Eros, is standing on the open right palm of a seated figure whose right arm is bent at the elbow, forearm stretched; Eros' arms are both, like our shade's, stretched towards the standing woman in whose direction he is facing. The pattern of appearance of this gesture suggests that on the Oxford lekythos it helped create the meaning 'Charon receives the shade benevolently', and also, given the funerary context, it evoked what seems to have been the gesture's specialized funerary use and thus connotations of mourning. On the lekythos Karlsruhe Bad. Landesmus. B 2663[191] the shade, again a small winged *eidolon*, stretches both arms towards Charon, in the same gesture as in the Oxford scene by the same painter. Clearly, in both scenes the shade's relationship to Charon is represented as being not simply unequivocally friendly, but also closely comparable to the relationship between child and parent.

Turning to the representation of shades of small children, on the lekythos Athens NM 1814[192] Charon stretches out his hand to the

[186] Cf. e.g. the gesture of one of the women in Bologna PU 362 (*ARV* 1000.202) towards the other.

[187] Cf. e.g.: Athens NM 1951 (CC 1755); *ARV* 1242.11; Kurtz 1975: pls. 40.2, 41.1 (if he did not hold a ribbon, which Kurtz 1975, 217 suggests as a possibility; but I think he is very slightly different in the angle of the forearm and of the hand from the comparable ones in which the hand is holding a ribbon or similar object such as that illustrated in Fairbanks 1914: pl. v; or Kurtz 1975: 32.1 left hand. If this is correct, it supports the view that the gesture on Kurtz 1975: 41.1 is also addressed to the stele and not to the woman on the other side of the stele). Cf. also Athens NM 12138 (*ARV* 855.1).

[188] Esp. close is the gesture on the calyx krater in Rome Vatican 16586 (*ARV* 1017.54; *Add.* 315) which is white-ground, but not a funerary lekythos, by the Phiale Painter who also painted some funerary lekythoi (cf. *ARV* 1022–3 nos. 138–41.). Cf. also the white-ground lekythos Berlin, Antiken Museum F 2443 (*ARV* 995. 118; *Add.* 312), where both arms are making a similar gesture.

[189] Cf. e.g. the lekythos New York 15.165 (*ARV* 1228.6; *Add.* 351).

[190] Vermeule 1979: 178 fig. 29; Fairbanks 1914: pl. 17.2.

[191] Sourvinou-Inwood 1986a: no. 2.

[192] Ibid. no. 23.

child on the shore who turns towards Charon and stretches out his hand to him. The child's stance and gesture corresponds to that of a child on the Charonian lekythos New York MMA 09.221.44,[193] looking towards, and stretching his hand to, his mother—and also in other scenes representing mother and child.[194] Interestingly, the two iconographical schemata on the two Charonian lekythoi with children are closely comparable. The chief divergence between them consists in the fact that the relationship between 'child–mother' and 'child–Charon' on the Athenian lekythos is the reverse of that on the New York one. On the former the child is sitting, its body turned towards its mother and it is turning its head and extending its arm, towards Charon; in the latter it is standing, turned three-quarter towards Charon in his boat, and is turning its head, and extending its arm (which, however, here is not bent, and is directed upwards) towards its mother. Charon's gesture towards the child on the Athenian lekythos belongs to a general category of friendly gestures involving arm and hand stretched. This particular version of the gesture is similar to that which Charon makes in the Oxford lekythos with the small *eidolon* discussed above. That it is a gesture of friendship (perhaps friendly urging) is also shown by the fact that the identical gesture is made by Hermes towards Charon on the lekythos Athens NM 17916.[195] Thus, the relationship between Charon and children is depicted in terms of (which entails that it was perceived as close to) that between small children and their parents, especially the mother.

The relationship between the shade and Charon is portrayed in terms comparable to those between children and their parents also in the case of adult shades depicted as full-scale human figures.[196] Often Charon's gestures towards other shades are the same as those we have observed towards children; other gestures are comparable

---

[193] Ibid. no. 13.

[194] Cf. e.g. a comparable (not the same) gesture on the white-ground lekythos Berlin 2443 (*ARV* 995.118; *Add.* 312) and a close parallel on the red-figure stamnos Louvre, MNB 1695 (G 188) (*ARV* 508.1; *Add.* 252). Cf. e.g. on grave reliefs: of Ampharete (Kurtz and Boardman 1971: pl. 31); of Philotera (Demakopoulou and Konsola 1981: pl. 38).

[195] Sourvinou-Inwood 1986a: no. 6.

[196] It is perhaps in the two lekythoi with a small *eidolon* that this iconographical closeness is most emphatic; perhaps because the *eidolon's* small size in interaction with the appropriateness of the model (the fact that the Charon–shade relationship was seen as similar to that between a child and its parents) led to a very close modelling on the child–parent schemata.

and belong to contexts in which friendly relationships pertain.[197] Some of the gestures made by figures towards the tomb in representations of visits to the tomb are also similar to gestures made by Charon towards the shades on some images.[198] This context is also funerary, but it involves gestures which may be ritual, and which in any case involve the interface of two spheres, of the living and the dead. They cannot therefore be assumed to be the same as those in the Charon scenes. However, it is clear that the contexts were perceived to be sufficiently close for the meanings to be closely comparable. For the broad semantic framework of gestures made by the Athenians towards the grave involved mourning and sorrow on the one hand and benevolent relationships between the living and the dead on the other, both of which fit the meanings established for Charon's other gestures.

Consequently, the gestures relating Charon and the shades on the white-ground lekythoi show that the relationship between them was represented as friendly, and that Charon was represented as benevolent and protective towards the shades.[199] Some scenes articulate more explicitly this benevolence and helpfulness through gestures which emphasize it.[200]

---

[197] For example, the arm bent at the elbow, forearm stretched, palm upwards, a gesture discussed above in connection with the Oxford lekythos by the Tymbos Painter (Sourvinou-Inwood 1986a: no. 3) is also seen on Charon on the lekythos Oxford 1889.827 (V.264) (Sourvinou-Inwood 1986a: no. 19). The following are a few more examples of gestures with friendly/parental type meanings. On the lekythos Brussels, Mus. Roy. A 903 (Sourvinou-Inwood 1986a: no. 25) the woman's right (her left is held by Hermes) is bent at the elbow and the forearm and hand is stretched towards Charon whose right is also bent at the elbow with the forearm and hand stretched towards Hermes and the woman, palm upwards, as is the woman's. This similarity of the gestures between ferryman and shade, which creates an effect of harmony between them, suggest a friendly relationship. On London D 61 (Sourvinou-Inwood 1986a: no. 37) Charon's whole arm is stretched towards the shade with his palm almost entirely facing the spectator; this gesture is similar to that of the mother receiving the child on the hydria London BM E 219 (*ARV* 1258; *Add.* 355).

[198] e.g. Charon's gesture towards the child on the lekythos Athens NM 1814 (CC 1662) (Sourvinou-Inwood 1986a: no. 23) is the same as that made by the bearded man on the left of grave stele towards the grave stele on the lekythos Athens NM 1941; Charon's gesture on the lekythos London D 61 (Sourvinou-Inwood 1986a: no. 37) is comparable, for example, to the visit to the tomb illustrated in Fairbanks 1914: pl. I.

[199] Other scholars have also perceived the infernal ferryman on the white-ground lekythoi as benevolent. Cf. e.g. Kurtz 1985: 325 who remarks of Charon: 'He is benevolent . . . and he is gentle with his charge, especially the very, very young.'

[200] When such gestures are not shown this relationship was not emphasized. However, unless these meanings were blocked, for example through the representation of contrary signs, which is not the case here, the viewers reading the images through their assumptions about the represented relationship (which we have reconstructed on the basis of their

(b) *Ideology and Gender Differences*

Given the alternation of women, youths, children, and the characterization of the shades discussed above, there can be no doubt that the Charonian scenes are not mythological, but represent an imagined 'everyday life scene', what was believed to be an unseeable reality. The shades facing Charon, we saw, are mostly women, less frequently adolescents or youths, very rarely children, and never adult male citizens. Since the sample is large enough to make the hypothesis of an accident extremely implausible, it follows that the meanings of the Charon scenes are appropriate for women, adolescents, and children, but not for adult men. Since the appropriateness is common to these three categories those meanings should pertain to something that differentiates these three categories from male adult citizens. In Chapter III § ii.3*d* we saw that the glorification of the war dead was a fundamental part of fifth-century polis ideology. This ideology pertaining to death in the service of the polis differentiates male adult citizens from all others. Because all male citizens were potentially war dead, this important differentiation between adult male citizens, who will or may die the good death glorified by the polis, and all others corresponds to the differentiation in the images. It is therefore in this ideology that the explanation of the absence of representations of Charon with adult males should lie. The hypothesis that this absence is dependent on the fifth-century ideology of 'good death' in war coincides precisely with my interpretation of the Charonian scenes as reassuring images of death, articulations of an individual perception of death in which the anxiety about death is somewhat lessened by the representation of death as a benevolent reception by Charon—a metaphor for 'good' not in the sense of glorious, but in the sense of personally not unpleasant, not frightening, death. If this interpretation is correct, such images were not appropriate for the war dead and potential war dead, whose death in battle was in the official ideology a proud occasion, the prospect of which was not supposed to generate anxiety and the corresponding need of reassuring images

articulation in those images which explicate the relationship) would have perceived it as benevolent. Of course, since the welcoming and protective figure was Charon, his friendliness could be seen as ambivalent, somewhat sinister when seen from the point of view of the living, but reassuring when seen from the viewpoint of the dead or in the context of these images in which, I suggested, the death of the other functioned also as a mirror for the death of the self.

of benevolent reception by Charon. Since all male citizens were (or, in old age, had been) potentially war dead, and their death (potentially) a 'good glorious death' they could not be associated with images which, on my analysis, were correlative with the perception of the death of the self as generating anxiety; for this would contaminate symbolically the image of the citizen's death and thus deconstruct the official ideology which presented death in the service of one's country as entirely positive, the optimum 'good death'. Thus my interpretation can explain why Charon is never shown with adult males.[201]

If this interpretation is correct, the symbolism associated with Charon, which reflected attitudes inappropriate for the male adult citizens, drifted towards the 'marginal' categories women, children, and adolescents (including the marginal ephebes), who became the vehicle for the articulation of these perceptions into images in which, in fact everyone, including men, and certainly the male artists who created them, could also see the prefiguration of their own death in terms of a reassuring image. For the emotional reality of the male citizens' attitudes towards the prospect of their own death did not necessarily correspond to the ideality. In other words, as the positive, 'heroic' values in the funerary ideology of fifth-century Athens focused on the male adult citizens, the attitudes of anxiety about one's death clustered around the marginal figures of women, children, and adolescents. Of course, the separation could never be complete and irreversible. For male citizens had been past ephebes, and ephebes were citizens-to-be.[202]

In these circumstances, I submit that the conclusion that these images represent Charon as a benevolent and reassuring figure is as

---

[201] The fact that male shades were shown with Charon in black-figure scenes at c.500 (Sourvinou-Inwood 1986a: nos. 1, 1a) is correlative with the fact that the coherent and systematic ideology of the good death of citizens in battle that does not involve mourning had not yet been elaborated at that time. It could be argued that the fact that men are not shown together with Charon is correlative with the notion of the war dead's heroization (on which Ch. III § ii.3d), which made it inappropriate for them to be shown crossing the Acheron. But the combination of two objections makes this hypothesis untenable. First, since not all Athenian males died in war during the period of production of white-ground lekythoi we would have expected the articulation with Charon to be an available option for those who did not—unless, as I am suggesting, there were ideological reasons blocking that option. Second, the image 'escaping Acheron's ferry' is used to express immortality, in Pindar fr. 143 Snell–Maehler and apotheosis in Theocr. 17. 46–50, and not heroization. This suggests that this escape was an image of immortality/apotheosis, not heroization.

[202] See a different but comparable drift concerning the parthenos–gyne relationship to the positive and negative values of 'woman' in King 1983: 110–11.

certain as can possibly be, given our limitations of access. It coincides
with the results of the semantic analyses conducted in the previous
section, and this convergence, in my view, confirms the validity of
these conclusions. If these analyses are right, we have also gained an
important insight into the relationship between official and private
polis ideology in fifth-century Athens: the latter had appropriated, in-
ternalized, important aspects of the official ideology; the two were not
in a conflictual relationship, they were in some ways complementary.

(c) *Conclusions*

These scenes, then, are propitiatory images seeking Charon's benevolence through the representation of that benevolence.[203] Given
Charon's function as a metaphor for death, the benevolent reception
by him can also be seen as a metaphor for 'having a good/easy
death', and its solicitation also a request for such a death. This in its
turn is a way of thinking about death in reassuring terms, and thus
channelling, displacing, some of the (potential or actual) anxiety
about one's own death and the grief at the death of the other.[204]

6. SCENES WITH CHARON: TYPES AND MEANINGS

Let us now consider the variations in the various types of Charonian
scenes. As we saw, type I with Charon and without Hermes is the
most popular. Scenes of Hermes alone with a shade, without Charon,
are extremely rare.[205] Hermes led the shades from the upper world to
the banks of Acheron/Acherousia; he was thus associated with the
transition from life to death, while Charon was connected with the

---

[203] The images of Charon are more explicitly benevolent in the 5th-cent. white-ground
imagery than at *c.*500. For the former were a popular genre of reassuring images, and thus
developed an iconography in which this aspect of Charon was developed and refined.
Charon's relationship with the shades, we saw, was already benevolent in the two early
lekythoi by the Tymbos Painter. Of the two black-figure scenes the phormiskos Tübingen
S./10 1507 (Sourvinou-Inwood 1986*a*: no. 1*a*) is extremely fragmentary and does not allow
any further comment. In the eschara, Frankfurt Liebighaus 560 (Sourvinou-Inwood 1986*a*:
no. 1) Charon's gesture towards the shades in his boat resembles that of Charon on the
lekythos London D 61 (Sourvinou-Inwood 1986*a*: no. 37). Thus the underlying mentality
seems to be the same, but with a progressively sophisticated iconographical expressiveness.

[204] The dominant dimension of these images signifies reassurance, but there is also
multivocality in some, where the winged *eidola* represent the otherness of death and thus
deconstruct some of the reassurance, reintroduce the element of anxiety and fear which
accompanies death, to a greater or lesser degree, in all collective representations.

[205] Cf. Kurtz 1985: 325; Garland 1985: 54–5.

final integration into the world of the dead. The actual death, and the transition from life to death, were traumatic when compared to the end of the perilous journey and the integration into Hades under the auspices of Charon. Thus the more traumatic part of the transition is compressed and passed over quickly, and the emphasis is on the final integration and Charon, who will help the shade over the final hurdle and towards the achievement of that integration. That is why representations of the beginning of the journey led by Hermes, and of the journey itself, are not popular. Scenes of type 2 in which Hermes is present evoke the whole transition from life to death, while scenes of type 1 concentrate on the final transition and Charon. Scenes of what may be called subtypes 1*c* and 2*c*, in which one shade is already sitting on Charon's boat while one or more shades are standing on the shore, contain elements of a descriptive/narrative mode. They are situated between the black-figure scenes in which several souls were ferried together in Charon's boat and the 'emblematic' one-to-one encounters of the other lekythoi.

The conflation of Charon with a 'visit to the tomb' represents death seen as both a personal experience and a family affair. Here the symbolic distance between the grave and the mourning of the living on the one hand and Charon and the infernal landscape on the other is significantly reduced through their combination into one scene in a constructed iconic space. This variant can be seen as a further development and intensification of certain versions of variant A, in which elements such as the fillet hanging on the reeds evoke the death-ritual in the infernal landscape. The scene on the lekythos Athens NM 1830[206] in which the themes of Charon and of Hypnos and Thanatos carrying a dead body are conflated, combines two images of good death: good death in the sense of the easy, not frightening experience, and the socially 'good death' symbolized by Hypnos and Thanatos.

7. THE ICONOGRAPHY OF THE INFERNAL FERRYMAN:[207] PERCEPTIONS OF CHARON, PERCEPTIONS OF DEATH

The texts always describe Charon as an old man, and it is as an old man that he is depicted on the two black-figure scenes. He may

---

[206] Sourvinou-Inwood 1986*a*: no. 31.

[207] I am discussing Charon's iconography here because there is no correlation between the type of Charon's face and the type of scene, or the sex or age of the shade.

have taken on the characteristics of those who would be his 'normal' customers in the ideality of the collective representations, old men[208]—as Aphrodite has the persona of a desirable young woman, Apollo of an ephebe, Artemis of a parthenos, and so on. On the white-ground lekythoi Charon is less unequivocally old; his iconography appears to fluctuate between the old and what we may call the ageless.[209] This was not inappropriate, since in these scenes Charon was also a metaphor for death, a figure through whom death was visually articulated, for whom agelessness is at least as appropriate as old age.[210]

Charon's face in the black-figure representations is a normal late black-figure face appropriate for an old man, with regular features. At about the middle of the fifth century a different type of Charonian face appears, sharply differentiated from the normal Greek face: it is rough and coarse, with varying degrees of coarseness and ugliness in the different scenes. Sometimes[211] he has a crooked nose, wrinkled skin, irregular eyebrow, and rough and unkempt and/or sparse beard. In other representations he continues to have regular features and a neat beard. The same painter can give Charon a different type of face on different vases.[212] In yet another set of scenes Charon's face lies between these two extremes: it is slightly irregular, in varying degrees and various ways, with one or more of the features that make up the coarse face elsewhere in a relatively attenuated form.[213] Thus, there are three main types of Charonian face in the white-ground lekythoi: the rough and coarse, the normal and regular, and the intermediate. The regular face was the earliest, the only one found in the black-figure scenes and the earliest white-ground lekythoi. In the black-figure scenes Charon is wearing a himation; on a few early white-ground lekythoi a chiton. From about the middle of the fifth century he acquires a garment which became his canonical costume in the white-ground lekythoi: the

---

[208] Because in the ideality of the representations it is mostly old people who die.

[209] Cf. Sourvinou-Inwood 1986*a*: 221–2. On the representation of Charon's age cf. also Papaspyridi 1923: 138.

[210] If, as I tentatively suggested, his old age was related to the persona of those who were considered to be his normal customers, we can easily explain why this characteristic was not deemed to be necessary in the white-ground lekythoi: the fact that only women, children, and adolescents were represented, and no men, entailed a loosening of the 'mirror image' model which, on this hypothesis, had perhaps helped determine Charon's old age.

[211] Cf. e.g. Pl. 9 (Sourvinou-Inwood 1986*a*: no. 5).

[212] Compare e.g. Sourvinou-Inwood 1986*a*: nos. 5 and 6 by the Sabouroff Painter.

[213] Cf. e.g. ibid. nos. 15, 19, 36.

exomis, the short chiton worn by slaves and labourers which leaves one shoulder bare. But the chiton does not disappear completely.[214] In the type which became canonical in the lekythoi the exomis is combined with a rustic pilos, which appears to be of the woolly or hairy or furry type worn by sailors, shepherds, fishermen. In a few early examples, before the canonical type was established, Charon is wearing a normal pilos,[215] a petasos slung at the back of his neck,[216] or no head-covering.[217]

Thus, Charon's pattern of differentiation from normal Greek males varies in the course of time. On the black-figure of *c.*500 he was not differentiated at all. In the white-ground lekythoi he begins with a 'normal' face and 'normal' dress, but the various elements that will eventually make up his canonical 'differentiated' type begin to appear early. In the minimally differentiated lekythos type Charon has an exomis and a rustic pilos.[218] In the maximally differentiated type he has a coarse, ugly, rough face as well as the exomis and rustic pilos. This new Charonian iconography developed around the middle of the fifth century within the lekythoi series, for we can observe the piecemeal appearance of the various elements that went into the making of the type. A regular face and dress would have been the obvious choice for Charon in the context of the conventions of black-figure vase-painting, provided the subject was thought of as a normal old male figure. Thus, the use of the normal male type to represent Charon tells us that at *c.*500 Charon was perceived as a normal old male. The elements which make up Charon's 'minimum differentiation schema' on the lekythoi, the exomis and the rustic head-covering, correspond to an established semantic facet of Charon, his 'banausic, manual, task'. They can be seen as choices inspired by, or at least made within the framework of, the tendency in the artistic idiom of the second quarter of the fifth century to differentiate the individual figures more significantly, moving away from the older generic 'types'. In that

---

[214] He is wearing it in ibid. nos. 8, 25, 30.

[215] Ibid. no. 1.

[216] Ibid. no. 2.

[217] Ibid. no. 1a. In some scenes (e.g. Sourvinou-Inwood 1986a: nos. 16, 17, 20, 21, 24) Charon is wearing a special type of rustic pilos, a very high variety which tends to give his head a rather strange 'alien' look, differentiating him even more sharply from normal Greek males.

[218] Though in a few cases he is not wearing an exomis or a rustic pilos even after the two had been established.

context, the desire to create a distinctive iconographical type for the old ferryman, in interaction with Charon's manual occupation, led to the representation of Charon with the dress which characterized those engaging in manual work. A factor in this choice may also have been the marginality of Charon, the frontier figure, since these clothes characterized especially marginal people. The exomis, though also worn by 'normal' central males on 'marginal occasions', characterized the slaves and the poor (and was also worn by women), and is opposed in iconography to the 'normal' male dress. The rustic pilos also characterized relatively marginal men of lowly occupations away from the polis. An additional contributory factor in this choice may have been the tendency to trivialize the representation of the shade's journey to Hades which, we saw, helped make Charon less frightening, thus reducing the anxiety of death.

A further series of choices led to the creation of the iconographical type of the ugly coarse Charon. Even after this creation the regular type continued to be used, sometimes by the same painters who elsewhere painted the ugly Charon. But this regular type, which had been previously neutral (in the sense that it was the obvious choice given the premise that Charon was perceived as a normal, non-monstrous, Greek male) inevitably acquired new meanings. For meanings are also determined by the relationship of the elements chosen to alternative elements which had been possible alternative choices and were not selected; thus the meanings of Charon's regular face were now also determined by its contrast to the coarse type and to whatever meanings were expressed in that type. The intermediate type acquired its meanings through its relationships to, and differentiation from, the other two types. Whatever may have been the impetus for the creation of the rougher iconographical type of Charon, even if it had been simply a further coarsening of the 'manual worker in exomis and rustic pilos' image, this type must have made sense in terms of contemporary perceptions of Charon. The fact that, as we saw, the three types of Charon face alternate, and the same painter may use any one of the three in different scenes, suggests that Charon's different faces do not correspond to different mythological perceptions of what he 'really looked like', that the ugliness and coarseness did not result from an attempt to represent Charon more realistically, to reproduce an established mental representation, a perception already articulated in literature or popular belief, but express some other perception pertaining to Charon. A series of further arguments will confirm that this is indeed the case. First, there is nothing in the surviving fifth-century literature to suggest that Charon was thought of as coarse-looking and ugly.[219] It is not until Theocritus that he is called grim; this is repeated in Latin texts which also describe him as ugly, a hideous old man, Charon with the frightful face.[220] Second, the lack of correlation between Charon's face and the type of scene, or the sex or age of the shade, shows that all types were appropriate to all types of scenes and of shades, and that therefore it is not a matter of easy simplistic divisions between Charon variants appropriate for different occasions. Finally, and most importantly, the fact that another figure intimately associated with death, Thanatos, whose face is usually of the 'normal' regular type, is sometimes also represented with a rough, ugly face[221] shows that this iconographical variation (the alternatives 'regular'/'coarse' face) pertains to, and is determined by, the semantic field of death. For while Thanatos' coarse face may have been based on Charon's, its selection would have been blocked if it had not been perceived as appropriate.

In order to recover the significance and meanings of these iconographical types of Charon we must first consider the significance of 'ugliness' and coarseness in fifth-century ceramic iconography. Both express negative connotations, a negative differentiation from the central 'norm', which characterized several conditions considered undesirable in contemporary mentality, such as old age, alienness and marginality, savagery. It is the context that tells us which of those negative connotations are expressed in the particular images. Another divine figure whose iconographical type in Attic ceramic iconography alternates, like Charon's, between the coarse, the normal, and the intermediate, is Boreas,[222] who, like Charon, is

[219] For the relevant literary sources cf. above and Sourvinou-Inwood 1986a: 210–12.

[220] Theocr. 16. 41; cf. also 17. 49. Cf. also: Verg. *Aen.* 6. 315; Tib. 1. 10. 36; Iuv. 3. 264–7; Apul. *Met.* 6. 18. Cf. also Sourvinou-Inwood 1986a: 210–12.

[221] Cf. e.g. for a face of the regular type the lekythos Athens CC 1654 (Bérard 1988: fig. 31.5); for a face of the rough type the lekythos London D 59 (*ARV* 851.272).

[222] Cf. e.g. for a rough and ugly Boreas the pointed amphora Munich 2345 (*ARV* 496.2; *Add.* 250); for Boreas with a regular face cf. e.g. the pelike in Rome, Villa Giulia (*ARV* 485.33; *Add.* 248); for an intermediary face cf. e.g. the oinochoe London BM E 512 (*ARV* 557.125; *Add.* 259). On Boreas cf. Kaempf-Dimitriadou 1979: 36–41 with bibliog. to which add Neuser 1982: 30–87.

sometimes shown with unkempt hair and beard, sometimes also a crooked nose, wrinkles, and overhanging brow. Boreas is a wild marginal god and has his unpleasant sides, but he was also benevolent and helpful towards the Athenians who instituted a cult to him in the fifth century to thank him for his help during the Persian Wars. In his case, then, the fluctuation between coarse, regular, and intermediate face relates to Boreas' ambivalent nature in the Athenian collective representations. Is the same true for Charon?

When we compare the images of Charon with the semantic field 'Charon' we find that the infernal ferryman's different faces do indeed correspond to an important aspect of his persona, his ambivalences. There are many dimensions of ambivalence in Charon. He is both the mythological ferryman who ferries the shades to their final destination in Hades and a metaphor for death. In his persona as helpful ferryman he is a reassuring image and a figure whose help and benevolence is sought. But at the same time he is ambivalent, for he effects the final passage into Hades and also guards the exit of Hades, and thus stands for the finality of death and the separation from life. Moreover, death itself is perceived as ambivalent. In so far as death is basically bad and frightening, the Greek images of death are negative. In so far as the Greek collective representations try to create reassuring images that allow the individuals to cope with death, and especially with the prospect of their own death, death also has a positive and kindly face. As we shall see in Chapter VI § ii.1*d*, death is sometimes represented as a deliverer from toil and pain. Moreover, there were certain models of good death constructed by official ideologies, such as that of death in battle in fifth-century Athens, in which death acquired a noble face, an image which inevitably also affected the general semantic field 'death'. Thus the different faces of Charon correspond to these ambivalences of Charon and of death.

Perhaps the development of Charon's ugly face and of his 'differentiated' iconography in general were made possible, and even encouraged, by the symbolic 'space' in which Charon was located: one of the semantic dimensions of his personality was his 'demonic' character, the fact that he was a marginal divine being who only existed at the frontier between the two worlds, a wilder, chthonic demonic, variant on the divine psychopompos Hermes Chthonios, situated in function, spatial location, and symbolic associations between Hermes and Cerberus.[223] The representation of Charon as banausic and ugly in a culture which values beauty very highly may at one level make him less frightening by devaluing him and in some sense trivializing him; trivialization, we saw, is one of the modes for making the awesome less frightening, and Charon was certainly one focus of the trivialization of the representations of the soul's journey to Hades. But at the same time, the differentiation from the ideal, and the ugliness, could have had—at least in some scenes—the effect of making Charon, and thus death, appear more sinister and frightening. All these facets, then, produced a complex play of signification in which Charon's face played an important part.

The different images of Charon in the different representations emphasize different aspects, are different articulations of his persona, which help articulate slightly different images of death, expressing or emphasizing different perceptions. The customer could take his choice. This interpretation of the different faces of Charon makes sense of the lack of correlation between the type of Charon's face and the type of scene or the sex or age of the shade. For all the images are possible ways of looking at Charon and death, and they pertain to everyone's encounter with the infernal ferryman, who, in these scenes, is always benevolent.

iii. *Shifting Attitudes and Eschatological Mythopoeia: The Emergence of Charon and Hermes Chthonios*

The differences between the Homeric representations of the transition to Hades and the ones involving Charon and Hermes that first appear in the archaic period correspond precisely to, and can be seen as particular manifestations of, the shift in the collective attitudes towards death which, we saw in Chapter IV, took place at that time. For one of the main aspects of this shift was the emergence (in certain circles) of a greater anxiety about one's own death and

---

[223] Cf. Rohde 1925: 237: in his function Charon is 'like a second Cerberus'. If my suggestion that the model 'older gods/monstrous beings in Tartaros' had a (limited) influence on Charon's creation is right, and if the similarity was 'heard' as part of Charon's persona, another whiff of the demonic may have become attached to him from that association.

the transition to the afterlife, which is the mirror-image of the reassuring representations which now fill the (elaborated) transition between life and death. The absence of details concerning the transition from life to death, which was adequate in the earlier nexus of attitudes, would contribute to the terror in the context of a more individual and anxious archaic visualization of one's own death; while in the new eschatology, Hermes Chthonios and Charon guide and support the shades during the (now more) awe-inspiring transition from life to death which is expanded and articulated in explicit familiar and reassuring terms. This correspondence between shifting attitudes and needs on the one hand, and the articulation of reassuring images on the other, the fact that the former is symbolically 'answered' by the latter, suggests that it was in the context of this shift in attitudes that the representations of death in which Hermes Chthonios and Charon function as psychopompoi was generated. The other trend in that shift that is relevant to the emergence of Charon and Hermes Chthonios is the desire to separate death more sharply from life; for it corresponds to the firmer, sharper and more secure, separation of the two worlds, separation between the two worlds involved in the eschatology in which Hermes and Charon are guarantors of the border between Hades and the upper world. Thus in this respect also, Hermes' and Charon's role can be seen as a manifestation of that general trend.

In these circumstances, it is clear that the eschatological changes involving Charon and Hermes correspond precisely to, and can be seen to be particular manifestations of, more general archaic trends, and to be fulfilling these new 'needs' which arose in the archaic period. Since the analyses pertaining to Charon and Hermes Chthonios were independent from this thesis of shifting attitudes,[224] the convergence of the results of the two sets of analyses provides, I suggest, some confirmation for the case put forward here.[225] This

---

[224] Some of my conclusions of the investigation of the emergence of Charon and Hermes Chthonios, reported very briefly in Sourvinou-Inwood 1981: 37–8 and Sourvinou-Inwood 1983: 46, were one very small part of the cumulative case I presented in favour of the thesis that a shift in attitudes took place; but there was no penetration of the argument in the other direction (from the shifting attitudes to the Charon and Hermes analyses), and thus no circularity.

[225] In theory, Charon's and Hermes' functions could have been the result of later change and reinterpretation; on this theory the fact that their emergence makes perfect sense as a response to the archaic shift of attitudes towards death would not necessarily entail that this

convergence offers a strong argument for concluding that it was this shift in attitudes that generated the conceptual framework in which took place the transformation of the earlier representations of the shades' journey to Hades; that in this context Hermes the divine crosser of borders assumed the role of guide of the shades to Hades, an articulation subsequently expanded further to include Charon, who played the role of a ferryman under the inspiration of the opportunity offered by the water-frontier, probably in conjunction with the model of an Oriental ferryman of the dead.[226]

My interpretation of the emergence of Charon and Hermes as psychopompoi, I submit, makes sense of all the data, including the pattern of their presences and absences in early texts. Different explanations can be offered—though less convincingly—to account for different sets of data. But, I submit, my interpretation makes sense of all the data and integrates them satisfactorily in the wider framework of Greek funerary ideology.

It may be asked, did the Greeks really believe that after their death they would go to Hades and Charon would ferry them there? Or was this 'just' a myth? In my view, the dichotomy 'belief'/'not belief' is culturally determined and misleading; more complex and ambivalent categories are needed.[227] The balance may have varied between different sections of society; but what is graspable[228] in this case is that the fifth-century Athenians—or at least a large section of them—believed in Charon in so far as this was a way of thinking

is the time at which they emerged. But the convergence of so many different sets of factors (the chronological pattern of appearance, the relationship of Hermes the guide of the souls and his wand to the Homeric Hermes and his wand, the pattern of the elaboration of the journey to Hades, the correlation between the appearance of Hermes as psychopompos and Charon and the lapsing of the 'rules' that unburied shades cannot enter Hades and that the shades, once in Hades, can never return to the upper world), when taken in conjunction with the perfect fit between the archaic shifting attitudes and the eschatology involving Charon and Hermes Chthonios, put this theoretical possibility beyond the bounds of even remote plausibility.

[226] It cannot be excluded that another, different, model may also have helped shape the new representations of the shade's journey and integration into Hades (in the context of the shift in attitudes): the institutionalization and greater structuring of life and society in the context of the polis. It is conceivable that behind Charon and Hermes we should also see the model of the magistrates presiding over the transition from one world to the other and safeguarding the separation between the two (and thus the cosmic order of which this separation is part) more securely than had been the case before.

[227] Aspects of the notions of 'truth' of, and 'belief' in, Greek myths are investigated in Veyne 1983: *passim*.

[228] It is a difficult enough question to answer whether Christians today (and which ones, other than fundamentalists) 'believe' in all aspects of Christian eschatology.

about life after death and the transition from life to death. For his appearance on the most important body of Athenian images of death (strictly speaking outside, but, we saw, not beyond, official polis ideology), and, even more strikingly, the fact that he is never associated with adult males, shows clearly that this figure had a very significant symbolic potency.

We may conclude that we have also found support for the view that the pattern of appearance in the surviving texts of this set of beliefs does correspond to the ancient realities; this shows that in this case (as, I believe, in all cases) poetic creativity and mythopoeia operate under the determining influence of the parameters formed by the society's beliefs, which interacted with a shifting ideology and collective attitudes. Thus privileging the doubting of the notion that our texts give us an approximation of the true picture is fallacious—though it appears deceptively rigorous, for the receptive bias of modern scholars favours the sceptical and the negatively formulated, even when, as here, scepticism masks a culturally determined manipulation of the data, which ignores the modalities of interaction between poetic creativity and established beliefs and collective representations and attitudes. Despite many scholars' gut feelings, not all scepticism, I suggest, is epistemologically healthy.

iv. *Other Views on Charon: A Critique*

Furtwängler[229] argued that Charon belongs to a primitive and genuinely popular complex of beliefs, despite his somewhat late appearance, his lack of genealogical connections, and the comparatively late advent of Charon's fees in graves[230]—a combination of circumstances which can more plausibly be interpreted as indicating that Charon was an archaic literary invention. It was precisely those considerations that had led Wilamowitz to suggest[231] that Charon had been invented by the author of the *Minyas*.[232] We cannot

---

[229] Furtwängler, 1905: 198–9.
[230] Kurtz and Boardman 1971: 166, 211, 216, 331, cf. also 204. On Charon's fees cf. also Rohde 1925: 237 and 245–6, n. 9; Waser 1898: 30–9; Garland 1985: 23. Cf. now esp. Stevens 1991: 215–29.
[231] Wilamowitz 1899: 166, 211, 227–30.
[232] Rohde also considered Charon an archaic literary invention (1925: 237).

determine whether Wilamowitz's guess is correct though we have found strong reasons for thinking that Charon was indeed an archaic 'invention'. But Furtwängler's case is far from compelling, even if we leave aside the positive arguments that lead to the opposite conclusion. He is right that in the surviving verses of the *Minyas* Charon is referred to in a manner suggesting that the public was already familiar with the figure, but this would only indicate that he had been invented before the *Minyas*, not that he was an old god; indeed, it cannot even be excluded that he had been invented by the poet of the *Minyas*, who had already described him earlier on in the poem.

Lawson suggested[233] that Charon was an old god because Hesychius calls him Akmonides, which, he thought, shows that Charon was earlier than Zeus by two generations, and that he had been the god of death 'among the old Pelasgian population of Greece'. As we saw, the ascription of the designation Akmonides to Charon is not absolutely certain; and if the designation does indeed belong to Charon it may be reflecting a genealogy modelled on that of the older gods because the latter may have helped shape the figure of Charon. Most importantly, the fundamental fallacy at the centre of this theory is that it relies on the mistaken assumption that the gods that are presented as pre-Olympian in the theology of historical Greece were gods who had been worshipped in an earlier historical period, that earlier divine generations represent earlier stages in Greek religion. I have discussed elsewhere[234] the fallaciousness of the assumption that myth reflects, and can be explained as and retranslated to, cultic history, and that succession myths reflect different stages of cultic history. Though such notions are now discredited, some theories that are based on them remain accepted without regard to their dependence on invalid presuppositions. A substantial part of Lawson's case and of those who follow him is based on an error: contrary to the assertion that lies at the centre of that case, there is no distinction between on the one hand Charon's conception in classical literature and art and on the other his identification with death. Lawson[235] failed to see that Charon's identification with death, which he perceived in expres-

[233] Lawson 1910: 116.
[234] Sourvinou-Inwood 1991: 217–43.
[235] Lawson 1910: 114, 116.

sions like *Charoneios thyra*[236] or *Charoneion*,[237] was the result of the development of the metaphor in which he was implicated, and thought that this identification was a popular belief, different from his conception in literature and art. While in reality, we saw, we can follow up the development of the metaphor in classical literature and art. On this false distinction was built the persona of Charon the old popular god.

The theory under discussion relies also on another discredited notion, that older popular figures were suppressed by certain poets, most notably Homer. Terpening[238] exemplifies this type of argument. He asserts[239] 'let me state that the fact that Homer does not mention Charon does not imply the late addition of the boatman to the pantheon of minor Greek gods'.[240] The argument on which he bases this assertion is that 'there are many ancient mythological figures and stories that find no place' in the Homeric poems. He cites as examples Herakles' labours other than the Cerberus adventure and additional features of other myths. This shows the confusion of categories involved in arguments of this kind. The selection of certain myths and certain versions and aspects of those myths is a very different thing from the omission of the two psychopompoi, whose presence or absence involves important eschatological differences. Even leaving aside the ways in which the creativity of a poet is shaped by the parameters of the established beliefs of his society, the notion that Charon, 'as part of folklore', 'may have been avoided as too common' first relies on the culturally determined notion, which is irrelevant to the circumstances of religious development in Dark-Age and eighth-century Greece, that Homer's pantheon is pure, noble, and lofty; it also involves crude distinctions like folklore and not-folklore, which are never explained but taken for granted and form the basis for making sense of the complex religious representations of early Greece.

Alexiou acknowledges that Charon's 'only claim to pre-Olympian antiquity is the epithet Akmonides' and then proceeds to put forward some further arguments in favour of this view. I have

---

[236] Suda s.v.

[237] Pollux 8. 102.

[238] Terpening 1985: 34–5.

[239] Ibid. 34.

[240] His credibility is not enhanced by his belief (Terpening 1985: 34) that in the *Iliad* Thanatos and Hypnos 'guided the soul from the living to the dead'.

considered this central argument and demonstrated, I hope, its fallacy. I shall now consider the rest of her case. She suggests that the following arguments offer support for the view that Charon was an older popular god ousted by Hades, suppressed by Homer and surviving in popular belief until he re-emerged, relegated to the role of ferryman. First, in her view, Charon's name, which she thinks is cognate with *charopos*, involves 'a reference to flashing eyes or fierce looks which do not seem compatible with the elderly ferryman of classical drama'. Whether or not this etymology is correct, Alexiou's judgement about compatibility is mistaken. Not only is it not the case that if one is an elderly ferryman one cannot have flashing eyes and fiery looks, but also and most importantly, Charon's anger, we saw, was a topos in literature, and, of course, anger and flashing eyes and fiery looks are correlative. Obviously, which aspect of Charon will be stressed in any particular (textual or iconographical) articulation depends on the particular choices in the particular context; contexts conducive to a reassuring presentation of Charon, discussed above, will not generally stress the more scary part of his persona that would be involved in the flashing eyes and fiery looks. It is their monosemic expectations that have led modern scholars to hive off the differently emphasized articulations of the complex nexus that was a mythological figure, and create separate phantom figures; their 'logical' culturally determined preconceptions prevented them from realizing that both were aspects of a complex and ambivalent nexus, and that in certain contexts one or the other aspect may be emphasized in a polarized manner.

A second hiving off of Charon, based on Alexiou's, is focused on the differences between the images in which Charon has a normal regular face and those in which he has an ugly coarse face. A version of the latter, not located primarily in the lekythoi images, has been made the pivot for this operation. Hoffmann argued[241] that the opposition between the regular-faced Charon and the figure on a head-vase[242] representing an old man whom Hoffmann identified as Charos[243] (rather than the opposition between the

[241] Hoffmann 1984: 65–9; 1986: 173–204, cf. esp. 179–80.

[242] Head-vase, from Spina, Ferrara Museo archeologico Nazionale Inv. 20401 (Hoffmann 1984: 66, figs. 1–3; 1986: fig. 8).

[243] As well as some other images, which in fact represent Thanatos, through the same iconographical schema as unambiguous Thanatos representations and in activities that are

regular- versus the coarse-faced Charon on the lekythoi), corresponds to two different mythological figures; for he believes that
the modern Greek Charos had existed in classical Greece and that
Charon is his tamed version. His starting point is Alexiou's thesis
about an old popular Charon, and in so far as that thesis is invalid—
which is what I have tried to demonstrate—so is Hoffmann's. But
the latter is also invalid on other grounds. On the lekythoi there is,
we saw, an opposition between a regular- and a coarse-faced
Charon, an opposition which Hoffmann plays down considerably;
if his thesis were right, this opposition on the lekythoi would have
been reflecting the two figures, Charos and Charon, in which case
we would have expected the two types to have involved two, starkly
differentiated, types of Charon and of images. In reality the opposite
is the case; first, there is no correlation between type of scene and
type of Charon, and second, the two iconographical types are at
two ends of a spectrum which includes intermediate types of
faces, which is incompatible with Hoffmann's thesis, while it fits
precisely the interpretation suggested above. Another argument
against Hoffmann's thesis is that, as we saw, exactly the same
spectrum of regular *versus* ugly is seen in the representation of
another figure with whom Charon is semantically comparable—
Boreas—even if we leave aside Thanatos, to avoid the circularity
implicated in Hoffmann's argument. Hoffmann is not exactly
wrong, he is mythologizing, he is telling the story of Charon's
ambivalence and complexity in terms of modern rationalizing
schemata.

Alexiou mentions Charon's wider association with death, but
admits that it is not legitimate to use evidence from late antiquity,
when the distinctions between Charon, Hades, and Thanatos were
no longer clear-cut, to support the theory that pre-classical antiquity
knew a Charon radically different from the ferryman figure.[244]

---

unambiguously associated with Thanatos; but this interpretation does not suit Hoffmann's
perception of Thanatos, and especially it does not fit his expectation that the fact that often
Thanatos is represented idealized entails that he cannot be depicted also as ugly. Thus,
the implicit assumption—that there cannot be figures whose iconography includes differently emphasized articulations—becomes the basis for constructing a different Thanatos
as well as a different Charon, and the former is deployed in support of the validity of the
latter.

[244] She correctly saw (Alexiou 1978: 221, 224–5) that in the modern Greek Charos are
conflated elements from both Charon and Thanatos: some of Charos' traits in ancient Greece
had pertained to Charon and some to Thanatos.

Indeed, as we saw,[245] the nature of religious development makes it illegitimate to project data from a later period into an earlier one, and should also induce caution against using aspects of the Etruscan Charun and the modern Greek Charos as evidence for the archaic and classical Charon. In this particular case, we saw, we can follow some of the stages of the relevant development in the surviving sources.

[245] In Ch. II § ii.2c.

VI.

Reading (Death) Otherwise:
The Case Study of an Archaic Epigram

---

i. The First and Second Reading Narratives

1. READING OTHERWISE

We saw in Chapter III §§ ii.2a and ii.3 that an archaic epigram from Teithronion in Phokis, if it was (as has been generally assumed) truly an epitaph, would constitute a unique exception to an otherwise consistent pattern of appearance, in epitaphs and elsewhere, of two important elements: the naming of the grave monument and the salutation *chaire* addressed to the dead. This epigram, of *c.*500 BC,[1] is inscribed on a limestone stele and is now in the Chaironeia Museum. The text is an elegiac couplet:

χαῖρε Χάρον. οὐδ⟨ε⟩ίς τυ κακὸς λέγει οὐδὲ θανόντα
πολὸς ἀνθρόπον λυσάμενος καμάτο.

The segment of the stone carrying the sigma at the end of *kakos* is now missing. The stele was first published by Klaffenbach.[2] According to the orthodox interpretation it is an epitaph for a doctor called Charon.[3] I hope to show that, for a series of strong independent reasons, this epigram cannot have been an archaic epitaph. If it were

---

[1] Jeffery 1990: 103 (on no. 11), followed by Hansen (1983: on no. 127) writes '500?'. This slight uncertainty does not affect my case, since even if the date is not exactly 500 it is very close to it, and this is the important point for our purposes; for the relevant changes do not take place until considerably later.

[2] Klaffenbach 1935: 702. Other publications: *GV* 1384; Peek 1960: 41; Pfohl 1967a: 146; Friedländer and Hoffleit 1948: 86; Jeffery 1990: 102, 103 no. 11, 403 pl. 13, pl. 13 no. 11; Hansen 1983: 127; 1989: p. 301. Hansen emends *lysameno⟨n⟩*.

[3] *Opp. citt.* (cf. references to the publications of the inscription in the previous paragraph). Cf. also Lattimore 1962: 287. There is, of course, no difficulty about the name Charon, which is known as a human proper name from other early contexts.

an epitaph every single one of its elements would be seriously and independently anomalous, with some of the anomalies involving serious conflict with the established attitudes, which would have blocked, for the archaic reader, the option to read it as an epitaph—even if we assume that it was conceivable for an archaic epitaph writer to compose it as such. In theory it could be argued that divergences do not prove that the epigram is not an epitaph, for it could have been an exceptional, aberrant, specimen, the product of local fashion; it is, after all, the only known archaic Phokian funerary epigram.[4] However, this hypothesis cannot stand. Not only is it the case that in the archaic period local fashions would not seem significantly to affect funerary epigrams, the character and style of which is international rather than determined by local peculiarities;[5] but also, and most importantly, it became clear in Chapter III that this is a highly codified genre whose codifications are motivated by important social attitudes.[6] The Teithronion epigram clashes with these attitudes, both by omission and by commission. Its divergences from the highly codified patterns, and, especially, its clash with the attitudes expressed in these patterns, place it outside the corpus of archaic epitaphs. The ideological conflict between the attitudes the epigram would have been expressing if it were an epitaph and the readers' attitudes made it, we shall see, impossible for it to function in that capacity. In Section ii of this chapter I will try to read this epigram through perceptual filters shaped by its society's assumptions and reconstruct the ways in which its contemporaries would have read it. Besides the importance of understanding that this epigram is not an exception to the patterns set out above, this investigation will also illustrate various important aspects of the Problematik of reading ancient texts. Because it is a short and simple text, but one to which the accident of time has given certain peculiarities, this epigram lends itself excellently to the role of case study, in which the mechanics of the traditional reading strategies applied to classical texts can be revealed; also, both the methods and the problems which preoccupy modern literary theory, especially reader-oriented criticism, can be observed

---

[4] The epigram Hansen 1983: no. 151, of the early 5th cent., is the epitaph of a *theoros* who died at Delphi.

[5] Cf. Wallace 1970: 97. The decision as to whether to have a verse epigram at all was influenced by local fashion (op. cit.).

[6] On the selectivity peculiar to each genre cf. Jauss 1974b: 224.

at their most elementary level of operation. For in this section I am trying to decode the text's elementary, determinate meanings,[7] to determine whether it functioned as an epitaph or as something else, and if so what? This 'reading story' can help ground some aspects of reader-oriented criticism somewhat more securely than do discourses pertaining to more complex texts and less elementary operations, involving complex, ambiguous and ambivalent meanings. What happens here openly and starkly, at the level of elementary decoding, may happen more subtly to other ancient texts, at higher levels of the reading operations.

I am setting out three reading narratives. First, the narrative pertaining to the orthodox reading of the epigram as an epitaph, which, I will try to show, is based on the implicit deployment of assumptions alien to those of *c.*500 BC Greece, the appropriateness of which has not been questioned because they were unconscious and had implicitly determined the perception of what constituted a 'reasonable' interpretation of the epigram. I argue that this reading is untenable; this is the second narrative, which is intertwined with the first in presentation, and which will show that the epigram could not have been conceived, or functioned, as an epitaph in the archaic period. The third narrative involves the attempt to reconstruct the meanings which the epigram's author had inscribed into the text and his contemporaries 'extracted' from it. I will argue that the reconstruction of the ancient reading process shows that the archaic reader would have inescapably been 'forced' to identify the epigram as not an epitaph, but as something else.

We saw in Chapter I that there is no linear progression from elementary to higher levels of reading operations, but a continuous coming and going between the different levels. In the realm that concerns us most directly here, that of epigraphy, Daux[8] has shown how the epigraphists' expectations when reading an inscription affect the actual reading of the stone as well as the articulation of the letters into words, because they are unconsciously guided by hypotheses formed while they are visually 'registering', perceiving an inscription, especially a badly preserved one. The fact that the formulation of hypotheses concerning higher levels affects the

---

[7] On determinate and non-determinate meanings see Culler 1983: 76 n. 12, 130.
[8] Daux 1971: 4–5.

decoding strategies at the lower levels is important for the reading of our epigram. For the circumstances of utterance, the context, is an important factor directing the formulation of the presuppositions which direct the decoding operations at the lower level. In our case that context, the stele's setting and function, is lost; we are thus missing a set of parameters that would have directed the text's reading by its contemporaries, and we must try to limit the potentially corrupting effect of this absence. We can only recover the missing contextual information by trying to reconstruct the meanings the epigram had for its contemporaries; despite the limitations of access, at the end of a proper reading the function and setting of the epigram should emerge and compel themselves upon us. But we must not allow any prior hypotheses to affect our reading; with a text of this kind, which does not slot unambiguously and without complications into a well-defined series, which does not belong to the standard form of a genre and does not incorporate a standard identifying formula, this would be especially dangerous methodologically. Any reading that starts with an intuitively formed hypothesis based on implicit comparisons to implicit models brings into the reading of the text prior (and possibly fallacious) assumptions, and distorts the evidence by implicitly organizing it around that already formulated central hypothesis, and so implicitly forcing it into a preconceived mould, so that the argument becomes self-validating. To put it crudely, if we ask 'What does this Telchronion epitaph mean?', we may be able to give an apparently satisfactory answer, but this answer will not necessarily correspond to the ancient reality. For the question was loaded and the (intuitively formulated) central hypothesis had determined the structuring of the evidence and the dominant direction of the investigation; it imposed certain selections and certain preconceived hierarchical patterns; thus, the enquiry was contaminated by the original hypothesis the validity of which one should have been testing in the first place. If we ask 'How can we explain this or that anomaly in this funerary epigram?' it is possible to give answers of the type 'exceptions/local peculiarities are always possible' which, though they can be shown to be improbable, cannot be conclusively disproved; for if it is difficult to prove a negative of any kind, it is especially so when that negative pertains to a society to which we have limited access. Thus, because the initial hypothesis is unconsciously taken to have established an implicit presumption that, unless it can be disproved, it is valid, this inability to disprove it conclusively is (implicitly or explicitly) taken to entail that the hypothesis is right.

In the case of our epigram, we shall see, when it is approached without any prior ideas about its character and meanings, and its elements read as much through the eyes of the archaic readers as possible, a very different interpretation from the orthodox one will emerge, in which all the elements fall naturally into place, and there is no need to allow for a series of (unrelated) anomalies, which can only be accounted for through a series of special pleadings, which only appeared convincing because the discourse had been centred on, and corrupted by, the initial hypothesis the validity of which should have been properly investigated. The fact that, we saw, a basic tendency in the cultural determination of perception is that selections favour what is familiar in the perceiver's tradition can provide the explanatory framework for the production of the orthodox reading of the Teithronion epigram: a text which (if I am right) belongs to a very rare type, of which we do not have other specimens (though the genre to which it would belong is common) was assimilated, through the activation of certain intertextual frames, to a well-established type—funerary epigrams functioning as epitaphs which address the deceased—despite the fact that a detailed analysis would have shown that it could not possibly have belonged to that type.

Archaic epitaphs, we saw, reflected the established, above all aristocratic, attitudes towards death and the dead. I will try to show that, if our epigram were an epitaph, it would have been in conflict with those attitudes, and with the common core of archaic funerary ideology, while at the same time soliciting, like all archaic epitaphs, the co-operation of its contemporary readers. Thus it could not have functioned as an epitaph; the serious discrepancies between its world and that of contemporary social reality would make it impossible for archaic readers to have read it as an epitaph, any more than it would have been possible for an archaic writer to have composed it as an epitaph. The reader's ideological bias, we saw, determines his perception of the text's ideological structures. Eco[9] brings an example from Ian Fleming's spy-stories which is especially illuminating: 'A reader of Fleming's stories who shares the ideo-

[9] Eco 1981: 22.

logical judgements expressed by the text at the level of discoursive structures is probably not eager to look for an underlying ideological scaffolding at a more abstract level; on the contrary, a reader who challenges many of the author's explicit value judgements is inclined to go further with an ideological analysis so as to "unmask" the hidden catechization performed at more profound levels.' Exactly the same thing happened with the Teithronion epigram. Because the ideological attitude underlying, for example, the notion that an epitaph can state 'nobody speaks ill of you even though you are dead'—that is, that it is normal (if, presumably, reprehensible) to speak ill of the dead—is not shocking in our own society, the modern readers did not conduct an ideological analysis which would have brought out the implied attitude towards the dead, and compared it to the archaic ideology, which would have revealed fundamental discrepancies and led to the questioning of the interpretation of the epigram as an epitaph.

The epitaph interpretation was (implicitly or explicitly) supported and sustained through comparisons to other superficially similar epitaphs, especially some post-classical doctors' epitaphs, which functioned as validating models for the interpretation of the Teithronion epigram as a doctor's epitaph. Of course, those reading operations are in conflict with the principle that it is illegitimate to use later inscriptions to help illuminate those of an earlier period,[10] especially since, we saw, formulations are motivated not just by fashion, but also by social attitudes and beliefs. Since meaning is ascribed in context,[11] the fact that attitudes changed entails that, even if an archaic epigram contains a formulation which appears to be similar to that of a Hellenistic epitaph, the two must not be assumed to be saying the same thing. Similarity has to be proved, through detailed analyses that take account first, of the whole text, not simply its isolated segments; and second, of the whole nexus of ideas and attitudes which gave meaning to each grave inscription, ascribed it value in its own age. In any case, the assumption of continuity is dangerous. For if it is fallacious it will inevitably distort the picture. Whereas not to assume continuity, but investigate whether or not, and where and to what degree there was any, is a

[10] Cf. e.g. Daux 1973: 251.
[11] Cf. Sourvinou-Inwood 1991: 3–23 *passim* with bibliog.

bias-free approach which does not contaminate the investigation with preconceived notions.

The orthodox interpretation of the Teithronion epigram relies on a grammatical decoding which appears to compel itself on us. However, as I will try to show, this was not necessarily the grammatical decoding that compelled itself upon the archaic readers. Grammatical analysis can never be entirely insulated from cultural assumptions, and I will argue that the 'obvious' grammatical decoding was not an option open to the archaic readers. The focus on the archaic readers helps dispose of a possible objection to my argument: what, it may be asked, if some odd person did compose this epigram as an epitaph, and did not care about the absence of social sanction and co-operation? I will leave aside the implausibility of such a state of affairs and imagine that the Teithronion epigram had indeed been conceived as an epitaph and set over a grave. Given that, as I hope to show, the archaic readers' assumptions excluded the possibility of their reading it as an epitaph, and inescapably led them to make sense of it as something else, which was in fact perfectly appropriate for a grave, we are still left with something that functioned not as an epitaph addressing the deceased, but something else, and the hypothesis that it could have been an epitaph can be seen to be untenable.

2. THE USE OF *CHAIRE*

The epigram begins with the salutation *chaire Charon*. On the orthodox interpretation the person addressed is a dead man called Charon. This reading depends on the activation of the wrong intertextual frame, '*chaire* addressed to the deceased', which was common in much later epitaphs, but which was inappropriate here. I hope to have shown in Chapter III § ii.3 that no archaic writer could have addressed a dead person with *chaire*, especially in an epitaph, and no archaic reader would have been capable of taking *chaire Charon* to be addressed to a dead person; even if the stele had stood over a grave their assumptions would have blocked that possibility.[12] *Chaire*, we saw, was (until the early fourth century) associated on the one hand with life and on the other with dead

---

[12] The interpretation I will be proposing would be valid, even if the stele had stood over a grave.

people of special status, in sharp contrast to the ordinary dead. Sectarian beliefs are not reflected in archaic epitaphs, but in any case, by no stretch of the imagination can our epigram be taken to be connected with heroization/immortality; on the epitaph interpretation itself it functions entirely at the level of everyday mundane reality. Thus it cannot be said to be addressing the deceased with *chaire* in the context of a heroization/deification ideology. Since attitudes towards the dead in the archaic epitaphs involve pity and sorrow, even leaving aside the connection of *chaire* with dead people of special status, the dead of the archaic epitaphs are not, in any case, appropriate recipients of the salutation *chaire* which included the wish 'rejoice', and no archaic reader would have understood it to be a salutation to a dead person. Even if the alternative addressee had not been obvious (and I will argue that he was) the fact that he was addressed with *chaire* would, I submit, have led an archaic reader to place him either among the living, or on a higher, heroic, demonic, or divine, plane.

3. NOT SPEAKING ILL OF THE DEAD?

If the Teithronion epigram were an epitaph, *oud⟨e⟩is ty kakos legei oude thanonta* would be praise for a dead doctor Charon. We shall see in § 4 that as an expression of praise this would be unparalleled among archaic epitaphs both in content and in form, and in § 5 that it would also be unparalleled among the expressions of praise for doctors in archaic and classical epitaphs. Here I will disregard all this, for I want to keep the different parts of my argument separate, and try to show that there is another fundamental objection against the view that this could be an expression of praise for a dead man.

The formulation could only have functioned as praise if in that society it was exceptional for people not to be spoken ill of after their death. Only then this would have been worthy of being recorded as praise in an epitaph; also, the structure of the expression, and in particular *oude*, raises expectations of exceptionality and/or unexpectedness. Thus, this formulation could only have functioned as praise if it was the normal practice, and was accepted to be the normal practice, in archaic Greece, for people to speak ill of the dead; especially since the values of archaic epitaphs were the established values of (aristocratic) society, and they represented the dead and the relationship between the dead and the living in an idealized light.[13] It might be argued that, while it is true that archaic epitaphs expressed the accepted social attitudes, this particular one was an exception which put things bluntly, as they really were. However, we saw, the notion of an epitaph which clashes with the norms, the assumptions by means of which epitaphs communicated with the living to ensure co-operation in activating the deceased's memory, is, at this time at least, untenable; no archaic epitaph writer could have composed such a formulation, or assuming that it had been possible for him to do so, would have sanctioned its use and persuaded the deceased's relatives to accept it. Thus, if speaking ill of the dead was not the accepted norm, if, on the contrary, it was prescribed that one must *not* do so, this epigram would be representing as praise what was no more than the prescribed attitude towards all the dead. This epigram could not have functioned as an epitaph. Whether the prescribed behaviour was actually followed in practice is irrelevant. I will now try to show that it was indeed the prescribed ethos in archaic Greece not to speak ill of the dead.

The legislation attributed to Solon (Plutarch, *Solon* 21. 1–2) forbade *ton tethnekota kakos agoreuein*. Plutarch presents this interdiction as laudable and lauded. But can we apply this evidence to the rest of the archaic Greece? I believe that we can. For the interdiction can be seen as part of the general phenomenon of increased concern with the positive survival of the deceased's memory in the archaic period discussed in Chapter III § ii.6. Or is this a culturally determined reading? The context of the legislation suggests that it is not. I mention Solonian and other archaic funerary legislation in the Appendix § 5 and suggest that it was responding to the shifts in the attitudes towards death which involved on the one hand the desire to distance oneself from death's physical reality, and on the other enhanced concern for the survival of one's memory. Certainly, Solon's legislation coincided with a striking increase in expenditure on grave monuments.[14] Thus the prescription not to speak ill of the dead can be seen to have been part of the new 'code' of relationships between the living and the dead, created when the old funerary system came under pressure from new attitudes and needs which it could not effectively fulfil. The

[13] Cf. above Ch. III § ii.2; cf. Lattimore 1962: 275; Pircher 1979: 11; Stupperich 1977: 67; cf. also Labarbe 1968: 331–5.
[14] Snodgrass 1980: 146.

tensions that necessitated funerary legislation of this kind were not
absent from Phokis, at least from the Delphic polis, since the phratry
of the Labyadai issued funerary regulations of precisely this type.[15]
Since (irrespectively of the question of the motivation of the funerary legislation) the interdiction against speaking ill of the dead seems
to have been part of the nexus of attitudes and responses to which
the archaic inscribed grave monument also belonged, we are jus-
tified in taking it as expressing attitudes that were widespread in the
archaic period in the circles that made use of the inscribed grave
monument, and not limited to Athens. Two fragments of Archilochos help enlarge the geographical context of the prescription and
thus offer further evidence in favour of this view. Fr. 134 West:

> οὐ γὰρ ἐσθλὰ κατθανοῦσι κερτομεῖν ἐπ' ἀνδράσιν

Related to this in meaning is fr. 133 West:[16]

> οὔτις αἰδοῖος μετ' ἀστῶν οὐδὲ περίφημος θανὼν
> γίνεται· χάριν δὲ μᾶλλον τοῦ ζοοῦ διώκομεν
> ⟨οἱ⟩ ζοοί, κάκιστα δ' αἰεὶ τῷ θανόντι γίνεται

These fragments can be considered the counterpart of the Solonian
prescription.[17] They testify to a certain indifference, in practice,
towards the memory of the dead,[18] which generates anxiety and
disapproval even from Archilochos, who was otherwise prepared to
take[19] a somewhat detached and rationalizing approach to grief and
mourning.[20] Thus, speaking ill of the dead, the negative presentation
of the memory of the dead, goes beyond even the challenges to the
accepted attitudes offered in archaic literature. While Semonides[21]
could say *tou men thanontos ouk an enthymoimetha, ei ti phronoimen,*

---

[15] *LSCG* no. 77; Rougemont 1977: no. 9, pp. 26–85, esp. 51–7. The surviving inscription
was inscribed in the late 5th cent., but at least part of it reflects earlier legislation (cf.
Rougemont 1974, 147–58, esp. 154; Rougemont 1977: 86–90). The case against the notion
that it was normal to speak ill of the dead does not depend on the validity of the proposed
shift in the archaic attitudes to death. The latter only provides the wider framework, and so
inevitably strengthens the case for thinking that the prescription was important, but that is all.

[16] On fr. 133 West cf. Lloyd-Jones 1971: 39

[17] Cf. also Stesichorus fr. 68 (*PMG* fr. 245; fr. 245 Davies), and cf. appar. crit. Compare
Eur. fr. 736N2

[18] A related, though not the same, idea, also pertaining to the 'failure of obligations' of
the living towards the dead in [Theogn.] 931–2.

[19] Cf. frs. 11 and 13 West.

[20] Cf. Sourvinou-Inwood 1983: 46.

[21] Fr. 2 Lloyd-Jones.

pleion emeres mies, speaking ill of the dead is never mentioned except to be castigated.

In these circumstances, the notion that the expression *oud⟨e⟩is ty kakos legei oude thanonta* was part of an archaic epitaph, an expression of praise for a dead man, proves to be untenable, and with it the view that the Teithronion epigram is an epitaph, which depends on it.[22]

4. PRAISE FOR THE DEAD

In Chapter III § ii.2*b* we surveyed the themes of praise of the dead on archaic epitaphs. Here I shall compare the alleged praise formulation *oud⟨e⟩is ty kakos legei oude thanonta* to the praise formulations in these epitaphs, and show that, even if we disregard the argument set out above in § 3, as an expression of praise the formulation is both unparalleled and odd. It diverges from the basic form in which praise is expressed in archaic epitaphs and also from the formulations pertaining to the theme to which *oud⟨e⟩is ty* etc. would have to belong if it were an expression of praise for a dead man, the theme that makes a (positive) statement about the deceased's reputation, not only in life and at the moment of his death, but by extension also after his death. This theme is extremely rare in archaic epitaphs. I know of only two instances. First, in the epigram for Alkimachos, from Athens[23] the deceased is told *eudochson se ch[yte k]ata gai' ekalyphsen . . .*, and then follow other, more usual epithets of praise. Second, in the epigram for Deines, from

---

[22] Friedländer and Hoffleit 1948: p. 89 quote both Solon's law and Archilochos fr. 134 in their comm. on the Teithronion epigram, but they miss the point that both testify to a prescribed attitude. Gentili (1968: 56) mentions 'l'accenno a un antico costume che vietava di parlar male dei morti' (and quotes *Od.* 22. 412 as well as Archilochos) but also misses the point that it is precisely because this is an established custom that it cannot function as a formulation of praise in an epitaph. On the Archilochos fragment and Solon's law, and the way they relate to the epitaphs cf. also, briefly, but on the right lines: Stecher 1981: 5. On the prohibition to speak ill of the dead cf. also Blech 1982: 98. The importance of the injunction not to speak ill of the dead in archaic funerary ideology also excludes the possibility that this could have been some kind of 'joke'. The 'joke' hypothesis is also invalidated by the nature of archaic funerary epigrams, and, most importantly, by the fact that, if the first verse of the Teithronion epigram had contained two jokes (the other being addressing the hypothetical dead doctor Charon with 'chaire') it would have clashed violently with the unambiguous seriousness, the sombre mood, of the second verse.

[23] Hansen 1983: 69; Willemsen 1963: 145–7 no. 12 pl. 61.

Apollonia on the Black Sea,[24] where *[d]okimotatos astoy is followed by ke⟨i⟩tai amometos terma la[ch]on thanato.* In these two formulations the positive nature of the reputation of the deceased is expressed in emphatic, and positive, terms: *eudochsos, dokimotatos astoy.* If the Teithronion expression is taken as praise its reference to the deceased's reputation would be neither positive, nor emphatic, it would be an absence of bad reputation rather than the affirmation of a good one. And this is unparalleled in any form. The negative formulation of the alleged praise diverges not only from statements about the deceased's reputation, but also from the basic form in which praise in general is expressed in archaic epitaphs. For in these epitaphs negative formulations are only used in order to describe something in which the deceased had the active role, and the negative formulation is used to express some positive quality possessed, or action taken, by the deceased. *Amometos,* in the epigram just mentioned, ascribes the normal kind of praise to Deines, by describing one of his virtues: he was blameless, his behaviour was unblem ished, it did not give rise to censure. This is a quality pertaining to the deceased in life, it does not describe the attitudes of others to wards his memory. This is made clear by the word itself and also by the whole expression, *amometos terma lachon thanato.* It does not pro vide a parallel for the Teithronion formulation. Another example is found in the epigram for Pyrrhiadas:[25] *hos ouk epistato pheugen.* I should note, to show the tenacity of the form, that this type of for mulation is quite frequently found in classical funerary epigrams, where they are also only used when the deceased had the active role.[26]

The praise that would be contained in *oud⟨e⟩is ty* etc. (if we disregard its clash with the established mentality discussed in § 3 above) would in any case be far too weak to count as praise when compared to the established archaic Greek topoi expressing the concept of good reputation as we can glimpse them in the epitaphs,

[24] Hansen 1983: 172; Jeffery 1990: 368, 372 no. 54, 416 pl. 72 no. 54; Friedländer and Hoffleit 1948: 78; Clairmont 1970: no. 8; Daux 1972: 521–2; Mihailov 1970: 405.

[25] Hansen 1983: 118; Lorenz 1976: 39–45 no. 2; Jeffery 1990: 98, 99 no. 4, 402 pl. 11 no. 4; Friedländer and Hoffleit 1948: 160. On the form of praise cf. also Stecher 1981: 22, 20, 68 n. 61.

[26] Cf. e.g. *oudena pemanas* (Hansen 1983: 83 l. 8; 5th cent.); *[ou]theni lype⟨r⟩a* (Hansen 1989: 569; Daux 1972: 550 4); *[ou]deni lypesasu, outhenu lypon* (Hansen 1989: 554; Clairmont 1970: no. 72; 4th cent.). On this theme cf. Skiadas 1967: 70–1; Tod 1951: 187; Pircher 1979: 44, 73. Cf. also the slightly different, because one-word, negative formulation *alypos,* with the same meaning, causing no pain or grief (cf. Pircher 1979: 73; cf. e.g. Hansen 1989: 684 (together with *amempton*)).

and see them clearly in literature. The following few examples from the latter source will show first, that our meagre sample of formulations of this theme from archaic epitaphs fits excellently in, and is typical of, archaic Greek literary formulations of this concept in general; and second, that these formulations are characterized by an expression of positive facets of a very positive reputation, and an emphatic, strong character. Consider, for example, the formulation in Tyrtaios fr. 12. 31 West:[27]

οὐδέ ποτε κλέος ἐσθλὸν ἀπόλλυται οὐδὲ ὄνομα αὐτοῦ

cf. l. 32:

ἀλλ' ὑπὸ γῆς περ ἐὼν γίνεται ἀθάνατος

Theognis 245–7

οὐδέποτ' οὐδὲ θανὼν ἀπολεῖς κλέος, ἀλλὰ μελήσεις
ἄφθιτον ἀνθρώποις αἰὲν ἔχων ὄνομα
Κύρνε

Ibykos *PMG* fr. 282. 47–8 (S151 Davies (*PMGF*))

καὶ σύ, Πουλύκρατες, κλέος ἄφθιτον ἑξεῖς
ὡς κατ' ἀοιδὰν καὶ ἐμὸν κλέος

Kleos aphthiton, and related expressions of imperishable glory, are well-established topoi in Greek literature from Homer onwards.[28] These, then, are the intertextual frames pertaining to the archaic Greek perception of good memory, good reputation after death, and they are very different from the Teithronion formulation. It might be objected that the latter adopts a more homely tone, that we should not expect high-flown concepts to be applied to a doctor.[29] There are several arguments against this view. First, the tone of the two epitaphs in which we found the instances of the theme under discussion, written for people comparable to the

---

[27] Which (Ch. III §iii) also includes *oud'* ... *oud* ..., on which cf. below, §ii.1*e*. This is, of course, a special case, in so far as Tyrtaios is glorifying death in the service of one's country, but the formulation belongs to a more general and wider category.

[28] Cf. e.g. *Il.* 9. 413; *Od.* 4. 584; *Il.* 7. 91; *Od.* 7. 333. Cf. also e.g. Bacch. 13. 59–66 (Snell). On *kleos aphthiton* cf. Floyd 1980: 133–57; Nagy 1981: 113–16; Finkelberg 1986: 1–5; Edwards 1988: 25–30; Nagy 1990: 147, 206, 225–7, 244–5 n. 126. On the relationship between the *kleos* of epic poetry and the *kleos* and *ainos* of praise poetry cf. Nagy 1986: 89–102; 1990: 147–53, 192–214. On the notion of *kleos* in Homer and archaic poetry cf. also Goldhill 1991: 69–166.

[29] On doctors' praise in epitaphs cf. §i.5 below.

alleged doctor Charon, is much closer to the literary formulations than to the Teithronion inscription. This argument can be supported further by the consideration of two comparable epitaph themes, which are based on precisely such a high-flown literary formulation. The first of these states that in life the deceased was *philos* or the like, in which the apparent, explicit emphasis is on emotions rather than judgement, so that the reference to the deceased's reputation is somewhat indirect. The epitaph for Menekrates (Hansen 1983: 143), a public epitaph for an individual, contains the expression *es gar proxenFos damou philos*. A similar expression is found in the epitaph for Phanes, from Thisbe:[30] *asstoi[s] kai chsenoisi Phanes philos*, followed by a mention of his glorious death in battle. Compare the formulation in Kallinos fr. 1 West 1. 16: *all' ho men ouk empes demoi philos oude potheinos*. Compare also to both Kallinos and the epitaph theme the expression in the epigram for Minades (Hansen 1983: 128) which was to become popular in classical epitaphs and which is related to the *philos* theme:[31] *andri pothenoi damoi*. The *potheinos* theme refers to the attitudes towards the deceased after his death and emphasizes the longing and desire which the living feel for the deceased;[32] the reputation of the deceased is represented as positive by implication.[33] In this theme, which is a variant of the grief/lament theme, the praise is constructed out of the lament, on the basis of the large number of people said to have been distressed by the death. As we saw, praise and lament are related.[34] The fact that similar emphatic positive statements about the reputation of the deceased are also found in the classical period and later[35] testifies to the tenacity of the schema governing these formulations and its related mentality.

A further argument against interpreting *oud⟨e⟩is ty* etc. as praise (in a more homely tone) is that we know what was the opposite of a good reputation after one's death in archaic Greek thought, and

[30] Hansen 1983: 112; Stecher 1981: 21–2.

[31] Cf. on this Stecher 1981: 22 and 68 n. 60. On the *philos* theme cf. also Stecher 1981: 24.

[32] On this cf. Vernant 1990: 41–50.

[33] Cf. also the 5th-cent. epigram for Gastron (Hansen 1983: 123): *hoss mala pollo[is] astois kai xeinois doke thanon anian*.

[34] Cf. Lausberg 1982: 106, cf. 117–18; Day 1989: 17–20, who privileges the praise element and understresses that of lament.

[35] Cf. e.g. Hansen 1989: 546, 531; *GV* 1388. On the form and vocabulary of praise in epitaphs see also Stecher 1963: *passim*; 1981: 23–4 and *passim*.

it was not what would be denied of Charon in the Teithronion epigram if the expression were praise of a dead man. The opposite of glory after death was to be forgotten.[36] This is in harmony with the generally manifested heightened concern for survival in memory as opposed to sinking into oblivion.[37] Thus the Teithronion formulation cannot be seen as the inversion of the 'negative memory' conceptual schema or intertextual frame.

The formulations we have just seen, and the mentality they reflect, expressed and shaped archaic Greek assumptions and expectations pertaining to statements about the deceased's reputation. When we consider the Teithronion formulation through the perceptual filters shaped by those assumptions and expectations, it becomes clear that it could not have been either written, or read, as praise by an archaic Greek.

5. DOCTORS' EPITAPHS: A COMPARISON

The interpretation of the Teithronion epigram as an epitaph depends on the assumption that the alleged deceased, Charon, was a doctor. This whole interpretation depends, implicitly, on the similarity of the expression in the pentameter to expressions contained in some later funerary epigrams for doctors. Here I will try to show that the superficial similarity conceals fundamental differences; and that there are also other reasons for seriously doubting the validity of the interpretation based on this similarity. The case based on the divergences between our epigram and the known epitaphs for doctors[38] is not wholly conclusive when it is considered entirely on its own;[39] not because the divergences noted are not significant, for some are, but because of the extreme scarcity of archaic examples for comparison.[40] None of the individual diver-

---

[36] Cf. Sappho fr. 55 L.–P.; this is also inherent in the literary passages quoted above.

[37] *Kleos dysphamon* in Pi. *N.* 8. 36–7 is something which primarily concerns the deceased's dependants.

[38] On doctors' epitaphs cf. L. Robert 1939: 163–73; 1946: 103–8; 1964: 175–8; Wilhelm 1931: 74–96; Benedum 1978: 115–21. Cf. also, on decrees for doctors: Pouilloux 1960: 64–70.

[39] That is, without taking any account of all the arguments against the view that this inscription is an epitaph, which is what I am doing in this section, in order to keep the different parts of my case separate, for methodological reasons.

[40] I am taking in classical doctors' epitaphs because, given the scantiness of archaic doctors' epitaphs, the divergence could be considered to be based on an (almost) *argumentum ex silentio*. The fact that the same (divergent from our epigram) characteristics are also found in the following period shows that the observed differences are indeed significant.

gences that make up this part of the argument is conclusive in itself;
but when taken together they make up a good cumulative case
which, even if it is not strong enough to disprove, on its own, the
interpretation of the Teithronion epigram as an epitaph for a doctor,
it is strong enough to confirm and reinforce the overwhelming case
built up on the basis of the inscription's other elements.

Despite the extreme scarcity of archaic specimens for comparison, it is on the very few surviving archaic doctors' epitaphs
that the greatest weight must be placed. For, we saw, it is not
legitimate to form expectations concerning archaic expressions on
the basis of later formulations. There are only two archaic epitaphs
for doctors, one epigram and one prose inscription. The epigram
(of *c.*510–500) is Attic and it is inscribed on a marble disc bearing
the painted representation of a seated bearded man.[41] The text reads

μνῆμα τόδ' Αἰνέο σοφίας ἰατρῶ ἀρίστο

The funerary character of this memorial for Aineias or Aineios[42]
has been doubted by some,[43] but on wholly *a priori* and, in my view,
unconvincing grounds.[44] Given the typology of the object and the
formulations of the inscription,[45] the grave monument interpret
ation is by far the most likely to be correct. But my argument would
not be significantly affected even if the disc had been votive. For if
the important formulation *iatros* was included in a votive inscription,
it would certainly have been included in an epitaph. This view is
confirmed by the fact that, we shall see, the designation *iatros*
appears regularly in, and characterizes, doctors' epitaphs of all
periods.

The second archaic epitaph for a doctor is a prose-inscription
from Megara Hyblaia, inscribed on a kouros of the Melos group

[41] Hansen 1983: 62; Jeffery 1962: 147 no. 66; Friedländer and Hoffleit 1948: no. 8; Berger
1970: 155–8; Clairmont 1970: no. 3; Daux 1972: 519–20; cf. also Krug 1985: 27. On the
formulation *mnema* etc. cf. also Simondon 1982: 86–7 and n. 28.

[42] Both forms are attested and possible (cf. Daux 1972: 520).

[43] Karouzos 1951: 98; Karouzos 1961: 89 n. 45; cf. Clairmont 1970: 17–20 and cf. 18–19
n. 31 for bibliog. on the controversy.

[44] When the doubts are not based on straightforward error as with Clairmont 1970: 20
(cf. on this Daux 1972: 520).

[45] Cf. Jeffery 1962: 147 on no. 64 and op. cit. n. 16; Hansen 1983: ad loc.; cf. also Stecher
1981: 20 and 66 n. 39.

(*c.*555–40);[46] the inscription is dated 'not much later than *c.*550'.[47] It is certainly an epitaph, for the kouros was found in the necropolis of Megara Hyblaia.[48] It stood over the grave of the doctor Sombrotidas[49] and reads as follows:

Σομροτίδα : τō hιατρō : τō Μανδροκλέος :

Both inscriptions, then, include the word *iatros*, an explicit mention of the deceased's profession. This is absent from the Teithronion epigram. But how important is this absence? Our sample is too small to allow us to make confident assertions, but three factors increase the significance of the absence. First, apart from the disputed Teithronion epigram, there is no archaic epitaph containing a periphrasis that may be taken to indicate that the deceased was a doctor. In other words, not only do the only two known archaic doctors' epitaphs share this feature, but also there is no possible specimen, however hypothetical and uncertain, that could conceivably fall into the category to which the Teithronion inscription would belong if it were indeed an epitaph for a dead doctor, in which the man's profession was indicated through a periphrasis expressing praise, with no mention of *iatros*. Second, our two specimens belong to different genres, so that the common feature is likely to be motivated by something stronger than genre tradition, which may suggest that it was the result of the attitudes associated with doctors operating across genres and localities. This suggestion is reinforced by a third consideration: these two mentions of *iatros* are the only examples, in archaic epitaphs, in which the dead man's profession is mentioned. The mentality behind this,[50] which makes the mention of this profession and of no other relevant, especially in a funerary context, is probably that expressed in *Il.* 11. 514–15:

ἰητρὸς γὰρ ἀνὴρ πολλῶν ἀντάξιος ἄλλων
ἰούς τ' ἐκτάμνειν ἐπί τ' ἤπια φάρμακα πάσσειν.

This may lead us to expect that a major element in all archaic

---

[46] Richter 1960: 112 no. 134; Bernabò Brea 1950: 59–66; cf. Jeffery 1990: 270, 276 no. 25, 411 pl. 52 no. 25; Berger 1970: 154–5, 191 n. 392; Guarducci 1967: 314; cf. also Krug 1985: 27.
[47] Jeffery 1990: 270.
[48] Cf. Bernabò Brea, loc. cit.; Jeffery 1990: loc. cit.
[49] Cf. Jeffery 1990: 270; Berger 1970: 155.
[50] On the mentality about doctors in Greece in different periods cf. Kudlien 1967: 15–30; Krug 1985: 70 and *passim*.

doctors' epitaphs[51] would be the explicit mention of that profession. First, because it would have been desirable to make this profession unambiguously clear, and to put stress on it, rather than have it indirectly deduced from a periphrasis. For archaic epigrams stress in their formulations the elements which are conceptually important. Second, because the single word *iatros* was both a more focused expression of the concept that would have been voiced by the periphrasis, and a more comprehensive one. The word *iatros* evoked a larger semantic field than a periphrasis such as *polos anthropon lysamenos kamato*. Of course, a formulation such as *polos anthropon lysamenos kamato* puts the emphasis directly on praising the doctor's ability rather than providing the information that he was a doctor. But I submit that in an archaic epitaph the inclusion of the theme of praise of his medical ability was not an adequate substitute for the designation *iatros*. An archaic epitaph would not omit the thematic focus of the professional designation, since in archaic funerary epigrams important concepts were referred to directly, either mentioned explicitly, or conjured up by means of established intertextual frames; and at this time there was no established tradition pertaining to doctors' epitaphs. The latter statement is not simply based on the scarcity of archaic doctors' epitaphs, but also on the comparative variety of forms in the doctors' epitaphs of the classical period and even later,[52] which suggests that it was in the classical period that an intertextual tradition began to be seriously built up. But even after the genre of doctors' epitaphs had been established, containing its own themes and formulations, and establishing its own intertextual frames, the explicit designation *iatros*, *ieter* and the like continued to be included more often than not in the epigrams. This testifies to the importance attached to the explicit inclusion of this designation in one's epitaph. As we shall see, the periphrases in later epitaphs which are comparable to *polos anthropon lysamenos kamato* are usually more explicit and stronger than the latter would be, despite the fact that they are supported by an intertextual tradition, while an archaic doctor's epitaph was not.

First let us look at the pattern of appearance of *iatros* and the like and of the periphrases that identify indirectly the dead man as a doctor at the same time as they praise him. There is only one

---

[51] We shall see to what extent and why things change later.

[52] Cf. e.g. the 3rd-cent. BC funerary epigrams for doctors *GV* 902 and *GV* 1699 (*IG* ii/iii2. 9052).

epigraphically attested fifth-century funerary epigram for a doctor, that for Euktitos (Hansen 1983: 103), and even this is not totally certain to have been a doctor's epitaph (for its meaning depends on a series of restorations); but it probably was. Three epitaphs for doctors who had lived and died in the fifth century have been handed down through the literary tradition; they were written at a later date, and thus reflect later practices. But it cannot perhaps be excluded that the assumptions through which they were written may have included knowledge of doctors' actual epitaphs from the epitaphs' putative period, and that some attempt may have been made to reflect something of the earlier models. In any case, even if they did not, this does not weaken my case; for the fact that the relevant elements persisted in the later period if anything makes the case about their importance in the archaic age stronger.

The epitaph for Pausanias was probably written in the fourth century.[53] It includes the designation *iatros* (as does the second epigram for a fifth-century doctor, that for Akron)[54] and combines it with the designation *Asklepiades*,[55] and also with praise for Pausanias' medical achievements. This praise is more emphatic than the alleged praise of the Teithronion epigram. The epigram for Hippokrates, the third of those mentioned which have reached us through the literary tradition, reads:[56]

> Θεσσαλὸς Ἱπποκράτης Κῷος γένος ἐνθάδε κεῖται
> Φοίβου ἀπὸ ῥίζης ἀθανάτου γεγαώς,
> πλεῖστα τρόπαια νόσων στήσας ὅπλοις Ὑγίειης,
> δόξαν ἑλὼν πολλὴν οὐ τύχαι, ἀλλὰ τέχναι.

The designation *iatros* is missing from this epitaph of the man who was the *iatros* par excellence; but *Phoibou apo rizes* etc. is a more elaborate form of 'descendant of Asklepios', that is, Asklepiades, doctor descended from Asklepios.[57] The epigram contains strong explicit praise for Hippocrates' medical skills.

The fragmentary epigram for Euktitos of *c.*400[58] mentioned above

---

[53] Page 1981: 152–3; *GV* 44; Pfohl 1967: 168; Diog. Laert. 8. 60–1; *AP* vii. 508. On the date of the source in which it was read by later writers cf. Page 1981: 152.

[54] On Akron's epigram cf. Page 1981: 153–4.

[55] On the designation 'Asklepiades' cf. Peek 1960: 298. On the guild of the Asklepiads cf. Kee 1982: 124–6; Phillips 1973: 29; Smith 1979, 216–19.

[56] *GV* 418; Pfohl 1967*a*: 144; *AP* vii. 135.

[57] In Eur. *Alc.* 970–1 Phoibos is mentioned as the patron and teacher of doctors referred to as 'Asklepiadai'.

[58] Hansen 1983: 103; Peek 1942: 124–5; Daux 1972: 548.

has been restored[59] to include the formulation (ll. 2–3):

[ὃς πλείσ]τος ἐξαν[έλυσε πό]νων βλαψιφ[ρόνων

The designation *iatros* is missing from the surviving part of the epigram; it may have been included in the missing part. Certainly, the designation *iatros* continues to be a focus at least in some doctors' epitaphs in the fourth century, as, for example, in that for Phanostrate: *maia kai iatros.*[60] Others seem to put the emphasis on periphrastic praise, as, for example, the epitaph for Maiandrios,[61] which does not include *iatros*, but does include the designation *Asklepiades*; the praise is spelt out, explicit and strong: (ll. 2–3):

ὃς

πολλοῖς θνητῶν τειρομένοισι νόσῳ εὗρεν ἄκη,
θανάτοιο δυσέλπιδος οἶτον ἀλέξων.

Even after the genre of doctors' epitaphs was established many doctors' epitaphs did not use periphrases to praise professional skills and success, but were focused on the designation *iatros*, normally accompanied by some comparatively simple form of praise.[62] There are also expressions such as (*GV* 785) *pikron ietora [nouson]*; (*GV* 584) *stygeron ietora nouson*; (*GV* 1034) *nouson d' ouk allos amino[n] ieter*. Finally, there are epitaphs in which there is no designation *iatros* or the like, only a periphrasis describing the deceased's professional achievements. To this type belongs, for example, the epigram *GV* 627 (*nouson stygeron pollous esaosa* (compare the expression in *GV* 584)) and the somewhat idiosyncratic epigram Kaibel no. 884 (*IG* ix. 1. 881):

ἐσθλὰ δαεὶς Παίωνος ἀλεξητήρια
νούσων οἷς πολλοὺς θανάτου ῥύσατο καὶ καμάτων.

This is the closest parallel known to me to the alleged praise

[59] Peek 1942: 124–5.

[60] Hansen 1989: 569; on this epitaph, and on Phanostrate and her profession cf. also Berger 1970: 160–2; Clairmont 1970: no. 53; Daux 1972: 550–4; Pircher 1979: 44–5 no. 15; King 1986a: 59–60, cf. also *passim*; Krug 1985: 195–6. Cf. also the epitaph for Aristokrates, which also designates him *iatros*: Peppas-Delmusu 1963: 154–5; Clairmont 1970: no. 78; Daux 1972: 563–4.

[61] Hansen 1989: 666; Peek 1960: 82.

[62] Cf. *GV* 1749: *Edyos iatrou* (L. Robert 1946: 103 comments that it 'n'utilise pas les thèmes les plus courants dans les épitaphes métriques des médecins'); *GV* 2040, 241, 686, 766, 1395.

expression of the Teithronion epigram.[63] A detailed analysis will show that the comparison is inappropriate, and that the later formulations cannot legitimately support the epitaph interpretation of the archaic epigram. Besides the fact that it is illegitimate to use later data to make sense of early epigrams, in this case, the fact that the later epitaphs relied on an intertextual tradition which was not available at *c.*500 means that in them each expression which had become an intertextual frame referred to, and called up (for its contemporaries) certain other concepts and formulations which (for them) belonged together with it; while an apparently comparable expression in an archaic epitaph did not. Thus, the two formulations that appear to us similar were read differently by the audiences for which they were written. Another variable, which also entails that an apparently similar phenomenon might have a different significance in each case, is the importance of the direct reference to the dead doctors' profession; in the later epitaphs this profession is no longer the only one judged worthy of mention, and this may have involved a shift of emphasis in medical epitaphs. Yet another variable is the difference in the style of the epitaphs. The later, and often much more elaborate, epitaphs can include an element of indirectness, which is at variance with the style of the archaic epitaphs, where the strokes of the discourse were bold. For all these reasons, it is illegitimate to use these late formulations as (implicit or explicit) models for reading, and for legitimating the reading of, the Teithronion epigram as the epitaph of a dead doctor. Furthermore, there are, we shall now see, observable differences between these late periphrastic formulations of praise for doctors and the alleged praise in the Teithronion epigram.

Given the structure of the expression, the main praise would have to be *oudeis ty kakos legei oude thanonta*, with *polos anthropon lysamenos kamato* in a subordinate position, providing the justification of the main praise.[64] Since I want to keep the different parts of my argument separate, I will disregard the case set out above which shows that this expression could not have functioned as praise in an archaic epitaph, and simply consider how the formulation

---

[63] Cf. also Wilhelm 1931: 76 no. III: *patren ryomenen nouson.*

[64] This is obscured in the translations: Peek (1960: 63 no. 41: the literal translation) connects the two with 'und': 'und viele Menschen hast du usw.' Friedländer and Hoffleit 1948: p. 89 separate the two with a semi-colon. But in the comm. the latter note the pentameter gives the reason why no one speaks ill of Charon even though he is dead.

compares with the expressions of praise in doctors' epitaphs. There is nothing among the praise formulations in epitaphs for doctors of any period that can be considered comparable to the formulation of the Teithronion epigram. The only comparable expressions resemble the subordinate part of the 'praise', the part which appears to motivate the formulation which would have to be considered as the main praise.

Let us then survey briefly the contents and forms of praise for doctors in epitaphs.[65] The archaic epitaph for Aineias already contains the themes (though not the formulations) which will predominantly characterize praise for doctors in the later epitaphs. It mentions Aineias' *sophia*, and it calls him *ariston iatron*. *Sophia* is the main virtue associated with doctors in Greek epitaphs.[66] The expression *aristos iatros* praises Aineias' *techne iatrike*, which is another, related, characteristic praise theme in these epigrams.[67] Such praise of the doctor's *techne* can be expressed by means of periphrases such as those quoted above, and it has been assumed that our epigram's *polos anthropon lysamenos kamato* falls into this category. But there are differences; the Teithronion formulation is shorter, less explicit, and less emphatic than most of them, and especially than those chronologically nearest to it.[68] The periphrastic praise in the funerary epigram Kaibel no. 884 cited above, which is the closest formulation of a doctor's praise to the Teithronion expression, is more explicit and emphatic and more analytically articulated than that of the Teithronion epigram, despite the fact that the latter had no intertextual tradition to reinforce its content. I suspect that it is this late epigram above all others that became activated during Klaffenbach's first reading of our epigram, and (perhaps implicitly) functioned as a model for its orthodox interpretation. This validating model helped obscure the fact that there are several unanswerable objections against interpreting our epigram as an epitaph.

---

[65] On praise for doctors cf. Stecher 1963: 197; 1981: 20, 66–7 n. 40; Pircher 1979: 44; Berger 1970: 155 and 199 n. 394; Kudlien 1967: 20–1, cf. 28, 29, and 31–47 on *techne iatrike*.

[66] Cf. Berger 1970: 155; Kudlien 1967: 20–1, 28, 29, 31; and examples in Stecher 1981: 66–7 n. 40.

[67] On *techne iatrike* cf. Stecher 1981: 66–7 n. 40; Kudlien 1967: 29, 31–47; Stecher 1963: 197.

[68] Cf. esp. the epitaph for Pausanias quoted above (*GV* 44) and that for Hippokrates (*GV* 148). Cf. also the one for Maiandrios (Peek 1960: 82) whose periphrastic praise was quoted above.

oudeis ty kakos legei oude thanonta differs from apparently comparable expressions relating to doctors in exactly the same way as it differs from other, non-specialized expressions referring to the dead man's reputation: in contrast to our epigram's alleged formulation of praise, the 'normal' epitaphs' praise expressions are positive, not negative, and emphatic, not faint. Compare, for example, the epigram for Hippokrates cited above (ll. 3–4): *pleista tropaia* etc., *doxan helon pollen* etc.; compare also the epitaph Hansen 1989: 717:

ἦν χρόνος ἡνίκα τόνδε σοφώτατον Ἑλλὰς ἔκλειζεν |
ἰατρῶμ Φαΐδαμ παῖδα Δαμασσαγόρα, |
ὦι πατ[ρὶς ἦν Τέ]νεδος, πρόγονοι δ' ὀνομαστοὶ ἀπ' [ἀρχ]ῆς |
ἔκγονοι Ἀτρειδᾶν Ἑλλάδος ἁγεμόνων.

Compare also *GV* 1034: *technes polloi martyres isin emes*; and also the epitaph for Phanostrate mentioned above (n. 60): *[ou]theni lype⟨r⟩a, pasin de thanousa potheine*. In these circumstances, we can conclude first, that *oudeis ty kakos legei oude thanonta* does not fit into the thematic category 'praise for doctors', indeed its content is at odds with the doctor-themes most directly comparable to it; and second, that *polos anthropon lysamenos kamato* differs significantly from the superficially comparable formulations in later doctors' epitaphs with respect to its position within the structure of the epigram: while they are straightforward expressions of praise, the Teithronion expression, if it were praise for a dead doctor, would be only secondarily praise, its primary function being that of motivating what is presented as the primary praise, *oudeis ty kakos legei oude thanonta*.

To sum up. Because of the extreme scarcity of archaic doctors' epitaphs the comparison of our inscription with the doctors' epitaphs that are directly relevant to it could not be conclusive. It showed a significant divergence, but the exiguity of the sample prevented us from concluding with confidence that this is significant. Later doctors' epitaphs appeared to confirm, though again not wholly conclusively, the importance of this deviation. Moreover, they also pointed to a few other differences which, while not necessarily significant in themselves when taken separately, nevertheless make up a clustering of irregularities, and show that the apparent similarity between the pentameter of the Teithronion epigram and later formulations in doctors' epitaphs is less real than at first appears. Consequently, this similarity cannot sustain the orthodox interpretation of this inscription as a funerary epigram for a dead doctor. On the contrary, the cumulative case derived from the detailed comparison of the Teithronion epigram with doctors' epitaphs, though it is not strong enough to disprove, on its own, the orthodox interpretation, helps confirm the overwhelming case built up on the basis of the analysis of the epigram's other elements.

6. AN ABSENCE OF GREAT IMPORTANCE

A fundamental objection to the view that the Teithronion epigram was an epitaph is that if it were an epitaph it would be unique among archaic epitaphs in omitting the naming the grave monument or burial, which, we saw, was perceived to be expressing the core function of the archaic grave monument, which entails that for as long as this mentality was alive it was inconceivable that an epigram-writer could have composed an epitaph lacking this element which characterized epitaphs in a most fundamental way, and which, therefore, for such a writer, would have been the indispensable underlying core for any funerary epigram composition. The only exception to this, the *oimoi* inscriptions from Selinous, far from providing support for the view that the Teithronion epigram could be an exception to the rule, on the contrary confirmed this rule's strength. For, even if it is correct that these Selinountine inscriptions (which were in any case the product of a very particular cultural environment) were not perceived as including any reference to the grave monument or burial, the fact that the formula was modified to include a naming reference whenever it was used outside Selinous, and most importantly in Phokis, where the Teithronion epigram belongs, demonstrates the tenacity of the mentality that demanded inclusion of a reference to the grave monument or burial in archaic epitaphs. In addition, there are also significant differences between the Teithronion epigram and the Selinous epitaphs that confirm further that the latter cannot provide support for the notion that the former was an epitaph. The *oimoi* inscriptions are formulations of lament, and thus, unlike the Teithronion epigram, fit perfectly into the corpus of archaic funerary inscriptions as regards their theme, their attitude towards the dead, and their perception of the condition of being dead. Also, these short, simple inscriptions consisting mostly of the exclamation *oimoi o* and the name of the deceased (though the word *phile* is added in one) can be seen as closely related to the simple name inscriptions, and as derivative from them, once lament established itself as a dominant feature in Selinountine epitaphs. Thus, we can imagine that from an inscription such as '*Theognis*',[69] through a hypothetical form '*oimoi. Gorgos (enthade keitai)*', the formulation *oimoi o Gorge* may have been created and perhaps sustained by its closeness to the simple name-epitaphs. Such a motivation of the absence of naming cannot apply to the longer, elaborate Teithronion epigram.

In these circumstances, the absence of any type of reference to the grave monument or burial from the Teithronion epigram would be sufficient even on its own to refute the interpretation of this epigram as an epitaph. No archaic epigram-writer could possibly have written it as an epitaph and no archaic reader could have read it as such—even if we leave aside, for the moment, all the other elements in this text which would have blocked such an interpretation and also the fact that a very strong case can be made for a totally different interpretation.

7. THE FIRST AND SECOND READING NARRATIVES: CONCLUSIONS

I hope to have shown that there are insurmountable objections to the interpretation of the Teithronion epigram as an epitaph: every single element in it would have involved either a (greater or lesser) irregularity or a major discrepancy when compared to the corpus of archaic funerary epigrams, and, in some cases, archaic funerary inscriptions in general; some of these discrepancies entail serious conflict with important aspects of archaic attitudes towards death and the dead as they are manifested in epitaphs and elsewhere. The interpretation of this epigram as an epitaph for a doctor called Charon has been shown to rely implicitly on a series of independent special pleadings; for the irregularities are not reducible to one central hypothesis. This in itself makes the interpretation implausible. In fact, at least two of the divergences analysed above are so significant, as to be each on its own capable of disproving the orthodox interpretation of the Teithronion epigram as an epitaph. Taken all together they make up an overwhelming and unanswerable

---

[69] Manni Piraino 1963: 137 no. 1, of the end of the 7th cent.

case, which will be further strengthened when the positive side of this argument is considered: as we shall now see, there is an alternative reading of the epigram in which all the elements fit well, and make excellent sense. It is my contention that, given the assumptions and expectations through which archaic Greeks wrote and read epitaphs and other texts, this was the only reading open to the epigram's contemporaries. I also tried to show how the orthodox interpretation of the Teithronion inscription as an epitaph came about, as a result of the (at first unconscious) activation of inappropriate intertextual frames which were (implicitly) used as models for the reading of this epigram, and which supported and reinforced the grammatical *lectio facilior* and obscured the many serious objections against it. The two main intertextual frames thus activated were, first, *chaire* addressed to the deceased in later epitaphs, and second, expressions of praise for the professional skills of doctors in much later epitaphs. I hope to have shown that these intertextual frames were inappropriate; and that it is because they imposed themselves in the minds of modern scholars, in combination with the fact that archaic attitudes towards death did not until recently form a prominent part of scholars' mental furniture, that the insurmountable objections against the epitaph interpretation did not immediately appear; for these objections only emerge in their full strength as a result of detailed analyses in the context of a systematic attempt to reconstruct the assumptions through which the text's contemporaries made sense of it.

I hope to have shown conclusively that the orthodox reading of this epigram cannot stand, and to have broken the mould of the expectations created by that reading. For unless it becomes absolutely clear that this epigram cannot be an epitaph, the obvious grammatical analysis will block the acceptance of any alternative, since there is always an implicit bias in favour of the grammatical *lectio facilior* that can distort the attempts at reconstructing the original reading. Once it is realized that the Teithronion epigram could not have been an epitaph, that it was impossible for its contemporary readers and its writer to make sense of it in that way, then it becomes possible to see the text through archaic eyes, and consider alternative readings without the interference of this culturally determined prejudice.

ii. *The Third Reading Narrative: Reading through Archaic Eyes*

1. READING THE TEXT

(a) *Introduction*

I will now propose a new reading for this epigram, based on an attempted reconstruction of the ways in which it was read by its original audience. The first stage of this reading operation involves the recovery of the assumptions which moulded the audience's (and writer's) perceptual filters; the second the attempt to reconstruct those filters and read through them, so as to make sense of the epigram as nearly through archaic eyes as possible. Some of the relevant assumptions have been discussed in other sections of this book; others will emerge for the first time here.

(b) Chaire Charon

We saw in Chapter III § ii.3 that an important function of *chaire* was its use for addressing deities and other superhuman beings. Thus, when an archaic reader was confronted with *chaire* in an inscription, one of the planes of reference called up would have been the supernatural sphere of divine/heroic/demonic beings; as we saw, the only two possible planes of reference were this divine/heroic/demonic plane and the world of the living. The juxtaposition of the former sphere and the name Charon would inescapably direct the ancient reader towards Charon the ferryman of the dead, especially since, we shall see, the context in which the epigram was set was almost certainly funerary. Thus the reading '*chaire* Charon (ferryman of the dead)' was the most compelling decoding hypothesis for the formulation *chaire* Charon in this epigram, and was confirmed, we shall see, by the rest of the epigram.

This reconstruction does not assume that there was an established intertextual frame *chaire* Charon (ferryman of the dead) when the epigram was written. But in reality, the process of reading *chaire* Charon in our epigram was probably much simpler. For it is very likely that such a frame had existed and was used by the writer of the epigram and activated by its readers who thus immediately understood both the *chaire* and the whole epigram to be addressed to the infernal ferryman. Leaving aside our epigram, the first

attested example of *chaire Charon* is found in a fragment of Achaios
(*TrGF* 20 F 11 (*Aithon*)):

> χαῖρ' ὦ Χάρων, χαῖρ' ὦ Χάρων, χαῖρ' ὦ Χάρων,
> —ἦ που σφόδρα θυμοῖ;

repeated by Aristophanes (*Frogs* 184). This is a pun.[70] Puns[71] create
a forced contiguity between two or more words and through it
suggest a series of possible relationships; in one main type of pun,
the one in our epigram, the similarity of the signifiers, of the words'
form, is made to suggest, through the forced contiguity, similarity
of meaning, a conceptual relationship, and in this way creates
possibilities for the emergence of new meanings. Here the pun
exploits the (probably) accidental similarity between *chaire* and
Charon to create certain effects. At one level *chaire* is an appropriate
salutation to Charon, who, as a superhuman (demonic) being,
is entitled to be addressed with *chaire*. At the same time Charon
belongs to a world, to a human experience, which involves the
antithesis of the rejoicing that is denoted by *chaire* and *chairein*. Thus,
by exploiting this similarity, by creating this contiguity (in the form
of an established and appropriate mode of address), the pun forces
to the surface the antithesis between life which, we saw, was characterized by *chaire*, and the grimness of death in which there is no joy
for the dead who, we saw, are not addressed with *chaire*. By jux-
taposing Charon's name to *chaire*, this address brings out the similarity between them, and so presents the name Charon as related to
the verb *chairein* and the salutation *chaire*. It thus stresses the contrast
between on the one hand Charon and his grim function and the
death he stands for, and on the other the joyous connotations which
his name is made to appear to be evoking. Charon is entitled to be
addressed with *chaire*, but *chairein* is not something which for
humanity is associated with Charon's activities and with the experiences he represents. Thus *chaire Charon* brings out and stresses the
grimness of death.[72] The relationship of semantic similarity between
Charon and *chairein* proposed by the pun, and the contrast between

---

[70] The term 'pun' does not involve a precise definition; it is a broad term covering a
variety of rhetorical devices involving play on words (cf. Redfern 1984: 6).

[71] On puns see Eco 1981: 72–8; Culler 1983: 91; Redfern 1984: *passim*.

[72] At the same time, the expression *chaire Charon* may have also been perceived—at least
in some contexts—as humorous because it is—in one way—incongruous. (Cf. a different
type of humorous use of *chaire*, because incongruous: Campbell 1984: 165.)

Charon and his grim function and the joyous connotations which his name is made by the pun's forced contiguity to appear to have, were articulated explicitly (thus showing that they made a deep impression on the Greek imagination) in the view that Charon had been named by antiphrasis.[73]

The contrast between *chairein* and Charon articulates the contrast between life, characterized by joy, and death, characterized by joylessness[74] which was deeply felt in Greek mentality: life = *chairein*, death = not-*chairein*. By conjoining one element from each of the opposing pairs, *chairein* and death, in the figure of Charon, this expression evokes this whole nexus of oppositions, and thus evokes the grimness of death, and also encapsulates a fundamental Greek perception of life and death. It might be argued that, at one level, this bitter pun in some ways challenges this established perception of life and death, makes a gesture of overcoming it, of extending, defiantly, as it were, the quality of joy, which characterizes life, into the domain of death, by applying it to Charon who here stands for the whole realm of death, for the concept of death itself. In this way, the values of life over those of death are asserted (at the level of imagery) and also life's strength, for it does go on despite death. Puns are sly and oblique[75] and slyness and obliqueness are not inappropriate ways of relating to death, especially to this figure signifying death who is located at the 'banausic' and trivializing level; attitudes towards Charon, we saw, were ambivalent and the pun expresses this ambivalence. It could be argued that, because it strikes a chord in a fundamental aspect of Greek collective representations, the conjunction between Charon and *chairein* would have been naturally made by the Greek mind, and so we

---

[73] Cf. Eust. Comm. Hom. Il. 16. 33–6) . . . *hos apo tou chairein, kaitoi charton ouden poion* . . . . Diod. 1. 92. 2–3 and 1. 96. 8 believes that Charon's name was imported from Egypt. The etymology of Charon's name is problematic (on this etymology cf. Chantraine IV-2 s.v. Charon 2). But this is not relevant. The dominant connotations of proper names are those of the important characters which bear them. The others are not felt except when they are brought out specially, as here, through puns and pun-like constructions, in which real or fictional similarities are brought out or created to make some specific point about the character and/or his actions. In this case, whatever the true origin of Charon's name the juxtaposition of *chaire* and Charon stresses the name's similarity with *chairein*. On etymological jokes on proper names in archaic and 5th-cent. Greek literature cf. Bonanno 1980: 65–88, esp. 76–7 and cf. esp. 82 on *kat' antiphrasin* names; cf. also 83–4. On significant names and rhetorical games on significant names cf. Calame 1986: 153–61. Cf. also Goldhill 1986: 19–21.

[74] Cf. esp. Od. 11. 488–91; and cf. Ch. III § ii.3.

[75] Cf. Redfern 1984: 26.

might expect it to have taken place as early as, or soon after the appearance of, the figure of Charon as ferryman of the dead. In *Frogs* Dionysos addresses Charon with *chaire* as soon as he sees him, so one could speculate that there may have been images of death (in literature) in which the dead were presented as addressing *chaire* to Charon when they arrived by his boat, marking the beginning of the final passage into Hades, as they had said *chaire/chairete* to their companions and to the world of the living at the moment of their death. In this way their passage from one world to the next may have been framed by two '*chaire*': *chaire* = farewell to life as they were leaving life to enter the liminal space between life and death, and *chaire* – hail to death in the person of Charon as they embarked on the passage between this liminal space and the Land of the Dead; a hail to death and a salutation to the infernal ferryman of the type addressed to divine and other superhuman beings when requesting protection and blessing. But this is speculation. There remains the possibility that the intertextual frame *chaire Charon* had become associated with the figure of Charon the ferryman of the dead early, and that therefore it had been established by the time of our epigram. But I hope to have shown that even if this intertextual frame had not been established at *c.*500, the archaic reader would nevertheless have been led towards the decoding *chaire Charon* (ferryman of the dead). Even if the expression *chaire Charon* had not yet been an established intertextual frame at that time, the juxtaposition of *chaire* and Charon would inevitably have activated, in that reader's mind, the nexus of contrasts mentioned earlier which underlies later juxtapositions of *chairein* and *Charon*; for this nexus formed a fundamental part of the Greek representations which shaped the perceptual filters through which this epigram was read by its contemporaries, and composed by its author. Through the activation of this nexus of contrasts, Charon would have been identified—even leaving aside all the other considerations—as Charon the ferryman of the dead; this identification, we shall see, was confirmed by the rest of the text.[76]

---

[76] As Prof. I. Rutherford pointed out to me, the arrangement of the inscription on the stone, with *chaire Charon* alone in the first line, puts special emphasis on this salutation. It thus emphasizes and strongly directs the whole reading of the epigram, directs the reader towards understanding it to be addressed to the infernal ferryman, a hypothesis which will be confirmed by the other elements. Consequently, by the time the reader has reached the problematic word *thanonta* the identity of the addressee had been firmly established as Charon

The meanings of the pun do not exhaust the meanings of *chaire Charon*. Because it is also a proper salutation/invocation/address to a supernatural being in the form in which mortals regularly addressed gods and heroes urging them to rejoice and requesting their protection,[77] this address is also an invocation, in which the addresser urges Charon to rejoice and requests his protection. Presumably Charon is urged to rejoice both at the dedication and at the statement made about him, that no one speaks ill of him, and all the rest.

(c) oud⟨e⟩is ty kakos legei

The expression 'nobody speaks ill of you', which made no sense when applied to a dead person, makes perfect sense when applied to someone for whom there is a definite expectation that he should be disliked and thus spoken ill of. Hence, it makes perfect sense when applied to Charon the ferryman of the dead who, we saw, came to symbolize death itself. Given the fundamental love of life and hatred of death which characterizes the mainstream archaic Greek attitudes towards death, the expectation would be that people would hate, and thus speak ill of, Charon. The fact that they do not (or so it is claimed in the epigram) invites mention and recording, and also Charon's rejoicing. Thus, the hypothesis which, on my reading, was formulated by the archaic readers on the basis of *chaire Charon*, that the epigram was addressed to the ferryman of the dead, would have been confirmed by the expression that follows, *oud⟨e⟩is ty kakos legei*.

Furthermore, the fact that the emphasis is on *oud⟨e⟩is ty kakos legei*, with the expression *polos anthropon lysamenos kamato* subordinated to it and providing the reason for the fact that nobody speaks ill of him, which did not fit the hypothesis of a dead doctor, makes perfect sense when the addressee is the ferryman of the dead. For it is the 'message' contained in the first expression that is primarily being communicated to Charon, the statement that (contrary to expectations) it is not hatred, but goodwill that governs the attitudes of men towards him.

---

the ferryman of the dead, and there was no possibility that the reader could take *thanonta* to refer to the epigram's addressee.

[77] On this cf. Bundy 1972: 49; Race 1982: 8; cf. also Miller 1979: 176.

(d) polos anthropon lysamenos kamato: *Death as a Deliverer*[78]

This expression gives the reason for, and thus also validates and reinforces, as well as elaborates, the previous statement. Side by side with the mainstream attitude of passionate love of life, and contrasting with it, we find, in certain archaic circles, the view that in certain circumstances death is preferable to life. This view, which appears in different forms, constitutes a challenge to the earlier belief[79] that life under any circumstances is preferable to death, a belief which was also dominant in the archaic period. This challenge emerged in the context of the shift in the attitudes towards death which crystallized in the archaic period. One of the contexts in which this attitude was manifested (see Appendix) was the hedonistic approach to life: Mimnermos (frs. 1–2, 4, 6 West) expresses the view that death is preferable to old age with its physical discomforts and loss of physical pleasures.[80] From another viewpoint, Theognis (vv. 181–2) expresses the view that death is preferable to the distress of poverty. The notion that it is better to die than to live in distress also underlies the expression of the desire to die because one is unhappy. This motif makes its first appearance in Homer, *Odyssey* 15. 353–60, in the context of a manifestation of grief otherwise unparalleled in the epics—which, in my view, is one of the elements that indicate the eighth century tentative beginning of the shift in the funerary attitudes. This motif is forcibly expressed in Sappho (frs. 94 L.-P.; 95.11–13 L.-P.). A different attitude, which goes very much further than all this in its 'anti-life' bias is expressed in [Theogn.] 425–8, where we are told that it is best not to be born, and once born to die as soon as possible.[81] We find half of this theme in Bacchylides (5.160–2 Snell): 'It is best not to be born.' All these themes have one thing in common: they imply a perception of death as cessation of trouble and unhappiness, as deliverer from trouble, toil, sickness and misery. This theme of 'death as a deliverer', which is almost explicitly formulated in Mimnermos (especially in fr. 6 West), was, then, an established intertextual frame in archaic literature. The notion that death delivers from pain is primarily

---

[78] I am leaving the discussion of *oude thanonta* until the end, because I want first to 'frame' that expression, to build up the framework against which it must be seen and understood.

[79] Cf. *Od.* 11. 488–91.

[80] Cf. Babut 1971: 35–9, 42; cf. also Sourvinou-Inwood 1983: 46.

[81] On this cf. Lloyd-Jones 1971: 52. We do not, of course, have to assume that these feelings were 'seriously meant'; what is significant is that such attitudes could be expressed.

inspired by, and manifests, a negative (as well as an extremely individual) view of life, rather than a positive view of death.[82] It is an image articulating, condensing, and illustrating forcefully through polarization man's bitterness about his lot, contrasting with the earlier attitude of acceptance. Its appearance is limited to certain literary circles in the archaic period.[83] It did not make an impact on the archaic collective representations as they are manifested in funerary behaviour and in the epitaphs.[84] The idea that life is not necessarily always preferable to death first appears in private epitaphs in the fourth century, with the motif which presents death in youth in a positive light.[85]

This theme appears very frequently in fifth-century tragedy in the form of four interconnected topoi.[86] There is considerable overlapping between the meanings conveyed by them, though there are differences in emphasis, depending on where the semantic focus lay in each case. The four topoi are the following. (i) Death as a deliverer from toil, pain, etc. This theme is also implicit in the other three. (ii) It is better to die than to live in distress.[87] (iii) Expression of the desire to die. This theme is quite common in tragedy.[88] (iv) It is best not to be born, and once born to die as soon as possible.[89]

---

[82] On the theme of death as deliverance from suffering cf. also Griessmair 1966: 98–101; cf. also Dover 1974: 267.

[83] Against Mimnermos' preference of death to old age and its miseries: Solon fr. 20 West.

[84] For the fragmentation of the attitudes to death and the horizons of expectation relating to them cf. Sourvinou-Inwood 1983: 45. Of course, these attitudes are significant for all archaic collective representations concerning death in so far as they show the frontiers of change from the earlier model, the new fluctuation parameters of social attitudes to death.

[85] Cf. e.g. Hansen 1989: 489. On death as a deliverer on much later epitaphs cf. *GV* 1329. 6–7, 533, 1812; and cf. Griessmair 1966: 97–101.

[86] Since these themes are firmly anchored in the archaic period, when it can be seen that the theme 'death as a deliverer' was an established intertextual frame, it is legitimate to consider the more plentifully available 5th-cent. evidence to form a fuller picture of the manifestation of the themes; though this does not entail that we are entitled to project the 5th-cent. formulations backwards—unless we find good reasons for doing so.

[87] Cf. Soph. *Ant.* 462–4; Aesch. *TrGF* iii. F 466 (classified among the 'dubia'); Eur. *Troad.* 632 (the passage (vv. 632–42) contains also the subtheme (cf. i.a.) 'the dead are not touched by pain and suffering').

[88] Cf. e.g. Soph. *OC* 434–6; *Electra* 821–2; *Philoct.* 797–8; Eur. *Suppl.* 85–6 (combined with the theme 'death as a deliverer'); *Hippol.* 1387–8; Aesch., *TrGF* iii. F 255 (combined with the themes 'death as a deliverer' and 'the dead are not touched by pain and suffering'). Cf. Soph. *Aj.* 854 (Ajax calls upon Thanatos just before he commits suicide; in fact, of course, his suicide itself is a manifestation of the attitude considered here). On the expression of the desire to die in archaic poetry cf. Boedeker 1979: 41–3, 49–52.

[89] Cf. Soph. *OC* 1224–38: the meaning here is: because life is full of trouble and toil and ends in the abhorrent old age; so the theme 'death as a deliverer' is almost explicitly included.

An attack on the notion that it is better to die than suffer is found in Agathon, *TrGF* i. F 7. Let us now consider theme (i), death as a deliverer from toil, trouble, pain and distress which is at the centre of our concerns. It is found in the following passages: Aeschylus, *TrGF* iii. F 353, F 255 (combined with the related subtheme 'the dead are not touched by suffering' and with the theme 'expression of the desire to die');[90] Sophocles, *Trach.* 1208–9; 1170–2 (cf. 1173: there is no more toil for the dead); Euripides, *Suppl.* 85–6, 1004–5; *Bacch.* 1361–2; *Hippol.* 599–600, 1047, 1373–7; *Heracl.* 595–6; *Troad.* 268–70; fr. 449 N²; Adesp. fr. *TrGF* ii. F 371.[92] A related subtheme says that the dead are not touched by pain and suffering: Aeschylus, *TrGF* iii. F 255; Sophocles, *Trach.* 1173 (no *mochthos*); cf. *OC* 955; Euripides, *Alc.* 937–8; *Troad.* 602–3, 632–42; fr. 833 N². Euripides, *Alc.* 669–72 makes the following comment on the notion that death is preferable to the troubles of old age:

> μάτην ἄρ᾽ οἱ γέροντες εὔχονται θανεῖν
> γῆρας ψέγοντες καὶ μακρὸν χρόνον βίου·
> ἢν δ᾽ ἐγγὺς ἔλθῃ θάνατος, οὐδεὶς βούλεται
> θνῄσκειν, τὸ γῆρας δ᾽ οὐκέτ᾽ ἔστ᾽ αὐτοῖς βαρύ.

An important version of the theme 'death as a deliverer' makes use of the imagery of healing, and death is presented as a healer, in an ironical reversal of the 'normal' realities (in which healing delivers people from the danger of death as well as from sickness) and attitudes which adds poignancy to the statements. Cf. Aeschylus, *TrGF* iii. F 255 from the *Philoctetes*:

> ὦ θάνατε παιάν, μή μ᾽ ἀτιμάσῃς μολεῖν·
> μόνος γὰρ εἶ σὺ τῶν ἀνηκέστων κακῶν
> ἰατρός, ἄλγος δ᾽ οὐδὲν ἅπτεται νεκροῦ.

Cf. also Euripides, *Hippol.* 1373: καί μοι θάνατος παιὰν ἔλθοι. Cf. also *Heracl.* 595–6: τὸ γὰρ θανεῖν κακῶν μέγιστον φάρμακον νομίζεται.[92]

In Eur. frs. 285.1–2 and 908.1 N2 we find the first part of this theme only (it is better not to be born) as in Bacchyl. 5.160–2.

[90] Cf. also *TrGF* iii. F 177. F 255 is from the *Philoctetes*.

[91] Cf. also Soph. *OC* 1224–38 (cf. supra in theme iv); and Eur. *Andr.* 1215–16. And cf. also Hdt. 1. 30–3 and the discussion in Arist, *Nichom. Eth.* 1. 1100ᵇ ff.

[92] *Akos* is not of predominantly medical use, so perhaps should not be included here, though it has also a medical sense. In Eur. *Hippol.* 599–600 we find: ... *katthanein hoson tachos ton nyn paronton pematon akos monon. Apolysis* (cf. Adesp. *TrGF* ii. F 371) can also be used in a medical sense (cf. LSJ *s.v.*).

In Sophocles, *Trach.* 1208–9 the imagery is transferred to Hyllos as a prospective giver of death:

> ... ὧν ἔχω παιώνιον
> καὶ μοῦνον ἰατῆρα τῶν ἐμῶν κακῶν

Sophocles, *TrGF* F 698 (*all' esth' ho thanatos loisthos iatros noson*) is a variant of this 'death as a healer' theme: death is the last and ultimate healer of diseases.

This medical imagery associated with the theme 'death as a deliverer' can explain the apparent similarity of the Teithronion formulation, which I take to be an expression of this theme, to later doctors' epitaphs. That similarity is not due to coincidence; it depends on the metaphor which presents death (in the theme 'death as a deliverer') as a healer, and thus a doctor. Charon often stands for, and symbolizes, death. This is his role in our epigram, in which he is said to liberate men from toil, trouble, and pain;[93] what is not explicitly stated, but was unambiguously understood by the archaic readers (given Charon's role and his symbolic equivalence with death and also the theme 'death as a deliverer') is that Charon delivered them from trouble/toil/pain by taking them to Hades. As, we saw, is the case in other texts, Charon's ferrying of the shades into Hades functions as a metaphor for death and Charon can be spoken of as a kind of agent of death. In the Teithronion epigram he is also (implicitly) presented as an agent of death, and hailed as a deliverer, through a version of the 'death as a healer' formulation of the theme 'death as a deliverer'.[94] Let us compare this Teithronion formulation to two tragic expressions of the motif 'death as a healer'.

Aeschylus, *TrGF* iii. F 353

> ὡς οὐ δικαίως θάνατον ἔχθουσιν βροτοί,
> ὅσπερ μέγιστον ῥῦμα τῶν πολλῶν κακῶν

Adesp. *TrGF* ii. F 371

> μηδεὶς φοβείσθω θάνατον ἀπόλυσιν πόνων

---

[93] *Kamatos* is a polysemic word the meanings of which cover the concepts toil, trouble, pains of disease and of childbirth, weariness, illness, and also the product of toil.

[94] Perhaps a further development of this metaphor in which death (and Charon as a metaphor for death) is presented as a healer may have contributed (together with other notions) to Charon's participation (with Plouton and Persephone) in a healing cult in a cave between Tralleis and Nysa (cf. Strabo 14. 1. 44 [649–50]).

The relationship between the Teithronion epigram and these two formulations can be presented as follows:

Aeschylus, TrGF iii. F 353	*Teithronion epigram*
ou dikaios	→ transformation into the opposite [*oudeis*]
thanaton	*ty*
echthousin	*kakos legei*
brotoi	*oudeis*
hosper megiston ryma	*lysamenos kamato*
ton pollon kakon	
[*brotoi*]	*polos anthropon*
[*pollon*]	

Adesp. TrGF ii. fr. 371	*Teithronion epigram*
medeis	*oudeis*
phobeistho	*kakos legei*
thanaton	*ty*
apolysin ponon	*lysamenos* [*polos anthropon*] *kamato*

Let us now compare the two tragic fragments:

Aesch F 353	*Adesp. F 371*
ou dikaios	→ transformation into the opposite
thanaton	*thanaton*
echthousin	*phobeistho*
brotoi	*medeis*
hosper megiston ryma	*apolysin ponon*
ton pollon kakon	

This comparison between the Aeschylean fragment and the adespoton shows that there is a close relationship between the two, and that it is extremely plausible that either one was based on the other or both were dependent on a third formulation of which they were transformations; in either case, they are versions of one intertextual frame, which is a variant of the 'death as a healer' formulation of the theme 'death as a deliverer'. The expression in the Teithronion epigram is closely related to this postulated intertextual frame. The network of similarities and differences between the three formulations is too intricate for the view that they are due to coincidence to be tenable. The hypothesis that best makes sense of these patterns of relationships is that all three are variants—the Aeschylean one a more original and forceful variant—of one intertextual theme which had the following approximate shape: (1) No one (2) Negative verb expressing hostility towards/fear of death (3) [who/for he is] a deliverer from pain/toil or the like.

If this hypothesis is correct, it would follow that this intertextual frame was already established by the time of our epigram, and that the Teithronion formulation was a variant of it, written, read and understood with the help, and by the means, of that frame. This would inevitably have imposed on the archaic readers the meaning (encoded by the epigram-writer through this frame) 'death as a deliverer from toil/trouble'. I submit that we can be certain that, first, the whole expression *polos anthropon lysamenos kamato* in the vicinity of 'Charon', and especially *chaire Charon*, activated that 'death as a deliverer/healer' frame, and imposed forcibly the reading 'the infernal ferryman addressed as a deliverer/healer'; and second, that no epigram writer could have selected the expression *polos anthropon lysamenos kamato* in the vicinity of the name Charon except to address the infernal ferryman and speak of death as a deliverer from toil. For in the assumptions he shared with his readers the juxtaposition of the two imposed the meaning 'infernal ferryman/death' and blocked all other possibilities. But even if the existence of this intertextual frame at the time of our epigram's composition is 'not proven', there can be no doubt that the expression *polos anthropon lysamenos kamato*, in the vicinity of *oud⟨e⟩is ty kakos legei* could not but activate the more general intertextual frame 'death as a deliverer' (which, we saw, had indeed been current at *c.*500 BC), thus confirming further the reading hypothesis formulated on the basis of *chaire Charon*, that the addressee was Charon the ferryman of the dead.

(e) Oude thanonta

Readings and Meanings.   There is one element in the Teithronion inscription which would *prima facie* appear to argue forcibly against the interpretation put forward here, and in favour of the orthodox reading: *oude thanonta*, which would appear to mean 'not even when/now you are dead' which in its turn would appear to support the interpretation of the epigram as an epitaph, and the hypothesis of the dead doctor Charon. However, this reasoning, I suggest, is fallacious. For the elements that make up a sentence and indeed a text are not read each in isolation from the others; nor is reading a purely linear process: it involves, we saw, a continuous coming and going across segments of the text—in this case the whole text—and also a continuous coming and going between lower and higher decoding/reading operations.[95] If it is correct that, as I hope to have shown, it was impossible for an archaic reader to take this epigram for an epitaph, and that he formulated the hypothesis, on the basis of *chaire Charon*, that the epigram was addressed to Charon the ferryman, a hypothesis which was confirmed by *oud⟨e⟩is ty kakos legei*, and further on by the intertextual frame referring to the theme 'death as a deliverer', it would follow that he was incapable of taking the subject of *thanonta* to be Charon, despite the agreement between *ty* as the object of *kakos legei* and *thanonta*. So, what seems to us the obvious reading was impossible for the epigram's contemporaries who, therefore, would have been obliged by their presuppositions to read *oude thanonta* in a different way. What other possibilities are there?

Presumably the author meant to say that no one, not even if dead, would reproach Charon.[96] How could this be said? *Oude thanon* was impossible because of the scansion. *Oude thanonton* was metrically possible but semantically weaker. The author wants to identify himself, and, more especially, if the stele was set over a grave, to identify the dead man (and also to allow the reader to identify himself) with the 'no one' he refers to, this would not be possible if 'no one' was entirely indefinite, both in form and meaning. It is possible that *oude thanonta* should be taken as an accusative absolute; parallels for this apparently ungrammatical construction are not lacking in Greek literature.[97] Failing that, we would have to assume that it is a mistake for the 'grammatical' *thanonton*.[98]

What support is there for either of these hypotheses? First, one

[95] Cf. Ch. I. The discussion is in Eco 1981: 3–43.

[96] *oud⟨e⟩is ty kakos legei oude thanonta* contains a version of a well-established intertextual frame, on which cf. below, 'The Intertextual Frame'.

[97] Cf. Kühner-Gerth 1898: 329–31; Schwyzer 1950: 403; cf. Buck 1955: 137 for dialectal inscriptions. An extra factor which may perhaps have increased tolerance of the accusative absolute in this case is the epigram's imitation of the superficial pattern of oral discourse, which may have led to the seepage of a little of the looseness of everyday speech—as dialogue writers used *anakoloutha* in imitation of that looser speech (cf. Kühner-Gerth 1904: 590–1).

[98] The letterer's inattention, manifested in his omission of the *e* in *oud⟨e⟩is*, would have allowed the preceding accusative to attract *thanonton* and change it to *thanonta*.

of them is inescapable if all that has been said so far is correct.[99] Second, the presence of *lysamenos* in the pentameter cannot be ignored. Klaffenbach[100] thought that the nominative instead of the expected accusative is due either to a mistake or to a possible agreement with the vocative *Charon*. Friedländer and Hoffleit[101] assume that it is unnecessary to emend *lysamenos* into *lysamenon*, but do not explain why. Grammatically, agreement with the vocative would be extremely odd, and can hardly be supported. Either the nominative is emended to preserve the correctness of the construction,[102] or it is explained as an example of *constructio ad sensum*. In the former case the presence of a 'wrong' accusative in the first line should not, then, surprise us. If the latter alternative is correct, my interpretation is preferable. For in the epitaph interpretation the nominative does not make sense. In my reading it makes excellent sense as a nominative absolute, giving the reason why no one speaks ill of Charon: the emphasis shifts back to Charon from *oude thanonta*, Charon is the main topic of the pentameter, and that explains the nominative. Either way, the orthodox reading of the epigram does not receive much support, and should, I submit, be abandoned.

The Intertextual Frame.   The expression *oud⟨e⟩is ty kakos legei oude thanonta* contains a version of a well-established intertextual frame. The following are some significant versions of it: Theognis 245: *oudepot' oude thanon apoleis kleos* etc., itself based on Tyrtaios fr. 12. 31–2 West: *oude pote kleos esthlon apollytai oude onoma autou all' hypo ges per eon* etc. Cf. also *Odyssey* 24. 93–4: *hos sy men oude thanon onom' olesas* ... Another version of this frame which is close to the Teithronion formulation is found in *Odyssey* 11. 553–4: ... *ouk ar' emelles oude thanon lesesthai emoi cholou* ... Cf. also, from the first half of the fifth century, Pindar, *Isthm.* viii. 56: *ton men oude thanont'*

---

[99] If the above analyses are correct, the straightforward construction was not a viable alternative for the archaic reader. Thus there would be no question of the *anakolouthon* construction being ambiguous, despite the vicinity of *ty* and the fact that *kakos legei* takes its object in the accusative. And, of course, *a fortiori* there would be no question of the *lectio facilior* imposing itself and not allowing the *anakolouthon* construction to be hypothesized in the reader's mind—as is the case with modern readers in the absence of a reconstructed archaic horizon of expectations consciously aiming at recovering the original reading.

[100] Klaffenbach 1935: 702.

[101] Friedländer and Hoffleit 1948: 89.

[102] Hansen 1983: 127 emends.

aoidai elipon; Aeschylus, *Cho.* 504: *houto gar ou tethnekas oude per thanon.* The expression in [Theog.] 931–2 ... *epei oude thanont' apohlaioi oudois, on mo ...* etc., does not belong to the type discussed here, and so it is not, as a superficial look might suggest, the closest formulation to that of the Teithronion epigram. It belongs to a related type, as does *Odyssey* 3. 258–9 (*to ke hoi oude thanonti chyten epi gaian echeuan, all' ara ton ge kynes kai oionoi katedapsan*).

There are, then, three variants of the main intertextual frame that is close to the Teithronion formulation: (1) *ou-* ... *oude thanon* with *sy* the subject of both the verb and *thanon*: Theognis 245; *Odyssey* 11. 553–4; (Post-500: Aeschylus, *Cho.* 504); (2) a 'synoptical' version of (1), capable of being analysed into *ou* ... *oude thanon*, with *sy* the subject of both verb and *thanon*: *Odyssey* 24. 93–4. (Post-500: Pindar, *Isthm.* viii. 56); (3) others, related, in which the intertextual frame has undergone a more radical transformation: cf. Tyrtaios fr. 12. 31–2 West. Thus, it is clear that by the time the Teithronion epigram was written, there was an established intertextual frame *ou-* ... *oude thanon* in which the semantic focus and addressee was the deceased—or prospective deceased—and *sy* was the subject of both verb and *thanon*. In the Teithronion epigram this frame was combined with the theme, 'death as a deliverer from pain/trouble', whether or not this theme had already crystallized into an expression 'oudeis hates death for he delivers many men from toil/pain' as I suggested earlier. When the frame *ou-* ... *oude thanon* was put to the service of the theme 'death as a deliverer' which it helps formulate in the Teithronion epigram, it was, of course, transformed; the semantic focus and addressee is no longer the deceased—or prospective deceased—but Charon, standing for death. We can perhaps take this further. The semantic content of the version of the frame *ou-* ... *oude thanon* in Theognis 245, and also in the variants in Hom. *Od.* 24. 93–4 and Tyrtaeus fr. 12. 31–2 West, which we may state generically as 'you will not be forgotten', 'your glory will not be lost', is related to the semantic content of the Teithronion expression 'no one speaks ill of you'. Both make positive statements about the reputation of the person spoken of; the former about the preservation of a positive memory of the deceased's social persona, the latter about the way in which people (perceive and) speak of, Charon. The latter, therefore, may have been inspired by the former. If the thematic intertextual frame 'death as a deliverer' had already crystallized into a frame of the approximate form 'no one hates (or the like) death, for he delivers etc.', it is conceivable that the Teithronion formulation arose out of the interaction between *ouk echthei* (or the like), which provided the controlling semantic direction, and the reputation motif associated with *ou- . . . oude thanon*.

(f) *The Reading*

If the analyses'set out here are correct, our epigram was composed, and read, with the help of the following intertextual frames: (i) *Chaire Charon*. This topos is attested in the fifth century; I suggested that it may have been established already at *c.*500 BC. (ii) *ou- . . . oude thanon*. This was an established topos by 500 BC. (iii) *Death as a deliverer*. This was an established thematic topos by 500 BC; I suggested that it might already have crystallized into the version 'no one hates (or the like) death, for he delivers many men from toil/trouble (and the like)'. (iv) *Charon stands for death*. As we saw in Chapter V, Charon stood for death in the fifth century; we do not know whether he had already done so by 500 BC, as the only other archaic literary reference to him, in the *Minyas*, cannot throw light on the matter. But there is some reason for thinking that he had. For if our reconstruction of his emergence and significance is right, it would follow that the nexus of ideas which gave rise to this metaphor, the association between the ferryman and death viewed as a personal experience, would have been present already at the moment of that emergence. But even if the metaphor had not been established by 500, it was (in the context of the Greek representations of death) an almost inevitable image. Even if we suppose that it was the writer of the Teithronion epigram who had invented it (not a very likely possibility!) the juxtaposition of 'Charon', especially of *chaire Charon*, and the expression *polos anthropon lysamenos kamato* would have inevitably activated for the archaic readers the theme 'death as a deliverer', even if the metaphor in which Charon stood for death had not previously been established. This metaphor gives concrete form to death; it allows death to become a subject, an animate entity with which men can constitute a dialogue.[103] This is what happens in our epigram, where Charon is invoked and propitiated.

---

[103] Thanatos is, of course, also a personification of death. On Thanatos cf. Vermeule 1979: 37–41; Hamdorf 1964: 41 ff.

2. RECONSTRUCTING THE MEANINGS

Even short texts have dense, complex and variable meanings; the reconstruction of the assumptions by means of which the Tei-thronion epigram was written and read has served us well in so far as the basic reading was concerned, the individuation of the topic and the 'first-level' meanings. But when it comes to more complex meanings things become more difficult. First, because there are large parts of the archaic horizon of expectations which elude us. Second, because there were diversities in that horizon which created divergences in the meanings perceived by the archaic readers. And such meanings are not determinate. What we can do is reconstruct the parameters determining the author's selections and the semantic fields of the 'material' that went into the making of the text, that is, reconstruct the main parameters within which its contemporaries made sense of it. Their full reading process cannot be properly reconstructed; we can try to re-create it, but at this level our own presuppositions inevitably intrude at least up to a point. I will try to read the epigram through the viewpoint provided by the horizon of expectations of the archaic age and recover the controlling images and directions that determined the selections that shaped its creation, and thus suggest certain readings. But the meanings that will be proposed will not necessarily (in fact, not probably) be all the meanings that its contemporaries would have extracted from the text, nor, necessarily, the meanings that all its contemporaries would have extracted from it. But I hope that they are all archaic meanings, that I have not interjected my own mental furniture and got back a reflection of my own presuppositions.

The epigram[104] is cast in the shape of direct address with Charon as the addressee, invoked at the beginning of the poem by means of *chaire* and his name in the vocative. The use of the vocative posits a relationship between two subjects;[105] as Charon here stands also for death, the vocative also establishes a subject to subject relationship

---

[104] I am not concerned with the question of whether it reflects an elegy. Friedländer and Hoffleit 1948: 89–90 claim that it 'may even be a pretty exact echo of a threnodic elegy'. Gentili 1968: 56 challenges that view. Both Friedländer and Hoffleit and Gentili interpret the epigram as an epitaph. I believe that the epigram was written for the purpose in which it was put—using established topoi. But whether or not this was the case, what matters here is how the writer composed this epigram in this particular form, for it to be inscribed on a stele, whatever its literary models may or may not have been.

[105] Cf. Culler 1981: 141.

between the speaker and death. But whose is the speaking voice? The statements about Charon are in free indirect speech; they are presented as objective truth emanating not from any one subject, but, the format claims, mankind. The implicit 'first subject' is mankind. Everyone who reads the epigram takes on the role of the narrator, embodies mankind, with regard to this address and its addressee, as the writer had done when composing the epigram. Mankind is also present in another form: *oudeis* is a refraction of mankind; so *oudeis* is also a refraction of the speaking subject. Because the reader embodies mankind as the speaker of the epigram, he also comes to embody, temporarily, *oudeis*. So that *oudeis ty* etc. comes also to mean 'I do not "hate" death' etc. Thus, at one level of the discourse, the epigram is concerned with the activities of the speaking subject as they reflect on the addressee. If the stele on which this epigram is inscribed had been set over an individual grave another embodiment of the universal speaking subject would have been perceived to have been the deceased over whose grave it stood, who might have been imagined as speaking the epigram. If it had been set up at the entrance of a cemetery the community of the living and of the dead buried in the cemetery would also have been perceived as refractions, embodiments of the universal speaking subject. In any case, this epigram can be considered, at one level, as an apostrophe in the discourse between the living and the dead conducted in the cemeteries by means of the epitaphs, visits to the grave and offerings proffered, and, generally, by means of the whole nexus of established funerary behaviour governing the relationships between the living and the dead.

This epigram, then, should be characterized also by the traits that characterize apostrophes in literary discourse. Indeed, the established characteristics of the apostrophe[106] are apparent in the epigram. The first characteristic of the apostrophe is that it makes the objects of the universe potentially responsive, sentient forces. This epigram, like all apostrophes, turns the object into a subject with which it attempts to establish a relationship. Apostrophes create a discursive time and space, a discursive now in which absent objects are present subjects. Our epigram turns into presence an absence which is by definition irreversible in empirical time. Charon could

---

[106] Cf. Culler 1981: 135–54. Cf. also Bergren 1982: 83–108, esp. 84–95 on the deployment of sacred apostrophe in the Homeric Hymns.

never be present among the living. He was, we saw, immovably
rooted to the water that forms the frontier between Hades and the
marginal place between Hades and the Upper World. He had no
established cult in early Greece,[107] so there was no time/space in
which men and Charon regularly 'met' in the cultic act. Though
any classification of this epigram is inevitably culturally determined
I will venture to suggest that one way of describing it is as an *ad hoc*
cultic act. Charon is addressed by means of an invocation used also
for deities, but the Teithronion epigram is not an invocation like
those addressed to deities. For Charon did not have an established
presence in cult and he did not stand towards men in the type of
relationship in which deities stood to them, which involved on the
one hand protection and on the other worship. This epigram then,
is an exceptional form of discourse, partly cast into the mould of
divine invocation, partly characterized by the traits pertaining to its
character as apostrophe in the discourse between the living and the
dead conducted in the cemeteries—though strictly speaking it is
not part of the discourse between the living and the dead but
between the living and death and the powers of death in the context
of the wider interactions between the living and the dead. Of
course, we saw, the relationship established by this epigram is not
simply between mankind/the reader and Charon, but also between
the former and death in the person of Charon, who here is both
himself, the infernal figure who plays a certain role in the transition
between life and death, and also a metaphor for death. And the
epigram is addressed both to the ferryman as an 'actor' in the
temporal sequence of events that come between one's death and
one's integration into Hades, and to death itself, the event and the
force that causes it.

The apostrophe, though it appears to be establishing a relationship
between the self and the other, can be seen as an act of 'radical
interiorization'[108] which either fills the world with fragments of the
self, or internalizes what might have been thought external, by
addressing the addressee only in terms of an activity that it/he
provokes in the addressing subject. This is the case here, a fact partly
masked by the fact that the activities of the speaking subject are
refracted by means of *oudeis*. *Polloi anthropon* belongs to a different

---

[107] For the Roman world cf. Sourvinou-Inwood 1986a: 225.

[108] Cf. Culler 1981: 146–8. On this aspect of the apostrophe cf. also De Man 1979: 28–30.

category: it is not another refraction of *oudeis* but a fragment of it, and of the speaking subject; a fragment that is part of a narrative element in the epigram, and which is located, not in the timeless present, as the speaking subject and *oudeis* are, but in the past. At the level of reading in which the reader embodies the speaking subject, *polloi anthropon* becomes an 'other' situated in the past, whose activities affect the speaking subject, of whom it might be perceived as a potential refraction (I too may one day be one of the *polloi anthropon* whom death will liberate from toil; or, if the stele stood over a grave, I too may be one of these people). The idea that the speaking subject addresses the addressee only in terms of an activity which the latter provokes in the speaking subject is certainly true here at the superficial level—involving the speaking subject as a whole in the hexameter, and a fragment of the speaking subject in the pentameter. But at a second, deeper, level, the real focus is indeed the addressee himself, for the activities of the speaking subject acquire focus and importance with reference to that addressee. However, at a yet deeper third level, the true focus and reference point of the epigram is indeed the speaking subject. For, as we shall now see, the positive statement addressed to Charon aims at creating a certain situation of interest and importance to mankind.

Since *chaire Charon* is an invocation the first message received by the archaic reader is that the epigram addresses Charon in terms of an invocation of a deity. Another connotation is salutation. We have seen that it is conceivable that the shades may have been thought to address Charon with *chaire* when they first met him on the shore. If this speculation were correct, the salutation here would have evoked that moment, and so transposed the reader to that situation, made him see himself as dead, which would have intensified his emotional involvement in the epigram. Another connotation carried by *chaire* is 'rejoice, be well'. Here this exhortation can be taken on its own and/or be causally connected with the statement that follows; 'rejoice because no one speaks ill of you' etc. Finally, *chaire Charon* brought up the contrast between Charon's grim function and the joyous connotations evoked by his name, which articulated the fundamental contrast, in the archaic representations, between life characterized by joy and death characterized by joy-lessness. But it also extended the quality of joy into the domain of death, thus asserting symbolically the values and strength of life

over those of death. For the archaic reader of this epigram these
connotations would have great force. They would again intensify
his emotional involvement with the epigram by bringing up vividly
the grimness of death, and its tragedy. In this way, the theme 'death
as a deliverer' contained in the pentameter is challenged in advance
as it is challenged by the assertion of the values and strength of life
over death contained in this expression.

The rest of the epigram, *oud(e)is ty kakos legei, oude thanonta,
pollos anthropon lysamenos kamato* is a propitiatory statement to, and
about, the infernal ferryman. It is claiming that men have a not
unfriendly attitude towards him, and is thus trying to establish a
friendly relationship between him and men, to placate him and win
his favour for men. The mentality involved here is the same as that
operating in the euphemistic appellations of terrifying supernatural
beings, such as Eumenides, Eubouleus,[109] and, strikingly similar in
content to this formulation, Eukles for Hades (the god).[110] It fits
perfectly the interpretation of Charon as a figure of reassurance.
Since in the Teithronion epigram he is both himself, the ferryman,
and he stands also for death, the propitiatory statement is addressed
both to the ferryman who guides the shade's crossing into Hades,
and to death. Charon, we saw, inhabited the frightening, anxiety-
creating passage between life and death. Winning his favour and
protection, or just taking the steps to do so, provided 'insurance'
for, and reassurance about, this terrifying passage. That is, the fact
that the reader (and, if the epigram stood over a grave, the deceased,
fictionally) addressed this propitiatory statement to Charon established, for the speaker (who was also the narratee), any other
narratees who may have been present, and, if it was part of a grave
monument, for those who had set it up, a friendly relationship with
the infernal ferryman; if it was set up by a community at the
entrance of the cemetery the relationship was established between
the ferryman and the living members of that community and the
collectivity of the dead buried in the cemetery. It established a
relationship in the same way that a sacrifice or a dedication does.
Sacrifices and dedications are established mechanisms for attracting
divine benevolence because they involve giving something to the
deity in the hope that this will attract a corresponding benevolence,

---

[109] On Eubouleus cf. Graf 1974: 172 and n. 72; Burkert 1975: 100.
[110] Cf. Burkert 1975: 100.

but also because through this act an actual relationship is established between devotee and deity. Thinking of death in terms of Charon allows the writer and the reader to manipulate symbolically the unfathomable concept of death and establish a dialogue between men and death. This is reassuring in itself and also allows this kind of propitiatory behaviour which is not only reassuring, but also hopes to ensure the interlocutor's benevolence—in this case the 'message' being, roughly, 'death, be kind to mankind/me'. Death cannot be avoided, but it can be long in coming, not painful, and so on. Ultimately, in reconciling oneself symbolically with death in this way, one can allay the anxiety and fear generated by the prospect of death (especially every time death strikes within one's immediate environment), and so live peacefully with it.

The form of the propitiatory statement is based on the theme 'death as a deliverer'. This, we saw, was not a mainstream collective attitude in the archaic period. But because it had established itself as a topos, an intertextual frame, it could become detached from the nexus of attitudes to which it had organically belonged, and be used on its own, in a different context, which, of course, inevitably affected its meanings. Here it is used as an element of praise in a propitiatory context; hence it does not convey an attitude about life and death, but makes what the epigram presents as a statement of fact which throws a positive light on death and which is presented as 'the truth'. This affected the form in which the theme was expressed. Compare the related expressions in the Aeschylean fragment *TrGF* iii. F 353 ... *thanaton ... hosper megiston ryma ton pollon kakon* and the adespoton fragment *TrGF* ii. F 371 ... *thanaton apolysin ponon*, which present the theme in universal and atemporal terms to *polos anthropon lysamenos kamato*. The latter does not speak of death as a deliverer from pain, but says, basically, 'o death, we don't feel hostility towards you because in fact you have delivered many men from toil'. Not necessarily 'I' will find, or 'everyone' finds, death delivers them from pain, but it has happened that death has delivered many people from pain—and this is a positive aspect of death. The theme 'death as a deliverer' is put here to the service of mainstream representations and attitudes, in a context of funerary behaviour concerned with coping with anxiety about death.

It might be argued that the fact that this epigram would be unique in the extant record of archaic funerary behaviour would constitute a serious argument against the interpretation put forward here. Leaving aside the questionable legitimacy of such an objection, I am now going to show that though this particular manifestation is unique, the mentality and type of funerary behaviour of which it is a manifestation is well established in the archaic period and takes different forms in different places. It has become clear, I hope, that the ultimate aim of the epigram is to ensure the protection of Charon and the benevolence of death for both the dead—those buried in the cemetery, or the person with whose grave the epigram was associated if it stood over a grave and the prospective dead that are the living who visit the cemetery and read the epigram. The act of addressing this epigram is not only aiming at securing that benevolence, but also in proclaiming that it is doing so, and thus establishing the claim as a reality at the level of discourse, of petition. The presence of the statement, the establishment of the claim, brings with it in the contemporary reader's mind the granting of the petition, and the presence of the inscribed epigram would also have been perceived as a sign of protection by the infernal powers invoked for the dead buried in the cemetery (or the grave).[111] This is an image of reassurance for the living with reference to the dead, and to themselves as prospective dead.

. The mentality, and funerary behaviour, which seeks to ensure the protection of the infernal powers for the deceased was, we saw, well established in archaic Greece, as was the practice of attempting to ensure the protection of the Underworld powers for the dead by setting up, on the grave, and perhaps also elsewhere in the cemetery, images of these powers and of the desired relationship of benevolence and protection between these powers and the dead, as well as shrines to those chthonic powers. The Teithronion epigram fits well into this series, for it is a verbal articulation of the same type of relationship. The Attic stelai surmounted by a sphinx in particular are very close to the Teithronion epigram, in so far as their protective aspect is concerned. The similarity is increased by the fact that the sphinx is also a death-bringer, an agent of death, and thus it is also an image of death. Since this practice is firmly rooted in the archaic period, it is legitimate to consider some later formulations of a comparable idea, which will illustrate some further

---

[111] A model for making this clear would be the presence of an icon in a modern Catholic or Orthodox grave being perceived not only as a petition for divine protection but also as a sign of this protection; that is, the icon both asks for, and grants, divine protection.

articulations of this concept that may be relevant to the Teithronion epigram[112] as illustrative models of a comparable practice, even though we cannot assume identity of belief, since they are part of a different nexus of funerary ideology. A third-century BC Thessalian grave is 'dedicated' to the other psychopompos, Hermes Chthonios, by means of the inscription, on a marble stele, *Damasias Timokleous. Hermei Chthonioi.*[113] On some other stelae, also from Thessaly, with a representation of Hermes, the inscription contains just the dedication, without the dead man's name: *Hermaou Chthoniou* or *Hermei Chthonioi.*[114] Another practice, also comparable to one of the aspects of the Teithronion epigram, is for funerary epigrams to formulate the theme 'introduction of the deceased to the powers of the Underworld, recommendation of the deceased to their benevolence'.[115]

Finally, though there are no exact formal parallels for the Teithronion epigram, its elements and characteristics can all be matched with those of other archaic epigrams belonging to the loose category 'dedicatory' to which our epigram should be ascribed.[116] First, the fact that the whole epigram consists of an address to Charon is paralleled in a group of archaic dedicatory epigrams in which the entire dedication has become an address to the god.[117] One of these epigrams[118] includes the address *chaire Fanax Herakles* and also a request for the granting of good reputation for its dedicator. Hence, despite the reference to the dedication—and the prose signature—there are formal similarities with the Teithronion epigram. It reads:

---

[112] It has been suggested (Papachristodoulou 1971: 94–9) that a stone found in a cemetery in Argos inscribed *Hagehidos*, of 475–50 BC bore the name of, and was dedicated to, a chthonic deity called Hagesis who was the protector of the grave; Johnston 1990: 444 s.v. C classifies it as a gravestone. On the 5th- and 4th-cent. inscriptions from near Cyrene which had been erroneously claimed as evidence for the identification of divinity and deceased cf. Forbes 1956: 235–52; Robert and Robert 1958: 209.

[113] *IG* ix. 2. 736. Cf. Lattimore 1962: 104.

[114] *IG* ix. 2. 999–1003, 1266, 1004–5, 1055. Cf. Helly 1978: 122–3.

[115] The following are some examples from the 3rd and 2nd cents. BC: *GV* 1572, beginning of the 3rd cent.; *GV* 1693, 3rd/2nd cent.; *GV* 1154 ll. 13–14 (GG 166), end of the 2nd cent.; *GV* 1179 ll. 7–8 (GG 216), 2nd cent.

[116] Loose, because I take it to include genuine dedications and idiosyncratic specimens like ours and the one from Thasos I will mention below.

[117] Cf. e.g. Hansen 1983: 418.

[118] Hansen 1983: 396; Friedländer and Hoffleit 1948: 111; Jeffery 1990: 255 no. 16, 261 no. 16: it is inscribed on a small clay pillar or pyramid (Metapontum, last quarter of 6th cent.).

Νικόμαχός μ' ἐπόε. |
χαῖρε Fάναξ ῾ηέρακλες· | ὅ τοι κεραμεύς μ' ἀνέθεκε· |
δὸς δέ F' ἰν ἀνθρόποις | δόξαν ἔχεν ἀ〈γ〉αθ〈ά〉ν

On a marble block built into the city wall beside a gate in Thasos
an epigram of the last quarter of the sixth century, which belonged
originally to two large reliefs depicting Herakles and Dionysos,
Zeus' sons and guardians of the city, of which only the one depicting
Herakles survives,[119] reads as follows:

Ζηνὸς καὶ Σεμέλης καὶ 'Αλκμήνης τανυπέπλο :
ἐστᾶσιν παῖδες τῆσδε πόλεως φυλαςοί.

It resembles the Teithronion epigram in the following ways. First,
the latter establishes a positive relationship between mankind and
Charon/death by means of addressing a positive statement to him.
The Thasos epigram describes a desired state of affairs as fact and
thus reinforces the strength of what is in this case a matter of
established religious belief—rather than, as in the Teithronion one,
of individual hope. It reinforces the guardianship of Herakles and
Dionysos and also the strength of the belief in it, so that it too
brings about reassurance. The statement in Thasos was expressed
iconographically as well as verbally. The surviving relief shows
Herakles as an archer, kneeling and ready to shoot. This representation, by the city gate, expressed the same concept: Herakles
is guarding the city. In the case of the Teithronion epigram, the
message is only verbal—though we cannot exclude the possibility
that the stele may have been connected with a more complex
monument which had included a representation of Charon.

In these circumstances, it is clear that the Teithronion epigram
interpreted in the way suggested here, though unique, fits perfectly
into the archaic funerary ideology and behaviour, and into the
formal structures of archaic dedicatory epigrams.

There is, we saw, a little evidence to suggest that at the time of
its inscription, at *c.*500, there may have been some interest in
Charon; his two earliest representations belong to this time, and
they are among his very few Greek images outside the series of
white-ground lekythoi. If there had been such an interest at this
time, conceivably as a result of the influence of a literary work, the

---

[119] Hansen 1983: 415; Jeffery 1990: 301, 307 no. 63, 412 pl. 58 no. 63. On this inscription
cf. also Lazzarini 1976: 156.

Teithronion epigram (or perhaps another epigram, of which ours is a reflection) may have been inspired by the convergence of this focus in the figure of the infernal ferryman on the one hand, and the feelings of anxiety about death on the other. The exact circumstances and context of its erection are beyond recovery. It was not found *in situ*, so we cannot know whether it had stood over a grave (perhaps combined with a base or structure inscribed with the name of the deceased) or elsewhere in a cemetery, perhaps at the entrance like the large upright slab which marked the entry to the cemetery area at Tsikalario on Naxos—the cemetery is mainly eighth century, with some archaic burials.[120]

I hope to have shown that this epigram was addressed to Charon the ferryman of the dead, who also stood for, and symbolized, death. And that it sought to propitiate Charon and ensure his benevolence for mankind, for the dead, and also for the living who, through the act of reading the epigram, saw themselves momentarily as prospective dead. Apart from seeking to ensure this benevolence, the epigram also established a friendly relationship between men and Charon, at the level of discourse and thus generated reassurance, like the images on the white-ground Athenian lekythoi. Indeed, these Charonian images on the fifth-century funerary lekythoi show that a propitiatory dedication to Charon (perceived also as a metaphor for death) is an entirely appropriate dedication in a cemetery of *c.*500 BC. Charon, as the lekythoi and the passage in Euripides' *Alcestis* show, can be invoked, a coming shade recommended to him, and he can be propitiated. It is in this semantic space that is located the dedication of the Teithronion epigram and its propitiatory address to Charon. The fact that the mentality articulated in, and articulating, texts like the *Alcestis* passage and the images on the lekythoi is of the same type as that which, on the interpretation set out here is reflected in the Teithronion epigram, shows, I submit, that this interpretation fits excellently within the nexus of beliefs and attitudes associated with the infernal ferryman between *c.*500 BC and *c.*400 BC; and this offers support for its validity.

---

[120] Cf. Kurtz and Boardman 1971: 179.

APPENDIX

Death, Burial, and Model-Testing: *A Critique*

1. INTRODUCTION

My thesis concerning the shift in the early Greek attitudes to death (cf. Ch. IV), set out in Sourvinou-Inwood (1981: 15–39 and 1983: 33–48), was challenged by Morris.[1] I shall answer his critique by subjecting it to a multifaceted, in-depth investigation, not only to show that it is invalid but also to address the important methodological problems that are involved in this disagreement.

2. THE METHODOLOGY OF INVESTIGATING DEATH

Morris believes (1989, 298–9) that the best methodology for investigating death is 'to build a simplifying model from prior probabilities, establishing which way the burden of proof lies, and then to examine it in the light of the evidence, modifying, adjusting or discarding the original hypothesis as necessary. The texts are so difficult that the most we can hope for is compatibility with a theory.' The fundamental flaw of this strategy is that, precisely because of the inadequacy of the evidence, it is especially vulnerable to radical distortion through the intrusion of culturally determined assumptions. While it is possible to devise methods to limit the distorting effects of cultural determination,[2] the model-building strategy imports them at the very centre of the argument, as I will try to show.

---

[1] Morris 1989. This article was supposed to be published in *JHS*, accompanied by an extremely brief version of my own reply. After seeing that brief reply Morris withdrew his article from *JHS* and published a revised version in *Classical Antiquity*. He gave no indication of this history.

[2] Sourvinou-Inwood 1987: 41–3; 1991: 3–23.

We make sense of data (of all data, but especially of data which are the few, obscurely seen, fragments of a now lost reality) by organizing them into 'structures': these letters are part of a poem, these stones are the remains of a temple. It is because of this organization, and not only because of its shape, that the function, the meaning, of a particular element—such as a stone—is identified. If the data are very fragmentary and problematic they can be organized mistakenly and still appear to fit; for they may make up a plausible 'structure', which, however, does not reproduce correctly the ancient reality. Thus, it is important to avoid organizing fragmentary data on the basis of wrong assumptions into the wrong 'structures'; we need to ensure that the investigation is not contaminated through the intrusion of the wrong 'organizing centres' (such as, for example, the assumption that a certain group of stones had made up one house when in reality there were two). Testing a preconstructed model against the evidence entails that the data are seen through *a priori* patterns which function as 'organizing centres' through which sense is made of fragmentary evidence. Like all such, these *a priori* models may or may not be accurate reconstructions of the ancient realities. If they are not, their deployment leads to falsification of the evidence and to mistaken conclusions. For when in theory they are being tested, in reality they function as 'organizing centres' which order the data into patterns which reproduce the model which is in theory being tested, by stressing some data and underplaying others, by connecting certain elements in certain configurations, and so on. For 'testing' a model means asking 'Can the data be arranged in a way that mirrors this model?' Thus the central assumption which is supposed to be tested in fact structures the data around itself in such a way that they are made to fit, and thus appear to validate it; while in reality they only do so because they have been structured by it in the first place. The fact that, as will become clear, Morris ignores completely whole sets of the evidence which had formed part of my case is one example of this type of self-validation of model-testing.

The exiguity and problematic nature of the evidence pertaining to early Greek attitudes to death entails that it is very difficult to reach incontrovertible conclusions. But it is desirable to undertake systematic investigations in this area; for otherwise the vacuum is implicitly filled by older orthodoxies and unexamined assumptions which are so subtly enmeshed into the scholarly discourse as to appear to be self-evidently correct, 'common sense'. However, the unfavourable circumstances make it imperative to base any such attempt on a rigorous and neutral methodology, the validity of which is not dependent on the validity of *a priori* assumptions, which does not involve casting the evidence into preconceived moulds, and in which the various parts of the argument are as little as possible dependent on, and so 'contaminated' by, the others. One of the implications of the problematic nature of our evidence,[3] is that we need to guard against the hidden assumption, the implicit structuring of the discourse dependent on the unstated (often unconscious) notion, that if a view contrary to one's own cannot be conclusively proven it can be presumed to be wrong, even when what evidence there is points in the direction of that view contrary to one's own.[4]

The methodology that governed my investigations, which I described in Chapter IV, can, it seems, be misunderstood; I will try to show that Morris misunderstood it seriously. Before I move on to the central argument I should mention another, not unimportant, misunderstanding. What I tried to describe in those two essays, and developed further here, cannot[5] be defined as 'a mass change in individual psychologies'. What I tried to do was to set out the parameters determining common assumptions and responses concerning death, and to show that these changed in certain circles under the influence of changed circumstances. For example, someone's (obsessive or not) fear of a nuclear war is an individual psychological phenomenon; this is different from the fact that the possibility, and the desire to avoid (certain types of) war because of the danger of a nuclear holocaust are part of our common cultural assumptions determining individual responses in interaction with a host of other things; both result from the fact that a new parameter 'change in war technology has produced the possibility of a nuclear

[3] Which should be a self-evident part of any rigorous methodology, but needs to be explicitly spelled out in this case, for Morris has fallen into its trap.

[4] Morris alleges (1989: 298) that I have made 'sweeping generalizations about "collective representations" on the basis of this patchwork of snippets' etc. and that I do not take account of the reading methodology behind a (hardly new or original) comment by Macfarlane which he cites. I hope that a reading of the original papers will convince that this allegation is unfair. Conceivably, the summary presentation (forced through restrictions of space) of some arguments may have misled those less familiar with what is taken for granted in the reading of ancient texts.

[5] As Morris believes (1989: 297).

holocaust' has entered our system of collective attitudes after 1945 AD. I did not use literary texts as evidence for what any particular author 'truly felt'; what I tried to determine was whether or not attitudes were expressed at this time in literature which are at variance, and in conflict, with the earlier ones; whether, that is, the parameters of the death discourse in general have changed. Let me bring an example from a later period. I do not agree with those who think that the fragment *TrGF* i. 43 F 19 (Kritias fr. 1 N) shows that tragedy challenged the religious discourse of the polis;[6] for comparable apparently 'subversive' statements in tragedies which survive complete can be seen to be subsequently deconstructed. But the fact that such a statement could be articulated in a tragedy is itself significant; it reflects the fact that the later fifth-century Athenian discourse encompassed such possibilities in a way that made it conceivable for such a statement to be articulated in a tragedy. That fragment would have been an index of this aspect of that discourse even if we had no other evidence.

On the central argument, I will now argue that the first part of Morris's critique is irrelevant to my case. Let me restate the steps in my argument and the logical hierarchy of my case. I began with the Greek data. On the basis of the study of these data I reached the conclusions about a partial shift in attitudes summarized in Chapter IV. Let me quote my formulation of this shift (for Morris has oversimplified my case radically, and then argued against that distorted schematic construct):[7] 'The shift in social attitudes to death in the archaic period was a very complex process ... what happened was not a drastic change, but a partial shift in the collective representations. The earlier model did not disappear: in some places and circles it became modified ... in others it lived on. Its "survival" was twofold: first as a living reality—sometimes perhaps slightly altered—in certain areas, circles and individuals ...; and second, as a consciously held and propagated intellectual position, derived from Homer and adapted to serve an emerging ideology of patriotism which glorifies death in the service of the city-state (cf. the poets Kallinos and Tyrtaios).' I also made clear (1983: 45) that this shift 'originated in aristocratic and intellectual circles'; and that

---

[6] Recent discussions have centred on authorship (on this fr. cf. most recently Davies 1989a: 16–32 with extensive bibliog.). This does not affect my argument, since my point concerns what can be said in a 5th-cent. tragedy, and these discussions do not affect the date.

[7] The quotation is from Sourvinou-Inwood 1981: 37; cf. also 1983: 45.

'collective representations change slowly, and ... even when they do, stratifications take place, so that old attitudes survive along the new ones' (1981: 16 and n. 6) and 'old attitudes can be found side by side with new ones in the same age, in different places and circles, but sometimes also within one individual' (1983: 33). My next step was to try to consider how this shift came about. For, in my view, if it could be shown that at the relevant period there were indeed circumstances likely to be conducive to the production of such a shift, this would offer some confirmation for the notion that that shift had taken place, by suggesting that it was not simply a mirage created by the fragmentary and problematic state of the evidence. Having considered the circumstances of eighth-century, and subsequently archaic, Greece I concluded that there was indeed a correlation between circumstances conducive to change and the shift in attitudes. I suggested that the changing circumstances of the Greek world in the eighth century affected the existing system of funerary behaviour and attitudes to death and afterlife beliefs. The increase in population,[8] urbanization and the rise of the polis,[9] and the sharp increase in communications inside and outside Greece and colonization expanded drastically Greek physical and mental horizons, and dislocated or destroyed many of the structures on which the 'familiar' death attitudes had depended. These changing demographic socio-economic, political, and intellectual realities in interaction with each other, affected, I suggested, the existing system of funerary behaviour, attitudes to death, and eschatology. They initiated a process of change, feedback, and interaction within

---

[8] Morris's criticism of Snodgrass notwithstanding (cf. e.g. 1989: 301–2; cf. Sallares' criticism of Morris's (1987) criticism of Snodgrass (Sallares 1991: 122–6; cf. also 50–107), and my answer to Morris's reply to Sallares in my review of I. Morris, *Death-Ritual and Social Structure in Classical Antiquity* (Cambridge 1992), forthcoming in *Man*), it is difficult to deny that at least some population increase took place, as indeed Morris accepts. The rate of growth does not affect my argument; for I had not suggested that the population increase affected attitudes to death directly, but through changes that we know happened anyway, primarily the emergence of the polis (cf. esp. Sourvinou-Inwood 1981: 15, cf. also 1983: 34), and also the expansion of communications and colonization; since Morris does not deny the reality of these phenomena the degree of the population growth does not affect this case.

[9] My use of the word 'urbanization' was probably wrong, but the substance of the argument is not affected: the change involved on the one hand the emergence of the polis as the central political, economic, religious, and social unit, and on the other the move—in at least some cases, and some cases is what I am talking about—from a small village to a 'town-like' settlement; even Morris's own numbers do not dispute this. Cf. on the spatial organization and 'urbanization' of early Greek cities: Vallet 1987: 133–63.

the interlocking parts of the funerary system and continued to fuel it through the following period, thanks to the continuing socio-economic and political fluidity and unrest and to intellectual developments. I suggested that these changed circumstances affected death-related behaviour and attitudes through four main channels, each interacting with the other, and with the death attitudes, and generating feedbacks and interactions. 'First, through the break-up of the earlier small, tightly-knit communities and the rise of the polis. Second, through the emergence of individualism, which affected the perception of one's own identity and death. Third, through the other intellectual developments of the archaic period, and especially philosophical speculation of an ethical and esch-atological nature. And finally, through the general mental tone of insecurity and fear of disorder resulting from the upheavals brought about by the dramatic expansion of horizons, the drastic and rapid socio-economic and political changes and the continuing unrest within the cities' (Sourvinou-Inwood 1983: 48; cf. 1981: 39).

To ensure that these analyses were not distorted by my own culturally determined assumptions, I used comparative material. I found that the Homeric and earlier nexus of death-related behav-iour and attitudes as I had identified it resembled to some extent in its general lines Ariès's 'Tamed Death' model, so I described it as 'a version of the "Tamed Death" attitude analysed by Ariès' (Sourvinou-Inwood 1981: 16–17; 1983: 34). But I also pointed out (cf. esp. 1981: 39) the considerable differences and spoke of general types of attitudes. The same is true of what I consider to be the shift away from the earlier type of death attitudes, a shift which I only described as 'broadly comparable' with the change in Europe in the Late Middle Ages.[10] In these circumstances, my case can only be invalidated if it can be shown that my analyses and conclusions concerning the *Greek data* are invalid; given the very particular and specific ways in which I used Ariès's models (cf. 1983: 33–4), it cannot be invalidated by the fact that there are differences in the

---

[10] Morris's quotations (1989: 300–1) from 'Sourvinou-Inwood 1981', are wrenched from their context in a way which obscures this very important point and significantly distorts my conclusions. In particular, the sentence preceding his second quotation reads 'There are also considerable differences, which is natural, given the different circumstances, but also the different eschatology and overall religious ideology and conception of man and the universe involved.' After the quotation I continue 'But the more complex the society, and the more developed its intellectual thought, the more individual and less "typical" its collective representations of and attitudes to death are likely to be.'

circumstances of early Greece and medieval Europe—which I had stressed myself. Morris's critique is fundamentally misconceived. He argues that my analyses are erroneous because the causes conducive to a shift in attitudes were not present in eighth-century Greece and there are not sufficient similarities between early Greece and late medieval Europe 'to expect *a priori* that there might have been comparable changes in attitudes towards death' (Morris 1989: 303). But this criticism would have been valid only if, like him, I had begun with the construction of a model 'from prior probabilities' and proceeded to test it; for in that case if he could show that any such model (which, on this misreading, would be at the centre of my case) was misconceived, that I had built my argument on a false analogy between the circumstances of early Greece and medieval Europe, he would have produced a case against my analyses and conclusions. But this is not what I did.

Morris's own position is as follows (1989: 299): 'The question is not whether Greek attitudes were the same in 500 as they had been ten generations earlier—they simply cannot have been—but whether the changes which took place are historically significant . . .' But who decides, and on what basis, what is a 'historically significant' change in attitudes to death? His question invites subjective judgements and *a priori* assumptions into the core of the investigation, to function as organizing centres. Indeed, the sentence just cited continues 'and the facts can only be called important or unimportant relative to a specific theory.' Obviously, any structuring of the continuum of experience depends on certain presuppositions, on the basis of which categories can be created. But the notion that this structuring should be governed by external categories and *a priori* assumptions deliberately imported into the investigation at an early stage is, in my view, misconceived, for these culturally determined presuppositions will corrupt the argument. Here the subjective perception that no circumstances conducive to a historically significant shift in attitudes obtained at the relevant period is assumed to entail that no such shift took place, a model is constructed on that basis, and then tested. I hope to have shown the dangers involved in this type of procedure. On my view, we need to try to construct a neutral methodology for reconstructing the funerary behaviour and attitudes of the Dark Ages, the eighth century, and the archaic age separately; and then to attempt to determine their relationship, making such (inevitably culturally determined) judgements as to whether there are 'historically significant differences'—if at all—at the very last stage, when they will not contaminate the whole investigation.

Morris's critique of my papers is also impressionistic. He simply states that because the city-state did not involve proper urbanization (while in fact it did already in the eighth century, at least in the case of the colonies), and because the analogies with medieval Europe are weak,[11] my thesis that the rise of the polis affected attitudes to death is wrong. He does not address the point, the specific modalities I discussed (cf. e.g. 1981: 28–9): the break-up of small communities,[12] the drastic expansion of the physical and mental horizons (in which colonization played a major role), or the general context of fluidity brought about by the rise of the polis and the continuous political and social fluidity in the archaic period. His critique of my discussion of 'the rise of individualism' consists of a series of dismissive statements. In fact, the notion that the rise of individualism took place in the archaic period is widely accepted and is not an *ad hoc* hypothesis I constructed under the influence of developments in late medieval Europe. Also, I did not suggest that individualism (which I perceive as a complex phenomenon which develops gradually, not as an 'essence' which is absent one day and present the next) is 'a cause' of the shift in the attitudes towards death; but that, in the context of a very complex interactive process, the circumstances which affected the attitudes to death also led to the gradual emergence of individualism, and that this in its turn

[11] Incidentally, in claiming that the circumstances in medieval Europe were too different from those of early Greece to be relevant Morris implicitly assumes that differences in scale in a few of the relevant factors are more important than the general correspondence in the general configuration of the two systems, and in their behaviour, which are interestingly comparable.

[12] I will illustrate my suggestions concerning the differences in the death-ritual and the relevant interacting attitudes between a small village on the one hand and a larger community on the other (cf. Sourvinou-Inwood 1983: 42–3; 1981: 28–9) with a quotation: An educated (anonymous) modern Greek woman living in Athens comments on the fact that after her father's death she wore black mourning garments when visiting her village of origin, but not when in Athens, and contrasts death-related behaviour and attitudes in villages to those in urban Greece (in terms that illustrate a fundamental *de facto* difference between very small communities and larger ones): 'In the village we accept death, we have become familiar with death, because when something of this kind happens (i.e. when someone dies) all the inhabitants of the village take part. In this way little by little they learn to accept him (i.e. death). It is not like here.' She had earlier spoken of the wake held for her father in the village and complained about the Greek legislation which forbids the corpse to be kept inside the house in the towns, which, she says 'is like they refuse to accept death' (*Pantheon* 862 (26 August 1986), 40–2).

reinforced and accelerated the shift in the funerary attitudes, which, I stressed, was very complex, a series of shifts over a long period (Sourvinou-Inwood 1981. 39, 1983. 48).

One of my conclusions concerning the death-ritual pertained to the role of the kin relative to that of the wider community. I suggested that in the Dark Ages the wider community, the village, participated in the death-ritual *de facto*, and that the emergence of the polis and the break-up of the old communities 'led to a loosening of the community involvement in each death, so that the burden shifted increasingly on to the family—except for aristocrats, who could call upon others to provide support' (1983: 42–3). I also argued that this restriction in participation was one of the many interacting factors that helped create a shift in the attitudes towards death. Morris thinks (1989: 303) that an objection against these conclusions is that 'even in the fourth century the obligations of the *anchisteia* in Athenian funerals were very like those of the near kin in Homer . . .'. He adds 'There is no evidence that a rise of the individual disembedded death from its communal context.' These views are based partly on a misunderstanding and partly on a blurring of important distinctions. I did not claim that the rise of the individual disembedded death from its social context, but that in the context of a complex shift in circumstances this social context became more restricted, a restriction in some respects enforced by law. In the archaic and classical period funerary legislation restricted participation (especially but not only of women) to a certain degree of kinship.[13] At some point the polis assumed the ultimate authority regulating the death-ritual, what can and what cannot be done, who cannot participate in what, and also obliging certain kin to take responsibility for the burial of their kin[14]—as well as making inheritance dependent on the performance of the burial rites.[15] In the case of the war dead and traitors the polis assumed responsibility for the disposal of the body, giving an honourable public funeral to the first while denying the second proper burial. In these circumstances, it is impossible to maintain that the role of kin in the

---

[13] On funerary legislation cf. [Dem.] 43. 62–4. See *LSCG* 77 C 24–8 and on the date Rougemont 1974: 147–58 esp. 154; cf. Rougemont 1977: 26–88; *LSCG* 97 A 24–9; cf. Cic. *De leg.* 66. Cf. also Sourvinou-Inwood 1983: 47–8 and nn. 84–5, 87 with bibliog.; add Garland 1989: 1–15; Toher 1991: 159–75 with further bibliog.

[14] Cf. e.g. [Dem.] 43. 58–9; 65; Guarducci 1950: no. 76 B.

[15] The body regulating funerals is normally the polis, in the case of the Labyadai (cf. Rougemont 1977: 26–88) the phratry.

death-ritual (especially the role of the kin relative to that of the wider group, the greater or lesser participation of the wider community, which is the question at issue here) is 'the same' in Homer and the classical period.

In Homer the grief for a death is assumed and expressed also by people not directly affected by the death. Interestingly, Homer feels that this fact needs some comment: he tries to explain why certain people weep who on the assumptions of a later age would not have been expected to, by supposing that they remember their own sorrows, and some other dearer dead, and it is for this that they really lament (cf. *Iliad* 19. 301–2, 337–8). He is right in so far as the (socially ordained) grief and lament does focus the emotions in such a way. But the fact that this can be articulated explicitly in this way may suggest that this assumption of grief by outsiders described in the traditional epic material was already less of a routine aspect of the ritual, and may even have started to recede in the eighth century, at least in areas like Ionia. It is parallel to the Homeric comment on the gift-exchange between Glaukos and Diomedes in *Iliad* 6. 234–6—that Zeus took away Glaukos' wits for he exchanged a valuable gold armour for a bronze one worth a fraction of its value; this is the comment of a society which does not share naturally in the earlier societies' mentality and assumptions pertaining to gift-exchange as a central way of relating to others, and tries to make sense of such situations contained in the inherited epic material through its own perceptual filters, which look at gift-exchange in different ways.

Morris concludes (1989: 303) that my 'causal model' is not persuasive, that 'the demographic and intellectual background in Archaic Greece cannot be said to be sufficiently like that in high medieval France for us to expect *a priori* that there might have been comparable changes in attitudes toward death. I will therefore proceed with the hypothesis that individual attitudes remained essentially constant.' I hope that it is now clear that this 'causal model' is entirely Morris's own creation, ascribed to me on the assumption that I followed the same model-building approach that he favours, an approach which I regard as methodologically flawed. Thus, I submit, he has not, as he claims, invalidated my case.

3. THE LITERARY EVIDENCE

Morris's conviction that he has shown that there was no change in attitudes by showing that the conditions for change as he understands them were not present in the eighth century, together with his methodological assumptions, led him to believe that all he needed to do to prove his case was to show that his views are compatible with the evidence. I argued that this is unsound, since the scarce and problematic evidence can be made to appear compatible with a variety of views—especially if it is not considered systematically and in its entirety. I will now refer to some of my earlier conclusions and attempt to retrieve them from Morris's misrepresentation.

I will only very briefly refer to the aspects of the afterlife explored in Chapter II above. Morris quotes (1989: n. 78) A. T. Edwards (1985: 218) for the view that the belief in a more fortunate existence after death was widespread before Homer, and also Edwards's criticism of my analyses. I discussed Edwards's own position in Chapter III of this book, where I hope to have shown that it is mistaken, both in its implicit assumptions about the nature of religious development and in the particular belief that a paradise for the select few originated in the Bronze Age. Edwards's claim that I required that evidence pertaining to the notion of a Land of the Blessed in the Homeric poems be removed as later insertions is based on a misunderstanding;[16] for, on the contrary, I stated unequivocally that in my view such stories are Homeric, but that their rarity and lack of organic integration when contrasted to the deeply routed theme 'all men must die and go to Hades' suggests that they belong to the last poets' own period, to the later, eighth-century forms of the epics.[17]

---

[16] If by 'later insertions' he means post-Homeric (which is the way Morris takes it, since he uses the word 'interpolations').

[17] Edwards also accused me of not taking account of the potential differences between a culture's poetic fictions and its religious practices and of not dealing adequately with the evidence of Minoan and Mycenaean influence. I addressed the last point in Ch. II. The discourse concerning the relationship between a culture's poetic fictions and its religious practices is complex. I indicated some aspects of my position in Ch. II. With regard to the Homeric poems I must stress again that they are not one man's fiction, but the end-product of the creativity of many successive generations of bards, who wove into the Homeric eschatological discourse different strands of beliefs which (I hope to have shown) originated in different societies—though they were perceived and presented by means of the perceptual filters formed by the assumptions of each of the creating poets.

Morris states 'we should not assume that differences between accounts are necessarily to be explained as an evolution through time.' Indeed we should not *assume* this. But in this instance, every facet of the pattern, investigated independently synchronically and diachronically, fits this hypothesis. In Sourvinou-Inwood 1981 and 1983 I cross-checked my (limited) conclusions about beliefs with the attitudes articulated in the Homeric death-ritual and with the archaeological evidence; I argued that the conclusions of each set of analyses prove to converge. In Chapter II of this book I suggested that the (archaeologically visible) growth of heroic cults in the eighth century is the exact archaeological correlative of the pattern of belief I proposed. Thus, it is perverse to deny that the data indicate that a change of the type proposed had indeed taken place. Scepticism always appears rigorous ('we cannot be sure that' sounds like scholarly caution); but in fact it relies on an implicit *a priori* assumption which is fallacious. For the fact that we cannot assume that A is always correct does not entail that it is more rigorous to presume that, unless the opposite can be conclusively proved, in an area where so little can be so proved, A is not correct, though all the evidence indicates that it is correct. The fact that the shift towards an individual destiny of the shade parallels comparable developments in the Late Middle Ages[18] which are associated with phenomena comparable to some of the phenomena with which the archaic Greek shift is associated, may also add a little—only a little—further confirmation to this reconstruction.

In discussing my argument that in the archaic period the movement towards a more individual destiny had developed and crystallized Morris isolates the notion of individual salvation and argues that, though it first appears in the *Homeric Hymn to Demeter* this does not entail that it was not an earlier idea. In fact, there are several good reasons for thinking that it was not. First, what I looked at was not simply the absence of the notion of individual salvation, but the fact that the pattern of absences and presences as it stands makes good sense: it is in harmony with a variety of other (independently considered) phenomena, which suggests that it corresponds to the parameters of the beliefs of the cultures that contributed to the creation of the texts under consideration. Second, it is true that some scholars had thought that the Eleusinian notion

[18] Cf. Sourvinou-Inwood 1983: 36 n. 17.

of a happy afterlife may have been earlier than the archaic period; but not only is there no evidence for such a view, but also, more importantly, recent work has shown that, contrary to what had previously been maintained, cult at the Eleusinian sanctuary did not begin until the later eighth century, and the notion of an earlier Mycenaean megaron surviving through the Dark Ages is a mirage.[19] Thus, the notion of Mycenaean Eleusinian Mysteries continuing into historical times—implicitly or explicitly sustaining the notion of an earlier existence of Eleusinian eschatology[20]—is extremely unlikely.

Morris further implies that my argument cannot stand in any case, because, as he sees it, the eschatological changes in question do not involve an innovation on anything like the scale of later eschatological innovations such as metempsychosis. This criticism illustrates the flaws in this type of approach. What a rigorous methodology demands is not to decide what change is or is not important on the basis of some arbitrarily chosen yardstick imported from a later period; but to determine the relationship between two systems, identify the differences, if any, and then consider those differences systematically and in context. On my thesis, the Eleusinian belief in a happy afterlife for the initiates is a particular version of an individual destiny after death, which became increasingly popular in the archaic and classical period, and which was absent from the Homeric poems—though there were, in those poems, the first seeds of the general category to which this happy afterlife belongs, the individual destiny of some shades after death, which contrasted with the dominant Homeric belief in the collective undifferentiated destiny of all shades.

I argued that there is a substantial strand of archaic literature reflecting attitudes to death that are not simply different from, but often in conflict with, the 'acceptance of a familiar death' attitude. Since I stressed that the latter nexus of attitudes also survived in the archaic period, my thesis cannot be invalidated by evidence showing that those older attitudes are found in archaic literature—which is what Morris cites. My conclusions would be invalidated only if it were shown that there are no new attitudes in archaic literature, or that any new attitudes there may be are not different from, and

---

[19] Darcque 1981: 593–605; cf. also Le Roy 1984: 167.
[20] Cf. Mylonas 1961: 32–59.

opposed to, the 'acceptance of a familiar death' type. This he has not done. His strategy is to postulate that there is no significant change between Homeric and archaic attitudes and test this hypothesis by looking for archaic statements that can be made to fit the Homeric attitudes. As we saw, this procedure involves serious methodological flaws. In addition, this argument cannot invalidate my own, since what is at issue here is not whether attitudes compatible with 'Tamed Death' can be found in archaic literature (this is part of my own thesis) but whether we can find in archaic literature beliefs and attitudes which not only were not encountered in Homer, but which are in conflict with the established Homeric attitudes. Morris has not succeeded in challenging my argument that while earlier attitudes were determined by the parameters of the 'familiar/Tamed Death' type, in the archaic period the parameters changed, the attitudes fluctuated within a wider spectrum and included some new and different attitudes, a type, apparently important in élite circles, which involved greater anxiety about death, especially one's own, and a desire to push death away, to limit its encroachment in life's spaces.

His discussion of Stesichoros involves a misunderstanding:[21] he takes the fact that varied attitudes are expressed in the different fragments to be an argument against my case about attitudes to death in archaic literature. This implication is wrong, since what I tried to determine was not what any particular poet 'truly felt', but whether or not attitudes were expressed at this time which are at variance, and in conflict, with the earlier ones, whether the parameters of the discourse in general have changed. Morris has further argued that in the following cases attitudes which I identified as being different from the Homeric ones are not in fact different but belong to the 'acceptance of a familiar death' type of attitude. First, he seems to deny that Mimnermos expresses attitudes of the new type I tried to identify. But the view that death is preferable to old age with its attendant ills and discomforts, clashes with two Homeric attitudes: that any life is preferable to death, and that (peaceful, normal) death in old age is a form of 'good death'. Whether Mimnermos 'meant it' is irrelevant, and the audience and circumstances of production simply tell us something about the ambi-

---

[21] Cf. now the apt comment on Morris's 'rather naïve approach' to literary evidence by H. Bowden in JHS 112 (1992), 200.

ence for which such attitudes were appropriate. The fact that Mimnermos' poems had different aims from those of Homer, Tyrtaios, and Kallinos cannot affect the argument, since what I was concerned with determining was the parameters of attitudes towards death, and what I hope to have shown is that the archaic funerary discourse encompassed attitudes that were in conflict with the earlier ones. Morris has misunderstood the argument. I did not suggest that Mimnermos shows fear of death, but that he expresses certain attitudes which are different from, and to some extent in conflict with, the Homeric attitudes. These different attitudes are, incidentally, comparable to attitudes which in other societies belong to a nexus involving a more individual perception of, and approach to, death.[22] Morris has not answered my point that Mimnermos expresses the hedonistic attitude towards life and death which is different from Homer's. The fact that it is the ills of old age that repel him, rather than old age itself, does not affect the argument. Such an attitude is entirely consistent with the 'hedonism' which I suggested was new in the archaic age.

His discussion of Anacreon is misleadingly selective: he does not mention fr. 395. 9–12 Page in which Anacreon articulates explicitly a fear of death and anxiety about dying, which, on my thesis, characterizes the more individual type of attitude towards death which crystallized in the archaic period. Another significant omission is the absence of any mention of the theme 'death as a deliverer from suffering', which, in its various versions, is determined by, and expresses, attitudes in sharp conflict to the Homeric ones. This theme, we saw in Chapter VI § ii. 1*d*, appears in archaic poetry and becomes an important topos in Greek tragedy. A combination of this theme with another attitude which is also in conflict with the Homeric is expressed in Bacchylides 3. 47 ff. While in Homer the foreknowledge of one's death, and the conduct of preparations for it are aspects of good death (cf. Sourvinou-Inwood 1983: 37; 1981: 25), Bacchylides 3. 52 ff. expresses the view that the most hateful death is the death that one sees coming;[23] this attitude is combined with the theme 'death as a deliverer' (Bacchylides 3. 47). Related to, but different from, 'death as a deliverer', is another theme which also expresses an attitude in conflict with the earlier hatred of death:

---

[22] Cf. Sourvinou-Inwood 1983: 46 n. 80.
[23] See Kenyon 1897: ad loc.; Maehler 1982: 51 *ad* 51–2.

'death as a pleasant image, yearned for' (Sappho 95 L.-P.).[24] 'Real' authorial feeling is not what is at issue here; it is the fact that attitudes in conflict with those reflected in Homer were conceivable and articulable.

One point on which Morris and I agree is in accepting that the ideology of good death in battle in the service of the polis included a Homeric type of attitude to death. But Morris understands this to be the result of a continuity in attitudes from the eighth to the fourth century, while I see it as the result of ideological manipulation by the emergent polis involving an adaptation of old attitudes to new purposes.[25] My view[26] is supported by what we know about the creation of the Spartan polis and its ideology, which, we shall see, involved the manipulation of attitudes towards death; to this we may compare the reuse and reshaping of initiatory ritual 'material' to create the *agoge*.[27] Morris oversimplifies the situation and ignores, for instance, the possibility of tensions between the emergent polis ideology and the individuals called upon to die for their country, such as appear to underlie the 'Lycurgan' legislation (cf. Sourvinou-Inwood 1983: 44). The notion that the creation of the ideology of good death in the service of the democratic polis in fifth-century Athens involved no change of attitude is *a priori* highly implausible and becomes especially unconvincing when we compare, as we did in Ch. III § ii.3*d*, archaic to fifth-century formulations pertaining to death in war.

My argument concerning the elaboration of the psyche's transition to Hades and the emergence of Charon and Hermes Chthonios is not based on Homer's silence, as Morris alleges (1989: 313). I hope that it became clear in Chapter V that my argument is much more complicated, though restrictions of space forced me to present it in an extremely summary form in the two essays, and to offer only the conclusions of some parts of the lengthy study which

---

[24] Cf. Vermeule 1979: 147; Boedeker 1979: 41–3, 49–52.

[25] For a comparable view cf. O. Murray 1980: 130–1.

[26] My view that Tyrtaios and Kallinos used the earlier attitudes as an intellectual position derived from Homer and adapted to serve an emerging ideology of patriotism which glorifies death in the service of the polis does not affect the central argument, which includes the view that in some circles earlier attitudes simply survived. My comments on Tyrtaios and Kallinos were *not* an attempt to 'explain away' an awkward fact—for even if my interpretation of these poets' attitudes were wrong, this would not create difficulties for my thesis. I was trying to bring out the diversity and complexity of archaic attitudes towards death, and to show that surface similarity does not necessarily mean absence of change.

[27] See Brelich (1969, ch. i), and *JHS* 91 (1971), 172–4.

is set out in this book. Morris also believes (1989: 309) that the attitudes to death in tragedy fit well into the Tamed Death nexus of attitudes. In my view, this belief involves the telescoping and oversimplifying of a long complex development, which included the construction of the ideology of good death in the service of the democratic polis. I will only mention two obvious reminders of this complexity, as indices of important facets which run counter to the simple schematic image Morris proposes. First, the theme of death as a deliverer, which began in the archaic period, is an important topos in tragedy.[28] An interesting instance is in Euripides, fragment 833 N (from *Phrixos*), where it is combined with the speculation that maybe what we call life is death and what we consider death is in fact life—also articulated in fragment 638 N (from *Polyidos*). This is in sharp contrast to the Homeric perceptions of life and death, the upper world and Hades (cf. esp. Sourvinou-Inwood 1981: 19, 21, 24; 1983: 35). Second, in the stichomythia between Pheres and Admetos in Euripides' *Alcestis*[29] attitudes are expressed which are impossible to accommodate within the Homeric-type nexus of 'familiar, accepting' attitude towards death.

In these circumstances, I submit that Morris's argument against the part of my case based on literary evidence cannot stand.

4. The Archaeological Evidence: Differential Burial of Children, Family Affiliation, Intramural Burial, Sacred Space, and Sanctuaries

I must begin by making clear the hierarchy of the argument based on the archaeological evidence and its place in the overall case I presented in the essays under discussion. Of the three phenomena I discussed, only one, the disappearance of intramural burial, was directly relevant to my central argument, part of the evidence that a shift in the attitudes towards death had taken place, and this is a phenomenon the reality of which Morris does not deny. The other two, the decrease in the differentiation of child burials and the visible incorporation of graves into groups signalling family affiliation, pertain to my suggestion that the burden of the death-ritual

---

[28] Again, it is not a meaningful question to ask whether the characters in the tragedy 'meant it'. What is significant is that the attitudes articulated in this topos are at variance with the Homeric attitudes.

[29] Eur. *Alc.* 629 ff.

increasingly shifted on to the family; this, in its turn, was not part
of the case showing that a shift in attitudes had taken place, it was
part of an argument suggesting that the framework which had
supported the familiar approach to death had begun to change.[30] It
may be asked why, since this is such a marginal part of my case, I
used archaeological evidence of such a problematic nature. My
reasons were methodological; ideally, in a study of this kind, there
should be cross-checks between the results of the different sets of
data; even when the archaeological evidence is problematic, and
cannot provide unambiguous answers, it can still suggest possibilities
and thus function as a partial control. And this is how I used it: I
tried to consider whether any changes could be detected in the
archaeological record in the eighth century and if so how these
related to my proposed reconstruction. It appeared to me that the
two phenomena mentioned above fitted well with, and could be
explained by, the notion that the family acquired greater importance
in the burial, as community involvement diminished, though I did
not consider this the exclusive or even main reason behind the
two phenomena under consideration; I saw it as only one factor,
interacting with the major factor that was the self-definition of the
aristocracy in the emerging polis. Thus, even if Morris had shown
that I was wrong in these two matters, my case for a shift would
not have been affected; only one facet of one argument pertaining
to the circumstances in which the shift took place would lose its
archaeological support. But as it happens, Morris has not shown
that my argument about these two phenomena is wrong.

With regard to the weakening of differential burial of children[31]
I argued that there was a sharp differentiation between adult and
child burials in most Dark-Age communities, a characteristic of
societies in which the death-ritual is a community affair, and that
in the eighth century the differentiation diminished: it was still the

---

[30] Though the modalities of the changes are very different, depending on, among other
things, the very different burial situation preceding them, it is interesting that the same two
dimensional distinctions pertaining to familial groupings and children's burials changed also
at Osteria dell'Osa in comparable historical circumstances (in Latium Vetus and South Etruria
changes took place between the 9th and the 7th cents. BC involving the passage from simpler
village-type societies to more complex communities with permanent social stratification and
'urban' settlements and the emergence of a gentilicial aristocracy); cf. Bietti Sestieri and De
Santis 1985: 35–45.

[31] Cf. Sourvinou-Inwood 1983: 45; 1981: 34–5. On the differential burial of children cf.
also Bérard 1970: 48–55.

case, in the eighth century and after, that less effort was expended on the burial of children than of adults, but this effort was considerably greater than before, and involved higher visibility. I suggested that this reflects the family's dominant role in the conduct of the death-ritual as the community involvement diminished; more energy spent on child burials is likely when the family becomes a main judge of what is appropriate. Of course the differential burial of children continues, as I myself stressed (Sourvinou-Inwood 1981: 31; 1983: 45). The adult *v.* subadult distinction is a major axis of mortuary differentiation in most societies[32] and certainly in societies like the Greek where adult *v.* subadult are very significant categories. What is at issue here is the *degree* of differentiation; my argument was that this changed in the eighth century, that from then on child burials involved more ceremony, and more energy was spent on them; this is seen in the fact that from the eighth century child graves appear in the main cemeteries, or in separate cemeteries; certainly they become highly visible and involve greater investment than before—as do some of the grave-goods accompanying some subadults.[33] The central point of my argument, that Dark-Age child burials involved little effort and ceremony, Morris concedes.[34] That from the eighth century the siting and other aspects of children's burials manifest more 'energy spent'—a significant criterion in mortuary differentiation[35]—is an undeniable fact. Thus, though my interpretation of the phenomenon must of necessity remain hypothetical, Morris's critique cannot invalidate it.

With regard to the incorporation of graves into groups, family plots, I obviously had not made sufficiently clear that I was talking about *the visible grouping of graves by physically clear means*, enclosures,

---

[32] Cf. O'Shea 1984: 42.

[33] Cf. e.g. Bérard 1970: 53, 33–47.

[34] I disagree with his claim that the decline in spatial differentiation was short-lived; for by weakening of the differentiation I did not only mean that the two categories were buried in the same cemetery, or even plot; but that while before the siting and other aspects of child burials indicated that very little effort was expended on them, the appearance of large numbers of children's graves in extramural cemeteries, including separate children's cemeteries, or separate plots within the cemetery, indicate that more effort was now expended on these burials. Certain 8th-cent. forms which stressed the child's family affiliation (e.g. the Athenian burials in the terraced plot in the Agora and the 'Plattenbau' (cf. Coldstream 1977: 120, 122, 135–7, 138 n. 27, 376) were presumably connected with the particular circumstances of the period, in which stressing the hereditary principle was very important (cf. below).

[35] O'Shea 1984: *passim*; cf. also ibid. *passim*, and esp. 94, 100, 105, 189–90, 247–8, 251 for some interesting modalities of adult v. subadult differentiation and its parameters.

tumuli and cairns, in areas where the tradition of collective burial had died out for centuries, the deliberate marking out of a visibly distinct group, stressing family affiliation.[36] On my thesis, from the eighth century onwards the death-ritual became more and more limited to the family, and I argued that this was one of the reasons behind the family's increased symbolic importance in the cemeteries, which, in interaction with the aristocratic process of self-definition in the emerging polis, inspired the trend to stress visibly family grave groupings. The latter category was not invented by me *ad hoc* to fit my theory: the eighth century trend to incorporate graves into groups has been commented upon by others.[37] Thus, the examples of inferred earlier family plots Morris cites as evidence against my case are not relevant; for it is not an implication of my argument that all family involvement in the arrangement of the graves, or family plots, began in the eighth century.[38] The stress of family affiliation was important in the emerging polis.[39] Even if the custom of incorporating graves into groups did fade away later this does not entail, as Morris suggests, that it had not had the proposed significance before. Particular dimensional distinctions may be very short-lived,[40] but they are still significant; they reflect particular historical circumstances: in this case, on my view, the stress on family affiliation and the inheritance principle in the context of the self-definition of the aristocracy at the formation of the polis. This could have become less important (at least in some places, depending on circumstances) after the aristocracy had defined itself as a class. In fact we do not know to what extent and when such fade-away took place. In Athens in so far as it is possible to judge, the trend towards the grouping of tombs continues in the archaic

[36] Cf. a comparable phenomenon in the Latium necropolis of Castel di Decima of the late 8th and 7th cents.: Bartoloni, Cataldi Dini and Zevi 1982: 268.

[37] Cf. e.g. Snodgrass 1971: 194–5; Hägg 1983: 29–30.

[38] Morris (1989: 314) states that 'there are clear groupings of ninth-century graves around stone constructions' in the Ag. Panteleimon cemetery at Anavyssos. Prof. P. Themelis (who has excavated part of the Ag. Panteleimon cemetery and published the central report on it (Themelis 1973–4), which includes the plan cited by Morris in n. 105 in support of his statement) was kind enough to confirm to me that there are no 9th-cent. groupings of the type relevant to my argument. In any case, I must stress again that what I was referring to was a general tendency towards physically marked groupings.

[39] Funerary ideology, especially that centred on the élite dead, was of great importance in the emerging polis, with the aristocracy effecting ideological manipulations involving the remains of their (real or claimed) ancestors: cf. Bérard 1982: *passim*, esp. 100–2.

[40] Cf. O'Shea 1984: 284.

period; often subsequent graves are grouped around the burial of a prominent ancestor.[41] The fact that family plots were encompassed within larger cemeteries is irrelevant; for my argument concerned the conscious stress of the affiliation by incorporating graves into family-plots in visible ways in larger cemeteries in the context of polis-formation.[42]

Morris does acknowledge the disappearance of intramural burial but rejects my interpretation of this phenomenon and offers a different one. Let me restate briefly my thesis. I suggested that the disappearance of intramural burial was part of a very complex process of interaction and feedback, in the context of a shift in attitudes to death which was itself part and result of a series of social, economic, political, and intellectual changes: 'the disappearance of intramural burial ... must be connected with the receding familiarity in the attitudes towards death and the dead apparent in other aspects of archaic death-related behaviour. The growing fear and revulsion generated by death expressed itself through the— inherited but flexible—concept of pollution, a conceptual and ritual mechanism for articulating boundaries. Much of the earlier trend towards greater use of extramural cemeteries was probably urbanistically inspired. But the diminished physical contact with, and proximity to the dead which ensued contributed to the shift from the familiar model of death, and so fuelled the tendency to remove burials outside the city, which again reinforced the recession of familiarity and so on' (Sourvinou-Inwood 1981: 36; cf. also 1983: 47). Morris's argument against my case consists of two main parts. First, he alleges that there is no other evidence for a shift in attitudes towards death; this part of his argument has already been addressed. Second, he claims that his own interpretation shows that the shift away from intramural burial can be explained in another way.

I would first like to stress that Morris's arguments are interdependent, while I tried to keep the different parts of my own argument separate. Consequently, the validity of his argument here depends on the acceptance of his case that there is no other evidence

---

[41] Cf. Humphreys 1983: 95–101. I do not use the treatment of Athenian mortuary evidence in Morris 1987, since I believe that it is deeply flawed.

[42] As to Morris's remarks concerning the size of the familial group involved (1989: 314–15), I had not spoken of individual nuclear family but of 'family', without attempting to determine the size and constitution of the socially significant familial grouping in the 8th-cent. poleis, which, *pace* Morris, is a problem of great complexity.

for a shift in attitudes—a conclusion which I hope to have shown to be wrong. But even if I have not convinced that it is wrong, the fact that it *may* be wrong means that it is not legitimate to base another (allegedly independent) part of the argument on that conclusion, and then (implicitly) use that second argument as independent evidence to support the overall case of which both arguments are part, and so also to support the validity of the first of the two interdependent arguments. Then, Morris is wrong to claim that there is nothing in the movement of cemeteries itself to indicate a change of attitudes to death. Plutarch, *Lycurgus* 27[43] provides some support for my interpretation; for it suggests that the cessation of intramural burial was indeed perceived to be connected with fear of death and aversion towards the grave, the desire to push death away, and that intramural burial was linked to familiarity with death and diminished death avoidance. A slight further support may be provided by the fact that the only model known to me of such a change from intramural to extramural burial (cf. Sourvinou-Inwood 1981: 36 n. 84; 1983: 44 and n. 62), though rationalized into concern for hygiene, was part of a shift in attitudes to death, relating to the desire to push death away. I am not, of course, claiming that this argument on its own can validate my hypothesis; but it does provide additional support to the case built on other arguments, and throws further doubt on Morris's belief that my interpretation of the cessation of intramural burial is unsupported by any evidence. Finally, it can be argued that Heraclitus fragment 96, which is roughly contemporary with what appears to be the culmination of the long and gradual process of the 'expulsion' of the dead from the living space, expresses precisely that attitude of desire to 'throw out' the dead.[44] I now turn to Morris's interpretation of the disappearance of intramural burial.

He admits that there is, as I suggested, a hardening of the boundaries between the living and the dead, and that the cessation of intramural burial is related to that hardening. But he sees this as due not to a change in attitudes towards death and the dead, but to

---

[43] On which cf. Sourvinou-Inwood 1981: 36; 1983: 47; cf. also below. On Spartan funerary legislation cf. also Garland 1989: 5–7, 13–14; Toher 1991: 169–73.

[44] Heraclitus' status as a particularly obscure exponent of 'intellectual' thought, the fact that he is clearly articulating his own particular vision here, and the fragmentary status of the statement, make it difficult to place this view precisely; but the fact that it could, at this particular time, be formulated at all is not without significance.

a general change in attitudes towards 'the sacred', gods as well as the dead, for which he finds evidence in the change he believes to have taken place in the eighth century in the relationship between sacred space and the living space of men. He claims that the relocation of the cemeteries is part, and the result, of changes in the boundedness of the spaces allotted to the gods, men, and the dead which, he believes, took place around 700 when the living space became 'more sharply differentiated from the sacred space of the gods and the dead'. This change in the articulation of space, he claims, suggests 'that a new system of classification was growing up'. He believes that (1989: 317) 'the main change in space was the rise of a discrete area for religious activity—the emergence of the Greek sanctuary.' For he thinks that in the Dark Ages 'cult activity was characterized by a certain spatial indeterminacy.' I have set out elsewhere (Sourvinou-Inwood 1993: 1–17) a detailed argument against the theory that there was spatial indeterminacy in cult in the Dark Ages, and that in the eighth century there was a change in the perception of sacred space in the context of which emerged the Greek sanctuary; I hope to have shown that the Greek sanctuary emerged in the Dark Ages and that there was no change of the type postulated by Morris in the perception of sacred space and its relationship to the profane in the eighth century.

However, even if we were to ignore the fact that the theory of the alleged eighth-century change is demonstrably mistaken, even if we were to suppose that that alleged change took place, it could not explain the shift away from, and final prohibition of, intramural burial. It could not explain why those discrete cemeteries were only situated outside the polis and never intramurally, while sanctuaries were to be found both inside and outside the settlement. I will also argue that, even if the above objections are momentarily set aside, Morris's model cannot explain a major datum, the Spartan exception, while my thesis explains it satisfactorily.[45] Morris

[45] There is another, more subjective, argument. In my view, the pattern of the decrease and ultimate disappearance of intramural burial (cf. Sourvinou-Inwood 1981: 35; 1983: 43–4 and n. 61) does not fit the notion of a change in the relationship between sacred and profane space and the relationships between men, gods and the dead; for in that case we would have expected first, a more drastic change, and second, one in which the pattern of any persistence was random, instead of predominantly involving child-burials, which suggests that the persistence related to the social persona of the deceased. This pattern of change is more likely to have been motivated by a change of attitudes to death rather than in religious beliefs pertaining to 'the sacred' in general; a change which was not uniform, and to which

acknowledges the existence of some extra-urban sanctuaries in the Dark Ages but tries to neutralize their significance for his theory by marginalizing them in ways that, I hope to have shown (Sourvinou-Inwood 1993: 1–17), are misconceived. But his overall thesis cannot stand even if we were to suppose for the sake of the argument that only extra-urban sanctuaries had existed in the Dark Ages, and that sanctuaries within the settlement only emerged in the eighth century. For even if that were the case, it would not entail that the sanctuary as a discrete religious space first emerged in the eighth century as a result of the redefinition of the boundaries between men and gods: it would be a perfectly tenable (indeed more plausible) notion to think that the communal separate sacred spaces, the sanctuaries, had hitherto been situated outside the settlement, and that it was only in the context of the creation of the polis, when the centre acquired a particular symbolic importance, that communal cult came to be practised at the centre of the polis— with the result that sanctuaries, which had hitherto (on this hypothesis) been extra-urban, emerged also within the settlement. On this view, the hypothesis that sanctuaries had existed only outside the living space before the emergence of the polis and then, in the eighth century, moved also inside the polis, far from supporting Morris's model, undermines it. For, since on Morris's model the behaviour towards the dead is determined by the same attitudes and changes in attitudes as that towards the gods, it would make it even more difficult to understand why, while the gods, on his thesis, had moved into the living space in a much bigger way than hitherto, the dead became excluded from that space. Thus, a special factor, pertaining to men's relationship with the specific category 'the dead', and not to a generic category 'the sacred', would in any case be needed to explain this difference, and the cessation of intramural burial. My thesis offers precisely such a factor. Furthermore, and most importantly, even if we were to ignore all the above considerations, Morris's notion that from *c.*750 onwards the living space of men is more sharply separated and differentiated from that of the gods, and that this signals a different symbolic articulation, is falsified by the existence of a very important

there was resistance and/or indifference. Compare, for example, the changes in Western Europe which related to a change of attitudes towards death and the desire to push death away, from the late 16th cent. onwards, with its various fictions, pressures, and resistance to the pressures to relocate cemeteries (Ariès 1977: 468–93, cf. esp. 489, 531–9).

Greek cultic modality: the presence of cultic foci (such as altars and Herms) all over the living space of the polis: in houses (the *hestia* and altars of *oikos* cult), in the streets, in public buildings, in gymnasia, and in the Agora (cf. Sourvinou-Inwood 1993: 9, 12–13). Far from there being a greater separation between the spaces of the gods and of men from the second half of the eighth century onwards, on the contrary, gods and heroes were installed at the very centre of the living space, of the polis and its institutions.

Thus, even if Morris's notion of a change pertaining to sacred space were right, it still could not have explained the shift away from, and the final prohibition of, intramural burial. Since sanctuaries and altars to gods and shrines/graves of heroes are found both inside and outside the settlement, if his view that the behaviour towards the graves of the dead was determined by the same attitudes as that towards the gods were right, an explanation would be needed more than ever as to why spaces were not allotted to the dead within the community's living space, as was the case with the gods and heroes, why cemeteries were excluded from the living space and intramural burial eventually forbidden. My contention that Morris's thesis cannot explain the exclusion of the dead from the living space is considerably strengthened when we consider heroic cults. For heroic cults, involving both the alleged graves of mythical heroes and, in the case of new foundations, those of the heroized, historical oecists, are instituted inside the emergent polis, usually at its very centre.[46] The fact that the categories 'recent dead' and 'heroes' drift nearer in the cult of the heroized recent dead whose graves are situated in the agora strengthens even further the expectation that if Morris's hypothesis were right there would have been corresponding similarities in the funerary sphere: there should have been walled cemeteries both inside and outside the polis, for this is the correlative of the situation pertaining to gods and heroes. Thus, there is a difference in behaviour towards on the one hand gods and heroes, installed not just inside the living space but also at the very centre of the polis, and on the other the dead, gradually excluded from that living space. This exclusion, then, clearly depends on factors pertaining to the relationship between the living

---

[46] Cf. the references in Sourvinou-Inwood 1981: 35 n. 83; 1983: 44, part of n. 61; add: Leschhorn 1984: 67–72, 98–105, 176–80; Kolb 1981: *passim*, and esp. 5–8, 19, 24–5, 47–52; Boehringer 1980: 7–8, 17–22; Bérard 1982: 89–105; De Polignac 1984: 127–57; Malkin 1987: 204–40, esp. 204–16.

and the dead specifically, not towards a generic category 'the sacred'. It is precisely such an explanation that my own interpretation offers.

The final argument against Morris's interpretation of the cessation of intramural burial is that it cannot explain why, in contrast to the other Greek cities, intramural burial was customary in archaic and classical Sparta.[47] It cannot explain why the Spartans did not cease to practise intramural burial, for their behaviour concerning sanctuaries was no different from that of the other Greeks. Plutarch, *Lycurgus* 27 provides an explanation for the Spartan exception: a Lycurgan law permitted intramural burial as a means of familiarizing youths with death, so that they do not shrink from it, fearing that they would become polluted if they touched a corpse or trod on a grave. We cannot know which, if any, part of this report was incorporated in the law, and so reflects seventh-century attitudes. However, not only is this report confirmed by archaeology, but it fits what we know about 'Lycurgan' legislation, which used and adapted elements of an earlier social system to serve new purposes, above all the transformation of Spartan citizens into an élite warrior corps. Here it tried to restore to those citizens the familiarity with death characteristic of the earlier society, and so reverse the trend towards death avoidance. Since the earlier attitude was perceived to

---

[47] For refs. cf. Sourvinou-Inwood 1983: 44 n. 64. It is clear beyond doubt (Christou 1964*a*: 124–31, cf. 131–59) that not only is it the case that what graves have been found in Sparta did not form part of a cemetery, but also that they were indeed interspersed with habitations and generally settlement structures (cf. the potter's kiln near the groups of graves excavated by Christou (1964*a*: 131–59; cf. 124–31)) *within* the Spartan villages, the *obai*. (Christou (1964*a*: 130) thinks that there was also an intramural public 'official cemetery' for the war dead and perhaps archons.) The Spartan practice provides the certain and important part of my case. But in Sparta's colony Taras intramural burial was also practised, at least since after the middle of the 5th cent. when the city expanded (inevitably, given its geography, towards the east) and new fortifications included the lower city and the necropolis (cf. Lo Porto 1971: 362–4, 377–82 (cf. also 357–82 on the important points of Tarentine topography in general); cf. also Martin 1971: 323–6. Cf. now further on the necropoleis of Taras: *Mus Tar* 123–72, 185–234, 313–450, 469–521, 559–610; cf. esp. 416–17 on the earlier burials). But the fact that the newly intramural cemeteries continued to be used, that new burials also took place within the newly expanded city, and that it was planned that it should be so, that the city would include new as well as the old burial areas, (cf. e.g. Lo Porto 1971: 380) entails and betrays indifference to intramural burial. For, whatever the circumstances that led to this, the Tarentines, unlike other cities, practised, and were perceived to have practised, intramural burial for centuries (Polybius 8. 28. 6), and this state of affairs was felt to be so extraordinary as to require not simply an explanation, but one which at the same time gave divine sanction for this practice, which is what the oracle cited by Polybius (loc. cit.) provided. Consequently, it is highly implausible that this acceptance was unrelated to the fact that the mother city Sparta practised intramural burial, and that this, on my interpretation, was perceived to have an important ideological significance.

have been linked with the physical proximity to the dead ensuing from intramural burial, the legislation set out to recreate the earlier circumstances in order to generate the old attitudes. This indicates that early Greek mentality associated intramural burial with diminished death avoidance, which supports the thesis that the accelerating archaic trend towards extramural burial is a manifestation of shifts in attitudes to death. Thus, my interpretation can explain the Spartan practice of intramural burial, in terms of the overall realities and ideologies of the early Spartan state as we know it from other evidence, and this explanation is supported by a text which makes precisely the connection between intramural burial and diminished death avoidance which I am postulating.[48]

Consequently, Morris's interpretation of the cessation of intramural burial has, I submit, been proved wrong, while mine is supported by strong evidence.

5. THE MISSING EVIDENCE: FUNERARY LEGISLATION AND OTHER MATTERS

Morris's critique of my papers does not even mention a series of phenomena which, I argued, indicate a shift in attitudes to death. This omission is methodologically fallacious. Moreover, all these attitudes, behaviour, and so on, form one system, of archaic funerary attitudes and behaviour, and each part helps define the others and

---

[48] In theory it could be argued that Plutarch's account was a later construct. However (even if we leave aside the fact that such a construct would be an extraordinary product for a much later society to achieve, to invent a nexus which—on other evidence—belongs organically together) a very strong argument against this view is that the notion that early Spartan ideology operated on that modality of conscious re-creation and adaptation of the Homeric 'familiar death' nexus of attitudes in the context of the creation of the emerging patriotic ideology glorifying death in the service of the polis, is not a simple hypothesis but a fact, for the same modality is clearly found in the poems of Tyrtaios (cf. also O. Murray 1980: 130–1). This convergence with an established early Spartan ideological modality suggests that it is highly implausible that Plutarch's account is a later construct. But my argument does not depend on the historicity of Plutarch's account. Tyrtaios testifies to the fact that early Spartan ideology operated on that modality of re-creation and adaptation of the Homeric 'familiar death' nexus of attitudes in the context of the creation of the ideology glorifying death for the polis; this, in conjunction with the Spartan practice of intramural burial, indifference to which had characterized the earlier Greek societies which had the 'familiar death' nexus of attitudes, makes it perverse to doubt that the exceptional burial practice is part of the exceptional ideological manipulation of the early Spartan polis—and therefore also that early Greek mentality associated intramural burial with diminished death avoidance: which supports my thesis that the accelerating trend towards extramural burial is a manifestation of shifts in the attitudes to death, the desire to push death away.

all are given value by the overall system. Consequently, the omission of a large part of the data falsifies that evidence at two different levels. First, at the level of investigation: the fact that the results of my readings of the archaic texts, for example, converge with the evidence of funerary legislation provides some confirmation for those readings of the texts; Morris's selective presentation of my argument conceals this. Second, at the level of the attempt to make sense of problematic and polysemic data: for example, my interpretation of the exclusion of intramural burial gains support from the fact that this exclusion of the dead from the living space took place at the same time as the encroachment of the death-ritual in the living space of the community was being limited by law. The following evidence has been ignored by Morris.

First, funerary legislation.[49] From the early sixth century on, in Athens and elsewhere, funerary legislation restricted death's encroachment on the community of the living, limited the expressions of grief during the funeral, and so also the disruption, and lowered the emotional tone of the ritual. This manifests the desire to restrict death's invasion of life, even to conceal partly its physical reality (as in the requirement to cover the corpse's face), to push death away. I argued that this legislation should not be seen exclusively, or even primarily, in sociopolitical terms, as it has been in the past, as a result of the modern overprivileging of the sociopolitical and underprivileging of the funerary-ideological in studies of death related phenomena, which, we saw in Chapter III § ii.6, is erroneous. In my view, its regulations (which require special pleading to be explained in purely sociopolitical terms), and the fact that such legislation was issued not only by different poleis but also by at least one phratry and at different periods, can be unproblematically explained in terms of funerary ideology and collective attitudes towards death. For such regulations are but one articulation of a desire to restrict death's invasion of life, which, I argued, is also observable in a series of other phenomena.

Second, Morris ignored my argument pertaining to the individualization of the grave and to the shift in the preferred images of death represented on grave monuments, which has been confirmed and radically extended, through the detailed analyses of the early Greek grave monument conducted above. Third, the time of

[49] Cf. Sourvinou-Inwood 1983: 47–8. Cf. above n. 13.

private funerals changed from daytime in the Homeric epics—and, I argued, in the societies of the periods which contributed to the creation of the epics—to night-time, before sunrise, in the archaic and classical period, that is to a time which involves a much less conspicuous presence of the death ritual into the realm of life. Finally, there are also some other phenomena which may conceivably have been manifestations of a shift in attitudes, such as the transfer of the funeral meal away from the grave and into the home (Sourvinou-Inwood 1983: 42); the predominance of primary cremations from the late eighth/early seventh century on, while until then secondary cremation had been the norm, may have been due to the tendency to reduce the handling of the physical remains, as may have been the shift of emphasis towards special offering areas, which may also indicate a shift of emphasis in the burial ceremony to the stage after the burial pit had been closed and the remains hidden from sight (Sourvinou-Inwood 1983: 47).

6. CONCLUSIONS

I submit that Morris's case against my essays is wrong, that it is based on misconceptions, a flawed methodology, and a highly selective use of data. I made clear (Sourvinou-Inwood 1983: 48) that I did not claim to have proved every interpretation of every feature of every facet of death-related behaviour and funerary ideology in each of the periods I discussed. But the case taken as a whole is strong; and it has been strengthened further by the detailed analyses conducted here of data that I had either not taken into consideration at the time, such as the content of the archaic epitaphs, or that I had investigated in a preliminary or relatively limited way. The case taken as a whole can often explain, and at other times provide an explanatory context for, a series of apparently disparate phenomena; and it does so through the independent investigation of the different phenomena and sets of data, considered in their full context. I agree with Morris's sentiment that each phenomenon of burial behaviour must be considered as part of a wider system which 'must be understood as a whole or not all'. But the whole that must be taken into account is bigger than he imagines.

7. APPENDIX TO THE APPENDIX: THE CHARGE OF
ATHENOCENTRISM

Another criticism which may appear relevant is the accusation of
Athenocentrism in my selection of the archaeological data, first
made by C. K. Williams after my paper was read out at the 1983
Symposium *in absentia*, and repeated by J. M. Hurwit.[50] This accusation is simply wrong. I did not limit my use of archaeological
evidence to Athens and I did give examples from other parts of
Greece (cf. Sourvinou-Inwood 1983: 44, 45). I stressed Athens
because, for example (cf. Sourvinou-Inwood 1983: 45), the change
in the differential burial of the children is most definite as well as
best documented in Athens. This misconception arose from the
fact that in the short version of the paper delivered to the Swedish
Symposium[51] it was not clear that my use of the evidence was not
Athenocentric, and I was not present in the discussion to explain.
But I made clear in the written version that (and why) it is not the
case, as Williams had thought, that the evidence from other parts
of Greece does not fit the picture I presented. For that view was
based on two erroneous notions which I clarified in the written
version: (*a*) when speaking of eighth-century incorporation of
groups of graves into family plots I meant visibly, deliberately
signalled groupings and (*b*) the existence of non-differential burial of
children in the Dark Ages did not affect the argument (Sourvinou-
Inwood 1983: 44). Moreover, it is *the general modalities and changing
trends that are at issue.* Thus, the fact that, for example, at Smyrna
subadult burials changed from intramural interments under the
floor of, or around, the house to burial in extramural burial grounds
separate from those of adults, outside, but at the edge of, the city,
a change which appears to have been completed in the second
quarter of the seventh century,[52] would only have constituted a
significant difference from the comparable situation in Athens if I
had proposed a schematic, linear, uniform change and simple
causal links; but what I had proposed was that circumstances,
funerary behaviour, and attitudes interacted, shifted, and crystallized
in *comparable* (not necessarily the same) configurations, with

[50] In his review of R. Hägg (ed.), *The Greek Renaissance of the Eighth Century BC: Tradition
Innovation* (Stockholm 1983) (= Proceedings of the Second International Symposium at the
Swedish Institute in Athens, 1–5 June 1981) in *AJA* 88 (1984), 602.

[51] Cf. bibliog. s.v. Sourvinou-Inwood 1983.

[52] Cf. Nicholls 1958–9: 44–6, 126.

variant rhythms in different places. Thus the Smyrna case supports my argument.

Most crucially, the one part of the archaeological evidence which is central to my argument, the disappearance of intramural burial, is well-attested all over Greece, with the exception of Sparta where, we saw, different factors pertained. With regard to the other two phenomena, which pertain not to the argument showing that a change took place, but to the conditions which I suggested were conducive to it, my case would not be invalidated even if my use of evidence were Athenocentric; for what I proposed was a partial shift which only happened in some places, in different ways, and with different rhythms, and Athens was one of the advanced places in which we would expect (on my thesis) to find the change sooner and more definitely than in most other places. Of course, if the archaeological evidence for the change (such as it is) were truly limited to Athens, this would bring into question the legitimacy of my bringing together Homeric and Athenian archaeological evidence; but it is not, and the same trends are observed in Ionia/Asia Minor, another advanced area.[53]

8. Epilogue

Proposing complex interpretations of complex phenomena is dangerous. Because not all readers invest the effort necessary to acknowledge their complexity and make sense of them in the interpretations' own terms, one is vulnerable to the danger of being misread, of one's arguments being made sense of through simplifying simplistic schemata, which are self-perpetuating because they are satisfactory to many, precisely because they are easy to grasp and correspond to modern assumptions—since they are the culturally determined product of such assumptions. Nevertheless, it is necessary to persist; to continue to try, through as neutral a

---

[53] Hurwit also states that there is an underlying assumption to my argument that the 8th cent. Greeks and Homer's heroes could not at the same time accept the fact of human mortality and resent their own death, which, he believes, shows a misunderstanding of human nature (on my part). Even leaving aside his innocent assumption of an unchanging, not culturally determined, 'human nature', the fact is that I did not claim that they did not 'resent' their death; 'resentment'—though a concept too vague to be especially helpful—is very different from the attitudes which I suggested characterized certain sections of archaic society.

methodology as possible, to reconstruct as faithfully as possible as many fragments as possible of the complex ancient realities—instead of allowing ourselves to be seduced by the reflections of our own minds.

REFERENCES

This list of references consists of all the books and articles cited in this volume except for sales catalogues, articles in lexica and encyclopaedias, excavation reports in publications such as *Notizie degli scave di antichità*, *Archaeological Reports* and the like, *SEG* entries, and also for reviews which are only cited once.

ABRAMS, M. H. (1971). *Natural Supernaturalism* (Oxford).

AHLBERG, G. (1971*a*). *Prothesis and Ekphora in Greek Geometric Art* (Göteborg).

—— (1971*b*). *Fighting on Land and Sea in Greek Geometric Art* (Stockholm).

ÄKERSTRÖM, A. (1988). 'Cultic Installations in Mycenaean Rooms and Tombs', in E. B. French and K. A. Wardle (eds.), *Problems in Greek Prehistory. Papers Presented at the Centenary Conference of the British School of Archaeology at Athens, Manchester April 1986* (Bristol 1988), 201–9.

AKURGAL, E. (1961). *Die Kunst Anatoliens von Homer bis Alexander* (Berlin).

ALEXIOU, M. (1974). *The Ritual Lament in Greek Tradition* (Cambridge).

—— (1978). 'Modern Greek Folklore and its Relation to the Past. The Evolution of Charos in Greek Tradition', in S. Vryonis (ed.), *The 'Past' in Medieval and Modern Greek Culture* (Malibu), 221–36.

AMANDRY, P. (1971). 'Armes et lébès de bronze. Collection Paul Canellopoulos (I)', *BCH* 95: 585–626.

ANDRONIKOS, M. (1956). '*Lakonika anaglypha*', *Peloponnisiaka*, 1: 253–314.

—— (1961/2). '*Hellenika Epitaphia Mnemeia*', *ADelt* 17: A. Meletai, 152–210.

—— (1968). *Totenkult*, Archaeologia Homerica Kapitel W (Göttingen).

—— (1984). *Vergina: Oi Vassilikoi Taphoi* (Athens).

ANGERMEIER, E. H. (1936). *Das Albastron: Ein Beitrag zur Lekythen-Forschung* (Diss. Giessen).

ARIÈS, PH. (1977). *L'Homme devant la mort* (Paris).

ARRIGHETI, G. (1966). 'Cosmologia mitica di Omero e Esiodo', *Studi classici e orientali*, 15: 1–60.

ASAD, T. (1983). 'Anthropological Conceptions of Religion: Reflections on Geertz', *Man*, 18: 237–59.

ATA, I. W. (1980). 'The Spread and Influence of Sufism in India—Historical Development', *Islamic Culture*, 54: 39–45.

446 *References*

AUSTIN, C. (1968) (ed.). *Nova Fragmenta Euripidea in Papyris Reperta* (Berlin).

AUSTIN, N. (1975). *Archery at the Dark of the Moon: Poetic Problems in Homer's Odyssey* (Berkeley, Calif.).

BABUT, D. (1971). 'Semonide et Mimnerme', *REG* 84: 17–43.

BALADIÉ, R. (1980). 'Le Styx, site et personnification', in J. Duchemin (ed.), *Mythe et personnification. Actes du Colloque du Grand Palais (Paris) 7–8 mai 1977* (Paris), 17–24.

BALDASARRE, I. (1988). *Archeologia e storia antica. Annali. Instituto Universitario Orientale. Napoli.* Dipartimento del mondo classico e del mediterraneo antico 10 (Sezione tematica: La parola l'immagine, la tomba. Atti del Colloquio Internazionale di Capri): 107–15.

BANTI, L. (1941–4). 'I Culti minoici e greci di Haghia Triada (Creta)', *Annuario*, 3–4: 9–74.

BARTHES, R. (1967). *Elements of Semiology* (London).

BARTOLONI, G., CATALDI DINI, M., AND ZEVI, F. (1982). 'Aspetti dell' ideologia funeraria nella necropoli di Castel di Decima', in G. Gnoli and J.-P. Vernant (eds.), *La mort, les morts dans les sociétés anciennes* (Cambridge), 257–73.

BAZANT, J. (1986). 'Entre la croyance et l'expérience: le mort sur les lécythes à fond blanc', in L. Kahil, Ch. Augé, and P. Linant de Bellefonds (eds.), *Iconographie classique et identités régionales*, BCH Suppl. 14 (Paris), 37–44.

BEAZLEY, J. D. (1938). *Attic White Lekythoi* (London).

BENEDUM, J. (1978). 'Zur lydischen Artzinschrift IGRR IV 1359', *ZPE* 29: 115–21.

BENNETT, E. L. (1961–2). 'On the Use and Misuse of the Term "Priest-King" in Minoan Studies', *KrChr*: 327–35.

BÉRARD, C. (1970). *L'Héroon à la porte de l'ouest. Eretria* 3 (Bern).

—— (1974). *Anodoi: Essai sur l'imagerie des passages chthoniens* (Rome).

—— (1982). 'Récupérer la mort du prince: héroisation et formation de la cité', in G. Gnoli and J.-P. Vernant (eds.), *La Mort, les morts dans les sociétés anciennes* (Cambridge), 89–105.

—— (1984). 'L'Ordre des femmes', in *La cité des images: Religion et société en Grèce antique* (Mont-sur-Lausanne), 85–103.

—— (1985). 'Argoura fut-elle la "capitale" des futurs Eretriens?', *MusHelv* 42: 268–75.

—— (1988), 'Le Cadavre impossible', *Archeologia e storia antica. Annali. Istituto Universitario Orientale. Napoli.* Dipartimento del mondo classico e del mediterraneo antico 10 (Sezione tematica: La parola l'immagine, la tomba. Atti del Colloquio Internazionale di Capri): 163–9.

BERGER, E. (1970). *Das Basler Arztrelief. Studien zum griechischen Grab- und Votivrelief um 500 v. Chr. und zur vorhippokratischen Medizin* (Basle).

—— (1990). 'Grabstele einer Frau', in E. Berger (ed.), *Antike Kunstwerke aus der Sammlung Ludwig. III. Skulpturen* (Mainz), 25–70.

BERGER, P., and LUCKMANN, T. (1971). *The Social Construction of Reality* (Harmondsworth; orig. pub. 1966).

BERGREN, A. L. T. (1982). 'Sacred Apostrophe: Representation and Imitation in the Homeric Hymns', *Arethusa*, 15 (1982), 83–108.

BERNABÒ BREA, L. (1950). 'Kouros arcaico di Megara Hyblaea', *Annuario*, NS 8–10 (1946–8): 59–66.

BESCHI, L. (1969/70). 'Divinità funerarie cirenaiche', *Annuario*, NS 31–2: 133–341.

BIETTI SESTIERI, A. M., and DE SANTIS, A. (1985). 'Indicatori archeologici di cambiamento nella struttura delle communità laziali nel 80 sec. A.C.', *DdA* 3. 35–45.

BLECH, M. (1982). *Studien zum Kranz bei den Griechen* (Berlin and New York).

BLOCH, M. (1987). 'The Ritual of the Royal Bath in Madagascar: The Dissolution of Death, Birth and Fertility into Authority', in Cannadine and Price (1987: 271–97).

BLOME, P. (1984). 'Lefkandi und Homer', *WurzbJb* 10: 9–22.

BOARDMAN, J. (1955). 'Painted Funerary Plaques and Some Remarks on Prothesis', *BSA* 50: 51–66.

—— (1974). *Athenian Black Figure Vases: A Handbook* (London).

—— (1975). 'Heracles, Peisistratos and Eleusis', *JHS* 95: 1–12.

—— (1977). 'The Parthenon Frieze: Another View', in U. Höckmann and A. Krug (eds.), *Festschrift für Frank Brommer* (Mainz), 39–49.

—— (1978). *Greek Sculpture. The Archaic Period. A Handbook* (London).

—— (1986). 'Leaina', in H. A. G. Brijder, A. A. Drukker, and C. W. Neeft (eds.), *Enthousiasmos: Essays on Greek and Related Pottery presented to J. M. Hemelrijk* (Amsterdam), 93–6.

—— (1988). 'Sex Differentiation in Grave Vases', in *Archeologia e storia antica. Annali. Instituto Universitario Orientale. Napoli*. Dipartimento del mondo classico e del mediterraneo antico 10 (Sezione tematica: La parola l'immagine, la tomba. Atti del Colloquio Internazionale di Capri): 171–9.

BOEDEKER, D. D. (1979). 'Sappho and Acheron', in G. W. Bowerstock, W. Burkert, and M. C. J. Putnam (eds.), *Arktouros: Hellenic Studies presented to Bernard M. W. Knox* (Berlin and New York), 40–52.

BOEHRINGER, E. (1959). 'Pergamon', in *Neue deutsche Ausgrabungen im Mittelmeergebiet und im Vorderen Orient* (Berlin), 121–71.

BONANNO, M. G. (1980). 'Nomi e soprannomi archilochei', *MusHelv* 37: 65–88.

BOND, G. W. (ed.) (1963). Euripides, *Hypsipyle* (Oxford).

BOON, J. A. (1982). *Other Tribes, Other Scribes: Symbolic Anthropology in the*

Comparative Study of Cultures, Histories, Religions and Texts (Cambridge).

BOUSQUET, J. B. (1964). 'Inscriptions de Delphes. Archédamos de Sélinonte', *BCH* 88: 380–2.

BOVIO MARCONI, J. (1961). 'Epigrafe funeraria selinuntina', *Kokalos*, 7: 109–12.

BOWIE, E. L. (1986). 'Early Greek Elegy, Symposium and Public Festival', *JHS* 106: 13–35.

BOWIE, M. (1979). 'Jacques Lacan', in Sturrock (1979: 116–53).

BOWRA, C. M. (1938). 'The Epigram on the Fallen of Coronea', *CQ* 32: 80–8.

—— (1952). 'Orpheus and Eurydice', *CQ* 2: 113–26.

BRANDT, E. (1965). *Gruss und Gebet: Eine Studie zu Gebärden in der minoisch-mykenischen und frühgriechischen Kunst* (Waldsassen and Bayern).

BRANIGAN, K. (1970a). *The Foundations of Palatial Crete* (London).

—— (1970b). *The Tombs of Messara* (London).

—— (1987). 'Ritual Interference with Human Bones in the Messara Tholoi', in Laffineur (1987: 43–50).

BRAUND, D. C. (1980). 'Artemis Eukleia and Euripides' *Hippolytos*', *JHS* 100: 184–5.

BRELICH, A. (1967). 'Situazione attuale degli studi di storia delle religioni', *Acta Classica Univ. Scient. Debrecen.* 3: 3–11.

—— (1969). *Paides e parthenoi* (Rome).

BREMMER, J. (1983). *The Early Greek Concept of the Soul* (Princeton, NJ).

BRISSON, L. (1976). *Le Mythe de Teiresias: Essai d'analyse structurale* (Leiden).

BROMMER, F. (1969). 'Eine Lekythos in Madrid', *MadMit* 10: 155–71.

—— (1986). *Herakles: Die zwölf kanonischen Taten des Helden in antiker Kunst und Literatur* (Darmstadt).

BRONEER, O. (1938). 'Excavations on the North Slope of the Acropolis, 1937', *Hesperia*, 7: 161–263.

BROUSKARI, M. S. (1974). *The Acropolis Museum: A Descriptive Catalogue* (Athens).

BRÜMMER, E. (1985). 'Griechische Truhenbehälter', *JdI* 100: 1–168.

BUCK, C. D. (1955). *The Greek Dialects* (Chicago).

BÜCHNER, W. (1937). 'Probleme der homerischen Nekyia', *Hermes*, 72: 104–22.

BUNDY, E. L. (1972). 'The "Quarrel between Kallimachos and Apollonios". Part I. The Epilogue of Kallimachos' Hymn to Apollo', *CSCA* 5: 39–94.

BURHENN, H. (1980). 'Functionalism and the Explanation of Religion', *Journal for the Scientific Study of Religion*, 19/4: 350–60.

BURKERT, W. (1961). 'Elysion', *Glotta*, 39: 208–13.

—— (1962). '*Goes*. Zum griechischen "Schamanismus"', *RhMus* 105: 36–55.

—— (1972) *Lore and Science in Ancient Pythagoreanism* (Cambridge, Mass.; first pub. in Ger., 1962).

—— (1975). 'Le laminette auree: da Orfeo a Lampone', in *Orfismo in Magna Grecia. Atti del XIVo Convegno di Studi sulla Magna Grecia. Taranto 6–10 ottobre 1974* (Naples), 81–104.

—— (1983). *Homo Necans: The Anthropology of Ancient Greek Sacrificial Ritual and Myth*² (Berkeley, Calif., Los Angeles, and London).

—— (1985). *Greek Religion: Archaic and Classical*² (Oxford).

—— (1987). *Ancient Mystery Cults* (Harvard).

BUSCHOR, E. (1933). 'Altsamische Grabstelen', *AthMit* 58: 22–46.

CALAME, C. (1977). *Les Choeurs de jeunes filles en Grèce archaïque* (Rome).

—— (1986). *Le Récit en Grèce ancienne: Énonciations et représentations de poètes* (Paris).

CALDER, W., III (1965). 'A New Verse Inscription from Selinous', *AJA* 69: 262–4.

CAMPBELL, D. A. (1984). 'The Frogs in the *Frogs*', *JHS* 94: 163–5.

CANNADINE, D. (1987). 'Introduction: Divine Rites of Kings', in Cannadine and Price (1987: 1–19).

—— and PRICE, S. (eds.), (1987). *Rituals of Royalty: Power and Ceremonial in Traditional Societies* (Cambridge).

CARLESS HULIN, L. (1989). 'The Diffusion of Religious Symbols within Complex Societies', in I. Hodder (ed.), *The Meanings of Things: Material Culture and Symbolic Expression* (London), 90–6.

CARPENTER, T. H. (1989). *Art and Myth in Ancient Greece* (London).

CATLING, R. W. V., and LEMOS, I. S. (1990). *Lefkandi II: The Protogeometric Building at Toumba. Part I. The Pottery* (London).

CHANTRAINE, P. (1980). *Dictionnaire étymologique de la langue grecque. Histoire des mots*. Tome iv. 2 (Paris).

CHRISTOU, C. (1964a). Spartiatikoi archaikoi taphoi kai epitaphios met' anaglyphon amphoreus tou lakonikou ergasteriou, *ADelt* 19: A. Meletai, 123–63.

—— (1964b). Ho neos amphoreus tis Spartis. Hoi alloi met' anaglyphon amphoreis tou lakonikou ergasteriou, *ADelt* 19: A. Meletai, 164–265.

CLAIRMONT, C. W. (1970). *Gravestone and Epigram: Greek Memorials from the Archaic and Classical Period* (Mainz).

—— (1983). *Patrios Nomos: Public Burial in Athens during the Fifth and Fourth Centuries B.C.* (BAR International Series 161; Oxford).

CLARK, R. J. (1970). 'Two Virgilian Similes and the Herakleous Katabasis', *Phoenix*, 24: 244–55.

—— (1979). *Catabasis: Vergil and the Wisdom-Tradition* (Amsterdam).

COLDSTREAM, J. N. (1976). 'Hero-Cults in the Age of Homer', *JHS* 96: 8–17.

—— (1977). *Geometric Greece* (London).

COLE, S. G. (1980). 'New Evidence for the Mysteries of Dionysos', *GRBS* 21: 223–38.

COOK, B. (1976). *Greek and Roman Art in the British Museum* (London).

CORDANO, F. (1980). ' "Morte e pianto rituale" nell'Atene del VI sec. A.C.', *ArchCl* 32: 186–97.

COUILLOUD, M.-Th. (1974). 'Reliefs funéraires des Cyclades de l'époque hellénistique à l'époque impériale', *BCH* 98: 397–498.

CROWTHER, N. B. (1991). 'The Apobates Reconsidered (Demosthenes lxi 23–9)', *JHS* 111: 174–6.

CULLER, J. (1975). *Structuralist Poetics* (London).

—— (1976). *Saussure* (Glasgow).

—— (1979). 'Jacques Derrida', in Sturrock (1979: 154–80).

—— (1981). *The Pursuit of Signs: Semiotics, Literature, Deconstruction* (London and Henley).

—— (1983). *On Deconstruction: Theory and Criticism after Structuralism* (London, Melbourne, and Henley).

CUMONT, F. (1922). F. Cumont, *Afterlife in Roman Paganism* (New Haven, Conn.).

D'AGOSTINO, B. (1982). 'Le sirene, il tuffatore e le porte dell'Ade', *Archeologia e storia antica. Annali. Istituto Universitario Orientale. Napoli. Dipartimento del mondo classico e del mediterraneo antico* 4: 43–50.

DAKARIS, S. I. (n.d.). *The Acheron Necromanteion: Ephyra—Pandosia—Cassope* (Athens, no date).

—— (1973). 'The Oracle of the Dead on the Acheron', in E. Melas (ed.), *Temples and Sanctuaries of Ancient Greece* (London), 139–49.

DALE, A. M. (1954) (ed.). Euripides, *Alcestis* (Oxford).

—— (1967) (ed.). Euripides, *Helen* (Oxford).

DARCQUE, P. (1981). 'Les Vestiges mycéniens découverts sous le Telesterion d'Eleusis', *BCH* 105: 593–605.

—— (1987). 'Les Tholoi et l'organisation socio-politique du monde mycénien, in Laffineur (1987: 185–205).

DARCUS, S. M. (1979). 'A Person's Relation to *Psyche* in Homer, Hesiod, and the Greek Lyric Poets', *Glotta*, 57: 30–9.

DAUX, G. (1962). 'Chronique des fouilles 1961', *BCH* 86: 629–978.

—— (1971). 'Reflexions sur l'épigraphie', *Acta of the Fifth International Congress of Greek and Latin Epigraphy, Cambridge 1967* (Oxford), 1–8.

—— (1972). Stèles funéraires et épigrammes. (A propos d'un livre récent)', *BCH* 96: 503–66.

—— (1973). 'Notes de lecture', *BCH* 97: 239–51.

—— (1973/4). 'Sur quelques stèles funéraires grecques d'époque archaique ou classique', *ArchCl* 25/6: 238–49.

DAVARAS, C. (1984). 'A Minoan Ship Model Carrying a Honeycomb from the Mitsotakis Collection', in Gk. with Eng. summary, *ArchEph* (1984 [1986]): 55–95.

DAVIES, M. (1987). 'Description by Negation: History of a Thought-Pattern in Ancient Accounts of Blissful Life', *Prometheus*, 13: 265–84.

——(1989a). *The Epic Cycle* (Bristol).

——(1989b). 'Sisyphus and the Invention of Religion ('Critias' *TrGF* i (43) F 19 = B 25 DK)', *BICS* 36: 16–32.

DAY, J. W. (1989). 'Rituals in Stone: Early Greek Grave Epigrams and Monuments', *JHS* 109: 16–28.

DE JONG, I. J. F. (1987). *Narrators and Focalizers: The Presentation of the Story in the Iliad* (Amsterdam).

DEMAKOPOULOU, K. (1990). 'The Burial Ritual in the Tholos Tomb at Kokla, Argolis', in Hägg and Nordquist (1990: 113–23).

——and KONSOLA, D. (1981). *Archaeological Museum of Thebes* (Athens).

DE MAN, P. (1979a). *Allegories of Reading: Figural Language in Rousseau, Nietzsche, Rilke and Proust* (New Haven, Conn., and London).

——(1979b). 'Autobiography as Defacement', *Modern Language Notes*, 94: 919–30.

DEMISCH, H. (1977). *Die Sphinx: Geschichte ihrer Darstellung von den Anfängen bis zur Gegenwart* (Stuttgart).

DE MOURGES, O. (1967). *Racine, or, The Triumph of Relevance* (Cambridge).

DE POLIGNAC, F. (1984). *La Naissance de la cité grecque* (Paris).

DERRIDA, J. (1967). *L'Écriture et la différence* (Paris).

——(1972). *Positions* (Paris).

——(1974, 1976). *Of Grammatology* (Baltimore and London).

DE RUYT, F. (1932). 'Le Thanatos d'Euripide et le Charun etrusque', *AntCl* 1: 61–77.

DESBOROUGH, V. R. d'A. (1972). *The Greek Dark Ages* (London).

DETIENNE, M. (1988a). 'L'Écriture et ses nouveaux objets intellectuels en Grèce', in Detienne (1988c: 7–26).

——(1988b). 'L'Espace de la publicité: ses opérateurs intellectuels dans la cité', in Detienne (1988c: 29–81).

——(ed.) (1988c). *Les Savoirs de l'écriture. En Grèce ancienne* (Lille).

DEUBNER, L. (1969). *Attische Feste* ³ (Vienna).

DE WAELE, F. J. M. (1927). *The Magic Staff or Rod* (1927).

DOHERTY, L. E. (1991). 'The Internal and Implied Audiences of *Odyssey* 11', *Arethusa*, 24: 145–76.

D'ONOFRIO, A. M. (1982). 'Korai e kouroi funerari attici', *Archeologia e storia antica. Annali. Istituto Universitario Orientale. Napoli*. Dipartimento del mondo classico e del mediterraneo antico 4: 135–70.

——(1986). 'Un "programma" figurativo tardo arcaico. (Le basi ateniesi con "Ballspielszenen" riconsiderate)', *Annali. Istituto Universitario Ori-*

entale. Napoli. Dipartimento del mondo classico e del mediterraneo antico 8: 175–93.

D'ONOFRIO, A. M. (1988). 'Aspetti e problemi del monumento funerario attico arcaico', *Archeologia e storia antica. Annali. Istituto Universitario Orientale. Napoli.* Dipartimento del mondo classico e del mediterraneo antico 10 (Sezione tematica: La parola l'immagine, la tomba. Atti del Colloquio Internazionale di Capri): 83–96.

DOUGLAS, M. (1973) (ed.). *Rules and Meanings: The Anthropology of Everyday Knowledge. Selected Readings* (Harmondsworth).

—— (1975). *Implicit meanings* (London and Henley).

—— (1980). *Evans-Pritchard* (London).

DOVER, K. J. (1974). *Greek Popular Morality in the time of Plato and Aristotle* (Oxford).

DREES, L. (1968). *Olympia: Gods, Artists and Athletes* (London).

DUCAT, J. (1976). 'Fonctions de la statue dans la Grèce archaique: *kouros* et *kolossos*', *BCH* 100: 239–51.

DURU, M. S. (1983). 'Continuity in the Midst of Change: Underlying Themes in Igbo Culture', *Anthropological Quarterly,* 56: 1–9.

EAGLETON, T. (1978). *Criticism and Ideology²* (London).

ECKSTEIN, F., and LEGHER, A. (1969). *Antike Kleinkunst im Liebighaus* (Frankfurt).

ECO, U. (1976). *A Theory of Semiotics* (Bloomington, Ind.).

—— (1981). *The Role of the Reader: Explorations in the Semiotics of Texts* (London).

EDMUNDS, L. (1987). *Cleon, Knights, and Aristophanes' Politics* (Lanham, New York, and London).

EDWARDS, A. T. (1985). 'Achilles in the Underworld: Iliad, Odyssey, and Aethiopis', *GRBS* 26: 215–27.

—— (1988). '*KLEOS APHTHITON* and Oral Theory', *CQ* 38: 25–30.

EDWARDS, M. W. (1991). *The Iliad: A Commentary,* v: bks. 17–20 (Cambridge).

EICHLER, F. (1914). '*Sema* und *mnema* in älteren griechischen Grabinschriften', *AthMit* 39: 138–43.

EISENBERGER, H. (1973). *Studien zur Odyssee* (Wiesbaden).

EITREM, S. (1909). *Hermes und die Toten* (Christiania).

ELAM, K. (1980). *The Semiotics of Theatre and Drama* (London).

ERBSE, H. (1972). *Beiträge zum Verständnis der Odyssee* (Berlin and New York).

ETTIG, G. (1891). 'Acheruntica sive Descensuum apud veteres Enarratio', *Leipziger Studien,* 13: 249–410.

EVANS, Sir A. (1935). *The Palace of Minos,* iv (London).

EVANS-PRITCHARD, E. E. (1965). *Theories of Primitive Religion* (Oxford).

—— (1973). 'Nuer Spear Symbolism', in Needham (1973: 92–108).

FAIRBANKS, A. (1907). *Athenian White Lekythoi,* i (New York and London).

—— (1914). *Athenian White Lekythoi,* ii (New York and London).

FARNELL, L. R. (1909). *The Cults of the Greek States,* v (Oxford).

—— (1932). *The Works of Pindar: Translated, with Literary and Critical Commentaries* (London).

FELTEN, W. (1975). *Attische Unterweltsdarstellungen des VI. und V. Jh. v. Chr.* (Munich).

FINKELBERG, M. (1986). 'Is *KLEOS APHTHITON* a Homeric Formula?', *CQ* 36: 1–5.

FINNEGAN, R. (1977). *Oral Poetry: Its Nature, Significance and Social Context* (Cambridge).

FLOYD, E. D. (1980). '*KLEOS APHTHITON.* An Indoeuropean Perspective on Early Greek Poetry', *Glotta,* 58: 133–57.

FONTENROSE, J. (1981). *Orion: The Myth of the Hunter and the Huntress* (Berkeley, Calif.).

FORBES, K. (1956). 'Some Cyrenean Dedications', *Philologus,* 100: 235–52.

FORREST, W. G. (1980). *A History of Sparta* (London).

FOUCAULT, M. (1972). *The Archaeology of Knowledge* (London; first pub. in Fr., 1969).

FRASER, P. M., and RÖNNE, T. R. (1957). *Boeotian and West Greek Tombstones* (Lund).

FRENCH, E. (1984). 'New Finds at the Phokikon', in *Studies presented to Sterling Dow* (Durham, NC), 89–96.

—— and VANDERPOOL, E. (1963). 'The Phokikon', Hesperia, 32: 213–25.

FREYER-SCHAUENBURG, B. (1974). *Samos ix. Bildwerke der archaischen Zeit und des strengen Stils* (Bonn).

FRIEDLÄNDER, P., and HOFFLEIT, H. B. (1948). *Epigrammata: Greek Inscriptions in Verse from the Beginnings to the Persian Wars* (Berkeley, Calif., and Los Angeles).

FRISK, H. (1970). *Griechisches etymologisches Wörterbuch.* Band ii (Heidelberg).

FRONTISI-DUCROUX, F. (1988). 'Figures de l'invisible: stratégies textuelles et stratégies iconiques', *Archeologia e storia antica. Annali. Istituto Universitario Orientale. Napoli.* Dipartimento del mondo classico e del mediterraneo antico 10 (Sezione tematica: La parola l'immagine, la tomba. Atti del Colloquio Internazionale di Capri): 27–40.

FURTWÄNGLER, A. (1905). 'Charon: eine altattische Malerei', *Archiv für Religionswissenschaft,* 8: 191–202.

GANSCHINIETZ (1919). *Katabasis,* RE x: cols. 2359–449.

GARLAND, R. (1981). 'The Causation of Death in the Iliad: A Theological and Biological Investigation', *BICS* 28: 43–60.

GARLAND, R. (1982). *Geras thanonton*: An Investigation into the Claims of the Homeric Dead', *BICS* 29: 69–80.

—— (1985). *The Greek Way of Death* (London).

—— (1989). 'The Well-Ordered Corpse: An Investigation into the Motives behind Greek Funerary Legislation', *BICS* 36: 1–15.

GARVIE, A. F. (1986). *Aeschylus, Choephori* (Oxford).

GEERTZ, C. (1966). 'Religion as a Cultural System', in M. Banton (ed.), *Anthropological Approaches to the Study of Religion* (London, Social Science Paperback, 1968; first publ. 1966), 1–46.

GENETTE, G. (1969). *Figures*, ii (Paris).

—— (1972). *Figures*, iii (Paris).

GENTILI, B. (1968). 'Epigramma ed elegia', in *L'épigramme grecque: Fondation Hardt pour l'étude de l'antiquité classique. Entretiens*, xiv (Vandœuvres and Geneva 1967 [1968]), 37–81.

GEORGOUDI, S. (1988). 'La Mer, la mort et le discours des épigrammes funéraires', in *Archeologia e storia antica. Annali. Istituto Universitario Orientale. Napoli.* Dipartimento del mondo classico e del mediterraneo antico 10 (Sezione tematica: La parola l'immagine, la tomba. Atti del Colloquio Internazionale di Capri): 53–61.

GILBERT, M. (1987). 'The Person of the King: Ritual and Power in a Ghanaian State', in Cannadine and Price (1987: 298–330).

GILLILAND, D. S. (1979). 'Religious Change among the Hausa, 1000–1800. A Hermeneutic of the Kano Chronicle', *Journal of Asian and African Studies*, 14 nos. 3–4, July–October: 241–57.

GIOVANNANGELI, D. (1979). *Écriture et répétition: Approche de Derrida* (Paris).

GLUCKMANN, M. (1949–50). 'Social Beliefs and Individual Thinking in Primitive Society', *Memoirs and Proceedings of the Manchester Literary and Philosophical Society*, 91: 73–98.

—— and EGGAN, M. (1966). 'Introduction', in M. Banton (ed.), *Anthropological Approaches to the Study of Religion* (London; Social Science Paperback, 1968; first pub. 1966), pp. xi–xlii.

GOLDHILL, S. (1986). *Reading Greek Tragedy* (Cambridge).

GOLDMAN, L. (1970). 'Structure: Human Reality and Methodological Concept', in R. Macksey and E. Donato (eds.), *The Structuralist Controversy: The Languages of Criticism and the Sciences of Man* (Baltimore and London, 1972; orig. pub. 1970 as *The Languages of Criticism and the Sciences of Man*), 98–110.

GOMBRICH, E. H. (1971). *Meditations on a Hobby Horse and Other Essays on the Theory of Art*² (London).

—— (1977). *Art and Illusion: A Study in the Psychology of Pictorial Representation* (Oxford).

—— (1982). *The Image and the Eye: Further Studies in the Psychology of Pictorial Representation* (Oxford).

GRAF, F. (1974). *Eleusis und die orphische Dichtung Athens in vorhellenistischer Zeit* (Berlin and New York).

—— (1982). 'Culti e credenze religiose della Magna Grecia', *Magna Grecia*, 18: 21–6.

GRAGG, F. A. (1910). 'A Study of the Greek Epigram before 300 B.C.', *Proceedings of the American Academy of Arts and Sciences*, 46: 3–62.

GRAY, D. H. F. (1947). 'Homeric Epithets for Things', *CQ* 61: 109–21.

—— (1954). 'Metal-Working in Homer', *JHS* 74: 1–15.

GREGORY, R. L. (1966). *Eye and Brain: The Psychology of Seeing* (London).

GRIESSMAIR, E. (1966). *Das Motiv der Mors Immatura in den griechischen metrischen Grabinschriften* (Innsbruck).

GRIFFIN, J. (1977). 'The Epic Cycle and the Uniqueness of Homer', *JHS* 97. 39–53.

—— (1980). *Homer on Life and Death* (Oxford).

GUARDUCCI, M. (1950). *Inscriptiones Creticae*, iv (Rome).

—— (1961). 'Epigraphical Appendix', in Richter (1961: 155–72).

—— (1966). 'Note di epigrafia selinuntina arcaica', *Kokalos*, 12: 179–99.

—— (1967). *Epigrafia Greca i. Caratteri e storia della disciplina: La scrittura greca dalle origini all' età imperiale* (Rome).

—— (1974). *Epigrafia Greca iii. Epigrafi di carattere privato* (Rome).

GUÉPIN, J.-P. (1968). *The Tragic Paradox: Myth and Ritual in Greek Tragedy* (Amsterdam).

GUIRAUD, P. (1975). *Semiology* (London; first pub. in Fr., 1971).

GUTHRIE, W. K. C. (1950). *The Greeks and their Gods* (London).

HÄGG, R. (1983a). 'Burial Customs and Social Differentiation in 8th-Century Argos', in Hägg (1983c. 27–31).

—— (1983b). 'Funerary Meals in the Geometric Necropolis at Asine?', in Hägg (1983c: 189–93).

—— (1983c) (ed.). *The Greek Renaissance of the Eighth Century B.C.: Tradition and Innovation* (Stockholm) (= Proceedings of the Second International Symposium at the Swedish Institute in Athens, 1–5 June 1981).

—— (1987). 'Gifts to the Heroes in Geometric and Archaic Greece', in T. Linders and G. C. Nordquist (eds.), *Gifts to the Gods* (Proceedings of the Uppsala Symposium 1985; Uppsala), 93–9.

—— (1992). 'A Scene of Funerary Cult from Argos', in R. Hägg (ed.), *The Iconography of Greek Cult in the Archaic and Classical Periods* (*Kernos* Suppl. 1, Athens and Liege), 169–76.

—— MARINATOS, N., and NORDQUIST, G. C. (1988). *Early Greek Cult Practice*. Proceedings of the Fifth International Symposium at the Swedish Institute at Athens, 26–29 June, 1986 (Stockholm).

—— and NORDQUIST, G. C. (1990) (eds.). *Celebrations of Death and Divinity in the Bronze Age Argolid*. Proceedings of the Sixth International

Symposium at the Swedish Institute at Athens, 11–13 June, 1988 (Stockholm).

HAINSWORTH, J. B. (1970). 'The Criticism of an Oral Homer', *JHS* 90: 90–8.

HALLPIKE, C. R. (1979). *The Foundations of Primitive Thought* (Oxford).

HAMDORF, F. W. (1964). *Griechische Kultpersonifikationen der vorhellenistischen Zeit* (Mainz).

HANSEN, P. A. (1983). *Carmina epigraphica graeca saeculorum VIII–V A.CHR.N* (Berlin and New York).

—— (1989). *Carmina epigraphica graeca saeculi IV A.CHR.N* (Berlin and New York).

HARARI, J. V. (1979). 'Critical Factions/Critical Fictions', in J. V. Harari (ed.), *Textual Strategies: Perspectives in Post-Structuralist Criticism* (Ithaca, NY), 17–72.

HASLAM, M. W. (1977), in A. K. Bowman, M. W. Haslam, S. A. Stephens, and M. L. West (eds.), *The Oxyrhynchus Papyri*, xlv (London).

HÄUSLE, H. (1979). *Einfache und frühe Formen des griechischen Epigrams* (Innsbruck).

—— (1980). *Das Denkmal als Garant des Nachruhms: Eine Studie zu einem Motiv in lateinischen Inschriften* (Munich).

HEBB, D. O. (1949). *The Organization of Behavior: A Neuropsychological Theory* (New York).

—— (1958). *A Textbook of Psychology* (Philadelphia).

HELLY, B. (1978). 'Quarantes épigrammes thessaliennes', *RPh* 52: 121–35.

HERTER, H. (1976). 'Hermes, Ursprung und Wesen eines griechischen Gottes', *RheinMus* 119: 193–241.

HESTER, D. A. (1971). 'Sophocles the Unphilosophical', *Mnemosyne*, 24: 11–59.

HEUBECK, A. (1972). 'Etymologische Vermutungen zu Eleusis und Eileithyia', *Kadmos*, 11: 87–95.

—— (1989). Books 9–12, in A. Heubeck and A. Hoekstra, *A Commentary on Homer's Odyssey. Volume ii. Books ix–xvi* (Oxford).

HICKEY, J. V., STAATS, G. R., and McGAW, D. B. (1979). 'Factors Associated with the Mecca Pilgrimage among the Bokkos Fulani', *Journal of Asian and African Studies*, 14/3–4, July–October: 217–30.

HIGNETT, C. (1952). *A History of the Athenian Constitution to the End of the Fifth Century B.C.* (Oxford).

HODDER, I. (1982a). *The Present Past: An Introduction to Anthropology for Archaeologists* (London).

—— (1982b). 'Theoretical Archaeology: A Reactionary View', in I. Hodder (ed.), *Symbolic and Structural Archaeology* (Cambridge), 1–16.

HOFFMANN, H. (1984). 'Charos, Charun, Charon', *OJA* 3: 65–9.

—— (1986). 'From Charos to Charon: Some Notes on the Human Encounter with Death in Attic Red-Figured Vase-Painting', *Visible Religion*, 4–5: 173–204.

HÖLSCHER, F. (1972). *Die Bedeutung archaischer Tierkampfbilder* (Wurzburg).

HOMANN-WEDEKING, E. (1966). 'Samos 1965', *AA*: 158–64.

—— (1969). 'Festvortrag, Winkelmannfest am 9. Dezember 1968', *AA*: 551–8.

HORNBLOWER, S. (1991). *A Commentary on Thucydides*, i: Books I–III (Oxford).

HULTKRANTZ, A. (1980). 'The Problem of Christian Influence on Northern Algonkian Eschatology', *Studies in Religion/Sciences religieuses* 9: 161–83.

HUMPHREYS, S. C. (1978). *Anthropology and the Greeks* (London).

—— (1983). *The Family, Women and Death: Comparative Studies* (London).

—— (1990). Review of I. Morris, *Burial and Ancient Society: The Rise of the Greek City-State* (Cambridge 1987), *Helios*, 17: 263–8.

HUNTINGTON, R., and Metcalf, P. (1979). *Celebrations of Death. The Anthropology of Mortuary Ritual* (Cambridge).

HUTCHINSON, G. O. (1985) (ed.). Aeschylus, *Septem contra Thebas* (Oxford).

IAKOVIDIS, S. (1969). *Perati: To Nekrotapheion* (Athens).

IMMERWAHR, H. R. (1967). 'An Inscribed Terracotta Ball in Boston', *CJOS* 0: 233 66.

JACOBSTHAL, P. (1933). *Diskoi* (93rd Winkelmannsprogramm der Arch. Gesellschaft zu Berlin; Berlin).

JACOBY, F. (1956) *Abhandlungen zur griechischen Geschichtsschreibung* (Leiden).

JANKO, R. (1992). *The Iliad: A Commentary*, iv: bks. 13–16 (Cambridge).

JAUSS, H. R. (1974*a*). 'Literary History as a Challenge to Literary Theory', in R. Cohen (ed.), *New Directions in Literary History* (Baltimore), 11–41.

—— (1974*b*) '*La douceur du foyer*: The Lyric of the Year 1857 as a Pattern for the Communication of Social Norms', *Romanic Review*, 65: 201–29.

JEFFERY, L. H. (1958). 'Review of GV', *JHS* 78: 144–5.

—— (1962). 'The Inscribed Gravestones of Archaic Attica', *BSA* 57: 115–53.

—— (1974). 'IG I, 1007: An Aiginetan Grave-Inscription', in D. W. Bradeen and M. F. McGregor (eds.), *Phoros: Tribute to Benjamin Dean Meritt* (New York), 76–9.

—— (1976). *Archaic Greece* (London).

—— (1990). *The Local Scripts of Archaic Greece*. Rev. ed. with Suppl. by A. W. Johnston (Oxford).

JENKINS, I. (1983). 'Is there Life after Marriage? A Study of the Abduction

Motif in Vase Paintings of the Athenian Wedding Ceremony', *BICS* 30: 137–45.

JENKINS, I. (1986). *Greek and Roman Life* (London).

——and WILLIAMS D. (1985). 'Sprang Hair Nets: Their Manufacture and Use in Ancient Greece', *AJA* 89: 411–18.

JOHNSTON, A. (1983). 'The Extent and Use of Literacy: The Archaeological Evidence', in Hägg (1983*c*: 63–8).

——(1990). 'Supplement 1961–1987', in Jeffery (1990: 423–81).

JOUAN, F. (1966). *Euripide et les légendes des chants cypriens: Des origines de la guerre de Troie à l'Iliade* (Paris).

——(1981). 'L'Évocation des morts dans la tragédie grecque', *RHR* 198: 403–21.

KAEMPF-DIMITRIADOU, S. (1979). *Die Liebe der Götter in der attischen Kunst des 5. Jhs. v. Chr.* (Bern).

KAHN, L. (1978). *Hermès passe ou les ambiguités de la communication* (Paris).

KAIBEL, G. (1878). *Epigrammata Graeca ex lapidibus conlecta* (Berlin 1878 [Hildesheim 1965]).

KAKAVOYANNI, O. (1989). *B' Ephoreia Proistorikon kai klassikon archaioteton: Anavyssos [ADelt 39 (1984) Chronika, 43–5]* (Athens).

KALLIGAS, P. (1981). 'Archaeological News from Euboea, 1981', *AAA* 14: 29–36.

KALOYEROPOULOU, A. G. (1974). 'Épitaphe mégarien', *AAA* 7: 287–91.

KAMERBEEK, J. C. (1978). *The Plays of Sophocles. Commentaries. Part III. The Antigone* (Leiden).

KANNICHT, R. (1969) (ed.). Euripides, *Helena* (Heidelberg).

KAPLAN, A. (1970). Referential Meaning in the Arts', in M. Weitz (ed.), *Problems in Aesthetics: An Introductory Book of Readings* (London) 270–91.

KAROUZOS, Ch. J. (1951). 'An Early Classical Disc Relief from Melos', *JHS* 71: 96–110.

——(1961). *Aristodikos: Zur Geschichte der spätarchaisch-attischen Plastik und der Grabstatue* (Stuttgart).

——(1972). *Perikalles agalma exepoies' ouk adaes*, in G. Pfohl (ed.), *Inschriften der Griechen. Grab-, Weih- und Ehreninschriften* (Darmstadt), 85–152.

KARUSU, S. (1961). 'Hermes Psychopompos', *AthMit* 76: 91–106.

KAROUZOU, S. (1968). *National Archaeological Museum. Collection of Sculpture: A Catalogue* (Athens).

KEARNS, E. (1989). *The Heroes of Attica* (London).

KEBRIC, R. B. (1983). *The Paintings in the Cnidian Lesche at Delphi and their Historical Context* (Leiden).

KEE, H. C. (1982). 'Self-Definition in the Asclepius Cult', in B. F. Meyer and E. P. Sanders (eds.), *Jewish and Christian Self-Definition*, iii (Philadelphia).

KENYON, F. G. (1897). *The poems of Bacchylides* (Oxford).
KERAMOPOULLOS, A. D. (1920). 'Eikones polemiston tis en Delio machis (424 B.C.)', *ArchEph*: 1–36.
KILIAN, K. (1975). 'Trachtzubehör der Eisenzeit zwischen Ägäis und Adria', *PZ* 50: 9–140.
KING, H. (1983). 'Bound to Bleed: Artemis and Greek Women', in A. Cameron and A. Kurht (eds.), *Images of Women in Antiquity* (London), 109–27.
——(1986a). 'Agnodike and the Profession of Medicine', *PCPS* NS 32: 53–77.
——(1986b). Review of R. H. Terpening, *Charon and the Crossing: Ancient, Medieval and Renaissance Transformations of a Myth* (London and Toronto 1985), *CR* 36: 355–6.
KIRK, G. S. (1962). *The Songs of Homer* (Cambridge).
——(1970). *Myth: Its Meanings and Functions in Ancient and Other Cultures* (Cambridge).
——(1990). *The Iliad: A Commentary*, ii: bks. 5–8 (Cambridge).
KITTO, H. D. F. (1956). *Form and Meaning in Drama* (London).
——(1961). *Greek Tragedy* (3rd edn. London)
KLAFFENBACH, G. (1935). 'Bericht über eine epigraphische Reise durch Mittelgriechenland und die ionischen Inseln', *Sitzungsberichten der Preussischen Akademie der Wissenschaft, Phil.-Hist. Klasse.* 19.
——(1966). *Griechische Epigraphik²* (Göttingen).
KNIGGE, U. (1988). *Der Kerameikos von Athen. Führung durch Ausgrabungen und Geschichte* (Athens).
KOCH-HARNACK, G. (1989). *Erotische Symbole. Lotosblüte und gemeinsamer Mantel auf antiken Vasen* (Berlin).
KOLB, F. (1981). *Agora und Theater, Volks- und Festversammlung* (Berlin).
KONTOLEON, N. M. (1970). *Aspects de la Grèce préclassique* (Paris).
——(1972). 'Anaskaphai Naxou', *Praktika*: 143–55.
KOUMANOUDES, S. N. (1969). 'Epigramma ek Kopon', *AAA* 2: 80–4.
KOUROU, N. (1987). 'Rhoa glykeia', in *Eilapine: Tomos timetikos yia ton kathegete Nicolao Platona* (Herakleion), 101–16.
——(1991). 'Aegean Orientalizing versus Oriental Art: The Evidence of Monsters', in V. Karageorghis (ed.), *The Civilizations of the Aegean and their Diffusion in Cyprus and the Eastern Mediterranean 2000–600 B.C.* (Larnaca), 110–21.
KRAIKER, W., and KÜBLER, K. (1939). *Kerameikos: Ergebnisse der Ausgrabungen i. Die Nekropolen des 12. bis 10. Jahrhunderts* (Berlin).
KRISTEVA, J. (1981). *Le Langage, cet inconnu* (Paris; first pub. 1969).
KRUG, A. (1985). *Heilkunst und Heilkult: Medizin in der Antike* (Munich).
KRUYT, A. C. (1973). 'Right and Left in Central Celebes', in Needham (1973: 74–91).

460   References

KÜBLER, K. (1954). *Kerameikos V.1 Die Nekropolen des 10. bis 8. Jahrhunderts* (Berlin).

KUDLIEN, F. (1967). *Der Beginn des medizinischen Denkens bei den Griechen von Homer bis Hippokrates* (Zurich).

KÜHNER–GERTH (1898). R. Kühner, *Ausführliche Grammatik der griechischen Sprache.* 3rd edn., by B. Gerth, i (Hanover and Leipzig).

——(1904). R. Kühner, *Ausführliche Grammatik der griechischen Sprache.* 3rd edn., by B. Gerth, ii (Hanover and Leipzig).

KURTZ, D. C. (1975). *Athenian White Lekythoi: Patterns and Painters* (Oxford).

——(1985). 'Vases for the Dead, an Attic Selection', in *Ancient Greek and Related Pottery: Proceedings of the International Vase Symposium Amsterdam 1984* (Allard Pierson Series, v. 314–28).

——(1988). 'Mistress and Maid', *Archeologia e storia antica. Annali. Istituto Universitario Orientale. Napoli.* Dipartimento del mondo classico e del mediterraneo antico 10 (Sezione tematica: La parola l'immagine, la tomba. Atti del Colloquio Internazionale di Capri), 141–9.

——and BOARDMAN, J. (1971). *Greek Burial Customs* (London).

KYRIELEIS, H. (1983). *To Heraio tes Samou* (Athens).

LABARBE, J. (1968). 'Les Aspects gnomiques de l'épigramme grecque', in *L'épigramme grecque. Fondation Hardt pour l'étude de l'antiquité classique. Entretiens,* xiv (Vandoeuvres and Geneva 1967 [1968]), 349–83.

LACROIX, L. (1982). 'A propos du sphinx des monnaies de Chios', *RA*: 75–80.

LAFFINEUR, R. (ed.) (1987). *Thanatos: Les coutumes funéraires en Égée à l'âge du bronze. Actes du Colloque de Liège (21–23 avril 1986)* [= Aegaeum 1] (Liège).

LAKS, A. (1982). 'Remarques sur *chairon ithi* et les formules apparentées', *Glotta,* 60: 214–20.

LAMBRINOUDAKIS, V. K. (1988). 'Veneration of Ancestors in Geometric Naxos', in Hägg, Marinatos, and Nordquist (1988: 235–45).

LANGDON, M. K. (1985). 'The Grave of Posthon at Sounion', *Hesperia,* 54: 145–8.

LATACZ, J. (1966). *Zum Wortfeld 'Freude' in der Sprache Homers* (Heidelberg).

LATTIMORE, R. (1962). *Themes in Greek and Latin Epitaphs*[2] (Urbana, Ill.).

LAUSBERG, M. (1982). *Das Einzeldistichon: Studien zum antiken Epigram* (Munich).

LAUTER, H. (1985). *Der Kultplatz auf dem Turkovuni* (Berlin).

LAWSON, J. C. (1910). *Modern Greek Folklore and Ancient Greek Religion: A Study in Survivals* (Cambridge).

LAZARIDIS, D. (1968). '*Eideseis ex Attikes*', *AAA* 1: 31–5.

LAZZARINI, M. L. (1976). *Le Formule delle dediche votive nella Grecia arcaica* (Rome).

LEACH, E. (1973). 'Structuralism in Social Anthropology', in D. Robey, (ed.), *Structuralism: An Introduction* (Wolfson College Lectures 1972; Oxford), 37–56.

—— (1976). *Culture and Communication: The Logic by which Symbols are Connected* (Cambridge).

LEBESSI, A. K. (1976). *Hoi steles tou Prinia* (Athens).

—— (1985). *To hiero tou Hermi kai tis Aphroditis sti Symi Viannou.* i.1 *Chalkina kretika toreumata* (Athens).

LEJEUNE, M. (1968). 'L'assibilation de *th* devant *i* en mycénien', *Atti e Memorie del Primo Congresso Internazionale di Micenologia* (Rome), 733–43.

LE ROY, Ch. (1984). 'Mémoire et tradition: réflexions sur la continuité', in *Aux origines de l'hellénisme: La Crète et la Grèce. Hommage à Henri Van Effenterre* (Paris), 163–72.

LESCHHORN, W. (1984). '*Gründer der Stadt*': *Studien zu einem politisch-religiösen Phänomen der griechischen Geschichte* (Stuttgart).

LESKY, A. (1971). *Geschichte der griechischen Literatur*³ (Bern).

LEVEQUE, P. (1982). '*Olbios* et la félicité des initiés', in L. Hadermann-Misguich and G. Raepsaet (eds.), *Rayonnement grec: Hommages à Charles Delvoye* (Brussels), 113–26.

LÉVI-STRAUSS, C. (1966). *The Savage Mind* (London; orig. pub. in Fr., 1962).

—— (1972). *Structural Anthropology* (Harmondsworth; first pub. in Fr., 1958).

—— (1975). *La voie des masques* (Geneva).

LEWIS, D. M. (1987). 'Bowie on Elegy. A Footnote', *JHS* 107. 188.

LISSARAGUE, F. (1990). *L'autre guerrier: Archers, peltastes, cavaliers dans l'imagerie attique* (Paris).

LLOYD-JONES, H. (1967). 'Heracles at Eleusis: P.Oxy. 2622 and P.S.I. 1391', *Maia*, 19: 206–29.

—— (1971). *The Justice of Zeus* (Berkeley, Calif., Los Angeles, and London).

—— (1973). 'Modern Interpretation of Pindar: The Second Pythian and Seventh Nemean Odes', *JHS* 93: 109–37.

—— (1981). 'Remarks on the Homeric Question', in H. Lloyd-Jones, V. Pearl, and B. Worden (eds.), *History and Imagination: Essays in Honour of H. R. Trevor-Roper* (London), 15–29.

—— (1985). 'Pindar and the After-Life', in *Fondation Hardt: Entretiens sur l'antiquité classique xxxi. Pindare* (Geneva), 245–79.

—— (1990). *Greek Lyric and Tragedy. The Academic Papers of Sir Hugh Lloyd-Jones* (Oxford).

LOESCHKE, G. (1879). 'Altattische Grabstelen', *AthMit* 4: 289–306.

LONG, C. R. (1959). 'Shrines in Sepulchres? A Re-examination of Three Middle to Late Minoan Tombs', *AJA* 63: 59–65.

462   *References*

LONG, C. R. (1974). *The Ayia Triadha Sarcophagus: A Study of Late Minoan and Mycenaean Funerary Practices and Beliefs* (Göteborg).

LO PORTO, F. G. (1971). 'Topografia antica di Taranto', in *Taranto nella civilta della Magna Grecia. Atti del decimo covegno di studi sulla Magna Grecia. Taranto, 4–11 ottobre 1970* (Naples), 343–83.

LORAUX, N. (1981). *L'invention d'Athènes: Histoire de l'oraison funèbre dans la 'cité classique'* (Paris, The Hague, and New York).

—— (1982). 'Mourir devant Troie, tomber pour Athènes: de la gloire du héros à l'idée de la cité', in G. Gnoli and J.-P. Vernant (eds.), *La Mort, les morts dans les sociétés anciennes* (Cambridge), 27–43.

—— (1985). *Façons tragiques de tuer une femme* (Paris).

—— (1989). *Les Expériences de Tirésias: Le féminin et l'homme grec* (Paris).

LORENZ, B. (1976). *Thessalische Grabgedichte von 6. bis zum 4. Jh. v. Chr.* (Innsbruck).

LUKES, S. (1973). *Emile Durkheim: His Life and Work* (London).

LYONS, J. (1977). *Semantics* (Cambridge).

—— (1981). *Language, Meaning and Context* (Fontana paperbacks, Glasgow).

McDONNELL, M. (1991). 'The Introduction of Athletic Nudity: Thucydides, Plato, and the Vases', *JHS* 111: 182–93.

MACLEOD, C. W. (1982). *Homer: Iliad Book xxiv* (Cambridge).

MAEHLER, H. (1982). *Die Lieder des Bakchylides: Erster Teil. Die Siegeslieder,* ii. *Kommentar* (Leiden).

MAIR, L. (1965). *An Introduction to Social Anthropology* (Oxford).

MALKIN, I. (1987). *Religion and Colonization in Ancient Greece* (Leiden).

MALTEN, L. (1912). 'Hephaistos', *JdI* 27: 232–64.

—— (1913). 'Elysion und Rhadamanthys', *JdI* 28: 35–51.

MANNI PIRAINO, M. T. (1963). 'Iscrizioni inedite e revisioni selinuntine', *Kokalos*, 9: 137–56.

—— (1964). 'Intervento' (on a paper by M. Guarducci), *Kokalos*, 10–11 (1964–5) (Atti del Primo Congresso Internazionale di Studi sulla Sicilia Antica), 481–4.

—— (1966). 'Quattro iscrizioni greche del museo di Palermo', *Kokalos*, 12: 200–6.

MARANDA, P. (1980). 'The Dialectic of Metaphor: An Anthropological Essay on Hermeneutics', in S. R. Suleiman and I. Crosman (eds.), *The Reader in the Text: Essays on Audience and Interpretation* (Princeton, NJ), 183–204.

MARKOE, G. E. (1989). 'The "Lion Attack" in Archaic Greek Art: Heroic Triumph', *ClassAnt* 8: 86–115.

MARTIN, R. (1971). 'L'Architecture de Tarente', in *Taranto nella civiltà della Magna Grecia. Atti del decimo covegno di studi sulla Magna Grecia. Taranto, 4–11 ottobre 1970* (Naples), 311–41.

MARTINET, J. (1973). *La Sémiologie* (Paris).

MASTROKOSTAS, E. I. (1972). 'Myrrhinous: la koré Phrasikleia, œuvre d'Aristion de Paros et un kouros en marbre', *AAA* 5: 298–324 (in Gk. and Fr.).

MATTHAIOU, A. (1986). '*Dyo archaikes attikes epitymbies steles*', *Horos*, 4: 31–4.

—— (1987). '*Erion Lykourgou Lykophronos Boutadou*', *Horos*, 5: 31–44.

MEIGGS, R. and LEWIS D. (1988) (eds.). *A Selection of Greek Historical Inscriptions: To the End of the Fifth Century B.C.*, rev. edn. (Oxford).

MERRY, W. W., and RIDDELL, J. (1886) (eds.). *Homer's Odyssey* (Oxford).

MIALL, D. S. (1982) (ed.). *Metaphor: Problems and Perspectives* (Brighton).

MIHAILOV, G. (1970). *Inscriptiones Graecae in Bulgaria repertae*, i.2 (Serdicae).

MILLER, A. M. (1979). 'The "Address to the Delian Maidens" in the *Homeric Hymn to Apollo*: Epilogue or Transition?', *TAPA* 109: 173–86.

MOMIGLIANO, A. (1978). 'Juifs et Grecs', in L. Poliakov (ed.), *Ni Juif ni Grec. Entretiens sur le racisme* (Paris), 47–63.

MOMMSEN, H. (1982). 'Irrfahrten des Odysseus: Zu dem Fragment Tübingen S./10 1507', in B. v. Freytag, D. Mannsperger, and F. Prayon (eds.), *Praestant Interna: Festschrift für U. Hausmann* (Tübingen), 205–12.

MORET, J.-M. (1984). *Oedipe, la Sphinx et les thébains: Essai de mythologie iconographique* (Rome).

MORETTI, F. (1982). 'The Dialectic of Fear', *New Left Review*, 136 (Nov./Dec.): 67–85.

MORGAN, L. (1988). *The Miniature Wall Paintings of Thera* (Cambridge).

MORRIS, I. (1987). *Burial and Ancient Society: The Rise of the Greek City-State* (Cambridge).

—— (1989). 'Attitudes toward Death in Archaic Greece', *ClassAnt* 8: 296–320.

MORTON-WILLIAMS, P. (1968). 'The Fulani Penetration into Nupe and Yoruba in the Nineteenth Century', in I. M. Lewis (ed.), *History and Social Anthropology* (London, Social Science Paperback ed., 1970; first pub. 1968), 1–24.

MOULTON, C. (1974). 'The End of the *Odyssey*', *GRBS*: 153–69.

MÜLLER, P. (1978). *Löwen und Mischwesen in der archaischen griechischen Kunst: Eine Untersuchung über ihre Bedeutung* (Zurich).

MURRAY, O. (1980). *Early Greece* (Glasgow).

—— (1983). 'The Symposion as Social Organisation', in Hägg (1983c), 195–9).

—— (1988). 'Death and the Symposion', *Archeologia e storia antica. Annali. Istituto Universitario Orientale. Napoli*. Dipartimento del mondo classico e del mediterraneo antico 10 (Sezione tematica: La parola l'immagine, la tomba. Atti del Colloquio Internazionale di Capri), 239–57.

MUTHMANN, F. (1982). *Das Granatapfel: Symbol des Lebens in der alten Welt* (Bern).

MYLONAS, G. E. (1961). *Eleusis and the Eleusinian Mysteries* (Princeton, NJ, and London).

—— (1962). 'Burial Customs', in A. J. B. Wace and F. H. Stubbings (eds.), *A Companion to Homer* (London), 478–88.

NAGY, G. (1973). 'Phaethon, Sappho's Phaon, and the White Rock of Leucas', *HarvStClPhil* 77: 137–77.

—— (1981). 'Another Look at *KLEOS APHTHITON*', *WürzbJb* 7: 113–16.

—— (1983). '*Sema* and *noesis*: Some Illustrations', *Arethusa*, 16: 35–55.

—— (1986). 'Ancient Greek Epic and Praise Poetry: Some Typological Considerations', in J. M. Foley (ed.), *Oral Tradition in Literature: Interpretation in Context* (Univ. of Missouri Press, Columbia), 89–102.

—— (1990). *Pindar's Homer: The Lyric Possession of an Epic Past* (Baltimore).

NAUERT, J. P. (1965). 'The Hagia Triada Sarcophagus. An Iconographical Study', *AntK* 8: 91–8.

NEEDHAM, R. (ed.) (1973). *Right and Left. Essays on Dual Symbolic Classification* (Chicago).

NEUMANN, G. (1965). *Gesten und Gebärden in der Griechischen Kunst* (Berlin).

NEUSER, K. (1982). *Anemoi: Studien zur Darstellung der Winde und Windgottheiten in der Antike* (Rome).

NICHOLLS, R. V. (1958–9). 'Old Smyrna: The Iron Age Fortifications and Associated Remains in the City Perimeter', *BSA* 53–4: 35–137.

NILSSON, M. P. (1950). *The Minoan-Mycenaean Religion and its Survival in Greek Religion*² (Lund).

—— (1967). *Geschichte der Griechischen Religion*³, i (Munich).

—— (1974). *Geschichte der Griechischen Religion*³, ii (Munich).

NOACK, F. (1907). 'Die Mauern Athens. Ausgrabungen und Untersuchungen', *AthMit* 32: 123–60; 473–66.

NOCK, A. D. (1972). Arthur Darby Nock, *Essays on Religion and the Ancient World*. Selected and edited, with an Introduction, Bibliography of Nock's writings, and Indexes, by Z. Stewart (Oxford).

NORDEN, E. (1970). *P. Vergilius Maro. Aeneis Buch VI* (Stuttgart).

NORTH, H. (1966). *Sophrosyne* (Ithaca, NY).

OLIVOVA, V. (1984). *Sports and Games in the Ancient World* (London).

ORANJE, H. (1980). 'Euripides' Protesilaus: P.Oxy. 3214. 10–14', *ZPE* 37: 169–72.

ORSI, P. (1892). 'Megara Hyblaea. Storia-Topografia-Necropoli e Anathemata [Topografia by F. S. Cavallari]', *MonAnt* 1: 698–950.

OSBORNE, M. J. (1988). 'Attic Epitaphs—A Supplement', *Ancient Society*, 19: 5–60.

OSBORNE, R. G. (1988). 'Death Revisited; Death Revised. The Death of the Artist in Archaic and Classical Greece', *Art History*, 11: 1–16.

O'SHEA, J. M. (1984). *Mortuary Variability: An Archaeological Investigation* (Orlando etc.).

PADEL, R. (1992). *In and Out of the Mind: Greek Images of the Tragic Self* (Princeton, NJ).

PAGE, D. (1955). *The Homeric Odyssey* (Oxford).

——(1981). *Further Greek Epigrams before A.D. 50* from the Greek Anthology and other sources, not included in 'Hellenistic Epigrams' or 'The Garland of Philip', ed. D. L. Page, revised and prepared for publication by R. D. Dawe and J. Diggle (Cambridge).

PAPACHRISTODOULOU, I. (1971). 'Dyo epigraphai ex Argous', *AAA* 4: 92 9.

PAPASPYRIDI, S. (1923). 'Ho "technites ton kalamon" ton leukon lekython', *ADelt* 8: 117–46.

PARKE, H. W. (1977). *Festivals of the Athenians* (London).

PARKER, R. (1983). *Miasma: Pollution and Purification in Early Greek Religion* (Oxford).

PARKER PEARSON, M. (1982). 'Mortuary Practices, Society and Ideology: An Ethnoarchaeological Study', in I. Hodder (ed.), *Symbolic and Structural Archaeology* (Cambridge), 99–113.

PEEK, W. (1934). 'Griechische Inschriften', *AthMit* 59: 35–80.

——(1941). 'Griechische Epigramme', *AthMit* 66: 47–86.

——(1942). 'Attische Inschriften', *AthMit* 67: 1–217.

——(1960). *Griechische Grabgedichte* (Berlin).

——(1970). 'Zu einem Epigram aus Kopai', *AAA* 31 87 9.

——(1978). 'Zum Epigram auf die bei Tanagra gefallenen Argiven', *ZPE* 30: 18–19.

PEIFER, E. (1989). *Eidola und andere mit dem Sterben verbundene Flügelwesen in der attischen Vasenmalerei in spätarchaischer und klassischer Zeit* (Frankfurt).

PEIRCE, C. S. (1931–3). *Collected Papers of Charles Sanders Peirce* (Cambridge, Mass.).

——(1958). P. P. Wiener (ed.), Charles S. Peirce, *Selected Writings* (New York).

PELON, O. (1990). 'Les Tombes à tholos d'Argolide: architecture et rituel funéraire', in Hägg and Nordquist (1990: 109–12).

PEPPAS-DELMUSU, D. (1963). 'Ein attisches Grabgedicht für ein Arzt aus Cypern', *AthMit* 78: 154–5.

PETIT, F. (1987). 'Les Tombes circulaires de la Messara: problèmes d'interprétation des pièces annexes', in Laffineur (1987: 35–42).

PETZL, G. (1969). *Antike Diskussionen über die beiden Nekyiai* (Meisenheim am Glan).

PFISTERER-HAAS, S. (1990). 'Ältere Frauen auf attischen Grabdenkmälern', *AthMit* 105: 179–96.

PFOHL, G. (1953). *Untersuchungen über die attischen Grabinschriften* (Diss. Erlangen).

—— (1967*a*). *Greek Poems on Stones*, i, *Epitaphs. From the Seventh to the Fifth Centuries B.C.*, ed. G. Pfohl (Leiden).

—— (1967*b*). *Poetische Kleinkunst auf altgriechischen Denkmälern* (Munich).

PFUHL, E. (1903). 'Der archaische Friedhof am Stadtberge von Thera', *AthMit* 28: 1–290.

PHARAKLAS, N. (1969). '*Daidalikos kormos ek Tanagras*', *ADelt* 24: A', Meletai, 66–73.

PHILLIPS, E. D. (1973). *Greek Medicine* (London).

PINI, I. (1968). *Beiträge zur minoischer Gräberkunde* (Wiesbaden).

PIRCHER, J. (1979). *Das Lob der Frau im vorchristlichen Grabepigramm der Griechen* (Innsbruck).

PLATON, N. (1954). '*Ta minoika oikiaka hiera*', *KrChr* 8: 428–83.

POLLITT, J. J. (1990). *The Art of Ancient Greece: Sources and Documents* (Cambridge).

POPHAM, M., SACKETT, L. H., and THEMELIS, P. (1979). *Lefkandi*, i (London).

POPHAM, M., TOULOUPA, E., and SACKETT, L. H. (1982). 'The Hero of Lefkandi', *Antiquity*, 56: 169–74.

POTTIER, E. (1883). *Étude sur les lécythes blancs attiques à représentations funéraires* (Paris).

POUILLOUX, J. (1960). *Choix d'inscriptions grecques* (Paris).

PRICE, S. R. F. (1984). *Rituals and Power: The Roman Imperial Cult in Asia Minor* (Cambridge).

PRITCHETT, W. K. (1985). *The Greek State at War*. Part iv. (Berkeley, Calif., Los Angeles, and London).

PROTONOTARIOU-DEILAKI, E. (1990). 'Burial Customs and Funerary Rites in the Prehistoric Argolid', in Hägg and Nordquist (1990: 69–83).

PUGLIESE-CARRATELLI, G. (1974*a*). 'Un sepolcro di Hipponion e un nuovo testo orfico', *PdP* 29: 108–26.

—— (1974*b*).'*Orphika*', *PdP* 29: 135–44.

RACE, W. H. (1982). 'Aspects of Rhetoric and Form in Greek Hymns', *GRBS* 23: 5–14.

RAUBITSCHEK, A. E. (1949). *Dedications from the Athenian Acropolis: A Catalogue of the Inscriptions of the Sixth and Fifth Centuries B.C.* (Cambridge, Mass.).

—— (1968). 'Das Denkmal-Epigram', in *L'épigramme grecque. Fondation Hardt pour l'étude de l'antiquité classique. Entretiens*, xiv (Vandœuvres and Geneva 1967 [1968]), 1–26.

REDFERN, W. (1984). *Puns* (Oxford).

REDFIELD, J. (1975). *Nature and Culture in the Iliad: The Tragedy of Hector* (Chicago).

REILLY, J. (1989). 'Many Brides: "Mistress and Maid" on Athenian Lekythoi', *Hesperia*, 58: 411–44.

RENFREW, C. (1972). *The Emergence of Civilization: The Cyclades and the Aegean in the Third Millennium B.C.* (London).

——(1982). 'Explanation Revisited', in C. Renfrew, M. J. Rowlands, and B. A. Segraves (eds.), *Theory and Explanation in Archaeology: The Southampton Conference* (New York, and London), 5–23.

RICHARDSON, N. J. (1974) (ed.). *The Homeric Hymn to Demeter* (Oxford).

RICHTER, G. M. A. (1942–3). 'Terracotta Plaques from Early Attic Tombs', *BMetrMus* NS 1: 80–92.

——(1960). *Kouroi: Archaic Greek Youths²* (London).

——(1961). *The Archaic Gravestones of Attica* (London).

——(1968). *Korai: Archaic Greek Maidens* (London).

—— and HALL, L. F. (1936). *Red-Figured Athenian Vases in the Metropolitan Museum of Art* (New Haven, Conn.).

RIDGWAY, B. S. (1977). *The Archaic Style in Greek Sculpture* (Princeton, NJ).

RIEZLER, W. (1914). *Weissgrundige Attische Lekythen* (Munich).

RIGBY, P. (1973). 'Dual Symbolic Classification among the Gogo of Central Tanzania', in Needham (1973: 263–87).

ROBERT, C. (1892). *Die Nekyia des Polygnot*, 16. HallWPr.

ROBERT, L. (1939). 'Hellenica, xi. Inscriptions relatives à des médecins', *Rev.Phil.* 13: 163–73.

——(1946). *Hellenica: Recueil d'épigraphie, de numismatique et d'antiquités grecques* (Paris).

——(1964). 'Index commenté des noms de personnes', in N. Farath, *Les stèles funéraires de Byzance gréco-romaine* (Paris), 131–89.

ROBERT, J., and ROBERT, L. (1958). 'Bulletin Épigraphique', *REG* 71: 169–363.

————(1978). 'Bulletin Épigraphique', *REG* 91: 385–510.

ROBERTSON, M. (1959). *Greek Painting* (Geneva).

——(1975). *A History of Greek Art* (Cambridge).

ROBERTSON, R. (1969) (ed.). *Sociology of Religion. Selected Readings* (Harmondsworth).

ROCCO, S. (1897). *Il mito di Caronte nell' arte e nella letteratura* (Turin).

ROHDE, E. (1925). *Psyche* (London; trans. of 8th edn.).

ROSE, H. J. (1925a). 'The Bride of Hades', *CP* 20: 238–42.

——(1925b). 'Antigone and the Bride of Corinth', *CQ* 19: 147–50.

——(1936). 'The Ancient Grief', in *Greek Poetry and Life: Essays presented to G. Murray* (Oxford), 79–96.

ROUGEMONT, G. (1974). 'L'Inscription archaïque de Delphes relative à la phratrie des Labyades', *BCH* 98: 147–58.

——(1977). *Corpus des Inscriptions de Delphes. i. Les lois sacrées et règlements religieux* (Paris).

ROUSSET, D. (1990). 'Les Doriens de la métropole. Nouveaux documents épigraphiques et prosopographie', *BCH* 114: 445–72.

RUDHARDT, J. (1958). *Notions fondamentales de la pensée religieuse et actes constitutifs du culte dans la Grèce classique* (Geneva).

—— (1978). 'A propos de l'hymne homérique à Déméter', *MusHelv* 35: 1–17.

RÜHFEL, H. (1974). 'Göttin auf einem Grabrelief?', *AntK* 17: 42–9.

RUSSO, J., FERNANDEZ-GALIANO, M., and HEUBECK, A. (1992). *A Commentary on Homer's Odyssey. Volume iii: Books xvii–xxiv* (Oxford).

RUTKOWSKI, B. (1968). 'The Origin of the Minoan Coffin', *BSA* 63: 219–27.

SACCO, G. (1978). 'Due note epigrafiche', *RFIC* 106: 75–7.

SAHLINS, M. (1976). *Culture and Practical Reason* (Chicago).

SAKELLARAKIS, J. A. (1970). 'Das Kuppelgrab A von Archanes und das kretisch-mykenische Tieropferritual', *PZ* 45: 135–219.

—— (1971). 'Elephantinon ploion ek Mykinon', *ArchEph*: 188–233.

SALLARES, R. (1991). *The Ecology of the Ancient World* (London).

SCALERA MCCLINTOCK, G. (1989). *Il pensiero dell'invisibile nella Grecia arcaica* (Naples).

SCHÄFER, J. (1957). *Studien zu den griechischen Reliefpithoi des 8.-6. Jahrhunderts v. Chr. aus Kreta, Rhodos, Tenos und Boiotien* (Kallmünz).

SCHIERING, W. (1974). 'Stele und Bild bei griechischen Grabmälern', Sitzung, Archaeolog. Gesselsch. zu Berlin 1973/4, in *AA*: 651–62.

SCHMALTZ, B. (1979). 'Verwendung und Funktion attischer Grabmäler', *Marburg Winckelmann Programm*: 13–37.

—— (1983). *Griechische Grabreliefs* (Darmstadt).

SCHMITT-PANTEL, P. (1990). 'Sacrificial Meal and *Symposion*: Two Models of Civic Institutions in the Archaic City?', in O. Murray (ed.), *Sympotica: A Symposium on the Symposion* (Oxford), 14–33.

SCHNAPP-GOURBEILLON, A. (1981). *Lions, héros, masques: Les représentations de l'animal chez Homère* (Paris).

—— (1982). 'Les funérailles de Patrocle', in G. Gnoli and J.-P. Vernant (eds.), *La mort, les morts dans les sociétés anciennes* (Cambridge), 77–88.

SCHNAUFER, A. (1970). *Frühgriechischer Totenglaube* (Hildesheim).

SCHREIBER, T. (1897). *Die Wandbilder des Polygnotos in der Halle der Knidien zu Delphi* (Leipzig).

SCHUCHHARDT, W. H. (1939). 'Rundwerke ausser den Koren. Reliefs', in H. Schrader (ed.), *Die archaischen Marmorbildwerke der Akropolis* (Frankfurt), 187–342.

SCHWYZER, E. (1950). *Griechische Grammatik, 2. Syntax und syntaktische Stilistik* (Munich).

SCUPIN, R. (1982). 'The Social Significance of the Hajj for Thai Muslims', *The Muslim World*, 72: 25–33.

SEAFORD, R. (1981). 'Dionysiac Drama and the Dionysiac Mysteries', *CQ* 31: 252–75.

——(1990). 'The Structural Problems of Marriage in Euripides', in A. Powell (ed.), *Euripides, Women and Sexuality* (London), 151–76.

SEGAL, C. P. (1962). 'The Phaeacians and the Symbolism of Odysseus' Return', *Arion*, 1: 17–64.

SHAPIRO, H. A. (1991). 'The Iconography of Mourning in Athenian Art', *AJA* 95: 629–56.

SHERRATT, E. S. (1990). '"Reading the Texts": Archaeology and the Homeric Question', *Antiquity*, 64: 807–24.

SHIBLES, W. A. (1971). *Metaphor: An Annotated Bibliography and History* (Whitewater, Wis.).

SIEBERT, G. (1981). 'Eidola. Le problème de la figurabilité dans l'art grec', in G. Siebert (ed.), *Méthodologie iconographique: Actes du Colloque de Strasbourg 27–28 avril 1979* (Strasbourg), 63–73.

SIMANTONI-BOURNIA, E. (1984). *Naxiakoi Anaglyphoi Pithoi* (Athens).

SIMON, E. (1972). 'Hera und die Nymphen. Ein böotischer polos in Stockholm', *RA*: 205–20.

——(1985). *Die Götter der Griechen* (Darmstadt).

SIMONDON, M. (1982). *La Mémoire et l'oubli dans la pensée grecque jusqu' à la fin du Ve siècle avant J.-C.* (Paris).

SKIADAS, A. D. (1967). *Epi tymbo: Symbole eis ten hermeneian ton hellenikon epitymbion emmetron epigraphon* (Athens).

——(1972). 'Epi tymbo. Ein Beitrag zur Interpretation der griechischen metrischen Grabinschriften', in G. Pfohl (ed.), *Inschriften der Griechen. Grab-, Weih- und Ehreninschriften* (Darmstadt), 59–84.

SMITH, W. D. (1979). *The Hippocratic Tradition* (Ithaca, NY).

SNELL, B. (1966). *Gesammelte Schriften* (Göttingen).

SNODGRASS, A. M. (1971). *The Dark Age of Greece* (Edinburgh).

——(1974). 'An Historical Homeric Society?', *JHS* 94: 114–25.

——(1980). *Archaic Greece* (London).

——(1988). 'The Archaeology of the Hero', *Archeologia e storia antica. Annali. Istituto Universitario Orientale. Napoli. Dipartimento del mondo classico e del mediterraneo antico* 10 (Sezione tematica: La parola l'immagine, la tomba. Atti del Colloquio Internazionale di Capri), 19–26.

SOURVINOU-INWOOD, C. (1973*a*). 'The Young Abductor of the Locrian Pinakes', *Bulletin of the Institute of Classical Studies*, 20: 12–21.

——(1973*b*). 'On the Lost "Boat" Ring from Mochlos', *Kadmos*, 12: 149–58.

——(1981). 'To Die and Enter the House of Hades: Homer, Before and After', in J. Whaley (ed.), *Mirrors of Mortality: Studies in the Social History of Death* (London), 15–39.

470   *References*

SOURVINOU-INWOOD, C. (1983). 'A Trauma in Flux: Death in the 8th Century and After', in Hägg (1983*c*: 33–48).

—— (1986*a*). 'Charon', in *Lexicon Iconographicum Mythologiae Classicae*, iii. 210–25.

—— (1986*b*). 'Crime and Punishment: Tityos, Tantalos and Sisyphos in Odyssey 11', *BICS* 33: 37–58.

—— (1987). 'Images grecques de la mort: représentations, imaginaire, histoire', *Archeologia e storia antica. Annali. Istituto Universitario Orientale. Napoli.* Dipartimento del mondo classico e del mediterraneo antico 9. 145–58.

—— (1988). *Studies in Girls' Transitions. Aspects of the Arkteia and Age Representation in Attic Iconography* (Athens).

—— (1989*a*). 'Assumptions and the Creation of Meaning: Reading Sophocles' Antigone', *JHS* 109: 134–48.

—— (1989*b*). 'Boat, Tree and Shrine: The Mochlos Ring and the Makrygialos Seal', *Kadmos*, 28: 97–100.

—— (1990*a*). 'Sophocles' Antigone as a Bad Woman', in F. Dieteren and E. Kloek (eds.), *Writing Women into History* (Amsterdam), 11–38.

—— (1990*b*). 'What is Polis Religion?', in O. Murray and S. Price (eds.), *The Greek City from Homer to Alexander* (Oxford), 295–322.

—— (1991). *'Reading' Greek Culture: Texts and Images, Rituals and Myths* (Oxford).

—— (1993). 'Early Sanctuaries, the Eighth Century and Ritual Space: Fragments of a Discourse', in N. Marinatos and R. Hägg (eds.), *Greek Sanctuaries: New Approaches* (London), 1–17.

SPARKES, B. A. (1991). *Greek Art* (Greece and Rome New Surveys in the Classics no. 22).

SPIRO, M. E. (1966). 'Religion: Problems of Definition and Explanation', in M. Banton (ed.), *Anthropological Approaches to the Study of Religion* (London; Social Science Paperback, 1968; first pub. 1966), 85–126.

SPYROPOULOS, TH. (1970). 'Excavation in the Mycenaean Cemetery of Tanagra in Boeotia' (Gk. with Eng. summary), *AAA* 3: 184–97.

STÄHLER, K. P. (1967). *Grab und Psyche des Patroklos* (Münster).

STANSBURY-O'DONNELL, M. D. (1990). 'Polygnotos' *Nekyia*: A Reconstruction and Analysis', *AJA* 94: 213–35.

STECHER, A. (1963). *Der Lobpreis des Toten in den griechischen metrischen Grabinschriften* (Diss. Innsbruck).

—— (1981). *Inschriftliche Grabgedichte auf Krieger und Athleten: Eine Studie zu griechischen Wertprädikationen* (Innsbruck).

STEVENS, S. T. (1991). 'Charon's Obol and Other Coins in Ancient Funerary Practice', *Phoenix* 45: 215–29.

STEWART, A. F. (1986). 'When is a Kouros Not an Apollo? The Tenea

"Apollo" Revisited', in M. A. Del Chiaro (ed.), *Corinthiaca: Studies in Honor of Darrell A. Amyx* (Columbia, Mis.), 54–70.

—— (1990). *Greek Sculpture: An Exploration* (New Haven, Conn.).

STINTON, T. C. W. (1987). 'The Apotheosis of Heracles from the Pyre', in L. Rodley (ed.), *Papers Given at a Colloquium on Greek Drama in Honour of R. P. Winnington-Ingram* (London), 1–16.

STUPPERICH, R. (1977). *Staatsbegräbnis und Privatgrabmal im klassischen Athen* (Diss. Münster).

STURROCK, J. (1979) (ed.). *Structuralism and Since: From Lévi-Strauss to Derrida* (Oxford).

SULEIMAN, S. R. (1980). 'Introduction: Varieties of Audience-Oriented Criticism', in S. R. Suleiman and I. Crosman (eds.), *The Reader in the text: Essays on Audience and Interpretation* (Princeton, NJ), 3–45.

SVENBRO, J. (1988). *Phrasikleia: Anthropologie de la lecture en Grèce ancienne* (Paris).

TAPLIN, O. (1992). *Homeric Soundings: The Shaping of the Iliad* (Oxford).

TERPENING, R. H. (1985). *Charon and the Crossing. Ancient, Medieval and Renaissance Transformations of a Myth* (London and Toronto).

THEMELIS, P. (1973–4). '*Anavyssos. Geometriko Nekrotapheio*', *ADelt* 29: Chron 108–10.

—— (1976). *Frühgriechische Grabbauten* (Mainz).

THIMME, J. (1964). 'Die Stele der Hegeso als Zeugnis des attischen Grabkultes', *AntK* 7: 16–29.

THOMAS, R. (1989). *Oral Tradition and Written Record in Classical Athens* (Cambridge).

TOD, M. N. (1951). 'Laudatory Epithets in Greek Epitaphs', *BSA* 46. 182–90.

TOHER, M. (1991). 'Greek Funerary Legislation and the Two Spartan Funerals', in *Georgica: Greek Studies in Honour of George Cawkwell* (London), 159–75.

TOUCHEFEU, O. (1968. Pub. as O. Touchefeu-Meynier). *Thèmes odysséens dans l'art antique* (Paris).

TRITSCH, F. J. (1968a). 'Tirynthia Semata', *Kadmos*, 7: 124–37.

—— (1968b). 'Bellerophon's Letter', *Atti e Memorie del Primo Congresso Internazionale di Micenologia* (Rome), 1223–30.

TSANTSANOGLOU, K., and PARASSOGLOU, G. M. (1987). 'Two Gold Lamellae from Thessaly', *Hellenika*, 38: 3–17.

TUCHELT, K. (1970). *Die archaischen Skulpturen von Didyma. Beiträge zur frühgriechischen Plastik in Kleinasien* (Berlin) [Istanbuler Forschungen 27].

VALLET, G. (1987). 'Le Fait urbain en Grèce et en Sicile à l'époque archaïque', *Kokalos*, 30–1 (1984–5) [1987] 133–63.

VANDERPOOL, E. (1964). 'New Inscriptions from the Phokikon', *Hesperia*, 33: 84–5.

VAN HOORN, G. (1951). *Choes and Anthesteria* (Leiden).

VASSILOPOULOU, V. (1987). 'Ekthessi yia ten anaskaphe sten odo Vassilikon kai Kratylou 56', Horos, 5: 149–52.

VERMEULE, E. (1965). 'Painted Mycenaean Larnakes', JHS 85: 123–48.

—— (1979). Aspects of Death in Early Greek Art and Poetry (Berkeley, Calif., Los Angeles, and London).

VERNANT, J.-P. (1965). Mythe et pensée chez les Grecs (Paris).

—— (1974). Mythe et société en Grèce ancienne (Paris).

—— (1976). Religion grecque, religions antiques (Paris).

—— (1982). 'La Belle Mort et le cadavre outragé', in G. Gnoli and J.-P. Vernant (eds.), La Mort, les morts dans les sociétés anciennes (Cambridge), 45–76.

—— (1990). Figures, idoles, masques (Paris).

—— (1991). Jean-Pierre Vernant, Mortals and Immortals: Collected Essays, ed. F. I. Zeitlin (Princeton, NJ).

VEYNE, P. (1983). Les Grecs ont-ils cru à leurs mythes? (Paris).

VIDAL-NAQUET, P. (1973). 'Valeurs religieuses et mythiques de la terre et du sacrifice dans l'Odyssée', in M. I. Finley (ed.), Problèmes de la terre en Grèce ancienne (Paris), 269–92.

VOKOTOPOULOU, I. P. (1973). Odegos Mouseiou Ioanninon (Athens).

—— (1986). Vitsa: Ta nekrotapheia mias molossikes komes (Athens).

V. BOTHMER, D. (1981). 'The Death of Sarpedon', in S. L. Hyatt (ed.), The Greek Vase (New York), 63–80.

VON DER MÜHLL, P. (1938). 'Zur Erfindung in der Nekyia der Odyssee', Philologus, 93: 3–11.

VON DUHN, F. (1885). 'Charondarstellungen', AZ 43: 2–23.

WALLACE, M. B. (1970). 'Notes on Early Greek Grave Epigrams', Phoenix, 24: 95–105.

—— (1984). 'The Metres of Early Greek Epigrams', in D. E. Gerber (ed.), Greek Poetry and Philosophy: Studies in honour of Leonard Woodbury (Chico, Calif.), 303–17.

WARDEN, J. (1971). 'Psyche in Homeric Death-Descriptions', Phoenix, 25: 95–103.

WARNING, R. (1975) (ed.). Rezeptionsaesthetik (Munich).

WASER, O. (1898). Charon, Charun, Charos (Berlin).

WEHGARTNER, I. (1983). Attisch Weissgrundige Keramik (Mainz).

WEIZSÄCKER, P. (1895). Polygnots Gemälde in der Lesche der Knidien in Delphi (Stuttgart).

WELCH, H., and CHÜN-FANG YÜ, (1980). 'The Tradition of Innovation: A Chinese New Religion', Numen, 27: 222–46.

WELLS, B. (1980). 'Death at Dendra. On Mortuary Practices in a Mycenaean Community', in Hägg and Nordquist (1990: 125–40).

WENZ, S. (1913). Studien zu attischen Kriegergräbern (Diss. Münster).

WEST, M. L. (1966) (ed.). Hesiod, Theogony (Oxford).

WEST, M. L. (1971). *Early Greek Philosophy and the Orient* (Oxford).

—— (1983). *The Orphic Poems* (Oxford).

—— (1985). *The Hesiodic Catalogue of Women: Its Nature, Structure and Origins* (Oxford).

WEST, S. (1988). In A. Heubeck, S. West, and J. B. Hainsworth, *A Commentary on Homer's Odyssey. Volume i. Books i–viii* (Oxford).

—— (1989). 'Laertes Revisited', *PCPS* 35: 113–43.

WHITLEY, J. (1988). 'Early States and Hero Cults: A Re-Appraisal', *JHS* 108: 173–82.

—— (1991). *Style and Society in Dark Age Greece: The Changing Face of a Pre-Literate Society 1100–700 B.C.* (Cambridge).

WILAMOWITZ-MOELLENDORF, T. v. (1917). *Die dramatische Technik des Sophokles* (Berlin).

WILAMOWITZ-MOELLENDORFF, U. v. (1899). 'Lesefrüchte', *Hermes*, 34: 203–30.

WILHELM, A. (1931). 'Ärtze und Ärtzerinnen in Pontos, Lykien und Ägypten', *ÖJh* 27: 74–96.

—— (1978). 'Bemerkungen zu den attischen Grabinschriften IG ii2', *ZPE* 29: 57–90.

WILLCOCK, M. M. (1990). Review of Heubeck and Hoekstra 1989, *LCM* 15/4: 63–4.

WILLEMSEN, F. (1963). 'Archaische Grabmalbasen aus der Athener Stadmauer', *AthMit* 78: 104–53.

—— (1970). 'Stelen', *AthMit* 85: 23–44.

WILLEY, G. R. (1974). 'A Summary of the Complex Societies Colloquium', in C. B. Moore (ed.), *Reconstructing Complex Societies*, Suppl. to BASOR 20: 145–53.

WINTER, E. H. (1966). 'Territorial Groupings and Religion among the Iraqw', in M. Banton (ed.), *Anthropological Approaches to the Study of Religion* (London; Social Science Paperback edn. 1968, first pub. 1966), 155–74.

WOYSCH-MÉAUTIS, D. (1982). *La Représentation des animaux et des êtres fabuleux sur les monuments funéraires grecs de l'époque archaique à la fin du IVᵉ siècle av. J.-C.* (Lausanne).

WRIGHT, J. C. (1987). 'Death and Power at Mycenae: Changing Symbols in Mortuary Practice', in Laffineur (1987: 171–84).

YALMAN, N. (1967). ' "The Raw:the Cooked: :Nature:Culture". Observations on *Le cru et le cuit*', in E. Leach (ed.), *The Structural Study of Myth and Totemism* (London; Social Science Paperback edn. 1968, first pub. 1967), 71–89.

ZANKER, P. (1965). *Wandel der Hermesgestalt in der attischen Vasenmalerei* (Bonn).

ZAPHEIROPOULOS, N. S. (1977). '*Anaskaphe eis Sellada Thiras*', *Praktika*: 400–2.

ZAPHIROPOULOU, Ph. (1983). 'La necropoli geometrica di Tsikalario a Naxos', *Magna Graecia*, 5–6: 1–4.

ZUNTZ, G. (1971). *Persephone* (Oxford).

—— (1976). 'Die Goldlamelle von Hipponion', *WSt* 10: 129–51.

INDEX

(This index is, by necessity, highly selective. The notion 'epitaph of' is subsumed into 'grave monument of'.)

INDEX OF PASSAGES

(This index does not include references to the Homeric epics (discussed in Ch. II) or to epigrams nor does it include references to passages in the footnotes. The precise passage is not given when several passages from one work are cited repeatedly in different places in the book.)

14899352R00272

Made in the USA
Lexington, KY
26 April 2012